Correctional Assessment, Casework, and Counseling

Third Edition

Anthony Walsh Ph.D.

Boise State University

Printed in the United States of America by Graphic Communications Inc., Upper Marlboro, Maryland.

For information on publications and videos available from ACA, contact our worldwide web home page at: http://www.aca.org

ISBN - 1-56991-133-9

This publication may be ordered from:
American Correctional Association
4380 Forbes Boulevard
Lanham, Maryland 20706-4322
1-800-222-5646

Library of Congress Cataloging-in-Publication Data

Walsh, Anthony, 1941-
Correctional Assessment, Casework, and Counseling / Anthony Walsh–3rd ed.
p. cm.
Includes bibliographical references and index.
ISBN 1-56991-133-9
1. Social work with criminals. 2. Criminals–Counseling of. 3. Criminals–Rehabilitation. 4. Parole officers. 5. Probation officers. I. Title.

HV7428 .W35 2001
365'.66–dc21

Contents

Foreword

Correctional theories and practices are always changing. To keep up with these changes, one has to be aware of recent research and emerging trends. This is why Dr. Anthony Walsh once again has updated *Correctional Assessment, Casework, and Counseling*. His book provides readers with a basic understanding of correctional psychology; examines the unique challenges of interviewing and counseling offenders; and offers counseling techniques that are helpful to those working in institutional and community corrections settings.

Walsh uses new data and updated research—including biological findings— for this third edition, and he expands on some ideas that have taken hold, in recent years, in the corrections profession. He devotes a new chapter to cognitive-behavioral therapy, a practice that has become increasingly popular. He also includes new *Perspectives from the Field* essays, so that these firsthand examples of "theory in practice" remain timely.

Walsh's book is exhaustive in its coverage of what professionals do to help their clients involved with the criminal justice system. Professors of criminal justice and social work can use this book as a practical manual for teaching, and students considering a career in counseling will find it fascinating reading. Additionally, experienced corrections practitioners will find a wealth of information in *Correctional Assessment, Casework, and Counseling* that is relevant to their work, as will probation and parole officers.

James A. Gondles, Jr., CAE
Executive Director
American Correctional Association

Introduction

In the introduction to the first edition of this book I wrote:

> Most social work and psychology texts to which many of us have turned to for guidance in interviewing and counseling do not respond to the special needs of criminal justice clients. These works proceed on the assumption that counseling clients are largely self-selected and are motivated to explore the problems that brought them to the counselor's office. Criminal justice clients, on the other hand, are almost always extremely reluctant to be in any counseling situation, are often impervious to the problems that led to such a situation, and typically have a congenital dislike for anyone who works for the system. This book assesses the special problems of interviewing and counseling under these conditions.

I cited those three sentences in the second edition, and now I'm doing it again because nothing has changed about offenders since then (they still do not like us very much). A number of publishers have discovered the need for interviewing and counseling texts specific to corrections since then, however. Good! Competition keeps us all on our toes and constantly improving; hence, the third edition of this book. Although the first edition was widely recognized as the most complete and comprehensive book of its kind, a number of improvements were made in the second edition, and more are made in this one. This edition has improved on the earlier editions in a number of ways:

1. It is extensively updated and revised using the latest research and data. Many exciting new ideas have emerged in criminality/corrections over the past few years.

2. The legal chapter has been extensively rewritten to cover legal issues in corrections that have emerged since the publication of the last edition. In our increasingly litigation-happy society, it has become imperative that correctional workers become aware of the rights of offenders and of situations in which they, the correctional workers, might be held liable for negligent treatment.

3. It contains more "Perspective from the Field" pieces, written by practicing professionals in corrections. These perspectives have been popular with students looking for that "practical" point of view from the trenches.

4. It pays more attention to case management techniques than was true in previous editions.

5. There is a brand new chapter on cognitive-behavioral therapy. Although previous editions addressed this increasingly popular form of therapy in a number of chapters, reviewers felt that the topic was worthy of a separate chapter.

The third edition, like the second, has benefitted greatly from reviews and criticism of prior editions. I have accommodated most of the suggestions made by these reviewers and critics, both academics and practitioners.

I continue to explore theories of criminal behavior, something which more and more "hard-headed" practitioners are realizing is important. The book begins with an exploration of criminal behavior from sociological, psychological, and biosocial perspectives. It is my belief that adequate assessment and counseling of any type of client, criminal or otherwise, must proceed from an adequate understanding of the presenting problem. As a former police officer and probation officer, I am aware that many practitioners distrust theory, but as an academic with practical experience, I also am aware of the links between theory and practice. Practice without theory is like a cart without a horse—it won't go anywhere. In writing these theory chapters, I constantly kept before me the question: "How does this theoretical discussion enhance the practitioners' understanding of criminal behavior they will experience in practice?"

Chapter 3 (Biosocial theories) has been completely rewritten, which largely reflects the tremendous growth in our knowledge of the biological underpinnings of much of our behavior in recent years.

The chapters on interviewing and counseling are geared exclusively to the correctional client. The chapter on interviewing contains a section on interrogation, and the counseling chapters address individual and group counseling in both community and institutional settings.

Unlike most counseling works, this one recognizes that proper assessment is a necessity before any type of counseling or other intervention is attempted. Thus, I have included two chapters on assessment and classification, which include numerous examples of the various instruments now used in corrections for this purpose. The professional assessment of clients has been a central part of the counseling course I teach, and I have always found it useful to use case studies. The instructor's manual (also updated) contains a variety of cases in presentence investigation report format. I use these cases to role play and to provide students with practice in using the various assessment and classification tools. I also include an essay written by Dr. Carl Clements, perhaps the foremost authority on correctional assessment and classification in the United States today.

I also recognize that correctional clients need more than counseling to turn their lives around. The correctional worker is as much a broker of community resources as a counselor or supervising agent. Consistent with that view, I include a chapter outlining how correctional workers can use community resources, including volunteers.

Recognizing and including the community in the goals of contemporary corrections work is at the heart of the philosophy of restorative justice.

This book encompasses a tremendous amount of material, all of which is available in more detail elsewhere. As I point out in the chapter on presentence report writing, the secret of professional report writing is the ability to glean from voluminous and diverse sources all that is necessary—not merely nice—to know. I hope that I have done that in this book.

I would like to acknowledge the input of the academics and correctional practitioners who reviewed the manuscripts for each of these editions. I also thank professors and students who informally have discussed with me the strengths and weaknesses of the previous edition, and the professionals who have shared their field experiences with us in their *Perspective from the Field*. Thanks also to my editor, Alice Fins, whose good-natured encouragement and advice helped get me through this extensive revision. All these people have contributed to making this edition a better one than it otherwise would have been.

Special thanks once again to my wife, Grace Jean (a.k.a. "Grace the face"). People sometimes ask me why I go around whistling and singing all the time like the village idiot. Grace's love has adorned me across the years and has made my heart sing and my mind dance, so if I'm a fool, I'm a fool for love. Thank you, Facie.

Chapter 1

Understanding the Need for Theory

There is nothing so practical as a good theory.

Kurt Lewin

The purpose of this book is to introduce students to the process of "correcting" the antisocial behavior of criminally convicted offenders. Correcting offenders' antisocial behavior means that some correctional agency or institution is charged with attempting to change undesirable behavior to desirable or appropriate behavior while offenders are in custody or under supervision. There is a great deal of skepticism and cynicism surrounding the corrective process, which is exemplified by the frequently heard lament that "nothing works." Such attitudes have some basis in reality, but often they are not warranted. If we believe that "nothing works," then we in the corrections field will operate consistently with this belief, and the outcome will justify our beliefs. If we believe that people can change, and that many do so every day, then we will act in accordance with that belief and also will find it vindicated—prophecies tend to be self-fulfilling. Of course, you will run into some people for whom it is true that nothing works. Realize also that no one thing works for everybody. Nevertheless, some things work for some people some of the time, and other things work for other people at other times.

Casework, Assessment, Counseling, and Criminal Justice

Casework, or *case management*, in corrections is simply the management of cases on a caseload. And, a "case" is the records and details of a particular offender's offenses, supervision history, and progress toward the goal of rehabilitation, or habilitation, since many offenders never have experienced anything approaching satisfactory social adjustment in the first place (Crow, 1998). Like everything else, casework can be accomplished well or poorly, depending on the personality, knowledge, and motivation the caseworker brings to the task. He or she can work the case by assuming a *reactive* posture by supervising and conducting surveillance of offenders until they do something wrong and then pouncing on them. This is better than nothing, but it is not nearly as productive as *proactive* casework in which the aim is to prevent that "something wrong" from ever happening. The motivating idea behind proactive correctional casework is not "bleeding-heartism," it is the recognition that the community is best protected through strategies that aid offenders in their efforts to live up to community standards. The community is safe to the extent that those who prey on it cease to do so.

Proactive case management involves the design and implementation of monitored programs of activity with the goal of assisting offenders to lead productive and law-abiding lives. Integral components of good proactive casework are assessment and counseling.

Assessment is the process of subjecting an offender to a formal evaluation and analysis of his or her deficiencies and needs, and the risks he or she poses to the community so that realistic counseling plans and strategies can be worked out. Assessment is accomplished with the use of well-researched and tested instruments, some of which are included or referenced in this book. Attempting to supervise, counsel, and otherwise help an offender without a thorough assessment is rather like a physician performing surgery without first conducting a thorough diagnostic work-up of a patient.

Counseling is a process in which offenders are led to explore their feelings and concerns; in the case of offenders, many of those feelings and concerns have led them to behave irresponsibly. We hope that the counseling process will lead offenders to an increased awareness of the self-destructive nature of their behavior and of alternative behavior choices. It aims at removing barriers to self-direction and personal growth and uncovering resources that offenders can use to forge a prosocial lifestyle.

Correctional counseling is different from general counseling in three important ways:

(1)   offenders, generally, do not seek counseling voluntarily, and so you are more likely to encounter more reluctance and resistance to the counseling process than you would have in other counseling settings;

(2)   offenders, in general, have fewer coping resources on which to draw than do clients in other counseling settings; and

(3)   offenders often have a psychological and economic investment in retaining their current lifestyle.

It was these differences that led to the writing of this book. Few general counseling texts address the special problems of dealing with offenders with their special needs.

We also enjoy an advantage in corrections that counselors in other areas do not have. This advantage is that we often possess a wealth of verified information about offenders' backgrounds and past behavior from a variety of sources such as juvenile files, police reports, and social and psychological evaluations. This information allows us to assess offenders more readily than counselors can in many other settings.

But even before a physician conducts a diagnostic work-up, he or she must have a grounding in the disease or condition that could account for the patient's complaint. Similarly, you should have a grounding in the causes of the type of behavior that you are trying to correct. Using this analogy, this author has structured his book around (1) *understanding* criminal behavior and its correlates, (2) *assessing* the individual problems and needs of offenders, and (3) *using* that understanding and knowledge to effectively counsel offenders.

Criminology is the study of the causes of crime. It is, or should be, an interdisciplinary study, encompassing genetics, neurology, physiology, psychology, economics, and sociology (Ellis and Walsh, 2000). Yet, much of criminology is limited to sociological analysis. Individual differences often are ignored, and one gets the impression from sociological criminology that everything is responsible for crime *except* the people who commit it. The problem is that while sociological insights are of tremendous importance in understanding crime, they do not exhaust the causal possibilities.

This is not a textbook on criminological theory, and no effort has been made to be comprehensive in this area. The theories of criminology that are briefly presented should help you to understand more fully the theories of counseling addressed later and should enhance the quality of your application of them in practice. In other words, *we are interested in criminological theories here only in so far as they provide a foundation upon which counseling techniques can be grounded.* We begin with a discussion of the usefulness of theory in general, and then go on to examine theories of the etiology (cause) of crime.

The Usefulness of Theory

Workers in any field must understand the nature of the phenomena with which they work. As a correctional practitioner, or as a student aspiring to be a practitioner, you must understand the phenomenon of crime and its causation so that you may deal more effectively with offenders under your supervision. As Goff and Owens (1999:25) put it: "Public policy and agency practice in the field of probation and parole must be guided by a theory of why people commit crime. In order to intervene [to prevent further offending] there must be an understanding of the causative factors of the original offense." Cullen and Gendreau (2000:145) augment this view when they write: "[C]orrectional treatments must be based on criminological knowledge." Theories of crime seek to offer plausible explanations of how the known correlates of crime are linked together. Empirically generated facts are silent, in themselves. Only theories of their interrelationships give voice to what otherwise would be a babble of unintelligible static.

A *theory* is an intellectual scaffold around which is constructed an edifice of useful knowledge. Empirical facts are the bricks of the edifice, each one slotted into its proper place to form a coherent whole. Given the numerous competing theories of crime causation, you may be forgiven for asking which one is "true."

Physicians do not ask which theory of disease is the true one, because they know that there are many different kinds of diseases for which there are many different causes. No physician ever treats a person for "illness." Rather, he or she treats a specific disease syndrome. Like disease, crime is not a unitary phenomenon explicable in terms of a single cause or set of causes. But, we tend to think and act as if it were when we treat all offenders for "criminality." Even treatment for specific disease syndromes often varies according to such things as age and gender, and are differentially successful according to how cooperative patients are, their personality type, and the level of psychosocial support they enjoy. Why should it be any different when dealing with criminals in all their diversity?

Theories about crime and criminality must be context-specific, but even then, theories never are considered true in any absolute sense. Truth for the scientist is tentative, relative, and open to qualification and falsification. If a theory generates useful empirical research and provides order and consistency within the domain of interest, we are more faithful to the spirit of science to call it adequate rather than to call it true. An *adequate theory* must conform to the pragmatic, correspondence, and coherence theories of truth as outlined by philosophers of science. That is, a theory is "true" to the extent that it (1) provides useful guidance for the further exploration of the phenomena of interest, (2) corresponds with the factual data already known about the phenomena of interest, and (3) fits those data into propositions to form a logically connected and coherent whole.

Thus, the usefulness of a given theory is context-specific. It would be of little help to a sociologist seeking to explain fluctuations in the crime rate over the past fifty years, for instance, to learn that neurophysiologists have discovered that a certain category of criminal shows a higher-than-expected frequency of dysfunction involving certain regions of the brain. Likewise, the neurophysiologist is little interested in the sociocultural variables alleged by the sociologists to account for differentials in the crime rate.

The sociologists and the neurophysiologists are simply dealing with different units of analysis: societies and brains, respectively. Criminal justice practitioners seeking to understand offenders, however, must be sensitive to the macro- (large-scale) analyses of the sociologist and the micro- (small-scale) analyses of the physiologist, as well as to all the disciplines in between that attempt to understand the phenomena of crime and criminality at their particular level of analysis.

Becoming sensitive to these perspectives does not mean that you have to become expert in them all, which is plainly impossible. It does mean that you should become acquainted with them and understand their language. Much of the heat generated by theorists of different macro and micro persuasions results from failing to distinguish between crime and criminality.

Crime refers to socially disapproved behavior, the rates of which fluctuate with various social, political, and economic conditions over time. Anyone can run afoul of the law and commit an out-of-character crime given a chance permutation of factors conducive to it. *Criminality*, on the other hand, refers to "stable differences across individuals in the propensity to commit criminal (or equivalent) acts" (Wilson and Herrnstein, 1985:23). Crime is thus a fluctuating property of sociopolitical systems, but *criminality* is a fairly stable property of individuals. It is fair to say that sociologists are more interested in crime, and other types of scientists are more interested in criminality.

As a correctional worker dealing with individuals, quite naturally, you will find theories dealing with individuals' behavior and their immediate environment to be the most suitable for your purposes. After all, these are the areas most accessible to perception and most amenable to change within the context of the correctional worker/offender relationship. Nevertheless, when you are engaged in interviewing, assessing, and counseling criminal offenders, you will be able to perform the task more professionally if you have an adequate understanding of crime causation at all levels of analysis. Therefore, we shall briefly examine five theories of criminality dealing with different levels of analysis ranging from the macrosociological to the psychophysiological..

Figure 1.1 is a schematic diagram representing the route or routes that may have led offenders to you. It begins with the forces in the larger sociocultural environment that are considered to be *criminogenic* (crime generating). Although there are a number of contending theories at all levels, we will consider the most well-known at each level. Anomie/strain theory illustrates criminological theory at its most comprehensive or at its macrolevel.

Figure 1.1
Criminal "Causal" Funnel and Explanatory Theories

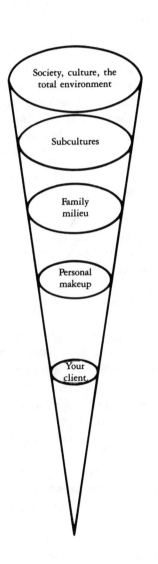

ANOMIE
Cultural values, norms, social structure, lack of legitimate opportunities

DIFFERENTIAL ASSOCIATION
Gangs, peer pressure to conform to subcultural values and beliefs opposed to lawful behavior

CONTROL
Unique personal experiences leading to lack of attachment and to criminal beliefs

PSYCHOPATHY/LOVE DEPRIVATION
Thinking and acting patterns of criminals

LIFESTYLE THEORY/BIOSOCIAL FACTORS
Inherited and acquired characteristics, such as differential autonomic nervous system functioning, possibly resulting from severe love deprivation in childhood

CHARACTERISTIC WAYS OF THINKING
Alcoholism, drug addiction, personal problems, "bad attitude"

Differential association theory provides a less inclusive analysis. The subcultural branch of this theory holds that all Americans share the larger sociocultural environment of the United States, but only a rather small portion of us share in subcultures declared criminogenic by differential association theory. Even individuals within a criminogenic subculture experience different socialization within the context of the family environment. These experiences are the subject matter of control theory, which focuses on the family. Taking the analysis one step further, we recognize that similar environmental experiences can have vastly different effects on different people.

Biosocial theories examine how individual biological differences interact with environmental factors to produce criminal behavior. Lifestyle theory, although concentrating on thinking patterns, incorporates concepts from many other theories to attempt to explain why criminals think the way that they do. Lifestyle theory will be examined in Chapter 11 when we discuss cognitive-behavioral treatment programs for offenders.

Please note that the diagram implies intimate connections among all levels of analysis. This does not mean that each of the theories cannot stand alone as a plausible explanation of crime at its respective level of analysis. Neither does it mean that a person who commits a crime because he or she lacks legitimate opportunity (as anomie theory sets forth) necessarily belongs to a gang (as differential association theory describes), or lacks family attachments (as control theory proposes). It simply means that the development of individuals cannot be viewed in isolation from the micro or macro environments that constitute their reality, nor can the effects of those environments be separated from the effects of the personal attributes and unique experiences individuals bring to them.

Correctional Philosophy and Restorative Justice

This book is about correctional *counseling* theory and practice, without a great deal of attention to the broader topic of *correctional theory* and practice. However, the area of correctional theory with broad applicability to our purposes is the ideology or philosophy of punishment and justice that is in vogue within the criminal justice system. After all, correctional workers' day-to-day practices and decisions relating to offenders are heavily influenced by the prevailing correctional philosophy whether they are aware of it or not (Lauen, 1997).

Two guiding philosophies have jockeyed for preeminence throughout the present century: the retributive and the rehabilitative (sometimes referred to as the just deserts and treatment models, respectively). Both philosophies are offender-driven (that is, what do we do with the offender?), and both have been severely criticized as ineffectual. Partly in response to these criticisms, a new philosophical model has arisen which, according to its supporters, has taken workable aspects from both older models, thrown out the unworkable, and added some concepts of its own. This new philosophy or guiding framework is called *restorative justice.*

The philosophy of restorative justice was formally endorsed as a policy on sentencing by the American Correctional Association (ACA) at the Congress of Correction in St. Louis in 1994 and reviewed and amended in 1999. This ACA policy statement avers that:

. . . sentencing should have as a major purpose restorative justice— righting the harm done to the victim and the community. The restorative focus should be both process and substantively oriented. The victims or their representative should be included in the 'justice' process. The sentencing procedure should address the needs of the victim[s], including their need to be heard and as much as possible to be and feel restored to whole again.

As we see from the American Correctional Association's policy statement, restorative justice should be as much victim- as offender-driven. The primary defining difference between restorative justice and previous models is its belief in the effectiveness of active community participation in the corrections endeavor. Correctional theorists long have contended that corrections cannot reintegrate the offender successfully back into the community without the community's active help and support (Bazemore, 2000). This philosophy has been applauded widely because it humanizes justice by bringing victim and offender together to negotiate a mutually satisfying way to correct the wrong done. Although developed for juveniles, restorative justice has been fruitfully applied to nonviolent adult offenders (Crow, 1998). Restorative justice principles are being implemented in correctional departments across the country. The Minnesota Department of Corrections has incorporated them into its mission statement, its training academy, and into its promotion requirements for all institutional and community corrections agents and officers (Pranis, 1996).

Just as the retributive model emerged (or more accurately, reemerged) after the alleged failure of the treatment or medical model, the restorative justice model has emerged with the apparent failure of such punishment-oriented efforts as "Scared Straight" programs, shock probation, and boot camps (Welch, 1996). Strong victims' rights/advocacy movements also have played a leading role in the emergence of the model (Shapiro, 1990).

Restorative justice differs from the other models in several important ways. Perhaps, most fundamentally, it "personalizes" crime by defining it as a harmful act committed by one person against another rather than an act committed against an abstraction called "the state." This recognition of concrete victims provides an entree for the offender to be actively involved in repairing the harm done and *restoring* the situation to its pre-crime status.

Under the older models, the "debt" incurred by the offender was owed to "society," and arguments about the extent of that debt took place (and still do, of course) between professionals standing in for the real victim and victimizer. The restorative justice model seeks to replace this method of obtaining justice with more direct involvement of victims to the extent that it is feasible and desirable. Make no mistake, this is not a new age "touchy feely" approach to corrections. It holds offenders fully accountable for their actions by applying appropriate punishment and adds the additional dimensions by requiring offenders to accept responsibility for taking action to repair the harm done (Bazemore, 2000).

Within the wide philosophical umbrella of restorative justice are a number of specific programs. The so-called *balanced approach* has the broadest scope. The balanced approach (to justice) is so named because it gives approximately equal weight to three important objectives in corrections work: (1) community protection, (2) offender accountability, and (3) offender competency. The community, the victim, and the offender are viewed as equal clients of the criminal justice system, and all are presumed to receive tangible benefits from the restorative process (Bazemore and Maloney, 1994).

The desired initial results of this balanced approach process are that victims' losses are restored and that victims and offenders become reconciled. The belief is that to the extent that both victim and victimizer come to see that basic fairness and justice is attained when a violation of one person by another is made right by the violator, the violator will have taken a step to reformation and the community will be a safer place in which to live (Coates, 1990:133).

You should realize that this is an idealized description, and that this approach no more "works" in every case than do more traditional punitive or treatment approaches. Some people are skeptical that such an approach, best applied in close-knit homogeneous communities, can work in our loosely knit heterogeneous urban society (Walker, 2001). It is true that much of the promise of restorative justice has yet to be proven, but it does have many unique properties that recommend it over the old models. Thus, correctional casework and counseling should take note of the aims of restorative justice. Frequent references to restorative justice are made throughout this book. Dr. Kay Carter, a pioneer in this approach, provides in her Perspective from the Field an excellent summary of the balanced approach.

Perspective from the Field:
Restorative Justice and the Balanced Approach
By Kay Carter, Ph.D.

Dr. Carter is the director of the Ada County, Idaho, Juvenile Court Services. She has been a pioneer in the development and teaching of the balanced approach in juvenile corrections. In addition to her work at the juvenile court, Dr. Carter is an adjunct faculty member of the criminal justice, social work, and dispute resolution departments at Boise State University.

The balanced approach was originally developed as a model for juvenile probation, but it also can be applied to probation work with adults. The application of this model has accomplished a great deal in juvenile justice, not the least of which is the reconciliation of historically opposing views. As an intern coordinator, it always has struck me that social work students tend to see juvenile justice issues in shades of gray, while criminal justice students tend to see juvenile justice issues only in black and white.

As criminal justice students move into the profession, it is necessary to provide them with training that will allow them to develop a more empathetic and understanding approach to working with delinquent youth, and to help social work professionals develop a better understanding and appreciation of the necessity for holding delinquent youth accountable.

Applying the balanced approach to juvenile probation has clarified and simplified the training for new probation officers. It also has reduced philosophical tensions within the agency, as everyone, regardless of their personal views, must endorse the values and goals of the balanced approach. Balanced approach training is so important that it is an upper division course elective for both criminal justice and social work majors.

The balanced approach model requires probation officers to assess youth and develop case plans giving equal consideration to community protection/public safety, youth accountability, and competency development. By doing so, probation officers and agencies no longer struggle with the age-old philosophical dichotomy of punishment versus rehabilitation, because each youth must be assessed individually within the context of the balanced approach, ultimately accomplishing punishment (accountability), rehabilitation (competency development), and community protection (detention, probation).

After the development of the balanced approach model, others built upon this model and overlaid or encircled it with the concept of restorative justice. The restorative justice concept is holistic, in that it views crime as harmful to victims, communities, and offenders and sees the primary mission of corrections as ensuring that harm is repaired, in other words restoring victims and communities, and making amends. Offenders who are individually assessed using the balanced approach might have a case plan, which requires them to give back to the victim in some way (through reparation, restitution, mediation, and so on); to participate in competency development designed to provide them new skills, and to assist in restoring them to a more productive lifestyle; and giving back to the community through community service.

The following case is an example of how a probation officer might apply the balanced approach with restorative justice to a youth who has committed a crime:

A. G., age fifteen, admitted to the court that he and two friends had committed petty theft and burglary at a local store. This was his first offense. His parents, though divorced, were supportive of A. G. and he was not judged to be at high risk to reoffend. His probation plan required the following:

1. Community Protection:
    a. Sixty days detention, suspended
    b. Serve one year of probation
2. Competency Development:
    a. Complete a decision-making class
    b. Pay for and complete a petty theft class
    c. Obtain a drug/alcohol assessment and complete the recommendations contained therein
    d. Abstain from any use of drugs/alcohol while on probation
    e. Complete a law-related education class
3. Accountability:
    a. Pay all petition fees
    b. Perform forty hours of community service
    c. Have no avoidable contact with the codefendants
4. Restorative Justice:
    a. Write a letter of apology to the store (victim)
    b. Attend a victim's panel
    c. Participate in victim/offender mediation, if desired by the victim

Many juvenile justice professionals believe that the community must be involved for justice truly to occur. The community is both a part of the problem as well as a part of the solution. If many delinquency issues grow out of problems in the community, school, or family, then it is clearly one-sided to focus the solution on the individual involved. Restorative justice, in the purest sense, requires institutions and individuals to change, to be accountable, and to participate in promoting strategies for safer communities.

This is an exciting time in juvenile justice because the system is shifting from its singular focus on offenders to a dual focus on offenders and victims. New victims' rights legislation has been instrumental in causing many of the changes the system is making, and heightened awareness of victims' needs has been the impetus for additional changes. Ada County (Idaho) Juvenile Court Services has implemented a victims' program, in which trained volunteers visit the home of all victims of juvenile crime to inform them about the court, its operations, its language, victims' rights, and programs for victims, which the court operates. The victim-impact program uses students and volunteers to provide many of these services, with one full-time paid coordinator. Victims now have a voice in how an offender should make amends, be held accountable, provide community protection, and develop competency.

To ensure that probation staff are fully using the balanced approach, every court report must address the three areas of the balanced approach. Additionally, probation officers are provided with intensive training in leading groups and are expected to facilitate or cofacilitate competency-development groups. This accomplishes many goals, such as allowing the probation officer to count the group session as a probation "contact," seeing youths in a group environment with their peers, assessing competency-development needs firsthand, and helping to prevent burnout by providing job variety and enhanced skill development for probation officers.

Probation officers within our juvenile court now have significant resources available to them as they use the balanced approach. Among the programs available at our court are the victims' program, community service program, weekend detention, an alternative school, and an employment program, as well as a variety of competency-building groups on such topics as anger management, decision making, and thinking errors. Additionally, the court now is focusing more attention on the parents of youthful offenders and involving them in competency-building groups. The parent project and parent-adolescent groups are being offered on a regular basis at the court, with some parents court ordered to attend.

Many of our programs such as the parent project, community service, and the victim-impact program are funded by grants, with grant funds used to pay trained mediators and facilitators. One of the unforeseen benefits of the balanced approach is that it also provides a funding road map for agencies. Resources must be allocated in a balanced way, with all three objectives (community protection, accountability, and competency development) being considered of equal importance.

Retributive justice has gained much public attention recently. Politicians and the public alike are concerned about crime, particularly juvenile crime, and demand a "just get tough" policy. However, public vengeance and provision of punishment through our traditional adversarial processes have not been shown to be particularly effective, and the cost both in terms of human beings and dollars is prohibitive. It seems more appropriate to approach corrections from a restorative framework, focusing on repairing the damage or harm done to victims and communities, while holding offenders accountable and helping them to develop more competencies.

Juvenile probation officers (care workers in other jurisdictions) in our department are required to assess the strengths and weaknesses of the family and to formulate a case plan to address them. The balanced approach takes an eclectic approach to probation practices and explanations of delinquency. The practice and application of the balanced approach seem to be acceptable to the general public, politicians, and practitioners—a rare achievement. Finally, the balanced approach and restorative justice model provide a logical framework for making funding decisions and allocating resources.

Summary

This author obviously believes that rehabilitation is possible with a thoroughly professional approach to the business of correcting the offender's behavior through proactive casework. Many negatives are associated with counseling offenders, foremost of which is the nonvoluntary nature of the offender/counselor relationship. However, there are also certain advantages not found in other types of client/counselor relationships such as the availability of a great deal of information about the offender, well-tested assessment tools, and the amount of control you can exercise over offenders' activities.

The usefulness of theory must be emphasized. Practitioners of any profession must be fully grounded in the knowledge available to that profession. Remember, theory is the jumping-off point for adequate practice. Without some theoretical understanding of the phenomena with which you are working, you will be floundering in the dark, making mistakes, and possibly thwarting offenders' chances of becoming useful citizens.

The philosophy of restorative justice recognizes both the need to involve victims (and their need for justice) and the offenders' need for reformation. This process strives to instill in both victims and victimizers the belief that they have attained fairness and justice, and thus, there is a rehabilitative effect on the offender.

References and Suggested Readings

Bazemore, G. 2000. What's "New" About the Balanced Approach? In P. Kratkoski, ed. *Correctional Counseling and Treatment*. Prospect Heights, Illinois: Waveland Press.

Bazemore, G. and D. Maloney. 1994. Rehabilitative community service: Toward restorative service sanctions in a balanced justice system. *Federal Probation*. 58:24-35.

Coates, R. 1990. Victim-Offender Reconciliation Programs in North America. In B. Galaway and J. Hudson, eds. *Criminal Justice, Restitution, and Reconciliation*. Monsey, New York: Criminal Justice Press.

Crow, A. 1998. Restorative justice and offender rehabilitation: A meeting of the minds. *Perspectives*. 22:28-40.

Cullen, F. and P. Gendreau. 2000. Assessing Correctional Rehabilitation: Policy, Practice, and Prospects. In *Criminal Justice 2000*. Washington, DC: National Institute of Justice.

Ellis, L. and A. Walsh. 2000. *Criminology: A Global Perspective*. Boston: Allyn and Bacon.

Goff, D. and B. Owens. 1999. Results driven supervision. *Perspectives*. 23:24-27.

Lauen, Roger. 1997. *Positive Approaches to Corrections: Research, Policy, and Practice*. Lanham, Maryland: American Correctional Association.

Pranis, K. 1996. Restorative justice catching on in Minnesota corrections. *Overcrowded Times*. 7:1-9.

Shapiro, R. 1990. Is Restitution Legislation the Chameleon of the Victims' Movement? In Galaway, B. and J. Hudson, eds. *Criminal Justice, Restitution, and Reconciliation*. Monsey, New York: Criminal Justice Press.

Walker, S. 2001. *Sense and Nonsense about Crime and Drugs: A Policy Guide*. Belmont, California: Wadsworth.

Welch, M. 1996. *Corrections: A Critical Approach*. New York: McGraw-Hill.

Wilson, J. and R. Herrnstein.1985. *Crime and Human Nature*. New York: Simon and Schuster.

Chapter 2

Sociological and Psychological Theories

Criminological theories are often not so much proven wrong as simply pushed to one side in favor of newer interpretations. The hope of the social sciences, of course, is to achieve an elegant simplicity, and perhaps in time the explanation of the crime will form a coherent whole.

Gresham Sykes

Anomie/Strain Theory

The term *anomie* is a French one meaning "lacking in rules" or "normlessness." It is a relative term, for no society is completely lacking in rules for the regulation of social life. French sociologist Emile Durkheim first used this term in his book *The Division of Labor in Society* (1951). His basic idea was that as societies become increasingly complex, the problem of maintaining social cohesion becomes more problematic. Crime (as well as other forms of deviance) grows in proportion to the loss of social cohesion. A loss of social cohesion means that there will be considerable ambiguity and contradictions regarding the rules and standards of moral behavior.

Durkheim, however, did not view crime as abnormal. He argued that because crime is found at all times and in all societies, it is a normal and inevitable phenomenon. What needs to be examined, according to Durkheim, are the social-structural conditions and contradictions that result in different levels of criminal activity in different nations and at different times (Durkheim, 1950). The 300 percent increase in Hungarian crime since the demise of communism (Gonczol, 1993) and the roughly similar figures reported from the former Soviet Union (Dashkov, 1992) attest dramatically to the criminogenic effects of rapid social change.

American sociologist Robert Merton expanded Durkheim's concept of anomie to develop a popular sociocultural explanation of crime, more commonly known as *strain theory*. Like all other macrosociological theories of crime, Merton's anomie/strain theory uses a frame of reference that involves three major elements: social structure, social values, and social norms. This theory views crime not as a symptom of personal inadequacies but rather as a "normal" response to the various ways that these sociocultural elements impinge on and limit the responses of certain groups of individuals.

According to anomie theory, the basic cause of crime is not to be found within individuals. Rather, it is structural contradictions within society that place *strain* on individuals, which may lead them to commit crimes. Merton identifies the structural contradiction or the disjunction or contradiction between the cultural value of material success and the lack of equal access to legitimate means of accomplishing it as the most important factor in terms of generating criminal behavior. As Merton (1957:146) put it:

> It is only when a system of cultural values extols, virtually above all else, certain common success goals for the population at large while the social structure rigorously restricts or completely closes access to approved modes of reaching these goals for a considerable part of the same population, that deviant behavior ensues on a large scale.

Although the theories presented here were formulated in an American context, they also apply to other societies that share to one degree or another similar values and social arrangements. American society has taken what traditionally morality considered to be base and evil—acquisitiveness and usury—and elevated them to the status of prescriptive (required or recommended) goals. Material things (SUVs, DVD players, and Tommy Hilfiger clothes) equal happiness, prestige, and self-worth in the American equation. If you do not possess at least a modicum of these visible trappings of self-worth, it is obvious to all that something is remiss in your character—you are not a participant in the "American Dream." Pause and reflect a moment: is this not the constant message you receive from all quarters on a daily basis? Are not the most popular heroes of the movies and television rich and powerful men and women playing with a lot of expensive toys? To maintain a sense of self-worth, then, individuals are exhorted to strive to achieve culturally approved goals.

According to this theory, however, certain groups of individuals are systematically denied access to the competition because of various structural impediments such as race and class. In other words, we all are encouraged to develop champagne tastes, even if we only have beer budgets. It is not the beer budget per se that generates the sort of dissatisfaction that may lead to crime, it is the size of one's budget relative to the size of one's culturally defined wants and needs. It is difficult to be happy, as Eastern philosophers long have maintained, if expectations exceed accomplishments or if wants and needs are not proportionate to means. As Durkheim himself dramatically put it (1951:246): "No living being can be happy or even exist unless his needs are sufficiently proportioned to his means." Happiness can be viewed as an equation:

$$happiness = \frac{accomplishments}{expectations \text{ or } goals}$$

To bring this equation into balance, individuals either have to increase their accomplishments or decrease their expectations. In other words, people have to adapt.

Modes of Adaptation

Merton identifies five modes or methods of adaptation to a social structure that exhorts us all to strive for accomplishments but which denies some persons legitimate access to the means by which they can be realized. This is due to the processes of conformity, ritualism, "retreatism," rebellion, and innovation.

CONFORMITY

Most of us are conformists in this Mertonian sense; if we were not, our society as it is now constituted would be in a lot of trouble. *Conformists* are individuals who accept the validity of the cultural goals and of the socially approved methods of achieving them. Such people quietly live out their lives and probably never will get themselves into any serious trouble with the law.

RITUALISM

The *ritualist* is the nine-to-five slugger who has long given up on ever achieving the prescribed cultural goals but who, nevertheless, continues to work ritually within the boundaries set forth as legitimate. Although Merton considered the ritualist adaptation as deviant because of the rejection of the cultural goals, it is not a criminal adaptation. The ritualist, satisfied with the security his or her job provides, is rarely in trouble with the law.

"RETREATISM"

The *"retreatist"* rejects both the cultural goals and the institutionalized means of attaining them. People in this category drop out of society and often take refuge in drugs, alcohol, and transiency. They are frequently in trouble with the law because of crimes committed to support a drug and/or alcohol habit. This type of individual often presents the greatest challenge to the criminal justice worker.

REBELLION

Rebels reject both the goals and the means of capitalist American society, but, unlike retreatists, they wish to substitute alternative goals and alternative means. They are committed to some form of sociopolitical ideal, such as socialism, which they believe will provide a more just and equitable society. You rarely will have to deal with rebels unless they become radicalized to the point of putting ideology into actions that break the law.

INNOVATION

Finally, we have the *innovator*. This individual fully accepts the validity of the cultural goals of monetary success but rejects (possibly because of having been denied access to them) the legitimate means of attaining them. The innovator best exemplifies Taylor, Walton, and Young's (1973:93) image of American society: "The desire to make money without regard to the means in which one sets about doing it is symptomatic of the malintegration at the heart of American society." Innovators do not work and stash a few dollars in the bank, and then watch it slowly gather interest; that is for suckers. It is a lot faster, takes a lot less effort, and is far more exciting to rob a bank. In other words, crime is an innovative avenue to success—a method by which deprived people get what they have been taught by their culture to want.

General Strain Theory

Criminologist Robert Agnew extended the Durkheimian/Mertonian concept of strain, which he considered too limiting, in a series of papers in the 1980s-1990s leading to what he calls *general strain theory*. Agnew's extension broadens the concept of strain to include many other strains besides being prevented from achieving goals. Agnew (1992:50) adds strain resulting from efforts by others to remove or threaten to remove things we value (such as the termination of a job or valued relationship), and strain resulting from others who present us with negative or noxious stimuli (such as being a victim of child abuse or sexual harassment).

More importantly, Agnew includes the variety of ways people respond to those strains, and the characteristics of individuals that might lead them to adopt one response rather than another. Identifying those who perceive a situation as a criminal opportunity and those who do not is obviously important. According to Agnew, the personal traits which may help us to differentiate between those who choose one option over the other include ". . . temperament, intelligence, creativity, problem-solving skills, interpersonal skills, self-efficacy, and self-esteem" (1992:71). Simply put, strain is likely to lead to crime or delinquency when the individual cannot effectively manage it.

Agnew (1997) has gone even further more recently to move strain theory from its original macrosocial context to include ADHD (attention deficit, hyperactivity disorder), impulsivity, and insensitivity to his list of individual differences that contribute to criminality. More recently, Walsh (2000) has attempted to place strain theory in a behavioral genetic context by pointing out that all the individual differences Agnew describes are moderately to highly heritable (the degree to which a trait is attributable to genetic factors). If the traits contributing to criminality are heritable, and if these traits are also negatively associated with the achievement of occupational success, they cannot be ignored. Figure 2.1 presents a diagrammatic representation of anomie/strain theory.

Figure 2.1
Anomie/Strain Theory

Success ("American Dream") upheld as goal; everyone in culture strives for it → Access to legitimate means to achieve goal denied to significant numbers in society

ANOMIE (disjunction between goals and means) → Individuals adapt to anomie in various ways →

	Goals	Means
Conformity	+	+
Ritualism	-	+
Retreatism	-	-
Rebellion	±	±
Innovation	+	-

+ = accepts;
- = rejects;
± = rejects prevailing goals and means but wants to substitute new goals and means

LESSONS AND CONCERNS

As useful as this theory may be to the macrosociologist, it has little practical utility for the correctional worker dealing with individual "retreatists" or "innovators." The correctional worker could derive few, if any, employable policy recommendations from it. In part, this is the reason why this, and many other sociological theories, often are rejected by those in positions of power within the criminal justice system (Gilsinan, 1990:103). The "cure" for crime logically derived from anomie theory is the expansion of legitimate opportunities and equal access to them. But every correctional worker can recount numerous instances in which he or she has labored to obtain employment for offenders only to see them "blow it" for one reason or another in short order. It is not enough simply to provide jobs for some offenders who may have come to prefer taking advantage of illegitimate opportunities.

As a criminal justice worker, you must convince such people of the ultimate futility of their short-run hedonism and the necessity of their becoming responsible human beings. Offenders have to be convinced to make a realistic assessment of their situations and to adjust their aspirations accordingly. Further, you must not be seduced into accepting the propositions of anomie theory as excuses for criminal behavior. Being a criminal does not necessarily mean that legitimate opportunities have not been made available, the assertions of Merton notwithstanding. In fact, one of the flaws in anomie theory is that it is tautologous (it argues circuitously). That is, it poses a cause of crime (lack of legitimate opportunity) and then uses the alleged effects of that cause (crime) as a measure of the opportunities one has not had (Nettler, 1978:252).

Agnew's extension of anomie/strain theory is more useful, although his concept of strain has expanded to include anything and everything that might frustrate a person. Is he really adding anything to the classical notion that humans are animals fundamentally motivated by the desire to maximize pleasure and minimize pain? The more useful part of his theory lies in pulling us back to the understanding that people are very different, and those differences determine whether strain (which we all experience in one way or another in Agnew's conceptualization) leads to criminal behavior. For instance, Merton makes much of strain generated by the lack of occupational success, but he views this lack as entirely the result of social discrimination. Agnew's inclusion of intelligence and temperament provides us with an alternate explanation of why some people do not achieve occupational success. Nothing predicts occupational success in an open society better than IQ and conscientiousness (reviewed in Walsh, 2000).

A lesson of anomie theory that is worth the attention of corrections workers is the notion that criminal behavior can be a rational response to social conditions as they are perceived by the offender. *Rational* means that there is a logical fit between a desired goal and the means used to attain it. Rational action in pursuit of a goal does not imply that the action is "right" or "moral." It merely means that those engaging in such action have sought a goal at a price they feel that they can afford. A criminal who risks life and limb in the illegitimate pursuit of legitimate cultural goals is certainly not behaving irrationally from the point of view of a middle-class observer. But rationality must be defined in terms of the actor, not the observer. The innovator simply has more to gain and less to lose through criminal activity than does the middle-class observer. Of course, middle-class folks themselves can be "innovators" if the price is right. Perhaps realization of this will lead you to develop a deficiency explanation rather than a pathological definition of criminal behavior. Therefore, you can view criminals as deficient in the attributes that produce lawful-behavior—not psychologically defective (unless proven otherwise).

Differential Association Theory

Differential association theory, first formulated by sociologist Edwin Sutherland in the 1930s (Sutherland and Cressey, 1978), focuses on subcultural elements (as opposed to personal characteristics) that may predispose an individual to one or another of Merton's adaptations. This theory stresses the potency of group pressures. It asserts that we all, like chameleons, take on the hues and colors of our environments. We blend in, we conform. We tend to like football, hot dogs, and apple pie rather than soccer, bratwurst, and strudel, not because the former are demonstrably superior to the latter but because we are Americans and not Germans. We view the world differentially according to the attitudes, beliefs, and expectations of the groups around which our lives revolve.

THE ASSUMPTIONS

For brevity, the nine propositions or components of differential association theory can be compressed into four general principles:

1. Criminal behavior is learned in interaction with other people. Criminal behavior, therefore, is not biologically inherited, the result of psychological abnormalities, or invented anew by each criminal.
2. For the most part, the learning of criminal behavior occurs within intimate personal groups. This learning includes specific techniques, motives, rationalizations, justifications, and attitudes.
3. The direction of the cognitive components of learned criminal behavior is derived from definitions of the legal code (the law) as favorable or unfavorable to violations of the law. Thus, people become criminals because they hold an excess of definitions favorable to the violation of the law over definitions unfavorable to violations of the law.
4. Associations with others holding definitions favorable to violation of the law vary in frequency, duration, priority, and intensity. That is, the earlier in life one is exposed to criminal norms of conduct, the more often one is exposed to them, the longer those exposures last, and the more strongly one is attached to one's mentors, the more likely one is to become a criminal.

The general validity of this line of thinking has been supported by a number of empirical studies (*see* Matsueda, 1982, for a review). The correlations found between association with delinquent peers and delinquency are some of the strongest found in social science. According to critics of this theory, however, various reviews of friendship patterns (Matsueda, 1982; Rodkin, et al., 2000) have shown that the propensity for a given pattern of activity (including antisocial activity) precedes association with like-minded individuals. "Birds of a feather flock together," and become more alike on the basis of association. According to critics, association with delinquent peers acts more as a "releaser" of delinquent behavior than as a stimulator for otherwise prosocial individuals to engage in criminal activity. This is not to say that associations do not increase the propensity, however.

The theory also has been criticized as both "true and trivial" because it reduces to the commonsense idea that people are apt to behave criminally when they do not respect the law (Nettler, 1978:265). It can be applied as a causal explanation to all sorts of values, attitudes, tastes, and behaviors as a general theory of socialization within subcultures. "Culture" explains everything in a global sense, and, therefore, explains nothing in a specific sense. The commission of crime is a specific behavior engaged in by a few individuals within cultural settings with varying degrees of tolerance for anti-social behavior, and in no sense is it a normative cultural expectation.

Differential association theory is a variation on the old social pathology theme. Criminal behavior is cooked up in the simmering caldron of pathological neighborhoods, stirred by morally bankrupt companions, spiced by trouble, toughness, and excitement, and dished up with an urban philosophy of "do onto others as they would do onto you—but do it first!" It is from this conflict with middle-class attitudes and values that "definitions favorable" to law violation are formulated and translated into criminal behavior. Figure 2.2 presents differential association theory in diagrammatic form.

Figure 2.2
Differential Association Theory

| Differential social organization in lower social class | ➡ | Values in conflict with mainstream society leading to definitions of the law favorable to its violation | ➡ | Differential association with others holding definitions favorable to law violation | ➡ | Learned definition and techniques are used in committing criminal acts |

LESSONS AND CONCERNS

Although we cannot deny the cogency of the line of thought presented to us by differential association theory, it contains little practical leavening to lighten the dense dough of theory. As a correctional worker, you will be able to do nothing to mitigate the pernicious effects of poor neighborhoods. You merely can help offenders to act responsibly within them. Nonetheless, you must be sensitive to the burden of peer pressures felt by criminal justice offenders. An awareness of those pressures will enable you to formulate realistic goals for treatment rather than moralize with offenders about the company they keep.

However, be aware that probation and parole conditions have regulations regarding their offenders' associations with other criminal types. Differential association theory dictates that this is a plausible prohibition, and that introducing offenders to activities that lead them to associate with prosocial others is a reasonable treatment plan. But life in the ghettoes and barrios of the United States often necessitates belonging to a gang and participating in its attitudes and activities. A young man, and sometimes a young woman, living in a ghetto who does not take advantage of the comradeship and protection of the local gang may not be acting in his or her best interest.

Nonparticipation in such groups leaves one naked to the preying designs of those more in tune with the reality of their existence. Thus, supporters of this theory (in answer to the criticism that people choose their associations based on personal predilections) insist that the area in which people grow up adequately accounts for the associations they have. It is only when delinquent and nondelinquent associations equally are available that we should evoke individual propensities to explain association patterns (Stark, 1987). You can take some comfort that quite often the simple acts of getting married and/or obtaining legitimate employment may distance many less criminally involved offenders from their former companions and place them in the company of others with a more prosocial set of values.

Other critics take issue with the basic assumption of differential association theory that antisocial behavior is learned, stating that it comes naturally to the unsocialized individual: "What is there to be learned about simple lying, taking things that belong to another, fighting and sex play" asks an early critic (Glueck, 1956:94). Assuredly, individuals learn to get better at doing these things because of their associations with other like-minded individuals, but they do not have to be taught such natural acts. What they have to be taught is how to curb them, what constitutes moral behavior, and how to consider the rights and feelings of others. We now consider a theory that recognizes this.

Control Theory

Whereas anomie and differential association theories focus on causes said to propel individuals into crime, control theory focuses on the conditions of the environment that restrain them from it. According to control theorists, criminologists do not need to explain why some of us behave badly but why most of us behave well most of the time. Control theory insists that self-interest is innate, that we are born asocial, and that we must learn painful lessons. We must learn that civilization is bought at the cost of the repression of natural urges and that our wants and needs are inextricably linked to the wants and needs of others. If we do not learn these lessons, we are heading for trouble.

IDENTIFYING THE "TYPICAL" CRIMINAL

The version of control theory examined here—that of Travis Hirschi (1977)—is compelling. It is consistent with what we are reasonably certain we know about the personal and demographic characteristics of those who commit crimes, as well as with the perceptions of crime causation held by most workers in the criminal justice field. Hirschi starts with the correlates of the "typical" criminal and finds him to be a young male who grew up in a fatherless home in an urban slum, who has a history of difficulty in school, and who is unemployed. Of course, there are also female criminals, but the following discussion uses the masculine pronoun to emphasize that we are talking about Hirschi's typical criminal.

Having defined the typical criminal, Hirschi makes a series of logical deductions flowing from the nature of crime. His first observation is that criminal activity is contrary to the wishes and expectations of others. From this he deduces that those most likely to commit crimes are those least likely to be concerned with the wishes and expectations of others. Criminal activity is contrary to the law and involves the risk of punishment. Therefore, those who commit crimes are least likely to accept the moral beliefs underlying the law, and are least likely to concern themselves with the risk of punishment. Finally, criminal acts take time and are engaged in by those who have the time that such acts require (they are unemployed).

What demands explanation are the conditions of the typical criminal's life that lead him to run roughshod over the wishes and expectations of others, his lack of belief in the moral order, his relative lack of concern for punishment, and his possession of the excess time that criminal activity requires. To state the question in terms more consistent with the theory: What are the controls existing in the environments of noncriminals which restrain them from criminal activity that are absent in the environments of criminals? These restraining controls are attachment, commitment, involvement, and belief.

THE FOUR CONTROLS

Attachment refers to one's psychological and emotional closeness to others. It implies a reciprocal relationship in which persons feel valued, respected, and loved, and in which they value the favorable judgments of others to whom they are attached. Sociologists use the concept of significant others and reference groups to refer to the people we consider important to us and whose good opinions we value. Significant others are close family members and friends, and reference groups are those groups of people who we admire and seek to emulate. These are the people to whom we look for guidance in our behavior, values, and attitudes. Much of our behavior can be seen as attempts to gain favorable judgments from our reference groups and significant others.

For many years, parents are the most important behavior-orienting significant others. It follows that those who do not care about parental reactions are those who are most likely to behave in ways contrary to their wishes. Risking the good opinion of another is of minor concern when that good opinion is not valued. Why that good opinion is not valued is a question that need not concern us at this point. In general, however, such a state results from the absence of a relationship between parent and child in which love, respect, value, and concern are constantly demonstrated.

Lack of attachment to parents and the attending lack of respect for their wishes easily spills over into a lack of attachment and respect for the broader social groupings of which the child is a part. Much of the controlling power of others outside the immediate family lies in the threat of reporting juvenile misbehavior to parents. If the child has little fear of parental sanctions, the control exercised by others has limited effect simply because parental control has limited effect.

The family is the nursery of human nature. If the family is in disarray, if there is little love, concern, or attachment within it, then the product will be defective. Children of such families will fail to form a conscience. They will lack the ability to sympathize and empathize with others. They will learn that the world is a cold and heartless place and will act toward it, accordingly. However, it is naive to posit that all life's ills have their origins in the lack of early childhood attachment. After all, numerous other life events intervene and impact on the probability of one becoming criminal.

Commitment refers to a lifestyle in which one has invested considerable time and energy in the pursuit of a lawful career. The pursuit of such a lifestyle is assumed to be rewarding to the individuals, who, therefore, have a valuable stake in conforming to the moral standards of their society. People who make this considerable investment, or who aspire to, are not likely to risk it by engaging in criminal activity. The benefit/cost ratio (what individuals stand to benefit from crime contrasted with what they stand to lose if caught) renders the cost of crime prohibitive for such persons.

However, the lower the stake with which one enters the criminal game, the more appealing are the possible prizes. The poor student, the truant, the dropout, and the unemployed risk less in the benefit/cost comparison. For example, although the bank president and the casual laborer equally may desire to engage the services of an under-age prostitute, the bank president probably is more likely to restrain the urge because he stands to lose far more than the laborer if caught and exposed. The successful acquisition of a stake in prosocial conformity, of course, requires success in school. Success in school requires disciplined application to tasks that children do not partic-ularly relish but which they nevertheless complete to gain the valued approval of significant others, especially parents. Again, if approval is not forthcoming or is not valued, children will busy themselves in tasks more congenial to their natural inclina-tions, inclinations that almost certainly do not include algebra or the principles of grammar. Attachment, then, would appear to be an essential prerequisite to any gen-uine commitment to a prosocial lifestyle.

Involvement is a direct consequence of commitment. It is a part of a convention-al pattern of existence. Essentially, involvement is a matter of time and energy con-strictions placed on us by the demands of our commitments. Involvement in lawful activities reduces exposure to illegal activities. Conversely, the lack of involvement in lawful activities increases the possibility of exposure to illegal activities: "The devil finds work for idle hands," moral considerations aside, is a cogent statement.

Belief refers to the ready acceptance of the social prescriptions and proscrip-tions regulating conduct. Those individuals who are free of the constraints on their behavior imposed by attachment, commitment, and involvement evolve a belief sys-tem shorn of conventional morality. It is a system of belief containing narrowly focused images of self-interest. Unlike differential association theory, control theory does not view the criminal belief system as causative in the sense that it generates criminal behavior. Rather, criminals act according to their urges and then justify or rationalize their behavior with a set of instrumental statements such as "Suckers deserve what they get," "Everybody does it—why not me?" and "Do onto others as they would do onto you—only do it first." These are the statements of alienated individuals— Merton's innovators, who are reflecting and rationalizing the lifestyle of the unattached. For control theorists, the behavior gives birth to the belief rather than vice versa.

Control theorists agree with differential association theorists that criminals are reinforced in their beliefs by like-minded individuals. However, it strongly disagrees with the proposition that such peer groups are intimately connected, loyal to one another, and bound by a prescriptive code of conduct. The criminality of group mem-bers reflects their weak bonds with conventional society more than their attachment to one another. Any worker in the criminal justice field will attest to the fact that when in a legal bind, criminals will trip over one another in the race to be the first to "cut a deal favorable to themselves to the detriment of their 'friends.'"

A point of central importance to understanding control theory is that the lack of attachment, commitment, and involvement to and with conventional others, *does not* constitute a motive for crime as an "excess of definitions favorable to the violation of the law" is alleged to provide in differential association theory. The lack of these controls represents *social deficiencies* (the lack of social bonds) that have the result of reducing the potential costs of engaging in criminal activity. Nor is a criminal belief system a motive for crime; it is merely an after-the-fact justification for antisocial behavior. The correctional worker, of course, should consider both the behavior and the alleged justification for it totally unacceptable. Figure 2.3 presents a diagrammatic representation of Hirschi's control theory.

Figure 2.3
Hirschi's Control Theory

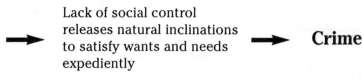

| The lack of attachment, commitment, involvement and belief constitutes the lack of social controls | → | Lack of social control releases natural inclinations to satisfy wants and needs expediently | → | **Crime** |

From Social Control to Self-control

With colleague Michael Gottfredson, Hirschi has moved from a focus on social controls in explaining crime to a focus on self-control; that is the "extent to which (different people) are vulnerable to the temptations of the moment" (1990:87). Gottfredson and Hirschi accept the classical idea that crimes result from natural human impulses to enhance pleasure and avoid pain. We all have these impulses, but most of us learn to express them in socially appropriate ways.

According to the theory, people with low self-control possess the following cognitive and temperamental traits that make offending more probable for them than for others (1990:89-90):

- They are oriented to the present rather than to the future, and crime affords them immediate rather than delayed gratification.
- They are risk-taking and physical as opposed to cautious and cognitive, and crime provides them with exciting and risky adventures.
- They lack patience, persistence, and diligence, and crime provides them with quick and easy ways to obtain money, sex, revenge, and so forth.
- They are self-centered and insensitive, so they can commit crimes without experiencing pangs of guilt for causing the suffering of others.

Crime affords such people quick and easy ways to satisfy their needs immediately, and their personal characteristics enable them to enjoy the satisfaction of their needs without experiencing the pangs of guilt or empathy.

Gottfredson and Hirschi trace the origin of low self-control, which they consider to be a stable component of a criminal personality, to poor parenting practices. Children do not learn low self-control. On the contrary, the defining traits of low self-control are the "default" options that occur naturally in the absence of adequate parenting. In other words, low self-control is not "caused;" high self-control is. Children must be taught self-control by parental warmth, nurturance, discipline, and vigilance. Thus, any set of family circumstances that make this type of parenting difficult to achieve negatively effects the development of self-control. Gottfredson and Hirschi list parental criminality, large families, and single-parent families as some of the major family circumstances that reduce parental supervision (Gottfredson and Hirschi, 1990: 100-105).

Low self-control is a necessary but not sufficient cause of criminal offending, for it must be paired with an opportunity to commit it. A criminal opportunity is a situation that presents itself in which an individual lacking in self-control can satisfy his or her needs with minimal mental or physical effort (Gottfredson and Hirschi, 1990). These criminal opportunities include an open window, a young woman walking alone in a dark alley, a car with keys in the ignition, and a distracted shopkeeper. A person with self-control would not construe the same situations as criminal opportunities.

Perspective from the Field:
Control Theory and Rehabilitation
By Robert M. Freeman, Ph.D.

Dr. Freeman earned his bachelor's and master's degrees in psychology from Indiana University of Pennsylvania. His doctorate is in criminal justice and criminology from the University of Maryland. Dr. Freeman is an associate professor in the Department of Criminal Justice at Shippensburg University in Shippensburg, Pennsylvania. From 1970 to 1990, he served as superintendent of two Pennsylvania Department of Corrections adult men's facilities, including the 2,600-bed Camp Hill Prison, where he served during the riots. He has extensive experience in every phase of correctional management.

During my first five years in corrections I was a psychologist involved in developing treatment plans for adult male offenders. The last fifteen years of my corrections career consisted of administrative duties, some of which involved initiating and monitoring a variety of specialized treatment programs. The foundation for both individual treatment planning and program development was the medical model of rehabilitation. The medical model of rehabilitation, which was so influential in corrections from the late 1950s to the mid-1970s and still forms the basis for most treatment planning for incarcerated offenders, has four basic tenets: (1) criminal behavior is a symptom of a personal deficiency; (2) these personal deficiencies can be identified through appropriate classification techniques; (3) deficiencies can be corrected by application of specific treatment programs and techniques; and (4) once deficiencies have been corrected, the symptoms no longer will occur.

My colleagues and I were taught that criminals should be viewed as people whose behavior was created by the inability to gain legal employment because of deficiencies in education and training. These deficiencies were to be corrected by enrollment in academic and job-skill development classes. Alcohol and/or drug dependency were symptoms resulting from a deficiency in self-esteem and coping skills and could be corrected by individual counseling and/or group therapy or placement in a therapeutic drug community. Assaultive crimes were symptoms of low-impulse control and/or low self-esteem to be corrected by participation in counseling programs focused on anger management and impulse control. Academic and job training programs were a generic prescription based on the belief that success in these activities would bolster self-esteem and teach self-discipline, as well as create employment opportunities. Counseling designed to bolster the offender's self-image was frequently added to the treatment plans under the assumption that all offenders, regardless of presenting symptoms, had a poor self-image. If the offender did well with in-house programming, then a variety of prerelease programs (work release, college, furloughs) could be made available for both reward and societal reintegration purposes.

Underlying the medical model is a belief in the propositions of control theory. Control theory postulates that people do not commit crimes when they are firmly attached to a conventional lifestyle because they have a "stake in conformity," which they cannot afford to lose. Those individuals attached to conventional individuals at an early age learn conventional behavior, spend their time in conventional activities, believe in conventional values, and function as law-abiding citizens. Criminals are not attached to a conventional lifestyle, have no stake in conformity, and are free to break the law because they have nothing to lose. The goal of the medical model is to provide offenders with a stake in conformity through attachment to conventional activities learned through participation in treatment programs provided by conventional members of society.

Control theory sounds plausible and can be used to help explain why many individuals drop out of crime when they get married, obtain a full-time job, or enter military service. Logically, a treatment approach based on control theory should produce impressive results. But one of the hardest lessons a beginning practitioner has to learn is that all theories have limitations. No matter how plausible the theory, failures will occur when they are applied in practice. An example follows:

During my third year as a psychologist, I developed a treatment plan for an inmate named George, a twenty-two-year-old white, unmarried male from a broken family, who had been in trouble as a juvenile, and was serving his first adult sentence for burglary. He had dropped out of school in the ninth grade, had no vocational skills, and sporadically had held a number of marginal jobs. Psychological testing with the Minnesota Multi Phasic Inventory (MMPI) showed a personality profile within normal limits. George was articulate, polite, very personable, had an I.Q. of 137, and had no history of alcohol or drug dependency. He expressed a sincere desire to improve his life and talked convincingly of his revulsion at the burglaries which had sent him to prison.

I put George in my therapy group, which focused on building self-esteem and gaining insight into the relationship between past experiences and current behavior, enrolled him in the General Equivalency Degree (GED) program, and carefully monitored his performance in the kitchen and on the cellblock. Six months later George had earned his GED, was tutoring other students, receiving exemplary reports from kitchen supervisors, and was showing an extraordinary level of insight in group. Block officers were unanimous that George should be an accelerated candidate for prerelease programming. I was delighted. The next step was to enroll George in a community college program. He had expressed a desire to receive an associate degree in computer programming, and the college admissions personnel agreed that he had the necessary aptitude. George did so well in the program that the college offered him a part-time job in their student records office. He met a conventional young woman while on weekend furlough, fell in love, and married her in the prison chapel shortly before parole was granted. George left prison with three months left in his college program and the offer of a full-time job after graduation. On the day of George's graduation, I knew George was a success story.

A year after graduation George walked into my office dressed in the blue clothing given to all new inmates. He had been convicted of stealing used car tires from a warehouse. I was stunned. According to control theory, George should have been a success. He had received his "stake in conformity:" a wife, a college degree, a good job, and the approval and acceptance of conventional members of society. What possibly could have gone wrong? "Why did you return to crime when you had so much going for you?" His answer, given after a minute of thoughtful reflection: "I got bored."

"I got bored!" The reality is that no single theory can explain, or be used to change, all human behavior. Would another approach, possibly one based on reality therapy, have worked with George? We never will know. The superintendent of the facility operated under the principle of "One and you're done." George had his "one," and two weeks later, he was transferred to a maximum-security prison where he became just another number.

LESSONS AND CONCERNS

The utility of control theory (both versions presented here) for the corrections worker is that it provides a certain amount of meaningful guidance in working with offenders. Obviously, nothing can be done about your offenders' levels of attachment to their families. You cannot visit the past and interfere with pathological family dynamics, unfortunate though that may be. You can take steps in your role as a counselor and a broker of community resources to involve offenders in a conventional lifestyle. Correctional workers have considerable power over the activities of offenders. That is to say, you can lead horses to water, and, with a little judicious use of authority, persuade them to sip a little. Perhaps they even may acquire a taste for it.

Contrary to the currently fashionable nihilistic "nothing works" philosophy, this author has witnessed many remarkable turnarounds by offenders who have had the guidance of caring criminal justice professionals, and many reviews of the rehabilitation literature (such as Gendreau and Ross, 1987; Latessa, 1999) substantiate this view.

Although control theory has something in the way of practical guidance to commend it over the other two theories examined, it is certainly not the final word in the understanding of criminal behavior. It does not account for those who simply appear to prefer a criminal lifestyle despite having been afforded numerous opportunities to forge a conventional one (*see* Dr. Freeman's case study, page 24).

Control theorists view criminal activity as a poor second choice made by unhappy individuals whose socialization has rendered them largely unfit to pursue conventional avenues to success. In the majority of cases, this is an accurate assessment. Most individuals caught up in criminal activity might well prefer acceptance into the "moral community," $90,000 a year from a straight job, a house with a white picket fence, and membership at the country club. Unfortunately, their experiences during their formative years have not prepared them psychologically, emotionally, or intellectually to accept the possibility that such a lifestyle could be a reality for them. They have a tremendous burden of inertia preventing them from taking that first step on the long journey to social respectability, and a stifling orientation to the here and now.

Control theory does not address that small percentage of criminals who have genuine contempt for the "straight life," those who, by their natures, find it extremely difficult to function in a conventionally acceptable way. There are individuals, who despite the best efforts of parents to teach them self-control, never learn it. Some children bring with them to the socialization process a temperament so difficult as to test the patience of saints. Self-control theory neglects children's effects on parenting, just as it neglects the fact that low self-control (impulsiveness) is related to serotonin, levels of which are primarily—though not entirely—under genetic control (Ellis and Walsh, 2000).

These are the people who enjoy hurting people, who crave the danger, excitement, and adventure provided by a life of crime. Life without the opportunity to hurt and dominate others, without drugs and alcohol, without violence and predation, without fast cars and faster women, would be unbearable to them. We call such people *psychopaths, sociopaths,* or *antisocial personalities.* Although they constitute a small minority of the criminal population with which you will have contact, it is important to have an understanding of them because they are engaged in a level of criminal activity out of all proportion to their numbers.

Summary

Anomie and differential association theories locate the causes of crime in the criminal's environment, and both theories would agree with the proposition that societies get the type of criminals they deserve. Anomie theorists believe that American socioeconomic conditions, which emphasize monetary success but at the same time deny access to legitimate avenues to this goal to a significant number of people, manufacture criminals. The retreatist and innovator modes of adaptation to this cultural disjunction are the modes that generate criminal behavior. The conformist and the ritualist modes of adaptation produce individuals who, in the main, are law abiding. Only under certain circumstances does the rebellious mode generate illegal behavior.

Differential association theory concentrates on specific subcultural environments that predispose individuals to adopt specific modes of adaptation. This theory emphasizes that criminal behavior is learned within subcultures where criminal behavior is more or less "normal" behavior. Differing levels of criminal behavior depend on the frequency, duration, priority, and intensity of association with criminals and criminal values and attitudes. Thus, differential association theory agrees with anomie theory that criminal behavior can be a rational adaptation to the conditions in which people find themselves. In short, theorists in both of these camps tend to give the impression that everyone is guilty of crime—except the criminal. Although these theories offer no policy recommendations that could be put into practice by the criminal justice worker, they do illuminate the relationship between criminality and the social arrangements in which it exists. Their main value to you should be that they lead you to a deficiency interpretation rather than a pathological interpretation of criminal behavior.

Control theory differs from the other two theories in that rather than looking at conditions that may lead people to commit crimes, it looks at conditions that isolate people from it. Those conditions, or controls, are attachment, commitment, involvement, and belief. The presence of the latter three controls depends to a large extent on the initial presence of attachment.

Criminal beliefs do not "cause" one to commit crimes, they merely serve as rationalizations for those who do. Control theory fits well with the perceptions of crime causation held by most criminal justice practitioners. Its later emphasis on self-control also fits well with the perceptions of criminal justice personnel. The important point to remember about self-control is that low self-control emerges in the absence of adequate parenting. Control theory recognizes that individuals' lack of controls (either social or self) are not entirely their own fault, but it does not attempt to justify irresponsible behavior by pointing to this lack as a cause. Control theory offers some useful practical guidance for correctional workers, both for understanding criminal behavior and for pointing to conditions that possibly may be rectified in the counseling and supervision process.

References and Suggested Readings

Agnew, R. 1992. Foundation for a general strain theory of crime and delinquency. *Criminology*. 30:47-87.

_____. 1997. Stability and Change over the Lifecourse: A Strain Interpretation. In T. Thornberry, ed. *Developmental Theories of Crime and Delinquency*. New Brunswick, New Jersey: Transaction Publishers.

Dashkov, G. 1992. Quantitative and qualitative changes in crime in the USSR. *British Journal of Criminology*. 32:160-165.

Durkheim, E. 1950. *The Rules of the Sociological Method*. Glencoe, Illinois: Free Press.

_____. 1951a. *The Division of Labor in Society*. Glencoe, Illinois: Free Press.

_____. 1951b. *Suicide: A Study in Sociology*. Glencoe, Illinois: Free Press.

Ellis, L. and A. Walsh. 2000. *Criminology: A Global Perspective*. Boston: Allyn and Bacon.

Gendreau, Paul and R. Ross. 1987. Revivification of rehabilitation: Evidence from the 1980s. *Justice Quarterly*. 4:349-406.

Gilsinan, J. 1990. *Criminology and Public Policy: An Introduction*. Englewood Cliffs, New Jersey: Prentice-Hall.

Glueck, Sheldon. 1956. Theory and fact in criminology: A criticism of differential association theory. *British Journal of Criminology*. 7:92-109.

Gonczol, K. 1993. Anxiety over crime. *Hungarian Quarterly*. 129:87-99.

Gottfredson, M. and T. Hirschi. 1990. *A General Theory of Crime*. Palo Alto, California: Stanford University Press.

Hirschi, T. 1977. Causes and prevention of juvenile delinquency. *Sociological Inquiry*. 47:322-341.

Latessa, Edward J., ed. 1999. *What Works: Strategic Solutions The International Community Corrections Association Examines Substance Abuse*. Lanham, Maryland: American Correctional Association.

Matsueda, R. 1982. Testing control theory and differential association: A causal modeling approach. *American Sociological Review*. 47:489-504.

Merton, R. 1957. *Social Theory and Social Structure*. New York: Free Press.

Nettler, G. 1978. *Explaining Crime*. New York: McGraw-Hill.

Rodkin, P., T. Farmer, R. Pearl, and R. Van Acker. 2000. Heterogeneity of popular boys: Antisocial and prosocial configurations. *Developmental Psychology*. 36:14-24.

Stark, R. 1987. Deviant places: A theory of the etiology of crime. *Criminology*. 25:893-909.

Sutherland, E. and D. Cressey. 1978. *Principles of Criminology*. Philadelphia, Pennsylvania: Lippincott.

Taylor, I., P. Walton, and J. Young. 1973. *The New Criminology*. New York: Harper and Row.

Walsh, A. 2000. Behavior genetics and anomie/strain theory. *Criminology*. 38: 1075-1107.

Chapter 3

Biosocial Theories

From the fact that crime is a phenomenon of normal sociology, it does not follow that the criminal is an individual normally constituted from the biological and psychological points of view.

Emile Durkheim

Durkheim's dictum that the causes of social facts "should be sought among the social facts preceding it" (1982:110) has been interpreted by many sociologists to mean that there are no other sources of human social behavior. The epigraph to this chapter, also written by Durkheim, reminds sociologists that his dictum is simply a definition of their discipline's boundaries, not an assertion of biological and psychological irrelevance (Udry, 1995). As indicated in Chapter 1, crime is a social fact, and its definition, spread, concentration, and prevalence are rightly within the domain or boundaries of sociology. However, criminality is a characteristic of persons possessing brains, genes, hormones, and personalities, which are the domains of psychology and biology. This chapter provides a brief overview of some of the contributions of these sciences that should be part of the correctional workers' repertoire of knowledge.

No researcher in these traditions posits the existence of "crime genes," but there are genes which, through a variety of neurohormonal routes, lead to particular traits and characteristics that increase the probability of criminal behavior. As one group of researchers put it: "The question is no longer *whether* but *how* genes influence behavior" (McGue, Bacon, and Lykken, 1993:107). This is not to say that genes influence behavior independent of the environment, or that one is more important than the other. To ask whether genes or the environment is more important to behavior is like asking whether the violin or the violinist is more important to the music. Both the qualities of the player and the instrument can be analyzed separately, but the music is the result of the interaction of both. The time is long past due to put the sterile nature *versus* nature debate out to pasture, and to acknowledge the reality of nature *via* nurture.

Psychopathy

Ever since French psychiatrist Phillipe Pinel introduced the concept of psychopathy to the world in the eighteenth century, it has had a checkered career. Conceptual and ideological arguments associated with the psychopathic syndrome moved Gibbons (1973:171) to state: "We regard any attempt to proceed further with the psychopathy/criminality line of inquiry a futile business." Numerous studies prior and subsequent to Gibbons' cavalier dismissal of the usefulness of the concept of psychopathy strongly suggest that his opinion was ill-considered. Such studies have shown rather convincingly that psychopaths can be distinguished from nonpsychopaths biologically, psychologically, and sociologically (Walsh and Petee, 1987; Mealy, 1995; Hare, 1996). Although the behavior of psychopaths and sociopaths is essentially identical, most researchers in this area reserve the term *psychopath* for those whose antisocial behavior is considered to be primarily genetic in origin, and *sociopath* for those whose antisocial behavior is mostly environmental in origin.

It is well known that a small number of recidivists account for the lion's share of serious crime. The classic study of a birth cohort of 10,000 males in Philadelphia found that 35 percent of the boys were arrested one or more times before reaching adulthood (Wolfgang, Figlio, and Sellin, 1972). However, a mere 18 percent of those arrested (6.3 percent of the total cohort) accounted for 52 percent of all offenses and 66 percent of all violent offenses known to have been committed by members of the cohort. Other cohort studies in various countries have shown essentially the same results; that is, a relatively small number of offenders are responsible for roughly two-thirds of all serious crimes (Tracy, Wolfgang, and Figlio, 1990; Farrington, 2001). Although the studies were interested in identifying recidivists, and not psychopaths per se, it is reasonable to assume that many of those chronic and violent recidivists possessed many of the descriptive features of psychopaths.

It is important to note that not all criminals are psychopaths, and not all psychopaths are criminals. However, while the estimates of the number of psychopaths in society range between 3 to 4 percent (Mealy, 1995), they make up 15 to 20 percent of our prison population (Hare, 1996). Psychopaths are also overrepresented in occupations that require ruthlessness and callous exploitation such as the highly competitive corporate world and elite military forces. Needless to say, the great majority of people in these occupations are not psychopaths.

THEORIES OF PSYCHOPATHY

From a variety of sources (Hare, 1993; Lykken, 1995; Mealy, 1995) it has been determined that the following descriptive features of psychopaths are the most common:

- Unable to profit from experience
- Lack of a sense of responsibility
- Inability to form meaningful relationships
- Lack of impulse control
- Lack of moral sense
- Consistently antisocial

- Punishment has no effect in changing their behavior
- Emotionally immature
- Glib and superficial
- Unable to experience feelings of guilt
- Extreme self-centeredness

The majority of researchers in this area tend to agree that psychopathy is the result of an interplay of genetic and environmental influences. Genes and the environments they find themselves in are positively correlated; that is, they are not random with respect to one another. The concept enables us to understand the indirect way (there is no direct way) that genes help to determine what aspects of the environment will be important and rewarding to us. Offenders, like the rest of us, take an active part in forging their own environment, and are not merely the pawns of it. Behavior geneticists speak of three kinds of gene/environment correlations: *passive, reactive,* and *active* (Plomin, 1995).

The basic idea behind passive gene/environment correlation is that parents provide children with genes for particular traits and an environment conducive to their development. For instance, athletic parents pass on genes related to athletic ability (strength, speed, coordination, and competitiveness) to their offspring and provide them with an environment (equipment, training, and the modeling and encouragement) that facilitates the expression of the genes underlying athleticism. The term *passive* should not be construed as implying that children do not actively engage their environment; it simply means that they merely have been exposed to it but have not been active in forming it. That is, the trait(s) in question develop independently of anything the child has done. The role of passive gene/environment correlation is limited to infancy and toddlerhood, after which the child's interactions with others outside the family begin to exert their influence.

Reactive gene/environment correlation picks up the developmental trajectory started by passive gene/environment correlation, and refers to the reactions of others evoked by the child's expression of his or her traits. A pleasant, outgoing, cooperative, and well-mannered child will evoke positive responses from parents, teachers, and peers, whereas a child exhibiting the opposite traits will evoke negative responses. The typical social science explanation of children's behavior—that it is shaped by the way others treat them—ignores the fact that the treatment of children by others is as much a function of children's evocative behavior as it is of the interaction style of those who respond to them.

The traits children bring with them to their interactions increase or decrease the probability of evoking certain kinds of responses from others. Some children may be so resistant to parental control that parents either resort to extreme forms of punishment or give up on the child altogether. Social scientists have a tendency to attribute the behavioral problems of such children to their parent's "harsh" or "permissive" parental style, ignoring completely that "parental styles" evolved, in large part, in response to the children's behavior. An extreme punitive or permissive parental response will tend to make such a child's antisocial traits worse and drive him or her to seek environments in which such behavior is accepted. These environments usually are populated by individuals similarly disposed: "Birds of a feather flock together."

Active gene/environment correlation refers to the seeking of environments compatible with our genetic dispositions. Our genes, within the range of cultural possibilities and constraints, help to determine what features of the environment will be rewarding to us, and what features will not. Active gene/environment correlation gains momentum as individuals mature and acquire the ability to take greater control of their lives and to construct their environments consistent with their innate dispositions. Daring and adventurous people are not likely to seek careers as accountants or bankers, and fearful and introverted people are not likely to become police officers or firefighters. The affects of genes on forming these environments can be gauged by studies showing that the intelligence, personalities, and attitudes of monozygotic (identical) twins are essentially unaffected by whether they were reared together. That is, identical twins reared apart construct their environments about as similarly as they would have had they been reared together, and considerably more similarly than dizygotic (fraternal) twins and nontwin siblings reared together (Bouchard, et al., 1990).

The second behavioral genetic concept is that of gene/environment interaction, which is different from, but related to, gene/environment correlation. It involves the reasonable assumption that, largely because of genetic differences, different people will interact with and respond to their environments in different ways. For instance, relatively fearless and impulsive children are genetically more vulnerable to opportunities for antisocial behavior in their environment than are more fearful and less impulsive children. The effects of parental scolding in response to poor behavior may have a positive effect on the future behavior for some children, no effect on some, and even a negative effect on others. Thus, identical environments may have radically different meanings for different individuals and thus result in quite different behaviors.

REWARD DOMINANCE THEORY

Reward dominance, or BIS/BAS theory, is a neurological theory of psychopathy and criminal behavior based on the proposition that behavior is regulated by two opposing mechanisms, the *behavioral activating* (or *approach*) *system* (BAS) and the *behavioral inhibition system* (BIS). The BAS motivates us to pursue things that are rewarding to us, and the BIS prevents us from going too far in that pursuit (Kruesi, et al., 1994). The BAS acts like an accelerator rushing us toward the fulfillment of some desire (food, drink, cognitive, physical, emotional, and sexual pleasures), and the BIS acts like a brake which, in response to punishment and cues from the environment, stops us from overdoing it. A normal BAS combined with a faulty BIS, or vice versa, may lead to a "craving brain" that can get us into all sorts of physical, social, moral, and legal difficulties, such as obesity, alcoholism, substance abuse, gambling and sexual addictions (Ruden, 1997).

The BAS primarily is associated with dopamine (one of a class of chemicals known as neurotransmitters) operating on an area of the brain known as the nucleus accumbens, a structure particularly rich in neurons (brain cells) that produce and respond to dopamine. The nucleus accumbens is a major "pleasure center" in the brain. The BIS is primarily associated with serotonin, another kind of neurotransmitter that often serves as a neuromodulator. Regardless of where it operates, dopamine facilitates goal-directed behavior, and serotonin generally modulates that behavior (Depue and Collins, 1999).

The BAS and BIS are balanced (in a state of dopamine/serotonin equilibrium) in most people most of the time. In other words, we are more or less equally sensitive to both reward and punishment (Ruden, 1997). For others, one system might dominate the other most or all of the time. Reward dominance theory asserts that criminals, especially chronic criminals and psychopaths, have a dominant BAS, which means that they tend to be overly sensitive to reward contingencies and relatively insensitive to punishment cues (Kruesi, et al., 1994; Lykken, 1995). Persons with a relatively strong BIS and/or a relatively weak BAS, are likely to suffer from obsessive compulsive disorder. Such persons are polar opposites of psychopaths, being wracked with unreasonable guilt and self-doubt (Kruesi, et al., 1994).

A third system of behavior control, the fight/flight system (FFS), has been added to the BAS/BIS model. The fight/flight is a subsystem of the autonomic nervous system (ANS) specializing in responding to threats. The autonomic nervous system has two complementary branches, the sympathetic and the parasympathetic. The sympathetic branch mobilizes the body's endocrine system to pump out epinephrine (adrenaline) in response to environmental threats. The sympathetic branch of the autonomic nerve system (specifically, the fight/flight system) responds to fear and mobilizes an organism to do something about it by changing numerous aspects of its physiology from its normal balanced state. Unlike the BAS, which activates us to seek rewarding experiences, the fight/flight system activates us to escape from actual and potential treats to our well being. The parasympathetic branch restores the body to equilibrium after the threat is over.

Just as individuals differ in terms of BAS/BIS functioning, they differ in terms of fight/flight system arousal, most having a fight/flight system that is neither too active nor too sluggish. However, there are a small number of people with a hyperactive fight/flight system. These people are very fearful and become conditioned very easily because fight/flight system arousal produces punishing visceral feelings associated with anxiety, guilt, and fear. They are very law-abiding because even the contemplation of nonconforming behavior arouses these uncomfortable feelings. Erasing or dismissing these antisocial thoughts provides the person with a visceral reward in the form of restoring the fight/flight system to equilibrium. The reduction of fear and anxiety is one of the most powerful rewards known to psychology. A hyperactive fight/flight system is thus a protective factor against criminal behavior, even among people at high environmental risk for crime. Brennan and her colleagues (1997) found that males in high crime environments who had highly reactive fight/flight systems were significantly less likely to exhibit antisocial behavior than males in the same environment who had a normal or a hyporesponsive fight/flight system (an example of gene/environment interaction). In fact, they even committed fewer antisocial acts than males in low crime environments with normal or hyporeactive systems.

Individuals with a hypo-arousable fight/flight system are relatively fearless and difficult to condition. They do not receive visceral reinforcement for conforming behavior because they are not viscerally aroused to fear, anxiety, and guilt in the first place, and thus cannot receive positive reinforcement in the form of a return to an unaroused state (Raine, 1997). Individuals with a relatively unresponsive fight/flight system are low in a neurotransmitter called norepinephrine, and are, by definition, relatively fearless, an attribute that can be quite useful when engaging in criminal activity (as well as when engaging in a number of prosocial activities such as acting in the role of police officer or firefighter). A review of forty studies of autonomic nervous system arousal and criminal and antisocial behavior found that thirty-eight (95 percent) supported the link and only two had nonsignificant results (Ellis and Walsh, 2000:282). Figure 3.1 presents a model of reward dominance theory. According to the theory, psychopaths or chronic criminals are high on novelty seeking (strong BAS), low on inhibition (weak BIS), and relatively fearless (hypoarousable fight/flight system). The acquisition of rewards is the dominant concern for them rather than the avoidance of punishment.

Figure 3.1
BAS, BIS, and FFS with Locations of Psychopaths and Obsessive Compulsives

SUBOPTIMAL AROUSAL THEORY

As the name implies, suboptimal arousal theory also concentrates on differential arousal levels, but focuses on a more primitive brain structure called the reticular activating system (RAS). The RAS is a finger-sized bundle of neurons extending from the spinal column into other brain areas and is a vital regulator of neurological arousal. Suboptimal arousal theory is based on the well-established finding that different levels of neurological arousal correlate with different personality and behavioral patterns (Ellis, 1996).

The theory basically states that in the range of everyday environmental situations, the level of stimulation most people find optimal, some find boring, and others find uncomfortably overstimulating. "Optimally aroused" means that the environment is neither too constant nor too varied. An optimal level of environmental stimulation for most of us will be stressful for some and boring for others.

Some individuals are *augmenters* of environmental stimulation; that is, they possess a RAS that is highly sensitive to incoming stimuli (more information is taken in and processed). Others are *reducers*, possessing a RAS that is unusually insensitive (less information is taken in and processed). Augmentation or reduction is solely a function of the differential physiology of the RAS; no conscious attempt to augment or reduce incoming stimuli is implied. Males tend to be reducers and females tend to be augmenters, although there is a great deal of overlap (Ellis and Coontz, 1990). Augmenters tend to prefer more constancy than variety in their world, and seek to tone down the level of environmental stimuli that most of us find to be "just right." Such people rarely are found in criminal populations. Reducers, on the other hand, tend to become easily bored with "just right" levels of stimulation, and continually seek to boost stimuli to more comfortable levels (Raine, 1997).

Relative to the general population, criminals, especially serious criminals, are chronically underaroused as determined by EEG brain wave patterns and resting heart rate and skin conductance measures (Ellis, 1996; Raine, 1997). Individuals who are chronically bored and continually seeking intense stimulation are not likely to apply themselves at school or work (much too boring!), and tend to find the level of stimulation they require in drug usage, risk-taking, sexual promiscuity, and criminal behavior. Antisocial behavior relieves miscreants of their suboptimally aroused (bored) state (*see* Dr. Freeman's Perspective from the Field in Chapter 2). Many criminals report that the primary reward they receive from their activities is the "buzz" or "high" they get from it rather than any monetary rewards, which often are far too meager to serve as motivators (Katz, 1988; Gove and Wilmoth, 1990).

CHEATER THEORY

Cheater theory (Mealey, 1995) is a theory based on evolution by natural selection. If you recall from biology 101, genes underlying any trait that somehow conferred an advantage in terms of survival and reproduction were selected for retention in future generations. *Reproductive success* refers to the number of offspring an animal produces that survive and reproduce themselves. Reproductive success can be achieved by fair means or foul. A small percentage of males in many nonhuman species follow what biologists call a *cheater* reproductive strategy (Mealey, 1995). Males following this strategy do not abide by the normal courtship rules of the species; rather, they achieve sexual intercourse by coercive and/or sneaky tactics (Alcock, 1998).

Although the traits conducive to cheating behavior normally are distributed in the population, there may be a small but stable percentage of individuals at one extreme of the distribution for whom cheating is a genetically obligatory strategy. An obligatory cheater strategy is likely to evolve alongside the more typical rule-based strategy (in which cheating behavior is environmentally dependent rather than genetic) when its reproductive gains are frequency-dependent. *Frequency-dependent* selection occurs when an alternative mating strategy enjoys high reproductive success when few practice it, but low success when it becomes more common. That is, when there are few cheats, each one enjoys numerous exploitation opportunities, but when many follow the strategy, there are fewer potential victims per cheat, and a greater awareness of the strategy. Thus, there is a lowered probability of its success

(Machalek, 1995). Cheaters in ancestral environments enjoyed enough reproductive success that the genes underlying the traits for this strategy were passed on.

What does all this talk about sex and reproductive success have to do with criminals? The answer is quite a lot, because cheater theory avers that psychopaths are the human analogs of cheater males in nonhuman species. That is, there is a small but stable number of human males for whom noncheating behavior (rule-based behavior) is almost an impossibility. This applies to any sort of behavior, not just sexual behavior, because the traits useful for pursuing a cheater reproductive strategy (manipulation; deceitfulness; aggression; lack of empathy, shame and altruism, and so forth) also are useful in following a criminal strategy.

A large body of evidence supports the relationship between criminal and promiscuous sexual behavior. Both male and female criminals have significantly more sex partners and begin having sex at an earlier age than do people in general. A review of fifty-two studies from seven different countries found that fifty-one reported a significant positive relationship between the number of sex partners and a variety of criminal/antisocial behaviors, and only one study found a nonsignificant relationship. Regarding age at the onset of sexual behavior, all the studies (thirty- one) reviewed on this topic found that the earlier the onset of sexual activity the greater the involvement in criminal behavior (Ellis and Walsh, 2000:227).

The probable adaptation aiding psychopaths in the pursuit of their goals is the muting of the neurohormonal mechanisms that regulate the social emotions so that psychopaths have little real understanding of what it is like to feel guilt, shame, anxiety, and empathy (Griffiths, 1990; Mealey, 1995; Nesse, 1990). Social emotions have evolved as integral parts of our social intelligence and serve to provide clues about the kinds of relationships (cooperative versus uncooperative) that we are likely to have with others (Walsh, 2000). Emotions animate, focus and modify neural activity in ways that lead us to choose certain responses over other possible responses from the streams of information we constantly receive. They cause positive and negative feelings when we survey the consequences of our behavior.

For instance, mutual cooperation evokes rewarding emotions such as a deepened sense of friendship and a heightened sense of obligation and gratitude that enhances future cooperation. By contrast, mutual cheating evokes negative emotions as both parties feel rejected and angry. When one party cooperates and the other cheats, the cooperator feels angry and betrayed, and the cheater feels anxiety and guilt. The more intensely we feel these emotions, the less likely we are to cheat, and the less we feel them the more likely we are to cheat. In short, emotions move us to behave in ways that enhanced our distant ancestor's reproductive success by overriding decisions suggesting alternatives to cooperation (in other words, cheating), which may have been more rational in the short term, but which ultimately were maladaptive.

The defining neurophysiological characteristic of psychopaths (the quintessential cheats) is their inability to "tie" the brain's cognitive and emotional networks together (Mealey, 1995; Patrick, 1994). Because psychopaths operate "below the emotional poverty line" (Hare, 1993:134), they do not reveal clues that would allow others to judge their intentions, making it easier for them to manipulate and deceive others. Lacking emotional self-regulation, they also tend to make social decisions exclusively on the basis of rational calculations of immediate costs or benefits (Mealey, 1995; Trivers, 1991). Thus, defective emotional controls, rather than low intelligence, are responsible for the psychopaths' inability to learn from experience. Punishment is also ineffective in altering their behavior.

PREFRONTAL DYSFUNCTION (PFD) THEORY

The prefrontal cortex (PFC) is a particularly prominent and important feature in the human brain. The prefrontal cortex is responsible for a number of uniquely human attributes such as making moral judgments; planning for the future; and analyzing, synthesizing, and modulating emotions, all of which are collectively referred to as *executive functions*. Given this important function, it is obvious that any dysfunction of the prefrontal cortex can result in antisocial behavior. Studies have found that individuals with lesions to the prefrontal cortex have reduced anxiety and fear and are less reactive to stressors of all kinds (reviewed in Raine, 1997). Prefrontal cortex damage need not be anatomically discernible to have a negative effect on behavior; damage could be at the cellular level and be the result of genetic factors that affect neurons during the earliest stages of frontal lobe growth and development, or caused by maternal substance abuse during pregnancy (Pihl and Bruce, 1995). Even slight damage to the prefrontal cortex, particularly to the left hemisphere, has been linked to a number of cognitive deficits (Reiss, et al., 1996).

Adrian Raine (1997) claims that prefrontal dysfunction theory can account for some of the physiological arousal factors observed in antisocial individuals by relating physiological functioning with psychological processes. For instance, reduced physiological arousal is associated with reduced arousal in certain areas of the prefrontal cortex. The evidence is most sound for criminals convicted of impulsive crimes, as we might expect given the executive function of the prefrontal cortex. A number of brain imaging studies find impulsive offenders to show less prefrontal cortex arousal, and those diagnosed with antisocial personality disorder to have less prefrontal gray matter, and to evidence reduced ANS activity (Raine, et al., 2000).

AROUSAL THEORIES AND CHILD ABUSE/NEGLECT

Human beings have powerful neurological and hormonal structures that demand the formation of bonds of affection (Fisher, 1998; Konner, 1982). Lacking the physical manifestations of love during infancy often produces people who are themselves unable to love (Kraemer, 1992; Walsh, 1995). People who lack the ability to love—to care, respect, nurture, give, and empathize—find it easy to victimize others. Glasser (1976:187), for instance, estimates that about 85 percent of those in constant and violent conflict with the law have not had these needs met. Abuse and neglect is a palpable indicator of unmet love needs, and these experiences are stamped on the brain (Glaser, 2000; Shore, 1997).

The brain is a marvelously plastic organ whose functioning, and even some aspects of its structure, is very sensitive to early environmental input (Kalil, 1989; Pinel, 2000). *Plasticity* essentially refers to the physiological calibration of the brain in response to environmental experience, especially early experience (Teicher, et al., 1997). The experiences that cultivate our beings are perceived, processed, and acted upon through intricate electrochemical interactions among some conservatively estimated 100 billion neurons. Our neurons are connected to each other through a maze of axons and dendrites, with the general structural pattern being contained in our genetic blueprints. However, there are not enough DNA molecules in the blueprint to provide specific information about how two neurons are to be connected. The patterning and organization of the brain cells are a function of habituated synaptic connections (a synapse is the interface between neighboring neurons).

Interneuronal connections are made when neurons send axons snaking out to seek other neurons that are the sources of certain chemicals needed to make the synaptic connection. Interneuronal communication occurs with greater facility the more often electrochemical synapses have been made. It consistently has been shown that organisms, including humans, raised in stimulus-enriched environments develop greater cortical density and greater quantities of essential neurotransmitter chemicals than organisms raised under less stimulating conditions (reviewed in Shore, 1997). Many more connections will be made in the young brain than will survive. Synaptic connections and neuronal pathways are selected for retention or elimination in use-dependent fashion in a process Edelman (1998) refers to as neural Darwinism. This is why early experience is neurologically so much more important than later experience. As Perry and Pollard (1998:36) point out: "Experience in adults *alters* the *organized* brain, but in infants and children it *organizes* the *developing* brain" (emphasis added). The stimuli associated with affection (touching, kissing, and cuddling) are tactile assurances for the infant that it is loved and secure, and appear to be very important for neural development.

The effects of a lack of tactile stimulation on the brain during its early development have been shown to have adverse effects (Glaser, 2000; Shore, 1997). For instance, the brain's emotional center, the limbic system, contains areas (the hippocampus and the amygdala) that appear quite vulnerable to damage by abuse and neglect. The possible affects of abuse and neglect on these limbic system structures have particular relevance to the operation of the BIS. The hippocampus is a crucial component of the BIS, and protracted abuse and neglect may alter the BIS's threshold setting so that it often may fail to perform its appropriate inhibitory role.

The damage is probably the result of the excessive production of stress hormones, called corticosteroids, in response to abuse (Teicher, et al., 1997). Similarly, frequent excitation of the amygdala in response to abuse and neglect eventually may lead to subconvulsive (as opposed to convulsive or epileptic) seizures (van der Kolk and Greenberg, 1987). Subconvulsive seizures in the amygdala (the most seizure prone area of the brain) often do not have any immediate environmental derivation. The term *episodic dyscontrol* is used to describe behavior resulting from subconvulsive seizures (Suchy, Blint, and Osman, 1997). Such seizures are related to impulsively violent and acting out behaviors, but not to any kind of planned criminal behavior (Ellis and Walsh, 2000).

Perry (1997) suggests that children who spend a great deal of time in a low-level state of fear tend to focus consistently on nonverbal cues of imminent danger because the brain has been habituated to do so. Perry further remarks that a cognitive profile in which performance IQ is significantly greater than verbal IQ (P>V) is a marker of this tendency. David Wechsler (1958:176) noted long ago that: "The most outstanding feature of the sociopath's test profile is the systematic high score on the performance as compared with the verbal part of the scale." One reviewer of the P>V/crime relationship writes: "This [PIQ > VIQ] relationship was found across studies, despite variations in age, sex, race, setting, and form of Wechsler scale administered, as well as differences in criteria for delinquency" (Miller, 1987:120).

A significant P>V discrepancy at the .01 probability level requires an approximate 12-point difference between the two IQ subscales. While the P>V profile has been consistently linked with psychopathy and chronic criminal offending (reviewed in Walsh,

1991), a significant V>P profile is often found to be a marker of prosocial behavior (Cornell and Wilson, 1992).

One study of more than 1,800 prison inmates found that V>P males were 29 times less likely to be found in prison populations than P>V males (Barnett, Zimmer, and McCormack, 1989). The possible affects of abuse and neglect on cognitive profiles were further evidenced in a study of 513 male delinquents. It was found that illegitimate boys raised by a single mother had higher abuse/neglect scores, higher delinquency scores, and both the highest mean PIQ and lowest mean VIQ scores (and hence the greatest P>V discrepancy) than boys born and reared under other circumstances (Walsh, 1990).

It is important to realize that a superior PIQ relative to one's VIQ is indicative of superior right hemisphere brain functioning relative to its left hemisphere functioning. Abused and neglected children may preferentially store their memories in the right hemisphere because abuse and neglect may be "associated with greater left-hemisphere dysfunction, which may lead to greater dependence on the right hemisphere. Increased right frontal function, in turn, may lead to enhanced perception and reaction to negative affect" (Teicher, et al., 1997:197).

Physiological arousal patterns also may be affected by childhood abuse and neglect. If a child experiences chronic stress during the organizational phase of brain development, the upshot may be the development of a hyporesponsive ANS as an "inoculation" to stress (Raine, 1997). It certainly appears reasonable that children who experience unusual levels of stress and emotional disturbance are likely to develop a mechanism for handling future stress. Experiments have shown that repeated aversive stimuli such as electric shock administered to laboratory animals has a steadily decreasing effect on ANS arousal until they become almost completely unreactive to stimuli that initially produced extreme symptoms of fear and anxiety, such as shaking, urinating, and defecating (Lykken, 1995; Solomon, 1980).

Good Guys Start Last and Finish First

Self-report studies long have told us that far more teens (especially males) commit delinquent acts than actually are caught and convicted. Indeed, boys who *do not* commit such acts have been considered "statistically deviant" (Farrington, Ohlin, and Wilson, 1986:40). However, after reaching a peak at around sixteen years of age, offending drops sharply, and by the age of twenty-eight about 85 percent of offenders desist from further offending (Moffitt, 1993:675). The vast majority who do not desist in early adulthood are offenders who commenced offending at an earlier age than those who do desist. Moffitt suggests that these two offender groups (early starters/late finishers and late starters/early finishers) represent two different etiological pathways to criminality. But what is it about adolescence that produces such a surge of antisocial behavior in many teenagers, particularly males?

First, males experience a ten-to-fifteen-fold increase in aggression-facilitating (not "causing") testosterone at puberty, which provides them with a lot of gas but nowhere to go. Females also get a slight increase, but males have about twenty times more of the activating testosterone than females. Second, MRI studies of brain development confirm what parents have always known, the adolescent brain, particularly the prefrontal cortex, is immature (Giedd, et al., 1999; Sowell, et al., 1999).

As noted earlier, the prefrontal cortex serves various executive functions, such as modulating emotions from the limbic system and making reasoned judgments and plans, something most teenagers are not very good at doing. Other MRI studies show that the link between the prefrontal cortex and the limbic system (the seat of our emotions) is not as well connected in adolescent brains as in adult brains (Baird, et al., 1998). Adolescence appears to be a period in which the fine-tuning of the brain is carried out. This may indicate that the adolescent brain, superimposed on an unfamiliar and diffused state of physiological arousal, may facilitate a tendency of the young to assign faulty and often negative attributions to the actions of others, which may result in antisocial responses.

Of course, all teenagers undergo this physiological maturation process, but only a few continue to commit serious antisocial acts after adolescence. Terrie Moffitt calls these *life-course persistent* offenders. Moffitt proposes that life-course persistent offenders have temperamental and neuropsychological problems that are evident in early childhood and initiate a number of cumulative negative interactions between them and their environment placing them on a developmental trajectory toward antisocial personality and behavior. As Moffitt describes this trajectory: "biting and hitting at age four, shoplifting and truancy at age ten, selling drugs and stealing cars at age sixteen, robbery and rape at age twenty-two, fraud and child abuse at age thirty; the underlying disposition remains the same, but its expression changes form as new social opportunities arise at different points of time" (1993:679).

A large number of studies have shown that life-course persistent offenders tend to be hyperactive, inattentive, negatively emotional, and have low-impulse control, and low IQ (Moffitt, 1993:680-681). All these traits are at least partially under genetic control via the operation of the various neurotransmitter and hormonal substances they produce. Hyperactivity and inattentiveness are related to sluggish RAS arousal and negative emotionality (Ellis and Coontz, 1990), and low-impulse control to low serotonin, a major mood modulating neurotransmitter (Spoont, 1992).

We also will see later that IQ is substantially inheritable. We can be quite confident, then, that the most serious and persistent of criminals have biological disabilities that put them at risk for offending. This observation does not mean that the social environment is not important to the understanding of life-course persistent offenders' behavior also. Negative emotionality and low-impulse control have also been related to rearing in abusive and discordant families (Caspi et al., 1994), as have ANS hypo-arousal and low IQ (reviewed in Walsh, 1995). However, behavior is the result of complex interactions between biological and environmental factors.

Moffitt calls juveniles who discontinue their offending in early adulthood adolescent-limited offenders. These offenders begin their offending at puberty, a biological event that suffuses them with boundless energy, strength, fragile confidence, and a strong desire to cut apron strings. Two or three generations ago, boys would have experienced puberty one or two years later, and probably would have obtained socially responsible roles, such as a relatively well paid full-time jobs shortly afterwards. Given the education required to participate responsibly in today's complex society, modern youth are trapped in a gap of about ten years duration between biological and social maturity rather than the one- or two-year gap experienced two or three generations ago. This gap is tailor-made to be filled with antisocial behavior.

According to Moffitt, many adolescent-limited boys gravitate to the excitement of antisocial peer groups led by "cool" life-course persistent males. Once in these groups, adolescent-limited offenders learn the techniques of offending by mimicking life-course persistent offenders and are reinforced for doing so by receiving material and psychological rewards. With neurological and social maturity (marriage, a job, parenthood, and so on), the vast majority of adolescent-onset offenders recognize the foolishness of their behavior and desist.

Note how Moffitt's theory differs from differential association, which posits a single causal route to criminality: association with delinquent peers. Moffitt asserts that for the great majority of offenders, association with delinquent peers leads only to temporary antisocial characteristics and offending, and is driven by a biosocial maturity gap. For life-course persistent offenders, association with delinquent peers is driven by their antisocial characteristics, which are the result of temperamental and neurological deficiencies combined with poor parenting. In other words, life-course persistent offenders possess *stable* antisocial characteristics, which *precede* and drive antisocial associations, while association with delinquent peers *precedes* the development of *temporary* antisocial characteristics for adolescent-limited offenders.

From Theory To Practice

Corrections workers may use information from these biosocial theories to aid in better understanding and assessing their charges. For instance, IQ information often is readily available from schools and/or clinical workups of offenders, and P>V discrepancy scores can be calculated. If psychologists discover a significant P>V, they often will point out that the P>V discrepancy is a marker of psychopathy in their clinical reports. However, you should not conclude that if a person has a significant discrepancy score (12 or more points) he or she is a psychopath; the P>V test is only a marker, not a definitive test. People who have superior visual/spatial skills, such as mathematicians and engineers, undoubtedly score significantly higher on PIQ than on VIQ. However, both sets of scores for such professionals would be in the superior range, whereas criminals with a P>V profile tend to have an average PIQ (around 100) coupled with a low (below 90) VIQ.

Another marker of violent behavior, favored more by psychiatrists than psychologists, is a history of enuresis (bedwetting), fire setting, and cruelty to animals, all of which are related to suboptimal arousal levels. The response to the necessity to void our bladders during sleep usually results in waking up and doing so. Parents of many violent and psychopathic individuals often report that their children wet the bed well into late childhood or adolescence. Not awakening in response to the urge to void (in the absence of any organic pathology, of course) may be seen as a function of a hyporeactive ANS failing to arouse the child and a general difficulty in the voluntary control of impulses. Ellis and Walsh (2000:242) found twenty-one studies supportive of the link between enuresis and antisocial behavior and three studies with nonsignificant results.

Setting fires and watching them burn is an exciting activity. Most of us limit this kind of activity to burning leaves and garbage, but some find setting fire to buildings to be intensely stimulating. Since psychopaths lack the attribute we call a conscience, there is little difficulty in accepting the idea that they may have few qualms about sacrificing someone's home in the pursuit of the visceral excitement they crave. Recall that this need for excessive excitement has been viewed as a function of sluggish reticular and autonomic systems, which inclines some to consider what many of us find exciting to be eminently boring.

The third behavior of the triad, cruelty to animals, is indicative of the lack of love and sympathy psychopaths have for other living things and their lack of empathy for the suffering of others. The budding psychopath finds cats and hamsters suitable targets for his cruelty until he gets big enough to take on humans.

Any one of these three behaviors taken alone requires a variety of interpretations that do not concern us. Taken together, they constitute an excellent diagnostic tool. Of course, there are many other variables that are predictive of violent behavior. This predictor (to include enuresis, fire setting, and cruelty to animals), unlike many other predictors, is included almost routinely in the psychiatric reports that you will be reading as correctional workers. To the extent that Moffitt's two-pathway model of offending is accurate, and studies from around the world support the belief that it is, offenders' rap sheets should tell you a lot about them. All other things being equal, the earlier they began offending, the less likely they are to discontinue, and the less likely they are to respond positively to correctional treatment.

LESSONS AND CONCERNS

What are the implications of biosocial theories for the correctional worker beyond an increased understanding of the problem of criminal behavior? Certainly, you can do nothing about the early developmental history of offenders. If abuse and neglect are reflected in the actual structure and functioning of the brain, the answer to the problem, if there is one, lies in social engineering related to child-rearing practices on a massive scale. We thus have returned to sociology and to the same sort of practical difficulties we encountered when examining sociological theories. Bryan Vila (1997) offers abundant evidence that money spent on what he calls *nurturant strategies* (good quality prenatal and postnatal care and child care, paid maternity leave, prevention of unwanted pregnancies, support for families, monitoring of infant development, home health care visits, and so forth) would be money well invested (*see also* Walsh, 1991; Walsh and Ellis, 1997). As corrections practitioners, we can only say that these things would be nice, but we have to adapt ourselves to conditions as they exist. We have the difficult job of trying to correct the damage done, allegedly by the failure to implement such strategies.

The psychopath (who may be fairly synonymous with Moffitt's life-course persistent offenders) is a poor candidate for rehabilitation. Robert Hare (1993:198-200) states that the psychopath is apparently incapable of the empathy, warmth, and sincerity needed to develop the type of emotional relationship required for effective therapy. Not only do psychopaths lack these attributes, they lack the anxiety that prods change, and see nothing wrong with themselves, anyway. Hare concludes that treatment often makes them worse (they learn how to better push others' buttons).

Andrews and Bonta (1998) are less pessimistic, insisting that early identification and family interventions such as those recommended by Vila may work. A corrections worker who is to achieve any success at all with such individuals must be prepared to set strict limits on their behavior and stand doggedly by them. He or she must be to some extent an authority figure, albeit a warm "parental" authority figure, with offenders assumed to possess this character disorder. Reality therapy (*see* Chapter 10) may prove to be the most effective method for dealing with the psychopath in a correctional setting.

Perspective from the Field:
The Relevance of Theory to Field Practitioners
By Kate King, Ph.D.

Dr. Kate King is an associate professor of Criminal Justice at Boise State University. She has been teaching criminal justice since 1990. Prior to her teaching career, Dr. King worked for eight years as a paralegal on death penalty cases in California. She also has taught various courses in prison, assisting inmates in their preparation for the high school equivalency test. Dr. King's primary areas of research include HIV/AIDS in prison, attitudes of correctional officers, and elderly inmates. She currently is collecting data about the experiences of families of murder victims and the experiences of families of death row inmates.

Criminal justice practitioners are asked to make resource allocations daily. Money, time, and programs are scarce commodities in the justice system. Spending available resources wisely is important and information can help. But what kind of information does one need? Would explanations of human behavior help us respond more appropriately to clients? Is it important to understand how people think to get the job done? Are early life experiences relevant to adult perceptions and behavior? I believe the answer is "Absolutely Yes!"

The goal of any theory in criminal justice is to create a model that will allow us to better understand criminal behavior and develop strategies to deal with it. Theory informs our decisions. We are able to spend our scarce resources where they are most likely to be beneficial. There are many theories that try to explain why crime occurs, or why certain people seem to be predisposed to commit crimes. Law-abiding citizens are often unable to understand criminal behavior that persists in spite of punishment because it does not seem rational. There is solid evidence that crime may not be the product of purely rational decision making. Biosocial theories suggest that genes and the environment combine to produce particular traits, some of which may lead to crime. This biological predisposition is triggered by environmental factors that produce different results in different people.

Theoretical development has not always gone smoothly. Much of the early biological research on crime has been discredited. Lombroso's ideas of the atavistic criminal with the ferocious instincts of primitive humans and inferior animals fell into disrepute. Gall's "lumps on the head" theory (phrenology) became extremely popular, but has not held up under scientific scrutiny. Despite Sheldon's conclusion that certain body types (endomorph, mesomorph, and ectomorph) are correlated with temperament and behavior, his theory has been dismissed by mainstream criminologists. Although body type has been consistently found to be related to delinquency and criminality (it is highest among mesomorphs), no direct link between body type and criminality has been established. The XYY chromosome theory, which suggested that chromosome abnormalities could result in overly aggressive males who were more likely to engage in criminal behavior, likewise has been discarded. It turned out that XYY individuals were no more likely to commit violent crimes than XY individuals, although they are significantly more likely to commit other forms of crimes. This propensity has more to do with their lower IQ scores than with their supposed aggressive tendencies. However, with the advances in medical science and technology, new biological theories are gaining recognition.

Today's researchers understand that inherited traits interact with environmental factors. Recent studies on twins have found more similarity between identical twins than between fraternal twins. Adoption studies have found similarities between the adopted individual and his/her biological parent, especially in the cases of chronic, violent behavior. Biosocial theories attempt to unravel the complex interactions between genetic inheritance and environment and explain how these factors influence behavior.

But what is the relevance of these theories to practitioners in the field? Being familiar with the different theories of crime helps us make sense of the otherwise nonsensical actions of our clients. It allows criminal justice workers to recognize and catalog offenders by their comments and patterns of behavior. It assists us in creating intelligent responses in the field and meaningful programs for offenders. For example, many offenders have extensive criminal histories, multiple incarcerations, and increasingly severe offenses. These people seem incapable of respecting other people. They seem unable to learn from their experiences, to form meaningful relationships, or to show guilt about the harm they cause. The theories of psychopathy tell us that these are the characteristics of psychopaths. Appealing to their sense of responsibility or social conscience is futile. Expecting them to respect the rights of others is unrealistic. These people are utterly self-centered and have no social conscience.

Of course, not all psychopaths are offenders and not all offenders are psychopaths, but these people do exist, and their behavior is predictable. Realizing this can be very helpful to criminal justice professionals when choosing candidates for treatment programs, suspended sentences, or community placement. As Walsh points out, psychopaths do not make good candidates for rehabilitation.

Some offenders seem to have no fear. Others are easily bored and stir up trouble just for something to do. They seek excitement regardless of the consequences. Biosocial theories help us understand that these traits are connected to the chemical makeup of the brain. A correctional officer familiar with suboptimal arousal theory, for example, could use this information in selecting job assignments for inmates. Some prison jobs offer more stimuli than others and assigning "stimuli cravers" to those jobs might lessen their need to cause disruptions within the prison environment.

Psychological theories have been very influential in establishing rehabilitative programs. Correctional counselors have used the tenets of psychology in intervention programs designed to change the offender from a maladapted individual to a normal person. Group therapy sessions are designed to help offenders get at the root of their problems and learn new ways to control their behavior. "Thinking errors" classes have been developed and sometimes are led by counselors, sometimes by correctional staff. The ideas behind the thinking errors classes come directly from psychological theories.

Learning reinforcement techniques have come from psychological theories as well. Learning reinforcement theory states that people respond to consequences and either persist or desist in different behaviors, depending on whether they are rewarded or punished for their acts. Because there are so many types of crime and offenders come from a variety of backgrounds and experiences, no theory explains every criminal act or person. Indeed, good theorists are careful to clarify their assumptions and specify their boundaries. But the criminal justice practitioners, armed with theoretical knowledge, can make more sense out of their environment. The professionals who understand the misbehavior of criminals and the possible causes of that misbehavior can make more informed choices about resource allocation, whether that resource is administrative detention, group therapy, a particular job assignment, or the penalty imposed for criminal acts. Scarce correctional resources should be used where they are most likely to produce results. Theory helps us understand offenders and devise strategies to handle, help, or simply cope with them in the course of our profession.

Summary

From the perspective presented in this chapter, the tendency toward crime is located in the individual. This does not mean that some people are born criminals or that crime is "in the genes." The first concepts we discussed were gene/environment correlation and interaction, noting that genes are constantly in a complex dance with their environments: neither genes nor environments "cause" behavior independently. We next explored the BIS/BAS concept and noted that inveterate criminals tend to have a dominant BAS; in other words, they tend to be far more sensitive to rewards than to punishment. We looked at psychopathy in terms of suboptimal arousal levels of ANS (specifically, the fight/flight system) and RAS functioning and the functioning of the prefrontal cortex. A person with a hyporeactive fight/flight system does not feel the same level of fear and anxiety that those with a more normally functioning one feel. Not being overly concerned with the punitive consequences of criminal activity, lacking a sense of guilt, and lacking sympathy for their victims, psychopaths tend to engage in crime with alarming frequency. Psychopaths and career criminals tend to have high dopamine and low serotonin and norepinepherine levels.

A person with a sluggish RAS is prone to boredom. He or she seeks higher levels of excitement than do most of us, a search that often ends in trouble. A person who is quickly bored is also not very likely to spend much time in academic pursuits that lead to a rewarding legitimate career. Such a person is also quite likely to seek artificial stimulation through the use of drugs and "thrill-seeking" crimes.

We then looked at the possible influence of child abuse and neglect on the structure and functioning of the brain. The experiences that we undergo during the phases of rapid brain cell growth influence the structure and function of our brains. Positive experiences in the form of plentiful stimuli, especially tactile stimuli, have the effect of wiring the brain to experience pleasure in the company of others. Negative early experiences have the opposite effect. Extremely negative experiences during infancy and childhood may lead to future violent behavior of psychopathic proportions.

Terrie Moffitt's dual-pathway model of the etiology of criminal offending was then examined. This model emphasizes that biological factors may be more important than environmental factors in explaining the small percentage of recidivistic offenders she calls life-course persistent offenders. On the other hand, environmental factors are probably more important for explaining the offending behavior of the majority of offenders who desist with social maturity (adolescent-limited offenders). Moffitt does not neglect environmental factors in the etiology of life-course persistent offenders, however. She emphasizes that inept parenting may interact with temperamental and neurological factors to produce antisocial characteristics.

References and Suggested Readings

Alcock, J. 1998. *Animal Behavior: An Evolutionary Approach*, 6th edition. Sunderland, Massachusetts: Sinauer Associates.

Andrews, D. and J. Bonta. 1998. *The Psychology of Criminal Conduct*. Cincinnati, Ohio: Anderson Publishing.

Baird, A., S. Gruber, D. Fein, L. Maas, R. Steingard, P. Renshaw, B. Cohen, and D. Yurgelun-Todd. 1998. Functional magnetic resonance imaging of facial affect recognition in children and adolescents. *Journal of the Academy of Child and Adolescent Psychiatry*. 38:195-199.

Barnett, R., L. Zimmer, and J. McCormack. 1989. P>V sign and personality profiles. *Journal of Correctional and Social Psychiatry and Offender Treatment and Therapy*. 35:18-20.

Bouchard, T., D. Lykken, M. McGue, N. Segal, and A. Tellegen.1990. Sources of human psychological differences: The Minnesota study of twins reared apart. *Science*. 250:223-228.

Brennan, P., A. Raine, F. Schulsinger, L. Kirkegaard-Sorenen, J. Knop, B. Hutchings, R. Rosenberg, and S. Mednick. 1997. Psychophysiological protective factors for male subjects at high risk for criminal behavior. *American Journal of Psychiatry*. 154:853-855.

Caspi, A., T. Moffitt, P. Silva, M. Stouthamer-Loeber, R. Krueger, and P. Schmutte. 1994. Are some people crime prone? Replications of the personality-crime relationship across countries, genders, races, and methods. *Criminology*. 32:163-195.

Cornell, D. and L. Wilson. 1992. The PIQ>VIQ discrepancy in violent and nonviolent delinquents. *Journal of Clinical Psychology*. 48:256-261.

Depue, R. and P. Collins. 1999. Neurobiology of the structure of personality: Dopamine,facilitation of incentive motivation, and extraversion. *Behavioral and Brain Sciences*. 22:491- 569.

Durkheim, E. 1982. *Rules of Sociological Method*. S. Lukes, trans. New York: Free Press.

Edelman, G. 1998. Building a picture of the brain. *Daedalus*.127:37-69.

Ellis, L. 1996. Arousal Theory and the Religiosity-Criminality Relationship. In P. Cordella and L. Siegel, eds. *Readings in Contemporary Criminological Theory*. Boston: Northeastern University Press.

Ellis, L. and P. Coontz. 1990. Androgens, Brain Functioning, and Criminality: The Neurohormonal Foundation of Antisociality. In L. Ellis and H. Hoffman, eds. *Crime in Biological, Social, and Moral Contexts*. Westport, Connecticut: Praeger.

Ellis, L. and A. Walsh. 2000. *Criminology: A Global Perspective*. Boston: Allyn and Bacon.

Farrington, D. 2001. Cross-national Comparative Studies in Criminology. In H. Pontell and D. Shichor, eds. *Contemporary Issues in Crime and Criminal Justice.* Upper Saddle River, New Jersey: Prentice-Hall.

Farrington, D., L. Ohlin, and J. Wilson. 1986. *Understanding and Controlling Crime: Toward a New Research Strategy*. New York: Springer-Verlag.

Fisher, H. 1998. Lust, attraction, and attachment in mammalian reproduction. *Human Nature.* 9:23-52.

Gibbons, D. 1973. *Society, Crime, and Criminal Careers*. Englewood Cliffs, New Jersey: Prentice-Hall.

Giedd, J., J. Blumenthal, N. Jeffries, F. Castellanos, H. Liu, A. Zijenbos, T. Paus, A. Evans, and J. Rapoport. 1999. Brain development during childhood and adolescence: A longitudinal MRI study. *Nature Neuroscience.* 2:861-863.

Glaser, D. 2000. Child abuse and neglect and the brain—A review. *Journal of Child Psychology and Psychiatry.* 41:97-116.

Glasser, W. 1976. *The Identity Society*. New York: Harper and Row.

Gove, W. and C. Wilmoth. 1990. Risk, Crime, and Neurophysiologic Highs: A Consideration of Brain Processes That May Reinforce Delinquent and Criminal Behavior. In Ellis, L. and H. Hoffman, eds. *Crime in Biological, Social, and Moral Contexts*. Westport, Connecticut: Praeger.

Griffiths, P. 1990. Modularity and the psychoevolutionary theory of emotion. *Biology and Philosophy.* 5:175-196.

Hare, R. 1993. *Without Conscience: The Disturbing World of the Psychopaths Among Us.* New York: Pocket Books.

_____. 1996. Psychopathy: A clinical construct whose time has come. *Criminal Justice and Behavior.* 23:25-54.

Kalil, R. 1989. Synapse formation in the developing brain. *Scientific American.* 76:85.

Katz, J. 1988. *Seductions of Crime: Moral and Sensual Attractions in Doing Evil*. New York: Basic Books.

Kraemer, G. 1992. A psychobiological theory of attachment. *Behavioral and Brain Sciences.* 15:493-541.

Konner, M. 1982. *The Tangled Wing: Biological Constraints on the Human Spirit*. New York: Holt, Rinehart and Winston.

Kruesi, M., H. Leonard, S. Swedo, S. Nadi, S. Hamburger, J. Lui, and J. Rapoport. 1994. Endogenous Opioids, Childhood Psychopathology, and Quay's Interpretation of Jeffrey Gray. In D. Routh, ed. *Disruptive Behavior Disorders in Childhood*. New York: Plenum.

Lykken, D. 1995. *The Antisocial Personalities*. Hillsdale, New Jersey: Lawrence Erlbaum.

Machalek, R. 1995. Basic dimensions and forms of social exploitation: A comparative analysis. *Advances in Human Ecology*. 4:35-68.

Mealey, L. 1995. The sociobiology of sociopathy: An integrated evolutionary model. *Behavioral and Brain Sciences*. 18:523-599.

McGue, M., S. Bacon, and D. Lykken. 1993. Personality stability and change in early adulthood: A behavioral genetic analysis. *Developmental Psychology*. 29:96-109.

Miller, L. 1987. Neuropsychology of the aggressive psychopath: An integrative review. *Aggressive Behavior*. 13:119-140.

Moffitt, T. 1993. Adolescent-limited and life-course persistent antisocial behavior: A developmental taxonomy. *Psychological Review*. 100:674-701.

Nesse, R. 1990. Evolutionary explanations of emotions. *Human Nature*. 1:261-289.

Patrick, C. 1994. Emotion and psychopathy: Startling new insights. *Psychophysiology*. 31:319-330.

Perry, B. 1997. Incubated in Terror: Neurodevelopmental Factors in the "Cycle of Violence,"J. Osofsky, ed. *Children in a Violent Society*. New York: Guilford Press.

Perry, B. and R. Pollard. 1998. Homeostasis, stress, trauma, and adaptation: A neurodevelopmental view of childhood trauma. *Child and Adolescent Psychiatric Clinics of America*. 733-51.

Pihl, R. and K. Bruce. 1995. Cognitive impairments in children of alcoholics. *Alcohol, Health and Research World*. 19:142-147.

Pinel, J. 2000. *Biopsychology, 4th edition*. Boston: Allyn and Bacon.

Plomin, R. 1995. Genetics and children's experiences in the family. *Journal of Child Psychology and Psychiatry*. 36:33-68.

Raine, A. 1997. Antisocial Behavior and Psychophysiology: A Biosocial Perspective and a Prefrontal Dysfunction Hypothesis. In Stoff, D., J. Breiling, and J. Maser, eds. *Handbook of Antisocial Behavior*. New York: John Wiley.

Raine, A., T. Lencz, S. Buhrle, L. LaCasse, and P. Colletti. 2000. Reduced prefrontal gray matter volume and reduced autonomic activity in antisocial personality disorder. *Archives of General Psychiatry.* 57:119-127.

Reiss, A., M. Abrams, H. Singer, J. Ross, and M. Bencla. 1996. Brain development, gender and IQ in children: A volumetric imaging study. *Brain.* 119:1763-1774.

Ruden, R. 1997. *The Craving Brain: The Biobalance Approach to Controlling Addictions.* New York: Harper Collins.

Shore, R. 1997. *Rethinking the Brain: New Insights into Early Development.* New York: Families and Work Institute.

Solomon, R. 1980. The opponent-process theory of acquired motivation. *American Psychologist.* 35:691-712.

Sowell, E., P. Thompson, C. Holmes, T. Jernigan, and A. Toga. 1999. In vivo evidence for post-adolescent brain maturation in frontal and striatal regions. *Nature Neuroscience.* 2:859- 861.

Spoont, M. 1992. Modulatory role of serotonin in neural information processing: Implications for human psychopathology. *Psychological Bulletin.* 112:330-350.

Suchy, Y., A. Blint, and D. Osman. 1997. Behavioral dyscontrol scale: Criterion and predictive validity in an inpatient rehabilitation unit population. *Clinical Neuropsychologist.* 11:258- 265.

Teicher, M., Y. Ito, C. Glod, F. Schiffer, and H. Gelbard. 1997. Early Abuse, Limbic System Dysfunction, and Borderline Personality Disorder. In J. Osofsky, ed. *Children in a Violent Society.* New York: Guilford Press.

Tracy, P., M. Wolfgang, and R. Figlio. 1990. *Delinquency Careers in Two Birth Cohorts.* New York: Plenum.

Trivers, R. 1991. Deceit and Self-Deception: The Relationship Between Communication and Consciousness. In M. Robinson and L. Tiger, eds. *Man and Beast Revisited.* Washington, D.C.: Smithsonian Institution Press.

Udry, J. R. 1995. Sociology and biology: What biology do sociologists need to know? *Social Forces.* 73:1267-1278.

van der Kolk, B. and M. Greenberg. 1987. The Physiology of the Trauma Response: Hyperarousal, Constriction, and Addiction to Traumatic Reexposure. In B. van der Kolk., ed. *Psychological Trauma.* Washington, D.C.: American Psychiatric Press.

Vila, B. 1997. Human nature and crime control: Improving the feasibility of nurtrant strategies. *Politics and the Life Sciences.* 16:3-21.

Walsh, A. 1990. Illegitimacy, child abuse and neglect, and cognitive development. *Journal of Genetic Psychology*. 151:279-285.

_____. 1991. *Intellectual Imbalance, Love Deprivation and Violent Delinquency: A Biosocial Perspective*. Springfield, Illinois: Charles C. Thomas.

_____. 1995. *Biosociology: An Emerging Paradigm*. Westport, Connecticut: Praeger.

_____. 2000. Evolutionary psychology and the origins of justice. *Justice Quarterly.* 17:4.

Walsh, A. and L. Ellis. 1997. The neurobiology of nurturance, evolutionary expectations, and crime control. *Politics and the Life Sciences*. 16:42-44.

Walsh, A. and T. Petee. 1987. Love deprivation and violent delinquency. *Journal of Crime and Justice*. 10:45-61.

Wechsler, D. 1958. *The Measurement and Appraisal of Adult Intelligence*. Baltimore, Maryland: Williams and Wilkins.

Wolfgang, M., R. Figlio, and T. Sellin. 1972. *Delinquency in a Birth Cohort*. Chicago, Illinois: University of Chicago Press.

The Self: Principal Tool
of the Correctional Helper

The most important factor effecting behavior is the self-concept. . . . The self is the star of every performance, the central figure in every act. Persons engaging in the helping professions, therefore, need the broadest possible understanding of the nature, origins, and functions of the self-concept.

Arthur Combs, Donald Avilla, and William Purkey

As Garrett points out, it is important that professional interviewers (and counselors) have more than a casual knowledge of human behavior and motivation, and that, "They should apply this knowledge, not only to an understanding of their clients' personalities, needs, prejudices, and emotions, but also to an understanding of their own. The wise maxim of the ancient Greeks, 'Know thyself,' applies especially to interviewers" (1982:5). Knowing yourself implies an honest self-appraisal of all your strengths and weaknesses with the intention of honing your strengths and working diligently to eliminate, or at least acknowledge and deal with, your weaknesses. The goal of this chapter is to get you to examine what you really think about yourself — to examine your self-concept.

The Self-Concept

There are many tools available to you to modify the behavior of offenders, but your own self-concept is the most important. A person can decline the use of other tools, but corrections work demands the use of the self. Effective helping behavior involves interaction between two selves. The offender's self, almost by definition, is deficient in some important aspects. His or her involvement in the criminal justice system demonstrates some degree of difficulty in behaving in a responsible manner. To compensate for the deficiencies of one-half of the interacting dyad (the offender), the other half (the criminal justice worker) must possess some extraordinary qualities if the relationship is to be an effective one. Before we discuss the interviewing process, it is a good idea to examine briefly the primary tool used in that process.

The importance of self-concept in understanding your behavior and that of the offenders is of the utmost importance. Your self-concept is who and what you believe that unique individual you refer to as "me" is all about. It is the central core of your existence, your focus of reality from which the world around you is experienced, understood, and evaluated. The self-concept is not the "real self" (whatever that is), it is rather the *picture* we have of ourselves in our heads. Your self-concept is both the product and producer of your experiences. If you are capable of giving and receiving love, if you consider yourself to be a worthwhile person, if you are confident in yourself, and if you behave responsibly, you will be able to bring positive feelings about yourself to the helping relationship.

You have developed these ideas about yourself through a lifetime of interacting with others and incorporating both their attitudes and feelings about you and their evaluations and expectations of you. Thus, your self-concept is the product of your experience. Since you do have a positive self-concept derived from the positive beliefs about you held by significant others, your behavior will tend to confirm their beliefs and yours in a kind of psychological version of the "rich get richer" spiral. As a famous author once said, "What a man [or woman] thinks of himself [or herself] contains his [or her] destiny." In this way, your self-concept produces your behavior.

Now, consider individuals whose experiences have resulted in a negative self-concept. Their behavior also will tend to confirm their self-perceptions derived from those unhappy experiences. If their experiences are such that they develop negative self-concepts, they are likely to view the world as an unfriendly place and to engage in behavior not likely to endear them to others. Such people may feel trapped in a way of life without much hope of improvement, being victims of their own self-perceptions, or "stinking thinking," as many counselors might refer to it. The psychological spiral now swirls in the opposite direction: "the poor get poorer." "I'm no good. I can't be—nobody loves me, wants me, or cares for me." "Who cares anyway? Not me; they can all go to hell!" "I can't get a job because I'm not very smart—everyone says so." "I'll just get what I need by taking it from all those suckers out there, and just let them try to stop me." This is the mind-set of many offenders caught up in the criminal justice system, and this is the mind-set that the correctional helper must wrestle with and overcome.

However, to accomplish this task, and it is an arduous and lengthy one, your own self-concept must be up to it. As Combs, Avila, and Purkey (1971:56-57) so well put it: Since new concepts of self are learned as a consequence of interactions with the helper, effective helpers must be significant people. They cannot be nonentities. One cannot interact with a shadow. The helping relationship is an active one, and a passive helper is unlikely to teach his [or her] client anything but his [or her] own futility. The personality of the helper must play a vital part in any helping relationship. It is the helper's use of his [or her] self which makes the interaction whatever it is to become.

Self-esteem

Although commonly considered so, the terms self-concept and self-esteem are not synonyms. The self-concept involves two separate motives: the motive to think well of the self—self-esteem, and the motive to protect the self from change—the self-consistency motive (Rosenberg, 1979:53). All counseling can be viewed as efforts to enhance offenders' self-esteem and efforts to get them to examine the self-consistency motive to get them to change the image of the self in positive directions.

It is pretty easy to recognize low self-esteem in people. People with low self-esteem are either "accepters" or "deniers." Accepters recognize the low regard that they have for themselves and constantly put themselves down, sometimes publicly, often privately. Deniers fight against their low opinions of themselves by constantly putting other people down so that they may feel superior by comparison. Accepters take little pride in their appearance or personal hygiene; deniers dress flashily and often outrageously. Both types are psychological traps that will lead to miserable unfulfilled lives. No one should have to face the complexities of modern living carrying around a picture of themselves as worthless failures.

However, because we have had plenty of experience with ourselves, we have a built-in bias against changing our self-image, even if we do not like the image. People need a sense of order and consistency in their lives, so what they have become used to doing and thinking becomes habitual and comfortable. This is as true of what they think of themselves as it is of what they think of baseball, chocolate pudding, or Madonna. To maintain this comfortable consistency, we often engage in selective-perception, which is seeing only what we want to see. We also may perpetuate our self-images by distorting reality, meaning that we find it difficult to really hear or under-stand the meaning of any message about ourselves, positive or negative, that do not fit the pictures we have about ourselves in our heads. This is why people's self-consistency motive must be challenged before they can build their self-esteem.

The desire for self-approval—to think of oneself as worthy—is perhaps the dom-inant force in a person's motivational system (Kaplan, 1982:139, Glasser, 1975). Many theorists firmly place the taproots of self-esteem in the ability to give and receive love, an assertion that has received much empirical support (Buri, Kirchner and Walsh, 1987; Walsh and Walsh, 1989; Walsh and Balazs, 1990). Criminals do not usually feel worthy, and this lack of self-esteem gets them into trouble with the law. They take drugs and alcohol in vain attempts to feel better, and seek out all other manner of de-viant ways to bolster their damaged self-esteem (Berman and Siegal, 1976; Buikhuisen, 1987). Yablonsky (1990:449) writes that violent youths (adults too) are, "because of their low self-esteem, acting out self-destructive behavior; they have limited concern about whether they live or die." It is part of your job as a criminal justice worker to help offenders to recognize their self-destructive behavior, to challenge their self-consistency motives, and to change their patterns of self-talk that contribute to their negative self-esteem. This is a tall order, but a challenging and exciting one for the ded-icated and effective correctional worker.

There is a shady side to the conventional wisdom that high self-esteem is conducive to prosocial behavior and that low self-esteem is conducive to antisocial behavior. Many highly antisocial individuals, especially psychopaths, have highly exaggerated opinions of their self-worth (Hare, 1993), and many even have a god-like attitude that they are the center of the universe (Sharp, 2000). On the other hand, shy, insecure, and self-deprecating individuals (those we have termed "accepters") are very much underrepresented in criminal populations (Baumeister, Smart, and Boden, 1996). Contrary to what Yablonsky asserts above, it has been found that most male/male assaults and homicides arise from trivial incidents that threaten bloated opinions of the perpetrator's self-worth rather than from low self-esteem (Anderson, 1999; Baumeister, Smart, and Boden, 1996).

Of course, we always can claim that such bloated self-esteem is really egotism, narcissism, conceit, and arrogance (typical of those we have called "deniers"), rather than "true" self-esteem, and that someone with "true" self-esteem would be immune to minor assaults on his or her self-worth. The kind of self-esteem earned on the streets ("juice") does not tolerate being "dissed," and is therefore dangerous self-esteem (Barash and Lipton, 2001). However, it has been earned in a way that is valued and respected in the streets, making it difficult to convince those who have it that it is worthless and damaging to them. Earning status and respect in a more prosocial manner makes little sense to those embedded in a criminal subculture, and who think their "bad ass" reputations entitle them to do as they please.

Qualities of Effective Correctional Workers

This chapter is about the correctional worker—you, or the potential you—not about assessment, casework, counseling, the criminal personality, and so forth. But you must become comfortable with all those things, as well as with yourself in correctional situations so that you may effectively use them. As Jeffrey Schrink (2000:58) puts it: "Counseling in a correctional setting with clients who may have long histories of failure demands a level of physical and psychological intensity that is unusual in the helping professions." Corrections is a fascinating but emotionally demanding line of work, and not everybody can do it. The rest of this chapter is designed to give you some feeling about whether you can become comfortable and effective in this line of work—to see if you have "the right stuff."

Much research has gone into determining what constitutes effective correctional supervision. And guess what? Most of it emphasizes the primary importance of the correctional worker's self. Andrews and Bonta (1998) summarize this research and provide what they consider to be the five dimensions of effective correctional supervision and counseling. These dimensions are briefly summarized here.

1. Relationship factors: Correctional workers should relate to inmates/offenders in an open, enthusiastic, and caring way.
2. Authority factors: Be firm but fair. Distinguish between rules and requests. Reinforce behavioral compliance, do not use dominance and abuse to force it.
3. Anticriminal modeling and reinforcement: Demonstrate and reinforce noncriminal styles of thinking, feeling, and behaving.
4. Concrete problem solving: Help offenders to build skills and remove obstacles to prosocial behavior in home, school, and work settings.
5. Advocacy and brokerage: Help offenders to help themselves by brokering services offered in the community that will help them with concrete problem solving (the prior dimension).

Meditate on those five dimensions for a while and realize that the kind of person you are means more to the success or failure of the endeavor than anything else except the kind of person the offender is. All this points to the conclusion that correctional workers must possess some extraordinary qualities if they are to have a meaningful part in changing the deficient self-concepts of so many offenders. In addition to a positive self-concept, other necessary qualities for an effective correctional worker include: a genuine liking for people, a good sense of humor (boy, does that help in this line of work!), and intellectual maturity. We will now briefly look at what those qualities are, and at some potential problems associated with unidentified areas of the correctional worker's self that may detract from the helping process.

The Correctional Worker Must Possess a Thorough Knowledge of Criminal Behavior and its Correlates. You should develop the interest and the patience to conduct an ongoing study of the forces and events affecting the lives of offenders. Knowledge of criminological theories, theories about substance abuse, and abnormal psychology enable you to view more objectively offenders' frames of reference. And, it lessens the impulse toward moralizing about *their* behavior based on your *own*. The subject matter of your field is people with problems that cause them to act irresponsibly. Individuals who aspire to be professionals must know their subject matter. However, no one expects you to be a specialist in all areas pertaining to criminal behavior. Think of your role as analogous to that of a physician in general practice. That is, you should know something about a wide range of crime-related subjects, but you should be wise enough to know your limitations and to refer to someone more knowledgeable—a specialist—when those limits are reached.

The Correctional Worker Must Be Realistic—Neither a Pollyanna nor a Cassandra: A *Pollyanna* is a person whose irrepressible optimism finds good in everything. Such a person often fails to see, or discounts, danger signals. He or she avoids or discourages negative feedback and is extremely reluctant to confront resisting or reluctant offenders. Pollyannas are gullible, take what offenders say at face value, and allow offenders to get away with too many minor infractions. They believe that this leniency marks them as nonauthoritarian and nondirective counselors. What they really are, however, are individuals who, lacking in self-confidence, provide no meaningful guidance or supervision to offenders whose personal and legal needs require it.

A *Cassandra* is a person who sees negativism in everything. He or she also lacks a sense of competence and feeds such a lack by discounting positive feedback. Cassandras are cynical, do not trust offenders at all, and attempt to avoid positive interactions with them. They also tend to set their goals and expectations impossibly high, thus ensuring offender failure. Whereas Pollyannas tend to provide unwarranted positive feedback when confrontation is required, Cassandras give feedback only when the offender has not lived up to expectations, but they will not reinforce positive behavior with positive feedback.

Both of these working styles are unrealistic and reflect attitudes about the self as well as toward offenders. The Pollyanna sees corrections work solely as social work and wants to "help," the Cassandra views it as police work and wants to control. Realistic corrections workers view their task as both and have sufficient understanding and self-confidence to know when the use of either role is appropriate. Lauen (1997:169) sums up this balance well when he writes: "Effective rehabilitative efforts involve workers who are interpersonally warm, tolerant, and flexible, yet sensitive to conventional rules and procedures."

Correctional Workers Do Not Use Offenders to Satisfy Their Needs: If the correctional worker has unresolved needs, the counselor/offender relationship is not the place to attempt to satisfy them. The insecure worker who needs to feel powerful, for instance, will overcontrol interactions. He or she will dominate the direction of counseling sessions, pose as an expert, and will try to convert offenders by preaching at them. Power-hungry counselors feel safe in pursuing their needs in this way with a captive clientele, but it is counterproductive and a misuse of authority.

Other correctional workers may attempt to satisfy their needs for warmth and acceptance through the offenders. Their interactions with the offenders are designed to elicit cues that they are liked and accepted. Like Pollyannas, they will blind themselves to negative cues because they fear rejection, and they are opening themselves to manipulation. It is quite alright to be friendly with offenders, but not friends (of course, not enemies either).

In contrast, there are unresourceful counselors who are fearful of control or fearful of closeness. Whereas the power-hungry and the acceptance-needers suffocate the offenders with attention, the weak and the distance-needers avoid contact as much as possible. Those who fear control will neglect to offer offenders advice and direction when needed and generally will be passive onlookers. Those counselors who fear closeness will act distant with the offenders, will avoid addressing offenders' positive feelings, and will not develop the involvement necessary for the helping process.

To put it another way, correctional workers must like people and enjoy frequent contact with them. They must like to solve different problems presented, and must take pride in doing a job that many people cannot do.

The Correctional Worker Inspires Trust, Confidence, and Credibility: Effective helping requires that offenders feel confident that they can share themselves with the helper. If they are to share their feelings, hopes, fears, and concerns openly, they first must sense a nonjudgmental acceptance on your part. They must come to view you as a credible professional, have confidence in your abilities and motives, and trust you to accept their feelings and concerns without criticizing, shaming, or ridiculing them. To be perceived this way, you must be this way. You cannot long feign openness, honesty, concern, and acceptance. You must cultivate these self-attributes. This does not mean that you should naively accept at face value everything offenders say anymore than you should always distrust them; but do have reality-based expectations of them.

The Correctional Worker Reaches Inward as Well as Outward: You should develop a commitment to nondefensive self-examination and awareness: "Who am I, what am I like as a person?" "Am I almost always honest, trustworthy, likable, accepting?" "Am I the type of person who inspires confidence and trust?" "Do I really make an effort to understand offenders and their environments?" "Am I a competent person?" "Do I find myself using people to satisfy my needs for power or for acceptance?" "Do I have the courage to change those aspects of myself that I do not like?"

As a correctional worker, you often will have offenders who are different from you. What are your attitudes about people who are different? Do you harbor racist or sexist attitudes and stereotypes? Can you accept and interact with individuals of a different race, sex, sexual preference, or socioeconomic background as easily as with individuals with whom you have these things in common? Do you value, or are you fearful of, diversity of attitudes and values? Do you accept different religions, political ideologies, and sexual lifestyles as being alternatives rather than regarding them as deviant? The more you learn about the various types of people with whom you will come into contact, and the more you explore your attitudes toward them and toward yourself with an open mind, the more you will become the sort of person who is an effective helper.

Perspective from the Field:
Pollyanna and Cassandra: Two Sides of a Bad Coin
By Robert M. Freeman, Ph.D.

Dr. Freeman is an assistant professor of criminal justice at Shippensburg University, Pennsylvania. His BA and MA degrees are in psychology and his Ph.D. is in criminology and criminal justice. For twenty years, he held a number of positions in the Pennsylvania Department of Corrections, including psychologist and deputy superintendent for treatment at the State Regional Correctional Facility at Greensburg, superintendent of the State Regional Correctional Facility at Mercer and the State Correctional Institution at Camp Hill. He is the author of *Strategic Planning for Correctional Emergencies* and *Popular Culture and Corrections*, both of which are available from the American Correctional Association.

During my twenty years as a corrections practitioner, I observed time and again the powerful impact of staff attitudes toward offenders and the quality of interaction between staff and offender and effective decision making. If we view attitude toward offenders on a positive-to-negative continuum, most correctional staff will be located somewhere in the middle. They understand the nature of the offender and the system within which they and the offender are interacting, have a balanced attitude toward offenders, and can be counted on to be realistic in their interactions and decisions. But there are a minority of staff located at both extremes of the continuum: on the left is the Pollyanna who sees the offender through rose-colored glasses; on the right is the Cassandra whose offender-perception is one of darkness and threat. Pollyannas and Cassandras are distinguished from each other by differences in their language and behavior. What they have in common is an inability to objectively and realistically interact with offenders, which invariably leads to flawed decisionmaking.

The Pollyanna operates with a deterministic philosophy, which stipulates that offenders are not bad people, and that the crime does not reflect the offender's true nature. Instead, criminal behavior represents an understandable response to societal victimization by a basically good person. Society makes criminals of good people by being racist, discriminatory, class-oriented, and unfair in the distribution of wealth and opportunity. As a food services instructor once told me: "There are no bad people. The people we call criminals are just the most vulnerable victims of this lousy society." The Pollyanna assumes that all offenders want to change their attitudes, behaviors, and lifestyles and eagerly will do so, if society is only willing to give them the opportunity. Offenders, regardless of crime, will respond to the willingness of staff to accept their basic humanity: "Extend the hand of trust and you will never be sorry," was the common expression of a social worker I once knew. If opportunity is not provided, the offender has no choice except to remain a criminal.

Pollyannas often come into conflict with other staff and administrators because of their willingness to ignore objective data and make high-risk decisions based on their belief that there is good in everybody. A typical supervisor-Pollyanna discussion might be as follows:

Supervisor: You've been recommending a disproportionately high number of inmates for prerelease programming very early in their sentence. I'm particularly concerned with one case: a twenty-four-year-old heroin addict with a history of rape beginning at the age of twelve who has received misconducts for poor kitchen work performance and disrespect to block officers.

Counselor: You mean John?

Supervisor: Yes, John has served nine months of the current sentence, so the sentencing criteria are met, but I am bothered by the criminal history.

Counselor: I guess I understand your concerns, if you just go by the paperwork. But, I go by the feelings John has been showing me. There's no reason to worry. John understands where he went wrong. He won't make the same mistakes again. He has enormous potential and is motivated to succeed.

Q: How do you know John isn't just blowing smoke?

A: Because we talk once a week and he gets very emotional when he talks about the harm he's done to his family by doing drugs. In one session, he actually cried.

Q: What about the rapes?

A: John says those happened when he was off heroin and drinking heavily. He lost control because of the alcohol, but says that won't be a problem on work release because he doesn't need to drink when he's working.

Q: John has been in trouble since he was twelve. Why do you think nine months in this prison have changed him?

A: Because he's finally found someone he can trust. He says he's never had a counselor so willing to help a man straighten himself out. When he looks me in the eye and promises he's a changed man, I know he's not lying.

Q: What about four misconducts for poor work performance and disrespect?

A: John is doing his best. If the supervisors and guards would let up on him, they'd find out just how good a man he can be. He just gets irritable when he's nagged.

Q: What about the psych evaluation? It describes John as a "stainless steel psychopath."

A: I don't trust tests. My gut-level feeling is better than any test. Besides, those tests were administered the week after reception and don't take into consideration the adjustment shock John was probably experiencing.

By refusing to confront the inmate with the reality of his past behavior, and uncritically accepting his platitudes that all is well because he has found someone to trust, the Pollyanna is not helping the offender. The Pollyanna actually sets the stage for future acting-out.

The Cassandra operates in accordance with a free-will philosophy that stipulates that all offenders are social parasites who are criminals because of a conscious decision to become criminals. Offenders have no hope of redemption because they derive far too much satisfaction from criminal activity and actively will manipulate those staff foolish enough to try to help them. As a counselor once confided to me: "Staff who trust inmates are the same people who trust lawyers and politicians. They deserve to get burned." The Cassandra has an almost paranoid fear of being "burned" by manipulative offenders and this fear results in a refusal to trust or take chances.

The supervisor of a counselor who is a Cassandra will tend to receive numerous complaints from inmates concerning the counselor's negative attitude, abruptness when they try to stop him or her in the hallway to ask questions, and reluctance to recommend inmates for prerelease status. A typical supervisor-Cassandra discussion will be similar to the following:

Q: I receive more inmate complaints about you than any other counselor. Why is that?

A: They all know I have their number. They figure if they complain to you, you'll get me off their backs and tell me to get with the program. They figure you'll push me into getting conned by them. But, I don't let anybody con me.

Q: Is that why you haven't recommended anybody on your caseload for prerelease placement in four months?

A: You got it. I have a bunch of trailer trash on my caseload. No way I'm letting any of them out of here before they've done their full minimum.

Q: Why aren't you running groups (counseling)?

A: The superintendent said group work was voluntary. No way, I have no time to waste listening to a bunch of crybabies whine about how tough they got it. What these guys need is to serve hard time. That's better than any counseling. I've been here longer than you. I know these guys better than you. Give an inch, they take a mile.

Q: The inmates are also complaining that you never see them in person. Do you see them when they request a meeting?

A: You know how busy we all are. If an inmate puts in a request slip, then I respond in writing. That's all I have time for. Besides, that way no inmate can accuse me of saying something I never said. What I say is always in writing. I always protect my back.

Q: With that attitude, why remain a counselor?

A: Because somebody has got to make these guys toe the line. I'm the only counselor you got who isn't afraid to say "no" and mean it. I leave and these guys will take over the place. I've been here nine years, and all inmates ever do is screw up every opportunity handed to them and then whine that their failure is somebody else's fault when the real reason they fail is because no one is willing to hold them accountable for not even trying. Well, I hold them all accountable. Nothing you say is going to change that.

Neither of these counselors is effective. Both have attitudes which interfere with objectivity and limit their ability to focus on the real issues the offenders are facing. Pollyannas and Cassandras are not just topics of theoretical interest to academicians. The decisions they make can have dramatic effects, especially if they are in a position of authority over other staff.

Early in this author's corrections career, he attended a counseling seminar designed to sharpen the diagnostic and treatment skills of a selected group of psychologists and counselors. The group was a mixture of novices, including himself, and veterans of many years of institutional work. On the afternoon of the second day, the instructor presented a case study of a nineteen-year-old inmate in a maximum-security institution who had been gang raped a month after reception. After three weeks in the prison infirmary, he was placed in protective custody in the Behavioral Adjustment Unit where his behavior deteriorated, and he began to receive misconducts for various forms of acting-out. After discussion, the group decided that the motivation for the acting-out was the anger and humiliation created by the rape. The instructor agreed and told us to develop a counseling plan of action. A variety of therapeutic interventions were suggested, with the general consensus being that the job of the counselor would be to help the young inmate understand how anger and humiliation were motivating his behavior and assist him in learning to substitute positive coping skills for the current self-destructive behavior.

Noting that one member of the group, a twenty-year veteran who was the chief psychologist of a maximum-security institution, had contributed nothing to the discussion, the instructor asked how he would respond to the situation. The response was: "What that punk needs is a good kick in the butt. That'll straighten him out better than all this talking." Clearly, this was the response of a Cassandra. One can imagine the damage that type of attitude was doing to vulnerable inmates under the jurisdiction of this psychologist's staff.

But Pollyannas in positions of administrative authority also can cause damage. An administrator at a facility with a highly successful work-release program made the decision to place an inmate recently received from a maximum-security institution on work-release status. The inmate's history was extremely negative: drug addiction and a high frequency of assaultive crimes. There were numerous contraindications to work-release placement, but the administrator, operating on the basic Pollyanna principle that "Everybody deserves a second chance," approved the inmate for work release. Weekend furloughs followed shortly thereafter. During one of these furloughs, the inmate murdered a young woman. The murder generated extensive publicity and calls for action.

The result? A work-release program that had successfully provided opportunity to hundreds of inmates was abolished overnight. Future inmates at that facility would have to pay the price of denied opportunity for one Pollyanna's mistake.

The Pollyannas and Cassandras are not limited to the ranks of treatment staff. They can be found in every category of correctional staff, from the block officer to the laundry supervisor to the clerk-typist. Regardless of their title and job, the Pollyanna and Cassandra represent a major challenge to supervisors, colleagues, and offenders.

The Benefits of Self-disclosure

One of the most important qualities that criminal justice workers should possess is the willingness to share themselves with others, including offenders, through self-disclosure. *Self-disclosure* means to communicate personal information to another who normally would not have that information. One may reasonably inquire what use it is for the correctional worker to communicate personal information to an offender: isn't the offender's self the focus of the offender/helper relationship—indeed, the reason for its existence? Yes, it is, and it was not until the advent of humanistic psychology that self-disclosure was considered appropriate and beneficial (Okun, 1987:261). However, the willingness of correctional helpers to share themselves serves some very useful functions.

First, it is a form of modeling behavior that encourages reluctant offenders to reveal intimate facts about themselves. The difficulty that offenders experience in revealing their most intimate feelings, thoughts, and valuations may be lessened by the helper's example. Remember, reciprocal self-disclosure is the basis of the success of various self-help groups such as Alcoholics Anonymous. Confession is good for the soul, and it yields an abundance of needed information for the assessment of the offender. Jose Arcaya puts the self-disclosure process in a criminal justice context when he writes: "For the ex-offender forced to present himself [or herself] before a probation officer, rehabilitation counselor, or psychologist, no meaningful dialogue will occur unless the client can identify a glimmer of his [or her] own humanity in the individual with whom he [or she] deals" (1978:231).

Second, self-disclosure gives the offender a new perspective on things derived from your personal experiences. Again, the sharing of personal experiences, the implanting of possibilities for alternative frames of reference in the minds of others, is part of the modus operandi of self-help groups in which offenders come to see reflections of themselves in others. This process of self-disclosure, of course, should be free of value judgments, moral exhortations, and self-serving and boastful exhibitionism. Besides being bad practice, it is not considered good taste to advertise what a great person you are. If the contrast between the offender's experience and yours is too great, he or she will not view your revealed frame of reference as being realistic. If you moralize and pass judgment, the offender is not likely to reveal any further personal information to you that could invite further denigration.

You always must be aware of the feelings and humanity of the offenders. If, for example, Bob reveals that he has experienced great difficulty obtaining employment because of his lack of a high school diploma and the vagaries of his lower-class upbringing, you may reply with sensitivity, revealing your own class origins, the possibility of obtaining a general education diploma (GED) and describe how you managed to acquire an education despite acknowledged early deficiencies. Rendered in this nonthreatening manner, your experience may strike a responsive chord of the possible within the offender. If you couch it in terms designed to emphasize your moral superiority ("I did it, why can't you?" "It takes guts, buddy." "You can get a job if you get off your lazy ass and start looking."), Bob is very likely to react negatively to such an assault on his self-concept, either by becoming hostile or by clamming up. Either way, you have lost the opportunity to further the meaningful interaction so necessary for an adequate assessment of the offender. You also have reinforced Bob's sense of hopelessness and his feeling that "nobody cares," and have revealed your own inadequacies as a helper. If such an exchange takes place during the initial interview, and if Bob is subsequently placed under you supervision as a probationer, parolee, or inmate, efforts to counsel him will meet with resistance because you have communicated to him that he is not worth much and that you are not really interested in him or his problems.

Some caveats about self-disclosure to an offender are in order at this point. The offender's problems must be the focus of any interview or counseling session. Therefore, the worker's self-disclosure should be infrequent, relevant, and focused. It should not give the offender the impression that you are working out your own problems with him or her. Chatty and unstructured conversations are inappropriate during a session designed to gather information about the offender, although they may have use in later counseling sessions if your motives are consistent with establishing a genuine atmosphere of informality. Gerard Egan's (1998:179-180) advice, which is paraphrased, is fitting here: Make sure your disclosures are appropriate, keep them selected and focused, and don't burden your client with too much. In short, be willing and able to disclose yourself in reasonable ways, but do so only if it is clear that such disclosure will contribute to the client's progress.

Other authorities discourage self-disclosure with criminal populations, asserting that offenders use this information to sidetrack the counselor, and even use tidbits of information to manipulate him or her (Sharp, 2000). This is very true in institutional settings in which counselors may have daily contact with inmates, and inmates have nothing better to do than play their games. Perhaps guarded self-disclosure is best only practiced in community settings where probationers or parolees may be able to put the disclosed information to some immediate use.

IMPROVING YOUR SELF-CONCEPT THROUGH SELF-DISCLOSURE

Training exercises in self-disclosure, such as those given at the end of this chapter, should be an integral part of the correctional worker's training. They are necessary for two reasons. First, they provide the helper with a gut-level understanding of the feelings of the offender as they are asked to reveal intimate information. Disclosing intimate information can be highly embarrassing and intimidating to the offender. Imagine the embarrassment of a fifty-five-year-old minister who has been found guilty of molesting a child as he is being asked to reveal details of his sex life to a probation officer or other correctional counselor young enough to be his grandson or granddaughter! The investigating or counseling officer must be highly sensitive to this embarrassment if he or she is to conduct a successful interview and make an adequate assessment. One of the best ways to learn this sensitivity is to experience the same sort of discomfort by self-disclosure in a classroom setting.

Of course, the classroom setting will not be as threatening to the student as the real-life setting is for the offender. Students easily can role-play rather than deal with real concerns. That is, they can manufacture fictitious problems that do not threaten them rather than exploring real problems that they may have. Only by realistically exploring problems can you gain insight into what it is like to be an offender. Remember, all prospective psychoanalysts have to undergo intensive psychoanalysis before they are allowed to practice their skills on others.

The second reason for engaging in realistic self-disclosure is to improve your greatest asset—your self-concept. As previously stated, people have a strong desire to preserve the picture they have of themselves—the self-consistency motive. If we protect the self from change, by definition, we cannot, grow psychologically. As paradoxical as it may seem, to preserve self-consistency some people may retain low self-esteem to protect the self-esteem they do have. People who expect little of themselves cannot fail. If expectations are low, a weak performance easily meets the meager expectations they have of themselves Psychological growth implies that we have the courage to test ourselves to our limits and to acknowledge the possibility of failure.

It is important for us to assess ourselves, to know what kind of people we are, to know our strengths, weaknesses, potential, and problem areas so that we can effectively operate in our environment. Some authorities consider wholesome self-disclosure to be as necessary for mental health as proper exercise and nutrition are for physical health. Fromm (1955) has written that to reduce our alienation from ourselves and from others, we must open ourselves to ourselves by disclosing ourselves to others. The more we know about ourselves, the better able we will be to understand others. Self-knowledge is desirable for all people, but it is vital for those in the helping professions because understanding others is a prerequisite to helping them. How can you help offenders come to terms with feelings that hinder their functioning if you have not confronted and dealt with similar feelings in yourself?

We must not harbor static images of ourselves. If we do, we will have unrealistic pictures of the world and our relationship to it. A static self-concept cuts us off from the fullness of the experiences that the world offers us, thus stunting our emotional and intellectual growth. Rather than building walls and defenses against life's fullness, we should accept all experiences and fit them into our self-concepts. We must adapt positively to the environment as it changes. To accomplish this successfully, we must receive information about ourselves from concerned others and use it for positive change. To receive information about ourselves from others, however, we must be strong enough to be willing to share ourselves with others. Both the receiving of information about ourselves and the sharing of ourselves is accomplished by meaningful self-disclosure. You will be asking the offenders to do all these things: adapt positively to their environments, experience lifestyles different from the one they have grown accustomed to, share themselves through disclosure, and receive information from you that you will expect them to employ fruitfully. If this is not a part of your personal operating philosophy, you will not be successful in imparting it to the offenders.

The Johari Window: An Aid to Self-Understanding

A useful framework for viewing self-concept and understanding how self-disclosure is valuable in improving it is the Johari Window (Luft, 1963). This device divides the self into four components or "cells," each representing aspects of the self ranging from those known by almost everyone to aspects which you yourself are not even aware. Positive self-disclosure should have the effect of enlarging Cell I (the public self) while shrinking the other three cells correspondingly. The following is a general discussion of the principles of self-disclosure, which should not be viewed within the context of the counselor/offender relationship. You certainly will not be asking offenders to help you to explore your intimate concerns.

Figure 4.1
The Johari Window
(adapted from Luft 1983)

	Known to self	Unknown to self
Known to others	I Public self	II Blind self
Unknown to others	III Private self	IV Unknown self

The *public self* is the self as it habitually is shared with others. It is an area of self-knowledge which one has no qualms about revealing.

The *private self* obviously has relevance to self-disclosure. You need not, and should not, burden others with excessive and exhibitionist disclosure of the private self: "If you only knew what I've accomplished in my life, and against what odds, you too would realize what a great person I really am." The idea is to disclose only those aspects of the private self that can help others with the exploration of those aspects that are of concern to you, such as values, weaknesses, and social and sexual identities.

The *blind self* is that part of the self that others see but which we do not. It is involved in self-disclosure only if others bring their images of you to your attention and if you are willing to acknowledge the validity of the transmitted information. The transmitted information may not be an accurate assessment of you, but it may be beneficial at least to recognize the possibility that it is. If the revealed information is negative, do not throw up fences and retreat from it. Instead, work with that aspect of the self to see how it can be improved. Never ignore traits or characteristics that others perceive and that may be negatively affecting your effectiveness as a helper or as a person.

The *unknown self* is the area of latent, inchoate, subconscious, and preconscious facets of the self. It is an area of shadowy fears and weaknesses, but also a reservoir of great untapped potential and talents that we all, including offenders, have. An unwillingness to explore unknown areas of the self is indicative of a frozen self-concept. In the process of exploring the blind self, it is possible that aspects of the unknown self will become accessible to you so that you may confront them and develop those that are desirable or deal constructively with those that are not.

Whereas it generally is agreed that self-disclosure (moving information contained in Cells II, III, and IV into Cell I) improves personal growth, it may result in growth-inhibiting outcomes. Whether self-disclosure is beneficial or harmful depends on the state of the receiver and the quality of the relationship shared by the receiver and the transmitter. Inevitably, self-disclosure involves a certain amount of risk-taking. A turtle never moves forward until it sticks its neck out.

Self-disclosure demands trusting and making an investment in the other person. As a professional criminal justice worker, you will be asking offenders to trust you and invest in you. If you are to perform your task in an effective and efficient manner, you must prove worthy of that trust and investment by responding to offenders in a sensitive, empathetic, and fully involved way. Furthermore, you also must be secure enough in yourself to be completely honest with the offender. Your honesty, openness, and acceptance do not guarantee that the offender will act likewise, but these characteristics certainly make it more probable.

APPLICATION TO THE OFFENDER

Although the Johari Window was conceived of as a strategy for self-exploration, it can be fruitfully adapted to serve as a model for the officer/offender relationship. For instance, the situation representing the immediate state of your "knowledge" of the offenders in your first meeting with them is presented in Figure 4-2. The major difference between exercises in voluntary self-disclosure for the purpose of self-growth and the officer/offender encounter is that the public self in this case is the self that the offender chooses to present to you, not the public self that he or she habitually shares with family, friends, and acquaintances.

Your knowledge of the offender's public self, for the moment, is limited to information written down in various official documents. Therefore, even getting to know offenders as others know them may prove to be an exacting assignment, for at this point you know only the *official offenders*. Your initial task is the melding of the two subsections of Cell I to form a unified picture of offenders as they normally present themselves to others. Offenders may have a number of aspects of the public self that they are unwilling to share with you. Consequently, they will erect barriers to protect those areas. The barriers can be scaled by an effectively conducted interview with the offenders and by collateral interviews with others acquainted with them.

Figure 4.2

The Johari Window
(Applied to the Client)

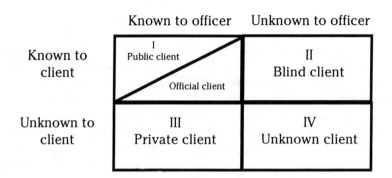

The private offender is that part of the offender's self that he or she wishes to keep unscrutinized by others, especially by the corrections worker. It represents the behaviors, feelings, and motivations that the offender habitually hides but that may be revealed when he or she chooses. These behaviors, feelings, and motivations, since the offender is aware of them, most probably will be the first target areas for mutual exploration. They are not necessarily problem areas. They just as well may be growth-promoting areas that, with a little support and encouragement, the offender could actualize. If aspects of the private offender are of this kind, he or she possibly may be more disposed to relating them to a relative stranger who is perceived as caring and accepting than to more familiar others from whom he or she may fear ridicule.

The blind offender represents those aspects of the self of which the offender is unaware but that the officer perceives and to which the officer is sensitive. The offender, just as the corrections worker, may be able to enhance the self by feedback in an atmosphere of openness and trust. Emphasis should be placed initially on the positive aspects of the offender's self of which the officer is aware, such as positive statements by others. If, for instance, an officer has access to school records indicating that the offender scored well on IQ tests, the officer may discuss the nature of IQ and potential possibilities open to the offender with such scores. This kind of information, needless to say, is most welcome and tends to spill over into congenial discussions of other aspects of the offender's blind self which he or she might not be so readily willing to accept.

The unknown offender represents those aspects of the offender's self that are unknown to officer and offender alike. Realistically, we know that many facets of the offender's unknown self will remain unknown. The initial interview, for whatever reason it is conducted, is not the place to attempt to probe into this area. Under supervision, however, the offender should be encouraged to explore it in order to discover the unknown potential that we all possess. You must have faith in this proposition if you are to be an effective correctional worker.

The Johari Window is a useful framework for conceptualizing the process and purpose of interviewing. However, we never should forget that offenders come to the interviewing process with vastly different biographies, motives, and attitudes. Each interview is a unique process between human beings who are far too individualized to be reduced to precise formulas. Interviewing is an art rather than a science. However, certain basic principles exist that enable the helper to conduct a successful interview. These are discussed in the next chapter.

The Mask

The following essay by an anonymous writer is an anguished cry for understanding and acceptance. It illustrates our discussion of self-disclosure, as well as the discussion of listening still to come. Notice how the writer has built a false self-image and barriers to protect it, and how painful the writer finds his or her inauthenticity. We all want to be accepted and loved, but many of us fight against what we so desperately need. The writer wants to be authentic by disclosing his or her true self and true feeling, but is so terribly afraid of rejection. This could have been written by any offender, perhaps even by some of your classmates (or even you). Remember it when you do your exercises in self-disclosure. Above all, remember it when you are working with real offenders.

The Mask—An Essay
Please Hear What I'm Not Saying
Author Unknown

Don't be fooled by me. Don't be fooled by the face I wear, for I wear a mask. I wear a thousand masks, masks that I'm afraid to take off, and none of them is me. Pretending is an art that's second nature to me, but don't be fooled, for God's sake don't be fooled. I give you the impression that I'm secure, that all is sunny and unruffled with me, within as well as without. Confidence is my name and coolness is my game, and I need no one.

But don't believe me. My surface is my mask. Beneath dwells the real me in confusion, in fear, in aloneness. But I hide this. I don't want anybody to know it. I panic at the thought of my weakness and fear being exposed. That's why I frantically create a mask to hide behind, to shield me from the glance that knows. But such a glance is precisely my salvation—that is, if it's followed by acceptance, by love. It's the only thing that can liberate me from my own self-built prison walls. It is the only thing that will assure me of what I can't assure myself—that I'm really worth something. But I'm afraid to tell you this; I'm afraid that your glance will not be followed by acceptance and love. I'm afraid you'll laugh, and that laugh will kill me. I idly chatter to you in the suave tones of surface talk. I tell you everything that's really nothing, and nothing of what's everything, of what's crying within me.

Please listen carefully and try to hear what I'm not saying, what I'd like to be able to say, what for survival I need to say. I'd really like to be genuine and spontaneous, and me, but you've got to help me. You alone can release me from my shadow-world of panic and uncertainty, from my lonely prison. It will not be easy for you. A long conviction of worthlessness builds strong walls. The nearer you approach me, the blinder I may strike back. I am irrational—I fight against the very thing that I cry out for. But I am told that love is stronger than strong walls. Please try to beat down those walls with firm hands, but with gentle hands—for I am very sensitive. Who am I, you may wonder. I am someone you "know" very well. I am every man you meet and I am every woman you meet.

Summary

This chapter emphasizes the primacy of the self in the helping process. Nothing is more important to the success or failure of a counseling relationship than the quality of the helper's self. The self-concept is the product and producer of experience. Positive experiences lead to a positive self-concept, and a positive self-concept leads to further positive experiences. The opposite progression, often found in offenders, is also true.

We looked at the various attributes that characterize the professional criminal justice worker. You should examine these attributes closely to determine how you measure up. Deficiencies and weaknesses in any of the areas can be explored in the process of self-disclosure.

To improve the self-concept, a person must accept a wide variety of experiences and integrate them into his or her self-concept. One way of doing this is through meaningful self-disclosure. Self-disclosure helps us to gain knowledge about ourselves by receiving feedback about ourselves from others. Every prospective counselor should experience self-disclosure in a number of sessions before actually practicing counseling, not only to gain valuable self-insight but also to experience the process in which he or she will be asking offenders to engage. The Johari Window is an excellent device for guiding self-disclosure of this type. There are few bits of advice more useful than the ancient injunction to "know thyself."

EXERCISES IN SELF-EXPLORATION THROUGH DISCLOSURE

The purpose of this activity is twofold: (1) to improve self-exploration by disclosing to a partner various aspects of yourself and (2) to give you some experience of what it is like to reveal oneself to a relative stranger. During the initial session, you may, out of fear, anxiety, or embarrassment, decide upon some relatively nonthreatening topic. Or, you may possess the self-assurance to pick a topic that is of real concern to you. It is preferable, of course, to choose aspects of the private self, especially those of an interpersonal nature, for exploration. The section asking you to explore values and attitudes toward various types of individuals should prove to be valuable in developing an empathetic understanding of them if both your disclosure and feedback are open and honest.

Exercises should be done in pairs, with frequent changes of partners. If your instructor chooses not to assign partners, it is preferable that you do not sit with the same person too often. Make an effort to sit with someone of a different race, sex, or ethnic background. You will find this to be a good learning experience and very rewarding. Each student should take turns in disclosing the chosen issue to the other. Remember, you are not engaging in a conventional conversation. The disclosing person should have control over the communication. The listener should listen, and pay attention to the techniques of active listening as outlined in the next chapter. The listener should speak only for the purposes of clarification and prompt further disclosure by the use of probes. Each of the following suggested topics is suitable for a discussion of about five to ten minutes.

TOPIC ONE: GENERALITIES

The kinds of people I like best are...
The kinds of people I like least are...
I try to avoid thinking about...
I think that the most important thing in life is...
I feel most competent when I...
I feel least competent when I...
My career goals are...
I would really like to be able to...

TOPIC TWO: VALUES AND ATTITUDES

My values are important to me because...
Here's how I REALLY feel that the relationship
    between the sexes should be ....
Here's how I REALLY feel about blacks/whites...
Here's how I feel about alcoholics...
Here's how I feel about drug abusers...
Here's how I REALLY feel about homosexuals...
Here's how I REALLY feel about criminals...
An open mind is desirable because...

TOPIC THREE: FEELINGS

I am happiest when ....
I get the most depressed when ....
I get embarrassed when ....
I get very angry when...
I feel guilty when ....
I am sometimes ashamed of...
I feel very hurt when...
I feel anxious when...

TOPIC FOUR: IDENTITY

Who are you? What kind of person are you? Odds are that you have never really thought too much about your identity. Try writing out ten separate answers to the question "WHO AM I?" Next, eliminate those answers that simply signify your various ascribed and achieved statuses, such as "American," "student," "male," or "nineteen years old." With your partners, explore those aspects of the self that you have left on your lists. You may have written, for example, "I am a shy person." Explore this aspect with your partner. Why do you think you are shy? What does your shyness do to your social life? How much more successful do you think you would be in life if you were not shy? How do you feel about your shyness? What do you think you can do about it?

TOPIC FIVE: STRENGTHS AND WEAKNESSES

Make a list of your five greatest strengths and five greatest weaknesses and discuss each one with your partner. These strengths and weaknesses should be developmental "feeling" topics rather than statements like "I'm a good/poor tennis player." For instance, how do you relate to other people, especially those close to you? Are you secure in your sexual identity? Are you a leader or a follower? Do you respect the feelings of others? Are you an autonomous person? Can you take constructive criticism?

TOPIC SIX: EFFECTIVENESS AS A CORRECTIONAL HELPER

Go back to the description of an effective correctional helper and rate yourself according to those attributes. Where are you weak? Where are you strong? What personal attribute do you possess that will aid you in becoming a more effective helper, and what personal attribute do you think will detract most from your ability to become an effective helper? Discuss these strengths and weaknesses with a partner.

References and Suggested Readings

Anderson, E. 1999. *Code of the Street: Decency, Violence, and the Moral Life of the Inner City*. New York: W. W. Norton.

Andrews, D. and J. Bonta. 1998. *The Psychology of Criminal Conduct*. Cincinnati, Ohio: Anderson Publishing.

Arcaya, J. 1978. Coercive counseling and self-disclosure. *International Journal of Offender Therapy and Comparative Criminology*. 22:231-237.

Baumeister, R., L. Smart, and J. Boden. 1996. Relation of threatened egotism to violence and aggression: The dark side of self-esteem. *Psychological Review*. 103:5-33.

Berman, A. and A. Siegal. 1976. A Neurophysiological Approach to the Etiology, Prevention, and Treatment of Juvenile Delinquency. In A. Davids, ed. *Child Personality and Psychopathology: Current Topics*. New York: Wiley.

Buikhuisen, W. 1987. Cerebral Disfunction and Persistent Juvenile Delinquency. In S. Mednick, T. Moffitt, and S. Stack, eds. *The Causes of Crime: New Biological Approaches*. Cambridge, England: University of Cambridge Press.

Buri, J., P. Kirchner, and J. Walsh. 1987. Familial correlates of self-esteem in young American adults. *Journal of Social Psychology*. 127:583-588.

Combs, A., D. Avila, and W. Purkey. 1971. *Helping Relationships: Basic Concepts for the Helping Professions*. Boston, Massachusetts: Allyn and Bacon.

Egan, G. 1998. *The Skilled Helper*. Monterey, California: Brooks/Cole.

Fromm, E. 1955. *The Sane Society*. New York: Rinehart and Co.

Garrett, A. 1982. *Interviewing: Its Principles and Methods*. New York: Family Services Association of America.

Glasser. 1975. *Reality Therapy*. New York: Harper and Row.

Hare, R. 1993. *Without Conscience: The Disturbing World of the Psychopaths Among Us*. New York: Pocket Books.

Kaplan, H. 1982. Prevalence of Self-esteem Motive. In M. Rosenberg and H. Kaplan, eds. *Social Psychology of the Self-concept*. Arlington Heights, Illinois: Harlan Davidson.

Lauen, R. 1997. *Positive Approaches to Corrections: Research, Policy, and Practice*. Lanham, Maryland: American Correctional Association.

Luft, J. 1963. *Group Process: An Introduction to Group Dynamics*. Palo Alto, California: National Press Books.

Okun, B. 1987. *Effective Helping*. Monterey, California: Brooks/Cole.

Rosenberg, M. 1979. *Conceiving the Self*. New York: Basic Books.

Schrink, J. 2000. Understanding the Correctional Counselor. In P. Van Vooris, M. Brasswell, and D. Lester, eds. *Correctional Counseling and Rehabilitation*. Cincinnati Ohio: Anderson.

Sharp, B. 2000. *Changing Criminal Thinking: A Treatment Program*. Lanham, Maryland: American Correctional Association.

Walsh, A. and G. Balazs. 1990. Love, sex, and self-esteem. *Free Inquiry in Creative Sociology*. 18:37-42.

Walsh, A. and P. Walsh. 1989. Love, self-esteem, and multiple sclerosis. *Social Science and Medicine*. 29:793-798.

Yablonsky. L. 1990. *Criminology: Crime and Criminality*. New York: Harper and Row.

Interviewing and Interrogating

It is not easy to achieve the ideal balance between relieving a client (offender) of the unbearable burden of what seem to be insurmountable difficulties and leaving him with essential responsibility for working out his own destiny. . . . One of the most important skills of the interviewer is a knowledge of his own limitations.

Annette Garrett

The interview is a focused process of communication by which you gather information for the purpose of assessing the interviewee. It is a structured and purposeful method of getting to know another person. Any interview, regardless of the context in which it takes place, is designed to help the interviewer make decisions, usually about the interviewee (is he or she suitable for the job, eligible for benefits, serious about this task, a good candidate for treatment?). Corrections workers spend the major portion of their time conducting interviews with offenders, victims, police officers, and many other people involved in some way with offenders' activities. Thus, it is necessary that you become informed about the basic principles of effective interviewing.

Interrogation is also part of the corrections worker's task. Like interviewing, interrogation involves information gathering, but the focus is more sharply delimited. As Vessel (1998:1) puts it: "Obtaining information that an individual does not want to provide constitutes the sole purpose of interrogation." Interrogation is conducted either to get an admission of guilt from a person or to eliminate that person from suspicion. The ability to conduct an effective interrogation is also a necessary part of your professional development.

Purpose of the Criminal Justice Interview

THE OFFENDER

Applied to the offender, interviewing is a diagnostic tool that will enable you to arrive at a preliminary understanding of offenders and their problems and to recommend and implement effective treatment modalities. A well-conducted interview also may be considered the first step in the counseling process if it creates an arena in which offenders can formulate an honest picture of their problems, and if they gain an understanding of the motives and resources of the helping person.

As former criminologist and prominent correctional administrator Paul Keve put it: "The most important step in the investigation process is the first interview with the defendant, and if you handle it skillfully, you not only have the basis for a truly competent report, but you also have gone a long way toward launching the treatment job that must develop later" (quoted in Hartman, 1978:309). The implication is that the interview can be the beginning of the rehabilitative process, or it can be merely a ritual in which uninterpreted demographic data are gathered and reported. The principles of interviewing are the same regardless of the specific purpose of the interview: preparing a presentence investigation report (PSI), meeting a newly assigned probationer or parolee, or conducting an intake interview for a new arrival at an institution.

THE VICTIM

A growing, but long-overdue, awareness of the victim as the "forgotten party" in the criminal justice system has prompted a number of states to require that victims have a more active part in the sentencing process. For instance, most states require that a "victim-impact statement" be included in each presentence investigation report, and that the judge consider these statements when making sentencing decisions. This requirement demands something more than the perfunctory telephone call to ascertain financial losses that used to be the norm. A telephone call will suffice, however, when the victim in a case of theft, burglary, or forgery is a business establishment (where no one individual has been personally victimized) and you merely wish to determine restitution figures.

In the case of personal victimization, however, victims should be given the courtesy of a face-to-face meeting with you. Both you and the victim can benefit from such an interview. You gather information that will help you to evaluate the offender; the victim can receive assurances of safety and a feeling that he or she has not been forgotten or ignored by the criminal justice system.

TECHNIQUES OF INTERVIEWING

The goal of interviewing is to gather information given voluntarily. It is not as difficult as you may think to obtain voluntary information from offenders. Most people like nothing better than to talk about themselves. Even reluctant, angry, or embarrassed offenders probably will succumb to the temptation to talk if they perceive that you are genuinely interested in them. For this reason, the development of genuineness, caring, and empathy are essential. Too much emphasis on technique detracts from the humanness of the interviewing process, and can be painfully transparent if not developed properly in a training situation.

ACTIVE LISTENING

This does not mean that techniques are not valuable; they are extremely valuable. The most valuable of these techniques is active listening. Active listening (the opposite of passive listening) is the key to effective communication. Active listening is different from hearing (or passive listening), which is simply the physiological registering of sound not requiring any intellectual effort on the part of the receiver (Gorden, 1992:82). Listening means paying complete attention (intellectually focusing on the sounds) to the information being offered by the offender, and conveying that attention to the offender both verbally and nonverbally. In other words, you must make a conscious decision to attend to the speaker.

To communicate to the offender that you are actively listening, maintain eye contact. In addition to conveying interest, eye contact enables you to observe the offender's nonverbal responses to uncomfortable questions. When does the offender avert his or her eyes, when does he or she flush, smile, or sneer? You cannot determine this if you are not watching. There are, however, certain subcultural differences attached to the meaning of eye contact. Middle-class people tend to view frequent eye contact as a sign of honesty and the averting of the eyes as indicative of furtiveness. Inner-city residents, especially blacks, feel that too much eye contact is a nonverbal challenge, so it may provoke hostility. Be very careful that your efforts to maintain eye contact do not inadvertently turn it into an attempt to stare down the offender. Additionally, in some American Indian cultures, individuals are taught that it is impolite to gaze directly at someone else.

When you are listening to the offender, you should be sitting about two arm-lengths apart (do not have a desk or other physical objects between you). Maintain a slightly forward-leaning posture. Leaning forward at certain points during the interview conveys an intensification of interest. Do not get so close to offenders as to make them feel uncomfortable—that is, so that they feel their personal space is being invaded. This is particularly important if the offender is of the opposite sex.

It is all too easy to convey unintended messages of a sexual nature this way. This author once had a female offender who started to cry during the PSI interview. He offered her a tissue and placed a comforting hand on hers. She took immediate advantage of this gesture of sympathy to grasp his hand and say: "I'll do anything to get out of this." This obvious sexual invitation was disquieting. Offenders who make such offers expect something in return (a favorable sentencing recommendation, easy supervision conditions, a blind eye to certain violations, and so forth). Had he succumbed to her invitation, he may well have found himself paying the $700 in restitution she owed, violating his professional code of ethics, and, not the least, facing a criminal charge. Needless to say, you must be very careful that your behavior is not open to this kind of misinterpretation.

QUESTIONING AND PROBING

Although the purpose of the interview is to listen to what the offender has to say, your job is to guide the communication toward relevant topics. You are interested in gathering information about offenders' backgrounds and lifestyles, about their attitudes about the offense and about concerns and problems which may have led to it. To get this information, you have to ask questions.

We will discuss two types of questions here: **OPEN** and **CLOSED**. According to Ivey (1983:41): "Open questions are those that can't be answered in a few short words.

They encourage others to talk and provide you with maximum information. Closed questions can be answered in a few short words or sentences. They have the advantage of focusing the interview and obtaining information, but the burden of talk remains with the interviewer." **PROBES** are indirect open-ended questions, which encourage the offender to explore some point to which he or she has alluded.

Offenders often will be unwilling to explore their personal lives and feelings with you. It is rare, however, that they outright will refuse to answer your questions. With reluctant offenders, it is necessary to encourage sharing through the use of probes. As indicated, probes are verbal tactics for prompting offenders to talk about themselves and to share their thoughts, feelings, and concerns with you in a specific and concrete way. For example, if Debbie indicates to you that her marriage is an unhappy one and that she "wants out," do not be content with that raw datum. Explore. Say something like: "So, you feel terrible about your marriage and feel trapped. About which do you feel worst?" You are encouraging Debbie to clarify her general statement by relating specific and concrete instances that give rise to her generalized feelings of dissatisfaction. Your probing may give Debbie the first real opportunity she has had to explore and vent these feelings regarding her marriage. Furthermore, Debbie's trouble with the law may be a direct or indirect consequence of her poor marital relationship. If this turns out to be the case, you will have discovered a starting point for your later counseling sessions with her if she is placed on probation.

Probing questions should be open-ended, meaning that they cannot be answered by a simple yes or no. Questions should be of the type: "Now that you know what the problem is between you and your husband, what do you plan to do about it?" They should not be of the type: "Now that you know what the problem is between you and your husband, do you plan to do anything about it?" A response of yes or no to this question will lead to further questions, giving Debbie the impression that she is being grilled. Using open-ended questions reduces the number of questions you ask and gives the offender some sense of control.

It obviously is desirable in some cases to use closed questions, which require simple answers, such as "What was the last school you attended?" Closed questions probably will be used most often in your follow-up to offender responses to open questions and in dealing with factual information such as whether an offender is married. Closed questions sometimes have to be used when open-ended questions would be preferable, such as when working with adolescents and with mildly retarded offenders who verbalize poorly. Sometimes you will run into streetwise offenders who make it a practice of not volunteering any information that is not specifically requested, which means that to get the information you want, you will have to rephrase your open question as a closed one. You never should stop trying, however, to get the offender to speak freely about himself or herself by the use of open questions.

Regardless of the type of question used, you should not rush offenders by throwing questions at them in staccato fashion. Your tone of voice and rate of speech indicate clearly how you feel about another person and whether you really have been listening to previous replies. Think of the many ways that you can say "I'm really interested in you." Give offenders ample time to think through their answers to your questions. Do not be embarrassed by silence or attempt to fill it in with small talk. The offender may be groping for ideas during such breaks in the conversation, and small talk will interrupt the flow of thought. If the silence becomes overly long, continue the interview by asking the offender to tell you more about the last point you covered. Do not attempt to break the silence by putting words into their mouths. They may grasp at your idea and agree with it in an effort to please you or to avoid saying what is really on their minds. Either way, you will be recording and evaluating offenders' responses as theirs when they are actually your own. "A good criminal justice interview," writes Alexander (2000:103), "permits silence."

LISTENING WITH THE THIRD EAR

Evaluating responses to questions requires active listening. Active listening requires a lot of practice. Some people are easy to listen to, and some are difficult. Prejudices and biases on the part of the officer will interfere with active listening to the offender, as will poor communications skills on the part of the offender. When either of these conditions is present, it is especially important to make an extra effort to listen to what the offender is saying. Active listening requires a great deal of alertness and flexibility. Be especially alert to any recurring thoughts or concepts that the offender presents and mentally flag them so that you can raise them later for further and deeper discussion.

Be flexible enough to deal with issues as the offender presents them. If you insist only on dealing with topics when you are ready for them, you may miss some vital information. The offender might be less agreeable to discussing a particular topic when you are ready, rather than when it first was broached. In short, active listening implies what psychologist Theodore Reik (1956) calls "listening with the third ear." This does not require the mere auditory recording of the offender's actual words so much as listening to what he or she is *trying* to tell you.

Offenders may be telling you things that they have no conscious intention of revealing. Does the offender reveal self-centeredness by the overuse of personal pronouns? Does the offender reveal overdependence or a lack of responsibility by constantly blaming others for every little misfortune? Does the offender bemoan his or her sins as vigorously as they are committed, thus perhaps revealing false remorse? What do the adjectives the offender uses to describe significant others reveal about the state of his or her interpersonal relationships? What kind of defense mechanisms (to be discussed later), such as rationalization, projection, and displacement, does the offender use to distort reality? This third-ear listening will tell you a lot more about the offender than face-value responses of the "what he did to me and what I said to her type."

However, you must restrain the urge to play Dr. Freud by reading too much into nonspecific responses at this stage. You simply do not yet have sufficient knowledge of the offender to make unsupported speculations in a report that has so much importance to his or her future. Third ear insights should be noted for your future use, but they should not be relayed to the sentencing judge as facts. When you begin to develop an empathetic understanding of the offender, and when a positive relationship has formed between you, then you may broach such issues. Of course, if you perceive something about an offender's responses that has direct applicability to the present offense (such as rationalizing or intellectualizing about the crime) and that has implications for sentencing and supervision, such responses should be explored with the offender then and there.

RESIST THE TEMPTATION TO INTERRUPT

Have you ever noticed while conversing with someone that instead of truly attending to what the other person is saying, you were thinking of the next thing you wanted to say or that you interrupted that person in midsentence? Have you ever noticed how annoying this can be when others do it to you and how it causes you to lose your train of thought? When you are interviewing an offender, you are not engaged in a debate in which your objective is to score points. It is all too easy to interrupt offenders when you perceive their verbal responses to your inquiries to be off the track. Do not let yourself become irritated and impatient with offenders' digressions. They may be approaching the topic you brought up in the most direct way they know how. There are limits, of course, to the amount of digression that you may tolerate, but an interruption made too soon may prevent the emergence of significant information. Some people simply need more time to arrive at their destination. Although side excursions can be time-consuming, a little extra time allowed during the initial interview actually can conserve time when you are attempting to establish a working relationship with an offender.

KEEPING THE OFFENDER IN THE FOREGROUND

Give the offender the lion's share of the "air time" during the interview. Goyer, Redding, and Rickey (1968:14) have suggested that if you find yourself talking uninterruptedly for as little as two minutes during an interview, you are failing to get through to the offender. It follows that it is a good idea to reduce interviewer talk time as much as possible. After all, we have agreed that the time is theirs. You must resist the temptation to thrust your opinions and advice onto offenders and talk them into a coma. Many offenders will be only too happy to allow the interviewer to babble on as a tactic to avoid exploring their own problems. Talk only when necessary to elicit information or to refocus or channel the interview in fruitful directions.

SOME FURTHER IMPEDIMENTS TO ACTIVE LISTENING

There are certain other impediments to active listening against which you should guard. These are **DAYDREAMING**, **DETOURING**, **ARGUING**, and **REHEARSING**. We all are guilty of each of these errors at one time or another. It is important in your chosen field to be aware of them and to take steps to reorient yourself to the content of offenders' communication when you perceive yourself to be drifting away from it.

Daydreaming occurs when you are bored with what you are hearing or when you have pressing needs unrelated to the present concerns. You may veer off on your own personal track and leave the offender behind, forgetting that the interview time belongs to the offender. You must never daydream during offender interviews. It soon becomes apparent to the offender that you are not interested in his or her problems, and you will experience failure in your efforts to establish a firm relationship. Frequent daydreamers are out of touch with their present reality. They fail in many tasks because they focus more on a future "could be" than on what actually is going on now.

Detouring occurs when some piece of communicated information reminds you of something not immediately relevant. You then may tend to let your thoughts wander off on tangents, coming back now and again to touch the actual line of communication. By the time your thoughts again make contact with the offender's, you never can be sure that the track you are on accurately corresponds to the offender's track. More often than not, it will not. Whether on the highway or in an interview, detours can get you lost. People who frequently detour are inclined to be scatterbrained; they have difficulty focusing on the problem at hand.

Arguing occurs when an offender makes a statement that rankles you in some fashion and you cut off the offender's line of communication to present your opinions.

You are forgetting that it is the offender's opinion and not yours that is the present concern. Allow offenders to express and explore their feelings fully without debating them. Do not argue with offenders, either by actually voicing your opinions or just by debating the offender in your mind. Arguers tend to be either self-righteous or contentious individuals who are overly concerned with their own viewpoints.

Rehearsing occurs when, instead of continuing to attend to the offender, you pause to consider how you will respond to an earlier statement. Rehearsers tend to be either unsure of themselves or perfectionists. They feel that responses are never adequate if they are not well formulated before delivery. They seek just the right word or example to make a point. The trouble is that, while you are thinking of that "perfect" response, you will have missed what else the offender has said, including things that might make your response irrelevant.

Regardless of counseling orientation or the purposes of an interview, the most crucial skill of all is listening. Listening is the prerequisite for all other skills. After all, if you have not really listened to what the offender has been saying, you cannot formulate meaningful follow-up questions; you cannot develop rapport; you cannot even begin to understand the offender, and your assessment will be sloppy at best. Poor listening will frustrate and alienate offenders, and you may become part of their problem rather than part of the solution.

RESPONDING: GUIDING THE OFFENDER'S DISCLOSURE

No matter how hard you have been listening, it often is necessary to verify an offender's message so that you do not jump to wrong conclusions. When you perceive a response to be somewhat ambiguous, you should ask for **CLARIFICATION**. Clarification involves a question of the type "Are you saying that. . . . ?" or "Do you mean that. . . . ?" Your request for clarification gives the offender the opportunity to confirm your understanding. **PARAPHRASING**, a simple restatement of the offender's message in the interviewer's words, is similar to clarification. Paraphrasing is used to restate messages with factual content, such as a description of a person, place, event, or situation, to clarify the message, to let offenders know that you have been attending, and to encourage them to focus more deeply on the content.

In contrast, **REFLECTION** is a rephrasing of the emotional content of the offender's message. Reflection is useful when you want to identify the offender's feelings about the factual message presented to you. Feelings are not always expressed verbally but may be identified by nonverbal cues such as rigid body posture, reddening of the face, pursed lips, tone of voice, and so forth. The purpose of reflection is to help offenders to become fully aware of their feelings and to encourage them to explore them.

A hypothetical dialog illustrates these techniques. A thirty-year-old single mother of three children, Betty, has been found guilty of child endangering. Her oldest son, Jason, age nine, was hospitalized with a broken arm. A physical examination revealed that he frequently had been physically abused. You ask her to explain why she abuses Jason. Some possible interviewer responses follow her reply. Try to think of some of your own replies by imagining what it would be like in Betty's shoes.

OFFENDER: I don't really know why I do these things to Jason. I do love him. I'd do anything to change things. I'm not proud of what I did. He's a beautiful boy. I guess I just get so frustrated having to bring up three children on what the welfare pays you. You know, it's no easy task trying to raise three kids. I can't get work because the kids are all so young. I just sit at home thinking about the future. I find myself drinking more heavily as time goes on. All that sitting and drinking hasn't done much for my figure. I weigh about 210 right now. Who would want to hire a slob like me? If only I could get a job I know things would be better for us all.

INTERVIEWER [Clarification]: Are you saying that one of the hardest things facing you right now is your inability to get work, which would enable you to make a better life for yourself and your children? Do you mean that your situation leads you to do these things to Jason?

INTERVIEWER [Paraphrase]: You love Jason, but your responsibility for raising your family by yourself is very difficult for you. You are having a tough time of it.

INTERVIEWER [Reflection]: You feel frustrated and angry about your inability to take care of your children as you would like. You feel terribly guilty about doing what you did to Jason. You feel embarrassed about your weight.

PREPARING TO INTERVIEW THE OFFENDER: THE PHYSICAL SETTING

The results of your interview probably will have a significant impact on the offender's future. Recognizing the importance of this process, it is vital that you give the offender your undivided attention during the time you are together. Although the physical facilities in many criminal justice agencies may not be ideal, it is important that the interview setting be as private and free of distractions as possible. The receptionist should be instructed to hold all nonemergency telephone calls, and a "Do not disturb" sign should be displayed on your office door. Some interruptions may be inevitable, but they must never be of the personal or frivolous kind. You must convey to offenders that this time belongs to them and that they are the only topic of importance to you during this period.

FAMILIARITY WITH THE CASE

Before interviewing the offender, thoroughly familiarize yourself with the case materials obtained from police and prosecutor's files. On the basis of these materials, formulate the questions that you plan to ask. A comprehensive semistructured interview schedule that is being used in probation and parole agencies nationwide is included and discussed in Chapter 7. It is an excellent tool for the beginning interviewer because it covers everything of importance for interviewing the typical offender.

While the schedule begins by asking questions regarding offenders' attitudes toward the offense, and offense patterns, questions pertinent to the crime and to the offender's criminal history are best left until last because these are the questions most likely to threaten the offender, and may require the use of interrogating rather than interviewing techniques. Offenders will answer questions about the offense and about any prior offenses more easily after friendly rapport has been established and they feel less threatened by the situation in which they find themselves.

Most probation departments use an intake form, which the offender fills out prior to meeting the probation officer. This form should request basic demographic data such as name, place and date of birth, current address and telephone number, names and addresses of family members and places of work, schools attended, and the offender's financial situation. It also should ask offenders for pertinent medical information, a recitation of prior involvement with the law, and should include a section that asks them to write out their version of the offense.

The use of such a form serves a number of functions: (1) it gives structure to the interview, (2) it sensitizes the offender to the kind of questions you will be asking in more detail, (3) it provides the offender with an opportunity to decide in private if he or she is going to be honest with you, (4) it gives you the opportunity to decide if the offender indeed has been honest with you by checking the written statement with "the record," (5) it gives you some insight into the offender's level of communication skills, and (6) it minimizes the recording of factual information (age, phone numbers, addresses, and so on) during the interview, which would detract from its smooth flow. A typical social history questionnaire is included in Chapter 7.

INITIATING THE INTERVIEW

A criminal justice offender's first contact with a community corrections agency is usually the result of a referral to a probation department for a presentence investigation report (PSI) after being adjudicated guilty of a crime. Because the PSI interview is perhaps the most important interview the offender will experience, we will assume in the following discussion that we are conducting such an interview. Given the circumstances of the PSI referral, it is necessary to realize that the offender probably will view it as punitive rather than as an opportunity to receive help and guidance. In light of the involuntary nature of the offender's presence, and in light of the offender's possible ingrained mistrust and disregard for authority, it is particularly important that the interview get off to a good start.

MEETING THE OFFENDER: RESPECT AND RAPPORT

The first contact with the offender is crucial. The offender may be anxious and nervous, and you should convey your respect and concern. First impressions certainly will color much of what will follow between you and the offender. It is essential, then, that you establish positive rapport at this time. Greet the offender by looking him or her straight in the eyes and offering a smile and a firm handshake. First names should not be used at the first meeting, especially with older offenders. Traditionally, the superordinate individual addressed the subordinate individual by first name, whereas the person in the inferior position was expected to use the presumed superior's full title and last name. This convention was designed to emphasize social distance, something you definitely wish to avoid. However, a more informal first-name relationship should be established as soon as you perceive that the offender is amenable to it. Your initial statement should be something like, "Good morning, Mr. Smith. My name is Joyce Williams. I will be your probation officer."

You now have introduced yourself and your role. Although your offenders are troubled individuals who you are seeing because they have committed some crime for which they may be deeply ashamed, there must not be any hint of a patronizing, condescending, or judgmental attitude in either your voice or your nonverbal behavior. You may have extremely negative feelings about the kind of behavior that has brought the offender to you. Any attempts to deny to yourself that the offender's behavior has elicited those feelings will result in an artificial, stilted, and unproductive interview. Acknowledge to yourself that these feelings exist and that they are normal and expected. However, also recognize that their expression in a professional goal-oriented setting is inappropriate. If you reveal your anger or embarrassment, even subtly or unconsciously, the offender will pick up on your cues and perhaps respond with his or her own anger and/or embarrassment. Negative emotions, either yours or the offender's, are not conducive to an effective interview. Professional recognition and control of personal feelings rather than denial and repression of them is a goal for which you should strive.

Early in this author's probation career, he had an offender whose appearance and whose crime had a very negative effect on him. The offender had paid a number of neighborhood boys to have sex with her over a period of several months. Although the author struggled to rid himself of the sexist attitudes acquired through socialization, he could not free himself of the notion that women simply "were not supposed to act that way." Consequently, he perceived her crime as somehow much more odious than he would have if she had been a man convicted of similar behavior. Furthermore, when he met her, her physical appearance made matters worse. She was an extremely obese woman with multiple chins thickly folded upon an expansive bosom, and she had a body odor too strong to ignore.

He tried hard to respond positively to her, but, on later reflection, realized how completely artificial he must have seemed to her. He ran through the interview and approached the embarrassing (both to her and to himself) question of her offense with insensitivity. In other words, he let his attitudes and feelings about the offender obscure her basic humanity. The interview was a simple ritual. She was placed on probation to him, but their relationship never did manage to overcome that disastrous first encounter. First impressions are indeed vital! He learned a lot about himself and his attitudes through that encounter, and tried hard to never make the same mistake again.

His experience with this woman underscores the desirability of examining your attitudes and prejudices relating to various kinds of people and their behavior before actually ever dealing with them in a field situation. Treat each person as a unique individual, not as a member of some larger group from whom you expect or do not expect certain ways of behaving. A colleague had a saying on her office wall, which she read every morning: "There is so much good in the worst of us, and so much bad in the best of us, that it ill behooves any one of us to find any fault with the rest of us."

EXPLAINING THE PURPOSE OF THE INTERVIEW

The actual interview should begin by asking offenders if they know the purpose of the interview. If an offender does not know—and many do not—then, the purpose should be fully explained. You should inform the offender of the type of information you wish to obtain, what it will be used for, and who will have access to it. Although an explanation of the uses to which a presentence investigation report will be put (to aid in sentencing decisions, and, if the offender is incarcerated, in prison classification and parole hearings) can raise the anxiety level of an offender, the honesty is appreciated. It is a good idea at this point to ask offenders if they understand what they have been told so far and if they have any questions. It is very important, however, not to respond with any opinion to such questions as "What do you think I'll get?" or "What are my chances?" Remember, you do not make the final sentencing decision, and you do not wish to raise false hopes or to generate needless anxiety. If you tell an offender that you are "sure" that he or she will receive probation, and the offender is incarcerated instead, that person surely will feel bitter and betrayed. One such incident may have a lasting negative affect on any subsequent dealings that offender may have with you or with any other correctional worker. Conversely, if you tell an offender that he or she is as good as on the bus to prison, but the offender actually is placed on probation, his or her attitude toward you could be one of smug contempt: "The judge didn't buy your recommendation. Just goes to show how valuable your opinion is, doesn't it?"

Some authorities disagree on this point, feeling that if incarceration seems probable, it is a humanitarian gesture to prepare the offender for it. This is rather like the physician's dilemma when asked, "How long have I got?" An honest appraisal in either case, so the argument goes, gives the individual the opportunity to prepare for it by saying goodbyes and putting personal affairs in order. However, in the case of an offender told that he or she probably will be sent to prison, the goodbyes may well be to the jurisdiction of your state. If you do offer the offender an opinion that turns out to be wrong, or if it leads the offender to abscond, you have only yourself to blame for the consequences. Instead, politely reply that you do not engage in second-guessing of judges and that it is not your place to speculate. You now are ready to begin the interview proper.

Conducting the Interview

THE INTERVIEWER'S LANGUAGE AND DEMEANOR

If you are using an offender intake form, the interview is to clarify and elaborate on the information the offender has written down. When questioning an offender, you are making contact with another human being. Questions must be geared both to the offender's vocabulary and to his or her pace. Legalistic or sociological jargon, street talk, and ten-dollar words should be avoided. The use of fancy phraseology will embarrass the offender whose vocabulary is limited and will not impress one who is as articulate as you are. Either way, it will distance the offender from you. Similarly, the use of street slang is unprofessional and will give the offender the idea that you either are patronizing or are playing buddy-buddy. Use conventional and easily understandable English. Just as importantly, do not adopt street mannerisms such as an artificially laid-back posture or the latest fad in handshakes. Do not say or do anything that is artificial to you; it will be blatantly visible to those used to being treated dishonestly.

THE USE OF AUTHORITY

A final concern is the officer's proper use of authority. Experts in the counseling field disagree on the issue of whether the use, or even the possession, of authority is detrimental to the helping process. Authority and helping can be incompatible, however, if you use and abuse it to emphasize the moral distance between you and your offender and to puff yourself up with your own importance. The bombastic "big stick" approach only will alienate offenders. They immediately will type you as "just another cop in social workers' threads," and will scoff at your insistence that you only want to "help" them.

Yet, authority comes with the job and it cannot be denied. The failure to use your authority when appropriate, will be viewed as weakness by offenders who value strength and who are adept at manipulating perceived weakness. Like feelings, officers' authority must be recognized and accepted, but used with professional restraint. Needless to say, the accouterments of force, such as guns or handcuffs, should not be on display at the first meeting with the offender.

DEALING WITH AWKWARD OFFENDERS

Some offenders will be fearful or angry and thus will act in a hostile way or refuse to answer certain questions. It may be that they are trying to maintain a sense of dignity and control in the only way they know. When such an attitude becomes apparent, do not continue with the interview as if you hoped that ignoring it would make it go away. Say something like: "Mr. Jones, I know that this is unpleasant for you and that you must be feeling a little uptight. It's quite natural for you to feel that way. Lots of people do. Why don't we agree to be civil to one another? What do you say?" This lets Mr. Jones know that you are aware of his feelings, that others have felt that way, that you accept his feelings as natural, and that you are willing to start over again on a new footing.

In those rare instances when offenders continue to refuse to answer questions, or when they continue to respond in a sarcastic, rude, or an abrupt manner, let them know in no uncertain terms that this kind of attitude is simply unacceptable. Inform them that if they continue in such a way, then the interview will be terminated and that it will be necessary for them to return to the department to try again after they have rethought their approach. You also may indicate that such an attitude will be conveyed to the sentencing judge if it continues. If this tactic does not work, try a phone call to the offender's attorney outlining the problem. This never fails to bring about a change in the offender's demeanor.

Most often, however, offenders are anxious to be cooperative and to convey a positive impression during the initial interview. They are feeling you out just as surely as you are feeling them out. Most offenders are aware that their attitudes will be reported to the judge and that they may influence your recommendation. Reluctance and uncooperativeness are much more common among offenders under actual supervision than they are prior to formal supervision. The presentence investigator and the parole board usually see offenders at their best.

It is the supervising probation and parole officers who most frequently are confronted with uncooperative offenders. For this reason, it is of the utmost importance that the groundwork be laid for the development of a trusting relationship at the initial interview, a period in which the offender's frame of mind is most conducive to it. (The problem of the reluctant offender is addressed in more detail in Chapter 10).

Regardless of the offenders' level of cooperation, their overall demeanor will provide valuable clues for your assessment. Someone who comes to the interview smelling of alcohol or under the influence of drugs is not taking the process very seriously and obviously will be difficult to supervise if placed on probation. A servile or arrogant manner also will provide clues to character assessment and possible supervision strategies.

These initial observations will assist you in designing a preliminary plan of treatment and will help you to decide if a referral to specialized treatment is in order. When you decide that a referral is advisable, discuss the matter with the offender and explain your reasoning. Do not antagonize offenders or put them on the defensive by flatly stating that they have a problem. Try to steer offenders toward that conclusion themselves. Ask them how the problem you perceive them as having affects their relationships with others and how they would feel if they could find support in controlling the problem. You then may discuss the services provided by the agency in question and the benefits they may derive from talking with a counselor there. Remember, the initial interview is positively your best opportunity to get your foot in the door to obtain offenders' cooperation and compliance.

TERMINATING THE INTERVIEW

At the end of the interview, summarize what has gone on during it. Your summary provides the opportunity to determine if anything important has been overlooked and gives the offender the chance to change, clarify, or add to transmitted information. Ask offenders if they have anything to add or anything else to ask. If not, you may conclude the interview, shake the offenders' hands, inform them that you will be in touch in the near future, and walk them to the door. Back in your office again, immediately go over your notes and write down additional impressions while they are fresh in your mind. The results of your interview also should help you decide what collateral interviews will be necessary.

Interviewing the Victim

PREPARATION

With the ascent of the restorative justice philosophy in criminal justice, a concern for victims' needs and feelings finally has emerged. Victims' input in plea bargain negotiations and sentencing and parole hearings may restore some of the confidence they may have lost in the criminal justice system, and also may help them restore some sense of control over their lives. Remember, under the philosophy of restorative justice, the victim is also your client, and you should do everything you can to make this component of the philosophy as meaningful and successful as possible.

Your first approach to the victim should be a phone call to make an appointment. Explain the reason for your wish to meet personally with the victim and set up a time at his or her convenience. To relieve victims of any further inconvenience, and as a courtesy, the meeting should take place in the victim's home unless he or she wishes otherwise. When you meet with the victim, identify yourself as an officer of the court by presenting your credentials. You then may go over the purpose of the interview again. Some victims welcome the opportunity to speak about the crime again in the informal and familiar setting of their own homes, but for others it is a nuisance that they rather would avoid. Let the victim know that your presence indicates the concerns the legal system has about his or her experience and that it is an opportunity to have some input into the sentencing process. This assurance tends to ease some of the pain and anger of all except the most cynical, and it returns a sense of control to those victims who feel that they have lost much of it by their victimization.

Personal criminal victimization is an intensely negative experience. Even if the crime is a nonviolent one in which the victim never had to confront the offender, the experience can leave a person with feelings of complete helplessness and violation. These feelings quite naturally tend to generate anger and a certain measure of self-blame, especially among victims of sexual assault. The typical experience of the victim as the case progresses through the courts sometimes involving interminable delays and postponements does nothing to mitigate these feelings. Some of that anger and self-blame may be displaced onto the presentence investigator. Be prepared to encounter such a natural reaction and deal with it in a sensitive manner. Your most trying experiences in the field may be to conduct interviews with parents who have lost a child to a drunken driver or with relatives of loved ones who have been brutally raped or murdered. Extreme sensitivity and understanding are absolute musts in such instances. In no case should you imply sympathy for the offender or make any suggestion that the victim may have contributed to his or her own victimization even if you think it, and never argue with a victim or the victim's survivors. Investigators should possess a self-concept strong enough to allow victims or their survivors to vent their anger on them without retaliation.

WHEN NOT TO INTERVIEW

The matter of interviewing child victims of sexual abuse is entirely different. Avoid any contact with such victims. It is not merely uncomfortable for a child to recount the episode; it may add to the psychological damage the child suffers. Henry Hartman, a criminal psychiatrist of many years experience, puts it this way (1978:217): "Intense emotional reactions on the part of the parents, repeated questioning by police, unpleasant appearances and cross-examination in courtrooms may all be as traumatic or even more traumatic than the offense itself." There is no point in risking further trauma for the sake of a little additional insight into the offense. There are children who, even after long-term sexual victimization by adults, have suffered no ill effects until the relationships were discovered and the children subjected to responses like those Hartman names. Such social reactions lead children to believe that much or all of the blame for what transpired belongs to them. Certainly it does not, and the investigating officer should not call up the child's residual feelings of guilt and shame in the pursuit of a "complete" PSI. Parents of the children, of course, should be interviewed and allowed to discuss the effects of the offense on their children.

Conducting the Interview

Asking for Details of the Offense

It is not advisable to request the details of the offense from victims in all cases. They have already recounted them numerous times to other officials, and the retelling may be quite painful for them. However, offer them the opportunity to speak about the offense if they desire to do so. Say something like "I know this has been an awful experience for you and you probably would like to forget it, but is there anything at all that you would like to add that you didn't tell the police or the prosecutor?" In posing the question this way, you have conveyed to the victim your recognition of his or her ordeal, and you have given the victim the option of elaborating. The decision must be entirely the victim's, and the officer should not press the issue in the face of obvious reluctance.

REASSURING THE VICTIM

One of the things that crime victims need most is reassurance of their safety. Many victims fear retaliation or worry that a burglar will come back. In the author's experience as a police officer and as a probation officer, he has never known perpetrators to retaliate against the victim after the case had been adjudicated, or a burglar to hit the same house twice. This is not to say that such things do not happen, but they are extremely rare. Make a clear statement to this effect to frightened victims. In the event that the victim and offender are known to each other, you even may indicate that in the event that the perpetrator is placed on probation, you will make it a condition of probation that he or she is to have no contact of any sort with the victim. Victims need to hear such reassurances.

PROMISES TO THE VICTIM

It is important that you not make any promises to the victim that you cannot keep or make statements regarding the defendant's probable sentence. Some states have made provisions for victims to have input into the sentencing of those who have offended against them. If your state has a statutory provision for a victim's recommendation for sentencing, you, of course, should request one. Whether these recommendations actually have an impact on sentencing decisions is a question awaiting research. Research indicates a statistically significant relationship between victim's recommendations and sentences imposed in sexual assault cases, but the relationship disappeared when the researcher controlled for the effects of seriousness of crime and offender's prior record (Walsh, 1986). Future research may show different results. Whatever the case may be, do not lead the victim into the belief that his or her recommendation necessarily will be heeded. Be as honest with victims as you are with offenders. Do not risk the victims' future anger and disrespect for the sake of their momentary peace of mind and satisfaction. Specific questions that you should ask the victim are listed in Chapter 6 on the PSI report.

TERMINATING THE INTERVIEW

Terminate the interview with victims by reiterating your assurances and thanking them for their cooperation. Give victims your card and tell them that they are welcome to call you with further concerns. This invitation probably will be viewed by the victims as a further indication that they are not the forgotten party in the criminal justice process. Finally, if it is not the practice of the prosecutor's office in your jurisdiction to apprise victims of sentencing dates, tell victims that you will notify them personally. At the very least, inform the victims of the final disposition of the case.

Interrogating the Offender

REASONS FOR INTERROGATION

Many jurisdictions legally define their probation and parole officers as law enforcement officers. As a law enforcement officer, you are responsible for monitoring the behavior of offenders. When offenders break the law or some condition of their supervision, or are suspected of doing so, it is your duty to question them. As you will see, your questioning under such circumstances will require a different strategy. This type of questioning is called **interrogation**. To those who enter the community corrections field with the notion that their only role is that of a helper, this definition is sometimes distasteful, probably because they associate interrogation with the third-degree tactics of yesteryear.

Do not lose sight of the fact that you are functioning both as a law enforcement officer and as a counselor, but those two roles do not necessarily conflict. As a law enforcement officer, you sometimes may have to use the techniques of interrogation. For instance, you may need to learn the truth about acts committed by offenders that place them in violation of their probation or parole. Offenders do not readily admit to violations. You are not doing justice to your role, or ultimately to offenders, if you do not learn and deal with details of their violations.

You also may need to interrogate offenders during a presentence investigation interview if they flatly deny having committed the crimes of which they have been convicted. This is not unusual. An unpublished study at the author's department found that 18 percent of a sample of 416 offenders denied their crimes during the PSI interview.

Since denial has implications for decisions about sentencing and treatment, it behooves the investigating officer not to report simply that the offender denies the crime and leave it at that. Many offenders will tell you that they are innocent and that they pled guilty on their lawyer's advice, or that they did so to obtain a plea bargain agreement. Although it is not unknown for innocent offenders to plead guilty because their lawyers have considered the case against them to be too strong, the fact that the case is now before you makes the possibility rather remote. Given the legal restraints on police questioning (restraints that you do not have in the presentence investigation situation), and the defendant's privilege of silence in court, your interrogation may be the first opportunity to get to the truth of the matter. Probably about one out of every four offenders who initially denies his or her guilt finally admits it under questioning, and at least two of the others make statements that are sufficient to dispel doubts of guilt.

DISTINGUISHING BETWEEN INTERVIEWING AND INTERROGATING

Interrogating is the act of making a thorough investigation of a specific allegation brought against a suspect through the use of systematic and formal questioning. There are two basic differences between interviewing and interrogating. The first concerns your relationship with the offender. You temporarily have discarded the helping attitude of the counselor and adopted the skeptical manner of the law enforcement officer. The second concerns purpose. Interviewing has the broad goal of gathering general information, whereas interrogating involves the drawing out of quite specific information, which the offender may be highly motivated to keep hidden—namely, whether the offender did or did not commit the act that you, the police, or some other party accuse him or her of committing (Vessel, 1998).

Interrogating is also different from the interviewing process in that it requires that the interrogator, not the offender, control the flow of activity. You must control the timing, content, and wording of your questioning with your singular purpose in mind. Suspect offenders must be given only enough initiative and control to allow them to relate their stories. They must come to understand that you mean business and that for the moment you are not interested in anything else but the question at hand.

On a legal note, if the matter for which you are conducting the interview involves a new offense, and if what you learn from the offender is to be used in a court of law for evidentiary purposes, you must inform the offender of his or her Fifth Amendment rights as required by *Miranda*. In *United States v. Deaton* (1972), the presiding judge stated that a probationer or parolee is probably under more pressure to respond to his or her probation/parole officer than to a police officer, and, therefore, the *Miranda* warnings should be given.

BEING CONFIDENT BY BEING PREPARED

Preparing yourself for an interrogation is both different from and similar to preparing for an interview. The major difference is that an interrogation is often a battle of wits and the atmosphere can be quite charged because the offender is aware of that fact. If you are to conduct an effective interrogation, one that will lead you to the truth regarding the matter at hand, you have to approach the task with confidence. Convey an impression of confidence to the offender. To achieve this level of confidence, be fully prepared. This means that you must be completely familiar with all of the evidence supporting the offender's guilt, and any evidence that might indicate otherwise. Depending on the situation, such evidence might include police reports, victim statements, or information from an informant. Not having all the information that is available to you will put you at a serious disadvantage once the interrogation begins.

CONDUCTING THE INTERROGATION

The interrogation may take place in your office or it may take place in a cell at the county jail. In any case, as the offender's supervising officer, unlike a police officer, you will have had an ongoing relationship with him or her. Consequently, you are able to dispense with the usual police lead-ins to interrogation like requests for demographic information such as name, address, and place of employment. You should greet offenders in a friendly but businesslike manner and inform them of your purpose by saying something like, "Jim, I've asked you to come to see me (or, I've come to see you) to get to the bottom of this matter that has come to my attention." You then may begin your questioning.

As indicated, confidence in your professionalism and in your preparation is of the utmost importance. A lack of confidence, reflected by frequently referring back to reports, hemming and hawing around, squirming in your chair, acting impatiently, and so forth, will convey the impression to the offender that perhaps the evidence against him or her is not all that strong. Demonstrate to offenders that the evidence that is in your possession leads you to the firm conviction that they are guilty. This conviction should be stated in a nonemotional and clinical manner. The credibility of the interrogator depends on these two points: his or her thorough knowledge of the matter under discussion, and the offender's perceptions of him or her as a competent professional. Do not "blow" the positive relationship with offenders that you have worked so hard to gain by becoming frustrated and angry because you feel that you cannot break down their defenses.

STYLE

Differences exist between interviewing and interrogating, but much that was said about interviewing also applies to interrogating. First and foremost, you must approach the task in a completely professional manner. Any attempts to borrow the techniques of the movie detective will prove disastrous. Do not put up a "tough guy" front. The typical criminal will see through this and match you verbal blow for verbal blow, a competition that could well end up being decided in favor of offenders who rely on such tactics to survive every day of their lives. If this happens, you reveal yourself as a phoney, and you can kiss good-bye any respect that your offender may have had for you.

Clifford Unwin, an experienced British police inspector, indicates that although the interrogator must control the psychological situation, it is not wise to adopt a role of complete psychological domination. "The problem is that if the interrogator limits himself [or herself] to displays of power he [or she] may find in certain situations that he [or she] is running the risk of doing exactly the opposite. It may cause the suspect to confirm his [or her] beliefs that the interrogator is the enemy and is someone to be defied, particularly with a hardened or seasoned criminal" (1978:1875).

As implied by Unwin, never adopt the attitude of "NIGYSOB" ("Now I've got you, you son-of-a-bitch") described by Eric Berne (1964) in his book *Games People Play*. If you project such an obviously self-satisfied attitude to offenders undergoing interrogation, in effect you are issuing a challenge and inviting resistance. You also imply that your objective all along has been "to get" offenders rather than to help them.

ASK LEADING QUESTIONS

Questioning within an interrogation context often will be of the **leading** type. A leading question is one in which the wording strongly encourages a specific answer (this kind of question never should be used in an interview). For example: you receive a complaint from Jim's estranged wife that he was drinking last night, and that he went over to her home and slapped her around. Jim's parole conditions include maintaining sobriety and staying away from his wife. You may confront Jim with: "You were in the Western Bar drinking last night weren't you? Isn't it also true that you became drunk and went over to your wife's home and beat her up?" Such questions, asked in a businesslike tone, have the psychological effect of making it more difficult to deny than a simple "Were you drinking last night?"

REVEAL A LITTLE INFORMATION

Reinforce both your confidence and the offender's anxiety by revealing some of the evidence you have indicative of guilt, or in a PSI situation, some of the evidence gathered by police agencies, taking careful note of how the offender deals with this information. However, do not reveal all evidence in one giant salvo. If the offenders successfully weather the initial attack, the officer has nothing left in reserve with which to surprise them. Always keep offenders on the defensive by letting them guess at the extent of the evidence in your possession. Point out inconsistencies in their stories and ask them to account for them (this cannot be done if you have not thoroughly assimilated the "official" version and paid complete attention to the offender's version).

Some offenders will respond to a straightforward statement from you indicating that alibis or protestations of innocence are "bullshit." On more than one occasion, this author has been confronted with a knowing smile, followed by the real story, after such a remark. This usually works with an offender who has been through the system before, and who tends to look upon what is going on between you as some sort of "game." This, of course, depends on the seriousness of the consequences to the offender of making such an admission. Other offenders will react defensively to a direct statement such as the above. With such offenders, it is preferable to state: "You haven't told me the whole truth," rather than to say: "You've been lying to me." The difference is subtle but real, nevertheless. Only experience will tell you when either approach is preferable. Usually, however, the latter method works best with the more "respectable" and less "streetwise" offenders.

LETTING OFFENDERS DAMN THEMSELVES

It is often a good ploy to allow the offender to make statements that you know are lies and for you to give the impression that you are accepting them at face value. The awkward thing about a lie is that it requires additional lies to support it. Eventually, this compounding of falsehoods should paint offenders into a very uncomfortable corner from which only truth will remove them. If the interrogator allows offenders to get themselves into such a psychologically uncomfortable position and then points out a series of inconsistencies, he or she has created a strong motive (the removal of psychological discomfort) for them to "come clean."

TAKING ADVANTAGE OF OFFENDER DISCOMFORT

If this does not provide the desired admission, signs of guilt, such as confusion, stammering, nervous sweating, an active Adam's apple, refusing to maintain eye contact, and other emotional reactions, point out to the offender that you take these signs as indicative of guilt. Take advantage of such signs of physiological discomfort by looking the offender squarely in his or her eyes and repeating some of your most threatening questions. You also may ask the offender to repeat his or her story three or four times at different points in the interrogation. It is easy to be consistent if the story is true, but it is very difficult to remember little details used to support a falsehood. That is, you can tell the truth in a dozen different ways, but it is hard to do the same with a lie. Knowing that you are aware of their discomfort often prompts offenders to unburden themselves by making a confession.

Often the use of morally neutral words rather than negatively emotionally loaded ones will also help guilty offenders unburden (Inbau and Reid, 1985). Think of the emotional differences between the statements given below:

Neutral: "John, I want you to *tell me the truth*."
Emotionally Loaded: "John, I want you to make a *confession*."

Neutral: "Alice, did you *take* those items?"
Emotionally Loaded: "Alice, did you *steal* those items?"

Neutral: "Did you *shoot* Mr. Brooks?"
Emotionally Loaded: "Did you *kill* Mr. Brooks?"

You will not be as far along in the interrogation as you may want to be if you ask "Did you *have sex* with Kathy?" as opposed to "Did you *rape* Kathy?" But, the greater likelihood that the offender will answer affirmatively to the more emotionally neutral question gives you a further advantage.

BLUFFING

Bluffing is a weak form of interrogation. Bluffing means conveying to offenders the impression that you have access to information that is damaging to them when, in fact, you do not. For instance, you may be interrogating Jack on the basis of police information that he has been trafficking in drugs. You may indicate to him that you have "accurate" information from "confidential informants" that he has been selling drugs. Bluffs such as this may pay off large dividends, but they are more likely to be "called." If Jack calls your bluff, all you can do is withdraw as gracefully as possible.

What if he really is not guilty of trafficking? Your crude "poker" tactics will offend him sorely and perhaps do irreparable damage to the supportive relationship you have been seeking to develop with him. The cost/benefit ratio of such tactics do not recommend their use. Be honest with offenders. It is always the best policy.

THE "BACK DOOR" APPROACH

Some authorities on police interrogation advocate a "back door" approach to interrogation (Napier and Adams, 1998; Unwin, 1978). That is, prompt a confession from a suspect by downplaying the seriousness of the offense the individual is suspected of committing, conveying sympathy and "understanding" of why such a crime would be committed under the circumstances, placing the burden of blame on victims or accomplices, or intimating that the act was perhaps accidental. Although such an approach may be used successfully by police interrogators, it is not advocated for the corrections worker. Confessions using this psychological ploy are obtained by lessening the guilt felt by the suspects by conveying to them that their actions were not really that bad, that others would do the same thing in their shoes, and by blame-sharing. While this suits police purposes by "clearing" crimes, it is counterproductive to the correctional goal. Rehabilitation is not accomplished by providing offenders with easy rationales for their actions. Correctional workers always must be aware of their dual role, and should not compromise one aspect of it to satisfy the immediate requirements of the other.

TERMINATING THE INTERROGATION

The way that you terminate the interrogation will depend on the circumstances. If the interrogation was necessitated by a technical violation of supervision conditions, such as associating with known criminals, continuing their substance abuse, failing to report to you, or any other violation of this kind, the action you take may be discretionary. You may feel it necessary to initiate formal proceedings for the revocation of probation or parole, or you may decide to resume your helping relationship.

If the interrogation resulted from an arrest for a new crime, any further action on your part has to await formal adjudication. In any case, the offender should be informed of your next step as soon as you have decided what it is to be. You may be able to inform the offender of your decision then and there, or you may feel it necessary to investigate further and think the matter over before declaring your intentions. In any case, explain your decision to the offender and give your reasons for making it. Regardless of what that decision might be, make every effort to reestablish your working relationship with the offender. Even if you have decided to initiate revocation proceedings, most offenders realize that you only are doing your job and they will not permanently alienate themselves from you if you have dealt fairly, honestly, and professionally with them.

Summary

This chapter has introduced the techniques of interviewing and interrogation. Prepare for both tasks by thoroughly familiarizing yourself with all the pertinent information available. An effective interview must begin by establishing rapport. This is particularly important in criminal justice where offenders are not exactly enthusiastic about being in your office. Offenders are convicted criminals, but they are also human beings who are deserving of consideration and respect. Make them as comfortable as possible, and show that you are concerned and are willing to listen to them.

Listening, really listening, is the most important aspect of an effective interview. Give the offender the "air time," and resist interruptions and debates. The interview time belongs to the offender. Offenders must be encouraged to explore themselves and their behavior. Encourage this exploration through the frequent use of probes and open-ended questions. Make sure that you understand what offenders are trying to tell you using paraphrasing, clarifying, and reflective techniques. Even the most awkward of offenders will settle down and provide you lots of valuable assessment information if you treat them with patience and respect, but also with firmness, when it is required. Interviewing victims requires a special sensitivity to their victimization. Any reluctance on their part to be interviewed or to approach certain subjects should be respected absolutely. Do not dig for details of sexual offenses (they are in the official record, anyway). It is extremely unadvisable to interview child victims of sexual assault. Never argue with victims about anything, and do not upset yourself if they sometimes use you as a convenient target for their verbal anger. Finally, reassure victims as much as possible, but, as with offenders, do not make any promises that are not within your power to keep.

Sometimes interrogation techniques are required. Any interrogation should be approached in a calm, clinical, and professional manner. Unlike the interview in which the purpose is to gather large amounts of general information, the interrogation is geared to one specific aim—"did you do it?" Also unlike the interview, you rather than the offender will control the content and pace of the interrogation. Know the evidence supportive of your offender's guilt, but do not jeopardize your relationship with the offender by coming on like a movie detective. Useful interrogation techniques such as letting offenders damn themselves and taking advantage of offender discomfort are included. Use these recommended techniques when it is necessary for you to interrogate, but above all, be honest and fair with the offender and be yourself.

EXERCISE IN LISTENING AND INTERVIEWING

This is an exercise in listening using the Client Management Classification (CMC) semi-structured interview schedule reproduced in Chapter 7. Although this exercise will familiarize you with the type of questions asked in a typical PSI interview, its main purpose is to provide an experience in listening. Divide students into groups of two, with one student taking the part of the interviewer and the other the interviewee. Rather than role playing, the interviewee should relate to the interviewer actual aspects of his or her life. For instance, when asked "How do (did) you get along with your father?", the interviewee should respond accurately with reference to his or her own father.

The main purpose of this interview exercise is to develop your ability to listen actively. Did you ever buy a lottery ticket or bet on a ball game and then listen for the results on the radio? Think back to that time and recall how you listened to the results. You sat close to the radio and faced it with intense interest. You leaned toward it, and you were impervious to all other stimuli surrounding you. That is how you should proceed with this exercise—with intensity and interest. Ask the questions provided in the schedule, but use, when appropriate, probes and open-ended questions; ask for clarification, and remember to paraphrase responses and reflect feelings.

On the basis of the interview, you should write a brief social history of your part-ner (a PSI without offense, criminal history, and evaluation and recommendation material) based on the information obtained. After writing this history, give it to the interviewee for evaluation. The interviewee should evaluate the history and your inter-viewing performance according to the following criteria:

1. Eye contact was maintained without gazing or staring. Yes✓ No__

2. Body posture was appropriate (relaxed, slight forward lean). Yes✓ No__

3. He or she made me feel comfortable and relaxed. Yes✓ No__

4. He or she made me really think about things which I have not thought about for some time by the use of probes. Yes✓ No__

5. He or she seemed to be genuinely interested in me. Yes✓ No__

6. He or she delivered questions without hesitations. Yes✓ No__

7. He or she often asked for clarification and paraphrased often. Yes✓ No__

8. I felt that I could tell him or her just about anything he or she asked about my personal life. Yes✓ No__

9. He or she accurately reflected my feelings. Yes✓ No__

10. On a scale of 1 to 10, with 10 being the best, I would rate his or her reported accu-racy of my social history as (circle one).

1   2   3   4   5   6   7   8 ⑨ 10

After each student has taken a turn at being both the interviewer and intervie-wee, share these ratings with one another. Ratings should be the honest evaluations of the rater, and not designed to ignore poor technique in the name of "smooth sailing." Constructive feedback should be viewed by the interviewer as just that. Think of it as another exercise in self-disclosure in which your partner has revealed something of your "blind self," in this case, your ability to conduct an effective interview. The bene-fits of these exercises will be enhanced greatly if you have access to a video recorder so that you will receive visual and audio feedback of your behavior during an interview. Lastly, do not forget that it is your first attempt. Learn from it.

References and Suggested Readings

Alexander, R. 2000. *Counseling, Treatment, and Intervention Methods with Juvenile and Adult Offenders*. Belmont, California: Brooks/Cole.

American Correctional Association. 1993. *Understanding Cultural Diversity*. Lanham, Maryland: American Correctional Association.

Berne, E. 1964. *Games People Play*. New York: Grove Press.

Cumming, G. and M. Buell. 1997. *Supervision of the Sex Offender*. Safer Society Press. Available from the American Correctional Association, Lanham, Maryland.

Garrett, A. 1982. *Interviewing: Its Principles and Methods*. New York: Family Services Association of America.

Gorden, R. 1992. *Basic Interviewing Techniques*. Itasca, Illinois: F. E. Peacock.

Goyer, R., C. Redding, and J. Rickey. 1968. *Interviewing Principles and Techniques*. Dubuque, Iowa: William. C. Brown.

Hartman, H. 1978. *Basic Psychiatry for Corrections Workers*. Springfield, Illinois: Charles C. Thomas.

Inbau, F. and J. Reid. 1985. *Criminal Interrogations and Confessions*. Baltimore, Maryland: Williams and Wilkins.

Ivey, A. 1983. *Intentional Interviewing and Counseling*. Monterey, California: Brooks/Cole.

Napier, M. and S. Adams. 1998. Magic words to obtain confessions. *Law Enforcement Bulletin*. 67:11-15.

Reik, T. 1956. *Listening with the Third Ear*. New York: Grove Press.

Unwin, C. 1978. Interrogation Techniques. *Police Review*. 85:1874-1877.

Vessel, D. 1998. Conducting Successful Interrogations. *Law Enforcement Bulletin*. 67:1-6.

Walsh, A. 1986. Placebo justice: Victim recommendations and offender sentences in sexual assault cases. *Journal of Criminal Law and Criminology*. 77:1126-1141.

Chapter 6

The Presentence Investigation Report (PSI)

The presentence investigation is the first step in the attempt to correct the offender's behavior. . . . It requires great skill in the study, evaluation, and supervision of offenders; familiarity with community resources; and an understanding.

Harvey Treger

The presentence investigation report (PSI) is the end product of the interviews you have completed with the offender, the victim, arresting police officers, and other interested parties. A comprehensive definition is provided by Dean Champion (1999: 74) who defines it as a:

> document, usually prepared by a probation agent or officer, which provides background information on the offender including name, address, occupation (if any), potential for employment, the crime(s) involved, relevant circumstances associated with the crime, family data, evidence of prior record (if any), marital status, and other relevant data such as the results of psychological examinations.

The quality and usefulness of the report depends on how well you have conducted your interviews, and how well you can summarize and communicate a voluminous amount of material, and make a reasoned selection of pertinent information from the mass available to you. You must learn to discriminate between information that is necessary to know and information that is merely nice to know. Too much unnecessary material will clutter the report and confuse the reader. Some reports are padded liberally with trivia that adds nothing to the understanding of the offender and clouds the issue of sentencing decisions. Studies exploring the decision-making process have shown an inverse relationship between the sheer weight of data and appropriate or useful decisions (Nettler, 1970). Would you, if you were the sentencing judge, want to read a fifteen-page report full of irrelevancies when you had to read perhaps ten other reports?

Good report writing is an art that flows from practice and feedback from classroom instructors, coworkers, supervisors, and judges. There is no easy substitute for the twin processes of practice and feedback. However, a discussion of specific content areas of the presentence investigation report should lay the groundwork for writing thorough, factual, concise, readable, and useful presentence investigation reports.

Uses of the Presentence Investigation Report

A brief review of the uses for presentence investigation reports, which fall primarily under the general areas of decision-making aids and treatment aids, will emphasize the importance of making sure that your reports exhibit attributes necessary for their function.

Judicial Sentencing Decisions. Presentence investigations for the purpose of aiding the judge in the selection of appropriate case dispositions serve the positivist philosophy of individualized justice. Probation officers are charged with the task of putting this philosophy into practice by presenting to the courts their assessments of "individualized" offenders and making sentencing recommendations consistent with those assessments. Numerous studies have shown that probation officers have been spectacularly successful in gaining judicial compliance with their recommendations (Abadinski, 1997; Myers, 1979; Walsh, 1984 and 1985a), although the advent of sentencing guidelines that indicate mandatory sentences based on the seriousness of the crime and prior record have diminished the importance of extralegal factors such as those outlined by Champion in the first paragraph of this chapter (Conaboy, 1997). Given that these recommendations, which should flow naturally from the information contained in the PSI, can have a profound effect on an individual's life, it is imperative that they accurately reflect the facts.

Departmental and Institutional Classification. Diagnostic information contained in the presentence investigation report is used by probation departments to determine the supervision level of offenders placed on probation. Information such as prior supervisions, arrest record, attitude, needs and risk assessments, and the nature of the crime are quantified on a scale (such as the risk and needs scales to be examined later) to determine the type and frequency of supervision. If the offender is incarcerated, his or her medical, psychological, and criminal history, as well as vocational and educational information are used by the institution as an aid in determining security level, work assignments, and vocational, educational, and counseling needs.

Parole Decisions. The presentence investigation report accompanies the offender to the institution and, in addition to classification, is used as an aid to parole-release decision. The parole officer to whom the offender is released also uses information contained in the presentence investigation report in formulating initial treatment and supervision plans. In the case of parole revocation decisions, presentence investigation information is used as a base line to gauge the offender's progress (or lack of it) since his or her initial assessment.

Counseling Plans and Community Agency Referrals. The treatment plans outlined in the presentence investigation report are used for the guidance of the probation officer that is supervising the offender (it may or may not be the officer who wrote the report). They also aid the officer in making appropriate referrals to agencies that deal with any specific problems of the offender that are beyond the officer's purview or expertise. The information contained in the PSI report is then used by the receiving agency as a planning guide, relieving the agency of the necessity of gathering duplicate information. Such information should not be provided to the agency, however, without the written consent of the offender.

Sample Presentence Investigation Report

An actual PSI investigation report is presented here to illustrate its areas of content. As you examine it, bear its uses in mind. Names, locations, and circumstances have been altered sufficiently to protect anonymity. This particular report was selected because of its excellent quality and because it illustrates some interesting applications of the criminological and/or counseling theories we have examined or will examine. This report is only one of several presentence investigation formats. Presentence investigation reports range from two to fifteen pages in length—the variability largely a function of agency requirements and case complexity.

THE ADRIAN COUNTY ADULT PROBATION DEPARTMENT
LOWMAN, IDAHO
PRESENTENCE REPORT

NAME: William (Bill) Bloggs   JUDGE: Joseph B. Lynch
ADDRESS: Currently in Adrian County Jail
    Formerly: 780 N 30th, Lowman, ID.
AGE: 28; DOB 7-25-73
SEX: male
RACE: white
PENDING CASES/DETAINERS: none
MARITAL STATUS: married
DEPENDENTS: none
OFFENSE:
INDICTMENT # 01-1234
  Aggravated Robbery
  IRC # 2911.01
INDICTMENT #01-3457
  Attempted Aggravated Murder
  IRC #2923.02
PROBATION OFFICER: Paul Corrick
ATTORNEY: S. Bonnetti

CIRCUMSTANCES OF OFFENSE

On 6-13-01, at approximately 1:30 am, the defendant entered the Big Man Restaurant, located at 1324 Main St., through an open rear door and announced his intention of robbing said establishment. Armed with a .38 caliber pistol, the defendant ordered the manager to fill a bag embossed with the Lowman College seal, which he had brought with him, with the day's takings. The manager, Barry Harbourne, complied with the demand and filled the bag with cash totaling $1,203.32. The defendant then picked up the bag and exited through the back door. As soon as he left the restaurant, Mr. Harbourne called the police to the scene. Upon leaving the scene, the defendant stopped to remove his sweater, gloves, and the face mask he was wearing. The police arrived as he was doing this and spotted him. At this point, the defendant saw them and started to run. The police ordered him to stop. He did not heed this warning and kept on running. The police were firing at him as he ran. The defendant returned the fire with two rounds, one shot hitting Patrolman Williams in the leg. The defendant was able to elude the pursuing officers at this time. However, the police found a 1976 Buick Special parked three buildings east of the Big Man registered to the defendant. In making good his escape, the defendant dropped the bag containing the money and a number of personal artifacts. The bag was the aforementioned Lowman College bag containing a man's wallet with the defendant's driver's license and other identification inside. The gun was found in the grass in a storm ditch across from Ray's Auto Supply Store, located at 1200 Main.

The defendant, accompanied by his attorney, turned himself into the Lowman police the next morning and made a full confession. He confessed to the present offense, as well as to two previous robberies of the same establishment, and one at the Big Man Restaurant at State and Glover on 4-12-99.

STATEMENT OF THE DEFENDANT

The defendant wrote out his statement for this officer. It is reproduced verbatim to preserve its flavor.

"On the morning of June 13, 2001, I robbed the Big Man Restaurant. In order to understand why I needed the money, first we should examine my childhood in order to find some underlying reason(s) for my behavior. Our family had a farm and a dog food processing business. The family hobby was hunting and trapping, totally our father's idea. The family businesses left very little time for our parents to be parents, they were most always in the position of boss.

During the years previous to meeting the woman who became my wife (she was not my first girlfriend), I did not see myself in any real one-to-one loving relationships. Even the pets I had would be taken from me, eventually I learned not to become attached to anything for fear it would be taken away. Death of something which I had compassion for never received mourning—the family was conditioned against it. The dog food processing experience also made me cold in the need for caring relationships with anything. The horses I saw were many times slaughtered, shot before my very eyes, then we as a family would skin, bone, grind up and package the meat. We even killed and trapped animals for "sport." The business would have been great if adults did all the work.

I never became close friends with any girls until after I graduated from high school. Never really finding anyone who cared as much for me as I cared for them until I met Susan, it became an obsession for me to please her, at times I probably ran her life. I hated her to work so she quit a good job as a secretary. I don't think she ever asked for anything that she didn't get. Now we both admit that our direction was wrong, and we have done something about it. We have sold many of our possessions and she has a job. She still does not want to work and I don't like the idea but it's part of reality—Bill cannot make enough money! Never again will I work third shift and regular weekends, I was so busy working I did not know what was happening to my brain. The more money I made the more I spent and the more I felt the need for money, which was not real but imagined.

Since my imprisonment, we have sadly learned the need for Susan to lose Bill, if not through imprisonment then through death. Shortly after I was arrested, Susan had a life reading, and one of the results has been this realization that she would lose Bill. In a past life she lost me through death very early, and has past Karma to overcome. I am sure of the need for Bill's punishment to correct the Karma he has for his crimes. I also know that Bill had the choice to do what he did or not to do it. What Bill does not know is this, how would Susan correct her Karma if I were not imprisoned. Would I die? This is a good question. What I have done is not easily forgivable, but I know that when I'm free, Bill will grow and hopefully will still have Susan to grow with him. I have been saved from a terrible future, no one was killed but many were hurt and hurt seriously and it will take a lot of hard work to correct the mistakes, I hope I have the chance to correct them—in this life."

We can glean from this statement that the defendant is interested in mysticism and paranormal phenomena. The "life reading" to which he refers is retrogressive hypnosis. This technique supposedly takes the offender back into his or her past to elicit memories buried in the subconscious. The true initiate apparently believes that this even extends to prior existences in other times and places.

The defendant believes that he lived before in what he calls the "horse and buggy" days. In that life, he and his wife reversed sex roles; in other words, the defendant was the female and his wife was the male. The defendant stated that he died of a brain tumor at the age of thirty-five on his last sojourn on earth. He or "she" was also a robber in that life. The combination of his early death and his antisocial career drove his wife or "husband" to alcoholism. (Is he projecting his perceptions of his wife's possible reactions to his current predicament into this story?) He feels that the "bad Karma" built up by their actions in the former life has to be worked out in this one.

Karma is an ethereal "something" which automatically adheres to the perpetrator of an evil act (something akin to sin). It must be canceled or "worked off" by a positive act which has a measure of good proportionate to the evil of the negative act. If this is not accomplished, the self is caught up in an endless cycle of birth and death. This belief, so the defendant states, enables him to tie everything he has done in this life to past lives of himself and his wife. He says that prison is necessary for him to equilibrate his "bad Karma." He wants to do volunteer work in the prison and upon his release to build up his reserve of "good Karma."

Although the defendant has a teleological view of life, he does not claim that he was "fated" to commit his crimes. He stated that "Bill has the free will that he was blessed with" (it is interesting to note that he often referred to himself in the third person. It is as though he disassociates himself and views himself as an object apart from himself). He did occasionally lapse into fatalistic explanations. For instance, when asked how he was able to elude capture and avoid getting hit by police fire, his eyes turned heavenward, and he replied with a cryptic "them." Who "them" are was not made clear. Notwithstanding the interesting story he tells, at bottom, the reason he committed the robberies was simply that he "needed" more money than he was making in order to indulge his wife's expensive tastes.

STATEMENT OF VICTIM (PATROLMAN FREDRICK WILLIAMS)

Patrolman Williams stated that he and his partner responded to a robbery call at the Big Man Restaurant at about 1:30 am on the morning of 6-13-01. As they came upon the scene, he noticed the defendant in a field taking off his sweater. The defendant fled as Williams and his partner approached, and he refused to stop when ordered to do so. Williams was chasing the defendant on foot when the defendant turned and fired two shots, one of which struck Williams in the leg. Patrolman Williams stated that his wound required six weeks off work and two weeks light duty.

When asked his opinion of the defendant, and what he thought should happen to him, Williams replied: "The guy's sick; he needs help. As far as I'm concerned, you can put him away for eighty years."

PRIOR RECORD   BIR # 234569   FBI # 356 953 V1

Juvenile:
Adrian County juvenile authorities report no juvenile record.
Adult:
6-14-01 LPD a) Attempted Murder b) Aggravated Robbery
Two other counts of Aggravated Robbery nolled (dismissed) in CR99-4357.
        One count of Aggravated Robbery nolled (dismissed) in CR99-4358
    LCPD, BCI, FBI, and Juvenile record checks made and received.

FAMILY AND MARITAL HISTORY

The defendant is the youngest of four children born to James and Mary Bloggs. The defendant, up until his marriage, lived his entire life on the family farm located at Box 3123, Rural Route 10, Elko, ID. Information received from the defendant's wife and certain of his siblings revealed that his childhood was characterized by excessive work demands, physical abuse, and forced incestuous relationships with his sisters. Details of the above are contained elsewhere in this report. It is quite clear that the entire Bloggs family was under the strict and uncompromising figure of Mr. Bloggs. The defendant had very little time to pursue any personal interests that he may have had, always having to acquiesce to the wishes of his father. His whole life evidently revolved around the family business, which he despised. The defendant's older sister related that her father was "absolutely livid" when he found out that her mother was pregnant with the defendant. He did not even visit his wife in the hospital during her confinement. She further stated that the defendant would often get blamed for things he did not do, and was made to feel unwanted. She went on to relate how both the defendant and his older brother were bed-wetters up to a relatively late age, and that her father would "hog-tie" them and keep them lying in bed in their urine all day. Interestingly, the defendant denied a history of enuresis to court psychologists as if to block out all memory of these extremely unpleasant occurrences.

The defendant left home at the age of twenty-two to take up residence with his girlfriend, now his wife, Susan Overton. This marriage took place on 9-15-99 in the Adrian County Jail. In an interview with Susan at this office, she described herself as an "old fashioned" type who did not wish to go out to work. She described the defendant as being "jealous and possessive," adding that he is prone to "snap in and out of an explosive temper." She stated that he felt like he owned her, and that he once hung and killed a kitten of hers when he suspected that she was seeing another man. When I inquired, in light of the above negative statements, and in light of the prison sentence that the defendant is facing, that she would marry him, she replied that they are "fated" to be together. She said that she could not cope with his death in their previous existence, and that she must now learn to cope with his absence in this one.

When asked why she thought that the defendant committed his crimes, she indicated the aberrant family situation previously mentioned. She stated that Mr. Bloggs slept with both of his daughters and had on numerous occasions forced them to instruct the defendant and his brother in sexual matters while he watched. On a second interview with the defendant I questioned him about this. He felt that this was no "big deal," and stated that he was about ten when these incestuous encounters began.

While Susan believes that this sexual deviance may have been a distinct influence, she felt that the more proximate cause for the defendant's criminal behavior was his desire to satisfy her request for a big wedding, which he could not afford. It is ironic that their desire for a conspicuous and grandiose wedding may have led them to nuptials in a barren jail cell with a corrections officer as a witness. Her final statement to me was "Don't send him to prison, he won't come back." The defendant's father and mother were interviewed at their family farm. Mr. Bloggs is fifty-four years old, has two years of college, and is a self-employed farmer. He is an impressive professorial-looking person who is obviously accustomed to being in control of any situation. He spoke slowly and deliberately, and appeared to take great pains to use just the right word. He stated that he is at a loss to explain his son's behavior, that he loved him, and will continue to support him. He denied any mistreatment of the defendant beyond what he called "normal chastisement." I did not feel it appropriate to raise the issue of the alleged incest with him in front of his wife.

The defendant's mother is fifty-five years old, has one year of college, and describes her occupation as "housewife." She is a timid-looking soul who complements her husband's personality with a passivity which approaches sycophantic proportions. She was never able to complete two successive sentences without her husband finishing them for her. She profusely praised her husband as a father and a provider, and also denied that he was excessively punitive. One wonders if she has any knowledge of her husband's sexual abuse of their children. A computer record check revealed no criminal history for either parent.

The defendant's oldest sister, Patricia Knowles, is a high school graduate who currently drives a cab for Black and White. Pat has been married and divorced twice, and has a ten-year-old daughter and a nine-year-old son. Pat has a criminal history of child endangering and drug abuse. Pat does not presently associate with her father, stating that "He f——ed all of us kids up. He's the one that should be in jail."

Ann, the defendant's second sister, has similar feelings about her father. She is a high school graduate. She stated that she ran away from home right after graduation, and openly admits that she went to Los Angeles to become a call girl. She eventually quit that occupation after becoming pregnant (she kept her child). She is currently on welfare in Los Angeles. A check with LAPD revealed numerous soliciting arrests for Ann.

Fredrick Bloggs, the defendant's older brother, could not be reached. However, Pat indicated that Fred dropped out of high school at the age of sixteen, has been married and divorced, and is now an "alcoholic bum" in Omaha, Nebraska. It would appear that the defendant is not the only victim of Mr. Bloggs' highly distasteful personality.

EMPLOYMENT HISTORY (SOCIAL SECURITY # 302-42-9988)

At the time of his arrest, the defendant was working for Lowman Cascade as a press operator. He has been employed there since 4-14-98. He works all the overtime that he can get, and frequently brings home in excess of $400 per week. The defendant's immediate supervisor characterized him as "a good and dependable worker who gave us no trouble." The defendant had taken the entrance examination to become a Lowman City police officer. Lt. Murdock of LCPD indicated that the defendant was to be called to the next class at the academy. The defendant relates no other employment except at his family business.

PHYSICAL HEALTH

The defendant is a white male, 28 years of age, 5' 7" tall, and weighs 155 lbs. He has dark blonde hair, blue eyes, and a fair complexion. He describes his current physical health as "excellent." He has suffered no hospitalizations or serious diseases, and relates no defects of hearing, speech, or vision. There is a family history of hypertension, and he feels that he is disposed to it himself. He is an infrequent consumer of alcohol, stating that the last time that he was drunk was over two years ago. He smoked marijuana rather heavily while in college, and stated that he frequently use amphetamines while working the night shift at Lowman Cascade in order to stay awake. He did not feel that he was addicted to them, however.

MENTAL HEALTH

The defendant graduated from Capital High School in 1992. He graduated 31st out of a class of 63, with a GPA of 2.27 on a 4.0 scale. School IQ testing saw the defendant obtain a full-scale IQ of 113, placing him in the 85th percentile of U.S. population IQ scores. Were his educational attainments commensurate with his IQ percentile ranking, the defendant would have placed ninth in his class. The defendant stated that he was too busy working on the farm to do justice to his studies.

Upon graduation from high school, the defendant entered Boise State University. He majored in, of all things, criminal justice. He was still attending BSU at the time of his arrest. He has obtained a cumulative GPA at BSU of 2.49. His criminal justice adviser stated that he was a "quiet student who participated very little in class, but his written work showed evidence of real independent thinking."

The Court Diagnostic and Treatment Center report indicates that their testing saw the defendant obtain a full-scale IQ score of 114, indicating a certain consistency in mental ability. It is noted that he scored significantly above average in tasks requiring nonverbal and short-term memory skills.

It is too easy to ascribe some form of mental abnormality to one who subscribes to the worldview described by the defendant. It should be remembered, however, that his views are a valid discourse for millions of people in the world. I am more inclined to view his neurotic materialism as indicative of mental instability than his new-found religious eclecticism. He himself views his seemingly insatiable acquisitiveness as being responsible for his criminal actions. He was socialized in a family seemingly obsessed with making money. Neither can we discount the incestuous behavior he was forced into as a generating factor. It is clear that love was not a prevalent quality in this man's life. This deficiency may explain his clinging, jealous, and paranoid attraction to the one person (Susan) who showed a loving interest in him.

Although the Court Diagnostic and Treatment Center report states that he is experiencing high levels of anxiety and depression, he now states to me that he is "more at peace" with himself. He spends much of his time in his cell these days reading the Bible and esoteric literature. He describes himself as "driven to achieve," and feels that he is very aggressive in a nonviolent way. Given his crime, the hanging of the kitten, and Susan's statement about his "explosive temper," one might well dispute this description. The CD&TC report also describes him as being "in the early stages of a schizophrenic reaction, specifically of a paranoid type." His frequent reference to himself in the third person perhaps augments the impression on disassociation. Overall, this officer gained the impression that the defendant is a very bright, knowledgeable, and articulate person. He has been completely cooperative, and was a pleasure to talk with.

Evaluative Summary

Before the Court is a 28-year-old married male facing his first criminal conviction. He is an extremely bright, articulate, and personable young man. He evidently had a childhood in which he wanted for nothing materially, but which was characterized by excessive labor, harsh punitive treatment, and forced incestuous episodes. It is evident from the defendant's own statements, and from information uncovered in the course of this investigation, that he was severely deprived of close and loving interpersonal relationships. His father was viewed by family members as the great patriarch, or as the defendant put it: "as a boss, not a father." His father bestowed praise and approval only when the defendant met his excessive demands. Love, if there indeed was any, was withdrawn on the slightest pretext. His mother was viewed as a good person, but also as a pusillanimous alter-ego to the father.

The defendant's lack of experience of loving relationships rendered him ill-equipped to function well within one when Susan came into his life. He was obviously obsessed with making good this deficit. His relationship with Susan, now his wife, appears to have been a clinging obsession with him. He was paranoid about the possibility of losing her, and hypersensitive to her "needs," which everyone concerned agrees were considerable. He wanted only the best for her, and often worked seven days a week, even while attending college, to get it for her. Even his considerable income was not sufficient to purchase all of the things he felt were necessary to ingratiate himself.

Nonetheless, we cannot overlook a string of armed robberies and the shooting of a police officer. It is evident that the robberies were well-planned and executed. In any objective sense, he was not in any desperate need of money, as he was earning a wage well in excess of average. He needed love, and his materialistic background told him that love was just another expensive commodity to be purchased with cash. His intelligence, desire to learn, and intensity of purpose will stand him in good stead upon his release from the institution. His new-found spirituality, coupled with psychological counseling, will, I believe, function to prevent any further criminality in the future. He is well aware of the terrible crimes he has committed, and stands ready to accept the consequences. The extreme seriousness of his crimes point to the necessity of imposing consecutive sentences.

STATUTORY PENALTY

IRC #2911.01	"...shall be imprisoned for a period of 4, 5,6, or 7
Aggravated Robbery	to 25 years and/or fined up to $10,000."
IRC #2923.02	"...shall be imprisoned for a period of 4, 5, 6, or 7
Attempted Aggravated	to 25 years and/or fined up to $10,000
Murder	

RECOMMENDATION

Regarding 01-1234, Aggravated Robbery, it is respectfully recommended that the defendant be sentenced to 4 to 25 years at the Idaho State Penitentiary and ordered to pay the costs of prosecution.

Regarding 01-3457, Attempted Aggravated Murder, it is respectfully recommended that the defendant be sentenced to 5 to 25 years at the Idaho State Penitentiary, and that he be first conveyed to the Idaho Medical and Reception Center for evaluation and classification. It is further recommended that said sentences be served consecutively, and that the defendant be ordered to pay the costs of prosecution.

Respectfully submitted,

_____

Paul E. Corrick, Probation and Parole Officer

Discussion of Sample Report

We will explain, section by section, the kind of information required in each section of the presentence investigation report. Then we will comment on each content area using examples from the Bloggs presentence investigation.

CIRCUMSTANCES OF OFFENSE

Approximately 90 percent of all felony cases are disposed of through plea negotiations rather than by trial (Robin, 1987:249). Consequently, the sentencing judge often is quite unaware of the circumstances that brought the offender before the bench for sentencing until he or she has read the presentence investigation. This section, then, should lay out the official (police) version of all pertinent details of the offense. It should contain basic information such as the place and time of the offense, the names of any codefendants, whether or not any weapons were involved, and the names and address of the victim, and it should report injuries or financial loss suffered by the victim. Additionally, you should report the circumstances surrounding the defendant's arrest: How was the defendant discovered? What was the defendant's condition at the time of arrest (drunk, high)? Did he or she resist arrest, or did the person voluntarily surrender to the police? Be concise but thorough.

STATEMENT OF THE DEFENDANT

A recitation of the offender's version of the offense assists you in filling in gaps in the official version. It is quite likely that the presentence investigation interview is the offender's first occasion to tell his or her side of the story. The police usually are concerned only with the question of commission and often do not care about the whys and wherefores of the case. As for defense attorneys, offenders often seem to think that their only interest is to "sell" them the plea agreement.

Nevertheless, you never must allow an offender's sob story to distract you from the facts contained in the official version. Your job is not to retry the case in your presentence investigation. Judges do not take too kindly to such efforts. Some interrogation techniques may be necessary, however, to attempt to reconcile any major discrepancies between the offender's story and the official version. Interrogation should not be carried out until you have listened objectively to the entirety of the offender's story. You must note discrepancies and go over them one at a time with the offender until you are satisfied that they are resolved.

Do not let your humanitarian impulses get in the way if you believe that the offender is trying to snow you. Note how the story is told. Is it just too slick and obviously memorized? Are there claims of memory loss (a favorite ploy with child molesters)? Are there major inconsistencies within the offender's own version of the offense? If you think that the story is untrue, come right out and say so. This may be all that is needed to get the real story. You can be burned badly if you succumb to the natural impulse to put your unconditional faith in the poor troubled human being sitting beside you. Not only will you be putting your credibility in jeopardy with the judge and your colleagues, but you also will be compromising it with the offender. Worse yet, you could be opening yourself up for a lawsuit if, as a result of your report, a dangerous offender is released on probation and subsequently harms someone else (Actually, the Presentence investigation investigator *qua* p[resentence investigation investigator has judicial immunity from lawsuits, but you still could get burned in other ways). Dig hard and dig deep. If you cannot reconcile the different versions, simply note them in your report. If you believe that unresolved discrepancies are the result of deliberate attempts at deception, report this in the presentence investigation and fully support your reasoning behind the belief.

An important variable to assess is the offender's attitude about the offense. Is there remorse? Is the remorse apparently genuine, or is it just sorrow for getting caught? Experience will sensitize you to signs of genuine remorse. Shame, as an indication of remorse, is signaled by blushing and sighing when the crime is discussed, attempting to avoid discussing embarrassing details of the offense, stuttering, stammering, showing apparent confusion, and avoiding eye contact previously established.

Similarly, guilty feelings are good indicators of genuine remorse. Behaviors consistent with a sense of guilt include voluntary confessions and the acceptance of complete blame, surrender to the police, a tendency to dwell on details of the offense, and the expression of a willingness to make amends in any way necessary. Offenders who display some or all of these indicators of shame and guilt are usually individuals who normally conduct themselves according to conventional moral standards. The interviewer should be sensitive to the inclination toward depressive states, and even suicidal ideation, among offenders of this type.

Such offenders are rare, however. Most will try to claim some sort of mitigation such as bad company, victim precipitation, or alcohol. In Walsh's unpublished study of

416 probation offenders, 52.7 percent of them tried to shift the blame for the offense in directions other than themselves. "Victim precipitation" is a favorite excuse in assaultive crimes, and alcohol or drug abuse in property crimes. In those cases involving multiple defendants, fully 92 percent placed the blame on bad company, neglecting to realize that each was the whipping boy of the other. This is not to assert that all claims of mitigation lack any substance. Your good judgment will help you decide what degree of credence you will give to such claims.

You also should discuss victims' losses with offenders and inquire about their attitudes for making restitution and their ability to do so. Restitution may include the victims' medical bills, time lost from work, or replacement costs for property lost or damaged. The court may order payment of restitution either directly to the victim or to his or her insurance company. The offender's willingness and realistic ability to pay restitution probably will be an important factor in both your recommended disposition of the case and in its actual disposition. Restitution cannot legally be ordered in many states, however, if the offender's plea was "no contest" rather than "guilty." This limitation displays a disregard for victim's rights and is one of the major injustices of the criminal justice system.

APPLICATION TO SAMPLE PRESENTENCE INVESTIGATION REPORT

Bill's version of the offense exactly mirrors the official one, and he doesn't attempt to deny any aspects of it. His statement written "in order to understand why I needed the money," however, is most instructive and interesting. His story is a psychiatric delight, that illustrates many of the ego-defense mechanisms that we discuss later. Constant themes throughout his statement are his severe deprivation of love and the pressures of life with an authoritarian father. His love for Susan was clinging, cloying, and jealous. He was willing to go to any lengths to buy from her the love he so desperately needed. He was painfully aware that he had grown up in a loveless environment, so much so that he "learned not to become attached to anything for fear it would be taken away." Susan was inadequately filling his desperate need for love, his deeply felt deficiency. His jealousy, and indeed his crimes, can be viewed as stemming from his unrealistic attempts to cling to someone toward whom he had finally developed a form of attachment. He had convinced himself (apparently genuinely) that this attachment extended back to a prior existence. We note that the processing probation officer did not disparage Bill's bizarre story but, instead, tried to understand it and fit it into the offender's frame of reference for the readers of the report. However, he correctly did not let this sway him from consideration of the extremely serious nature of Bill's crimes. To understand is not to excuse. The probation officer also perceptively picked up on Bill's use of the third person when discussing himself and nicely tied it in with evidence from the examining psychiatrist, who indicated that Bill may have been in the "early stages of a schizophrenic reaction."

Was Bill remorseful, and if so, was his remorse genuine? He did turn himself in to the police, and he did make a full confession. However, given that he left behind so much identifying evidence at the scene of the crime, we can hardly assume that his cooperation was indicative of remorse. Further damaging to any interpretation of genuine remorse is the fact that the present offense was his fourth such robbery within a short period of time. But he did accept full responsibility for his crimes ("Bill has the free will that he was blessed with"), and he did accept the legitimacy of his impending punishment. The overall impression one gains is that Bill would have continued his crime spree had he not been caught. His apparently genuine remorse was late in coming, was related to the situation he was in at the time of the interview, and could not be viewed as a mitigating factor when considering sentencing.

STATEMENT OF VICTIM

As already noted, under the influence of the philosophy of restorative justice, more and more jurisdictions are requiring that a victim-impact statement be included in the presentence investigation report. Such a statement is worth including even in the absence of a legal requirement. The statement should include the victim's version of the offense and the physical, psychological, and financial impact of the crime on him or her. You also should obtain an itemized statement of any financial losses from the victim or the victim's insurance company. It is not unusual, although it is understandable, for victims to inflate the extent of their losses. This author always solicits a statement of the victim's feelings and a recommendation on the disposition of the case.

APPLICATION TO SAMPLE PRESENTENCE INVESTIGATION REPORT

Given the seriousness of this offender's crimes, it was obvious from the onset that incarceration had to be the recommended disposition. Therefore, no attempt was made to ascertain financial losses to Patrolman Williams or the police department (notwithstanding the defendant's inability to pay restitution if incarcerated, the courts can not monitor payments if the defendant is under the jurisdiction of the Department of Corrections). Since Officer Williams' version of the offense was an integral part of the official version, his additional statement throws no more light on it. His understandably negative response to his opinion of the defendant, and what he thought should happen to him, was of no value in the formulation of a sentencing recommendation.

PRIOR RECORD

Before you interview the offender, a complete criminal history should be available to you. This should include juvenile, local police, state bureau of criminal investigation, and Federal Bureau of Investigation (FBI) arrest sheets ("rap sheets"). Most of these records should be included in the prosecutor's case file. Immediately upon receiving the case, however, you should run your own computer check for an updated history. A computer check also will reveal any outstanding warrants for the offender. If you discover that the offender is wanted, you should make inquiries with the issuing clerk of courts concerning the particulars of the warrant. It is your duty to place the offender under arrest if the warrant indicates a serious crime. For obvious reasons, do not reveal your knowledge of the warrant until the interview has been conducted. Telling an offender that he or she will be arrested at the conclusion of the interview will not make for a very productive interview. If the warrant was issued for something as innocuous as nonpayment of traffic fines, it is probably a better idea to tell the offender to take care of them before you see him or her again rather than making an arrest. At this point, avoid confrontation about relatively unimportant matters.

Having gathered arrest records as well as any previous presentence investigation reports and records, review this history of criminal activity with the offender. Ask the offender to explain any particularly serious prior arrests and convictions, and try to discern any pattern among the arrests. For instance, are the crimes all of a similar type (property, sex, violent), or is the record one of a polymorphous deviant? Do they reveal a pattern of increasing seriousness? At what point in life did the offender start acquiring a criminal record? Are any or most of the crimes related to alcohol and/or drug abuse? Is the pattern one of planned criminality, or do the crimes seem mostly those of opportunistic spontaneity? Finally, are all crimes readily admitted to you, or does the offender attempt to rationalize away the majority of them?

APPLICATION TO SAMPLE PRESENTENCE INVESTIGATION REPORT

The lessons to be learned from a perusal of the offender's criminal history are many and valuable. In Bill's case, it is very instructive that he had no previous arrests, either as a juvenile or as an adult. Yet, his offenses were extremely serious. In the normal progress of a criminal career, one graduates over a period of years from committing far less serious crimes to the types of crimes Bill committed. It is so extremely rare to find an offender who, at the age of twenty-eight, begins a criminal career with armed robbery that you immediately should be alerted to the fact that there are some very special circumstances involved.

FAMILY AND MARITAL HISTORY

Although not necessarily reported in the presentence investigation, a family history should contain the names and addresses of parents, siblings, children, spouse, and any former spouses and indicate the current status of each family member (deceased, divorced, retired, imprisoned, whereabouts unknown). These data will yield important information about the offender's family dynamics. Inquire into the offender's relationship with his or her parents during the formative years. Were they divorced early? With whom did the offender live? Did either or both of the parents remarry, and what type of relationship did the offender have with his or her stepparents? What are the offender's current relationships with his or her parents and significant others—supportive or rejecting? Exploration of parental reactions to the present predicament will provide access to the type of moral environment in which the offender was raised. Collateral interviews with parents, if time allows and the seriousness of the case warrants, can be used to validate and expand on the offender's perceptions. It may be instructive to inquire into offenders' friendship networks. Do they associate with known criminals? If so, ask why. How is leisure time spent with friends—in productive or nonproductive ways?

Then, obtain the offender's marital history, if any. How many times has the offender been married? Frequent marriages, common-law or otherwise, indicate an inability to form lasting relationships and a certain lack of responsibility. If the offender has been divorced, what was the reason for divorce? Placing the blame on the spouse may reflect an overall pattern of blaming others for negative outcomes. Find out if the offender has any children from former relationships. And, if the offender is a male, if he is living up to his financial support obligations.

The quality of the relationship with the current spouse should be examined next. If there are any major difficulties, explore their nature and extent. Is the offender responsibly supporting dependents, or does his or her lifestyle demonstrate neglect? Again, a collateral interview with the spouse may prove useful. You may conduct a collateral interview by telephone, although you lose much of the flavor if you do. You certainly would want to find out the spouse's attitudes about his or her criminal activity and how he or she would cope if the offender were to be imprisoned.

APPLICATION TO SAMPLE PRESENTENCE INVESTIGATION REPORT

Officer Corrick's collateral interviews with Bill's wife, his parents, and selected siblings certainly paid off in terms of insight into the origins of Bill's criminal behavior. Although Bill's family was comfortably middle class and demonstrated commitment to, involvement in, and belief in typical American success values, beneath the veneer of respectability lay an abominable family situation. Attachment, genuine reciprocal love, was obviously absent. Bill appeared to have tried very hard to gain his father's love and approval. His father, however, seems to have been a patriarchal, sadistic, sexually perverted, and over-demanding individual. His absolute control over the family is quite in evidence in the report. His mother "complements her husband's personality with a passivity which approaches sycophantic proportions." Note that she never mentioned anything to Corrick regarding the incestuous behavior that went on for so many years. It is not at all unusual for wives to deny, even to themselves, that such behavior is taking place. This behavior first came to light during the collateral interview with Susan. It was then incumbent on Officer Corrick to verify the information, which he did with Bill himself and with two of his siblings. Such potentially damaging information should never be included in a report on the basis of one individual's statement.

The effects of growing up under the conditions that existed in the Bloggs family have resulted in many negative outcomes for Bill's siblings as well. Pat has had two broken marriages in four years and has a record of child abuse and drug abuse. Ann has one illegitimate child and was a prostitute for a period of time with numerous soliciting arrests. Fred is a high school dropout, was divorced after one year of marriage, and is an admitted alcoholic. All this, in spite of having access to all the "objective" advantages of a white, middle-class status, supports Officer Corrick's analysis of the origin of Bill's behavior as presented in the evaluation section of the presentence investigation report.

Susan's statements indicate that she shared Bill's unusual interpretation of their relationship ("they are 'fated' to be together"). She quit her job when she and Bill started living together, and she was evidently quite happy to allow Bill to work all hours of the day and night to satisfy her considerable material wants. Her comments about Bill's "explosive temper" and his hanging of her kitten provide all those who will use the presentence investigation report in the future with valuable insight not gleaned from either Corrick's or the diagnostic center's interviews with Bill.

Very few collateral interviews will ever be as valuable to you as the ones presented here. Further, for less serious cases, time constraints usually will prohibit going to the extraordinary length which Corrick went here. Nor would it be especially productive if the offender fit the profile of the typical armed robber. The typical armed robber would fit a certain profile which, by definition, is associated with most others who commit such crimes (lower-class, poorly educated, broken home, unemployed, and so on). It was the atypicality of Bill's criminal profile which led Corrick to dig as deeply into Bill's past as he did.

EMPLOYMENT HISTORY

The section covering employment history explores the offender's employment or other sources of income such as welfare, social security, or disability income. A complete and verified employment history is a vital part of any offender assessment. As the theories we have examined have informed us, a steady work history, evidence of prosocial commitment, involvement, and access to a legitimate avenue of success are incompatible with serious criminal involvement. Of the 416 offenders in this author's unpublished (1983) study, only 55.8 percent were working at the time of the presentence investigation interview. Of those working, 86.6 percent were in unskilled dead-end occupations. Only 2.8 percent were in managerial, technical, or professional occupations, and all of those were first-time sex offenders.

The name, address, and telephone number of the offender's current place of employment is the first item on the agenda. To avoid putting the offender's jobs in jeopardy, verify their employment by having them bring in their most recent paycheck stubs. Verify length of employment through the offenders' tax records. Ask offenders what type of work they do and if they enjoy it. Are there opportunities to move up in the company? Do they feel that their present income is sufficient to meet their basic needs? Do they criticize the company excessively? Why?

Verify former employment directly. A standard form should be sent to former employers asking them to indicate type of work, length of service, reason for leaving, and an evaluation of an offender's work performance and of his or her general character. What is the offender's pattern of movement in the workforce? Does the offender work steadily and quit employment only to obtain a better position, or does the offender quit on any pretext after minimal periods? This information will give you a general picture of the offender's level of responsibility, his or her ability to get along with others, and his or her general persistence. You should fully explore all gaps in employment history. You also should ask the military for a copy of the offender's service record, if any, although you may not receive it until long after sentencing.

APPLICATION TO SAMPLE PRESENTENCE INVESTIGATION REPORT

Bill's employment history is an atypically good one. At the time of his arrest he had been working for more than two years for the same company. He worked hard and earned a good income. Management at his place of employment was very positive toward him, even to the extent of planning to promote him to supervisor. He also worked part time on the family farm and had passed the examination to become a police officer. Bill's exemplary work history obviously impressed Officer Corrick and further alerted him to dig beyond surface demographics to explain Bill's behavior.

PHYSICAL HEALTH

An assessment of offenders' physical health (self-reported, or, if necessary, verified by a physician), noting how their social and vocational functioning could be affected by it, should be included. Recent hospitalizations and diseases, use of medications or prosthetic devices, drinking habits, and drug abuse should be noted in this section. Substance abuse should be the central concern of this section because of its association with many criminal acts. Drugs and alcohol are chemical substitutes for the lack of love and meaning in many offenders' lives—a method of temporarily shutting out the cruelties and responsibilities of life. Inquire into the extent and frequency of offenders' drinking, noting if they have any alcohol-related offenses, such as drunk driving, on the rap sheet.

Next, address extent, frequency, and type of drug abuse. Not all offenders will be willing to admit abuse, but with careful observation you will know when to probe. Physical indicators of drug abuse are examined in Chapter 16. A word of warning here: some offenders will exaggerate the extent of their substance abuse in the hope that blame will be shifted from them to the substance and that they will touch a sympathetic cord in the officer. This author's (1983) study found that 13.5 percent blamed substance abuse for their crimes. If offenders claim drug dependency, or if you suspect it, immediately refer them to a drug dependency clinic for a complete workup and evaluation.

APPLICATION TO SAMPLE PRESENTENCE INVESTIGATION REPORT

Nothing unusual was uncovered in Bill's physical health history that is pertinent to decisions on his sentence, classification, or treatment. He did report heavy use of marijuana while in college and current use of amphetamines. However, given the ubiquity of marijuana use among the young and his stated reason for taking amphetamines, there is no cause for undue alarm. We do note that the use of amphetamines is favored by those seeking intensified stimulation.

MENTAL HEALTH

The first item for consideration under the heading of mental health is the offender's education. Names and locations of all schools attended, including dates of attendance, should be listed and records requested from the offender's last high school or college. From school records you should note grade point average, class standing, IQ, vocational testing, and attendance and behavioral history. If the offender dropped out of high school, inquire about the reason. If you feel that your sentencing recommendation will be probation, explore the possibility of the offender attending General Equivalency Degree (GED) classes. Offenders' responses to this and similar ideas will give you some idea of their motivation to better themselves. IQ and vocational testing results will provide you with an offender's range of possibilities, but do not be misled by low scores and dismiss an offender as a hopeless case. A recent study showed that probationers attending General Equivalency Degree classes at a probation department had significantly fewer arrests, and committed significantly less serious crimes, than a matched group of dropout probationers not attending classes (Walsh 1985b).

Any psychiatric or psychological workups done on offenders should be discussed with them and integrated into your own assessment. Discuss any discrepancies that may exist between the stories they have told you and those they have related to mental health professionals. Lies told have an awkward tendency to be soon forgotten. Do not be afraid to disagree with or add your own opinions to those of the mental health professionals—you are a professional in your own right. Studies have shown that when the recommendations of probation officers conflict with those of mental health professionals, judges are somewhat more apt to agree with the officers (Walsh, 1990).

Remember, the training and role expectations of mental health workers lead them to see mental pathology in nearly all cases they review. Although real mental illness does exist, a deficiency view rather than a pathological view of criminal behavior is both more productive and less stigmatizing. Never contend with mental health professionals, however, if they advise psychiatric hospitalization. Such recommendations are not rendered lightly, and you must respect boundaries of expertise.

When discussing aspects of their mental functioning with offenders, concentrate on how they feel about themselves, their aspirations, their goals, and their usual ways of coping with stress and adversity. If you feel that a particular offender has some special problems that require the assistance of mental health professionals, refer him or her for a workup, indicating the areas you wish the diagnostic center to explore.

Application to Sample Presentence Investigation Report

We already have addressed many of the possible underlying reasons for Bill's criminal behavior. It is interesting to see how Officer Corrick added and integrated his own findings into those of the Court Diagnostic and Treatment Center. However, he did not step beyond the boundaries of his professional expertise to contest the findings and opinions of the center's personnel. He merely added to their insights and provided additional light. His collateral interviews with family members made him privy to information unavailable to court diagnostic personnel. We know that enuresis and cruelty to animals are two of the childhood and adolescent behaviors predictive of violent behavior and that Bill exhibited two of them. We do not know if Bill was also into fire-setting, so perhaps we should not make too much of this since it is the three behaviors taken together that are considered predictive. Nevertheless, Corrick was aware of Bill's late enuresis (we note that Bill denied it to the examining psychiatrist) and his hanging of Susan's pet kitten; court diagnostic personnel were not aware of these facts. Would they have labeled Bill passive aggressive (shooting a policeman and hanging a kitten is certainly aggressive, but hardly passive) had they known? Nor were they aware of the sexual perversities into which Bill's father forced him and his siblings. This is an excellent example of the use of collateral interviewing when appropriate. The court diagnostic center's other diagnosis of Bill as being "in the early stages of a schizophrenic reaction" was supported by Officer Corrick's observation that Bill often spoke about himself in the third person.

Other revealing pieces of information contained in this section help us gain a clearer picture of Bill. Whereas Bill's high school GPA of 2.27 is respectable, it, as well as his class standing, is considerably below what one would expect from someone with an IQ in the bright-normal range. Is this indicative of an underachiever or of someone kept too busy working for his father to do justice to his studies, as Bill claimed? The consistency of IQ test scores taken seven years apart reveals that regardless of what other mental problems Bill may have had, he suffered no deterioration of intellectual functioning.

Alert students will have noted an important piece of information that Officer Corrick reported but on which he did not comment: Bill "scored significantly above average in tasks requiring nonverbal and short-term memory skills." We noted in the section on psychopathy that the performance IQ is determined by performance on such tasks, and that many authorities consider performance IQ clearly in excess of verbal IQ as a clear marker of psychopathy. Unfortunately, Corrick did not report the performance and verbal IQ subscales but only the full-scale score. We do not know, therefore, if Bill's performance IQ was "clearly in excess" of his verbal IQ. However, this piece of information in conjunction with Bill's enuresis, cruelty to animals, apparent inability to form close loving relationships, and history of deprivation of love renders the application of the psychopathic label plausible. Had Corrick picked up on this (assuming that he was aware of the theory behind it), he may have been led to investigate further along those lines. This observation again underscores the necessity for criminal justice workers to be conversant with criminological theory. Finally, it is clear that Officer Corrick was very much impressed with Bill, but he did not let that reaction cloud his judgment when he made his sentencing recommendation.

EVALUATIVE SUMMARY

The evaluative summary is the most challenging section of the presentence investigation report to write. You are summarizing the facts contained in your report and drawing reasoned conclusions from them. This section represents the distilled wisdom of the investigator and separates the true professional from the data gatherer. It is the product of a disciplined effort to organize, synthesize, and analyze your collected data. No new data should be included in this section; your sole task here is to draw meaning from what you already have reported.

Since this section requires the inclusion of value judgments, make every effort to minimize any emotional feelings you may have for or against offenders and/or their behavior. Fully appraise your subjective feelings by asking yourself: "Why do I feel this way?" The tone of your report can convey impressions of the offender to the reader that may have a major impact on the offender's future. Emotion-laden terms, such as "morally bankrupt" or "a picture of womanly virtue," reveal more about the investigator's attitudes than about the offender's and should not be a part of a professional report. If you find that your offender evokes this kind of heavy emotional response, it is a good idea to consult with your supervisor or your colleagues before writing this section in order to clarify and objectify your thoughts.

This does not mean that you should not take a firm and positive stand. Indeed, as a professional this is your duty. Ambiguous, "wishy-washy" hedging statements are indicative of investigators who are uncomfortable in their role and uncertain of their expertise. Such beating around the bush undermines the authority of the entire report, and causes the reader to have doubts about the advised plan of action.

Of course, all strong statements should be firmly grounded in the information uncovered and set down in other sections of the report. Of the utmost importance is your evaluation of the offenders' strengths and weaknesses, their patterns of criminal behavior, their potential for reform, and their amenability to various kinds of treatment and training. This evaluation requires a thorough knowledge of available community resources as well as of the offender. This knowledge serves as the basis for a treatment plan, which is the logical conclusion of the evaluative summary. The treatment plan should be realistic and rendered with full knowledge of the possibilities.

The recommendation of a treatment plan that cannot be implemented is frustrating to the person who must act on your recommendations. One offender with a string of armed robberies to his name had been released on parole after serving ten years and was in jail for a parole violation for yet another robbery. He received a recommendation from his officer that he be allowed to go to another state under the care of a Christian youth camp. The officer had been convinced by the offender and by the offender's spiritual counselor that he was a "born-again Christian." The officer skillfully sold his recommendation to the sentencing judge, who allowed the offender to go. After this fifty-three-year-old man found himself surrounded only by youths and discovered that he was expected to work for his daily bread, he left the camp and committed further crimes before he was apprehended. Needless to say, that officer found his credibility seriously compromised.

In formulating a treatment plan, give the threat that the offender poses to the community equal consideration with the offender's rehabilitative needs. Clues to this threat are provided by the nature of the present offense and by the length and seriousness of the person's criminal record. Weigh various alternative plans in terms of their advantages and disadvantages for the offender and the community. Give reasons for plans that you decide to reject, and show complete justification for the accepted plan in terms of both offender and community concerns. Formulate treatment plans that involve other agencies in concert with them. Their special expertise may uncover deficiencies in an offender's character or motivation that in their opinion renders him or her unsuitable for the plan you have in mind. If this is the case, respect their professional evaluation and concentrate on an alternative plan.

APPLICATION TO SAMPLE PRESENTENCE INVESTIGATION REPORT

Officer Corrick begins his evaluative summary by reiterating the fact that the present offense is Bill's first conviction, and he rendered his positive feelings about the offender based on objective criteria and on his dealings with him. He then launched into a thoughtful examination of the possible origins of Bill's behavior. He emphasized the lack of love, the punitive and incestuous milieu in which Bill grew up, and the excessive acquisitiveness of both Bill and Susan. After you read this evaluation, you feel that you "know" Bill fairly well without ever having seen him. This is the ideal for which you should strive.

Officer Corrick did not outline a treatment plan for Bill because he felt that the seriousness of Bill's crimes warranted incarceration in spite of Bill's "first-offender" status. He seemed to feel that the experience of being caught, incarcerated, and having the opportunity to examine his behavior would deter Bill from future criminality.

RECOMMENDATION

Like the denouement of a mystery novel, the recommendation should flow logically from all the information preceding it. It also should be consistent with the legal requirement of the state. Certain crimes, such as murder, rape, and aggravated robbery, are not probationable, and certain crimes outside that category may contain elements that render them non probationable. The officer must be aware of the penal codes of his or her jurisdiction.

The recommendation should state concisely the number of years the offender is to spend in prison or on probation (some jurisdictions, however, require that the investigator only recommend probation or prison without specifying a time to be served). If you recommend probation, state special conditions of probation, such as amount of restitution and the name and address of payee, attendance at alcohol or drug centers, fines to be paid, amount of time that you feel that the defendant should serve locally in jail or in a work release program), and so forth.

APPLICATION TO SAMPLE PRESENTENCE INVESTIGATION REPORT

Corrick's estimation of community feelings, the possible threat Bill posed to the community, and the extreme seriousness of the offense led him to recommend that Bill serve two consecutive prison sentences of four to twenty-five years and five to twenty-five years. The judge imposed those sentences. What would you have recommended?

PRESENTENCE INVESTIGATION CHECKLIST

The most useful summary of this chapter takes the form of a checklist of factors that should be considered in any presentence investigation. Styles and formats of presentence investigation reports vary from department to department, and some areas we have discussed such as victim's statement and officer's recommendation may be optional inclusions at your department. Remember one thing above all: the presentence investigation will have a significant impact on the offender's future. Accuracy is of the utmost importance.

1. *Circumstances of present offense*(s). This should be a concise summary of all the relevant details of the offense(s) for which the offender is to be sentenced.

2. *Offender's version*. How does the offender's version differ from the official version? What is the offender's attitude about the offense, and what type of attitude does her or she have overall? The officer should evaluate and make judgments about these questions.

3. *Prior record*. This should be a complete and verified criminal history of the offender, noting patterns of criminality.

4. *Family history*. This includes: family demographics, characteristics, conflicts, migrations, child-rearing practices, marital history, and so on.

5. *Employment history*. This includes a complete and verified history of the offender's employment and financial situation.

6. *Physical and mental health*. This includes recent hospitalizations and diseases; drug and/or alcohol abuse; level of intellectual functioning (school grade completed, GPA, IQ); vocational training, and psychological information.

7. *Evaluative summary*. This is a capsulated version of the entire report, evaluating its overall meaning. It contains the officer's professional assessment of what is to be done to amend the offender's behavior.

Perspective from the Field:
A Few Words About Interviewing in Presentence Investigations
By Marilyn West

Marilyn West is a presentence investigator with the Fourth District (felony) Court, Ada County, Idaho. She is a graduate of Northwest Nazarene College, and is active in many community organizations aimed at criminal rehabilitation, including the Fourth Judicial District Sexual Abuse Task Force

In most jurisdictions, presentence investigations are prepared by probation officers. In some jurisdictions there are people whose work consists solely of doing presentence investigation reports. This author is one of those people.

A presentence investigation is a necessary and vital function of the criminal justice system, but due to its confidential nature, few people outside of the criminal justice system know that these reports exist. This makes being a presentence investigator a real conversation starter. People are intrigued to hear that someone is in charge of gathering all sorts of background information on felony criminals and presenting it to the court. People who have served on juries often express concern that the criminal histories of defendants are not made known to juries. Former jurors are relieved to learn that there is a point in the process where these histories are taken into consideration.

Because our presentence investigation reports make sentencing recommendations, we have to make sure that our information is factual and our conclusions are well grounded. This involves interviewing large numbers of people who know the defendant, including friends, relatives, and professional contacts. Presentence investigation reports are also a conduit for defendants and victims to express their feelings to the court.

Normally, the investigator has contact with the defendant for about three weeks following a guilty verdict or guilty plea. The goal of the presentence process is not to conduct rehabilitation, it is to do a diagnostic workup. Of course, a good workup can go a very long way toward beginning the ultimate goal of rehabilitation. Strong interviewing skills are an absolute necessity if you are to perform a good diagnostic workup. You can not simply "ask questions" and expect to get meaningful answers in criminal justice settings. You always will get answers to your questions regardless of how they are asked, but they will not necessarily be helpful or truthful. You must establish a relationship in which the defendant can feel comfortable in revealing intimate information to you. That is quite a challenge.

We are obliged to be objective in our reports. This requires a special effort because a lot of emotions can surface during the investigation. The victim's side of the story often arouse our feelings, and oftentimes we discover traumatic or tragic circumstances in the defendant's past which stir our sympathies as well. This type of emotional information rarely comes to light in police or prosecutor's investigations, and is of little concern to them. But we have to decide how much of this information is necessary to us in the formulation of our recommendations to the court. Overall, our goal in constructing the recommendation is the same as that of the sentencing judge: to protect society.

Perhaps one of the most valuable functions the presentence investigator performs is that of making specific recommendations. It is not enough to simply recommend that a person be treated for some problem. We have to recommend the specific resource, keeping in mind such practical matters as the appropriateness of treatment, cost, and availability. To make these recommendations, we must keep ourselves current on what is available in the treatment community. This means that we have to become "quasi-experts" in many treatment fields. Several people in our office are active in community treatment organizations for such problems as alcohol and drug abuse or sexual abuse. We also are charged with offering our opinion to the court as to whether an individual is capable of being rehabilitated. As you can imagine, this is sometimes a tough question. We have to supply ample information to show the basis for our opinions. Again, this underscores the absolute necessity of strong interviewing techniques.

It is a challenge to obtain a valid profile of an individual's life in the space of a few weeks. It makes me feel pleased when my recommendations are confirmed by judges, or when probation officers come up to me and say something like, "Your report on so-and-so was right on the money. Now maybe we can draw his attention to some of the things he's doing to get himself in trouble, and maybe we can show him some of the ways to stay out of trouble." That is the essence of our role.

References and Suggested Readings

Abadinsky, H. 1997. *Probation and Parole: Theory and Practice*. Upper Saddle River, New Jersey: Prentice-Hall.

Administrative Office of the United States Courts, Division of Probation. 1978. *Presentence Investigation Report*. Washington, D.C.: Government Printing Office.

Champion, D. 1999. *Probation, Parole, and Community Corrections*. Upper Saddle River, New Jersey: Prentice-Hall.

Conaboy, R. 1997. The United States Sentencing Commission: A new component in the federal justice system. *Federal Probation*. 61:58-63.

Myers, M. 1979. Offended parties and official reactions: Victims and the sentencing of criminal defendants. *Sociological Quarterly*. 20:529-540.

Nettler, G. 1970. *Explanations*. New York: Harper and Row.

Robin, G. 1987. *Introduction to the Criminal Justice System*. New York: Harper and Row.

Walsh, A. 1984. Gender-based differences: A study of probation officers' attitudes about, and recommendations for, felony sexual assault cases. *Criminology*. 22:371-387.

_____. 1985a. The role of the probation officer in the sentencing process: Independent professional or judicial hack? *Criminal Justice and Behavior*. 12:289-303.

_____. 1985b. An evaluation of the effects of adult basic education on rearrest rates among probationers. *Journal of Offender Counseling Services and Rehabilitation*. 9:69-76.

_____ 1990. Twice labeled: The effects of psychiatric labeling on the sentencing of sex offenders. *Social Problems*. 37:375-389.

Assessment Tools and Guidelines in Community Corrections

Justice consists of treating equals equally and unequals unequally according to relevant differences.

Aristotle

Aristotle's epigraph signifies the philosophy of individualized justice. Individualized justice is achieved by responding to specific offenders with respect to their needs and to the risk they pose to the community, as well as with respect to the nature of the crimes they have committed. To do this we rely on actuarial models that make statistical predictions based on the observed outcomes of similarly situated offenders in the past. Corrections workers thus attempt to operationalize justice (define it in terms of the operations used to measure it) by assigning numeric scores on assessment scales. These tools attempt to determine Aristotle's "relevant differences" so that justice can be done as equitably as possible (Walsh and Hemmens, 2000). Everyone benefits from the more structured and reasoned approach to decisionmaking made possible by research-grounded tools such as those presented in this chapter (*see also* Lauen, 1997). The assessment tools presented in this chapter apply mainly to presentence evaluations and to community corrections. (Assessment and classification of prison inmates is discussed separately in Chapter 8.)

Offenders benefit by being treated more justly and consistently than was previously the case, and the community is better served by a more accurate assessment of the risks offenders pose to it. The assessment and guideline approach is used in many jurisdictions to set bail, and in prosecutors' offices to screen cases for dismissal or prosecution, and to guide plea bargain arrangements. Some argue that hundreds of millions of tax dollars could be saved, with little additional risk to the community, if adequate numerical guidelines were developed to stem this nation's burgeoning jail and prison crowding problem (Carlson, et al, 1999; Pollock, 1997).

This chapter provides instruction on the various assessment tools used in many probation and parole agencies. These forms and scales are filled out by the processing officers on the basis of their evaluation of the offender. If your instructor assigns practice presentence investigation interviews, he or she will provide you with actual cases for practice interviews and assessments. If you are role-playing the offender, you will have access to information supplied by the offender. It is the "officer's" task to elicit this information from the "offender" using the interviewing techniques described in Chapter 5.

If you are role-playing the interviewing officer, you will be presented only with case materials that normally are provided from sources other than the offender. These include circumstances of the offense, criminal record, victims' statements, and school records. Drawing on the information provided by the offender and other sources, perform an evaluation of the offender, make a realistic recommendation, and formulate a treatment plan. There are no "correct answers." There are only good or poor evaluations, realistic or unrealistic recommendations, and workable or unworkable treatment plans. When considering each section in the practice presentence investigation reports, reread the appropriate section in Chapter 6 to determine if you have considered everything pertinent before deciding on an evaluation and recommendation. Do not hesitate to recommend imprisonment if you feel that the case warrants such a disposition. However, for the purposes of formulating a treatment program, assume probation placement even if you recommended imprisonment. All the assessment tools covered in the following discussion appear in the Appendix.

The forms and scales in this chapter are presented in the order that they are encountered by officers in the field.

Social History Questionnaire

The first tool you should become familiar with is the Social History Questionnaire (SHQ) (found in the Appendix). The social history questionnaire asks for relevant demographic information such as the offender's address, educational level, family and work history, and so forth. An intake officer or the agency receptionist hands this questionnaire to the offender referred for a presentence investigation. Offenders are requested to fill it out completely before they meet with the presentence investigator. For conducting presentence exercises, students role-playing offenders should complete copies of the form using the data provided by their "offender" presentence investigation reports. Each item is self-explanatory.

Felony Sentencing Worksheet

The first instrument typically used by the presentence investigator is some sort of sentencing guideline used to assist him or her to make a sentencing recommendation. The Felony Sentencing Worksheet (FSW) (*see* the Appendix) is one of several sentencing guidelines used throughout the nation. Developed in Ohio, sentencing guidelines were developed as a compromise between factions in criminal justice who believe either that the punishment received by an offender should "fit the crime" or that punishment should fit the offender and be appropriate to rehabilitation. Both of these positions are addressed in the guideline, with the seriousness of the offense being weighted more than the character of the offender. The Felony Sentencing Worksheet is consistent with the American Correctional Association's (ACA) policy statement ratified in 1994 and amended in 1999, which states, in part, that sentencing should be based on "multiple criteria." It also states that sentencing should "allow for recognition of individual case differences" and "should provide the framework to guide and control discretion according to established criteria and within appropriate limits, but must allow for tailoring of sentences within those limits to fit each case presented to the court."

Guidelines also were developed to attempt to minimize wide sentencing disparities for similar crimes and similarly situated individuals. They are aimed at structuring judicial discretion in sentencing and promoting consistency by providing judges with sentencing norms based on the past practices of their peers. Implicit in the idea of guidelines is the notion that disparity flowing from legitimate variation (relevant differences) among different crimes and different offenders is acceptable, but disparity shorn of just or coherent reason is not (Walsh and Hemmens, 2000). Consider sentencing guidelines as an application of Aristotle's definition of justice as relying on relevant differences.

The processing probation officer scores the Felony Sentencing Worksheet by assigning the indicated numerical scores on the basis of the legal and social factors addressed in each subsection. Some sections simply require the recording of factual data, such as the degree of the offense, multiple offenses, prior convictions, and repeat offenses. Other sections, covering culpability, mitigation, and credits, require a great deal of interpretation. If you are assigned a case to assess for sentencing, do not be confused if you and your classmates arrive at different FSW scores. Since judgments are called for, the FSW allows for the intrusion of ideology in its scoring. One study showed that the FSW is differentially scored by practicing probation officers according to their ideological convictions, with conservative officers assigning significantly higher scores (Walsh, 1985).

Sentencing by arithmetic is not impervious to ideological intrusion, but it does constitute an improvement on unstructured sentencing. An earlier study of the effects of the guideline on sentencing found a predictive accuracy of 85 percent; that is, judges imposed the suggested sentence in 85 percent of the cases, with 8 percent being harsher than indicated and 7 percent being more lenient than indicated (Swisher, 1978). This study was carried out a year after implementation of the guidelines. Judges may have been more willing to abide by sentencing guidelines initially because of the novelty effect. This author believes that it is of utmost importance to develop value-free guidelines and to make it mandatory that sentences suggested by them be heeded except under special circumstances that are fully justified in writing.

After scores have been assigned and added for both the offense and the offender categories, they are applied to a grid on the reverse side of the FSW at the point at which they intersect. The grid indicates a suitable sentence for offenders whose crimes and whose criminal histories fall into it. These are suggested sentences only. Do not be hesitant to recommend sentences that are not consistent with the grid if you feel there should be alternatives and can justify them. In fact, it is probably a good idea for practice purposes to ignore the scoring of the FSW until after you have decided on a recommendation. You then may score the FSW and see how close your decision comes to the suggested sentence.

As a quick exercise, score Bill Bloggs on the FSW. He was a first offender and thus is scored zero on the "offender rating" section of the sheet. In the "degree of offense" subsection Bill would receive the maximum points (four) because both of his crimes were first-degree felonies. In the "multiple offenses" category, he would receive two points because he was convicted of aggravated robbery and attempted aggravated murder. In the "actual or potential harm" category he would receive two points for his wounding of the police officer. His eight points thus far already put him beyond the FSW's range for probation. This author also would assess two points against Bill in the "culpability" section for "shocking and deliberate cruelty," but could not justify deducting any points in the "mitigation" category. Bill, therefore, would get ten offense-rating points assessed against him, a score that places him in the upper-left hand square of the grid.

Sentencing guidelines can be a major tool in more just and sensible sentencing, or they can serve as "scientific" rationales for more draconian penalties. For instance, while federal sentencing guidelines have reduced disparities within the federal system, they have done so by incarcerating more and more nonviolent criminals (particularly drug users) at tremendous expense to taxpayers.

The number of inmates in federal prisons increased by 164 percent from 1985 to 1995 (Bureau of Justice Statistics, 1995), and there has been an average annual growth of 6.4 percent each year since (Bureau of Justice Statistics, 2000). The guidelines per se are not responsible for this increase, but they do provide a sort of justification (Schmalleger, 1993). This author remains convinced of the utility of sentencing guidelines, and agrees with Roger Lauen, former state director of community corrections in Colorado, who writes:

The passage of sentencing guidelines legislation has been an effective tool in reducing prison use for selected offenders. However, without widespread public support, sentencing guidelines, sentencing grids, and sentencing commissions are unable to maintain their organizational independence and stay removed from the "get tough" political rhetoric (1997:113).

Client Management Classification Assessment Instrument

The second tool is the Client Management Classification Assessment Instrument (CMC) (also in the Appendix). This semistructured interview schedule is reproduced in its entirety in the Appendix. Developed for the Wisconsin Bureau of Community Corrections, it is the end product of much study and research (Crooks, 2000). Whereas the social history questionnaire deals primarily with factual demographic data, the CMC offers guidance for exploration of offenders' attitudes and feelings and for supervision and treatment planning. When using this schedule, do not feel bound to repeat the questions exactly as they are printed on the page. There is sufficient leeway to incorporate your own style into the questions and to allow for unusual situations. However, the meaning of each question should be preserved even when you translate it into your own words. Also, leave the issues addressing the crime and criminal history until the end of the schedule, at which time sufficient rapport should have been generated to make these questions less threatening to offenders.

In actual practice, the CMC is scored so that probation and parole officers can assign offenders to one of four treatment modalities (selective intervention, environmental structure, casework control, and limit setting). This scoring, a rather complicated procedure for the uninitiated, is accomplished by using eight templates (cardboard sheets with holes punched in them that fit over a scoring guide). Probation and parole officers attend three-day workshops and receive extensive follow-up training before they are able to use this system to its fullest. Explaining the system in its entirety is well beyond the scope of this book. In fact, the training material used in these training sessions constitutes a book in itself. Thus, consider the interview schedule included here simply as a guide to the type of questions you should be asking your offenders and as an introduction to the CMC system of offender classification. The classifications obtained from scoring the CMC are highly correlated with the classification scheme obtained from the far more succinct risk and needs scales, which we now discuss.

Client Risk and Need Assessment Survey

The client risk and need assessment survey (in the Appendix) is part of the client management classification system, and is designed to be used in conjunction with the CMC interview schedule. The system consists of two separate scales—one that assesses an offender's "risk," and the other, an offender's "needs."

Offender risk refers to the probability of reoffending and/or the threat the offender poses to the community. Assessment is accomplished by assigning numerical scores on variables known to correlate with recidivism. The earlier that one begins a criminal career, the more involved one becomes in it, the frequency with which one turns to chemical substances, the less one is legitimately employed, and the more negative one's attitude is, the more likely one is to reoffend. The more likely offenders are to reoffend, the greater their risk to the community, and the more closely they must be supervised. In many jurisdictions, offenders are moved up one level of supervision if they have a history of assaultive offenses. The risk and need assessment, and complete scoring guides, are reproduced in the Appendix.

Offender need refers to deficiencies in offenders' personal repertoires and lifestyles that may be preventing them from making any commitment to a conventional moral pattern of behavior. Scores on the risk and on the needs sections of the scale tend to be highly correlated. That is, an offender who is high risk tends to have high needs, and offenders with few needs are not high risk. The needs section constitutes the area in which the probation and parole officer's counseling skills and knowledge of community resources are of great value. Whenever completing such scales, you always should be mindful of the need for complete accuracy. The safety of the people of the community and the rehabilitative needs of the offender depend on your accurate assessment. Read the instructions carefully before making any assessment.

Let us see how Bill Bloggs would do on the risk and needs scales. Going over the risk scale, Bill would be assessed only three points (he was between the ages of eighteen and twenty-nine at the time of the current offense). However, the "assault factor" automatically would place him up one level of supervision in most departments.

In the "emotional stability" section of the needs scale, this author would assign Bill two points. On the one hand, given some of his weird behavior and statements, he should be assessed more than two. On the other hand, his symptoms do not prohibit adequate functioning, so this author also would assess three points against him in the "living arrangements" category. The only other assessment against him is one point for "situational or minor difficulties" under "financial status," but this author would assess five points under "officer's impressions," for a total of eleven points.

If we turn to the supervision level matrix (Figure 7-1), we discover that Bill's level of supervision without the assault override, would have been minimum. Such a supervision level is clearly untenable for someone who committed the type of crimes that Bill did. (This level might be fine if he were being classified for parole rather than probation and if information from prison authorities justified it). Such a possible classification problem underscores two points: (1) that Bill was clearly an atypical case and (2) that the suggestions of these scales, based as they are on the "typical" criminal, are not cast in stone. In the extremely unlikely event that Bill had been placed on probation, you would have been seriously remiss if you had followed these guidelines unquestioningly.

Figure 7.1
Risk and Needs Supervision Level Matrix

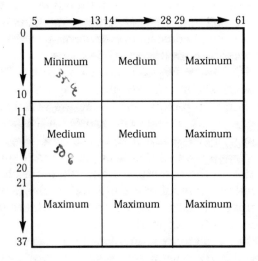

The kind of risk and needs scale we are discussing is one of a number of others that have been called "third-generation" scales because they are based on empirical research and because they incorporate more (and more sophisticated) indices of risk, as well as treatable needs. As Lauen explains:

> Third-generation risk instruments allow practitioners to measure dynamic risk factors and better illuminate where and how the change process might be enhanced for a particular offender. Offender-assessment data derived from well-integrated risk/need tools organizes and profiles populations according to various 'criminogenic' need areas, as well as risk levels. Multiple scales are used so that the assessment can differentiate which need areas are the most urgent and, in so doing, establish case-management priorities, which, in turn, are most likely to result in real reductions in criminal behavior (1997:126).

A perusal of the risk/need assessments contained in the Appendix will reveal that they address the major nonbiological risk factors for offending identified by multiple researchers and summarized by Weibush, Baird, Krisberg, and Onek, 1994. These major factors are (1) age at first adjudication or conviction, (2) criminal history (number and type of arrests, incarcerations, probation/parole periods prior to current offense), (3) history of extent of drug and alcohol use, (4) education and vocational skills, (5) employment history and potential, (6) family stability, (7) emotional stability, and (8) intellectual ability. If used in conjunction with the CMC, the correctional worker also will be able to identify offenders' friends and social network, as well as their attitudes and beliefs regarding crime and life in general.

Supervision Level Matrix

On the basis of scores obtained in both sections of the assessment scale, offenders are placed under minimum, medium, or maximum supervision. These levels of supervision closely correlate with the case management classification system derived from the CMC. Correct assessment of offenders contributes greatly to the efficient use of officers' time. The time not wasted in "overservicing" low-risk and low-needs offenders can be fruitfully spent with those who require more attention.

Five cells of the supervision-level matrix represent maximum-supervision, three represent medium, and only one cell represents minimum supervision. Only offenders with ten or fewer risk points and thirteen or fewer needs points fall into this minimum category. Do not be alarmed by the number of cells calling for maximum supervision. It has been empirically determined that only about 15 percent of probation and parole offenders fall into these five cells. About 50 percent of the offenders will fall into the medium level of supervision, and the remaining 35 percent will require only minimal supervision (Idaho Department of Corrections, n.d.:19). These figures will vary according to the probation/parole granting practices of a given jurisdiction. If, for whatever reasons, a jurisdiction relies heavily on community-based corrections, the number of offenders requiring maximum and medium supervision will be a lot greater than in jurisdictions that only reluctantly grant probation/parole. In the latter type of jurisdiction, the number of offenders requiring minimum supervision may be perhaps 60 to 70 percent.

Case Management

Effective case management is an integral part of corrections work. The techniques of case management have been borrowed from social work. Social workers have long experience in trying to connect (or reconnect) their clients to their communities by securing services for them from a variety of sources, coordinating the efforts of the various agencies providing those services, and monitoring their clients' use of them. According to Healey (1999:2), case management can be distilled into five sequential activities: (1) assessing a client's needs, (2) developing a service/treatment plan, (3) linking the client to services, (4) monitoring his or her progress, and (5) acting as an advocate for the client. This chapter focuses on activity numbers 1, 2, and 4. The remaining two activities will be addressed elsewhere in this book.

Healey (1999) also identifies general models for implementing these activities: the "strength-based" and "assertive" models. The strength-based model delivers services and makes expectations about results based on the client's strengths. The client's strengths are first identified (with the help of the client) and a management plan is formulated so that the client can build on those strengths. Andrews and Bonta (1998:245) refer to this as the *responsivity principle* of treatment delivery, and define it as providing treatment "in a style and mode that is consistent with the ability and learning style of the offender." The assertive model basically means that the worker delivers the needed services to clients assertively (even aggressively) rather than simply offering those services to them. Applied to correctional "clients," case management must be both strength-based and assertive.

Some commentators view this emphasis on case management as a radical departure from previous models of probation and parole practice. There have even been suggestions that the Probation Service in the United Kingdom be renamed the Offender Risk Management Service (Robinson, 1999:420). Nellis (1995:27) appears to decry the trend, arguing that the rehabilitative ideal of earlier models focusing on offender needs has been replaced by a soulless quest for "accurate prediction and effective management of offender risk."

Effective management of offenders must be, of course, the first and foremost concern of correctional personnel, with offender needs being of secondary importance. After all, rehabilitation is desirable primarily because it reduces risk to the community, and only secondarily because the offender will benefit from it personally. There is no real antithesis between the rehabilitative ideal and reinscribing it in a risk-management model. After all, an accurate assessment can help determine "*who* warrants the investment of probation resources (according to the logic of risk) and *what* needs to be changed in order to reduce the risk of reoffending" (Robinson, 1999:429, emphasis original).

When the offender is placed in the appropriate supervision level, case management proper now begins. Based on all the information you have gathered, you now have to formulate a plan aimed at his or her rehabilitation. It is of the utmost importance that treatment plans represent a balance between the offender's treatment needs and the offender's present coping resources. This is an example of strength-based case management, and we will return to this issue in Chapter 10. You have identified the offender's needs, so the next task is to prioritize them according to their importance relative to his or her legal difficulties. The supervision planning form will aid you in this endeavor. It asks you to list the offender's strengths/resources and problems/weaknesses. In rank-ordering problem areas, give extra weight to the problems most amenable to speedy change so that the offender can begin to develop an orientation of success.

The officer should be particularly alert to what may be a primary or "master" problem, a particularly debilitating one that may be the source of most of the offender's other problems. For instance, lack of education and employment, poor financial status, and poor spousal relationships are highly interdependent areas that possibly may be mitigated by meaningful vocational training and subsequent employment. Perhaps all these areas, as well as others such as the influence of criminal companions, themselves are dependent on some form of substance abuse. If an evaluation of the offender's problems leads the officer to believe that most of them are secondary to substance abuse, then the obvious plan is to rank substance abuse as top priority for change.

With the offender's rehabilitative needs identified and prioritized, draw up a tentative supervision plan according to the form Supervision Planning, reproduced in the Appendix. The tentative supervision plan includes a problem statement, a long-range goal, short-range objectives, a probationer/parolee action plan, and an officer/referral plan. For instance, the officer may identify alcoholism/problem drinking and vocational training as the problems needing immediate attention. A second problem that may be identified is an offender's lack of marketable skills, which keep him or her from obtaining worthwhile full-time employment.

The long-range goals, therefore, would be to maintain sobriety and complete vocational training. As we will see in Chapter 10, a good case management plan should be simple, specific, and something the offender must do as soon as possible rather than something he or she should stop doing. The officer may state the short-range goal to be two days of sobriety and attendance at the next AA meeting for alcoholism. Then, the officer will formulate a probationer action plan and request that the offender indicate commitment to it by signing it. The officer/referral action plan may state the officer's commitment to the plan by indicating that he or she will attend the first AA meeting with the offender, and that the offender is to be referred to an alcohol treatment facility for further evaluation of the extent of his or her drinking problem and for treatment recommendations. The procedure for the second problem area is, likewise, simple and focused.

The reassessment plan is implemented after the outcomes of the tentative plans have been determined. For instance, the information received from the alcohol treatment facility may have advised more intensive treatment, or concluded that the offender's drinking problem perhaps had been overemphasized by the officer. In either case, the officer will plan the next supervision phase accordingly. Assuming that the offender had been referred for vocational training, and that this training was successfully completed, the long-range plan now may be to secure and maintain full-time employment, and the short-range plan may be for the offender to file a designated number of applications for employment every day until he or she has secured a job. Supervision plans must be reassessed and changed frequently as circumstances dictate.

After six months, and semiannually thereafter, there should be a reassessment of the offender's risk and needs. Reassessment may result in a higher or lower supervision category on the basis of the offender's progress or lack of progress in the preceding six months. Let us examine some of the characteristics of the offenders who fall into each of four classifications described by the CMC.

SELECTIVE INTERVENTION

Offenders in the selective-intervention category require the least time and present the fewest supervision problems. As the term implies, the supervising officer will intervene in the offender's life only on an "as needed" basis. Offenders in this category almost always fall into the low-risk category as determined by the risk and needs scales. Generally, they have relatively stable, prosocial lifestyles, and their current offense is frequently their first involvement with the law. Their offenses can be viewed as a temporary lapse or suspension of an otherwise normal value system. They often show strong indications of guilt and embarrassment. Avoid increasing guilt and criminal identification in these offenders without allowing them to intellectualize or minimize their criminal acts.

These offenders respond best to a warm, supportive relationship with their officers and to the use of rational problem-solving approaches to counseling. Avoid giving the impression to such offenders that you are trying to run their lives for them or that you lack trust in them. There is some research evidence that low-risk offenders actually may become worse if they are overly restricted and "treated" by well-meaning correctional workers (Bonta, 1991). If your agency uses a system of minimal contact, such as allowing low-risk offenders to report into the agency by mail or by telephone, make sure that offenders know that you are available to help them through temporary crisis situations or emotional problems that may prompt further criminal activity. These offenders should not be put on minimal supervision or write-in status until you satisfactorily deal with their treatment needs, but remember that less intrusive supervision strategies tend to work best for these offenders.

ENVIRONMENTAL STRUCTURE

Offenders who need environmental structure generally fall into the low end of the medium-risk category and require regular supervision. Intellectual, vocational, and social deficits contribute considerably to their criminal activities. They tend to lack foresight, to have difficulty learning from past mistakes, and to be overly dependent on like-minded individuals for acceptance and approval. Usually, they are not committed to a criminal career, and malice as a motivation for criminal activity is rare.

The typical goals to seek with these offenders are to develop and/or improve intellectual, social, and work skills, to find alternatives to associations with criminal peers, and to increase control of impulses. Be more directive and concrete with these individuals than with your selective-intervention offenders. Move slowly to build a success identity for the offenders by balancing your expectations of them with their present coping resources. Initially, you often may have to do things with and/or for them (such as taking them job hunting), but take care that you do not foster overdependence. Many of the offenders in this category can become productive citizens with a warm and accepting officer who knows the available community resources.

CASEWORK/CONTROL

Casework/control means that offenders placed in this category require more intensive casework and that their activities should be more tightly controlled. Offenders in this category are at the high end of the medium-risk and needs scale. They evidence a generalized instability in their lifestyles. They lack goals in their lives and have difficulty with interpersonal relationships and in finding and keeping employment. They tend to have had chaotic and abusive childhoods, which they repeat with their own families. Alcohol and drug abuse is frequently found among these offenders, and many of their criminal convictions reflect this abuse.

The basic goals to be achieved with this group are much the same as those outlined for the environmental structure offenders but are more difficult to achieve because of their substance abuse and greater emotional problems. These offenders require a great deal of your time, and considerable coordination of auxiliary programs. Attendance and involvement with outside programs must be monitored strictly, and they should be allowed to suffer the consequences of their noncompliance, such as short periods in the county jail. In short, use all the leverage at your disposal to promote offender compliance. These offenders will try your patience and professional competence, but they can be turned around by a knowledgeable, caring, and no-nonsense officer.

LIMIT SETTING

Offenders who need strict limits set for them by their officers are high risk on the risk and needs scale. They are quite comfortable in their criminal lifestyles and demonstrate a pattern of long-term involvement with criminal activities. They delight in their ability to beat the system and tend to minimize or deny any personal problems. They see themselves as normal individuals who simply have chosen a criminal lifestyle for themselves. Indeed, in comparison to the structured-environment and casework/control offenders, they often show quite superior ability to function normally (if not morally) in society.

Offenders in the limit-setting category typically are assigned to a special intensive supervision officer. Intensive supervision officers usually enjoy small caseloads, enabling them to devote the time necessary to supervise high-risk offenders. Protection of the community through surveillance and strict control (often with the aid and cooperation of the police) of the offenders is of primary concern. Such offenders are extremely manipulative and frequently will test your resolve. Any failure on your part to act assertively will be interpreted as weakness. Thus, you always must be prepared to confront them with even minor infractions of the rules. If you do not, you will not be respected, and you can be sure that they will escalate their violations.

These offenders respond best to the techniques of reality therapy described in this chapter, and to rational discussion, because their criminal behavior is often more a function of choice than of emotional or intellectual deficiencies. Figuring the cost/benefit ratio of crime as explained in Chapter 12 may be beneficial to these offenders. Since they also tend to be quite energetic and to possess adequate native intelligence, they have capabilities that can be channeled into profitable and legal endeavors. Attempt to develop challenging and innovative opportunities to provide them with satisfying alternatives to a criminal lifestyle.

For offenders who have defeated all your best efforts, who repeatedly have sabotaged treatment plans and exhausted existing programs, and who plainly lack any sort of motivation to change, it may be appropriate to discontinue major efforts to restructure their lives. When all else has failed, but you have not initiated formal legal action against them, expect nothing more than legal conformity from them. Make it crystal clear, however, that any legal violation, no matter how minor, will result in official action.

A FINAL WORD ABOUT THE CMC SYSTEM

It is important that neither the seasoned officer nor the student see the CMC system as just bureaucratic paper-pushing. It may seem like a lot of extra work to the officer used to supervising offenders in accordance with his or her "intuition" or "experience." The CMC system is actually an efficiency-enhancing device that ultimately will save time. A study (Lerner, Arling, and Baird, 1986) found that high-risk offenders on CMC supervision experienced 8 percent fewer parole revocations than regularly supervised ("seat of the pants") high-risk offenders. Medium-risk CMC offenders experienced 6 percent fewer revocations than non-CMC medium-risk offenders. Both these differences were statistically significant. The substantive difference represented by these percentages was ninety-five fewer parole violation reports, and that is a lot of time spared. More importantly, it meant that ninety-five offenders were saved from the futility of the revolving prison door because their needs had been identified and efficiently serviced. CMC supervision of low-risk offenders resulted in only 1 percent fewer (6 percent versus 7 percent) revocations than the regularly supervised low-risk offenders. This seemingly insignificant difference is more a function of the generally good performance of low-risk offenders than the inapplicability of the CMC system to them. Michael Schumacher, Ph.D., Chief Probation Officer of Orange County, California, is an enthusiastic supporter of CMC.

Probation programs . . . can no longer rely upon the assertions of "doing good" for people based upon a subjective model of human behavior. The risk/needs approach provides an objective look at offenders based on characteristics that have been shown to have some predictive value for the success or failure of other probationers. It supports a healthy balance between the peace officer role [and the] social work role. It is a tool that has been a long time coming and shows promise for probation supervision as a major factor in the resocialization of offenders. Longitudinal research conducted in jurisdictions where this system has been fully implemented has shown encouraging results in the reduction of criminal behavior by probationers. If this system is properly implemented, I am convinced reductions in recidivism rates will result (1985: 454-455).

Objective Approaches to Offender Assessment
By Carl B. Clements, Ph.D.

Carl Clements is a clinical psychologist who has been on the faculty of the University of Alabama since 1971. His work in the field of corrections includes consultation and testimony in several landmark prison crowding cases, development and evaluation of objective offender classification methods, and training of psychologists for work in the justice system. He has written several articles and chapters on offender classification and is the author of *Offender Needs Assessment* (1986) published by the American Correctional Association.

Within the criminal justice system, we are asked to collect what seems to be an enormous amount of information about offenders. This information presumably shapes our decisions and recommendations—pretrial, presentence, prerelease, and postincarceration. No doubt, each piece of information is potentially useful (or was once thought to be); the data range from nuts and bolts demographics (age, race, employment, and crime history) to educational, medical, and psychological profiles. Our purpose spans the dimensions of risk assessment, needs identification, supervisory placements, and treatment assignment. Although the assessment-decision sequence rarely has operated smoothly or in a systematic fashion, recent advances have improved the link between these two processes.

The fundamental goal of assessment in the criminal justice system is the identification of relevant offender characteristics from which to formulate differential responses. Except for basic identification and tracking purposes, there is no need to conduct assessments unless they lead to improved decision-making. This rationale, then, forces us to examine both the accuracy (reliability) and the value (validity) of the information being collected. Does this or that psychological test really predict who will respond to drug treatment? Does an offender's risk scale score accurately reflect the level of supervision needed?

Increasingly, the answers are likely to be, "yes." In recent years, improved instruments and processes have been developed to assess salient offender characteristics, background, current adjustment, and the like. In turn, these tools increase our ability to match offenders to the best available options. The reality of scarce resources demands that we use them wisely. Of course, we cannot conduct all the necessary experiments to ultimately test the validity of an instrument (nor should we expect error-proof assessments). For example, we cannot randomly assign a group of presumably high-risk offenders to the community just to see if they really will reoffend. More often, such tests have occurred through "natural experiments." For example, a selected group of offenders may be released to the community through judicial order or in response to prison crowding. These "low-risk" offenders (as assessed by objective instruments) typically prove to recidivate at a predictably low rate.

At the other end of the spectrum, in a classic study involving mentally disordered offenders, a federal court found unconstitutional the commitment law under which "dangerous, mentally ill" patients were being held. After release, this group evidenced quite low crime and violence rates despite their previous diagnoses. Reoffense in such groups is typically more accurately predicted by past crime and violence history than by mental illness status. In this case, the prediction of dire consequences was off the mark.

Both in the field of clinical psychology and within the workplace, broadly defined, we have clung to the questionable belief that intuition, "clinical judgment," experience, and clever interviews provide the best predictors of success, or that all we need to know is something about the traits of an individual, giving no thought to environmental factors that promote or inhibit the behaviors we hope to predict and manage. To address the first of these concerns, techniques of risk and needs assessment have moved out of the purely subjective, highly discretionary realm into a more objective, empirically based approach. This trend has proven to be an improvement for at least four reasons:

- Important offender characteristics can be consistently identified by diverse staff.
- Those features can be evaluated against outcomes.
- If done correctly, the information necessarily points to a preferred response or package of services across a range of offender management issues.
- Assessment results can be assembled for large groups of offenders, allowing an agency or system to better know its offender base and the correlated demand or need for particular correctional resources.

To some, the use of structured interviews, point systems, and checklists (such as those noted in this chapter as well as in Chapter 8 — Assessment and Classification in Institutional Corrections) may unnecessarily inhibit or minimize the case manager's personal feel for the offender. What becomes of the rapport believed to enhance candor and positive influence? In fact, no such conflict exists. Conducting structured assessments is not automatically a coldly impersonal process. While a major benefit is to remove subjectivity, the offender typically can participate in reviewing findings and learning about the rationale for recommended interventions. Indeed, well-developed assessment packages may confer more credibility and fairness to the process and the resulting dispositions.

However, it is also the case that a few "points," one way or the other, can make a difference in an offender's institutional custody rating, for example, or in the stringency of recommended parole supervision. Thus, expect offenders often to debate or challenge certain facts that lie behind these calculations.

At the same time, the accuracy of formulations based on objective systems repeatedly have been shown to be superior to clinical intuition or individual "experience." (Interestingly, the experience factor often shows up in objective or data-driven approaches; yet, some of the variables included in most models were derived from accumulated wisdom.) In several correctional systems in which this author has consulted or served as part of a technical assistance team, the move to objectifying assessments and decision-making was directly tested against existing classification methods. With respect to security and supervision in prison settings, for example, somewhat less restrictive alternatives typically were recommended for a sizable group of offenders. In virtually every instance, neither increased risk to the community (such as escapes) nor disruptions of facility routines were observed. In some cases, sweeping recalculations of offender custody ratings sometimes underscored the statewide need for more minimum-security and community-based alternatives.

To be sure, this "correction" in course often has taken place in the context of acknowledged crowding of facilities and a general reliance on highly secure housing for most offenders. Objective classification systems, however, are policy neutral and just as easily can result in recommendations for more stringent supervision if criteria are met. Nevertheless, the negative repercussions of further crime by an offender who was prematurely released or inadequately constrained tends to make the risk assessment and decision-making process quite conservative.

Assessments must be connected firmly to decision making. As an example, consider the question, "Should we give a particular personality test to all offenders?" The answer should be based on a series of conditions:

- Will specific decisions, dispositions, assignments, or intervention strategies be determined or influenced by the results of this test (or structured interview, or risk scale)?
- Does this test validly measure the traits or behaviors that are relevant to this (or these) choice(s)?
- Are those offenders "selected" or identified by this test significantly more likely to benefit from X (respond to Y, commit less violence, and so forth) than those with different scores?

"No" answers to any of the questions suggests that the instrument or scale is irrelevant, invalid, or both.

On the other hand, an instrument may be valid for one purpose but not another. Do not expect a treatment-oriented assessment to predict an offender's inclination to escape from custody. Few multipurpose instruments exist, although the recently developed Levels of Supervision Inventory (LSI-Revised) used in the Canadian system addresses several elements of both risk and needs (*see* Lauen, 1997).

The most deficient aspect of the assessment-planning-intervention link is the storehouse of available intervention regimens and validated treatments. As exemplified by the Client Management Classification (CMC) system described in this chapter, a "diagnosis" should be directly linked to a differential response or tailored package of interventions. Not only are such connections likely to promote community supervision success, for example, but more expensive resources also can be concentrated on those offenders who need and are most likely to benefit from intensive or highly structured (and typically more costly) interventions.

Similarly, within correctional settings, the classification process should go well beyond basic assignments to the traditional "minimum," "medium," and "maximum" custody designations. Research clearly supports the value of additional layers of differentiation to promote more homogeneous groupings of offenders who, in turn, can be matched to compatible and effective supervision strategies. However, developing differential approaches for different offender subgroups remains a challenge.

A final benefit of objective assessment systems is the potential to communicate the rationale and elements of the process. Justice personnel, whether in probation or institutional corrections, are more likely to trust the assessments, understand the derived profiles, and participate in (or support) the prescribed interventions when they see the connections across these steps. Involvement in such a proactive process also can be expected to reduce professional burnout and cynicism.

Summary

The proper assessment of correctional offenders has become increasingly important in criminal justice. The various scales, forms, and questionnaires found in this chapter constitute efforts to classify and treat offenders in a more rational and equitable way.

The Social History Questionnaire and the Client Management Classification Interview Schedule are interviewing and assessment aids. They are used prior to sentencing. The felony sentencing worksheet assists you in making sentencing recommendations by providing you with sentencing "norms" based on past experience.

The risk and needs assessment scales are supervision aids. These scales provide you with information relating to the risk offenders pose to the community, and the needs they have in order to lead a more productive life. They also provide you with the information you need to develop treatment plans for offenders. Treatment plans begin by identifying major problem areas and devising a "tentative treatment plan" based on the need to alleviate these problems. These plans should be reassessed as frequently as necessary, or at least every six months. The use of the tools contained in this chapter has resulted in a remarkable improvement in corrections supervision over the old "seat of the pants" methods of supervision.

References and Suggested Readings

Allen, H. and C. Simonsen. 2001. *Corrections in America*. New York: Macmillan.

American Correctional Association. 1999. *Public Correctional Policy on Sentencing*. Lanham, Maryland: American Correctional Association.

Andrews, D. and J. Bonta. 1998. *The Psychology of Criminal Conduct*. Cincinnati, Ohio: Anderson.

Bonta, J. 1991. Correctional halfway houses: The evidence on effectiveness. *Second Annual Corrections Research Forum Proceedings*. Ottawa: Correctional Service of Canada.

Bureau of Justice Statistics. 1995. *Prisoners in 1994*. Washington, D.C.: U.S. Department of Justice.

———. 2000. *Prisoner Statistics*. www.ojp.usdoj.gov/bjs/.

Carlson, N., K. Hess, and C. Orthmann. 1999. *Corrections in the 21st Century*. Belmont, California: West/Wadsworth.

Crooks, C. H. 2000. The Case Management System in Ohio. In Kratcoski, P., ed. *Correctional Counseling and Treatment*. Prospect Heights, Illinois: Waveland Press. pp. 269-275.

Healey, K. 1999. *Case management in the criminal justice system*. National Institute of Justice Research in Action. Washington, D.C.: U.S. Department of Justice.

Lauen, R. 1997. *Positive Approaches to Corrections: Research, Policy and Practice*. Lanham, Maryland: American Correctional Association.

Lerner, K., G. Arling, and C. Baird. 1986. Client management classification: Strategies for case supervision. *Crime and Delinquency*. 32: 254-271.

Nellis, M. 1995. Probation values for the 1990's. *The Howard Journal*. 34:19-44.

Pollock, J. 1997. *Prisons Today and Tomorrow*. Gaithersburg, Maryland: Aspen.

Robinson, G. 1999. Risk management and rehabilitation in the probation service: Collision and collusion. *The Howard Journal*. 38:421-433.

Schmalleger, F. 1993. *Criminal Justice Today, Second Edition*. Englewood Cliffs, New Jersey: Prentice-Hall.

Schumacher, M. 1985. Implementation of a client classification and case management system: A practitioner's view. *Crime and Delinquency*. 31: 445-455.

Swisher, T. 1978. *Sentencing in Ohio*. Columbus, Ohio: Ohio State Bar Research Foundation.

Walsh, A. 1985. Ideology and arithmetic: The hidden agenda of sentencing guidelines. *Journal of Crime and Justice*. 8:41-63.

Walsh, A. and C. Hemmens. 2000. *From Law to Order: The Theory and Practice of Law and Justice*. Lanham, Maryland: American Correctional Association.

Weibush, R., C. Baird, B. Krisberg, and D. Onek. 1994. *Risk Assessment and Classification for Serious, Violent, and Chronic Juvenile Offenders*. San Francisco, California: National Council on Crime and Delinquency.

Assessment and Classification in Institutional Corrections

by J. Arthur Beyer, Ph.D. and Thomas C. Balster

Through its diagnostic and coordinating functions, classification not only contributes to the objective of rehabilitation, but also to custody, discipline, work assignments, officer and inmate morale, and the effective use of training opportunities.

presiding judge in *Morris v. Travisono* (1970)

This chapter is written by J. Arthur Beyer, Ph.D. with significant contributions from his graduate assistant, Thomas C. Balster. Dr. Beyer is an assistant professor of criminal justice at Mankato State University in Minnesota. He is a former sergeant with a city police agency in Idaho, and a former housing unit counselor involved in the classification of inmates. Later, he served as a security lieutenant at the Idaho State Penitentiary. He also has had experience as a probation and parole officer and he has published a number of articles on juvenile delinquency, rural youth threat groups, and prison classification.

Mr. Balster is a graduate student in public administration at Mankato State University in Minnesota. He received his bachelor's degree in law enforcement and political science from Mankato State University in Minnesota. He has worked as an intern, updating policies and procedures for the Law Enforcement Department of the City of Faribault, Minnesota.

Classification is simply a method of ordering the way in which we relate to or deal with objects, situations, or people. For example, virtually all of us classify the weather as warm and sunny or cloudy and cold, thus permitting us to make reasoned decisions pertaining to our clothing and activities. Within a prison setting, classification is a management tool, which allows prison administrators to maintain institutional order and safety through the allocation of resources and the provision of inmate services.

We classify people as well. We call them Republicans, Democrats, conservatives, liberals, alcoholics, criminals, and so on. We subjectively may classify individuals and groups on the basis of our personal experiences, perceptions, and prejudices. Regardless of the methods we use to arrive at our classifications, we tend to respond to the object classified in a manner consistent with our beliefs and classifications.

Professional practitioners within their respective disciplines have developed elaborate systems of classification relating to the phenomena of their disciplines. These practitioners have gone beyond subjective methods to embrace more objective ones. For instance, psychologists and psychiatrists classify various systems of behavior in a manual called the *Diagnostic and Statistical Manual of Mental Disorders* (DSM-IV). The multiaxial system allows for the classification of individual characteristics in terms of clinically important factors, and provides a common bond of understanding within the family of mental health professionals. This facilitates the management of caseloads and the implementation of treatment modalities.

Unfortunately, the classification of institutionalized offenders is not yet quite so neat and tidy as that provided by the DSM-IV. Although the causes and treatment of criminal behavior have been important items in the criminal justice agenda since it was first suggested that there just might be alternatives to flogging, mutilating, and torturing, several reasons exist for the lack of consistency in prison classification.

To facilitate and standardize inmate classification on a national level and to address court mandates, the American Correctional Association (ACA) has established a set of standards for classification. *The Principles of Classification* (in the Appendix) are excerpted verbatim from *Prison Classification: A Model Systems Approach*, 1981, pp. 20-26, reprinted with permission from the National Institute of Corrections (NIC) (1984). They were developed by the National Institute of Corrections based on research conducted by professional practitioners.

First, classification (prediction) procedures are of three types: (1) *anamnestic*, which are based solely on an individual's past behavior, (2) *clinical*, which are based on expert diagnosis and evaluation, such as the DSM-IV, the Minnesota Multiphasic Personality Inventory (MMPI), and other tools to be reviewed in this chapter; and (3) *statistical or actuarial*, which are based on individual behavior patterns in comparison with similar behavior patterns of others (Morris, Miller, and March, 1987).

A second problem deals with false positive (Type I or Alpha Error) and false negative predictions (Type II or Beta Error). If we predict that an individual poses a risk to a society, when, in fact, that person does not pose the predicted risk, we have made a false positive prediction. Thus, the individual unjustly is deprived of rights or privileges. Conversely, if we predict that an individual does not pose a risk to society, when, in fact, that person does, then we have made a false negative prediction.

The false-positive situation can be illustrated by the assessment of an excessively long prison sentence based on the offender's past behavior (anamnestic) without regard to other factors such as age, type of crime, and actuarial information.

Subsequently, we compound this error when we predict that the offender will continue to pose a risk when the risk is no longer present. The false-negative situation (Beta Error) is illustrated by the Jeffery Dahmer homicides in Milwaukee, and the failure of police to intervene as a result of a false-negative prediction. They did not believe that he posed a risk.

Legal and ethical issues develop from the question of false-positive and false-negative predictions. If offenders who pose a real and present risk to the prison population are not classified in a manner that affords protection to others (false negative), institution security and order are threatened. On the other hand, if we err and deprive offenders of rights and privileges (false positive) afforded under the U.S. Constitution and correctional agency policy, we become excessively punitive at a greater fiscal cost to society at large. In either circumstance, violations of the Eighth (cruel and unusual punishment) and Fourteenth Amendments (due process) to the U.S. Constitution often are alleged. Correctional agencies then may become involved in lengthy and costly litigation, which ultimately must be borne by the public.

Another closely related problem deals with predicting individual behavior. The complexity of the human organism precludes 100 percent accuracy in predicting individual behavior. We can classify an individual as belonging to a particular group whose members have the same characteristics. For example, we know that young males have a greater propensity to commit crime than other groups, and we know that the early onset of criminal behavior, the seriousness of the first offense, and the frequency of offending predict future criminality. Thus, the group (as an entity) may present a significant risk to a society; however, the individual offender as a separate subentity may not. In fact, studies indicate that the best formal predictions of individual criminality are little improved over chance predictions (Farrington, 1987; Steadman, 1987). Consequently, it is very risky, regardless of the classification tool, to predict that a given individual will behave in a particular manner in any given instance.

Finally, unlike "free world" classifications, predictions within the criminal justice system tend to deprive individuals of their liberty and access to goods and services. We have suggested that the decision process for the assignment of individuals to various classification levels is far from perfect. Because of the possibility of diminution or loss of freedom, it is necessary to develop and use classification procedures that remove as much subjectivity as possible so as to be less capricious and arbitrary. Standardized procedures encourage uniformity and fairness for the offender, for the institution, and for the public.

The problem is one of objective classification versus subjective classification. Traditionally, the validity of the various methods used by administrators to assess levels of security or custody to which inmates were assigned has relied on the more subjective evaluation of the *Diagnostic Statistical Manual* (DSM) criterion, interpretation of the MMPI, and other diagnostic tools used by trained professionals. However, the interpretation of offender characteristics depicted by the criteria presented, and the interpretation made can vary among evaluators. Even minimal differences can result in classification to custody and security levels, which dramatically limit inmate choices and liberty.

The objective classification of inmates using models that attempt to evaluate inmate characteristics through standardized criterion and other variables enhance the validity of inmate classification (Proctor, 1994). By developing an objective model, we are able to reduce the incidence of error and avoid legal challenges under 42 USC § 1983.

42 USC § 1983, The Civil Rights Act of 1871

Every person who under color of any statute, ordinance, regulation, custom, or usage of any state or territory, subjects or causes to be subject, any citizen of the United States or other person within the jurisdiction thereof to the deprivation of any rights, privileges, or immunities secured by the Constitution and laws, shall be liable to the party injured in an action at law, suit in equity, or other proper proceedings for redress.

42 USC § 1983. A violation of this U.S. statute by a public official can result in a civil action against those officials and their supervisors when acting under the color of state law if they deprive an individual of his or her constitutional rights. There are two conditions that must be met to make a valid claim under 42 USC § 1983: (1) the public official must have acted under the color of law that is in the capacity of his or her assigned duties, and (2) the person who was wronged was deprived of some right or immunity guaranteed by the Constitution or laws of the United States.

Classification to specific levels of security and custody determine to a great extent the amenities that an offender will be afforded. In *Rhodes v. Chapman* (452 U.S. 337 [1981]), the court held that the constitution "does not mandate comfortable prisons" but neither does it permit inhumane ones. It is now well settled through court cases that "the treatment a prisoner receives in prison and the conditions under which he or she is confined are subject to scrutiny under the Eighth Amendment" (*Rhodes v. Chapman*, 349).

In its prohibition of "cruel and unusual punishments," the Eighth Amendment places restraints on prison officials, who must provide humane conditions of confinement. Prison officials must ensure that inmates receive adequate food, clothing, shelter, and medical care, and "take reasonable measures to guarantee the safety of the inmates," *Hudson v. Palmer* (468 U.S. 517 [1984]); *Washington v. Harper* (494 U.S. 210 [1990]); and *Estelle v. Gamble* (429 U.S. at 103 [1976]). Indeed, a prison official's "deliberate indifference" to a substantial risk of serious harm to an inmate violates the Eighth Amendment *(Helling v. McKinney*, 509 U.S. 25 [1993]) and thus raises a section 1983 action. One of the purposes of classification is to assign the inmate to the appropriate security and custody level consistent with the risk that is presented to the institution, staff, and other inmates, as well as to respond to the needs of the inmate.

Historical Overview

To understand and appreciate offender classification as it is practiced today, it is important to have a basic knowledge of historic developments in penology that are related to classification. Early attempts at classification consisted simply of separating men from women and children within prisons. In the late 1700s, the Walnut Street Prison in Philadelphia inaugurated a classification process to separate serious offenders from others. Those classified as serious offenders were placed in isolation and were not allowed to work or interact with other prisoners (Lewis, 1967:17).

Some fifteen years later, in 1804, the Charleston Prison in Massachusetts established a trilevel system of classification based on prior convictions of offenders. Each of the three groups was identified by distinctive uniforms, and groups were segregated from one another. On the basis of this classification, offenders were assigned quarters, prison work, and differential access to various amenities. First-time offenders were given the best quarters, job assignments, and food. Second-time offenders were allowed only two meals per day and performed the less desirable work. Third-time, or habitual offenders, did the most menial tasks and received the worst food (Lewis, 1967:71).

In the early 1800s, prison administrators experimented with a variety of new custodial and classification systems. One such system, which was to provide the model for most prison construction for the next 150 years, was the Auburn Prison, opened in New York in 1819 (Allen and Simonsen, 2001). Prisons based on this model were invariably maximum-security with harsh conditions of confinement. Little effort was extended to establish inmate classification as an integral part of prison administration.

In 1959, criminologists Richard Korn and Lloyd McCorkle (1959) provided a broad classification of crime and criminals according to legal designation, personality types, the ways criminals organized their lives, and offense types (such as sex offenses and drug offenses). This text set the scene for later and more sophisticated typologies. But it was the intervention of the courts, as much as anything else, that provided the impetus toward better classification systems.

As late as 1966, the courts generally avoided interfering in specific classification decisions, recognizing "that discipline and the general management of such open institutions are executive functions with which the judicial branch will not interfere" (*Cohen v. U.S.*, 25 F. Supp. 679, at 688 [1966]). However, as a result of a court action in Rhode Island in 1970, the Federal District Court issued the first order that a meaningful, nonarbitrary classification system be designed and implemented. The court further recognized that inmate classification is a management tool that enables the prison administrator to allocate scarce resources to areas where the greatest good may be achieved. As stated by the court (*Morris v. Travisono*, 310 F. Supp. 857 at 965 [1970]):

> Classification is essential to the operation of an orderly and safe prison. It is a prerequisite for the rational allocation of whatever program opportunities exist within the institution. It enables the institution to gauge the proper custody level of an inmate, to identify the inmate's educational, vocational, and psychological needs, and to separate nonviolent inmates from the more predatory . . .

Thus, the courts have charged correctional administrators with the task of minimizing the risk of injury to the public, to inmates, and to the correctional staff. This is to be accomplished while placing each offender in the least-restrictive setting consistent with the stated goals and with the needs of the offender. As you may well imagine, inmate classification is perhaps the most involved and all-encompassing aspect of inmate supervision where we are addressing the issue of "security, treatment, incapacitation and organizational maintenance" (Gottfredson and Gottfredson, 1989: 204).

Figure 8.1
Physical Security Levels

SECURITY LEVELS

SECURITY ELEMENTS	I (MINIMUM)	II (MEDIUM)	III (MAXIMUM)
Housing	Dormitories, cubicles, or rooms	Rooms and/or multiple cells	Single cells, very secure, with heavy duty hardware
Perimeter Security	None, or single fence; occasional patrol	Double fence; electric alarm system; patrol of perimeter or towers	A combination of double fence; wall; towers; constant armed perimeter surveillance; and electronic alarm system
Internal Security Measures	Inmate census taken at least 3 times daily	Inmate movement controlled by pass system; formal census at least 4 times daily, plus frequent informal census	Frequent informal census; capability to quickly separate the inmates into groups of 50 or less; directly supervised and/or escorted when outside cellhouse or living area; formal census taken at least 6 times daily

Figure 8.2
Custodial Levels

CUSTODY LEVELS

ACTIVITY	MINIMUM	MEDIUM	MAXIMUM
Observation by staff	Occasional; appropriate to situation	Frequent and direct	Always supervised when outside cell
Day movement inside facility	Unrestricted	Observed periodically by staff	Restricted; directly observed or escorted when outside cell
Movement after dark	Intermittent observation	Restricted, with direct supervision	Out of cell only for emergencies. In restraints when outside cellhouse, or as approved by watch commander
After evening lockdown	Intermittent observation	Escorted and only on order of watch commander	
Meal periods	Intermittent observation	Supervised	Directly supervised or in cell
Access to jobs	Eligible for all, both inside and outside perimeter	Inside perimeter only	Only selected day jobs inside perimeter, or directly supervised within the housing unit
Access to programs	Unrestricted, including community-based activities	Work and recreation, inside perimeter; outside perimeter only as approved by C.E.O.	Selected programs/activities inside the facility perimeter, as approved by C.E.O.
Visits	Contact; periodic supervision, indoor and/or outdoor	Contact, supervised	Noncontact or closely supervised (1-1)
Leave the institution	Unescorted/escorted	Direct staff escort; handcuffs, with chains and leg irons (optional); armed escort (optional)	Minimum of two escorts with one armed, full restraints; strip search prior to departure and upon return
Furlough	Eligible for unescorted day pass and furlough*	Eligible for staff-escorted day pass or furlough*	Not eligible

*DEFINITION: Day Pass—Permits inmate to be away from institution only during daylight hours. A furlough authorizes overnight absence from the facility.

This custody classification system is used as a guideline to determine the following:
1. Assignment is made to an institution that provides the level of security consistent with the inmate's custody requirement.
2. Assignments are made to institutional programs that are consistent with custody needs. These assignments include housing, work, and other programs such as education, visiting, and any activity that involves risk to staff, other inmates, or the community.

SECURITY AND CUSTODY

As you will note from Figure 8.1, security levels are of a physical nature. They refer to the environmental factors of perimeter security and use of towers, patrol, and other detection devices. Custodial levels (Figure 8.2) refer to the degree of supervision the inmate/offender receives. Programs refer to the activities that are provided, such as educational and vocational opportunities, counseling services, and activities such as recreation and hobbies. Figure 8.2 makes it clear that access to jobs and programs is an inherent function of custodial classification.

Classification Data

STANDARDS AND PRINCIPLES OF CLASSIFICATION

Classification of behavior in the DSM-IV provides an organized, systematic, and established procedure for assessing offender characteristics. This classification, in turn, allows for differential treatment modalities. In institutional corrections, not all criminals exhibit the same behavior or present the same security risk. For example, the criteria for diagnosis of the antisocial personality (DSM-IV, 1994:360) is specific, yet provides diagnostic discretion for the trained professional to evaluate the individual offender's risk to society.

In the past, we have not normally observed differential approaches to offenders; rather, we have tended to treat all inmates in a similar manner. Now, we have the tools to make distinctions and the rationale of cost savings for doing so (Lauen, 1997).

There are three general schools that tend to provide the explanations for the etiology of crime: the sociogenic, the psychogenic, and the biogenic or sociobiological school (Steel and Steger, 1988). Our parent discipline, sociology, provides a home for the sociogenic school, in which environmental factors explain aberrant behavior. It tends to downplay individual differences that are not explicable in terms of environmental variation. Sociology, according to Jeffery (1979:113), assumes equipotentiality, meaning in effect that we all have the same potential for both good and evil. This school attributes crime causation to society. What we eventually become is the product of variation in the environment, with individual differences being constant.

Psychology, or the psychogenic school, looks at the individual proclivity and motivation to engage in criminal behavior. Although not discounting environmental influences, this school appeals to the individual's mental processes to explain "acting out" behavior.

The third approach, the biogenic or sociobiological school, looks to physical, neurological, biological, and chromosomal abnormalities to provide explanations for crime. In this school, pre- and postnatal trauma, chemical imbalances, endocrine abnormalities, and other biological dysfunctions are believed to be a major factor in criminal behavior.

At one time, each of these opposing perspectives on criminal behavior has been predominant in corrections. Yet, criminology, as an emerging discipline, is developing new ways to examine corrections. Jeffery (1979) feels that by drawing on chemistry and biology, as well as the work being done on nutrition, and incorporating sociological and psychological insights as well, we will arrive at a greater understanding of criminal behavior, and thus a greater understanding of the correctional process. A number of theorists (for example, Nigg and Goldsmith, 1998; Walsh, 2000) argue for the influence of heritable factors in the development of criminal behavior. A number of other studies suggests a robust relationship between neurohormonal and frontal lobe dysfunction and criminal behavior (Reiss and Roth, 1993; Brennan, Mednick, and Volavka, 1995; Raine, 1997). Indeed, many of the criteria (lack of attention to details, carelessness, being easily distracted, impulsiveness, and hyperactivity) which are used in the DSM-IV diagnosis of Attention Deficit/Hyperactivity Disorder (AD/HD) are the same ones that we have observed in delinquents for several years. Much of the Attention Deficit/Hyperactivity Disorder behavior is now treatable with medication, that stimulates or retards the neurotransmitter function at the synapse.

RECEPTION AND DIAGNOSTIC UNIT

Following a sentence of imprisonment, offenders are transported to the designated facility. For offenders being sentenced to prison for the first time, this is very likely the most frightening experience of their lives. Consider for a moment the confusion and fear that the offender must be experiencing as he or she tries to come to grips with the consecutive ordeals of trial, conviction, sentencing, and arrival at the "big house."

Upon arrival at the institution, all offenders are considered close-custody inmates pending initial classification. The function of the security staff at this point is to instill the reality of prison security in the newly committed inmate. Armed guards are present, orders are given, and immediate compliance is demanded. Inmates are stripped naked, all property is seized, and a strip search is conducted. Based on who conducts the search, the policy of the institution, and security considerations, this may include a body cavity search. The strip search is very likely the greatest known intrusion of one's privacy. Inmates are then ordered to shower, with instructions to apply a delousing agent to all areas of body hair. At no time during these initial orientation processes is an inmate allowed out of the sight of correctional staff. Following the shower, inmates are issued a drab prison uniform and a number. All vestiges of individuality are removed. The inmate has effectively become a nonentity, totally vulnerable and dependent upon his or her keepers. This process is demeaning, but it is unfortunately necessary as both a security and a sanitation precaution.

Inmates stay at the reception and diagnostic unit from two to three weeks, during which time they will be closely observed by security and programming staff. Their observations of adjustment and behavior are forwarded to the classification committee for inclusion in their assessments and evaluations.

TESTS

During the reception and diagnostic period, inmates are examined by medical staff and are tested in accordance with the policies of the particular state or institution. These tests may include the Nelson Reading Skills Test, the General Aptitude Test Battery (GATB), the Wechsler Adult Intelligence Scale (see Chapter 3), the Minnesota Multiphasic Personality Inventory (MMPI), the Human Synergistics Lifestyle Inventory, and the Myers-Briggs Type Indicator (MBTI). We will take a brief look at each of these tests.

Nelson Reading Skills Test. The simplest of these tests in terms of inmate understanding is the Nelson Reading Skills Test. It is designed to evaluate the offender's reading and vocabulary grade level. This test tends to establish offender eligibility for participation in subsequent testing. If the offender does not read and understand written communications at least at the sixth-to-eighth grade level, the results of subsequent testing are invalid.

General Aptitude Test Battery. The General Aptitude Test Battery is often administered by governmental employment services and is designed to measure aptitudes that have been found to be significant in many occupations. Developed in 1947, the GATB is not normally administered to anyone who does not read at least at the sixth grade level. Although it was designed to test adults and high school seniors, conversion tables have been devised for converting scores obtained by those reading at less than the twelfth grade level.

Areas for which scores are obtained are presented below. Combining specified scores provides a composite score, which is then cross referenced with specific occupational areas, indicating a general aptitude for that field.

1. *General learning ability* (G). The ability to understand instructions and underlying principles; the ability to reason and make judgments.
2. *Verbal aptitude* (V). The ability to understand the meanings of words, the ideas associated with them, and the ability to use them effectively. The ability to comprehend language, to understand relationships among words, and to understand meanings of whole sentences and paragraphs.
3. *Numerical ability* (N). The ability to perform arithmetic operations quickly and accurately.
4. *Spatial ability* (S). The ability to comprehend forms in space. Frequently described as the ability to visualize objects of two and three dimensions.
5. *Form perception* (P). The ability to perceive pertinent details in objects or in pictorial or graphic material.
6. *Clerical perception* (Q). The ability to perceive pertinent details in verbal or tabular material.
7. *Motor coordination* (K). The ability to coordinate eyes, hands, and fingers rapidly and accurately in making precise movements with speed.
8. *Finger dexterity* (F). The ability to move the fingers and manipulate small objects with them rapidly and accurately.
9. *Manual dexterity* (M). The ability to move the hands easily and skillfully.

Combining the G, V, and N scores provides a score related to cognitive abilities. A functional "performance" score is obtained by combining the S, P, Q, K, F, and M scores. Although comparing results from instruments designed for different purposes is a risky business, it is interesting to note the similarity of criminal profiles obtained by the GATB and Wechsler IQ (WAIS) tests. As indicated in Chapter 3, criminals tend to score significantly higher on the performance test of the (WAIS) than on the verbal test. Likewise, inmates tend to score significantly higher on the functional areas than on the cognitive sections of the GATB. These significant differences are not reported when either the GATB or the WAIS is administered to noncriminal samples.

Minnesota Multiphasic Personality Inventory. The MMPI, developed in the 1930s, is one of the most widely used personality inventories in corrections. It consists of 550 affirmative statements to which the test taker responds with "true," "false," or "cannot say." A MMPI-based typology of criminal offenders is one of five psychological classification systems used by the Federal Bureau of Prisons (Van Voorhis, 1988).

The MMPI has ten scales relating to ten different clinical disorders:

- Hypochondriasis (Hs) (morbid concern over one's health)
- Paranoia (Pa)
- Depression (D)
- Psychasthenia (Pt) (neurotic state with irrational phobias, obsessions, and compulsions)
- Hysteria (Hy)
- Schizophrenia (Sc)
- Psychopathic deviate (Pd)
- Hypomania (Ma)
- Masculinity-femininity (Mf)
- Social introversion (Si)

Three additional control scales are built into the inventory. The Lie (L) scale is designed to assess a person's tendency to try to "look good." The Validity (F) scale is intended to reveal confusion and carelessness. The Correction (K) scale is more subtle than the L or F scales. A high K score tends to indicate that the respondent either is highly defensive or is attempting to "fake good." A low K score is indicative of either an attempt to "fake bad" or a tendency to be overly self-critical.

In 1979, Edward Megargee constructed a classification system for youthful and adult offenders based on the MMPI profiles. The scales that he developed allow administrators to obtain computer-generated classifications of offenders arranged in hierarchical models from least to greatest risk. Rather than using the scales of the MMPI, the Megargee model constructs an aggregate composite based on the analysis of scale. Since the University of Minnesota released a new version of the MMPI, Megargee and his team have adapted his model to the new (MMPI-2) version (Van Voorhis, 1994). Some studies have found the Megargee/MMPI-2 to predict prison assault and misconduct, but in terms of postrelease behavior, it has been found to be weak or of no support (reviewed in Andrews and Bonta, 1998).

Human Synergistics Lifestyles Inventory. The Human Synergistics Lifestyles Inventory (HSLI), developed by Dr. C. Lafferty, is another self-report test. People taking the HSLI test are asked to select which statement of two is more descriptive of them. A series of paired statements is presented to the respondent. Each statement is repeated often, with alternative pairings. A profile is developed of individual lifestyle preferences from the responses. Here are brief descriptions of those preferences.

1. *Humanistic.* Enjoys helping, developing, and teaching others. Regards people as inherently good and accepts them unconditionally. Likes people and understands them. Needs to establish and maintain open, warm, and supportive relationships.
2. *Affiliative.* Cooperative, friendly, and open with others. High need for relationships with many friends. Wants to like and be liked.
3. *Approval.* Overly concerned with being liked. Bases own opinion of self and things on what others think.
4. *Conventional.* A conformist, takes few risks, covers mistakes, and follows rules.
5. *Dependent.* Does what is expected without question. Compliant and eager to please. Highly influenced by others.

6. *Avoidance*. Tendency to stay away from any situation that may pose a threat. Needs to protect self-worth rather than experience life and growth.

7. *Oppositional*. Needs to question things, including resisting authority. Critical tendencies may be a reaction against the need to be close to others. Behavior can be antagonistic, causing defensiveness in others.

8. *Power*. Tends to be hard, tough, bossy, and aggressive. Needs to gain influence and control over others to maintain personal security. Authoritarian and dictatorial as a leader.

9. *Competitive*. Self-worth is based on winning. Turns many situations into contests. Strong need for commendation and praise. Can be self-defeating because failure is unacceptable.

10. *Competence*. Driven, needs to appear independent and confident. Selects high expectation for self to the point that it is unreasonable. Failure to meet perfectionist standards results in self-blame.

11. *Achievement*. Feels that personal effort makes the difference in the outcome. Needs to set own standards of excellence and pursue set goals. Willing to take some risks if they may produce positive results.

12. *Self-actualizing*. Concerned with personal growth and development. Responsible, confident, relaxed, and unique. Motivated by internal need to accomplish set goals. Perceptive and understanding of others, and accepts life in all its fullness.

High scores in a specific series can provide a composite of specific traits. Individuals scoring high in areas 1, 2, 11, and 12 tend to have a realistic view of themselves. Such people are extremely rare within prison walls. Individuals scoring high in areas 3, 4, 5, and 6 are insecure, but mask it to gain approval. They avoid risks and are easily influenced. High scorers in areas 7, 8, 9, and 10 tend to keep people at a distance and show an inability to deal with their feelings and emotions. They have a strong distrust of others. This group is heavily represented in institutional settings.

The Lifestyles inventory not only is designed to generate personality profiles but also is useful in identifying oppositional aspects of respondents' personalities. If an individual scores high on opposing lifestyle areas for example, Humanistic/Oppositional, Affiliative/Power, or Approval/Competitive, he or she is attempting to meet competing and incongruent needs. Such attempts probably will result in debilitating intrapersonal conflicts and stress.

Myers-Briggs Type Indicator (MBTI). Developed in 1962, the Myers-Briggs Type Indicator (MBTI) is based on psychoanalyst Carl Jung's theories of judgment and perception. Jungian theory proceeds from the premise that, from an early age, people are predisposed to react to the world in different ways. These preferences of interaction will tend to direct the use of judgment and perception and will influence both what people direct their attention to and the conclusions they draw from their interactions. The MBTI identifies four separate preference categories. The interaction of the preference categories provides sixteen separate groupings or "types" of individuals. These are the four categories.

1. **Extroversion-Introversion (EI).** This category reflects the individual's basic attitudes or orientation. An extrovert is oriented to the outer world and tends to focus perceptions and judgments on people and things. An introvert is oriented inwardly and tends to focus judgments and perceptions on concepts and ideas.

Extrovert (E): The extrovert's interests tend to flow to the outer world of actions, objects, and persons. They have a breadth of interest. Thus, they like variety and action and often are impatient with long, slow tasks, preferring to get the task accomplished so that they may see the results of their efforts. They tend to work fast, often acting quickly, sometimes without thinking; because of the spontaneity, there is a dislike for complicated procedures. Since they are people oriented, they are interested in how other people would accomplish a task; they enjoy the company of others, are good at greeting people, and communicate well.

Introvert (I): Introverts have interests that mainly are directed to the inner world of concepts and ideas. They like to know the idea behind their job, and dislike sweeping statements. Where the extrovert has a breadth of interest, the introvert has a depth of concentration, which lends itself to detail work, and long periods of uninterrupted work on a single project. They prefer quiet environments where they may work contentedly alone; they like to mull things over before they act and sometimes fail to act. Being introspective, and preferring their own company, there is a tendency to have trouble remembering names and faces, and they experience some problems in communicating.

2. **Sensing-Intuiting (SN).** The SN category indicates the individual's perception functions. The sensing process is dependent on observable objects and occurrences, which are processed through the senses. Intuition is based on "gut feelings" about relationships, things, and occurrences and is beyond the scope of the conscious mind.

Sensing (S): The sensing preference places a great deal of reliance on facts, and persons with this orientation seldom make errors of fact and are good at precise work. The person who is a sensing type prefers to deal with the immediate, real, practical facts of experience and life. There is a dislike for problems unless a standard and routine solution exists; they are seldom inspired and rarely trust inspiration. They prefer established routines using skills that they already have learned, in preference to learning new skills. There is a tendency to work steadily through a task to reach a conclusion, and there is a realistic idea of the time involved to finish the task. Although patient with routine details, when the details of a task become complicated, sensing types become frustrated and impatient.

Intuitive (N): The intuitive individual likes solving problems and prefers to perceive the possibilities, relationships, and meanings of experiences. There is a strong dislike for routine details and repetitive tasks especially if the routine or repetitive task requires the expenditure of time to accomplish precision undertakings; however, they are challenged and patient with complicated nonroutine situations. The intuitive type enjoys learning new skills, but not necessarily the use of a new skill. There is a tendency to pursue a task for a short period with a high level of enthusiasm and energy followed by a slack period of low production. The intuitive type follows inspiration, good or bad, often makes errors of fact, and frequently jumps to conclusions.

3. **Thinking-Feeling (TF).** The TF category is the judgmental index. Thinking allows the individual to reflect on the probable consequences of choices made. Feeling, in contrast, will provide the basis for personal or social values.

Thinking (T): The thinking type relies on logic and analysis to make objective and impersonal judgments and decisions while considering both the causes of events and where decisions may lead. The thinking preference types are relatively unemotional and uninterested in the feelings of others. Thus, they make decisions on an impersonal basis, sometimes ignoring the wishes and hurting the feeling of others without knowing it. They are able to reprimand people and fire them, when necessary; thus, they seem to be hard-hearted. Although the thinking type relates well only to other thinking types, they do have a need to be treated fairly.

Feeling (F): A feeling person subjectively and personally weighs the values of choices and how the choices matter to others when making judgments and decisions. The decisions, therefore, may be influenced by their own or other people's likes and wishes. They tend to be very aware of other people and their feelings, and enjoy pleasing others if even in small unimportant ways; thus, they relate well to most people. Feeling-oriented people are sympathetic and dislike telling people unpleasant things; they also require occasional praise. They have a strong preference for harmony, and their efficiency can be badly disturbed by discord.

4. **Judgment-Perception (JP)**. This category relates directly to the extroverted function of a person's life—how he or she deals with the outer world. A person who prefers to use judgment in these dealings will assign either the thinking or the feeling process to situations. However, if the individual reports a perception preference, the perceptive functions of sensing and intuition will dominate in relating to outer-world activities.

Judgment (J): A judging type tends to rigid organization and prefers to live in a decisive, planned, and orderly manner, aiming to regulate and control events. Judging persons work best when they can plan their work and follow the plan. Once they have reached a judgment on a thing, person, or situation, they tend to be satisfied. They want only the minimum essentials needed to accomplish a task so that things may be settled and wrapped up; however, they may decide things too quickly, may not notice new things that need to be done, and may dislike interrupting a current project for one with a higher priority.

Perception (P): Perceptive people are ones who live their life in a spontaneous, flexible manner, attempting to understand life and adapt to the changing situations of life. They may have problems making decisions and may postpone unpleasant tasks. They do not mind leaving things open for alterations. They tend to be curious and welcome new perspectives on things, situations, or people; however, the curiosity causes them to start many new projects which they have difficulty finishing. When beginning a new task, they want to know all about it.

Each of the sixteen possible groups, referred to as "types," is derived from factor analyses of the category scores. Each type has particular characteristics associated with it depending on which of the bimodal attributes are dominant, auxiliary, tertiary (meaning "third most important"), or inferior functions.

The purpose of the JP index is to identify the visible and extroverted function, and by doing so allows us to identify the dominant, auxiliary, tertiary, and inferior functions of the type indicator. Each letter indicates preferences in a fixed order; the first letter indicates the E-I preference; the second refers to the preference for the perceptive function (S-N), the third for the judgment function (T-F), and the fourth letter, the JP index points to the function that is typically extroverted; thus, the other preferred function will be introverted. By identifying each function, we are more readily able to understand the dynamics of behavior.

The dominant function is the function which is most used, most developed, and most allowed the freedom to shape the life of an individual. The individual may use auxiliary functions as the need arises and, on occasion, will resort to tertiary and inferior functions.

For example, an ENTJ is an extrovert whose dominant method of relating to the external world is as a thinking type. The J points to the third letter, which is the judgment function, thinking and feeling, in this case T. The N, on the other hand, points to the second letter which is the perception function, sensing and intuition. Thus, an ENFP would take an intuitive (N) approach as the dominant method of relating to the external world.

In the case of the first example, ENTJ, since the dominant function is extroverted T, the auxiliary function would be introverted intuitive (N). The third function is the opposite of the second and thus would be sensing (S); the inferior function is therefore the opposite of the dominant function, and is feeling, F. By using the same logic, the ESFP functions would be S (dominant), F (auxiliary), T (tertiary), N (inferior).

This may be translated into an offender profile which depicts the offender as decisive, ingenious, and good at many things. The ENTJ offenders are usually good at whatever they attempt, tend to be well organized, and rely on reasoning, logic, and analysis to control their world. Sometimes they are more positive and confident than their experience in an area warrants. They tend to use their intuitive function to look at the possibilities and relationships beyond what is known. The intuitive function hones the thinking function, but tends to negate the sensing function. It is often necessary for the ENTJ to rely on a sensing type to provide the relevant facts and details. Feeling is the least developed process, and the ENTJ consciously may use and manipulate others without regard for their feelings.

The introspective dynamics differ in identifying the dominant and auxiliary functions. Recall from above, that the JP index points to the visible and extroverted function. Thus, if the attitude (E-I) preference is introverted, and the JP index points to the extroverted function, the other preferred function will be introverted. Thus, an ISFP would have a dominant preference of feeling. P points to the perception functions S-N. Since the JP index points to the extroverted, that is, the visible outer-world function, S in this case, the other preferred function, F, must be introverted. Insofar as the E-I attitude is introverted, the dominant preference also must be introverted. The dominant function then is F. Using the same formula and logic described for the extrovert, we can determine that the auxiliary preference is S, the tertiary N, and the inferior is T.

Any further explanation of the MBTI is beyond the scope of this book. Yet, it is very helpful in identifying and understanding offenders' personalities. Once this is achieved, the counselor can assist the offender to develop the tertiary and inferior functions of his or her personality in a wholesome direction. In the case of an ENTP offender, for example, by assisting the offender to deal with routine assignments until completed and by helping to identify flaws in his or her logic, which justify aberrant behavior, offender personality development may be enhanced. For further information, please refer to the references and suggested readings at the end of this chapter, specifically, Myers and McCaulley (1985), and for an abbreviated version, Keirsey and Bates (1984).

The results of all of this testing (in conjunction with information extracted from the presentence investigation report, reports submitted by custodial and other staff, and the offender's criminal history) are consolidated by the classification committee to provide a comprehensive profile of the inmate.

Risk and Needs Assessment

Once all the data has been gathered and consolidated, a classification interview is arranged for the new inmates. The factors that establish the inmates' risk and custody level are explained to them. The psychological, educational, and vocational needs that have been identified during the assessment period also are explained. Inmates are told about available programs and how to get into them.

The final step is the establishment of any override considerations. An override means that unusual factors not addressed in the classification instruments are considered important enough to overrule the determined custody level in favor of another custody option. Areas of concern related to security and maintenance of order include any gang or organized crime affiliations. Areas of concern related to the custodial safety include consideration of any suicidal gestures, the protection of any inmates known to be informants, or the protection of those inmates whose crimes make them targets for abuse, such as child molesters.

The override option provides for both objective and subjective considerations not addressed in the classification instruments. Use care in the exercise of overrides. The committee chairperson should be required to justify in writing the reason for the override action. If the classification instrument is overridden with some frequency, either the classification committee is not properly using the instrument, or the instrument itself is defective and thus invalid. Either condition may result in judicial action to correct the problem.

In the years following the *Morris* decision, referenced earlier in this chapter, several classification models have appeared. The actuarial prediction model summarizes statistical data to predict future behavior. Consensual classification is an incremental process conducted by prison administrators that weighs classification criteria for implementation with individual inmates. Clinically based systems employ psychological test data as predictors of behavior and adjustment. Decision-tree models are sequential. Each decision is based on the evaluation immediately preceding the current choice. Figure 8.3 illustrates the decision flow. It is not to show the ultimate decision, but it displays the beginnings of the decision flow and its progression. "Further decisions" are based on the criteria being met at each level and will lead the decision makers to the custody level appropriate for the individual inmate. The additive model combines both actuarial and statistical data to provide cutoff scores along a continuum.

A common feature among models is the relative simplicity of the instruments used to deal with a complex problem. The issues they address are of the utmost importance, first and foremost being the risk that an inmate presents to society and the institution, as well as the needs of the inmate, which should be met, to minimize that risk. The risk and needs models discussed below offer a closer look at the classification process. They are the National Institute of Corrections' *Model for Custody and Need* and the *Adult Internal Management System* (AIMS).

Figure 8.3
Custody Classification Decision Tree

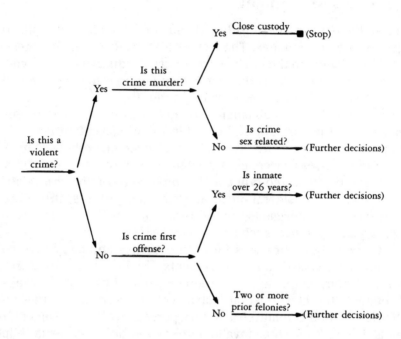

THE NIC'S MODEL

Custody Classification. The instrument identifies eight areas of assessment that, when properly scored, provide for objective custodial placement. To accurately assess the new inmate, the classification committee needs to refer to the detailed classification manual that accompanies the instrument. After becoming thoroughly familiar with the manual and instrument, committee members need to refer to the manual only to verify adherence to and use of appropriate criteria. As we go through the custody classification sections, we will apply them to Bill Bloggs using the information contained in his PSI report (*see* Chapter 6).

1. *History of Institutional Violence.* Assault and battery is any overt act toward another person, including another inmate, in which contact was made and injury attempted. If a weapon were used or serious injury occurred, this section is scored 7. In the event of two similar offenses, only the more serious is scored. Bill Bloggs had no previous institutional history. Therefore, unless he assaulted someone at the reception center, he would have a score of 0.
2. *Severity of Current Offense.* A severity of offense scale is provided on the reverse side of the instrument. Although an inmate may be committed for several offenses, only the most severe is scored, for a maximum of 6 points. Bill would get 6 points assessed against him because he committed armed robbery.
3. *Prior Assaultive Offense History.* This section reflects offenders' propensity for frequent violent behavior. Attempts to commit battery (simple assault) are scored

regardless of the degree of contact or injury. The maximum score is 6. Bill's assaultive history is minimal in terms of frequency. However, shooting a police officer to avoid capture is extremely serious and indicates that Bill can be dangerous when cornered. An assessment of 4 or 6 points is rather discretionary. In light of the seriousness of his assault, this author would assess Bill 6 points.

4. *Escape History.* Any documented escape or attempt within the time framework provided is scored. Any adjudication by an institutional disciplinary hearing committee is sufficient for assessment regardless of any court prosecution. The maximum score is 7. Bill has no escape history. Assess him 0 points.

The first four areas are the primary indicators of the risk that an inmate presents to the security of the institution and the welfare of other inmates and staff. A maximum score of 26 may be obtained. A score of 10 or more requires that the inmate initially be classified to close-custody supervision. A score of 9 or less on the first four classification criteria requires that the last four areas be scored. Bill has had 12 points assessed against him. Thus, he will be placed initially in maximum custody. Assume for the purposes of the exercise that he had 9 or fewer points and score him on the following.

5. *Alcohol/Drug Abuse.* Abuse causing occasional legal and social adjustment problems is defined as any abuse that has resulted in five or fewer misdemeanor convictions, or interruption of employment within the last three years. Six or more alcohol or drug convictions during an offender's lifetime, or commitment to jail or treatment facilities within the last three years for substance abuse is considered serious abuse. The maximum score is 3. Bill has no history of drug or alcohol abuse causing him legal and social adjustment problems. He gets 0 points here.

6. *Current Detainer.* A detainer is a legal hold that another jurisdiction has placed on an inmate. Prior to releasing the inmate on parole or at the expiration of a sentence, the institution notifies the jurisdiction that holds the detainer so that the agency, which issued the detainer, can make arrangements to transfer the inmate to their jurisdiction. The maximum score is 6. Bill has no current detainers. He gets 0 points here.

7. *Prior Felony Convictions.* This is a simple summation of prior felony convictions. Do not include the current offense. The maximum score is 4. Again, Bill is not assessed any points since the current offense is his first.

8. *Stability Factors.* Each item should be verified prior to scoring. This is the only area in which the scores are cumulative, thus resulting in a possible score of "minus" 4. Bill would receive the maximum points for stability factors. He was twenty-six or over at the time of his offense ("minus" 2), he is a high school graduate ("minus" 1), and he had been employed for more than six months at the time of his arrest ("minus" 1). If this section were scored regardless of the custody score, Bill would have a total of 12 "minus" 4 = 8 points. This would place him in medium rather than maximum custody. The classification committee well might decide to override the custody classification score and place him in medium custody.

After sections one through eight of the instrument have been completed, sum the scores to provide a score that is used to determine custody level. Recall that a score of 10 or more points in sections 1 through 4 results in close-custody classification. If the score in sections 1 through 4 is 9 or less, the score is totaled with the scores in sections 5 through 8. If the final score is 7 or more, the inmate will be assigned to medium custody. If the score is 6 or less, the assignment will be to minimum custody.

Needs Classification. Identification of the inmate's needs is based on all gathered data, and the inmate's own perceptions of his or her programming needs. During initial assessment interviews and testing, staff should elicit from inmates their ideas of what they need to become productive citizens. Areas of primary concern are educational, vocational, and medical needs, mental abilities, psychological problems, and substance abuse problems. The instrument reflects the fact that an individual's perceptions of his or her needs are somewhat subjective. For this reason, it is imperative that a high-quality classification interview is conducted by personnel thoroughly trained in the process (see the Initial Inmate Classification in the Appendix).

Following the risk and needs classifications, the classification committee will summarize the findings. Included in the summary will be the custody level and score, any override considerations and justifications for them, a final custody level assignment, and program and job assignment recommendations (*see* the Initial Classification Summary, which is part of the Initial Inmate Classification in the Appendix).

ADULT INTERNAL MANAGEMENT SYSTEM (AIMS)

Herbert C. Quay developed a classification system called the AIMS model that differs substantially from the National Institute of Corrections' (NIC) model. Quay's model relies on observable behavior patterns as assessed by correctional staff and integrates the documented behavioral history addressed by the NIC model. This system of classification was adapted from an earlier model designed by Quay for use in the Florida juvenile corrections system, and has been used in the form discussed here, by the Federal Bureau of Prisons as well as by some states.

Figure 8.4
Characteristic Behaviors by Group

I ——————Heavy—————— II		III Moderate	IV ——————Light——————V	
Aggressive	Sly	Not excessively aggressive or dependent	Dependent	Constantly afraid
Confrontational	Not directly confrontational	Reliable, cooperative	Unreliable	Anxious
Easily bored Hostile to authority	Untrustworthy Hostile to authority	Industrious Do not see selves as criminals	Easily upset Clinging	Passive Seek protection
High rate of disciplinary infractions	Moderate-to-high rate of disciplinary infractions	Low rate of disciplinary infractions	Low-to-moderate rate of disciplinary infractions	Moderate rate of disciplinary infractions
Little concern for others	Con artists, manipulative	Concern for others	Self-absorbed	Explosive under stress
Victimizers	Victimizers	Avoid fights	Easily victimized	Easily victimized

The AIMS model establishes five groups based on the behavioral characteristics of inmates (see Figure 8.4). These groups are identified as Groups I and II ("heavy"), Group III ("moderate"), and Groups IV and V ("light"). The terms "heavy," "moderate," and "light" allude to prison jargon that describe a perceived risk, threat, or the propensity to victimize other inmates or to be victimized. The basic idea behind the AIMS model is that classifying inmates according to behavioral characteristics can greatly enhance differential treatment modalities.

Under the risk classification model already examined, all five of the AIMS groups may be represented in each custody level. The unspoken assumption behind custody classification based on type of crime is that those who commit similar crimes are similar in terms of more general behavioral traits. At all custody levels, there are a wide variety of behavioral types. There are those who are victimized and those who victimize. The vast majority of inmates, however, are found between these extremes. Also, within each custody level, it is necessary to provide programs that are duplicated at other levels. AIMS classification is an attempt to discriminate more meaningfully among prisoners so that mixing victimizers and victims does not occur and so that programs are not unnecessarily duplicated. This should result in a reduction of prison violence and an increase in program effectiveness.

CORRECTIONAL ADJUSTMENT CHECKLIST

Dr. Quay has devised two very simple checklists, the Correctional Adjustment Checklist (CACL) and the Checklist for Analysis of Life History (CALH), (both shown in the Appendix) that, when transferred to appropriate scoresheets (also shown in the Appendix) provide a raw classification score. The raw score then is converted through the use of conversion tables into what statisticians call T-scores. This is not the place to go into detail about the derivation of T-scores. Suffice it to say that they are raw scores that have been mathematically standardized to achieve comparability of scores from distributions of raw scores that are dissimilarly shaped. Quay (1984:34) says: "The intent of the checklist is to cover adequately as possible the domain of behaviors that might forecast adjustment and program participation in correctional settings."

To develop the Correctional Adjustment Checklist (CACL), Quay solicited behavioral descriptions from professional correctional practitioners and from mental health professionals with correctional experience. He also incorporated descriptions developed from his own research with juveniles. The checklist contains forty-one behavior descriptions. The CACL tends to identify behavioral extremes of aggressiveness or submission.

In practice, line correctional personnel—that is, the staff that has the most contact with inmates—complete the CACL. Then, the form is submitted to the classification staff for scoring. The scores place inmates in either the "aggressive-manipulation" group (Groups I and II) or the "passive-inadequate" group (Groups IV and V). Group III inmates are not identified by the CACL instrument inasmuch as their behavior is generally acceptable within the prison environment.

Checklist for the Analysis of Life History

The source of data for the Checklist for the Analysis of Life History (CALH) is the presentence investigation report. Quay asserts that the descriptions that should be readily available from the PSI report and from the casework interview can be used to gauge the degree of institutional adjustment and program participation of the inmate (1984:36). The classification staff completes the CALH and assigns inmates to groups on the basis of their scores.

After completing both the CACL and the CALH raw-score forms, the classification committee transfers the data to the Classification Profile for Adult Offenders and converts the raw scores to T-scores (see these forms in the Appendix). Then, the T-scores are combined to provide a final classification of the inmate.

As a correctional practitioner, this author believes that the AIMS classification method provides an excellent management tool for the differential assignment of inmates to programs. Studies have shown that it discriminates very well among the inmate behavioral types. Group I inmates are involved in serious disciplinary problems more often than those in other groups, and Group III inmates generally are not involved in violent disturbances and present fewer management problems overall. However, this author would be loath to substitute it entirely for the risk classification tools provided by the NIC's model.

For example, an inmate convicted of homicide, having no prior contact with the criminal justice system, would be classified as a close-custody inmate under the NIC's model. However, it is conceivable that the same inmate could qualify as a Group III inmate (equated with minimum-custody level) solely on the basis of the AIMS criteria. Given the current public mentality regarding incarceration, it is extremely doubtful that we could justify placing a convicted murderer in minimum custody at initial classification.

Figure 8.5 summarizes the process of classification starting with the presentence report and ending with the initial classification of an inmate to custody level, job assignment, and various programs aimed at his or her institutional adjustment and personal improvement.

Figure 8.5
The Process of Classification

Summary

In this chapter, we briefly looked at what prison classification is, why we classify prisoners, and how it is accomplished. Classification of prisoners is the differential assignment of people to varying levels of security: maximum, close, medium, and minimum. The determination of custody level is influenced primarily by the risk that the prisoner presents to the safe and orderly operation of an institution. Custody classification is related to security classification, and the classification level affects an inmate's access to various counseling, educational, vocational, and recreational programs. A general observation is that program access varies inversely with security and custody levels—as security is increased, program access is decreased.

Professional organizations such as the American Correctional Association and the National Institute of Corrections have been influential in the development of classification standards and models for implementing those standards.

Modern classification procedures have been influenced by the judiciary and by the various human sciences. These influences have resulted in some classification procedures that go beyond the concern for institutional security. Various testing and assessment tools have been developed, which can be used by correctional administrators to evaluate prisoners in terms of their personalities, needs, and potentialities. We briefly examined the GATB, WAIS, MMPI, HSLI, and MBTI instruments.

There are numerous classification methods in use, most of which are hybrids of the two models (NIC and AIMS) presented here. As new data become available through research, we will see the development of more efficient and effective classification systems, just as evolution occurs in the more advanced fields.

REFERENCES AND SUGGESTED READINGS

Allen, H. and C. Simonsen. 2001. *Corrections in America*. New York: Macmillan.

American Correctional Association. 1981. *Classification* (monograph, series no. 1). Lanham, Maryland: American Correctional Association.

_____. 1982. *Classification as a Management Tool: Theories and Models for Decision Makers* . Lanham, Maryland: American Correctional Association.

_____. 1990. *Standards for Adult Correctional Institutions*. Lanham, Maryland: American Correctional Association.

American Psychiatric Association.1994. *Diagnostic and Statistical Manual of Mental Disorders, 4th edition*. Washington, D.C.: American Psychiatric Association.

Andrews, D. and J. Bonta. 1998. *The Psychology of Criminal Conduct*. Cincinnati, Ohio: Anderson Publishing.

Brennan, S. A., S. A. Mednick, and J. Volavka. 1995. Biomedical Factors in Crime. In J. Q. Wilson and J. Petersilia, eds. *Crime*. San Francisco: ICS Press.

Farrington, D. 1987. Predicting Individual Crime Rates. In M. R. Gottfredson and D. M. Gottfredson, eds. *Decision Making in Criminal Justice: Toward the Rational Exercise of Discretion*. New York: Plenum Press.

Jeffery, C. 1979. *Biology and Crime*. Beverly Hills, California: Sage.

Keirsey, D. and M. Bates. 1984. *Please Understand Me: Character and Temperament Types*. Del Mar, California: Prometheus Nemesis.

Korn, R. and L. McCorkle. 1959. *Criminology and Penology*. New York: Holt, Rinehart, Winston.

Lauen, R. 1997. *Positive Approaches to Corrections: Research, Policy and Practice*. Lanham, Maryland: American Correctional Association.

Lewis, O. 1967. *The Development of American Prisons and Prison Customs, 1776-1845*. Montclair, New Jersey: Patterson-Smith.

Morris, N., M. Miller, and P. March. 1987. *Predictions of dangerousness in the criminal law. Research in Brief*. Washington, D.C.: National Institute of Justice.

Myers, I. and M. McCaulley. 1985. *A Guide to the Development and Use of the Myers-Briggs Type Indicator*. Palo Alto, California: Consulting Psychological Press.

National Institute of Corrections. 1984. *Prison Classification: A Model Systems Approach*. Washington, D.C.: National Institute of Corrections.

Nigg, J. and H. Goldsmith.1998. Developmental psychopathology, personality, and temperament: Reflections on recent behavioral genetics research. *Human Biology*. 70:387-412.

Proctor, J. L. 1994. Evaluating a modified version of the federal prison system's inmate classification model: An assessment of objective and predictive validity. *Criminal Justice and Behavior*. 21:256-272.

Raine, A. 1997. Antisocial behavior and psychophysiology: A biosocial perspective and a prefrontal dysfunction hypothesis. In D. Stoff, J. Breiling, and J. Maser, eds. *Handbook Of Antisocial Behavior*. New York: John Wiley. pp. 289-304.

Reiss, A. and J. Roth. 1993. *Understanding and Preventing Violence*. Washington, D.C.: National Academy Press.

Steadman, H. 1987. How Well Can We Predict Violence for Adults? A Review of the Literature and Some Commentary. In F. Dutile and C. Foust, eds. *The Prediction of Criminal Violence*. Springfield, Illinois: Charles C Thomas.

Steel, B. and M. Steger. 1988. Crime: Due Process Liberalism Versus Law-and-Order Conservatism. In R. Tatalovich and B. Daynes, eds. *Social Regulatory Policy: Moral Controversies in American Politics*. Boulder, Colorado: Westview Press.

Quay, H. 1984. *Managing Adult Inmates.* Lanham, Maryland: American Correctional Association.

Van Voorhis, P. 1988. A cross classification of five offender typologies: Issues of construct and predictive validity. *Criminal Justice and Behavior.* 15:109-124.

_____. 1994. *Psychological Classification of the Adult Male Prison Inmate.* New York: SUNY.

Walsh, A. 2000. Behavior genetics and anomie/strain theory. *Criminology.* 38:1075-1107.

Nondirective Counseling:
Theory and Practice

Love is the increase of self by means of other.

Spinoza

Robert Martinson's article "What Works? Questions and Answers about Prison Reform" (1974) provided much grist for the mills of those who subscribe to a "lock 'em up and lose the key" philosophy. Many politicians were so excited about Martinson's alleged findings that the rhetorical "what works?" was translated into the nihilistic "nothing works." Thus, the Martinson report was interpreted as a justification for terminating all efforts to rehabilitate criminals in favor of punishing them, preferably by long periods of incarceration.

Disregarding the fact that Martinson (1979) had the courage to admit that he was wrong in 1974, and disregarding the fact that to incarcerate all convicted criminals is financially prohibitive (*see* Walker's (2001) excellent analysis of the financial waterfall needed to implement this philosophy), to consign all convicted criminals to prison is both morally inhumane and socially insane. Nearly all incarcerated felons will leave prison someday, and they will emerge harder, crueler, more savage, and more bitter than they were before they went into prison. We already incarcerate more people in the United States than does any other country (Reuters, 2000). Yet, the call for longer terms of punishment for more people continues to fall on receptive ears. In 1999, American taxpayers spent almost $24 billion on institutional corrections for approximately 2 million inmates.

Of course, many correctional programs did not work for a variety of reasons. Addressing this issue of program failure, Gendreau and Ross, two researchers in the forefront of efforts to revive the rehabilitation ideal, write:

> The programs recorded in the literature which have failed (and earned treatment a bad name) did so because they were derived from conceptual models (e.g., psychiatric, nondirective counseling methods, clinical sociology) that made little sense in terms of offender populations or were applied to inappropriate target populations or sought to effect behaviors which were unrelated to crime. They failed because they were badly managed, because they were not sufficiently intensive, and because they employed staff who were inadequately skilled, who exerted insufficient effort or who were not aware or supportive of the program's techniques and goals (1981:47).

What Gendreau and Ross are saying is that rehabilitative efforts must be based on "tried and true" theories and methods geared to the specific clientele (which does not mean that the methods they mention as ineffective have nothing at all to offer), and must be conducted by caring individuals who fully believe in what they are doing. A review of studies assessing probation success rates found tremendous variability in success rates ranging from a low of 35 percent to a high of 70 percent (Morgan, 1995). Other reviews of studies with stricter criteria for success find recidivism rates lowered by between 8 and 10 percent (Palmer, 1994; Andrews and Bonta, 1998). At least some of that variability was attributable to the diverse treatment styles of individual probation departments, but most was attributable to supervision styles (how tolerant the department was of minor violations, and so on) and to the differing levels of probation eligibility in each jurisdiction.

Before we can determine that something does or does not work, we first have to define thresholds. A rehabilitation program is not a machine that either works or does not when the switch is pulled. Where human beings are concerned, nothing works for everybody, and nothing will ever work for everybody all the time. If it did, we would not be the kind of beings that we are; we would all be programmed robots. So, when we make statements about programs working or not working, we certainly are not demanding that they work for everybody all of the time.

What rate of success is acceptable before we say a program works: 90 percent, 80 percent, 50 percent, 10 percent? Of the 231 studies that Martinson included in his review, he found that 48 percent reported *some* degree of success. If your criterion for success is a demanding 100 percent, then, indeed, nothing works. For this author's part, a 48 percent success rate (however "success" was defined in the original studies) is cause for optimistic celebration.

Walker (2001) reports that other reviews of the kind of studies reviewed by Martinson found success rates between 67 and 77 percent. In a later review of rehabilitative programs, Gendreau and Ross (1987) found evidence for a great deal of success. They conclude their review by stating that "it is downright ridiculous to say that 'Nothing works.' This review attests that much is going on to indicate that offender rehabilitation has been, can be, and will be achieved" (1987:395). Other commentators have stated the belief that properly run community based programs could possibly result in a 30 to 50 percent reduction in recidivism (Van Vooris, Braswell, and Lester, 2000). Such figures probably are overly optimistic on the basis of major meta-analytic reviews, which tend to suggest reductions more in the 10 to 20 percent range (reviewed in Cullen and Gendreau, 2000). Nevertheless, we have enough evidence to dismiss the pessimism of the "nothing works" crowd and explore counseling theories designed to help those caught up in the criminal justice system come to grips with their problems.

Counseling

WHAT CORRECTIONAL COUNSELING IS NOT

"Beware of helpers. Helpers are con men who promise you something for nothing. They spoil you and keep you dependent," according to John Stratton, an experienced supervising probation officer, in his insightful essay on "counseling con men" quoting Fritz Perls (1975:125). It is a statement that all who aspire to a helping profession should consider. We enter the so-called helping professions with noble motives, and it makes us feel good to "help" the troubled and the less fortunate. But the point of helping is not to make us feel good; rather, it is to help offenders to help themselves to feel better and to become more productive members of society. We never should do for offenders what they are capable of doing for themselves, or we risk fostering offender dependence, an inability to be responsible and to stand on their own two feet, and, to use a current buzz word, we "enable" them to persist in their self-destructive and immature behavior. This is not true helping or counseling behavior.

Certainly, offenders can be allowed to lean on us, but only if they lean on us to lift themselves. However, too many corrections counselors view their role as designed to "straighten out" offenders' behavior and to "adjust" their attitudes. They attempt to do this via a series of directives and well-meaning "advice." There is indeed much about correctional casework that is coercive in the sense that we must restrain and constrain offenders. But in exercising such restraint and constraint, we will be far more successful if we treat offenders with respect and enlist their cooperation, just as we would if we were engaged in counseling in a noncoercive setting, say, in marriage counseling where there is no authoritative relationship between counselor and clients.

Advice giving also must be avoided in a counseling situation unless specifically requested. As Meier states: "Friends and family give advice; counselors generally don't, particularly in the initial stages of relationship building" (1989:19). Even advice from family and friends is usually not too well received or attended to unless it is requested—uninvited advice often irritates and angers. As authority figures, we can force our advice on offenders and even force them to follow through with it, but meaningful and lasting results only can be achieved if offenders are personally convinced of its usefulness. Learning and discovery ultimately can come only from within; that is the real task confronting the counselor.

WHAT COUNSELING IS

Our first task is to differentiate between the terms counseling and psychotherapy. Some claim that there is no essential difference between the two terms since their definitions and roles are interchangeable. Further, the theories presented in a text in counseling are the same theories contained in a text on psychotherapy. However, in keeping with this author's early advice to respect boundaries of expertise, he stresses the differences between the two.

Psychotherapy is practiced by psychiatrists or clinical psychologists with many years of highly specialized training. True, they employ many of the same techniques used by those engaged in counseling, but they have a deeper theoretical understanding of causality pertaining to the conditions they are treating.

The term *treating* delineates another important distinction between psychotherapy and counseling. Psychotherapists operate with a pathological interpretation of their patients' problems; counselors are advised to operate with a deficiency interpretation of offenders' problems. Psychotherapy differs from counseling in the depth and seriousness of the problems dealt with and in the intensity of the treatment. If we laid all the psychiatrists and psychologists in the world out couch to couch, we would not have near enough to treat all our criminals, the vast majority of whom do not require "treating." That is why we need counselors.

Counselors attempt to help offenders with specific life-adjustment problems and to develop the personality that already exists. Psychotherapists attempt to help their patients by a restructuring of the basic personality over a long period of time. Another way of stating this difference might be to say that psychotherapists deal primarily with intrapersonal conflicts, whereas counselors deal primarily with interpersonal conflicts. When an offender is obviously in need of treatment that exceeds your capability as a counselor, you should not hesitate to relinquish the further handling of the case to those more qualified to deal with it.

SIMILARITY BETWEEN INTERVIEWING AND COUNSELING

Counseling is a series of concerned responses offered to offenders who have concerns and problems that adversely affect their functioning. Counseling is essentially an extension of the interviewing process and uses the same communications skills and techniques. However, "techniques" are secondary to the warmth, acceptance, and understanding the counselor brings to the task. Open, warm, accepting, and empathetic counselors operating with different theoretical perspectives are more similar to each other than are good and poor counselors with the same theoretical perspective (Austin, 1999). In other words, all the counseling methods and theories we will examine are only as good as the person putting them into practice. If you work on improving the quality of the self you bring to the counseling process, then the techniques should come easily to you.

DIFFERENCES BETWEEN INTERVIEWING AND COUNSELING

Although counseling is an extension of the interviewing process, certain differences between interviewing and counseling in a criminal justice setting should be emphasized. First, you are more likely to encounter offender resistance during the counseling process than during the interviewing process. During the presentence investigation interview or parole hearing, offenders are fairly anxious to reveal a contrite and cooperative demeanor because they know that you make recommendations. After a case has been disposed of, offenders tend to lose some of their motivation to cooperate along with the anxiety about the disposition of the case. This tendency is a good reason to make the best possible effort to establish a working rapport during the initial interview. If you do not establish such a relationship when the offender is fairly amenable, you will find rapport much more difficult to develop later. Do not be disheartened if you do perceive a change in some offenders' demeanor following case disposition. Accept it as a professional challenge.

Second, assuming that you are successful in establishing a working relationship with offenders, you are ready to communicate with them at a deeper level in successive counseling sessions by carefully developing an empathetic understanding of them. You no longer have to gather large amounts of data from them, so you are free to concentrate on specific problem areas. Therefore, counseling differs from interviewing in its depth.

So, what is correctional counseling? William Lewis, a psychologist with many years of experience counseling offenders, defines correctional counseling to be "ongoing, positive, interpersonal relationships as the vehicle through which a variety of systematic verbal techniques can be applied to increase the counselee's *feelings* of self-satisfaction, *and* improve his [or her] *actual* social adjustments" (1989:71, emphasis in original). The correctional worker who can follow these requirements has a positive and integrated sense of self and can serve as a model of growth-inducing interpersonal relationships.

Counseling Theories

With this brief introduction to counseling, we turn to five of the most popular theories of counseling, two in this chapter, two in the next, and one with a chapter of its own. Important aspects of counseling will be illustrated in the context of the theories that most strongly emphasize those aspects. Special attention will be paid to the processes of generating rapport and empathy and to the techniques for dealing with reluctant/resisting offenders.

You may view the large number of theoretical orientations to counseling (and there are certainly far more than the five presented here) in two ways. You may consider it to be so much clutter, indicative of a lack of scientific rigor in the field. Alternatively, you may regard it positively as a rich mine of possibilities in which you can dig for counseling gems. No one theory is applicable to all problems and concerns with which you will deal, and no one theory exhausts the uniqueness of each offender. Remember what a sage once said: "Each person is like all other persons, like some other persons, and like no other person." It follows that certain insights from one counseling theory may be universally applicable, be applicable only some of the time, or not be applicable at all on some occasions. The more theoretical insights you have in your repertoire, the better you will be able to respond successfully to the diverse offenders and problems you will encounter. Loyalty to any one theory may severely limit your effectiveness by leading you to stretch everything to fit it and/or to ignore whatever will not work. Good counselors develop a unique, flexible, and workable style of their own.

Studies of professional counselors find that the plurality of them (30 to 40 percent) think of themselves as eclectic or "integrative" counselors (reviewed in Austin, 1999). By developing an eclectic approach, picking and choosing those elements that fit your style and serve your needs, you will begin to discern some of the common threads woven into all theories. It is my contention that the agreement of greatest importance among all theories is the vital necessity of all human beings to love and be loved.

The present chapter focuses on psychoanalysis and client-centered counseling. Psychoanalysis and client-centered counseling are nondirective forms of counseling. They put great faith in their patients' or clients' ability to discover their own capabilities and find their own directions. Counselors play a relatively passive role and are reluctant to impose their values on patients/clients and provide them with direction. Psychoanalysis and client-centered therapy rarely are used in a correctional setting, primarily because they are too nondirective, and because the terminology and concepts are too abstruse, and the methods are difficult for the nonspecialist to apply. They have been included, nonetheless, because of certain unique aspects, to be outlined as we continue.

Psychoanalysis → Role of past

Psychoanalysis is the seminal therapy/counseling theory from which all others evolved. Although psychoanalysis is beyond the boundaries of expertise for the nonpsychiatrist or nonpsychologist, it contains some very useful insights into the nature of human beings. Whereas the other four theories focus primarily on the present, psychoanalysis puts great emphasis on the role of the past in shaping current behavior. Since so many emotional and behavioral difficulties stem to a large degree from past experiences, it is important to be aware of and explore offenders' pasts as a vehicle for understanding their present. However, this author rejects the notion that the past *determines* present behavior or that people are "victims" of their past.

According to Fine, "The technical task of psychoanalysis has been to elucidate the nature of love" (1973:16). Freud himself has stated that happiness exists in "the way of life which makes love the center of everything, which looks for all satisfaction in loving and being loved" (1961:29). The psychoanalyst explores patients' childhoods to uncover underlying reasons for their inability to love.

The psychoanalytic theory of the tripartite structure of the personality—the id, the ego, and the superego—is too well known to warrant extensive treatment here. The id is the biological source of the organism's energy and the driving force of the personality. Its only goal is to seek gratification of its urges—to seek pleasure and to avoid pain. The superego acts as the counterforce to the id by exercising socially derived moral prescriptions and proscriptions. We call individuals who give free reign to the id nasty names such as "psychopaths" or "criminals," and we call individuals with a powerful superego slightly less offensive names such as "neurotic" or "conformist." The ego synthesizes the biological and social demands on the organism. Well-balanced people have strong egos and are able to obtain gratification of their id drives within the bounds of moral restrictions placed on them by their superego (their conscience).

The value of Freud's theory of personality lies in the recognition of both the "beast and the angel in man." The bestial side of humanity is the side that most concerns the criminal justice worker. As a criminal justice worker, you are striving to assist offenders in understanding themselves, and to enlist that understanding in the task of strengthening the rational ego "so that it can appropriate fresh portions of the id. Where an id was, there shall ego be" (Freud, 1965:80). This emphasis on the ego's control of impulses emanating from the id is reminiscent of Gottfredson and Hirschi's (1990) emphasis on the importance of self-control.

PSYCHOSEXUAL STAGES development of personality

Psychoanalysis stresses the great importance of the so-called psychosexual stages involved in early character development. There are three such stages: oral, anal, and phallic (other stages have been identified, but the first three generally are considered the most important in terms of their effects on personality development). Each stage represents the child's first encounters with external restraints on natural urges coming from the id. These encounters generate negative feelings in the child, such as hostility, hatred, anger, and destructiveness. Since the display of these feelings invites negative reactions from other people, the child learns to repress them, resulting in a later inability to accept and express his or her real feelings. This barrier to self-knowledge must be breached in any counseling session.

ORAL STAGE: FROM BIRTH TO AGE ONE *love/security* *if this does not happen could have problems*

The oral stage encompasses the first year of life. This is the period of life in which the child learns love and security and in which the template for the child's basic personality is formed. At the mother's breast, the infant satisfies its hunger and needs for tactile stimulation. These are unconditioned needs (needs which do not have to be learned), the satisfaction of which the infant "loves" because they are intrinsically rewarding. When the infant identifies the source of its pleasure, it develops a love for that source that is stronger than the love of the pleasures the source affords. In this sense, love for mother is a sort of conditioned response due to the continual associations made between her and the pleasures she provides.

According to this theory, negative behaviors, such as acquisitiveness and aggression, are substitutes for what the individual really needs—love. Unloved individuals feel unworthy, unwanted, and unaccepted and are mistrusting and rejecting of others. They cannot accept either themselves or others because they have not experienced acceptance. Early love experiences are a safeguard against this type of negativism. This does not mean, of course, that all people who exhibit these negative characteristics have experienced an unloving childhood, or that individuals who did experience an unloving childhood necessarily will exhibit them. The theory merely asserts that negative adult behaviors are more likely to characterize those individuals who experienced a childhood marked by a lack of love than to characterize those individuals who did not.

Reread the early life experiences of Bill Bloggs in the presentence investigation report. Can we not see his extreme materialism and bursts of aggressive behavior as stemming from his lack of love during the oral stage of his life? By his own admission, he was quite socially isolated and sought to win Susan's love by purchasing things?

ANAL STAGE: AGE ONE THROUGH THREE *discipline* *potty training → first time f* *discipline*
self control & accomplishment

In the anal stage, the child first encounters discipline. The child has received a series of admonitions prior to this stage, such as "Don't touch that oven!" or "Stop biting the cat!" But children encounter "real" discipline in the anal stage. They learn disciplined self-mastery by learning control of bodily functions through toilet training. Toilet training is given such importance in psychoanalytic theory because it is the first time that the children have to suppress natural urgings until they can be satisfied in the appropriate way and in the appropriate place.

While the child tends to rebel against the unnaturalness of toilet training, when the training is completed, he or she takes pride in the mastery of accomplishment. Parents should encourage this sense of mastery by allowing the child to explore and to make mistakes. They should emphasize that it is okay to make mistakes if one learns from them. If parents are constantly critical of mistakes that the child makes, the child will be reluctant to explore and expand. If parents show exaggerated concern and do everything for the child, the child will not develop a sense of independence

Self-esteem comes from this stage

and autonomy. The children of such parents may be stuck forever in a "no-can-do" mode, lacking the self-confidence to expand their horizons and possessing poor self concepts.

It is easy to view Bill's parents, especially his father, being hypercritical of him during his formative years, given the description of their personalities provided by Officer Corrick. Bill's whole life seemed to revolve around doing things to please his father. He did not leave home until he met Susan, indicating a strong sense of dependency. His hanging of the kitten, his bursts of extreme temper, and, not the least, his shooting of a policeman point vividly to his inability to express his feelings appropriately.

PHALLIC STAGE: AGES THREE THROUGH FIVE

[handwritten: entcounters Pleasure w/ body to catching child masturbating] *[handwritten: Depends on how mother responds]*

The phallic stage is a period of early development of conscience and sex-role identification. During this stage, children become aware of their genitals. Masturbation commonly is begun during this stage, and parental response to the discovery of this activity can have serious consequences. If parents are overly moralistic, defining masturbation as something that "nice boys and girls don't do," they are setting the stage for the overcontrol of the superego. Such a rigid conformity to puritanical morality also may preclude the enjoyment of intimacy with others later in life because of inadequate sex-role identification.

We have no information about Bill's experiences during this stage in his life, but it takes no great flight of imagination to see Bill's father as a real authoritarian moralist where the behavior of others was concerned. Bill did have a great deal of difficulty forming intimate attachments with others, and perhaps his belief that he was a woman in his "previous existence" is indicative of sex-role ambiguity. Bill's later forced incestuous experiences would have conflicted seriously with any early development of a moralistic conscience. Bill did have, to say the least, a quite unusual view of reality.

DEFENSE MECHANISMS

[handwritten: Part of psychoanalysis is D.F. We suppress things that are uncomfortable. e fine there to protect us.]

The identification of a patient's defense mechanisms is an important part of the psychotherapeutic process. Defense mechanisms, which operate at an unconscious level (the individual is unaware of them), function to protect the ego from a threatening reality by distorting it. Defense mechanisms are not necessarily pathological. We all use some of them to some extent, and they even can be psychologically adaptive. Only when they become an integral part of a pattern of life leading one to avoid facing reality do they become matters of great concern. Numerous defense mechanisms are listed in the psychoanalytic literature. Any comprehensive listing of them is beyond the scope of this book. We will discuss only those most commonly seen in a criminal justice setting.

Denial is the blocking out of a portion of reality that is threatening to the ego. Sexual feelings and activities often are subject to this defense mechanism. Otherwise quite respectable child molesters often will attempt to deny to themselves that the incident ever occurred. This is not simply "forgetting" (repression), but rather refusing to recognize that it happened. Bill's denial of his enuresis may be seen as an attempt to deal with the residual anxiety felt about being "hog tied" and whipped when he wet his bed, and his statement that his incestuous experiences were "no big deal" can be seen as an attempt to divorce himself from the possibility that he could have welcomed them.

Rationalization is the process of providing oneself with acceptable reasons for one's behavior or one's experiences in order to soothe a damaged ego. This is a definite favorite of offenders. Bill recited a litany of experiences to make Officer Corrick understand "some underlying reason(s) for my behavior," thus creating the impression that he was more wronged than wrong. Rationalization helps us to maintain an acceptable self-image by downplaying our own badness and/or inadequacies. We parcel out blame or devalue what we may want but cannot get ("I didn't get the job because this is a racist society and I'm black. Who wants that stupid job anyway?").

Fixation is being immobilized at an earlier stage of personality development because the more appropriate stage is fraught with anxiety. Many offenders have a childlike attachment to the present because stepping into the future is stepping into the great unknown. Many have developed a pattern of helplessness through their dependence on the welfare system, which is the only financial "parent" many have ever known. To go out and expand one's capacities and explore one's potential is not one of the lessons imparted by the culture of poverty. As a criminal justice helper, you are charged with helping offenders to develop a realistic orientation to the future by attempting to enlarge their sense of self-worth and their sense of the possible.

Displacement is the transference of feelings about someone or something onto another person or object because the original person or object is either inaccessible or too powerful. Anger or aggression often is displaced onto the innocent. Wife and child battering frequently is displaced aggression generated by others too powerful to attack directly. All too often one finds that offenders have much pent-up anger, the source of which they find difficult to identify. Further, they have not learned to express their feelings in appropriate ways, so they vent them on "safe" targets. Bill's explosive temper and the hanging of the kitten would be interpreted by the psychoanalyst as an expression of the anger he felt toward his father being displaced on nonthreatening targets.

Intellectualization is a process of using arguments to deflect the blame from themselves by pointing out how others should be blamed. Some of the better educated offenders are quite adept in the use of intellectualization. They often will attempt to assail legal reality by intellectualizing their crimes away. The marijuana dealer who launches into a monolog accusing society of hypocrisy, the petty forger who cites chapter and verse on white-collar crime, and the thief who discourses plausibly on corporate irresponsibility are all examples of people trying to avoid the reality of their own malfeasance. You certainly may accept the legitimacy of their position, but you also must impress on such offenders that the issue is their behavior and not that of others, and that they cannot avoid confronting their behavior by trying to refocus the discussion elsewhere. *somebody else did something worse. helps w/ legal*

Projection is the mechanism by which people attribute to others the feelings they refuse to see in themselves. One is often most troubled by the behavior of others when it mimics one's own repressed urges. The rough treatment of child molesters in prisons may be viewed as an attempt by other inmates to convince themselves that they could not possibly harbor such evil urges themselves. Offenders who feel that no one understands or likes them, who harbor hostility toward others, are projecting onto others their negative feelings about themselves, thereby protecting the ego by confusing self with other. So many expressions of hostility and hatred of the world by criminal justice offenders are really expressions of self-hatred. If you can aid offenders to develop more positive feelings about themselves, you will find that they will develop better attitudes toward the world. *lacking sympathy for others.*

LESSONS AND CONCERNS

The primary usefulness of psychoanalytic theory for the criminal justice worker is that it provides insights that lead to a better understanding of offenders' struggles with themselves and with the outside world. An understanding of the defense mechanisms is particularly useful in understanding offender resistance to the helping process.

A little knowledge, it has been said, is dangerous. The criminal justice helper lacks the depth of training necessary to put the techniques of psychoanalysis into practice. To attempt to do so could result in negative consequences. Besides, it is too time consuming and involved. It is an approach better suited to folks seeking professional absolution for their sins and peccadillos, and who enjoy richer vocabularies and fatter wallets than the typical offender. Many psychiatrists and psychologists themselves have turned to more simplified methods to deal with the problems presented to them by the typical offender—methods that generally have been found to be more productive of change because few offenders require total personality restructuring. Sometimes the use of psychoanalysis for relatively minor life-adjustment problems is like swatting flies with a baseball bat. This is not, however, to belittle the often profound theoretical insights into human nature provided by this theory.

Client-centered Approach →client counselor relationship

Carl Rogers developed his client-centered (or person-centered) approach to counseling in response to the deficiencies he perceived in psychoanalysis. According to Austin (1999:16) Rogers' theory is favored over any other single counseling theory by professional counselors, and he has been ranked as the most influential psychotherapist by these same professionals (Ellis, 1996). Being an existentialist/humanist thinker, Rogers rejected the determinism of Freud's psychoanalytic theory in favor of self-determination and what he considered the natural goodness in humankind. Rather than viewing individuals as driven by irrational biological impulses (which Rogers saw as an intimation that humans were basically antisocial), this approach sees human beings as basically good, self-driven, and possessing an innate capacity for self-actualization (the tendency to become all that we are able to become). Self-destructive behavior and attitudes arise from faulty self-concepts and an inability to grasp the fundamental truth that we are free agents in charge of our own destinies. Although this type of thinking is somewhat Pollyannaish in that it refuses to see the beast in man, it is ennobling in its enunciation. The basic goal of client-centered therapy is to improve the self-concept.

Rogers' definition of counseling is as follows: "The process by which the structure of the self is relaxed in the safety of the relationship with the therapist, and the previously denied experiences are perceived and then integrated into an altered self" (1952:70). Client-centered therapy eschews searching for causes and the teaching of counseling techniques in favor of asserting the absolute primacy of the nature of the offender/counselor relationship (Austin, 1999). What counselors bring to the relationship in terms of the quality of the self is far more critical than what they do with it in terms of technique.

The absence of loving human relationships is the basic reason that isolated, alienated, lonely, and self-destructive offenders require the counselor's assistance. It follows that the offender must form such a positive relationship with at least one other person if anything meaningful is to be accomplished. That one other person is the counselor. Although the burden of discovering the true goodness of the self is placed squarely on the shoulders of the offender in this essentially nondirective form of counseling, the burden of establishing the kind of relationship in which it may be accomplished is placed on the counselor: "If I can provide a certain type of relationship, the other person will discover within himself the capacity to use that relationship for growth and change, and personal development will occur" (Rogers, 1961:33). The counselor functions as a midwife, wresting out of the offender the goodness that is already present and awaiting birth.

Can the correctional worker provide the "love" that Rogers feels so important? Unfortunately, the English language is such that the term *love* is either confined to romantic love or used indiscriminately as an intense form of liking ("I love golf," or "I just loved that movie."). William Lewis tells us how we can meet offenders' need for love: "A correctional worker can meet the need for love, for example, at the young adult level through such means as courtesy; showing genuine interest and concern; giving instructions in a friendly, respectful way (as opposed to grumpy or profane barking); giving honest praise for work well done; and asking for opinions and respecting them as worthwhile (1989:28). Let us define *love* in the corrections context as "an active concern for the well-being of another."

The only techniques of client-centered therapy are those we talked about before (Chapter 5): active listening, clarifying, and reflecting of feelings. Evans *et al.* (1989:3) characterize Rogers as the "listening counselor." If you were to watch a client-centered counselor at work, you would probably get the impression that nothing is occurring. The counselor simply listens intensely to the offender while making occasional verbalizations such as, "Yes, please go on,"Uh, huh," "Uhm," and "Once again, please," and with other signs of approval such as smiles and head nods. What is going on here is counselee reinforcement in the form of verbal and visual signs of approval, and such reinforcement is considered vital in the counseling process. Offenders tend to talk about those topics that are reinforced, and not to talk about topics that are not. Experiments demonstrate that people's verbal and nonverbal behavior can be shaped systematically in desired directions by such simple acts of reinforcement as these (Evan et al. 1989:5-6).

Rogers is much more concerned with the client/counselor relationship and the personal attributes of the counselor than with techniques. The three main attributes that the counselor must bring to the relationship are *unconditional positive regard, genuineness,* and *empathy.*

UNCONDITIONAL POSITIVE REGARD

According to Rogers, many negative self-feelings and psychological problems develop because others place conditions on their acceptance of us. They like us or love us "if" we are or "if" we do what they would like us to be or do. Since we all want to be liked, loved, and accepted, we tend to conform to these conditions. Our conformity to the expectations of others leads us to an inauthentic self-image. To function as psychologically healthy people, we must set our own standards of behavior and self-acceptance. We have the ability to be fully authentic human beings, but we first must experience this unconditional positive regard from at least one person. For Rogers, the counselor fills that role.

Unconditional positive regard occurs when the counselor communicates to the offender a full and genuine acceptance of his or her personhood, warts and all.

Acceptance must be uncontaminated by judgments of the offender's attitudes, feelings, or behavior as being wrong or bad. This does not mean that the counselor approves or accepts illegal or immoral behavior; it means that the offender's essential humanity is accepted and valued in spite of his or her attitudes and behavior. This acceptance allows offenders to be free to examine their own behavior in a nonthreatening setting. Thus, they themselves may arrive at the conclusion that their attitudes and behavior are self-defeating. Officer Corrick appears to have had a positive feeling about Bill Bloggs while at the same time soundly condemning his behavior in the presentence investigation report.

"Unconditional positive regard" is an ideal to be striving for and it is not an all-or-nothing requirement. It is most unrealistic to think that you can develop this type of relationship with all offenders, or even most of them. Any relationship between two people is a chemical mix that may blend or explode. Some offenders are downright determined to make your life as difficult as possible, and they will read only weakness or patronization into your efforts to establish a positive working relationship. Most, however, will respond to your warmth with warmth of their own. The degree to which you can achieve the kind of positive regard that Rogers talks about is largely the degree of success you will achieve in your efforts to turn around an offender's life. At the very least, you should respect the basic humanity of the offender. Be cautious, however, that the relationship does not become one in which the offender depends on you, or that you do not use the relationship possessively to fulfill your own needs for positive regard.

GENUINENESS

Counselors must be genuine (be completely themselves) with offenders. Counselors must accept and deal with all feelings, whether positive or negative, generated by their interaction with the offender. In short, counselors must be authentic in the presentation of self to the offender. Pretensions, game playing, and facades must be avoided. The displaying of false fronts means that the counselor feels a lack of congruence between the real and the public self, which is, according to this perspective, precisely the vulnerable state of the offender. Since it is the task of the counselor to help the offender become more aware of internal incongruities, is it highly desirable that the counselor present an integrated self to the offender. The ultimate aim of self-disclosure exercises for the neophyte counselor is to develop an authentic and congruent sense of self. The goal is that the counselor's authentic self should permeate freely into the offender.

Human genuineness or authenticity exists only on a continuum and must be developed. It is interesting to note the agreement among the giants of the human sciences on this subject of human authenticity. Freud, Marx, and Maslow, despite radically different ideological and theoretical orientations and concerns, all agree that the ability to love and be loved is the key to human authenticity (Walsh, 1986).

EMPATHY

Empathy is the counselor's capacity for participating in the feelings of the offender. Empathy implies more than an intellectual understanding of the offender's feelings. It goes beyond cognitive knowledge about the offender to fuse with the offender, and causes the counselor to experience the offender's feelings as if they were the counselor's own. This implies the kind of gut-level subjective understanding that is granted only to those who have walked in similar shoes. Mayeroff (1971:41-42) describes the empathetic ability thus:

> To care for another person, I must be able to understand him and his world as if I were inside it. I must be able to see, as it were, with his eyes what his world is like to him and how he sees himself. Instead of merely looking at him in a detached way from the outside, as if he were a specimen, I must be able to be with him in his world, "going" into his world in order to sense from the "inside" what life is for him, what he is striving to be and what he requires to grow.

This definition of empathy is like the definition of unconditional positive regard—beautiful in its conceptualization but probably impossible to attain in any absolute sense. Yet, many books on counseling contain statements such as "Respond to the client with empathy." This gives the beginning counselor the mistaken impression that "getting into" a client's frame of reference is not much more difficult than following instructions such as "Place block A on block B and click into place." This could be dangerously misleading and falsely reassuring.

DEVELOPING ACCURATE EMPATHY

Is empathy possible between persons of different races, social strata, and educational backgrounds? For example, can a white, middle-class, female, college-educated corrections worker really "participate" in the mind-set of a semiliterate street male who is of another race and social class? I believe that it is possible, but only in a limited sense. Such an ability does not come naturally or easily. You must work very hard to develop it, both by examining your own values, prejudices, and stereotypes and by assimilating as much knowledge as you possibly can about the causes and reasons why offenders live and behave the way they do. Your ability to empathize with offenders will increase in direct proportion to the time you spend in these endeavors. Even then, it may be counterproductive to convey to offenders the idea that you "understand" their problems until you have had a number of sessions with them in which you actively have listened to what they have to say. For this reason, empathy was not stressed in the chapter on interviewing, but listening was: active listening is the essential prerequisite to empathy.

Egan (1998) distinguishes between what he calls *basic* and *advanced* empathy, both of which he subsumes under the general term "accurate empathy." "Basic empathy involves *listening* to clients, *understanding* them and their concerns to the degree that this is possible, and *communicating* this understanding to them so that they might understand *themselves* more fully and act on that understanding" (1998:81, emphasis in original). For instance, basic empathy might involve communicating understanding of an offender's anger, depression, and anxiety, since these feelings are common to all people, regardless of their unique experiences.

Advanced-level empathy concerns not only what clients say but also what they imply or leave half-expressed. Skilled counselors "often see clearly what clients only half see and hint at" (Egan 1998:170). This is what Reich (1956) means by "listening with the third ear." However, we should distinguish between its use in an initial interview setting and in a counseling setting. In an interview setting, your primary task is the "assessment of offenders," and your secondary task is to prepare the groundwork for future counseling sessions. You are listening to what offenders are implying or leaving half-expressed to gain the best initial understanding you can of their background. In the initial interview, it is too early in your relationship to challenge offenders about what you think they are implying or half-expressing. You have very limited knowledge of offenders at that point, trust is not established, and you could be completely wrong in your judgments and interpretations. Even if you are right, offenders may not be ready to verify your insight at this time and may deny it. Once some facet of the offenders' deeply private self has been denied, it becomes more difficult for them to admit it at some later date. It is threatening and frightening to be forced to confront a negative feature of the self that formerly has been repressed. Do not risk erroneous assumptions or provoke the offender's denial by premature attempts at advanced empathy.

Empathy, then, is a series of responses rendered by the counselor with a developed sensitivity to the offender's unique set of feelings about the world and his or her place in it. In effect, you are thinking with offenders rather than about them. We will examine some responses using both forms of empathy in a criminal justice counseling session.

EXAMPLES OF EMPATHETIC RESPONSES

Remember, your responses are never neutral; they are either constructive or destructive. This is particularly important for offenders since they are stuck with you, for better or worse, during their period of correctional supervision. Constructive responses are those that involve offenders in self-exploration so that they may arrive at solutions to their troubles themselves. Fully involving offenders means accepting the reality of their problems and reflecting them back on them. For example, suppose that Fred comes to you and states that he finds his job (let us say he is a factory assembler) boring, unsatisfying, and unsuitable for his talents and ambitions. Furthermore, he tells you that he wants to quit. You want him to keep his job, knowing that jobs are difficult to find, that he has financial obligations, and that "the devil finds work for idle hands." You respond by saying: "Fred, you feel that your job makes you feel depressed and less than worthy and productive. I can understand that because I've had jobs that made me feel that way too. What is it in particular about your job that makes you feel depressed, Fred?"

What have you accomplished in these three sentences? First, you have recognized the reality of Fred's problem and the fact that it is a genuine concern for him. Second, you have reflected his feelings about the problem, thereby making him aware that you have correctly understood him. Third, you have shown empathy by self-disclosure of your similar experiences. This reinforces Fred's perception of your acceptance of the reality of the problem and gives him a feeling of commonality with you. This also will make Fred more receptive to the plan of action you will decide upon together, since you have modeled the plan in your own life experience. Fourth, you have probed further by the use of an open-ended question asking Fred to identify specific conditions, circumstances, or situations that arouse his negative feelings. Your response has generated a positive atmosphere, which will allow further discussion and exploration, leading, you hope, to a mutually acceptable plan of action for dealing with the problem. In short, you have made excellent use of accurate primary empathy.

Contrast the positive response to Fred's concern with the following negative response: "Fred, you're always complaining about something. This business about your job is all in your head. It does you no good to dwell on it. How can you expect a better job with your education? Besides, you can't quit without my permission, so relax and forget it, buddy."

What have you accomplished here? First, by responding from your frame of reference rather than Fred's, you have denied the reality of the problem and of his feelings about it. Second, you have denigrated him by calling him a complainer and belittling his education. Third, you have distanced yourself from him by (1) showing a lack of concern and understanding, (2) emphasizing differences in educational levels, and (3) emphasizing the relationship of authority that exists between you. Furthermore, by telling him to "relax and forget it," you have guaranteed that he will not. Instead, you will have exacerbated his negative feelings and left him to deal with them in a possibly destructive manner. You can bet that he will not come to you again with his concerns. In short, Fred will be influenced by the second response just as he would be influenced by the first. The second response, however, generates feelings in Fred that will be destructive to your relationship with him. Your lack of professional concern will make your job more difficult and demanding, and may cause Fred to quit his job despite your warning that he cannot. This, in turn, may lead to a technical violation or further criminality. The golden rule of counseling is "Treat offenders as you would wish to be treated."

Suppose Fred responds to your primary-level empathy with the following statements and nonverbal behaviors.

Fred is sitting with his folded hands resting on his thighs and looking at you (in a nondefensive, open, and trusting demeanor). "Well, Terry, I didn't mind the job so much when I was on days. It's this night shift stuff." Fred now straightens up, looks away, and raises his voice slightly (some defensiveness, embarrassment, and anger creeping in). "My wife complains that I don't spend enough time with her. We used to go out dancing once or twice a week, but now I can't because either I'm working, or I'm too damn tired on the weekend."

Fred sits up straight and grasps the arms of his chair. His face reddens a little, and his speech becomes faster and louder (a strengthening of his defensiveness, embarrassment, and anger). "She goes by herself, though. I don't like that, and I tell her so. We've had quite a few arguments about that crap."

You now come to realize that Fred's job is not the real cause of his depression. His more substantial concern is his wife's dissatisfaction, and his statement contains some significant intimations that he is concerned about the possibility that she may be doing more than just dancing with other men. You might engage in the following dialog with Fred.

> **Counselor:** Are you saying that it is not the job itself that you want to quit but, rather, you would like to get off the night shift? (Clarification)
> **Fred:** Yes, I think things might be better if I went back on days.
> **Counselor:** The night shift leaves you without much time or energy to devote to your wife, and this is causing some friction between you. (Paraphrase) You are angry and upset because she goes to the dance by herself. (Reflection)
> **Fred:** You bet I am! I've told her that it's not right for a married woman to go dancing by herself.
> **Counselor:** Fred, I can understand your annoyance with your wife, and I know that the two of you have talked about it. Why do you think she continues to go when you have told her that you dislike it? (Probe)
> **Fred:** I don't know. We get so mad at each other when we talk about it that I think she does it out of spite. (Angry arguments do have a way of leading one of the participants to act in uncharacteristic ways to "get back.")

Counselor: What do you think she would do if you let her know your feelings without getting upset? (Open-ended question designed to get Fred to think about his wife's possible reaction to a rational discussion of the problem rather than an emotional confrontation.)

Fred: I don't really know. We don't argue that much about other things. I don't mind her having some fun, but dancing? My wife's an attractive woman—I see the way that men look at her. (Fred's reply indicates, that except for this one issue, quarreling is not a major feature of his marriage. He quickly disposes of your question and gets down to his real concern.)

Counselor: You like your wife to enjoy herself, but you find it unsettling for her to do it in this way because she is in the company of other men. (Paraphrasing and reflecting) Am I hearing you say that you are concerned that one of her dance partners may make a play for her? I wonder if she realizes that she is hurting you this way. (Clarifying your perception of Fred's underlying feeling and using advanced empathy.)

Fred: I guess I'm kind of jealous. I really love Carla, and it eats me up inside to think that she might be playing around behind my back. I haven't admitted this to myself before today. I suppose I wasn't too eager to think about it. What do you think I should do, Terry? You've made me realize that I don't really want to quit my job—it pays good money and I have my restitution and fine to finish paying—but I don't want to lose Carla. (Fred is now asking for your advice, which up until now you have resisted giving. He will be more receptive now that he has explored the problem himself and has explicitly requested advice. You also have led him to identify for himself what he was feeling—jealousy. This is much better than simply coming out and asking him, "Do you feel jealous?" He may have denied the embarrassing feeling if you rather than he had approached the issue directly.)

Counselor: I do not think it's a question of either quitting your job or losing Carla. I might suggest two courses of action for you to think about. First, you could speak with your boss at work to see if there is any possibility at all of getting back on days, even if it means a different job and less pay. Regardless of whether or not this is possible, you could discuss your feelings openly with Carla as you have done with me. Do this without any hint of accusation or anger, and you will find that, more than likely, she will respond the same way. Since you seem to enjoy dancing yourself, try to arrange it so that the two of you can go together at least once a week. What do you think about these suggestions, Fred?

This exchange illustrates both basic and advanced level empathy. You went beyond the initial problem that Fred presented to you and probed for a deeper concern. You skillfully led him to explore feelings that he was reluctant to admit to himself, and you offered him, at his request, some helpful suggestions for dealing with them. It took a great deal more time than it would have taken to tell him to stop complaining, but you may have gone a long way in helping Fred to save his job and his marriage. Also, you probably have saved yourself time and trouble in the long run.

WHAT ACCURATE EMPATHY IS NOT

Now that you have a good idea of what accurate empathy is, it is important to understand what it is not. Empathy does not mean that you should condone wrong behavior. If Fred were to tell you, for example, that he goes out and gets drunk because he can't stand Carla's imagined infidelities, nagging, and denigrating him, and then he asks you what you would do in a similar situation, he has put you in something of a spot. He is asking for your sympathy, understanding, and self-disclosure. It is a poor kind of empathy to reply, "I guess I'd do the same thing," even if, in fact, you think that you might do so. Such a reply would imply that you are condoning his behavior. But, if you reply that you certainly would not do so, Fred will perceive you as being critical and judgmental. It would be better for you to say, "I'm sure that your wife's behavior makes you feel terrible. I'm not sure what I would do myself. I think perhaps that I would seek marital counseling. Do you think that's a possibility for you?" This reply relieves you of the appearance of condoning the offender's behavior while at the same time recognizing his feelings and offering a constructive alternative to the bottle.

LESSONS AND CONCERNS

The primary reason for including the client-centered approach in this discussion is its emphasis on the offender/counselor relationship. It goes without saying that we all attend more to the concerns of those whose good graces we value than of those about whose judgments we do not care. Objective understanding and special techniques and stratagems are not necessary to bring about change in the type of relationship Rogers emphasizes.

Although client-centered counseling can be fruitfully applied in some counseling settings, as evidenced by its great popularity among counselors in general, we have to ask ourselves if it is practical in the criminal justice setting. Andrews and Bonta's (1998) review suggests too much focus on the relationship dimension to the exclusion of establishing anticriminal contingencies is ineffectual and may be harmful. It seems to this author that unconditional positive regard, genuineness, and empathy as described here are the qualities we manifest only in a very real intimate love relationship with people who are truly special to us. Not being in such a relationship with offenders we counsel, is there a major conflict between being genuine and expressing the idea to offenders that we accept them unconditionally? Is there also a real danger that we will avoid necessary confrontation with an offender so as not to upset the close relationship deemed to be so important? Do we need to set conditions on our acceptance? Consider substituting "active concern for the well being of another" for "unconditional positive regard," when using the client-centered approach.

As a criminal justice counselor, you must allow positive regard for offenders to be conditional. This does not mean that you refuse to accept the basic humanity of offenders or that you pass unnecessary judgment on their past behavior. What it does mean is that you must place unambiguous conditions on their future behavior and not be afraid to confront them and let them suffer the consequences when they fail to meet those conditions. Empathy, too, must be guided in responsible directions.

Nevertheless, establishing a positive working relationship with offenders is important. Unconditional positive regard, genuineness, and empathy are continuous variables that you present to offenders in varying degrees. The degree to which you do present them depends on the quality of your concept of self in interaction with the self-concepts possessed by offenders. While you cannot always be your "genuine self," you should not suffer a sense of personal failure if you feel a lack of acceptance of the offenders or an inability to empathize fully with their view of the world.

A final point about the powerful influence of establishing positive relationships with offenders comes not from criminal justice or counseling research but from medical research. William Knaus and his colleagues at the George Washington University School of Medicine set out to discover what variable is most important to survival of patients in intensive care units (ICU's). Using advanced statistical techniques, they looked at such variables as technological sophistication, levels of professional expertise of physicians and nurses, prestige of the hospital, research funding, and patient/caregiver ratio. Their examination of 5,030 intensive care unit patients in a variety of hospitals across the United States over a period of five years found that none of these nominated variables was the crucial one. The crucial variable was the quality of the relationships that existed between doctors and nurses and between nurses and patients. The hospitals that allowed nurses to function semi-autonomously and to interact with patients at an emotional level were the hospitals with the best intensive care unit survival rates (Holzman, 1986:56). The researchers expressed their surprise at this finding; Carl Rogers would have responded with a knowing smile.

Perspective from the Field:
Getting Back in the Race
By Lindsey Whitehead

Lindsey Whitehead is the chief probation officer of the Lucas County Probation Department, Toledo, Ohio. He was a probation officer and unit supervisor for seven years before becoming chief. He holds master's degrees in guidance and counseling and public administration. He is also a Certified Alcoholism Counselor (CAC).

A few days ago as I was returning from lunch, I saw a young man who looked vaguely familiar to me leaving the probation department. As he approached me, he smiled and asked, "How are you, Mr. Whitehead? You don't remember me, do you?" I wasn't very sure of what the relationship between us had been, but after talking with him for a few moments, the memory was clear. The last time I had seen him was in 1978 when I was his probation officer. He was eighteen or nineteen years old at the time, and was on probation for his first felony conviction as an adult. He had been convicted of robbing a carry-out store. This young man's social history was very typical of those who are in trouble with the criminal justice system. He was from a broken home, lived in poverty, was inadequately educated, unemployed, and his spirit had been demoralized.

During the time that he was on probation, he obtained his General Equivalency Diploma and enrolled in a vocational school to learn welding. Upon completion of training, he was immediately hired as a welder by a local company.

"But why is he here at the probation department?" I wondered. "Is he in trouble again?" He explained apologetically that he had been caught with some cocaine and was now serving another term of probation. He further explained that this was the first time that he had been in trouble with the law for nine years and that he was still working as a welder with the same company and trying to be productive.

A few years ago, a young mother of beautiful twin girls was placed on probation for forgery. She had little motivation to do anything to try to improve her pathetic situation. But through the persuasion and leverage of the probation department and the court, she enrolled in the department's General Equivalency Diploma program. At first she didn't like it, but in time she became enthusiastic and was a willing participant. At the graduation ceremony, as her daughters looked on, she was extremely proud as she walked across the stage to be recognized for having completed her GED. She had come to realize that her efforts could result in positive changes in her life, and that, at the very least, her probation officer considered her worthwhile and cared for her.

There is nothing unique or unusual about these two cases. Similar experiences are repeated daily in probation and parole departments throughout the country. Pencil and paper no doubt can demonstrate a lack of success in the community corrections function, and perhaps this is so. But those of us who are in the trenches often have the opportunity to see the human spirit triumphant over what could have been lost lives. A probation or parole officer cannot run the race for those who have dropped out, or for those who never got into the race in the first place. But it is encouraging, if only occasionally, to see people pick themselves up and get into the race of life through the help of caring and professional probation and parole services.

Perspective from the Field:
On Rules and Crisis Intervention
By Charles L. Miller

Chuck Miller spent six years as a police officer before entering the corrections' field. His corrections experience includes supervision of maximum-security and death-row sections and command of the SWAT team at the Idaho State penitentiary. He is a certified self-defense instructor. He holds a master's degree in human relations from Abilene Christian University, in Texas.

The supervision of a high-security prison unit will provide numerous opportunities to practice and experiment with different aspects of crisis intervention. A crisis may occur at any time and for any reason. The key to good crisis intervention in an institutional setting begins long before a crisis ever occurs. The counselor involved with the crisis intervention must have developed a great deal of credibility with the inmates. He or she must demonstrate a willingness to enforce the rules of the institution consistently, equally, and fairly, and at the same time demonstrate a genuine concern for the welfare of the inmates.

My experience leads me to the belief that inmates have an unrecognized desire to be controlled. While they try all sorts of devious things to circumvent the rules, and even may riot when rules become too oppressive, they desire some sort of structure. A great many of them desire rules to make up for the self-control that they personally lack. Lack of self-control probably got them into prison in the first place. They lack the controls necessary to live within the boundaries established by society and its laws. Many come to see the prison rules as a sign of caring on the part of those who enforce them.

I remember a young man I dealt with when I was a street cop. "Ted" had served time in a juvenile facility and had been released to live with his sister. His sister lacked the ability or desire to enforce any rules. Ted soon found himself in all kinds of trouble with the law again. The funny thing is that it seemed as though he wanted to be caught. He either turned himself in or made it extremely easy for us to catch him. The upshot was that he was returned to the juvenile facility.

About nine months later, I was sitting in a coffee shop on a break when Ted walked in with a friend who had been incarcerated with him. They sat down with me and we talked about a number of things. I asked Ted if he hadn't been trying to get caught for his crimes in order to be returned to the institution nine months before. He proudly explained that he was. I asked him why—wasn't it a prison? I'll never forget his answer: "I liked it there because the people there cared enough about me to tell me what I could and couldn't do." His friend chipped in "Yeah, that's right." It appeared that Ted had become institutionalized at an early age—unable to function in open and free society as a result of his juvenile incarcerations.

Ted proved me wrong for a while. He had married an older woman who kept him in line. But she left him, tired of playing mother as well as wife, after he came home stoned one day.

I next saw Ted as an inmate in prison. He was a model prisoner who never caused any trouble. Ted is on parole now and seems to be doing well. What will happen when he is no longer supervised will be interesting.

Another way that a person demonstrates a genuine caring is through the art of listening. Far too often we see counselors acting before they really have listened. When a crisis threatens, we often see them taking strong security actions or opening their big mouths to make matters worse. We all could be more effective and demonstrate more caring if only we would listen. Listening is a skill that we must work on. It is more than simply hearing what a person says. The listener must demonstrate that he or she understands the implications of what is being said. I have always tried to be a listening supervisor. I have found that at those times when I have not taken the time to really listen, the level of tension on the tier increases. I have never been an inmate, but I can understand how their frustrations and impotence to change their environments can lead to violence. Many potentially dangerous crisis situations can be averted by empathetic listening.

Crises in prisons occur with disquieting frequency. They occur when inmates are thrown off emotional balance by the various frustrations of inmate life. The best way to deal with crises is to anticipate them by being sensitive to precipitating conditions and by listening empathetically to complaints. When they do occur, remain calm and project self-confidence. Listen to the complaint, and with the inmate(s), examine what can be done about it. However, never promise anything you cannot produce, and produce what you have promised. Through conscious efforts to show a caring attitude, a great number of potentially major incidents can be defused.

Summary

Janning ✳

Counseling differs from psychotherapy primarily in the depth and intensity of treatment. Psychotherapists attempt to restructure the basic personalities of patients with intrapersonal conflicts, whereas counselors deal with interpersonal conflicts and problems of everyday living. You should be alert to those offenders whose problems go beyond your professional ability.

There are similarities and differences between interviewing and counseling. Many of the techniques they use are the same. The quality of the self—your warmth, acceptance, and understanding—is the most important ingredient in both situations. In essence, counseling is an extension of the interviewing process. Counseling requires communication with offenders at a deeper level about more specific issues. You will accomplish this more easily if you have developed a positive relationship with them during the initial interviews.

Freudian psychoanalysis is a theory that offers some profound insights into human nature. It emphasizes the importance of the psychosexual stages of development, especially the importance of love at the earliest stages. The identification of defense mechanisms is useful in criminal justice, particularly denial, rationalization, fixation, displacement, intellectualization, and projection. You never will use the techniques of psychoanalysis in your dealings with offenders in the same way that you will use the techniques derived from other theories. Its usefulness to you as a criminal justice worker lies in its illumination of human nature.

Client-centered therapy shares with psychoanalysis its passive and nondirective approach. This theory asserts the absolute primacy of the offender/counselor relationship. Client-centered counseling rests on three attributes which the counselor should possess and offer to offenders: unconditional positive regard, genuineness, and empathy. Since many psychological problems are the result of conditions that others attach to their acceptance of a person's self-worth, it is vital that counselors accept those offenders with whom they work, unconditionally as individuals of worth. The counselor also must be genuine (be completely himself of herself); and avoid pretensions, dishonesty, and game playing. The counselor's authenticity will provide a model for the offender to emulate. Counselors always should strive to improve their own authenticity.

The final necessary attribute is empathy. It is very difficult to achieve because it implies the ability to participate actively in the mind-set of another, to actually walk in the person's shoes. Primary empathy is the communication to offenders of an initial basic understanding of what they are saying. Advanced empathy implies a deeper understanding, a reading between the lines. Empathy is something that is developed only by experience, by learning all you can about human behavior, and by really caring about what the offender is trying to communicate.

References and Suggested Readings

Andrews, D. and J. Bonta. 1998. *The Psychology of Criminal Conduct*. Cincinnati, Ohio: Anderson.

Austin, L. 1999. *The Counseling Primer*. Philadelphia: Accelerated Development Group.

Camp, C. and G. Camp. 1999. *The Corrections Yearbook*, Middletown, Connecticut: Criminal Justice Institute.

Cullen, F. and P. Gendreau. 2000. Assessing correctional rehabilitation: Policy, practice, and prospects. *In Criminal Justice 2000*. Washington, D.C.: National Institute of Justice.

Egan, G. 1998. *The Skilled Helper*. Pacific Grove, California: Brooks/Cole.

Ellis, A. 1996. *Better, Deeper, and More Enduring Brief Therapy*. New York: Brunner/Mazel.

Evans, D., M. Hearn, M. Uhlemann, and A. Ivey. 1989. *Essential Interviewing: A Programmed Approach to Effective Communication*. Pacific Grove, California: Brooks/Cole.

Fine, R. 1973. Psychoanalysis. In R. Corsini, ed. *Current Psychotherapies*. Itasca, Illinois: Peacock.

Freud, S. 1961. *Civilization and its Discontents*. New York: Norton.

———. 1965. *The New Introductory Lectures on Psychoanalysis*. New York: Norton.

Gendreau, P. and R. Ross. 1981. Offender rehabilitation: The appeal of success. *Federal Probation*. 45:45-48.

———. 1987. Revivification of rehabilitation: Evidence from the 1980s. *Justice Quarterly*. 4:349-407.

Gottfredson, M. and T. Hirschi. 1990. *A General Theory of Crime*. Stanford, California: Stanford University Press.

Holzman, D. 1986. Intensive care nurses: A vital sign. *Insight*. 56 (December).

Lauen, R. 1997. *Positive Approaches to Corrections: Research, Policy and Practice*. Lanham, Maryland: American Correctional Association.

Lewis, W. 1989. *Helping the Youthful Offender: Individual and Group Therapies that Work*. New York: Haworth.

Martinson, Robert. 1974. What works? Questions and answers about prison reform. *The Public Interest*. 35:22-54.

———. 1979. New findings, new views: A note of caution regarding prison reform. *Hofstra Law Review*. 7:243-258.

Mayeroff, M. 1971. *On Caring*. New York: Harper and Row.

Meier, S. 1989. *The Elements of Counseling*. Pacific Grove, California: Brooks/Cole.

Morgan, K. 1995. Variables associated with successful probation completion. *Journal of Offender Rehabilitation*. 22:141-153.

Palmer, T. 1994. *A Profile of Correctional Effectiveness and New Directions for Research*. Albany, New York: State University of New York Press.

Reich, T. 1956. *Listening with the Third Ear*. New York: Grove.

Reuters. 2000. *U.S. Prison Population May Pass 2 Million Next Year*. October 4. www.reuters.com

Rogers, C. 1952. Client-centered psychotherapy. *Scientific American*. 187:66-74.

———. 1961. *On Becoming a Person*. Boston: Houghton Mifflin.

Stratton, J. 1975. Correctional Workers: Counseling Con Men. In E. Peoples, ed. *Correctional Casework and Counseling*. Pacific Palisades, California: Goodyear.

Van Vooris, P., M. Braswell, and D. Lester. 2000. *Correctional Counseling and Rehabilitation*. Cincinnati, Ohio: Anderson.

Walker, S. 2001. *Sense and Nonsense about Crime and Drugs: A Policy Guide*. Belmont, California: Wadsworth/Thompson.

Walsh, A. 1986. Love and human authenticity in the works of Freud, Marx, and Maslow. *Free Inquiry in Creative Sociology*. 14:21-26.

Directive Counseling: Theory and Practice

To love and to be loved is as necessary as the breathing of air. Insofar as we fail in loving, we fail in living. The most important thing to realize about the nature of human nature is that the most significant ingredient in its structure is love.

→ are more cognitive
→ more emotional

Ashley Montagu

The theories we examined in the last chapter could be described as passive and nondirective: the counselor helps offenders to give birth to their own solutions for what ails them. The theories presented in this chapter are very active, directive, and didactic, with equal involvement of the counselor and the offender. These theories—transactional analysis and reality therapy—were both formulated by traditionally trained psychotherapists who were dissatisfied with the passive methods of traditional psychoanalysis and the extraordinary length of time required for that type of treatment. Both theories were designed to identify and deal with problem areas quickly, and are oriented toward cognitive rather than emotional approaches. The creators of the theories realized that most offenders must be actively assisted in their endeavors to become rational, responsible, whole individuals.

Transactional Analysis

Transactional analysis (TA) is the brainchild of Eric Berne, a psychiatrist best known for his book, *Games People Play* (1964). Transactional analysis stresses the cognitive and behavioral aspects of personality and places very little emphasis on emotions. If a person gains emotional insight from transactional analysis, it is through

Interpersonal vs counseling

185

the process of gaining intellectual insight and/or changing their behavior patterns. Any type of insight or change is achieved by examining transactions between the offender and others. A *transaction* is simply the act of two or more people interacting together; *analysis* refers to the process of exploring and explaining those transactions. Transactional analysis shares with psychoanalysis the assumption that human behavior is influenced rather profoundly by the events of early childhood, particularly events which told the child that he or she was loved or unloved.

Berne feels that the greatest strength of transactional analysis lies in its use of colloquial, simple, and direct terms that are easily understood by all. As Berne himself put it (1966:214):

> Transactional analysis because of its clear-cut statements rooted in easily accessible material, because of its operational nature, and because of its specialized vocabulary (consisting of only five words: Parent, Adult, Child, Game, and Script), offers an easily learned framework for clarification.

Offenders using transactional analysis soon acquire an easily understood vocabulary by which they can interact with the counselor to identify problem transactions.

SCRIPTS

Scripts are "memory tapes" that we all carry with us in our heads. The most important scripts are recorded in early childhood because children tend to accept messages unquestioningly, lacking the maturity to do otherwise. The messages communicated by our parents during this critical period contribute strongly to our future evaluations of ourselves as worthy ("OK") or unworthy ("not OK") people. By the time we become mature enough to question verbal and nonverbal messages regarding our OKness, any questioning is directed and influenced strongly by the powerful scripting we received in our most impressionable years. If the preponderance of messages told us that we were loved, respected, and appreciated, we will see ourselves as OK. If the preponderance of childhood messages were in the opposite direction, we will see ourselves as not OK. These evaluations of OKness tend to persist throughout our lives regardless of the messages we receive in later life because of the deeply etched early recordings.

Related to these early recordings is the intense human need for what Berne calls strokes. People hunger for strokes, to be touched both physically and emotionally. If they do not receive these strokes, they will not develop into psychologically healthy human beings. According to Berne, much of our time is structured around the pursuit of *positive strokes* (seeking assurances that we are loved). Positive strokes lead to positive scripting tapes, and negative strokes lead to negative ones. Transactional analysis theorists believe that to change negative scripts into more positive ones, clients require direction from a strong "parent" figure in the form of a counselor.

Four basic life positions issue from our scripting and act as backdrops throughout our lives in our interactions with others.

1. "I'm not OK; you're OK." This is a position commonly found in children. When they are punished for some transgression, they often feel "not OK." But their godlike parents, upon whom they depend, are naturally OK in their little minds. You will find this life position in many offenders, especially among substance abusers. They frequently are depressed and will have what Glasser calls in reality therapy

get through proper [handwritten margin note]

a failure identity. At least an offender with this life position will consider you OK, so you can concentrate on building up his or her own OKness.

2. "I'm not OK; you're not OK." This is the scripted life position of an abused child who was led to question the OKness of his or her parents rather early in life. A person like this views the world as a hostile and futile place, for the person is unloved and unloving.

3. "I'm OK; you're not OK." This, too, is the position of abused children who have questioned the OKness of their parents. However, they somehow have come to view themselves as OK from their own circumscribed perspective of OKness. They tend to be loners and to project blame for all their problems and actions onto others. The "psychopath" operates from this life position in its extreme.

4. "I'm OK; you're OK." This is the life position from which correctional workers must operate. To do your job adequately, you must be convinced of your OKness; to do it well, you must strive to generate the offender's OKness. The goal of transactional analysis is a relationship between counselor and offender with mutual convictions of "I'm OK; you're OK." That is, offenders must divest themselves of the negative scripts left over from childhood and find their own power and OKness.

GAMES   *we get strokes by playing games* [handwritten]

Transactional analysis views games as exchanges of strokes that are unauthentic because they have ulterior motives. *Games* are the result of individuals interacting with one another from one of the first three life positions. The ultimate payoff in a game-playing relationship in which one's time is structured around getting strokes (or giving them to those in positions of authority) is a storehouse of bad feelings that serve only to reinforce negative life scripts. It is only from an authentic "I'm OK; you're OK" position that individuals can engage in a meaningful, game-free interpersonal relationship. *strokes are anything positive.* [handwritten]

Games are very much a part of criminal justice supervision and counseling. You quickly must learn to identify and expose them, for they are dishonest and destructive. You even might find yourself playing games with the offenders. We already have mentioned one that officers might play in their law-enforcement role in the section on interrogation: ("Now I've got you, you son-of-a-bitch") when they are using offenders for power strokes. Another one often heard is "I'm only trying to help you," used by those gentler souls seeking acceptance strokes. Both of these games, of course, issue from an "I'm OK; you're not OK" position.

Offenders are very good at playing games—they have had lots of practice. You quickly will find out that they are much better at it than you are (take that as a compliment). A real value of transactional analysis for correctional workers is the ability it gives them to expose these games. Games that you will run into with frequency are "Poor me" (reaching for sympathy and "understanding"), "If it wasn't for . . ." and "Ain't it/I awful" (false remorse). Corrections workers who are acceptance seekers or who are ineffectual will easily fall for KIUD ("Keep it up, doc'). Such workers are suckers for offenders who tell them that they are doing a great job while continuing to behave irresponsibly. The payoff for KIUD offenders is that their counselors probably will let them get away with an awful lot of misbehavior in exchange for their dishonest strokes.

Yet another game, often seen in prison settings, is HDIGO ("How do I get out of here?"). Offenders soon learn to tell counselors just what they think they want to hear.

They learn the latest social science explanation for their behavior and spew it back while shaking with "self-understanding" and "remorse." Of course, self-understanding and remorse are very much a part of your goals for each offender in your charge. But it is imperative that they learn to distinguish the real goods from self-serving manipulation of the counseling setting. It is easy, and very human, to accept the game as the real thing because it gives you a feeling of success and a verification of your effectiveness as a counselor. Do not fudge the data for quick and easy self-strokes. If you accept the game as the real thing, the offender will have won the battle but will lose the war against his or her criminality.

PARENT, ADULT, CHILD → *Interpersonal*

Parent (P), Adult (A), and Child (C), or PAC, are ego states: three distinct systems of feelings and thinking related to behavior patterns. Each ego state perceives reality differently: the parent judgmentally, the adult comprehensively, and the child prerationally. We all slip into and out of these states as we engage in our various transactions, with one usually being dominant over the others.

The Parent is critical, controlling, and moralizing, just like Freud's superego. There is a good side to the Parent, though. The good Parent is the nurturing Parent who reacts to others with care, dignity, and respect and makes demands that are not overbearing. This is the kind of parental figure that the transactional analysis counselor is supposed to be. The critical or examining Parent is domineering, self-righteous, and authoritarian. The person who always operates in the parental mode (the constant Parent) excludes the reality of the adult mode and the playfulness of the child. Freud would call such a person "neurotic." You probably will not find the constant Parent represented much among offenders. If you do, they almost inevitably will be sex offenders against children.

The Adult is logical, realistic, and objective. *only judgmental when we have to* He or she is much better able to judge the appropriateness of when to allow the less characteristic ego states of their expression than is either the Parent or the Child because of a comprehensive and realistic integration of past experiences. Like the Parent, though, the constant Adult will enjoy little feeling or spontaneity. Almost by definition, you will not find the Adult among criminal justice clientele. You will find many among your colleagues.

The Child is spontaneous, fun-loving, and irresponsible. Many offenders will be of this type. It is perfectly OK to be an Adapted Child, one who enjoys fun and laughter in appropriate ways and in appropriate settings. The problem is the Constant Child, one who consistently excludes the Adult and Parent and refuses to grow up and behave responsibly. The exclusion of these restraining influences means the exclusion of conscience, the total absence of which is psychopathy.

One or another of these ego states predominates in each individual. The apparent equivalence of the ego states to the Freudian id (Child), ego (Adult) and superego (Parent) has been denied by Berne (1966). Berne's ego states are aspects of only the Freudian ego. Further, he states that whereas the id, ego, and superego are "theoretical constructs" (inferred entities not amenable to observation), his ego states are "phenomenological realities" (amenable to direct observation). Let us see how we can go about making these direct observations.

STRUCTURAL ANALYSIS

The process of making these observations is known as *structural analysis*. Structural analysis is a tool used by transactional analysis counselors to make offenders aware of the content and functioning of their ego states. A goal of transactional analysis is that all offenders become an expert in analyzing their own transactions. If offenders become adept at identifying their characteristic ego states, they can understand better their options for change.

Ideally, the Parent, Adult, and Child should be distinctly separate states with clear-cut boundaries, as they are in part one of Figure 10.1. Like the Freudian ego, the Adult holds the executive position but admits the Parent and Child, when appropriate. Two types of problems arise in personality structure as viewed in structural analysis: exclusion and contamination.

Figure 10.1
Ego States

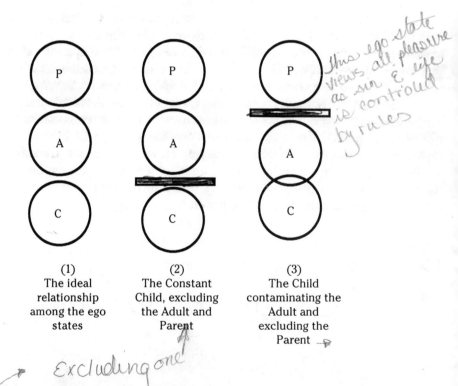

(1)	(2)	(3)
The ideal relationship among the ego states	The Constant Child, excluding the Adult and Parent	The Child contaminating the Adult and excluding the Parent

[handwritten note in right margin: this ego state views all pleasure as sin & life is controlled by rules]

[handwritten note at bottom: Excluding one]

Exclusion occurs when ego-state boundaries are drawn so rigidly that free movement across them at appropriate times does not occur. The fundamentalist puritan who views all kinds of sensuous enjoyment as sin, or who lives out his or her life bound by unexamined rules and strictures, is an example of the Constant Parent excluding the Child and the Adult. But we do not worry much about puritans in our business. We do have to worry about the Child who excludes the Adult and Parent. The individual is the complete opposite of the Constant Parent, doing everything that the Constant Parent would not and doing nothing that the Constant Parent does do. This exclusion is illustrated by part two of Figure 10.1.

Contamination occurs when the content of one ego state gets mixed up with the content of another ego state. We think of contamination in terms of the intrusion of either or both of the parent or child states into the rational boundaries defining the Adult state. Contamination of the Adult by the Parent often involves assumptions left over from our early scripting, which distort objective thinking. In the chapter on interviewing, this author related how his prejudices regarding proper behavior for women intruded into his Adult when he interviewed the woman charged with sex crimes against children. This contamination ruined the effectiveness of his interview and his subsequent relationship with her. Bill Blogg's Adult certainly was contaminated by his Child. He wanted success, Susan, a grandiose wedding, and lots of money. Not too much wrong with that, only Bill wanted it "right now!" The childlike nature of his actions hardly needs belaboring. Contamination is illustrated in part three of Figure 10.1. *On the same level lines are parallel*

COMPLEMENTARY AND CROSSED TRANSACTIONS *Not parallel*

Transactions between and among individuals can be either complementary or crossed. The ideal transaction is a complementary one. A *complementary transaction* occurs when a verbal or nonverbal message (the stimulus) sent from a specific ego state is received and reacted to (the response) from the appropriate, or complementary, ego state of the receiver. In transactional analysis communication, complementary transactions occur when stimulus and response lines on a PAC diagram are parallel.

The lines representing a crossed transaction in a PAC diagram are not parallel. *Crossed transactions* occur when a stimulus sent from one ego state meets a response from an ego state other than the expected one. Crossed transactions usually cause trouble in our interpersonal relationships. However, crossed transactions sometimes are called for and are beneficial if the unexpected ego-state response leads the stimulus sender to adjust his or her ego state to a more appropriate one. Figure 10.2 illustrates some complementary and crossed transactions. *Complementary would also be parent to chil[d]*

Figure 10.2
Complementary and Crossed Transactions

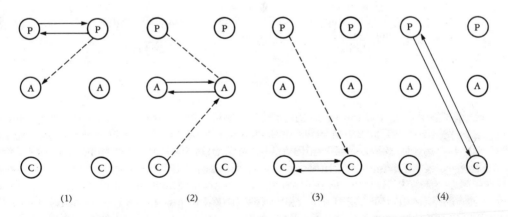

(1) (2) (3) (4)

In part one we have Parent-Parent communication. This might be two new probation officers discussing the "ignorance" and "immorality" of "welfare mothers cheating on the system." The Adult may never enter into their conversation to explore the whys of the behavior. If one of the officers suddenly shifts into the Adult mode (indicated by the dotted line), the conversation may not be as congenial as when they were engaging in transactions at the same level. However, the shift may bring the conversation to a more appropriate Adult-Adult state, at which point the ego states are again complementary. Do not engage in complementary transactions just for the sake of congeniality when you know that some other ego state is more appropriate. As Carl Rogers would say, "be genuine, be yourself."

Part two represents Adult-Adult communication. This could involve a prison counselor and the offender discussing a problem that the offender may be experiencing from a mutual "I'm OK; you're OK" position. The counselor does not contaminate the Adult by talking down to the inmate from the Parent ego state nor making light of the problem by joking about it from the Child ego state. These problematic crossed transactions are illustrated by the dotted lines.

Part three illustrates a Child-Child transaction. An example of this would be you and your colleagues planning a Christmas party. Obviously, you should never interact with offenders at this level unless the occasion is something innocuous, such as sharing a joke. A crossed transaction in this context could be something like refusing to take part in the office festivities because they are "frivolous," or responding to the offender's well-meaning attempt at levity with a cold stare. These responses would both reflect a Critical Parent ego state intruding on what should have been an appropriate Child-Child transaction.

Part four illustrates a complementary transaction even though the parties are interacting from different ego states (the lines are still are parallel). An example of this type of transaction would be a parole officer chastising an offender about some instance of irresponsible behavior. The officer confronts the offender from a parental ego state, and the offender responds as a child might when caught with a hand in the cookie jar: "You're always picking on me." This transaction is complementary because a Parent-Child stimulus has evoked a Child-Parent response. Had the officer confronted the offender from the Adult ego state and asked him or her simply to explain the behavior in question, and had the offender responded from the child state, the transaction would have been crossed.

Remember, any crossed transaction can lead to difficulties in interpersonal relations unless the crossover is purposely designed to shift the transaction to a level that is more appropriate to the immediate situation. In general, crossed transactions usually follow when one party or the other in the transaction operates from one of the first three life positions, which include various combinations of negative "not OK" attributions.

LESSONS AND CONCERNS

Transactional analysis simply and effectively illustrates the consequences of feelings one has about the self or about others in everyday transactions. Berne's genius was his ability to transform complex ideas into colloquial language and easy-to-follow diagrams. These ideas can be relayed with relative ease to offenders so that they may analyze their own feelings and behaviors. The emphasis on manipulation and game playing is especially useful for criminal justice workers. Finally, transactional analysis nicely describes in a neat linear fashion how early deprivation of love leads to poor self-concept, how a poor self-concept usually leads to a negative image of others, and how these negative feelings lead to poor interpersonal relationships, a common criminal justice phenomena.

On the other hand, transactional analysis may possess all the vices of its virtues. There is a danger that an inexperienced counselor simply may see counseling as an intellectual exercise consisting of identifying life positions and doing structural analyses. The very simplicity of the theory invites this type of truncated counseling. It is too easy to hide beneath covers stitched from nifty diagrams and clichéd phrases such as "strokes" and "games." You have to involve the offenders' emotions and feelings in the counseling process as well as their heads. It is also a theory that makes it easy for manipulative inmates and offenders to con inexperienced (and sometimes even experienced) counselors.

Therefore, use an eclectic approach to counseling. They all have something to offer. Although some offer more than others, none of them offers everything. Used in conjunction with client-centered therapy's emphasis on the nature of the client/counselor relationship and the other theories we will discuss, transactional analysis could prove to be a powerful counseling tool for you.

REALITY THERAPY

Reality therapy, founded by William Glasser (1972; 1975), has become a favorite counseling approach among those who work in community and institutional corrections. In fact, Glasser developed the basic ideas of reality therapy in a correctional setting while he was a staff psychiatrist at the Ventura School for delinquent girls in California. Thus, and unlike other counseling models, it was developed around the realization that corrections workers have a professional responsibility to hold offenders accountable for their irresponsible behavior. Reality therapy also shares with transactional analysis the happy quality of being relatively easy to understand.

> The principles of reality therapy are common sense interwoven with a firm belief in the dignity of man and his [or her] ability to improve his [or her] lot. Its value is twofold: it is a means by which people can help one another, and it is a treatment technique, applicable regardless of symptomatology. It is simple to learn albeit somewhat difficult for the novice to practice. Experience, not extensive theoretical grooming, is the key to accomplishment (Rachin, 1974: 52).

Reality therapy takes the outstanding features of the other approaches we have examined and integrates them into a single theory that can be applied without modification to offenders. Its basic goal is for clients (to use the vernacular) to "get real," and see themselves in charge of their own lives. In agreement with psychoanalysis, reality therapy recognizes that people have basic needs that must be met for healthy functioning. It also agrees that these basic needs are love and a sense of self-worth.

However, reality therapy does not dwell excessively on these deficiencies. Rather, like cognitive-behavioral therapy (to be discussed in the next chapter), it moves the offender away from bemoaning past privations and concentrates on present self-defeating behavior while teaching the offender how to become a more worthwhile person. It is also similar to cognitive behavior therapy in that it is didactic, concerned with the present, and action oriented. Unlike cognitive behavioral therapy, however, it recognizes the problems inherent in calling antisocial behavior "irrational" and

*cannot be ~~responsible~~
but can be rational*

substitutes "irresponsible." This is not just a semantic disagreement. Rationality is seen in terms of positive or negative consequences of individuals' behavior for themselves. In contrast, responsibility is seen in terms of positive or negative consequences of individuals' behavior both for themselves and for others. As we have seen, one can be rational and engage in criminal activity; but one cannot be responsible and do likewise. The reality counselor will not hesitate, however, to point out self-defeating irrational thinking, just as the cognitive-behavioral counselor will not hesitate to point out irresponsible behavior.

It follows that the reality counselor follows a hard-nosed, no-nonsense approach to offenders: behavior is either responsible or irresponsible, period. But, in common with client-centered counseling, reality counseling recognizes the importance of developing a warm, sensitive, and open relationship with the offender as a prelude to effective counseling. Positive regard (not "unconditional"), genuineness, and empathy are stressed without the somewhat syrupy and abstruse connotations attached to them by client-centered therapy.

THEORETICAL BACKDROP

William Glasser believes that those who engage in any type of self-defeating behavior, including criminality, suffer from the inability to fulfill basic needs adequately. If these needs are not met, the person will fail to perceive correctly the reality of his or her world and will act irresponsibly. (By "reality," Glasser means that individuals realistically perceive not only the immediate consequences of their behavior but also the remote consequences). To act responsibly, offenders have to be helped to face the reality of the world in which they live, and to face reality, they must be helped to fulfill their basic needs. These basic needs are the need to love and to be loved and the need to feel that we are worthwhile to ourselves and to others. Glasser goes on to describe how these two needs are interrelated: "Although the two needs are separate, a person who loves and is loved will usually feel that he [or she] is a worthwhile person, and one who is worthwhile is usually someone who is loved and can give love in return" (1975:11). The person who has these needs met develops a "success identity" and the person who does not develops a "failure identity," which results in irresponsible behavior.

*automa-
feel worth*

A failure identity is analogous to what Berne calls in transactional analysis an "I'm not OK" life position, and a success identity is analogous to an "I'm OK" life position. Glasser feels that a person's basic identity (success or failure) is developed by the age of four or five. If we are loved, and if we are allowed and encouraged to learn, explore, and experience, we will have a success identity. If we are not loved, and if we are neglected and stifled, we will have a failure identity. The whole process of reality therapy can be seen as an effort to help offenders to develop a success identity, to enhance their self-esteem by guiding them from success (however small) to success.

Glasser's theory nicely ties in at the psychological level with the sociological insights of Hirschi's control theory (1977). The lack of a loving relationship with significant others (attachment) leads to a generalized lack of concern for the expectations and values of the larger society. This unconcern leads to a lack of commitment to a prosocial lifestyle, failure in school and in the job market, and a failure identity. Lacking this commitment, the individual is not involved with enough people with success identities who could model responsible behavior patterns for him or her. Rather, he or she is involved with others with failure identities who justify themselves and their behavior by developing a set of beliefs that are contrary to conventional morality. If early deprivations are severe enough, the individual may develop a psychopathic personality.

Although reality therapy refers to causes of behavior, it stresses that the causal understanding of behavior should not be viewed as excuses for that behavior. Reality therapy agrees with the client-centered perspective that individuals ultimately are responsible for their own "identity." In common with client-centered therapy, reality therapy asserts that there is a "growth force" within us all that strives for a success identity. Reality counseling attempts to activate that force by helping offenders to learn who they are, how to interact with others in a responsible fashion, and how they can be accepted more fully by others. It charges the counselor to be a continuing model of personal responsibility for the offender. This means, once again, that counselors must work on themselves with the objective of becoming the best kind of person they are capable of becoming.

In an interview with Evans (1982), Glasser enumerates seven steps that the counselor must take to effect meaningful changes in an offender's behavior. These are paraphrased below:

1. Get involved with offenders; develop warm rapport; show respect.
2. Understand offenders' personal histories, but deemphasize them in favor of what they are doing now.
3. Assist offenders to evaluate their attitudes and behavior, and help them to discover how they are contributing to their failure identities.
4. Explore with them alternative behaviors that may be more useful in developing a success identity.
5. After decisions have been made regarding alternatives, get a commitment in writing to a plan of change.
6. Once the commitment has been made, make it clear that excuses for not adhering to it will not be tolerated. Emphasize that it is the offender's responsibility to carry out the plan.
7. Do not be punitive with offenders, but allow them to suffer the natural consequences of their behavior. Attempting to shield offenders from these natural consequences reinforces their irresponsibility and denies the self-directedness of their actions.

THE RELUCTANT/RESISTANT OFFENDER

The attitudes and techniques of reality therapy are particularly useful in counseling reluctant and/or resistant offenders. Most counseling theories assume a voluntary client who has actively sought out help with various problems, although studies indicate that most clients, even self-referred ones, exhibit some reluctance or resistance at times (Paradise and Wilder, 1979; Harris, 1995). Some authorities even consider voluntary and welcomed interaction with the counselor as an essential prerequisite to the helping process. Reality therapy makes no such assumption. It recognizes that the majority of offenders are inclined to demonstrate resistance to various degrees, and it hardly needs to be said that none of them is in your office by choice.

Recognizing Reluctance and Resistance. Offender resistance can range from a sullen silence, through game-playing by telling you only what they think you want to know, to outright hostility. Most verbal resistance does not take the form of angry name calling and challenges. It is more often a series of responses like "I don't know," "maybe," "I suppose," and "you're the boss." In the vocabulary of transactional analysis, the offender is acting from a hostile child ego state. Nonverbal resistance can reveal itself in frequent finger and foot tapping, negative nodding, smirky smiles, and arm folding (a gesture of defiance and barrier erection). This kind of verbal and nonverbal behavior can be very disconcerting to the beginning counselor who "only wants to help" (transactional analysis' nurturing parent) and who is desperately trying to be liked.

Since the counselor's intentions are good, and he or she is doing all the right things learned in Counseling 101 to establish rapport, the counselor finds it very difficult to accept the offender's reluctance and negativism (the transaction is crossed). All of us enjoy positive feelings, and few of us are very good at dealing with negative feelings, either our own or those of others, because it requires confrontation. Rather than acknowledging and dealing with negative feelings, the beginning counselor often tries to deny, downplay, or redirect them (trying to maintain an inappropriate complementary transaction). The negative feelings must be acknowledged and worked through with the offender (temporarily crossing the transaction so that it can be reinitiated at a more appropriate Adult-Adult level). The process requires extra effort on the counselor's part; it is all too easy to coast and avoid uncomfortable issues. A counselor with a strong and integrated self-concept is not afraid to encounter negativism and confrontation.

Reasons for Resistance. Why do offenders resist well-meaning attempts to help them? For one thing, they do not come into your office asking themselves what you can do for them. They are much more concerned about what you can do to them. You are a symbol of something that many offenders have spent a good proportion of their lives resisting: authority. To cooperate with you may well be an admission of weakness, in their way of thinking, and they are not overly anxious to admit weakness, especially to a representative of "the system."

Resistance is a form of a defense mechanism designed to protect the ego from the disconcerting feeling of the loss of autonomy. They also may not want to cooperate because what you want and what they want are two totally different things. You want them to act responsibly and obey the law; they want to get out of your office and out of your life. The very fact that offenders are in your office involuntarily is enough to generate resistance. The principle of psychological reactance tells us that whenever people's sense of autonomy is threatened by forcing them in some way to do something, even if they would otherwise have done it voluntarily, their natural inclination is to resist. Finally, you should ask yourself why offenders should want to surrender themselves to a person whom they do not yet trust and to a condition they see as manipulative, for purposes with which they do not, at least for the present, agree.

Dealing with Resistance. The first thing that you must do with resisting offenders is to acknowledge their feelings by reflecting them back and giving offenders the opportunity to vent them. You need not share an offender's views of you or "the system" in order to acknowledge the offender's right to hold them. Arguing back and forth with offenders at this point only will serve to strengthen their resolve. You even may inform them that you do not particularly mind if they feel the way they do as long as they behave responsibly.

Offenders must be reminded that probation or parole (if this is the setting for the relationship) is a conditionally granted privilege and that they cannot be allowed to abuse it. You can inform resistant offenders that you understand their desire to get out

self control best for social control

of your office and out of your life and that you share this desire with them. That joint objective provides a mutually agreeable starting point. You then can begin to delineate the conditions under which your mutual goal can be successfully achieved. Emphasize that you are responsible for implementing the conditions of probation or parole and that noncompliance will not be tolerated. You also should state that both of you have a vested interest in successful completion of probation or parole, that it therefore should be a cooperative endeavor, and that a negative and/or hostile attitude could seriously impede your mutual goal: "Let's help each other out." In the vocabulary of transactional analysis, the laying down of expectations is a Parent-Child transaction, and the treatment contract to be negotiated is an Adult-Adult transaction.

This approach is the one that a reality counselor would take. Such a counselor has not punished the offender by returning hostility for hostility, but has let it be known that the offender will be allowed to suffer the natural consequences of behavioral noncompliance. The counselor has been strong enough to deal with negative feelings in a constructive way by a judicious use of authority. They have been straight with the offender without being overly authoritarian. The offender has been allowed the dignity of possessing and expressing attitudes contrary to the counselor's but has been told up-front that nonapproved—that is, irresponsible—behavior is not permitted. Most offenders much prefer and respect directness rather than sweet-talking and beating around the bush. The counselor has enlisted the offender's help to accomplish a goal desired by both parties. Involving the offender in a shared purpose gives meaning to the relationship. The ability to involve offenders in their own rehabilitation is the major skill of doing reality therapy (Glasser, 1975:25).

This area of general agreement between yourself and your reluctant or resisting offender is then channeled to specific areas of concern by the implementation of a concrete plan of action. Initial plans should be microscopic in their breadth so as to maximize the probability of successful completion. They also should be formalized in writing and signed by the offender and by yourself in the manner described by the tentative supervision plan. This step says to the offender, "Your signature attests to your commitment to achieve this goal, and mine attests to my commitment to support you in your endeavor." Adherence to such a plan begins the process of the development of a "can do" success identity and engenders a sense of responsibility for living up to agreements. Glasser himself has emphasized the importance of commitment: "Commitment is the keystone of reality therapy. It is only from the making and following through with plans that we gain a sense of self-worth and maturity" (Glasser and Zunin, 1973:303). Moreover, keeping the expectations of the action plan modest often overcomes an offender's reluctance to comply.

TREATMENT AND SUPERVISION PLANS

Balance. To minimize reluctance, resistance, and the probability of failure, treatment and supervision plans should be balanced with the offenders' present coping resources. These resources—intelligence and educational levels, financial situation, self-concept, strength of interpersonal relationships, and so on—are known to you from previous interviews and the needs assessment scale. Similarly, you should be aware of problem areas to be addressed in the treatment and supervision plans. Balanced plans are those whose demands on the offender should neither undertax nor overtax the resources they have available to implement them. The principle of balanced plans is illustrated in Figure 10.3 with some hypothetical clients.

Figure 10.3
Balancing Treatment Goals

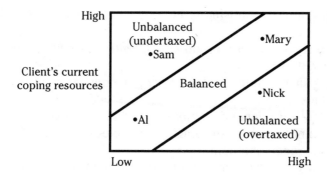

Treatment and supervision
expectations (Goals)

The diagram is divided into three sections: one balanced and two unbalanced. The upper-left triangle represents an unbalanced condition in which high coping resources are paired with low treatment expectation. The lower-right triangle represents the opposite condition. Sam is in the undertaxed section because he has high coping resources but low demands have been placed on his resources. Sam will be quite happy and content if you allow him to slide right along without having to do anything toward correcting problems that led to his criminal behavior. Of course, Sam may be a first offender who needs no treatment plan and who is best left alone. But if there are clear problem areas that may lead him to reoffend, you must take advantage of whatever strengths are represented by his relatively high-coping resources for his growth toward responsibility.

Nick's situation is the opposite of Sam's. Heavy treatment demands have been made on his limited coping resources. The dilemma here is that Nick's low level of resources is the very reason that more intense treatment is required. That is, Nick's coping resources are low. Therefore, heavy demands are made on him to correct the deficit. But the lack of resources indicates that he probably will not be able to meet those demands at present. Thus, Nick is in a kind of "Catch-22" situation. If you insist on maintaining Nick's present level of treatment, you will be setting him up for resistance and failure, and the consequences that go with them. Present treatment demands on Nick must be lowered so that they are commensurate with his present capacities to cope with them. As his capacities increase, you then may renegotiate more demanding treatment goals with him.

The treatment goals set for Al and Mary are balanced with their present coping resources. Mary is considered to have coping resources equal to Sam's, but she is being challenged to use them for personal change and growth. Al has extremely low coping resources and thus probably needs a higher level of treatment than Mary. However, his present resources are not sufficiently strong to allow for the same level of treatment. As his resource strength increases (that is, as he slowly builds up a success identity) the demands that you negotiate with him may increase as well. Do not undertax or overtax the offenders' coping resources. Rather, move them slowly toward the ultimate goal one simple step at a time.

Simplicity. To change a failure identity to a success identity, a good plan should have the following qualities and be

- Uncomplicated, simple, unambiguous, concrete, to the point: "Attend AA tonight at 6 o'clock."
- Active—something to do, not stop doing: "Attend AA tonight at 6 o'clock," not "Stop drinking alcohol."
- Something that can be done as close to "right now" as possible. "Attend AA tonight at 6 o'clock."
- Entirely dependent on offender's actions for fulfillment, not contingent on the actions of others: not "Attend AA tonight at 6 o'clock if your wife/husband lets you off doing the grocery shopping."
- Something that can be done everyday, or as often as possible: "Attend AA tonight at 6 o'clock, and every Tuesday and Thursday at the same time and place for the next month."
- Specific as to what, where, when, how, and with whom it is to be done: "Attend AA tonight at 6 o'clock at St. Anthony's Church on Pine Street. You (the counselor) will pick me up at my home for the first meeting to introduce me to other members."

The first plan need not be quite so active as this example. It can be something as simple as being on time for the next appointment. Whatever the plan may be, put it in writing and get it signed by both you and the offender.

Orientation toward Progress. Subsequent plans should be designed to build on the offenders' strengths rather than on their obvious weaknesses. Again, the idea is to build a success identity. Too early an emphasis on major weaknesses creates too great a chance of failure, thus reinforcing the offenders' failure identity and generating further reluctance and resistance. For instance, if JoAnn lacks a high school diploma and all indications are that she could successfully complete a General Equivalency Diploma program, show her that you have confidence in her capabilities and try to secure an agreement from her to enroll in such a program. Do not forget, though, that this goal must be balanced with her capacities. Do not insist that she commit herself if she is overly reluctant. Instead, you must persuade her to at least take a placement test She may well be more receptive to the entire program if the test shows that she could do well. A recent study comparing rearrest rates between probationers enrolled in a GED program and a matched group of probationers not enrolled found that those enrolled in the program were significantly less criminally involved over a three-year period.

> The sense of personal accomplishment, the sense of participating in a socially valued endeavor, the anticipation of legitimate employment, and the idea that the 'system' finds one worthy enough to make an investment in time and resources to provide one with a second chance, may be sufficient to put the scotch to an incipient criminal lifestyle (Walsh, 1985:76).

The secret of counseling in criminal justice, then, is to temper your necessary authority to direct your offenders' actions along acceptable avenues while always being aware of, and showing a concern for, their basic humanity. Try to view offender resistance as a normal response to coercion, perhaps even a psychologically healthy one. Examine your own resistance to self-growth and development, and examine your own behavior with offenders to see if you are perhaps doing something to generate resistance. For instance, you may be a little too directive, too authoritarian, or in too much of a hurry to accomplish your goals. Especially examine the possibility that your goals for the offender are not balanced with the offender's present level of coping resources. As Newman has put it (1961:38): "One of the first major accomplishments of treatment comes about when the offender becomes aware, both intellectually and emotionally, that the officer represents not only authority with the power to enforce certain restraints and restrictions but that he [or she] is also able to offer material, social and psychological aids."

We must not forget that counseling is a very difficult and sometimes draining enterprise. You cannot expect to be an expert at it by simply reading a book, but with experience and caring you will become better and better at it and begin to develop your own style. As Peoples puts it, treatment is often a "maze," but

> The significant point to emphasize is do *something*. Shelve the paper work, for-get the coffee, get out of the office—and counsel. Risk a little involvement with the human beings on your caseload. Learn, teach and grow with them in expe-riencing the most vital quicksilver of all, human behavior (1975:372).

LESSONS AND CONCERNS

Reality therapy is a relatively simple method of counseling that stresses respon-sible behavior, and it can be applied fruitfully by professionals. Its "one small step at a time" approach to developing offenders' success identities is particularly useful. Also very useful is its direct and assertive stance that fosters a no-nonsense, but warm and offender-involved relationship. Its assertion is that, at bottom, the origin of many offenders' problems lies in early and protracted deprivation of love.

Finally, a number of studies have concurred with Rachin's (1974: 53) conclusion that "Correctional clients who have proven least amenable to conventional treatment methods respond well to reality therapy." For instance, a study from Hong Kong (Chung, 1994) showed that reality therapy for three to six months prior to release sig-nificantly increased self-esteem and a sense of responsibility among incarcerated juve-niles who received therapy compared with a matched group who did not. At times it may be necessary to resort to the vocabulary of transactional analysis when explain-ing reality therapy. By doing so, the concepts are brought home more strongly. Offenders also will better understand the supervision and counseling process if they are introduced to this simple vocabulary, which is the great strength of transactional analysis. The integration of this vocabulary into the reality therapist's repertoire should prove very useful.

Dismissal of mental illness as merely "irresponsible behavior" is overly facile. Increasingly, we are coming to the realization that much of what we have termed men-tal illness does have origins in chemical and endocrinal imbalances. To treat individu-als with such problems as merely irresponsible when they are demonstrably ill does them a disservice, to say the least. Criminal justice counselors must learn to recognize when offenders are behaving "irresponsibly" due to no real fault of their own and refer them to a mental health specialist.

Reality Therapy → Needs Resources
They need to do something

EXERCISES IN PRIMARY AND ADVANCED EMPATHY

The exercise in interviewing emphasized practice in listening to what your partner had to say. In these exercises in counseling, you will be taking a more active part. Not only will you be intensely listening to your partner, but you will be communicating to him or her that you understand his or her perspective. You will use all of the techniques outlined in the chapter on interviewing, including the use of paraphrase, clarification, and reflection of feelings. Do not be content with vague statements from your partner; make him or her cite specifics.

If you are the student being counseled, choose for discussion a topic that is of concern to you. It should be one with emotional content, such as the loss of a loved one, the breakup of a romantic relationship, the inability to get along with someone of importance to you, or a perceived personal defect. Such topics make for realistic counseling sessions for both partners. You will gain experience of an offender's feelings when revealing intimate information, and the counselor will gain some experience in attempting to pull out deep feelings that the offender may be reluctant to express. However, please do not feel obligated to choose a topic that is too painful to discuss with an inexperienced counselor. This exercise should be both productive and relatively safe. Therefore, you should be given ample time to decide on a topic.

After you have been through a short counseling session, you and your partner should put your heads together and try to identify strategies for understanding and/or ameliorating the problem discussed. Perhaps you could do some structural analyses on your important relationships. Do you see a pattern of crossed transactions? What is your typical ego state? Does the person being counseled agree? Is his or her usual state consistent with what Berne would predict from the person's history of strokes? How about irrational ideas that he or she may be harboring? If the counselor did not identify them, maybe you now can do it together as a team. Finally, can you together define a simple plan to work on eliminating the problematic behavior or feelings experienced by the individual. You should find these exercises fun if approached from a mutual "I'm OK; you're OK" position.

COUNSELING "REAL" OFFENDERS

The location of both male and female correctional institutions close to Boise State University affords this author and his students the luxury of going to these institutions to interview and counsel real offenders. However, those not enjoying such proximity also can get the feel of counseling real offenders. If you have written presentence investigations (PSIs) as interviewing and assessment exercises, your instructor may wish to use them as the basis for providing practice in counseling with a criminal justice flavor. The student who initially wrote the PSI again can team up with the same partner to explore more fully the problems and concerns discovered during the PSI process. These problems are many: alcoholism, child molestation, drug abuse, negative self-concept, anger and aggression, and so forth. The student counselor should determine what referrals, if any, might be beneficial for the offender. Explore these problems in turn from each of the three counseling perspectives in this chapter, and then devise some simple "success identity" plans appropriate to the offender.

If you are role-playing the offender, then prior to the counseling session you should think deeply about being in the offender's shoes (empathy) so that you can present a realistic challenge to your partner's developing counseling skills. Much of your partner's success in this exercise will depend upon how well you are able to capture the feelings of the offender. An added bonus for you will be a greater ability to view the world from the offender's perspective.

Perspective from the Field:
When Cultures Clash: Resistance and Persistence
By Roman C. Pena

Mr. Pena received his bachelor's and his master's degrees in Public Administration from Idaho State University. He spent four years with the Utah Department of Corrections as a correctional counselor at a halfway house. He is currently a probation and parole officer with an intense supervision caseload.

I only had been in the intensive supervision program for three weeks when I was notified that I would be getting a new parolee, "Casey Jones." Reviewing Casey's inmate file and conversing with various sources, I became aware of Casey's Aryan Brotherhood affiliation. The Aryan Brotherhood is a white supremacist group that is very active and powerful within prison walls. Well, here's Roman, very much a non-Aryan, going to be this racist's parole officer. Although Casey's involvement in the Brotherhood was minimal, just the fact that he chose to identify with this group and their values was enough for me. Hence, I immediately contrived ways of defending myself in the event of a confrontation.

Sure enough, seated across the interviewing table the next day was Casey. His face and mannerisms displayed hate and anger. I knew that he knew about me from his own sources. As I asked him the required questions and advised him of his responsibilities, he would respond with abrasiveness and sarcasm. It was tempting to retaliate, but I knew that it was necessary to maintain a professional demeanor.

The first two months of continual daily face-to-face visits were uneventful. Casey's attitude did not improve, and I often hoped that he would abscond from supervision. Nevertheless, he was content in doing as little as possible in most areas of concern, and he managed to stay within the "gray zones" of behavior and attitude. His welcoming remarks to me at home visits were, "Ya, what do you want?" and "Not you again!" His acquisition of a guard dog (which once nipped the back of my leg) became an object in our power struggle. Casey enjoyed watching my approach to the front door, as I tended to proceed with some trepidation. His enjoyment was short-lived as the dog befriended me.

Two more months passed until Casey experienced the setback of being laid off from his job. I could not help feeling that his negativism was a factor in his layoff. Casey started showing signs of worry. Christmas was only three weeks away and the job market was stagnant. One day an employer from a local mobile home factory called me up and asked me if I knew of someone who would like a job installing mobile home windows. I quickly went and notified Casey. He got the job. From that point on, he began to be more friendly. He would even greet me at the door with a friendly "Hello!" He began to share personal problems. I listened intently and offered guidance when possible. He thought I was "one of a kind." Casey completed his six-month intensive parole period and was transferred to regular parole supervision.

Casey's new parole officer was—are you ready for this?—a Mr. Rodriguez. Mr. Rodriguez was firm yet fair with Casey. He told him that there would not be any side-tracking on cultural issues. Compliance with supervision standards was to be the priority. Casey agreed to cooperate with him the best that he could. One day Casey called Mr. Rodriguez on the telephone. Mr. Rodriguez's face showed concern and empathy as he consoled Casey on the death of his newly born son. This was a major turning point in Casey's life. He became increasingly receptive to assistance and cooperative in matters of supervision.

As I now submit Casey's final recommendation for discharge to the parole board, I remember our first two months in the program together. I've witnessed a miracle in human relations, not only in Casey but also in myself. Casey's departing comments to me were, "You know, you're not so bad after all—for a Mexican. Thanks for everything." For some reason, his Aryan values and my Mexican culture seemed so insignificant.

SUMMARY

This chapter has outlined two counseling approaches often used in criminal justice settings. These theories have found a place in corrections because they are relatively easy to understand and apply. They emphasize the offender's own responsibility for change and include equal involvement of the offender and the counselor.

Transactional analysis is built around five simple words: Parent, Adult, Child (the ego states), game, and script. Much of our behavior is a playback of scripts laid down during infancy and childhood. The kind of scripts we have in our heads depend on the quantity and quality of the strokes (love) we received early in our lives. Our scripting leads to the four basic life positions from which we carry out our transactions with others: "I'm not OK; you're OK," "I'm not OK; you're not OK," "I'm OK; you're not OK," "I'm OK; you're OK." The large majority of offenders will be operating from one of the first three life positions. We must strive to conduct all of our transactions from the "I'm OK; you're OK" life position.

Parent, Adult, and Child are three distinct ego states we slip into and out of during our various transactions. Offenders tend to operate mostly from the Child ego state. Many of them exclude the Parent altogether, and their Adult states frequently are contaminated by the intrusion of the Child. When interacting with offenders, you should be operating from the Adult ego state. You also should strive to get offenders more involved with their adult state.

Reality therapy views self-defeating behavior as the result of not having one's basic needs adequately met. These interrelated needs are the need to love and be loved and the need to feel worthwhile. People who do not have these needs met tend to develop a failure identity. Your task is to assist offenders to develop success identities by becoming actively involved with them.

Reality therapy is especially useful in dealing with resistant and reluctant offenders. You often will run into this type of offender in the criminal justice field. Offenders resist your help because you are a symbol of authority, and they have spent much of their lives resisting authority. They also resist because they are not in voluntary association with you. You must recognize and confront their resistance rather than ignoring or downplaying it. Allow them the dignity of their opinions, but make it clear that behavioral nonconformity simply will not be tolerated. Indicate that you will allow them to suffer the natural consequences of nonadherence to the conditions of their supervision.

To minimize resistance, and to develop offenders' success identities, treatment plans must be balanced with their present coping resources. Neither overtax nor undertax offenders' coping resources. Overtaxing invites resistance, and undertaxing is not growth producing. Treatment plans should be as simple and as concrete as possible, and they should be made in writing and signed by both parties.

References and Suggested Readings

Berne, E. 1964. *Games People Play*. New York: Grove Press.

_____. 1966. *Principles of Group Treatment*. New York: Oxford University Press.

Brown, J. and R. Pate, eds., 1983. Being a Counselor: *Directions and Challenges*. Monterey, California: Brooks/Cole.

Chung, M. 1994. Can reality therapy help juvenile delinquents in Hong Kong? *Journal of Reality Therapy*. 14:68-80.

Evans, D. 1982. What are you doing? An interview with William Glasser. *Personnel and Guidance Journal*. 61:460-462.

Glasser, W. 1972. *The Identity Society*. New York: Harper and Row.

_____. 1975. *Reality Therapy: A New Approach to Psychiatry*. New York: Harper and Row.

Glasser, W. and L. Zunin. 1973. Reality Therapy. In R. Corsini, ed. *Current Psychotherapies*. Itasca, Illinois: F. E. Peacock.

Harris, G. A. 1995. *Overcoming Resistance: Success in Counseling Men*. Lanham, Maryland: American Correctional Association.

Hirschi, T. 1977. Causes and prevention of juvenile delinquency. *Sociological Inquiry*. 47:322-41.

Newman, C. 1961. Concepts of treatment in probation and parole supervision. *Federal Probation*. 25:34-40.

Paradise, L. and D. Wilder. 1979. The relationship between client reluctance and counselor effectiveness. *Counselor Education and Supervision*. 19:35-41.

Peoples, E. 1975. Sorting from the Treatment Maze. In E. Peoples, ed. *Readings in Correctional Casework and Counseling*. Pacific Palisades, California: Goodyear Publishing.

Rachin, R. 1974. Reality therapy: Helping people help themselves. *Crime and Delinquency.* 20:45-53.

Walsh, A. 1985. An evaluation of the effects of adult basic education on rearrest rates among probationers. *Journal of Offender Counseling Services and Rehabilitation.* 9:69-76.

Chapter 11

Cognitive-Behavioral Approaches
Albert Ellis

"There is nothing either good or bad, but thinking makes it so."

Shakespeare's *Hamlet*

This chapter deals with cognitive-behavioral approaches to offender treatment. The techniques of cognitive-behaviorism has been around a long time. Albert Ellis (1989:5) claims that great religious leaders such as Buddha and Jesus were basically cognitive behavioral therapists, "and their followers were, in a sense, clients." These and other great religious leaders essentially were trying to get people to change their behavior—from short-run hedonism to prudence, from cruelty to compassion, from hate to love, and from immoral behavior to moral behavior—by appealing to their rational self-interest (make these changes and you will go to Heaven/attain Nirvana, and you will feel pretty good about yourself as well). Changing antisocial and self-destructive behavior into prosocial and adaptive behavior by appealing to offenders' best interests is the nuts and bolts of correctional treatment.

Unlike psychoanalysis, transactional analysis, client-centered therapy, and reality therapy, the cognitive behavioral approach is difficult to define. It might be said that cognitive behavioral therapy is a systematized eclectic theory. As Vennard, Sugg, and Hedderman (1997:5) put it: "Cognitive behaviourism is not a unified, distinct psychological theory or method but a term given to a range of interventions derived from the following three psychological theories." They then go on to identify *behaviorism, cognitive theory*, and *social learning theory* as the component parts of cognitive-behavioral therapy. Let us briefly look at these component parts.

Behaviorism is a theory that asserts that behavior is determined by its consequences. The consequences of any particular behavior are either rewarding or punishing to various degrees. If a behavior is rewarding, it is said to have been reinforced and therefore is likely to be repeated. If a behavior is punished, it is less likely to be repeated. Future behavior thus is contingent on the ratio of rewards to punishments a person has experienced following a particular behavior in the past. Criminal behavior has many consequences that are both rewarding and punishing, but as we saw in Chapter 3, many criminals are overly sensitive to rewards and relatively insensitive to punishments. The behavioral theorist, however, maintains that the level of sensitivity has been shaped by previous experience and thus can be changed by shaping it in the opposite direction.

Many of the techniques of pure behaviorism (classical and operant conditioning) cannot be implemented by correctional workers, particularly community corrections workers, because they depend primarily on the ability of the therapist to shape behavior by rewarding or punishing such behavior as soon as possible after it is performed. This ability, of course, requires that the therapist have almost complete control of the environment in which the shaping is to take place (such as so-called token economies in institutional settings, therapeutic communities, or halfway houses).

Such control is perhaps achievable to some extent inside prisons, but not in community corrections. However, the principal behavior is governed by its consequences. That is, offenders must come to understand the maladaptive consequences of their behavior. Glasser's use of contracts discussed in the previous chapter is an example of the application of this principle. The feeling of accomplishment, rewarded by the positive response of the corrections worker for fulfilling it, is reinforcing, just as allowing the natural consequences of not fulfilling the contract is punishing. In other words, the offender's *behavior* is the focus, what he or she has *done*, not what he or she thinks or believes. The assumption is that changes in thinking will follow behavioral change.

Cognitive theorists agree that at the ultimate level of analysis, maladaptive behavior has been shaped by experience. However, they assert that at a more proximal level, self-defeating behaviors are the result of unproductive thought patterns relating to these past experiences (Austin, 1999). We can do nothing about past experiences, but we can do something to put the way we think about those things into proper perspective. After all, thinking, not a series of old experiences, is the most immediate precursor of our behavior. We may be able to trace a straight line from those experiences to the way we think about certain situations, but we still can change our behavior in those situations by changing our thinking. Criminal behavior is the result of faulty thinking (dwelling on the past, egocentric thinking, and "I can'tism," among numerous others), or as we like to say in corrections, "stinking thinking."

Social learning theory is essentially a sociological view of socialization. Behavior is not only learned in stimulus/response/reward/punishment fashion as behaviorists assert, but also learned by modeling and imitation. That is, people observe the behavior of others and come to deem it appropriate or inappropriate for themselves. This has more to do with the status of the person or persons we model ourselves on than with rewards or punishments, although the psychological rewards of successful imitation of valued others cannot be overlooked. A major difference between social learning and cognitive theory is that the former consider cognition as only one "link in a behavior-cognition-environmental loop that gives primacy to none of these components . . ." and that "cognitions are mediators, whereas in cognitive therapy they are causes as well" (Arkowitz and Hannah, 1989:152-153). The primary contribution of social learning theory to cognitive-behavioral therapy is the teaching of social skills and problem solving training (Vennard, Sugg, and Hedderman, 1997).

Although behaviorist and social learning concepts are incorporated into cognitive-behavioral counseling, what actually is practiced is cognitive therapy with some behavioral and modeling techniques applied, when possible. The theories, both directive and nondirective, that we have examined so far can be seen as cognitive behavioral in some sense, since they all engage in "talk therapy" with the aim of changing their clients' thought patterns and behaviors.

What differentiates cognitive-behavior therapies from the others is that uncovering, challenging, and changing maladaptive thought patterns takes on a central role in treatment. Cognitive behaviorists acknowledge that we may be driven to some extent by unconscious processes (as claimed by psychoanalysts), and that our behavior is shaped to some extent by external contingencies (as claimed by behaviorists). However, they assert that most of our behavior is guided by processes of which we easily can be made aware, even though they normally are not a part of our awareness. These processes are simple thought processes.

Changing Criminal Minds

Criminals think differently than the rest of us—who ever doubted it? The idea of criminals thinking differently from the rest of us, however, was something of a radical idea in the 1970s when blaming criminal behavior on factors entirely external to the offender was in vogue. The idea of criminal thinking patterns originated with psychiatrist Samuel Yochelson and psychologist Stanton Samenow, whose failed treatment methods based on "outside circumstances" models with institutionalized offenders led them to abandon them and develop their own model. In a series of books (Samenow, 1998 and 1999; Yochelson and Samenow, 1976) they developed treatment theories based on the tactics and thinking errors of people who make crime a way of life. Samenow (2000:xii) states that: "Once we understood the world from the criminal's point of view and stopped imposing our own theories and explanations, we were able to understand how they perceive themselves and the world." This approach struck a responsive chord with corrections workers in daily contact with offenders, especially incarcerated offenders.

According to Vanstone (2000:172), cognitive behavioral methods in corrections are "used to address issues such as self-control, victim awareness and relapse prevention, and to teach among other things critical reasoning and emotional control." Adding to this, Chavaria (1997) points out that cognitive-behavioral programs must teach offenders to recognize (1) their patterns of thinking, feeling, and perceiving, (2) how these patterns support their criminal/dysfunctional behavior, (3) how to make the decision to change these patterns to change their lives, and (4) how to follow the decision to change with a program aimed at developing social competency. This, of course, is easier said than done given what we know about criminal thinking patterns.

Boyd Sharp (2000:3) cites a Calvin and Hobbs' cartoon to illustrate a typical line of criminal "stinking thinking." Calvin is speaking to his father, saying:

> I have concluded that nothing bad I do is my fault . . . being young and irresponsible, I'm a helpless victim of countless bad influences. An unwholesome culture panders to my undeveloped values and it pushes me into misbehavior. I take no responsibility for my behavior. I'm an innocent pawn in society.

No doubt this cartoon produced some chuckles from its readers, but such thinking is no laughing matter. If Calvin continues thinking this way, you might see him on your caseload one day. From where does such thinking arise? We might start by noting that mainstream criminology seems to have made an industry (not intentionally, of course) of making excuses for criminals—"It's society, poverty, racism, capitalism, *et cetera* and *ad infinitum*, that is to blame." These nostrums are repeated in the news media for all to read and digest, and criminals and their defenders are certainly happy to make a meal of them. Defense lawyers pick up the remaining slack by coaching their clients in denial and advising them not to admit anything. Of course, it is natural to want to deny something that can have negative consequences, and lawyers are only doing their jobs, but when respected professionals reinforce criminal denial and excuse-making by encouraging it, it becomes very difficult to change. It is this kind of ingrained pattern of denial that is primarily responsible, according to Sharp (2000), for making criminal thinking so difficult to change.

Sharp devised a therapeutic community treatment program based on cognitive-behavioral principles within prison walls in Baker City, Oregon. It is a strict, no-nonsense program for mainly alcoholic and drug abusing offenders based on the premise that offenders are liars, manipulators, sneaks, and egotists. Of course, staff members do not call participating offenders these things directly. However, participants know that staff members perceive them this way because each participant is given a list of thirty-six thinking errors characteristic of the criminal personality, and a list of tactics criminals use to obstruct their own treatment. These lists let participants know that the staff are well aware of their thinking patterns and behavioral characteristics, and thus they would not likely be able to pull the wool over the eyes of any staff member.

The program uses a lot of inmate/counselor contracts, standard educational programs, social skills training, and individual and group counseling. Inmates are in the program from between six to fifteen months, and Sharp claims a great deal of success in meeting most of the program's goals. Unfortunately, the only goal not met was a reduction in rearrest rates, which is, of course, the one goal that really matters. Changing criminal behavior is indeed very difficult.

RATIONAL EMOTIVE BEHAVIOR THERAPY

Because cognitive-behavior therapy is not a unified and distinct theory, the approach will be discussed further by focusing on a well-defined theory that defines itself as cognitive-behavioral: rational emotive behavior therapy (REBT). This theory was formulated by Albert Ellis, who first called it rational therapy, then rational emotive therapy, and finally rational emotive behavioral therapy in 1993. Ellis is an extremely well-respected person in the counseling field. In 1991, he was ranked as the most influential psychotherapist by Canadian clinical psychologists, and second (behind Carl Rogers) by American clinical psychologists (Ellis, 1996:xii).

Ellis takes issue with the assumptions and practices of both psychoanalysis and client-centered therapy. Psychoanalysis is concerned with the darkness of the unconscious mind and nonrational biological drives. Client-centered therapy zeroes in on the emotional rapport of the client/counselor relationship. Rational emotive behavior therapy fully recognizes that we share biological drives and emotional states with other species, but relegates them to minor importance in favor of cognition, a unique quality of humankind. It also relegates the client/counselor relationship while acknowledging that it is important, nevertheless.

According to rational emotive behavioral therapy, problem behaviors arise from faulty thinking and irrational beliefs, and they can be corrected by helping offenders to understand and acknowledge that their beliefs are at odds with logic. It follows from this assumption that the rational emotive behavioral therapy counselor takes a very active role in the counseling process and considers the quality of the offender/counselor relationship to be secondary to what takes place within that relationship. Rational emotive behavioral therapy counseling is highly directive, didactic, challenging, and often confrontational and painful for the offender. Before we get into the meat of rational emotive behavioral therapy counseling, it is necessary to learn something of Ellis' ideas about human personality.

THE A-B-C THEORY OF PERSONALITY

Rational emotive behavioral therapy counseling revolves around Ellis' A-B-C theory of personality (actually, this concept is more a *proposition* about, or *model* for explaining, people's faulty perceptions than a *theory* of personality, but we will endure the accepted phraseology). A is the experience of an objective fact, a so-called *Activating event*, B is the subjective interpretation of or *Belief* about that fact, and C represents the *Consequence,* that is, emotional content accompanying the meaning (B) that the experience of the fact (A) has for the individual. Most people view an activating event as causing the emotions they are experiencing ("I'm happy, sad, depressed, suicidal, because he/she asked me for a divorce") in the following way.

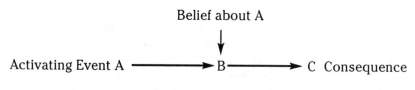

Activating Event A ————————————→ C Consequence
      objective fact   A leads directly to C
                              Belief

Ellis says no; there is always an interpretive process that goes between A and C that really determines the consequences as follows:

Belief about A
↓
Activating Event A —————→ B————→ C Consequence

A leads to B which leads to C

The important point for the rational emotive behavioral therapy counselor is that A is not the direct cause of C, but rather that B, the individual's belief about A, causes C. If A caused C, then everyone experiencing the same A would experience the same C, which obviously is not the case. The reason that everyone experiencing the same activating event does not experience the same emotional consequence is that the intervening belief about A is different from person to person. As Shakespeare had *Hamlet* say: "There is nothing either good or bad, but thinking makes it so."

The rational emotive behavioral therapy counselor sees problems of living as resulting from illogical and negative thinking about experiences (the interpretive processes) which the offender reiterates in a self-defeating monologue. The offender is reluctant to let go of irrational beliefs because they serve to protect a fragile ego.

disputing what you already believe

("She's to blame for my depression because, after all, she was the one who asked for the divorce."). This process resembles the Freudian defense mechanism of rationalization—a mechanism that serves the self-consistency motive. Empathizing with the offender's definition of reality in the Rogerian manner, according to Ellis, only serves to reinforce faulty thinking and is counterproductive. Passive listening to an offender's monologue, as in psychoanalysis and client-centered counseling, is replaced by an active and assertive dialog between counselor and offender. Counseling is not a warm relationship of relating partners; it is more akin to a teacher/student relationship, complete with lectures and homework assignments, which is the behaviorist aspect of the theory.

It is the counselor's task to strip away self-damaging ideas and beliefs by attacking them directly and challenging the offender to reinterpret experience in a growth-enhancing fashion. Ellis (1996) has recently added D (Disputing) and E (Effective new philosophy) to his ABC model. Disputing dysfunctional ideas and beliefs and replacing them with a new, healthy philosophy, was always part of rational emotive behavioral therapy, but by "letterizing" those components, Ellis has placed them on par with A, B, and C. Thus, after uncovering a dysfunctional idea or belief, the next stage is to dispute it.

The rational emotive behavioral therapy counselor operates from the assumption that no matter how well offenders come to understand the remote origins of their behavior, they often are unable to make the vital link between those origins and current behavioral problems. Rational emotive behavioral therapy counselors will rapidly cut short any offender's attempt to "explain" his or her behavior by asking, "But what are you doing to correct it?" Rational emotive behavioral therapy counselors quickly cut through the quagmire of reasons, causes, explanations, and rationalizations, to nail offenders down to one or two basic irrational ideas considered to be the "real" reason for their disturbed behavior. After those ideas are identified, the rational emotive behavioral therapy counselor challenges the offender to validate those ideas. When the offender cannot, the counselor points out the lack of a reality basis for those irrational ideas.

It goes without saying that this business of tearing into offenders' irrational ideas should not be done in a dogmatic or condescending way — "God, what a damn stupid idea! How can you be so dumb?" It must be accomplished in a way that does not move the offender to dig in defensively or to completely cut you off: "Alex, do you really believe what you're saying is true?" It is better if the counselor can guide the client to dispute the irrational idea himself or herself by saying something like, "Do you really mean that? Can you think of some other way to interpret what went on that perhaps would not make you feel as if it is a catastrophe?"

If the rational emotive behavioral therapy counselor needs backup, many will suggest bibliotherapy, the practice of having offenders read books that the counselor knows will challenge their views (*see* the use of bibliotherapy with a sex offender discussed in the case study later on in this chapter). Some offenders also will be asked to keep journals of their relevant daily activities and thoughts. The whole idea is that individuals have indoctrinated themselves with false and irrational ideas about themselves that lead to self-devaluation. The task of the rational emotive behavioral therapy counselor is to reindoctrinate offenders with more realistic thoughts about themselves, which may include the deflation of an overly inflated image based on their antisocial behavior, through the medium of reality-based logical thinking.

We dont want to know why you did it we want to know what your going to do to change it. Dont dwell on the past

"MUSTURBATIONS" → *you feel like you must have they rule your life*

Ellis has identified eleven ideas that he considers to be pervasive in our society. These ideas are highly irrational and lead to "widespread neurosis." He calls these ideas MUST*urbations* and sums them up thus: "I now see that I have given up any addiction to MUSTurbation many years ago—to thinking that I must do well; that others must treat me considerately or fairly; and that the world must provide me with the things I want easily and quickly" (1982). Most of us are addicted to certain of these MUSTurbations to some degree or another. An examination of some of these ideas will help to identify self-defeating "musts," "shoulds," and "oughts" in both your own thinking and that of the offender. Here are six of these ideas adapted from Ellis' delightful book *A New Guide to Rational Living* (1975). These six are especially applicable to offenders (and sometimes to corrections workers as well).

1. *It is essential that one be loved or approved by virtually everybody.* We all would like our desires for universal approval to be satisfied, but we do not really need them to be. You would hardly be human if you did not derive intense satisfaction from the positive judgments of others, but preoccupation with your own demands for love and approval prevents you from seeing the lovable traits in others. Put otherwise, by not concentrating on your demands that you be loved, you free your psychic energies so that you are able to love. Furthermore, if you believe that you are not a worthy person unless you are universally liked, you guarantee that you will be an insecure and self-devalued person because you are chasing an unattainable rainbow.

2. *One must be perfectly competent, adequate, and achieving to be considered worthwhile.* This is a trap into which the beginning criminal justice counselor often falls. You have taken on a very difficult task. A fair percentage of offenders will reoffend regardless of all your efforts to rehabilitate them. If you regard that circumstance as a personal failure, you denigrate yourself and the offenders' capacity to be responsible for their own lives. A perfectionist will never cut it in correctional work. As long as you have done your best, you are a worthwhile person. We all must develop the courage to be imperfect and not to experience failure as catastrophic.

3. *Unhappiness is caused by outside circumstances over which we have no control.* We allow ourselves to be emotionally upset about outside circumstances caused by our mental interpretations of them. Some outside circumstances constitute such a powerful assault on our lives that it is unreasonable not to expect a negative emotional consequence. However, other circumstances are only as defeating as we let them be. The rational person avoids exaggerating unpleasant\outside circumstances and looks for the growth potential in them. Many offenders find themselves overwhelmed by relatively innocuous unpleasant experiences and turn to the chemical comforts of the bottle or the pill.

4. *It is easier to avoid personal responsibilities than to face them.* You can hide from your responsibilities only for a short while. When your head does emerge from the sand, the responsibility still is there and may have grown. The rational person knows that it is less painful to attend to a responsibility than it is to deny or avoid it. Offenders are masters at avoiding their personal responsibilities

because they often lack the self-confidence to attend to them. It is the counselor's task to make offenders see the logic of the rolling-snowball effect of nonattendance to responsibility.

5. *One must have someone stronger than oneself on whom to depend.* Many offenders are in a dependency mode. They lack the self-reliance to live a responsible, self-motivated life. An overdependence on others (including a dependence on chemical substances) places individuals at the mercy of life's clutches. Rational people, while they may occasionally depend on others, minimize dependence on others and take charge of their own lives.

6. *Past experience determines present behavior, and the influence of the past cannot be eradicated.* Although it is true that our values are largely programmed by our experiences and that it is difficult to overcome their influence, our behavior is not bound by them. We have the capacity to transcend our experiences (and the mind-sets they engender) by accepting and analyzing the effect they have on us and by refusing to be determined by them. Typically, offenders have not recognized their capacity for self-directed change and allow themselves to be blown hither and thither by past and present environmental conditions. It is your job to encourage offenders to examine their experiences, make them realize how they have influenced their negative attitudes and behavior, show them that those past experiences are not acceptable as excuses for present behavior, indicate that they possess the human capacity to break the chains of experience, and activate them toward the goal of self-responsible behavior.

WHAT ABOUT EMOTIONS? *emotions – irrational*

Many people have taken rational emotive behavioral therapy (and cognitive-behavioral therapies in general) to task for not being concerned enough with emotion. Self-talk and logic may work fine for "cold" cognitions, but not for "hot" cognitions (thoughts with high emotional content). The problem with this is the belief that cognitions and emotions are completely separable phenomena, which they are not. We know from EEG studies that thoughts automatically engage emotions (Buss and Schmidt, 1993). Thus, all cognitions have an element of emotion attached to them, and vice-versa. It is emotions such as shame, empathy, and guilt that prevent many of us from following what might be economically more rational, at least in the short term, and it is cognitions that tame and modulate less noble emotions such as anger and hatred. Ellis himself wrote that: "RET assumes that human thinking and emotion are not two disparate or different processes, but that they significantly overlap and are in some respects, for all practical purposes, the same thing" (1984:216).

Nevertheless, critics do have a point: Illogical thought processes are doubtless dealt with more easily when they have little emotional content (are cold) than when they are suffused with emotion (are hot). Yet, a criminal hardly has a deep emotional attachment to his or her lifestyle in the same way that, say, a son has to his mother, a patriot to her country, or religious fundamentalists to their God. Rational emotive behavioral therapy counselors disputing the primacy of one's mother, country, or God would be confronted with probably insurmountable emotional barriers to change, whereas confronting criminals with the illogical and self-defeating nature of their criminal lifestyle engages thoughts only slightly tinged with emotion. Thus, because thoughts automatically engage emotions, changing beliefs, attitudes, and perceptions also should automatically change the emotional contents of these things. This is why Ellis (1996) changed his original rational therapy to rational *emotive* therapy in 1961.

The following case study illustrates the successful use of rational emotive behavioral therapy with an offender supervised by the author. Other examples of specific rational emotive behavioral therapy techniques are given in the chapter on group counseling.

Case Study
Rational Emotive Behavioral Therapy With a Sex Offender

[handwritten annotation: activating event → raped, made fun of in prison actually did not do it.]

Marc was a tall, good-looking man with an IQ of 119. He also had an attractive wife and a five-year-old son. Nevertheless, his work record was extremely poor. He was mainly a casual laborer. He never kept a job very long because he always seemed to get into an argument with his bosses and get fired or quit. After losing a job, he would go on short drinking binges and then go on to indecently expose himself (he had two prior convictions for indecent exposure). Despite his rather quick temper, his wife said that he was never abusive to her or their young son.

I first met Marc after his conviction for gross sexual imposition. He had been driving around one day in the rain after a minor drinking bout when he came upon two children—a girl age twelve and a boy age eleven—standing at a bus stop in the rain. Marc stopped and offered them a ride, which they accepted. The children later said they had accepted because they had just missed one bus, it was raining heavily, and they apparently felt there was safety in numbers.

After some small talk, Marc took the children into an alley and told them both to take their clothes off. The children refused and started to cry. Marc then verbally abused the children and proceeded to force his hand up the dress of the girl and stick his fingers in her vagina. He also fondled the boy's penis and told them both to keep quiet. The young boy was able to escape and shout for help from a nearby construction team, who apprehended Marc and held him for the police.

Marc told me during his PSI interview that his initial motive was simply to get the children out of the rain (he was trying to make me hear, "I'm really a nice guy, I tried to be helpful"). Once the children were in the car "I felt an overwhelming urge to expose myself to them" ("I couldn't help myself; I'm a victim of my urges; I need treatment, not punishment"). He admitted frequently exposing himself to children standing at bus stops in the past, and he had two prior convictions for such behavior. He admitted telling the young girl to remove her blouse: "It gave me a feeling of mastery. But I knew she wouldn't do it because of modesty." He denied (there's that awful word) touching the girl's vagina or the boy's penis.

My investigation led me to discover a rape conviction in another state that was not on Marc's FBI rap sheet. He reluctantly admitted this conviction to me, but said that he was wrongfully convicted. This turned out to be the truth, much to my surprise. He has been granted a full governor's pardon and $2,000 compensation for the three years he spent in prison for his conviction. Marc's wife informed me that he had told her that he had been frequently raped in prison, which he described as "a whorehouse

213

where the only thing missing was the women." She felt that many of his sexual problems stemmed from his prison experience.

Marc had referred himself to a private psychiatrist after his arrest and bail. This psychiatrist wrote that Marc's pedophilia was of recent origin, and that with "intensive psychotherapy it would never reach a stage of chronicity." He felt that Marc's desire to expose himself to children was caused by "deep-seated resentment of his mother's early rejection of him," and that he was essentially "thumbing his penis" at his mother. The psychiatrist recommended that Marc be placed on probation and that the county pay for his therapy. Marc never told his psychiatrist about his imprisonment, if he had, I wonder if the psychiatrist's focus on Marc's mother (a favorite whipping boy of classical psychoanalysis) would have changed?

For my part, I reasoned that Marc had kidnapped, terrified, and sexually molested two young children and that nothing less than incarceration could be justified. The judge reasoned otherwise, and placed Marc on probation on the condition that he continue treatment and spend sixty days in jail. Marc did not continue therapy with his psychiatrist. Instead, he opted to attend group counseling at the county court diagnostic and treatment center.

For a variety of reasons, not the least, I suppose, being his ability to make intelligent conversation, Marc's case fascinated and challenged me. During one session in which we were discussing his prison experiences, he told me that other inmates had ridiculed him about the size of his penis and how this used to devastate him. Further discussion led to his telling me that he had measured his erect penis at what was to him an unsatisfactory five inches. As Albert Ellis might have put it, Marc was "catastrophizing" the size of his penis. Ellis might have gone on to say something like: "Yes, I'm sure you would like to have a bigger penis, but there's nothing you can do about it. It's not your penis size that's getting you into trouble, it's your belief that I must have a bigger penis to be a man. You are miserable and feel inadequate, but you make yourself feel that way by irrational and dysfunctional thinking. Your irrational thoughts are leading you to continue your criminal behavior, and that will land you back in the prison environment where you say all your problems stemmed from."

Not being in Ellis' class, I went on to play Dr. Freud (a definite "no-no" for an untrained person) and suggested the possibility that his urge to expose himself to children may have stemmed from an exaggerated concern for the size of his penis. To a young child, an erect adult penis seems gigantic. Marc acknowledged that perhaps he was trying to reassure himself about the adequacy of his penis by shocking his victims with its erect enormity to compensate for the cruel hazing he received about it from his fellow inmates.

Latching onto what I thought might be a crucial piece of information, I assigned Marc some rational emotive behavioral therapy "homework." I instructed him to go to the public library and check out three textbooks on human anatomy and physiology. From these books, he was to look up information on the size of the normal erect penis. He signed a plan saying that he would do this the following morning. This assignment led to Marc's discovery that 95 percent of all males have an erect penis of between five and one-half and six and one-half inches, meaning that Marc was just one-half inch short of being within the average range.

This discovery provided for a fruitful evaluation of just how irrational it was for Marc to get himself into so much trouble for the sake of one-half inch of flesh that no one but his wife and he would ever see if he did not expose himself. He was guided to view his self-esteem in terms of his good looks, his high intelligence, and the love of his supportive wife and dependent child.

Ellis would have added that he will experience anxiety about his perceived inadequacy from time to time and to just accept it as normal. Anxious people tend to get anxious about their anxiety, telling themselves over and again, "I must not be anxious, I must not be anxious!" Being anxious about not being anxious is a self-defeating "musturbation" ("I must be totally in control of my emotions"). Marc has to learn to accept himself and his anxieties; all that he has to disown are his irrational thoughts and his anxiety will disappear.

Over the next few months, Marc reported that he had experienced urges to expose himself again. However, he had not done so because he reminded himself of the irrationality of the act and of his responsibilities to his family. Marc successfully completed three years of probation without further trouble with the law. I monitored the daily arrest sheet for the two remaining years I spent in probation without ever seeing his name on it. I ran into his wife one day at a shopping center. She told me that everything was going fine, that Marc had been at his job for over a year, that he had drastically cut down on his drinking, and that there did not seem to be any residual sexual problems. Marc's case was the kind that made me feel proud to have been a probation officer, and, for once, glad that my recommendation to the court perhaps had been wrong.

Lifestyle Theory

The interesting thing about the cognitive behavioral treatment approach is that it is the only approach to have a full-blown criminological theory based on its principles. The theory is known as the *lifestyle theory*, and has been primarily developed by Glen Walters (1990), a senior psychologist at the U.S. Penitentiary at Leavenworth, Kansas. Walters' theory is more psychological than sociological, and since it was developed in a prison setting, it is of particular interest to corrections workers. The term "lifestyle" appears to have been chosen to let us know that criminal behavior is not just another form of behavior, but rather it is a lifestyle.

Much of the foundation for Walters' theory was laid by Albert Ellis' rational emotive behavioral therapy and the "criminal mind" or "criminal personality" concept of Samuel Yochelson and Stanton Samenow. Walters borrowed Ellis' ABC concept of personality, which makes the point that people wrongly attribute causal power to situations and circumstances when it should be attributed to our beliefs or perceptions about those events. People respond to events according to the meaning that those events have for them, not according to any intrinsic quality of those events. Walters also borrowed and further systematized Yochelson and Samenow's list of fifty-two "thinking errors" that help to constitute the criminal personality.

Lifestyle theory contains three key concepts: *conditions, choice,* and *cognition.* A criminal lifestyle is the result of *choices* criminals make, although it is acknowledged that choices take place "within the limits established by our early and current biological/environmental *conditions*" (Walters and White, 1989:3). Note that while biological and environmental conditions lay the foundation of future behavioral choices, they do not determine it. Among the most important biological and environmental conditions affecting behavioral choices stressed by Walters are temperament and IQ, as stressed in Agnew's general strain theory, and <u>attachment</u>, as stressed in Hirschi's social control theory.

The third concept, *cognition*, refers to cognitive styles people develop as a consequence of their biological/environmental conditions and the pattern of choices they have made in response to them. According to this theory, lifestyle criminals display eight major cognitive features, or *thinking errors* that make them what they are (Walters 1990, Walters and White, 1989). Very little can be done to change criminals' behavior until they change this pattern of thinking. Each of these eight interrelated thinking errors is briefly described:

- *Mollification* refers to criminals' rationalizations and excuses designed to mollify (soften) the response of others toward them. Mollification is not simply a ploy to fool others; criminals often believe their own rationalizations.
- *Cutoff* refers to the ability of many criminals to discount the suffering of their victims. Feelings of guilt, sympathy, or empathy would render it difficult for them to victimize others, so they cut off such feelings. Firefighters, police officers, and many other professionals who deal with pain and suffering every day also must "steel" themselves to it if they are to do their jobs properly.
- *Entitlement* refers to criminals' feelings that they are entitled to that which they take from others. Being self-centered creatures, criminals consider themselves "special" people to whom the rules do not (or should not) apply. They believe that the world owes them a living and that they are simply taking their due.
- *Power Orientation* refers to criminals' propensity to view the world in terms of weakness and strength. They desire and understand strength and fear and exploit weakness. They want to dominate and control, and they carry a scorecard into every situation to figure who wins and who loses. They may do whatever they have to not to lose, but if they do lose, they will compensate by exploiting weaker individuals.
- *Sentimentality* refers to criminals' efforts to convince themselves and prosocial others that they are basically good people: "Sure, I've made mistakes, but I've never meant to hurt anyone."
- *Superoptimism* refers to criminals' exaggerated sense of self-confidence in their ability to get away with anything. Many criminals retain the adolescent's notion of personal invincibility (nothing will happen to me), which is why they have a strong tendency to discount or downplay the possibility of punishment.
- *Cognitive Indolence* refers to criminals' mental laziness. They are present oriented and concrete in their thinking. They have difficulty understanding abstract moral reasoning, are intellectually immature, easily bored, and crave excitement to fill the shallowness of their inner world.
- *Discontinuity* refers to criminals' inability to integrate their thinking patterns. Their thinking is so compartmentalized that they are overly sensitive to environmental pressures and changes, viewing them as unconnected to any integrated whole. This is why they have difficulty committing themselves to a long course of action such as schooling, training for a skilled occupation, or marriage.

These thinking errors resulting from arrested development of cognitive processes lead to four interrelated behavioral patterns or styles that almost guarantee criminality: *rule breaking, interpersonal intrusiveness* (intruding into the lives of others when

[Handwritten margin notes top left: "what ... own lies; unable to tie (L) & (R) side of the brain"]

not wanted), *self-indulgence*, and *irresponsibility*. Thus, criminality is the result of irrational behavior patterns, which are the result of faulty thinking, which arises from the consequences (reward and punishment) of choices in early life, which are themselves influenced by the individuals' biology and their early environmental conditions. Figure 11.1 illustrates the lifestyle progression towards criminal behavior.

FIGURE 11.1
Criminal Lifestyle Story

[Handwritten: "blames for our criminal behavior"]

Conditions	Choices	Cognition	Cognition	
Early biological and environmental experiences and personal traits and characteristics	→ Differential choice options resulting from interaction of conditions and the response of others to them	→ Cognition style formed by choices: cutoff, power orientation and cognitive indolence	→ Patters of behavior: rule breaking, interpersonal impulsiveness, self-indulgence, irresponsibility	→ **Crime**

LESSONS AND CONCERNS

Rational emotive behavioral therapy emphasizes that problems arise from the faulty operation of that which is unique to humankind: the capacity to think. Ask yourself, however, are emotional problems easily assuaged by pointing out that they are the result of faulty thinking? One philosophical wag opined that the sole function of the neocortex (the thinking brain) is to justify and rationalize the emotions and behaviors generated by the mammalian and paleocortices (the emotional and instinctual centers of the brain, respectively). Freud himself was said to believe that his "talking cures" were effective only with educated, middle-class patients having well-developed capacities for rational thought. This is not an apt description of the typical offender. Nevertheless, rational emotive behavioral therapy has found a home in corrections, particularly with alcoholic offenders (Trimpey, 1989; Ellis and Velten, 1992) and sex offenders (Hall and Osborn, 1994; Marsh and Walsh, 1995).

Are cognitions really more basic and potent than emotions, as Ellis seems to think? How often have you realized how utterly stupid it was to feel a certain way, wished very much that you did not, but continued to do so anyway? As Ellis himself frequently points out, we think and emote practically simultaneously, but do we feel bad because we think bad, or do we think bad because we feel bad? Certainly, we can change our thoughts regardless of whether they are preceded or followed by our emotions, but we need to address emotions a little more strongly than rational emotive behavioral therapy does. One way of doing this is to acknowledge that the past is more important to the understanding of the present than is admitted in rational emotive behavioral therapy. It is absolutely and obviously true that we cannot change the past, but invariably it insinuates itself into the present through our memory tapes. Unless we understand why this happens, confront it, and move on, we will continue to think irrationally.

Some (but certainly not this author) may criticize rational emotive behavioral therapy for insisting that rationality and irrationality always be defined from a law-abiding middle-class point of view. The insights of anomie and differential association theories tell us that under certain conditions, crime is a quite rational response (a fit between a goal and the means by which it is sought). Nevertheless, Ellis feels that the counselor's values and attitudes are legitimate therapeutic tools. Many offenders, but by no means all, can learn valuable self-insights from an active and didactic counselor. This is especially true if the counselor also draws lessons from client-centered therapy and establishes a warm relationship before attempting to confront the offender. Finally, rational emotive behavioral therapy, with its teacher/student relationship, is more realistic and genuine than client-centered therapy in a criminal justice setting, provided that the teacher is not confused with the preacher.

Lifestyle theory's solid concentration on individuals rather than their past and present environments is welcomed by many practically oriented correctional workers. It provides us with a starting point with which to attack criminal behavior with the weapon we know best—talk. We can do nothing about offenders' early conditions or the choices they made in response to them. We, however, can challenge their cognition. We can attack their thinking errors formed from the rewards and punishment they have experienced in response to their early choices. Lifestyle, and other similar theories stressing cognitive aspects of the individual, also have been welcomed because "they give permission for punishment of offenders, because offenders are responsible for their actions and make purposeful decisions to commit crime" (Williams and McShane, 1994:226)

Note the different conclusions we might draw from anomie/strain theory and lifestyle theory regarding the rationality of offending. The former maintains that offending is fully rational from the offenders' point of view because it is a means by which they attain goals that are (presumably) otherwise unattainable. Lifestyle theorists would not deny that criminal behavior is *logical* in the sense that it provides means/ends that follow from certain premises. Nevertheless, it is *irrational* because the premises themselves (the faulty cognition) are seriously flawed. Theories that locate the blame for crime outside the criminal do serious harm to society by providing criminals with authoritative rationalizations for their harmful and irresponsible behavior. If criminals can point to external "causes" of their behavior, they may deny and resist any efforts to correct it.

As welcome as the emphasis on the individual is to the correctional worker, lifestyle theory has its problems. Research in this theoretical tradition has been based overwhelmingly on prison inmates, a focus that excludes nonincarcerated felons and noncriminals. We might wonder how many noncriminals evidence the same thinking patterns. We also might wonder if thinking is not overemphasized at the expense of emotion. Some people are suited temperamentally to quietly "thinking things out," while others are impulsive hotheads. Additionally, moral or prosocial thinking is positively correlated to IQ (Kohlberg, 1984). Thus, IQ and temperament may effect the probability of criminal behavior beyond their effects on early life choices. It is all very well to demonstrate that criminals think differently from noncriminals, but science would like to know why they do. However, lifestyle theory is a strong "working" theory, and judged on that basis, a good one.

Perspective from the Field:
Cognitive Skills Programs in Correctional Settings
By Bruce L. Bikle, Ph.D.

Bruce Bikle is an assistant professor in the Division of Criminal Justice at California State University at Sacramento. He began his corrections work as a unit manager in the Hawaii correctional system and has worked in Oregon, Washington, and California in both prisons and jails. He received his Ph.D. from Portland State University in Public Administration and Policy. His areas of specialization are inmate programs, administration and management of correctional facilities, and direct supervision jails.

Most cognitive skills programs have as their principal goal to teach offenders to think and act in a prosocial manner. While many cognitive skills programs are used as stand alone programs, many jurisdictions have integrated cognitive skills programming into larger and more comprehensive program activities. The doctrine of cognitive thinking or cognitive skills programs center around the belief that it is "criminal thinking" that leads to criminal acts. Therefore, these programs work toward teaching offenders both the thinking skills and awareness about how thinking influences action. One such program is the Oregon SUMMIT Boot Camp, which has been in operation since 1994. SUMMIT stands for Success Using Motivation, Morale, Intensity and Treatment. The SUMMIT program is located at the Shutter Creek Correctional Facility on Oregon's central coast. While many boot camps around the country stress the military model, the SUMMIT program stresses the therapeutic and rehabilitative nature of the cognitive skills program in the context of military bearing and discipline (*see* Beers and Duval, 1996).

Setting up a program did not come quickly. The 1993 Oregon legislature mandated a program that would accommodate prisoners who were not sex offenders, or those with mandatory minimum sentences to serve. All participants in SUMMIT are volunteers and both men and women are admitted to the program.

Prior to the arrival of the first platoon of inmates, an extensive amount of research and training went into the program. Staff from Shutter Creek traveled to New York to observe that state's program. Feeling a need to stress rehabilitation, and encouraged by the success of other cognitive-based programs in Oregon (*see* note on page 221), the planning staff of the program decided on the "Options" cognitive program, developed by Jack Bush of Vermont. The Options program originally had been designed for the U.S. Navy and was adopted by Bush and the National Institute of Corrections for the offender population. Bush came to SUMMIT and trained the staff in the principles and practices of the Options program.

The doctrines of the Options program are as follows:

Choice and noncoercive use of authority: Accountability is stressed and offenders are held accountable in a constructive manner designed to challenge the offenders and motivate them toward change.

Objectivity: SUMMIT participants are expected to make thinking reports detailing their feelings and thoughts. These are presented without excuses or blame, and are designed to avoid defensiveness and excuse making.

Thinking Controls Behavior: The program is designed to get offenders to see how their own thinking can shape their behavior

Cognitive Change is Changing the Thinking Behind the Behavior: The process works by identifying the behavior to be changed, identifying the thinking, that influences the behavior to be changed, learning how to stop or interrupt this thinking, and replacing it with new thinking, and then practicing this new thinking, until it becomes ingrained in the individual.

Self-awareness and Self-responsibility: These traits are developed throughout the program through reports, counseling, group meetings and journals kept by the participants.

The Shutter Creek staff also underwent another cognitive skills enhancement program when all the staff involved with the program attended the "Breaking Barriers" sessions designed to improve the staff acceptance of the boot camp and to develop teamwork. Breaking Barriers has been used in a number of correctional facilities to rehabilitate offenders, and in private industry to improve operations and build a team spirit. Further, since the SUMMIT program was designed to release inmates to parole supervision, parole officers were encouraged to take the training as well. Many of the parole officers attended staff training and participated in military drill and physical training activities so they would know what their charges had experienced at Shutter Creek.

Bill Beers, the superintendent of the Shutter Creek facility, was determined that this boot camp program would provide the best chance for success on parole for the graduates, and strongly emphasized the necessity of the cognitive skills piece of the program. Beers states that "the development of cognitive skills to reduce criminal thinking is the primary emphasis of this program."

The first inmates arrived at Shutter Creek in March, 1994 and began their six month program. The regimen is tough—the day goes from 5:30 AM until 9:30 PM, seven days per week, and includes work, physical training, cooperation, teamwork, military bearing, decision making, education, reentry planning, twelve-step classes, alcohol and drug treatment, and daily assessment meetings with staff and each inmate's squad where issues are discussed and lessons are learned in the context of teamwork and self-responsibility.

From March, 1984 to April, 2000 more than 2,000 inmates entered the SUMMIT program. Of these, 1,172 inmates graduated from the institutional (Shutter Creek) portion of the program and 940 participants completed the community portion of the program. Completion rates were 58 percent for the institutional portion and 49 percent for the entire program.

The program has been successful on several counts. Information provided by the Oregon Department of Corrections shows that the thirty-two platoons who graduated from the program and completed the community reentry phase of the program have demonstrated a lower recidivism rate (measured as a lack of new felony convictions) than individuals who were closely matched to the successful SUMMIT graduates in terms of eligibility for program participation.

The numbers provided by the Oregon Department of Corrections speak for themselves: In the first year following release SUMMIT graduates recidivated at 8.7 percent. The comparable rate for SUMMIT eligible inmates who did not take the program was 18.1 percent. After two years, SUMMIT graduates showed a 20.4 recidivism rate while the comparison group showed a rate of 31.7 percent. And, at the three-year mark, SUMMIT graduates recidivism rate was 28.2 percent while the comparison group was 40.2 percent.

Not only did SUMMIT graduates stay out of trouble more often and longer than their peers, they also saved the state significant sums of money. Even after accounting for the fact that the SUMMIT program is more expensive to run than the general population program, due to increased program costs, the Department of Corrections estimates that from inception to April, 2000, the state had saved more than 14 million dollars with the SUMMIT program (Oregon Department of Corrections).

Lessons From the Oregon Experience About Cognitive Skills Programs:
First, an administrative commitment is essential to a successful program outcome. Oregon invested a lot of time, effort, and money in the development of the cognitive skills program that is used at SUMMIT, and invests in the Cognitive Skills Network noted below. Cognitive skills programs are found in most Oregon Department of Corrections' institutions. One might also look at the Correctional Service of Canada, which has adopted a cognitive skills program at many of their institutions and in many of their community corrections centers.

Secondly, we also might look at the SUMMIT program, which closely follows the New York boot camp model, which makes cognitive skills the centerpiece of the program. Programs that teach how to recognize thinking errors and how to correct them are of primary importance and demonstrate higher rates of overall success. Thirdly, both the Oregon and Canadian experience support the idea that a successful cognitive skills program needs to involve the staff (all the staff ideally) in the program; thus, "everyone is playing from the same sheet of music."

The Oregon SUMMIT boot camp program is one example of how a cognitive skills based program can contribute to lower recidivism, lower costs, and inmates who have learned how to better manage and control their lives. The success of these programs is contingent on support by administration and a motivated staff to implement the program. Oregon has demonstrated that the hard work is worth the effort.

Note: Oregon has implemented a number of Cognitive-based Programs, including:

- The "Reasoning and Rehabilitation" program developed by Robert R. Ross and Elizabeth A. Fabiano, which also is used extensively in the Correctional System of Canada
- Aggression Replacement Training, developed by Arnold Goldstein and Barry Glick
- Breaking Barriers or Framework for Change, developed by Gordon Graham
- Pathfinders, a transition and workforce development program that relies heavily on cognitive skills in the context of preparing inmates for release from prison

As a result of the popularity of the various programs, a "Cognitive Skills Network" of program providers, facility personnel, counselors, probation and parole officers, program planners, and ex-offender graduates of the programs meet several times a year to share information, conduct training, and review programs. For more information on cognitive skills program, check out the webpages of the National Institute of Corrections (www.nicic.org), the Oregon Department of Corrections, (www.doc.state.or.us) or the Correctional Service of Canada (www.csc-scc.gc.ca).

References and Suggested Readings

Arkowitz, H. and M. Hannah. 1989. Cognitive, Behavioral, and Psychodynamic Therapies. In A. Freeman, K. Simon, L. Beutler, and H. Arkowitz, eds. *Comprehensive Handbook of Cognitive Therapy.* New York: Plenum.

Austin, L. 1999. *The Counseling Primer.* Philadelphia: Accelerated Development Group.

Beers, W. and C. Duval. 1966. The Oregon Summit Program. In American Correctional Association, ed. *Juvenile and Adult Boot Camps*: Lanham, Maryland: American Correctional Association.

Buss, D. and D. Schmidt. 1993. Sex differences in jealousy: An evolutionary perspective on human mating. *Psychological Review.* 100:204-232.

Chavaria, F. 1997. Probation and cognitive skills. *Federal Probation.* 61:57-60.

Ellis, A. 1975. *A New Guide to Rational Living.* Hollywood, California: Wiltshire.

_____. 1982. *A Guide to Personal Happiness.* Hollywood, California: Wiltshire Book Company.

_____. 1984. Is the unified-interaction approach to cognitive-behavior modification a reinvention of the wheel? *Clinical Psychology Review.* 4:215-218.

_____. 1989. The History of Psychotherapy. In A. Freeman, K. Simon, L. Beutler, and H. Arkowitz, eds. *Comprehensive Handbook of Cognitive Therapy.* New York: Plenum.

_____. 1996. *Better, Deeper, and More Enduring Brief Therapy.* New York: Brunner/Mazel.

Ellis, A. and E. Velten. 1992. *When AA Doesn't Work for You: Rational Steps to Quitting Alcohol.* Fort Lee, New Jersey: Barricade Books.

Hall, K. and C. Osborn. 1994. The conduct of socially sensitive research: Sex offenders as participants. *Criminal Justice and Behavior.* 21:325-340.

Kohlberg, L. 1984. *The Psychology of Moral Development: The Nature and Validity of Moral Stages.* New York: Harper and Row.

Marsh, R. and A. Walsh. 1995. Physiological and psychosocial assessment and treatment of sex offenders: A comprehensive victim-oriented approach. *Journal of Offender Rehabilitation.* 22:77-96.

Samenow, S. 1998. *Straight Talk about Criminals.* Livingston, New Jersey: Jason Aronson.

_____. 1999. *Before It's Too Late: Why Some Kids Get into Trouble and What Parents Can Do About It*. New York: Times Books.

_____. 2000. Introduction. In B. Sharp. *Changing Criminal Thinking: A Treatment Program*. Lanham, Maryland: American Correctional Association.

Sharp, B. 2000. *Changing Criminal Thinking: A Treatment Program*. Lanham, Maryland: American Correctional Association.

Trimpey, J. 1989. *Rational Recovery from Alcoholism: The Small Book*. Lotus, California: Lotus Press.

Vanstone, M. 2000. Cognitive-behavioural work with offenders in the U.K.: A history of influential endeavour. *The Howard Journal*. 39:171-183.

Vennard, J., D. Sugg, and C. Hedderman. 1997. The Use of Cognitive-Behavioural Approaches with Offenders: Messages from the Research. In C. Lewis, ed. *Changing Offenders' Attitudes and Behavior: What Works?* London: Home Office Research and Statistics.

Walters, G. 1990. *The Criminal Lifestyle: Patterns of Serious Criminal Conduct*. Newbury Park, California: Sage.

Walters, G. and T. White. 1989. The thinking criminal: A cognitive model of lifestyle criminality. *Criminal Justice Research Bulletin*. Huntsville, Texas: Sam Houston State University Press.

Williams, F. and M. McShane. 1994. *Criminological Theory, Second Edition*. Englewood Cliffs, New Jersey: Prentice Hall.

Yochelson, S. and S. Samenow. 1976. *The Criminal Personality: A Profile for Change*. Livingston, New Jersey: Jason Aronson.

12,15,16

7. Empathy training means
    1. Teaching inamates
B ☞ 2 Put in victim shoes & reveal how they feel
    3. more sensitive
    4 dwell

15. Most criminal deny alcohol problem because

    1. dont have problem
    2 get more sivrious pu
    3.
    4 Free to go into prison

11. 1st metabilitie
    1 acietra THC
    2 anta
    3 Teta
    4 Urine

Group Counseling in Institutional Settings

When the prison gates slam behind an inmate, he does not lose his human quality, his mind does not become closed to ideas, his intellect does not cease to feed on a free and open interchange of opinions; his yearning for self-esteem does not end; nor his quest for self-realization conclude. If anything, the needs for identity and self-esteem are more compelling.

Justice Thurgood Marshall

The Power of the Group

Jails and prisons are not very nice places. They were never meant to be, and they never can be. Whatever euphemisms we dream up for them, they still exist to punish lawbreakers and to separate them from "decent" society. They are prime examples of what Goffman (1961) has called "total institutions." *Total institutions* can be mental hospitals, army training facilities, or any other institution where large groups of people live together under tightly restricted and scheduled circumstances and under the control of a central authority. Total institutions are divided into "managers," who control, and "subjects," who are controlled. It is the function of the managers to restrict social interaction between the subjects and the outside world. The consequence of such an authoritarian and coercive situation is the development of two antagonistic subcultures within the institution. Social distance between the controllers and the controlled is great, and each group tends to develop hostile attitudes toward the other.

THE INMATE CODE

The hostility toward the managers is expressed in an informal set of rules known as the *inmate code*, which includes the game playing we discussed in the section on transactional analysis. One of those rules is "Don't be a sucker," a rule that warns

225

inmates against granting overt respect and prestige to prison officers and staff and against trusting them. This rule does not mean that inmates openly defy prison officials and regulations, because overt acts of defiance may bring down the wrath of the managers on the entire group. Rather, it means never be openly friendly to officials unless you can use them for your own ends, never cooperate at a level beyond that which is necessary to avoid trouble, never volunteer for anything simply for the good of the institution, and never show subservience.

Unfortunately, the noncooperative inmate code extends to noncooperation with those members of the prison staff whose function it is to aid and counsel inmates. No wonder it has been said that trying to rehabilitate criminals in prison is like trying help alcoholics maintain sobriety in a brewery. Institutional counseling is, therefore, the ultimate challenge for the criminal justice helper.

THE ORIGINS OF THE INMATE CODE

When we discussed differential association theory, we noted that many criminals develop a set of values and attitudes in opposition to lawful behavior through the frequency, duration, priority, and intimacy of their associations with individuals of like mind. The individuals with whom they most associate, either by choice or by necessity, become their reference group, the group around which they orient their lives, and against whose standards they evaluate themselves. When criminals are incarcerated, the power of the reference group over their lives increases considerably because now it is the only group with which they are able to associate. Within this closed community, anti-establishment values are refined and reinforced. In prison, compliance with anti-establishment values and attitudes can become much more of a survival imperative than it ever was on the outside. This is an important point for any new member of the treatment staff working in a prison.

PRISONIZATION

Not all inmates enter prison with a ready-made set of antisocial attitudes. However, new prisoners, like new immigrants, face a painful process of assimilation into a new culture from which it is difficult to remain aloof. The process of assimilating the norms and values of the prison subculture has been termed *prisonization* by Clemmer (1958). The basic premise of prisonization is that people who share a common experience, especially one imposed upon them, develop a sense of "we-ness" buttressed by a set of legitimizing attitudes in opposition to those professed by "them."

The first steps in the prisonization process are simple acts of behavioral conformity, which occur regardless of how the inmate feels about performing them. The inmate watches and follows the examples of other inmates because conformity makes life easier, avoids conflicts, and enables the inmate to fit in without being conspicuous. Before the inmate knows it, he or she is speaking the language of fellow inmates and beginning to define the inmate world in their terms. It requires only a subtle and minute change to make a stated attitude become a "taken-for-granted" perception of reality. When this process is completed, inmates become "cons."

The prison subculture often satisfies the inmates' needs to belong, a need that we all have. To belong, an inmate must be accepted, and to be accepted he or she must live by the inmate code whereby a "wrong" by the standards of the straight world becomes a "right." To the extent that an inmate abides by that code, he or she becomes a "good convict," and is accepted. For an inmate not to be accepted by fellow inmates could be a very dangerous thing indeed for the inmate.

According to Gordon Graham, a hard-nosed ex-con who spent nearly twenty years in various prisons and now is president of the Human Development Training Institute, this need to belong by conforming to the inmate code is the biggest stumbling block to inmate rehabilitation (1992:62). Through hard experience, observation, and much study, Graham concluded that the establishment of a strong personal identity as a "good convict" in prison becomes more strongly etched into the person's self-concept the longer he (or she) remains in the prison environment.

We all develop what Gordon calls a "comfort zone," which is a set of situations, settings, and circumstances in which we feel confident and comfortable. For instance, a "take charge" police officer might tremble at the thought of giving a lecture, and an erudite professor might tremble if he or she is thrust into the professional world of the police officer. When we are outside of our comfort zones, we get feedback telling us that we are "out of place," and we often retreat back to the psychological safety of the known. Inmates develop a "comfort zone," too, but a very constricted one. When they get back onto the streets, they do not fit in; their much sought after reputations as "good convicts" now become liabilities, their worlds have turned upside down (Graham, 1992:158).

Although all prisoners have to conform behaviorally, not all, perhaps not even most, will conform attitudinally in the sense that they will internalize the inmate code as right and proper. Ways to avoid attitudinal assimilation on the part of prisoners suggested by Clemmer (and seconded by Graham) are shorter prison sentences and more frequent contact with the outside world.

Prisoners with strong personalities and those who actively strive to remain aloof from the prison subculture do not succumb to prisonization to the same extent that more pliable individuals do, although trying to remain aloof may subject the inmate to "dangerous ostracism (Schmalleger, 2001:493). Some take on the values and attitudes surrounding them only as a measure of convenience, being fully aware all the time that their conformity is a temporary condition of their confinement. We can help these individuals to counteract the insidious process of prisonization, and even perhaps those who have already succumbed, by well-run group counseling sessions. Remember, all counseling is designed to challenge what Graham calls our comfort zones. Becoming a better person (attaining psychological growth) requires that we extend those zones as far as we possibly can so that we can be reasonably confident and comfortable in even the most unusual of circumstances.

Group Counseling

A major obstacle to effective institutional counseling is the oppositional stance of the inmate code. Inmates do attend counseling sessions, Alcoholics Anonymous, and Narcotics Anonymous meetings, and vocational and educational programs. Attendance at these sessions is not a violation of the inmate code. Indeed, much banter is heard in prisons about the necessity to "get into a program." Unfortunately, the concern for getting into a program is more often than not motivated by efforts to impress the parole board rather than a genuine concern for self-improvement (Berne's "How do I get out of here?"). If the possibility of the ultimate reward for participation, that of early release, were not a reality, inmates who attended such sessions would be violating the inmate code and branded as "suckers" or "ass kissers." Consequently, inmates who attend sessions aimed at reforming criminal behavior patterns may spend a great deal of time telling other inmates how they are exploiting the sessions for their own ends.

Group counseling is an effective way to combat the negative group pressures that hinder rehabilitative efforts. Group counseling may be viewed as a kind of intellectual jujitsu in which the strength of the group is used against itself. Group counseling uses peer pressure to combat the criminal attitudes and values that many of the group members hold as individuals. The differential association theory of crime stresses the power of peer group pressure to lead the individual into conformity with antisocial values. Why not use the same pressure for the opposite purpose? If an individual's behavior is an intrinsic part of groups to which he or she belongs, if we want to change that behavior, we must direct our efforts at those groups.

However, do not imagine that this is an easy task. How does one change the criminal attitudes of individuals in a group that, with the exception of the group leader, consists of criminals? Although it is extremely difficult, and realistically you can expect at least as many failures as successes, it is not impossible. Think about the gratifying success rate of Alcoholics Anonymous (AA) groups. Do you think that it is more difficult to rehabilitate the typical alcoholic or the typical criminal? Objectively, the alcoholic presents the more difficult case. After all, there is no biological urge to commit crimes (not that we currently know of, anyway) in the same sense as there is for the alcoholic to drink. The criminal who desists from committing crime does not suffer painful physical withdrawal symptoms that are alleviated only by committing one. Criminals are not physiologically punished for stopping their activities the way alcoholics are. On the contrary, they run the risk of punishment for continuing with the activity.

Many criminals enjoy the thrills and excitement of the criminal lifestyle just as alcoholics enjoy drinking. But neither alcoholics nor criminals like the negative consequences of their respective activities. Significant emotional events in their lives, the loss of jobs, spouses, and self-respect, and the loss of long periods of freedom constitute powerful motivations for change.

Whatever motivations exist for change must be brought into full consciousness and be sharply focused. They then must be carefully cultivated and nurtured. In other words, dissonance and tension must be generated in the minds of those whose attitudes are to be modified by forcing them to confront the reality of their behavior. Many criminals are so present-oriented that they fail to consider what five years in prison actually mean. It is the group counselor's task, with the cooperation of the group, to bring each member to the realization that powerful motivations for change do exist in every one of them. Specific strategies for achieving this in a group setting are presented later in this chapter. If Alcoholics Anonymous can achieve respectable success rates in groups consisting of members who have all experienced the pleasures and the pains of alcohol, there is no reason to feel that groups consisting of those who have experienced the pleasures and pains of crime could not enjoy similar success.

THE POWER OF THE GROUP

A group consists of "a number of persons who communicate with one another often over a span of time, and who are few enough so that each person is able to communicate with all others, not at secondhand, through other people, but face-to-face" (Homans, 1950:1). The prison community is not a group in this sense, but merely an aggregate of people in the midst of which the individual could feel terribly alone. None of us likes to feel alone, and we often will go to great lengths to become part of a group.

We are very social animals. Group counseling takes advantage of this human need for social interaction by offering inmates a constructive alternative to the antisocial cliques that form in prisons.

Groups possess dynamics of their own that are relatively independent of the sum of the individual attributes of their members. Much of sociology and social psychology revolves around issues of how group life affects individual behavior. Numerous studies attest to the ability of groups to generate a general conformity to their norms, even among reluctant members. Here we cannot consider in detail the question of why groups possess powers that appear to be greater than the sum of their constituent parts.

Suffice it to say that group conformity is more likely if goals are shared, and goals are more likely to be shared if they are democratically determined. As the group leader, meaning the person who initiates the process and who gives the initial direction and initial suggestions, the counselor is in a position to strongly influence the nature of the goals. Inmates realize, of course, that the ultimate goal is to reeducate them into conformity with society's standards and expectations. Therefore, they are not likely to choose topics that they perceive as being too directly related to this end. As a group counselor, you must make haste slowly. If inmates are to learn new values and unlearn old ones, they will do so only by the process of self-exploration that is of their own choosing.

Planning for Group Counseling: Goals and Operating Philosophy

The first task in the planning for group counseling is to formulate in your own mind the specific aims and goals that you want the group to pursue. Your operating philosophy should be something like that of a professor who has a certain core content of knowledge to impart to the class but who remains flexible enough to let the students dictate the pace of the class. Much student interest and participation is lost in classes where professors refuse to follow a train of thought brought up by a student because "We have to finish Chapter 10 by Thursday." Group interest and participation similarly can be stifled if you do not maintain an attitude of structured flexibility.

SELECTION OF MEMBERS

Your next task is the selection of group members from the pool of volunteers. For various reasons, there is rarely any lack of volunteers for group counseling in prisons (Juda, 1984:48). You simply should not throw people together to see what will happen, an all-too-frequent practice in prison settings. Rizzo suggests a "loose homogeneity" in such settings (1980:29). An examination of the offenders' classification scales and their psychological profiles obviously will aid you in this endeavor. Needless to say, if the group is to be centered around a specific problem, such as alcoholism, drug addiction, or sexual offenses, then inmates should be selected on the basis of problems they have in the specific area rather than on other considerations.

Each prospective member of the group then should be given an individual screening interview. This practice is laid down as one of the ethical guidelines of the Association for Specialists in Group Work (ASGW, 1980):

The group leader shall conduct a pre-group interview with each prospective member for purposes of screening, orientation, and, in so far as possible, shall select group members whose needs and goals are compatible with the established goals of the group; who will not impede the group process; and whose well-being will not be jeopardized by the group process.

Corey (1983:102) indicates that the following questions concerning suitability can be explored in about a half-hour interview with each candidate:

1. Why does this person want to join the group?
2. How ready is the person to become actively involved in the process of self-examination that will be part of group?
3. Does the candidate have a clear idea about the nature and purpose of the group?
4. Does he or she have a view of what is expected?
5. Are there any indications that the person might be counterproductive to the development of the cohesion in the group? Might this group be counterproductive to the person?

Such a screening interview not only permits you to choose group members who you feel will strengthen the group's possibilities of success, but it also allows you and individual offenders to become acquainted with one another. Moreover, it gives offenders the opportunity to decide for themselves whether they want to be part of your group after all. Thus, you have a double screening process, yours and theirs. Without the dual check-out process, you and the offenders are on a blind date, and we all know how disastrous blind dates can turn out to be. Except when counseling is mandated, inmates never should be forced into a group against their will. To do so will prove very counterproductive (Alexander, 2000).

COMPONENTS OF GROUP COUNSELING

Gazda, Duncan, and Meadows provide the best definition of group counseling:

Group counseling is a dynamic, interpersonal process focusing on conscious thought and behavior and involving the therapy functions of permissiveness, orientation to reality, catharsis, and mutual trust, caring, understanding, acceptance, and support. The therapy functions are created and nurtured in a small group through the sharing of personal concerns with one's peers and the counselors. The group counselees are basically normal individuals with various concerns which are not debilitating to the extent of requiring extensive personality change. The group counselees may utilize the group interaction to increase understanding and acceptance of values and goals and to learn and/or unlearn certain attitudes and behaviors (quoted in Mahler, 1973:101).

By analyzing the component parts of the definition, we can get a feeling for the process of group counseling, what it is and how it should be conducted.

"Group counseling is a dynamic, interpersonal process" alerts you to the fact that the process is active, productive, forceful, and energetic. It is not static, but full of continuous verbal movement toward purposeful goals. It can be dynamic only if real concerns and problems are put before the group for open evaluation and discussion by members of the group.

"Interpersonal" means that it is an activity that takes place between or among two or more people. Advocates of group counseling feel that members learn and/or unlearn attitudes, values, and perceptions better in a group setting because it is more similar to their natural interpersonal world. Relating to peers is more consistent with normal socialization experiences than relating to a counselor in a situation that can be reminiscent of the teacher/student relationship. Most of all, "interpersonal" means sharing.

"*Focusing on conscious thought and behavior*" indicates that the topics explored are attitudes and behaviors of which the group members are fully aware and which are problematic. Group counseling is not group therapy. Group therapy is more likely to deal with unconscious motivations, and it is usually conducted by individuals with advanced degrees in psychiatry, psychology, or psychiatric social work. The difference is analogous to the distinction made earlier between psychotherapy and individual counseling. Like psychotherapy, group therapy goes into great depth, and it is a process that may last months or years. Group counseling is very short, by comparison, and may be conducted by individuals with minimal specialized skills. Remember, the most successful group counseling in the world is conducted by the concerned amateurs of Alcoholics Anonymous. Remember also that the personal attributes of the counselor are more important to success than the depth of the counselor's knowledge of the complexities of mental health.

"*Permissiveness, orientation to reality, catharsis, and mutual trust, caring, understanding, acceptance and support*" are attributes that the counselor must strive to foster in the group. This is no easy task with a prison group! Permissiveness does not mean that the group is allowed to act out, to bully weaker members, or to be otherwise disruptive. It means that the group should be democratic in its choice of problems to discuss, that no one member should be allowed to monopolize the floor, and that no relevant topic should be denied a hearing. *→ structure but allow them to expl*

Neither does "*permissiveness*" mean that the group is run without some basic ground rules. As with the formulation of treatment plans in community corrections, the rules should be determined in concert with the group. However, group counseling is a guided-group experience. Accordingly, during the initial screening interview, the counselor will indicate a series of expectations about what will go on in the group. The counselor basically wants group members to examine their impulses in an atmosphere of acceptance to help them make connections between those impulses and their criminal behavior. Groups function much more effectively if each member is aware of the expectations and has been given an opportunity to participate in their formulation. A democratically determined group structure outlining purposeful goals goes a long way toward developing a feeling of "we-ness" in the group. The essential elements of group interaction—each individual "I," the "we" of the group, and the "it" of the goals—must form an integrated "I-we-it" triangle if the process is to be useful (Anderson, 1984: 13-15).

Take care, however, that democratically derived decisions regarding group topics and issues are not at odds with institutional requirements, are socially acceptable, and are fit for individual members of the group. Neither group nor counselor pressure should be used to cajole individual members into conformity. As Bennett, Rosenbaum, and McCullough (1978:89) put it: "We cannot continue to coerce offenders into conformity. We must provide those experiences necessary to individual adjustment and a meaningful life. For most people this comes through opportunities for intellectual and emotional growth. Why not for offenders?" Why not indeed?

"*Orientation to reality*" refers to an awareness on the part of all group members that the goals of the group are directed toward the rejection of unrealistic and irresponsible values and behavior and the substitution of realistic and responsible values

Not looking @ long term goals
they only look @ short term feel and things

231

and behavior. Realistic and responsible here are consistent in meaning with Glasser's usage in his reality therapy. The general goals of a prison group are improved self-awareness, genuine problem sharing, an awareness of the self-defeating nature of a criminal lifestyle, improved coping skills, and an understanding of the benefits and possibilities of the straight life. Specific goals are determined by the makeup of the group (for example, alcohol abusers, exhibitionists, and so forth).

"*Catharsis*" refers to the release and ventilation of repressed emotions associated with painful experiences. Psychoanalysts feel that much guilt, anger, aggression, and hostility are the result of repressed emotions. If these pent-up emotions can be liberated—that is, brought into consciousness and explored—then, much of the negativism they generate will dissipate. → Never going to get bu strive to.

"*Mutual trust, caring, understanding, acceptance, and support*" are attributes conspicuously absent among prison inmates at anything beyond a superficial level. However, they should not be considered impossible to generate in a prison setting. By and large, inmates do not possess these attributes because they rarely have encountered them in their lives. If you, by your example, can foster such an environment, if you can demonstrate acceptance, understanding, and caring, chances are that some of it will rub off. Here is one inmate's report of her experience in group counseling: "I have felt needed, loving, competent, furious, frantic, anything and everything, but just plain loved. You can imagine the flood of humility, release that swept over me. I wrote with considerable joy, 'I actually felt loved.' I doubt that I shall soon forget it" (quoted in Jarvis, 1978:197-198).

"*The therapy functions are created and nurtured in a small group*" says that the size of the group is an important consideration. A group of too few members, say three, is comfortable for the group leader to handle, but it is not very practical in terms of the efficient management of time and resources. Groups this small also have two additional disadvantages that often seem to occur: two members forming an alliance against a third, or members feel too much pressure to speak and thus feel uncomfortable (Jacobs, Harvill, and Masson, 1998). Having too many members renders the group unmanageable for the leader. The group begins to act like a class in school, directing communications primarily at the group counselor. This tendency defeats the whole purpose of being in a group. The more people there are in a group, the easier it becomes for some members to hide and avoid discussing their problems. Even if no one wanted to hide, there is just so much "air time" to go around, and the multiplicity of topics may prevent focusing where it is desirable. A generally accepted optimal group size is between five and eight members (Jacobs, Harvill, and Masson, 1998).

Even a group of this size can be intimidating and difficult to manage for new counselors. In a one-on-one situation, counselors have the feeling of being in control, because they have to attend to only one individual. It is not unusual for inmate groups to test new counselors by ganging up on them. Having something of a vested interest in maintaining current self-concepts, in demonstrating independence and noncooperation, and in displaying bravado, group members often feel that the best defense is offense. Confident and self-assured counselors recognize and deal with this obvious game-playing by indicating to the group that they know what is going on, and asking the members why they feel that they have to do it. Counselors never should go on the defensive, but rather, should toss the ball right back at the group, without emphasizing their moral authoritative superiority over the group.

"*Through the sharing of personal concerns with one's peers and the counselors*" points to the exchange of self-disclosure and feedback among members of the group.

This is the essence of group counseling. The success or failure of the group depends almost entirely on the meaningfulness of the self-concerns disclosed and the nature of the feedback.

But prison is a place where it is often necessary to shut off one's emotions, where inmates are supposed to "do their own time," and where to reveal personal concerns is to open oneself up to possible abuse, derision, or even blackmail. Consequently, inmates in a group session may go to great lengths to lead the group communication away from themselves and toward others, or to general topics. Such ploys may be in evidence in any group setting, but they are especially so in the prison setting. You must learn to identify them and confront members with them, at the same time recognizing the motivations behind them. A prison group is not an encounter group for which members have paid considerable sums of money to seek "self-actualization." You will be setting yourself up for disappointment and failure if you fail to empathize with the special concerns about self-disclosure within a prison setting.

There are several ways to handle the lack of self-disclosure within the group. It is wise not to expect or to attempt to facilitate self-disclosure at all during the first session. Simply give the group members an opportunity to warm up to intergroup communication by venting general nonthreatening concerns. Inmates must sense at least a modicum of trust and acceptance before they will risk self-disclosure.

An excellent institutional counseling strategy is to begin the first session with an explanation of Berne's theory of structural analysis (Lester, 2000). Its easy terminology and simple diagrammatic presentations of Parent-Adult-Child (PAC) interactions provide a useful shared framework from which all participants can analyze what will go on during future sessions. The various ego states and their transactions can be drawn and explained on the blackboard. You may be surprised how much more easily group members will pick up on game playing and how it quickly will improve understanding when you use this very powerful anchor of shared discourse. However, some experienced prison counselors feel that the transactional analysis approach is not very useful in prison settings beyond the early sessions that introduce terminology. The very simplicity of the approach is tailor-made for inmates who may want to use it to manipulate fellow inmates, and even counselors.   A never cause of B it's what you think of B that is the cause

After one or two "getting acquainted" sessions, you may make a statement to the group something like the following: "You know, we've been talking for quite some time together now, but I haven't heard any of us touch on the topics of 'self' or 'I' yet. Will somebody volunteer to explore the question 'Who or what am I?' with us?"

The first attempt at self-disclosure should be reinforced positively by the use of nonthreatening and nonjudgmental feedback from the counselor. Feedback should reflect the feelings of the person making the disclosures, making sure that the reflection is based on accurate perceptions rather than on inferences. If, for instance, Frank responds to your request to explore the question "Who am I?" with the response, "I suppose that by society's standards I am a failure, a no-good screw-up," he is making a statement about his perceptions of how others on the outside view him. You should not infer that he perceives himself that way by asking him why he is a "screw-up." Rather, you should ask him if he agrees with that perception and why he does or does not. Such feedback could lead to an animated group discussion of values and attitudes held by group members.

As a member of the group, the counselor should be prepared to model self-disclosure for the group. Needless to say, the counselor must feel that he or she is fair game in any session and must be prepared to answer uncomfortable questions in an honest and forthright manner. It is not unusual for inmates to test the counselor by asking pointed questions such as "Did you ever steal anything?" Almost everybody has stolen something at one time or another, even if it was only a candy bar or a company pen. You must not attempt to give the impression that you are a "goody two-shoes" by denying that you have, thereby modeling dishonesty for the group. You could take advantage of such a question by describing how guilty you felt afterwards and asking other members of the group how they feel when they steal and how they themselves have felt when others have stolen from them. You also can use the opportunity to describe your ideas of responsibility, emotional maturity, respect for self and others, and discuss how your values have enabled you to lead a basically happy life. Again, this should not be delivered in a preachy style calculated to impress the group with your moral superiority.

"*The group counselees are basically normal individuals with various concerns which are not debilitating to the extent of requiring extensive personality change*" is a reminder to respect the humanity of the group members. Do not think of them as being sick, evil, beyond help, or radically different in any way from yourself. They are basically unloved individuals with deficiencies that prevent them in one way or another from functioning in a socially acceptable way. Inmates who do have crippling and debilitating concerns do not belong in group counseling. Think of all group members as possessing wholesome potentialities that only need to be recognized and developed. The distortions of reality you encounter are the result of faulty thinking rather than pathological blockages. Your basic task is to reeducate inmates toward responsibility, not to psychoanalyze.

"*The group counselees may utilize the group interaction to increase understanding and acceptance of values and goals and to learn and/or unlearn certain attitudes and behaviors*" simply restates the goals of any counseling session, group or individual. It is a guided effort to change a failure identity into a success identity through self-disclosure and feedback. The only difference emphasized here is that group counseling makes use of peer feedback and modeling.

Specific Topics and Strategies for Group Counseling

The goal of group counseling is to guide offenders toward change by exploring and assessing their values, attitudes, and behaviors. What follows are some specific strategies for getting started. Additional exercises may be similar to the exercises at the end of some of the chapters in this book, such as exploring general attitudes and values.

COUNTING THE COST OF A CRIMINAL LIFESTYLE

From the perspective of some criminals, crime may be considered a rational pursuit in the sense that there is a logical fit between the attainment of ends and the means used to achieve them. That is, it gets them what they want at a price that they think they can afford. This group exercise is designed to challenge that perception of rationality through certain cognitive-behavioral techniques. From any objective viewpoint (that is, going beyond the offender's subjective perception of immediate rationality), for all but the "kingpins" of crime, crime simply does not pay in the long run.

You can help your group members discover this for themselves by having them make out an inventory of their estimated criminal gains (assuming they were property offenders) obtained for the crime(s) for which they are doing time. You might go even further by asking them to list their gains from undetected crimes committed during the period between their current arrest and any previous arrest. The list should contain actual cash gains and the "fenced" value of any property taken. A list compiled by an offender who did forty months in prison for three burglaries is presented below. This individual also included in his inventory ten other burglaries for which he was not caught.

Cash	$400
Stereos	$150
TV's	$ 75
Jewelry	$200
Tools	$ 20
Miscellaneous	$180
Total	$1,025

After these lists are completed, divide the monetary gains from crime by the amount of time spent in prison (take along a calculator). For instance, the person in this example received a "pay check" from his criminal activity of $1,025, for which he did forty months in prison. Therefore: $1,025/40$ months = $25.62 per month, $0.82 per day, or $0.10 per hour. The group members will be quite surprised when they discover how little they have been "working" for per hour! Few of the offenders, if any at all, have ever thought along these lines. You then may proceed with what should be an animated discussion of just how smart it is to work for ten cents per hour.

Drive the point home by calculating the possible gains the person would have if he or she had spent forty months in noncriminal activity. Ask each individual to speculate about what portion of his or her prison sentence he or she reasonably could have been expected to work at a regular job on the outside. If our individual doing forty months stated that he would have worked only about one-quarter of the time, multiply this time by the take-home pay he would have received at minimum wage (about $400 per month). Thus, $400 times 10 months = $4,000. Add to this approximately $100 per month he could have received in welfare during his periods of unemployment, and we reach a total of $7,000. This is hardly a princely sum, but considerably in excess of his $1,025. Even if you add the fruits of a criminal lifestyle in the form of prison wages (an average of about 80 cents per hour) for those lucky enough to have a prison job, the contrast will be only slightly diminished.

Other less tangible, but sometimes more important, costs and benefits associated with a criminal lifestyle can be discussed in the group. To start this discussion rolling, have each member divide a sheet of paper into two equal sections. Have them label one column Benefits, and the other Costs. Rather than doing this on an individual basis, consider dividing the group into two sections, one to brainstorm about the benefits of crime and the other to do the same about the costs of crime. They might arrive at a set of costs and benefits like that shown in Figure 12.1 (page 236).

Other costs and benefits are possible, but almost invariably you will find that members will be able to think of a lot more costs than benefits. Discuss this discrepancy with them, as well as the inconsistency of such items as "being free to be my own man," on the one hand, and having every movement dictated by the "screws" on the other. You even may go further and invite them to rate each item on a scale of one through ten according to how positive they consider each benefit of crime and how negative they consider each cost of crime. They then can sum the columns to arrive at their own numeric evaluation of the costs and benefits of their lifestyles. Since they will have listed the items themselves, as well as deciding what numeric score to assign to them, this exercise can be a powerful tool in getting your group members to realize how destructive to themselves their lifestyles are.

Figure 12.1
What Do I Gain and Lose From a Life of Crime?

Benefits	Costs
Lots of leisure (not working)	No regular paycheck, little money to spend
The street reputation	The boredom of sitting in a cell
Doing what I want, being free to be my own man	The worry caused to my parents
Lots of girls think I'm cool	Having the screws decide almost all I do and when I should do it
The laughs	No women in the joint
Putting one over on the system	Police hassle and arrest
Money for nothing	Can't get a job because of record
	The whole prison experience
	Appearing in court and paying fines
	This prison is a long way from home, so I rarely see my parents
	My wife divorced me and married another guy while I was away

ROLE REVERSAL AND EMPATHY TRAINING

Criminals rarely think of the feelings of their victims. One of the ways to encourage such thought is to ask them to compile a list of feelings that they think the victims of their latest crimes may have experienced as a consequence of those crimes. The lists may contain such feelings as anger, revenge, fear, and outrage. Ask the group members if they feel that these responses of the victims are justified. This exercise should not be conducted in the spirit of "How would you like it if. . . ?" Most members long ago will have been inured to such moralizing.

Yet, it is highly likely that most group members will have been victims of crimes themselves in the past. Ask them to recall the feelings that they had about their victimizers on those occasions. Also, have them explore feelings they had when a family member or close personal friend was victimized. Such a discussion should lead to the general conclusion that even criminals value justice and "law and order" when the offender/victim roles are reversed.

SENTENCING EXERCISES

Without being explicit, you can further emphasize their beliefs in conventional morality by engaging in the type of sentencing exercises you have been asked to do as students. That is, you could provide the group with hypothetical criminal cases and have the group decide on appropriate penalties for them. You will find that inmates will present arguments similar to those of probation officers at sentencing staffings (meetings at which officers decide together on an appropriate sentencing recommendation) and that they often can be considerably more punitive in their sentencing decisions! What group members will be doing implicitly in these exercises, without fully recognizing it for the moment, is revealing and reflecting on some of their anticriminal and prosocial values.

REATTRIBUTING RESPONSIBILITY AND INCREASING SELF-ESTEEM

Criminals share with the rest of us a penchant for systematically biasing causal attributions of responsibility for what happens to them. It is generally true that when something good or praiseworthy happens to us, we locate the causal agent in ourselves: "I was able to accomplish this goal because I'm a pretty dependable and neat kind of person." When something bad or blameworthy happens to us, we tend to attribute it to circumstances beyond our control: "I'm branded a criminal because I was never given a chance. My parents beat me and never took an interest in me. Nobody'll give me a job, so I have to steal." In the first instance, we take a free-will perspective by offering "reasons" located within the self for having accomplished a goal. In the second instance, we tend to take a determinist position by offering "causes" external to ourselves that guarantee "it could not be otherwise."

Such attributions of responsibility are normal, albeit not desirable. They function as defense mechanisms to protect our self-images. Like all other defense mechanisms, they can become pathologically destructive if we deny all responsibility for the negative things that happen to us. Unfortunately, many criminals are remarkably creative in inventing and exaggerating the power of circumstances deemed beyond their control to justify their criminal behavior and their inability to follow the straight and narrow. Your task is to demonstrate the irrationality and lack of responsibility inherent in this attitude. We are not dead leaves blown hither and thither by environmental winds. We do have a hand in what happens to us, and we do possess the capacity to bring those events under our control.

To explore this way of thinking with your group, ask them to draw a large four-celled square like the one in Figure 12.2. Instruct them to list in the windowed cells (1) what good things in their lives are the results of their own actions, (2) what good things in their lives are the results of circumstances outside their control, (3) what bad things in their lives are the results of their own actions, and (4) what bad things in their lives are the results of circumstances outside their control.

The odds are that you will see the great majority of responses in the upper-left and lower-right cells of the square. You might begin the discussion by asking members to volunteer reasons why they have placed a given event in a given cell and then open up those reasons for discussion. You can steer the discussion around to the concept of human autonomy, guided by the insights of Ellis' rational emotive behavioral therapy. Emphasize that the subjective reality of free will is extremely useful for individuals if they are to believe that they are capable of initiating actions that will lead to self-improvement. Individuals who insist that they are the directors of their own lives, that they alone are responsible for what they will become, and that they can overcome almost anything through sheer acts of will, are people who will achieve far more than their less active peers who seek excuses for their failures outside of themselves.

Figure 12.2

Reattributing Responsibility (adapted from McGuire and Priestly, 1985)

	MY LIFE	
	Good things that have happened to me	Bad things that have happened to me
The result of my own actions		
The result of circumstances beyond my control		

Of course, things do happen to us that are beyond our personal control. Individuals who blame themselves for events that are clearly outside of their power to influence suffer from low self-esteem (Ickes and Layden, 1978). The objective of this exercise is not to move everything into the top two cells. It is rather to explore ways in which some of the bad events could have been brought under the individual's control. The exercise also is designed to enhance the self-esteem of those who masochistically attribute all negative events to themselves and who may tend to attribute the positive events in their lives to outside influences. The idea is expressed in Reinhold Niebuhr's "Serenity Prayer": "God grant me the serenity to accept the things I cannot change, the courage to change the things I can, and the wisdom to know the difference."

DIFFICULT GROUP MEMBERS

Despite the screening process designed to gather together a relatively homogeneous group, and despite all the other things you have done to assemble a smoothly running group, you probably will run into members who will be disruptive and/or uncooperative in one way or another. Their behavior may not necessarily be intended as disruption or noncooperation. To prevent such members from hindering the progress of the other members of the group, quickly identify and deal with disruptive behavior. Even if noncooperative behavior affects only the person not cooperating, you also should identify and deal with it. Some of the more usual types of difficult members are described below. Although we begin with the resister as a separate type, all other types are also resisters in one or more respects. Yet, some resistance to change is natural, and as previously pointed out, necessary for health and stability (Harris and Watkins, 1987; Harris, 1995).

THE RESISTER

Since all group members have volunteered and all have had the opportunity to screen themselves out of the process, you can assume that the resister is experiencing ambivalence about the process. He or she has made a commitment in theory to explore himself or herself but finds it difficult to do so in practice. Because we dealt at some length with resistance when we discussed reality therapy, we will not explore it in detail here. Most authorities on group counseling feel that resistance is easier to deal with in a group setting than it is in an individual setting. This will be particularly true if you have provided the group with a common discourse for identifying resistance, such as structural analysis as outlined in transactional analysis. For instance, in a piece about resistance in groups that has not been said better in the half-century since it was made, Bry states:

> The first and most striking thing in handling of resistance in groups is that frequently resistance does not have to be "handled" at all, at least not by the therapist. The group is remarkably effective in dealing with this phenomenon. Early in the experience of each group, considerable effort is directed toward demonstrating what resistance is and how to become sensitive to its appearance in others as well as oneself. The group members as well gradually develop ideas as to how to deal with resistance and how to use it productively. In cases of protective talking, sooner or later a group member usually gets sensitive to its resistance character and starts complaining about the "beating around the bush" (1951:112).

THE "EXPERT"

The "expert" in a group knows the answer to everyone's problems in the group and is not above liberally dispensing advice on how to deal with them. This behavior can be intimidating to the group leader if the advice giver really is an expert, or if everyone believes him or her to be. This author once had a physician in a group of child molesters who knew what was wrong with everyone in the group but himself. He had a doctoral degree, versus this author's master's degree (at the time). The author felt himself relinquishing the group direction to the doctor. Rather than trying to understand his motivations, the author eventually confronted him with a reminder of who was the group leader and of the fact that he was an offender, and that, unlike the doctor, the author had "dealt with hundreds of sex offenders." In other words, the author reduced himself to the doctor's level by puffing up his sense of importance as an "expert" in his own right. This was a very poor way of handling the situation.

Instead, the author should have realized that this man's conviction as a child molester had severely damaged his self-respect and that he was trying to regain some of it by demonstrating his superiority. An empathetic recognition of this would have led to a more sympathetic and understanding resolution of the problem he posed to the group. It is highly likely that he used advice giving to divert attention from his own problems, from letting others help him face and cope with his painful situation. Perhaps, he genuinely even felt that his advice would be helpful to his fellow members.

We all know how unwelcome unsolicited advice is. The group is not meeting for exchange of advice but for self-exploration. When a group member offers advice to another member, you might say something like this to the advice giver: "Charlie, it is obvious that John's problem is of concern to you, and you are concerned enough to offer some suggestions about what he might do."

Without pausing, you could then address John as follows: "John, when you have difficulty in coping, do you like to have someone who cares enough to suggest what you might do? Do you feel that Charlie's suggestion could be of use to you?" These responses indicate to Charlie that you have interpreted his offered advice as a genuine attempt to help John with his problem; you have not put him down. You also have given John an opportunity to respond to Charlie's advice giving, plus a chance to explore his problem further. John probably will put Charlie in his place if he feels he needs to; that is part of the group process of getting feelings out into the open. It is important that any necessary putting down be left to the group members rather than to the group counselor. Only after "experts" are confronted with the unacceptability of their behavior will they start to explore their own problems.

THE MONOPOLIZER

The monopolizer shares many of the characteristics of the resister and the expert. He or she tends to be a self-centered recognition seeker who wishes to rule the group. Motivations for monopolizing the group discussion are very similar to the motivations of the expert. Monopolizers really may feel that they are the only ones present with anything meaningful to contribute. However, the monopolizing may be a conscious tactic to steer the group away from discussing uncomfortable topics and toward topics of the monopolizers' choosing: "the best form of defense is offense." Either way, the negative effects on the group are the same.

Bry's statement about the resister is likely to be applicable here. Sooner or later, someone will pipe up with "Why don't you give somebody else a chance to speak?" When a statement such as this emerges, say something like the following to the protester: "Debbie, you feel angry at Sue because you feel that she is not interested in what others have to say and that she may be avoiding topics that are not comfortable for her. Am I right?" If Debbie indicates that you have accurately reflected her feelings, you might go on to say to Sue: "Sue, do you see yourself as monopolizing the conversation? Wouldn't you really like to listen to what others have to say and perhaps learn more about yourself and about others?" Monopolizers lack the important skill of listening. They need feedback from the other members about how their behavior is affecting others, even if the feedback results in a temporary sullen withdrawal from group participation.

THE WITHDRAWN MEMBER

Withdrawn group members either are engaging in passive resistance or may be lacking in confidence and/or the verbal skills to express themselves effectively. They hide in the group and are quite content to let the monopolizer, or anyone else, have the limelight. The group counselor should resist putting such persons on the spot by calling on them as a teacher calls on students in a classroom. As part of the group, however, withdrawn members are fair game for other members to approach. Be ready to help out the withdrawn person on such occasions so that being on the spot does not become too painful.

You might decide that you have made a mistake in allowing the withdrawn person to participate in the group or that the person has made a mistake in deciding to participate. The fact that the person is present, however, can be taken as a sign that he or she desires some form of counseling. You can determine this by the use of a session evaluation form containing the question: "Would you like an individual session with me?" If the answer is "yes," that person can withdraw from group counseling and enter individual counseling. If it is "no" and he or she continues in the group, make every effort to include that person in the discussions.

THE MASOCHIST AND THE SADIST

Masochists are persons with low self-esteem and ingrained dependency needs who purposely set themselves up as targets for the displaced aggression of others. They doubt their ability to be loved, respected, or accepted by others. Since they desire companionship and relationships, however, they feel that the only strategy available to them is to put themselves into the hot seat where they are the victims of bullying, teasing, sarcasm, and being the butt of bad jokes. They often become welcome targets for sadistic members of a group, and others may follow the sadist's lead to avoid personal exploration.

Both the masochist and the sadistic bully should be identified quickly by the group leader. The feelings of both parties should be reflected so that other group members can suggest better methods for each to relate to others. Under no circumstances should you allow a group member to be set up as a constant target for unproductive criticism and hurtful comments. When other group members realize that such bullying is not acceptable to you, they will rally to the defense of the masochist. They can be relied on to put down the offending party. Allow them to do this for as long as it seems useful. However, if fisticuffs threaten to replace the spoken word, as they may well do with an individual who relies on bullying to get his or her way, bring the put-down to an end. You may offer the offending party an "out" by suggesting that he or she perhaps really did not mean to be hurtful: "Isn't that true, Mike?"

ADVANTAGES AND DISADVANTAGES OF INSTITUTIONAL GROUP COUNSELING

There are, then, a number of theoretical and practical reasons why group counseling may be considered superior to individual counseling in an institutional setting. It will not be preferable for all offenders, for some clearly benefit more from private individual sessions. Likewise, many corrections workers are more comfortable conducting private rather than group sessions. Summarized in the following box are the major advantages and disadvantages of group counseling in an institutionalized setting.

Exercises in Group Counseling

One of the best exercises for getting the feel of group counseling is to repeat the exercise in reattribution of responsibility. Since social psychologists tell us that almost everybody has the tendency to systematically bias causal attributions, this exercise will be more realistic for you than exercises such as counting the cost of a criminal lifestyle because you will be dealing with real issues rather than role playing criminals.

The instructor may wish to act as the group leader, or he or she may wish to assign this task to someone. Just as in a real group situation, the group leader can begin the process by asking one of the other members to volunteer to explain a life event and to state where he or she has placed it in the two-by-two square. The discussion among group members then can begin to explore whether that event (good or bad) could have been brought more under the control of the individual.

SOME ADVANTAGES OF GROUP COUNSELING IN INSTITUTIONS

1. Time constraints and personnel shortages make it an efficient method for counseling a number of individuals with similar problems at the same time.
2. Groups with prosocial purposes offer inmates a constructive alternative to antisocial inmate cliques that form in response to the need of human beings for social interaction.
3. Because of the sharing of problems with the group members, members learn about alternative coping strategies.
4. Inmates can learn these alternative strategies, which also can be tried out in the abstract by involved discussions with those others who have experienced them.
5. Well-led and democratically run groups tend to develop a feeling of togetherness and "we-ness."
6. This sense of belonging can enable group pressure to change the attitudes of individuals in the direction of the group's purposes—to change antisocial attitudes into prosocial attitudes.
7. Unlike one-on-one counseling sessions with a representative of the "system," group counseling lessens the possibility that an inmate will be intimidated by a perceived authoritarian relationship.

SOME DISADVANTAGES OF GROUP COUNSELING IN INSTITUTIONS

1. Some offenders may be reluctant to explore intimate feelings in the company of peers, although they desperately may want to do so. Some individuals feel much more comfortable speaking in private with an authority figure. Handle this situation by passing out evaluation forms that contain a question such as "Would you like to arrange an individual session with me?" Concerns that have surfaced in the offender's mind during a group session then can be given voice in private.
2. A lot of time can be wasted pursuing meaningless topics. The snag here is that we can realize that they are meaningless only after they have been fully expressed. Only experience will tell you when to cut off such topics and redirect the session along more meaningful avenues. However, this lost time is more than compensated for by the time saved in counseling a number of individuals at one time.
3. Closely allied to point two is the danger that the means become accepted as the goals. If the group counselor succeeds in generating discussion without reference to where the discussion is leading, nothing much is accomplished. The discussion is the means, not the goal. Group counseling always must be geared to realistic goals.
4. Some group members may take advantage of the numbers of people in the group in order to hide. We all are aware of students who select large classes and then sit at the back of the room to avoid class participation. They are missing out on much of the educational experience by doing this. Likewise, offenders who hide miss out on much of what could be meaningful to them. By the use of the same evaluation form, the counselor can determine if a given person is merely a hider or one who really wishes to address problems but who is shy in groups.

This is obviously a time-consuming exercise, and it is likely that not everyone in the class will have the opportunity to offer a life event or serve as the group leader. Given the time constraints, go into some depth with one or two individuals rather than to try to cover everybody superficially. Therefore, the instructor may wish to examine everyone's summary of life events prior to commencing the exercise, and select one or two of the more interesting ones, and ask those people to volunteer.

Perspective from the Field:
Group Counseling: Change as a Process, Not an Event
By Jeff Lane

Jeff Lane is a program manager at the Idaho State Correctional Institution. He has a master's degree in psychology from the University of Illinois, and almost thirty years working in the counseling/mental health/program field with eleven years as a clinician in the Idaho Department of Correction.

Group counseling in a prison setting is considerably different from group counseling in the community. Individuals in a community setting generally have a prosocial stance and want to deal with a problem. In a prison environment, the motivation can be more complicated. Completing a group or program may be a way to get a parole date or a commutation. There may be a genuine desire to change, or it may be part of a scheme to gain something else. Although most offenders do not come into groups with a strong motivation to change, it may occur a little bit at a time. It is very difficult to effect change of the criminal personality. Many different types of programs have been developed and tried, but few have obtained any long-term success.

In determining what groups are to be offered in prison, I have focused on those behaviors that have brought offenders into conflict with society: anger, problem-solving, sexual behaviors, substance abuse, and the basis for these behaviors which is criminal logic and criminal thinking. Stanton Samenow and Samuel Yochelson began in the 1950s to develop insight into criminal thinking and the values and belief systems that are the foundation of such thinking. The framework of criminal thinking, or cognitive distortion (thinking errors), gives a good framework for dealing with offenders in groups.

Anyone who has worked in drug and alcohol groups understands that alcohol is a disease of denial. Although criminal behavior, in all of its forms, is not a disease, it is maintained by keeping it secret, calling it something else, rationalizing the effects, or simply pretending it does not exist. This is a type of denial, and presents the biggest challenge in working with offenders. In groups that deal with problems from anger to child molestation, the participants generally will avoid dealing with the behavior and spend time dealing with everything but their own accountability. The best way to deal with this is by group structure. Without a well-defined and understood structure, a group facilitator can spend a good deal of time redefining boundaries, refocusing on goals, and explaining the process. Offender self-absorption can be counterproductive to the group's goals. In prosocial groups, individuals usually have problems but do not know why. In offender groups, members know they have problems and tend to blame others for those problems. This is counter to the goal of accepting responsibility. If the offender is generally unwilling to talk about his or her problem behavior by using denial, rationalizations, or misrepresentation, then taking responsibility only can occur when an offender remains open to the group process, open to looking at his or her behavior in a different way than is normal. This different view may involve employing empathy, seeing the cost of the behavior to the offender, and evaluating what the behavior has actually given the offender versus his or her perceived gains.

Most groups within the prison system of Idaho are voluntary. We identify what someone wants to get out of the group and what they most value. Examples of what can be valued are family, freedom, recovery, dependent children, helping others, and much more. A person's progress in group can be measured (by themselves) by how their openness and behavior brings them closer to or further away from what they say they value. Does their behavior in the group—how they deal with anger, for example—take them closer to their family or further from it? Does this behavior take them closer to their children and the parent they want to be or further from that? This is important in that most offenders are very concrete and look to short-term goals. The "big picture" is usually something that is not seen, since their values usually get them tied up in the moment. Participant interaction requires offenders to use the words "I" or "me." Their role in groups is to relate their own experience. Lecturing or advising others is not part of the process.

The staff's role is to facilitate. When I have shared in a group, it has been very general and as a way to make a point. Staff roles in prisons are critically important and need to be well-defined. In offering programs, I know that all change is self-change and groups offer an opportunity to change. That change can be a long process taking years. Each group, each class, each effort to change can be a vital step in the process. Even efforts that may be viewed as failures at the moment may be critical elements that support a later change.

This change process that groups offer is probably the most difficult task that an offender has ever undertaken, and the struggles that most offenders go through are normal and not the exception. Supporting them and being aware of where they are in the process is a critical element of any prison group because it is vital to any success that offenders may achieve.

Summary

Time and cost considerations make group counseling in institutionalized settings attractive. This does not mean that group counseling is "second best" to individualized counseling. Group counseling actually can be more beneficial for some offenders than individual counseling. Group counseling uses the power of the group to achieve its aims. Group counseling offers inmates a constructive alternative to the antisocial cliques that develop in prisons and can function to offset the power of the inmate code. Through the process of sharing, inmates can learn about alternative coping strategies from others who have "been there." A properly run group can develop a feeling of "we-ness," which is not always possible in individual counseling.

In almost any group setting, there will be members who are disruptive. You can minimize their effect through the proper selection of members based on assessment information and one-on-one interviews with prospective members. But disruptive members, intentional or otherwise, will remain. Group members themselves will take care of much of the disruption, but you retain the ultimate responsibility for recognizing and dealing with disruption. Disrupting members should be dealt with in a dignified and caring manner. It is possible that disruption is a clear signal that the person doing the disrupting should not be in the group. Approach that person with an offer of individual counseling with you. The insights of transactional analysis, rational effective therapy, and reality therapy were presented as discussion topics. The "counting the costs" exercise may be particularly beneficial. Include predetermined topics like this in your counseling strategies. It is too easy to mistake animated discussion on irrelevant topics for progress. Group counseling must have a goal to aim toward. However, any relevant topic raised by a group member should be explored. And, do not forget, you as a member of the group are fair game for discussion.

References and Suggested Readings

Alexander, R. 2000. *Counseling, Treatment, and Intervention Methods with Juvenile and Adult Offenders*. Belmont, California: Brooks/Cole.

Anderson, J. 1984. *Counseling Through Group Process*. New York: Springer.

Association for Specialists in Group Work (ASGW). 1980. *Ethical Guidelines for Group Leaders*. Falls Church, Virginia: Association for Specialists in Group Work.

Bennett, L., T. Rosenbaum, and W. McCullough. 1978. *Counseling in Correctional Environments*. New York: Human Sciences Press.

Bry, T. 1951. Varieties of resistance in group psychotherapy. *International Journal of Group Psychotherapy*. 1:106-114.

Clemmer, D. 1958. *The Prison Community*. New York: Holt, Rinehart and Winston.

Corey, G. 1983. Group Counseling: Being a Counselor: Directions and Challenges. In J. Brown and R. Pate, eds. *Being a Counselor*. Monterey, California: Brooks/Cole.

Goffman, E. 1961. *Asylums*. Garden City, New York: Anchor.

Graham, G. 1992. *The One-Eyed Man Is King*. Seattle, Washington: Graham and Graham Company.

Ellis S. 1993. *Short-term Group Counseling*, 3rd edition. Lanham, Maryland: American Correctional Association.

Harris, G. 1995. *Overcoming Resistance: Success in Counseling Men*. Lanham, Maryland: American Correctional Association.

Harris, G. and D. Watkins. 1987. *Counseling the Involuntary and Resistant Client*. Lanham, Maryland: American Correctional Association.

Homans, G. 1950. *The Human Group*. New York: Harcourt, Brace and World.

Ickes, W. and M. Layden. 1978. New Directions in Attribution Research, Vol. 2. In J. Harvey, W. Ickes, and R. Kidd, eds. *Attributional Styles*. Hillsdale, New Jersey: Lawrence Erlbaum Associates.

Jacobs, E., E. Harvill, and R. Masson. 1998. *Group Counseling: Strategies and Skills*. Pacific Grove, California: Brooks/Cole.

Jarvis, D. 1978. *Institutional Treatment of the Offender*. New York: McGraw-Hill.

Juda, D. 1984. On the special problems of creating group cohesion within a prison setting. *Journal of Offender Counseling, Services and Rehabilitation*. 8:47-59.

Lester, D. 2000. Group and Milieu Therapy. In P. Van Vooris. M. Braswell, and D. Lester, eds. *Correctional Counseling and Rehabilitation*. Cincinnati, Anderson.

Mahler, C. 1973. Group Counseling: Theory, Research, and Practice. In J. Lee and C. Pulvino, eds. *Group Counseling*. Washington, D.C.: American Personnel and Guidance Association.

Rizzo, N. 1980. Group therapy: Possibilities and pitfalls. *International Journal of Offender Therapy and Comparative Criminology*. 24:27-31.

Schmalleger, F. 2001. *Criminal Justice Today*. Englewood Cliffs, New Jersey: Prentice-Hall.

Chapter 13

Case Management, Community Agencies, and Volunteers

Corrections personnel must do more to discover how community and societal resources can be brought to bear on the problems of offenders, bearing in mind that the community is the corrective aspect of the correctional process. . . .what helps the offender protects the community.

Louis Radelet

Community Resources

Individual and group counseling of offenders is not enough. Often the process of changing offending behavior requires accurately assessing offenders' concrete needs and knowing how to go about helping them to meet these needs—not necessarily deconstructing faulty thinking and attitudes. The professional criminal justice worker knows that more concrete help for the offender is often needed. Attempting to move the offender toward a more responsible lifestyle is a difficult task, which you need not bear alone. Indeed, no single professional has the expertise needed to provide all the services required by all offenders.

According to the philosophy of restorative justice, corrections is a community problem, and you should consider yourself to be in partnership with the various community-supported agencies in this rehabilitative endeavor. Probation and parole departments simply do not have the resources to provide for all the needs of offenders. As Carlson and Parks see it:

It is the task of the probation [or parole] officer to assess the service needs of the probationer [or parolee], locate the social service agency which addresses those needs as its primary function, to refer the probationer [or parolee] to the appropriate agency, and to follow up referrals to make sure that the probationer [or parolee] actually received the services (1979:120).

Carlson and Parks (1979:121) go so far as to assert that the criminal justice workers' relationships with community service agencies are more important than their relationships with offenders. In other words, they see criminal justice workers more as brokers of community services than as counselors. The broker and counselor roles may be of equal importance, although in some cases, one role may be more important than the other. In terms of the emerging case management emphasis in corrections, corrections workers should find themselves as a member of a team of professionals bringing their skills and expertise to bear on creating treatment and service plans for offenders (Healy, 1999). The corrections worker, having legal authority over the offender, must be the lead person and coordinator of these services.

Unfortunately, many correctional workers are unaware of the help that is available to offenders (and to themselves) within the community. To make proper use of community agencies, you should gain a thorough knowledge of them and an understanding of their functions before you need them. Only with this knowledge and understanding can you decide on the appropriate referral for the specific need. Corrections workers' ability to provide extended and effective services to offenders is proportional to the scope of their knowledge of available resources in the community. This kind of knowledge is helpful in the supervision of all offenders, but it is particularly important for parolees. They have to be integrated back into the community after long absences. Here is a brief overview of the types of community resource agencies available in most cities.

MENTAL HEALTH CENTERS

The mental health center is the community resource with which the criminal justice worker is probably most familiar. Many jurisdictions have a diagnostic and treatment center staffed by social workers, psychologists, and psychiatrists, specifically to assess offenders' mental health and functioning. They deal with competency testing, presentence and postsentencing evaluations, and parole testing and treatment. Specialized individual, group, and family counseling also are provided at many of these centers.

In addition to centers run for and by the court system, there are the more general mental health centers. These centers may be the preferred referrals for the offender because they are not a part of the criminal justice system. Whatever the case may be, you must develop the ability to recognize symptoms of mental illness and/or specific diagnostic and treatment needs that may be best dealt with by a referral to a mental health professional. Never underestimate or downplay symptoms displayed by offenders that lead you to suspect serious mental problems. You may be right or you may be wrong, but err on the side of caution and refer.

SUBSTANCE ABUSE CENTERS

Substance abuse centers can be either private or public agencies. They include hospitals, chapters of Alcoholics Anonymous, Volunteers of America, methadone centers, halfway houses, and often residential centers specifically designed for offenders. For offenders who are veterans of the U.S. armed forces, various Veterans Administration hospitals provide excellent inpatient substance abuse treatment free of charge. Many health insurance policies cover the cost of drug and alcohol treatment. If you have offenders who have either of these problems and who are lucky enough to still have a job, check out their insurance with them. It is amazing how often this possibility is overlooked by both officers and offenders.

EDUCATIONAL AND VOCATIONAL GUIDANCE

Since most convicted criminals tend to be unemployed high school dropouts, education and vocational training should be high on the list of offender needs. Community high schools offer General Equivalency Diploma (GED) preparation classes free of charge, as well as offer some vocational training for minimal fees. One drawback of GED classes at local high schools is their use of traditional teaching methods. Usually, students are taught as a group without much attention paid to individual levels of ability. Because of this problem, some departments set up their own GED programs based on individualized instruction in which students are able to proceed at their own pace without regard to classroom norms. One such program was evaluated and found to significantly reduce recidivism (Walsh, 1985). All probation and parole departments should start a program such as this. Money to employ a part-time teacher need not come from tight departmental budgets. The evaluated program was funded adequately by small grants from local churches and other concerned organizations.

The Bureau of Vocational Rehabilitation, a state and federally funded program, provides many opportunities for vocational testing and on-the-job training, counseling, and a number of valuable services for qualified applicants. Since this program operates within the prison system and in the community, it is sensitive to the special needs of offenders. It provides offenders with counselors who can assist them with job interviewing and other work-related skills. Correctional workers should become fully acquainted with this particularly useful agency.

State employment agencies duplicate, with somewhat less success, many of the functions of the Bureau of Vocational Rehabilitation. Additionally, they maintain lists of currently available employment in the area. In this age of technology, however, it is becoming increasingly difficult to take advantage of the employment office's ever-decreasing job list without adequate vocational preparation (see, 9 to 5 Beats Ten to Life: How to (Re)Enter Society by Mike Davis, 1996, for other suggestions to help offenders).

WELFARE AGENCIES

The local welfare department administers various federal, state, and local welfare programs. Most offenders are better acquainted with "welfare" than are their officers, but many are not aware of the range of programs available, although recent welfare reforms have severely restricted available funds. In addition to general relief and food stamps, this agency administers aid to the disabled, medical assistance, aid to the aged, and offers family counseling, to name just a few programs. It is useful for probation and parole officers to have a contact at the welfare department who will expedite matters when the need for offender assistance is acute. Such an occasion may arise when a homeless and penniless offender has been released from jail or prison or when young men or women are thrown out of their family home with only the clothes on their back.

Most communities have an agency that specializes in finding accommodations for the homeless. In cooperation with the welfare department, it may provide the offender and his or her family with permanent or temporary accommodation. It often is able to provide the offender or spouse with homemaking skills, such as family planning and balancing a tight budget. Temporary shelter for the real down and out can be found at various religious and secular "missions." These places offer meals, counseling, and companionship as well as accommodations.

SOME REGIONAL AND NATIONAL VOLUNTEER GROUPS

There is a wide variety of regional, national, and even international volunteer groups that either specialize in correctional helping or have programs and supply services useful for correctional clientele. Some of these organizations almost definitely have branch offices in your area. If they do not, perhaps a real service you could provide for your department and your community would be to contact these organizations and find out how you might start one. A list of a few such organizations are presented below with a brief description and contact addresses.

The Alston Wilkes Society is a nonprofit South Carolina agency that offers services to offenders, former offenders, and their families. The society helps offenders with employment, housing, family assistance, parole assistance, prison visitation, and court mediation. [This society has 5,000 volunteers and an annual budget of about $2,000,000 (Walker, 1993:94)]. For more information, contact The Alston Wilkes Society, Anne Walker/Executive Director, 3519 Medical Drive, Columbia, South Carolina 29203, (803) 799-2490.

Association on Programs for Female Offenders. Operating since the 1960s, this organization has been a pioneer in stimulating awareness and identifying the unique needs of female offenders. In addition, the Association endeavors to communicate with individuals, agencies, and organizations who are dedicated to the improvement of services to female offenders, and provides support to professionals committed to the improvement of services to female offenders. For more information, contact Mary V. Leftridge Byrd, President, 500 East 4th Street, Chester, Pennsylvania, 19013, (610) 490-5412.

Family and Corrections Network. Founded in 1983, the mission of the Family and Corrections Network is to uphold families of offenders as valued resources to themselves and their communities to help the criminal justice system, other institutions, and society become supportive of family empowerment, integrity, and self-determination. With their focus on families of offenders, this organization publishes information on children of prisoners, prison visiting, and incarcerated fathers, among other topics. For more information, contact Jim Mustin, President, 32 Oak Grove Road, Palmyra, Virginia 22963, (804) 589-3036. www.fcnetwork.org

The International Association for Justice Volunteerism is a nonprofit membership association serving justice volunteers, volunteer managers, and other justice personnel. It works to enhance the image of justice volunteerism by serving as an advocate for citizen volunteers, developing relationships with organizations with similar goals, and building the efforts of local programs in the United States, Canada, and abroad. For more information contact The International Association for Justice Volunteerism, P.O. Box 786, Milwaukee, Wisconsin 53201, (404) 963-6092 or www.justicevolunteers.org.

The National Center for Victims of Crime is a nonprofit organization that promotes victims' rights and victim assistance. The center provides programs and services to organizations helping victims and criminal justice-related organizations, and provides information and resources to the media and the public. For more information, contact: The National Center for Victims of Crime, 211 Wilson Blvd., Suite 300, Arlington, Virginia 22201, (703) 276-2880 or www.ncvc.org.

Prison Fellowship is a nationwide evangelical prison ministry that provides seminars and Bible studies focusing on spiritual renewal. Inmates also are offered a correspondence program with pen pals on the outside, and postrelease mentoring, which pairs a volunteer with an ex-offender. For more information, contact Prison Fellowship, c/o Burt Rosen, Vice President of Field Operations, P.O. Box 17377, Pittsburgh, Pennsylvania 15235-0377, (412) 829-7866 or www.prisonfellowshipintl.org.

The Salvation Army, working in ninety-seven countries, provides spiritual and practical assistance to inmates and ex-offenders. The Salvation Army offers Bible studies and individual counseling to inmates and provides support services to inmates' families through its corps community centers. Ex-offender services include drug aftercare, employment services, General Equivalency Degree preparation, parenting skills, English as a second language, AIDS counseling, and mental health programs. For more information, contact The Salvation Army National Headquarters, 615 Slaters Lane, P.O. Box 269, Alexandria, Virginia 22313, (703) 684-5500 or www.salvationarmy.org.

Volunteers of America provides inmates throughout the United States with spiritual guidance and opportunities for success. Volunteers of America services include a restitution program, a program for female offenders that houses them with their children, and electronic monitoring for pretrial defendants. For more information, contact Volunteers of America, Chuck Gould, President, 1660 Duke Street, Alexandria, Virginia 22314, (703) 548-2288 or www.voa.org.

RESOURCES FOR VICTIMS

For too long, victims have been the most neglected part of the criminal justice system. The concept of restorative justice has brought them once again to our attention. Although corrections workers are not trained to address the concerns of victims, one of the things that you can do is to put them in touch with professionals who are aware of the various resources available to them. The following is a list of toll-free numbers of various victims' rights groups.

Battered Women's Justice Project	www.vaw.umn.edu/BWJP/	800-903-0111
Childhelp USA National Hotline	www.childhelpusa.org	800-4-A-CHILD
Mothers Against Drunk Driving	www.madd.org	800-438-MADD
National Center for Missing and Exploited Children	www.missingkids.org	800-843-5678
National Clearinghouse on Child Abuse and Neglect	www.calib.com/nccanch/	800-394-3366

National Domestic Violence Hotline	www.ojp.usdoj.gov/vawo/newhotline.htm	
		800-799-7233
National Organization for Victim Assistance	www.try-nova.org	800-TRY-NOVA
Parents of Murdered Children	www.pomc.org	888-818-POMC

IN AND OUT REFERRALS

You will not always be able to determine the offender's needs and problem areas by yourself. Quite often other agencies—the police, courts, prosecutors, ministers, neighbors, family members, and concerned citizens—will provide information regarding their needs and problem areas. Your task is to act as a broker or go between matching the complaint or concern referred to you with the appropriate action. The appropriate action often will be a referral of your own to another specialized agency. Figure 13.1 is a flowchart illustrating the in-and-out flow of referrals.

Figure 13.1
Flowchart of In-and-Out Referrals

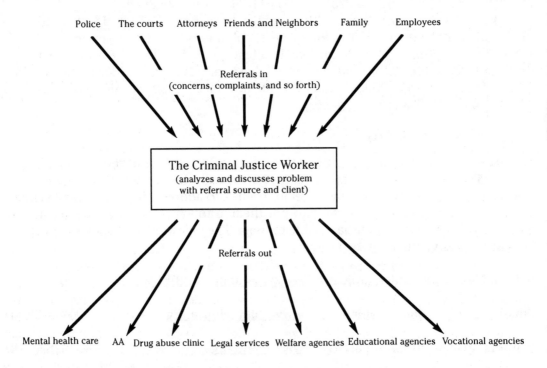

Using and Engaging the Community

The criminal justice system cannot fight the war against crime alone. The police have long recognized that the greatest asset any police department has in its battle is the confidence and cooperation of the community (Thurman, Zhao, and Giacomazzi, 2001). Police departments also have discovered that certain members of the community are willing, and often anxious, to aid the police by forming neighborhood watches, engaging in citizens' patrols, or even acting as volunteer officers (police reserves or auxiliaries).

Although the possible roles that members of the general community may play in corrections are not so readily identifiable as their roles in law enforcement, they exist and are much more diverse. We in corrections should follow the example of law enforcement and recognize the tremendously valuable resources that lie untapped in the ordinary men and women who live in our communities. While many agencies and institutions make good use of volunteers, there is always room for new programs and new volunteers. These individuals usually want nothing more out of their efforts than to know that they are helping their community to be a safer place to live by helping those who have victimized it.

VICTIM-OFFENDER RECONCILIATION PROGRAMS

Victim-offender reconciliation programs (VORPs) are an integral component of restorative justice philosophy. Many crime victims are less vindictive than commonly supposed and are seeking fairness, justice, and restitution *as defined by them* (restorative justice), rather than revenge and punishment as defined by the state (retributive justice). In many cases, this can be reasonably accomplished to the satisfaction of all involved. Central to the victim-offender reconciliation process is the bringing together of victim and offender in face-to-face meetings mediated by a person trained in mediation theory and practice (Trenczek, 1990). These meetings are designed to iron out ways in which the offender can make amends for the hurt and damage caused to the victim. The participation of both offender and victim must be voluntary for the process to work, although there is considerable underlying pressure for offender participation in their realization that formal court procedures are the default option for failure to participate.

Victims participating in victim-offender reconciliation programs gain the opportunity to make offenders aware of their feelings of personal violation and loss and to lay out their proposals of how offenders can restore the situation. Offenders are afforded the opportunity to see firsthand the pain they have caused their victims, and perhaps even to express remorse. The mediator assists the parties in developing a contract agreeable to both, which is signed by them and by the mediator, laying out the terms arrived at (such as a schedule of payments). The mediator will monitor the terms of the contract and perhaps schedule further face-to-face meetings. At the satisfactory completion of the contract, the mediator will make a report to the court.

Rarely are victim-offender reconciliation programs used for personal violent crimes—it would be difficult, for instance, to imagine any degree of restoration for the survivors of a murder victim. Such programs work best when the crimes involved are property crimes such as burglary, theft, fraud, and vandalism. A typical finding is that about 60 percent of victims invited to participate in victim-offender reconciliation programs actually become involved, and that a high percentage (mid-to high 90s) result in signed contracts (Coates, 1990). Further, 97 percent of victims involved in victim-offender reconciliation programs in Indiana and Minnesota indicated that the experience was satisfying to them and they would do it again (Coates, 1990). Similar positive results have been reported in Britain (Marshall, 1990), Germany (Trenczek, 1990), and Canada (Pate, 1990). Mark Umbreit (1994) sums up the various satisfactions expressed by victims in his study:

1. Meeting offenders helped reduce their fear of being revictimized.
2. They appreciated the opportunity to tell offenders how they felt.
3. Being personally involved in the justice process was satisfying to them.
4. They gained insight into the crime and into the offender's situation.
5. They received restitution.

Victim-offender reconciliation programs are an excellent method of involving the community in the corrections process. Volunteers trained in mediation techniques can relieve overburdened professionals of much of the work of formally dealing with relatively minor property offenders as well as gain personal satisfaction in helping reconcile the offender and the victim. According to Coates, "This participation fosters a significant community stake in VORP as a way of dealing with crime, as well as sensitizing community members to the human nature of crime" (1990:130). In other words, crime signifies a breakdown of social bonds; victim-offender reconciliation programs are efforts to repair those bonds by bringing people together to work on them.

A COMMUNITY-RESOURCE VOLUNTEER SPEAKERS' PROGRAM

Some years ago the Lucas County (Ohio) Adult Probation Department instituted a successful program to help offenders deal with various problems of living. It provided some useful services for offenders. The program was modeled after the Texas Pre-Release Program designed to prepare inmates for release into the community. Both the Texas program and the Lucas County Adult Probation Department's programs are based on the recognition that much recidivism could be traced to an inability to cope with what most of us would consider relatively mundane problems. Inability to cope in turn was traced to simple ignorance rather than any lack of native ability or debilitating mental health problems. Consequently, the department developed a Citizens' Volunteer Speakers' Bureau to provide probationers with much-needed guidance and advice on matters of daily living. Volunteers, and the department itself, never experienced any difficulty recruiting specialists in their field. The department's easy successes in getting concerned speakers points to the vast amount of talent "out there" just waiting to be tapped.

The program worked by first identifying offenders with simple problems of living and getting them to agree to attend a four-week cycle (two nights per week) of informal "resource information" talks conducted by the specialists. If such a program is initiated in your department, you should not require or demand that offenders attend. Insistence could be counterproductive. You should intimate, however, that you will view their attendance very positively as being indicative of their desire to help themselves. Typical topics and sources of speakers are presented in Figure 13.2.

Unfortunately, the program was never formally evaluated for its effectiveness, but the general consensus was that it was extremely helpful to offenders dealing with the problems of living addressed by the various speakers. Officers also learned a great deal about the community resources available to help them help offenders. However, the original Texas Pre-Release Program was formally evaluated. According to Clark (1975:240), it significantly reduced recidivism among former inmates of the Texas prison system. It is a system well worth instituting in your department or agency.

VOLUNTEER OFFICERS IN CORRECTIONS

Being a volunteer officer is quite different from being a volunteer who provides some useful service to inmates and offenders. As is a reserve police officer, the volunteer probation/parole officer is invested with many (sometimes, all) of the powers and responsibilities of the professional officer. (In some jurisdictions which define probation and/or parole officers as law enforcement officers, volunteer officers are deputized or sworn in (McShane and Krause, 1993:394). The practice of probation began with volunteers, and to a somewhat lesser extent, so did parole (Allen and Simonsen, 2001). Volunteers in probation and parole can be a tremendous aid to the professional officer going far beyond filing cases and licking stamps. This author began his career in probation as a volunteer before accepting a paid position. With proper screening for suitability, initial and ongoing training, and proper matching of offenders and volunteers, volunteers can be a most useful addition to any community corrections endeavor.

Figure 13.2

Community Resource Information Speakers' Program

Week #	Subject	Speaker or source
1.	Job opportunities and employment aids	Employment bureau
	Finding and keeping a job	Local employers
	Social Security benefits	Social Security Administration
	Unions and employment	Union representative
2.	Sensible spending and budgeting	Financial counselor
	Sensible borrowing	Credit union representative
	Insurance needs	Insurance representative
	Your welfare department	County welfare department
3.	The family	Family counselor
	Human relationships	Human relations counselor
	Reponsible citizenship	Leaders in civic affairs
	Veteran's benefits	Veterans Administration
4.	Personal health	State and county health departments
	Alcohol and drug abuse	AA and NA members
	Educational and vocational opportunities	Bureau of Vocational Rehabilitation
	Mental health and general assistance agencies	Mental health Community Chest Professionals

Of course, the successful volunteer program must be well planned and must have the support of the professional staff. As McCarthy and McCarthy (1984:377) put it: "poor staff-volunteer relations are a frequent cause of program failure," and "positive staff-volunteer relations are essential for program success." As with many areas in which volunteers are involved, the professional staff may view volunteers as "amateurs" sticking their noses in areas in which they have no expertise. There should be a good training program for volunteers and education for the professionals about the positive things that volunteers can do to help them. Such a program can take care of any staff-volunteer relationship problems.

When good staff-volunteer relationships exist, professional staff tend to be quite positive about volunteer involvement. One evaluation of a volunteer program offered the following conclusion:

> Overall, officers were quite pleased with the quality of volunteers' performance. Their ratings suggested satisfaction with VIC [Volunteers in Corrections] service in every activity included in this assessment. While all of the areas examined received average performance ratings of "good" or better, officers were particularly pleased with volunteer services directly delivered to offenders (e.g., high ratings for operation of treatment programs and counseling), as well as volunteers' direct interactions with officers regarding offender progress (Lucas, 1987:73).

What kind of person is a volunteer, or what kind of person should the volunteer be? According to Henningsen (1981:119): "Typically, the volunteer is a sensitive and concerned individual with maturity and control over his or her own life. The volunteer relates well to others and is usually a warm and caring person capable of giving and receiving love." In other words, the volunteer's self must be as much "together" as the professional's—neither a naive Pollyanna nor a cynical Cassandra. After all, if volunteers are to be used efficiently and meaningfully by professionals, they have to be very much like professionals. A noncaring and immature dilettante is of no use to either you or the offenders. If such a person manages to slip through the selection net, he or she will not stay long, but can do a lot of damage in the meantime.

What can you as a professional corrections worker expect to gain from the services of volunteers? According to Scheier (1974), the two biggest gains lie in the areas of amplification and diversification of services. The volunteer frees professional workers from dealing with a number of less problematic cases so that they can increase meaningful contact time with the remainder of the caseload. Often, offenders accept volunteers more readily than they accept professionals because they see volunteers as less threatening. Some also may view volunteers as more concerned precisely because they receive no financial remuneration for their time and services. Shields, Chapman, and Wingard (1983) see a whole host of other benefits for departments and offenders alike accruing from volunteers.

Volunteers can be especially well accepted if you do your best to match offenders and volunteers according to the needs and abilities of each (Lauen, 1997). Lauen actually recommends matching professional officers with offenders, but practical considerations preclude such large-scale matching. Although matching treatment modalities and officer/offender types would be an ideal solution, Cullen and Gendreau (2000:129) opine that this would lead to "an unending permutation of offender-treatment type-setting interactions." We can never "customize" treatment for each offender, but matching is a valid option for volunteers who can devote considerable time to selected offenders.

For example, an older volunteer who is the "nurturing parent" type could be matched with young offenders who have lacked such a person in their own life. Perhaps another offender would be more comfortable with a peer volunteer who is of the same sex and age, who could serve as a role model.

Figure 13.3 shows the matching criteria employed in a highly successful volunteer probation officer's program in Lincoln, Nebraska. Notice that the importance of the criteria varies according to the type of offender/volunteer relationship desired. For example, if an adult role model relationship is desired, matching for ethnicity is considered "essential;" if a friend/companion relationship is desired, ethnic matching is seen as "very useful," but it is considered to be only "useful" if a supervisory or counseling relationship is desired. In contrast, counseling skills are essential if a counseling relationship is desired, but "useful" only if any of the other three types of relationships is desired. Such a table may prove valuable to you in matching offenders with volunteers.

Figure 13.3
Matching Clients with Volunteers by Type of Relationship

Volunteer/ client match	Relationship desired by usefulness of match			
	Adult role model	Friend/companion	Supervisor	Counselor
Ethnicity	Essential	Very useful	Useful	Useful
Sex	Essential	Essential	Irrelevant	Irrelevant
Age	Essential	Essential	Useful	Irrelevant
Education	Very useful	Very useful	Irrelevant	Irrelevant
Community contacts	Useful	Useful	Very useful	Irrelevant
Interests	Very useful	Essential	Irrelevant	Irrelevant
Social class	Very useful	Very useful	Irrelevant	Very useful
Counseling skills	Useful	Useful	Useful	Essential

With respect to the diversification of services, Scheier (1974:263) cites one report that indicated that a court system made use of fifty different types of skills brought to it by citizen volunteers. Volunteers from all walks of life provide offenders with everything from spiritual guidance to jogging classes. These valuable services, most certainly, could not have been supplied by the professional staff. As for the benefit to the department, one retired volunteer with the department at which this author worked put in as much time as any of the paid staff for about ten years. He supervised all of the department's welfare fraud cases, as well as supervised a number of other volunteers.

Volunteers with the Oakland County (Michigan) Adult Probation Department handle about 15 percent of the department's total caseload. Most certainly, this does not mean that potential professional officers are being "robbed" of a job by amateur "dabblers." The typical Oakland County volunteer brings to the position a host of talents and life experiences that young professionals cannot match (Smith, 1993). Any corrections agency is remiss if it fails to recognize and use the tremendous variety of skills available in any community. To use volunteers effectively and efficiently not only magnifies the efforts of professional workers, but also can assist the rehabilitative possibilities of the offender. Isn't that what it is all about?

A word of warning is necessary at this point. Make quite sure that offenders are not manipulating volunteers and that volunteers are holding offenders responsible for living up to their conditions of supervision (*see* Bayse, 1993). Problems in these areas can arise with some frequency if volunteers are not screened for suitability, if they are not adequately trained and told what is expected of them, or if they are not well matched with offenders. You retain the ultimate responsibility for monitoring the offender's progress. Thus, volunteers should submit a monthly progress report on each of the offenders they supervise for you. Volunteers expect and appreciate this. Volunteers need the feedback to improve their services to offenders and to let them know that they are being taken seriously.

Community involvement in corrections is a time that has come. Such involvement is part of the restorative justice ideal and is beneficial to all parties. Lauen calls community involvement "a win-win deal," and adds that: "Lay citizens win by becoming more knowledgeable about crime, corrections, and offenders. In so doing, they reduce their crime fears and increase their power. They begin to take charge. Community corrections offenders, staff, and programs win by building a broader base of support, living and working with people who are more knowledgeable and thereby more supportive, and gaining insights, advice and direct services from citizen volunteers" (1997:218).

EXERCISES IN COMMUNITY RESOURCE USE

Nearly all communities have a clearing house (sometimes referred to as the Community Chest) where you can obtain information about the various types of resources available to help the unfortunate. Identify the needs of the offender on whom you have written a practice PSI report and match them with appropriate agencies. Then, find out if your community has an agency that could deal with the offender's particular problem. If your community does not have such an agency, what would your second-best referral or plan of action be?

Devise a resource information speakers' program based on the resources available in your community and on the needs of offenders as you perceive them. What additional resources not included in this chapter do you think offenders would find useful?

Find out if the community corrections agencies located in your community have volunteer programs. If so, call and ask them about their criteria for volunteer selection, the training offered to volunteers, and whether they make attempts to match volunteers with offenders. What did the person you spoke with consider to be the most useful attribute of a prospective volunteer?

Perspective from the Field:
Volunteer Probation Work
By Dr. Stephen B. McConnell

Dr. McConnell is a professor of sociology at the University of Toledo in Ohio. His fields of specialty are criminology and social stratification. He began as a volunteer probation officer with Lucas County supervising adult offenders in 1983. Dr. McConnell also has field experience working in a large California prison.

Many things are too important to be left to the professionals alone: defense to the Pentagon, medicine to the M.D.s, and law to legislators and attorneys. If any truth lies in this observation, there well may be a point for volunteerism in criminal justice. For, after all, an array of professional personnel implements correctional policy.

The value that volunteer probation officers bring has little to do with saving a jurisdiction money or sparing regular staff even bigger caseloads. The central contribution of volunteer probation officers derives from the inclusion of ordinary citizens, albeit civic-minded ones, in the operation of justice proceedings. The professionalism of full-time staff is leavened with the innocence of volunteers.

There is a well-documented tendency for police officers to develop cynicism as an occupational necessity. Similarly, but to a much lesser extent, probation officers can develop a less-than-sanguine view of offenders and rehabilitation. Volunteers, who have developed value systems and understandings outside the criminal justice system, for whom criminal cases have not become routinized affairs, can—and occasionally do—challenge the orthodoxy of the prevailing professional views and ideology. In short, volunteers can ask fresh questions, even provide new insights that do not occur to veteran professionals.

So much of corrections work pivots on anticipating which offenders will or will not repeat crime. Predicting human behavior is a crapshoot at best, and this is especially true concerning criminal recidivism. Some psychologists would have us believe that prediction is a science, but the facts are otherwise. Nobody has a monopoly on predicting what another will do postconviction/postprobation-parole. On this count, the volunteer probation officers whose mature understanding of behavior stems from coping with life itself is on an equal footing with the professionals.

The justice system involves a number of somewhat technical and arcane practices that obscure the big picture of the reality of criminal justice. Informed volunteers can demystify and demythologize the system for a public for which such matters are remote and alien. Likewise, volunteers can step beyond the "trained incapacities" (the inability to see beyond the taken-for-granted realities imposed by professional role socialization) of professionals-as-professionals.

The motivations of volunteers in criminal justice are very broad. Most of the college students are amassing experience to ease their transition into paid positions upon graduation. Older volunteers have more altruistic and diverse motivations. In this author's own case, the motivation was twofold: he had been teaching in the city for over a decade and wanted to repay in some fashion the community from which he extracted a living. Equally important, he wanted to gain some hands-on experience with offenders, for it has been nearly twenty years since he worked in the field. Direct experience contributes much to the rethinking and refining of the theoretical ideas he teaches in his criminology and corrections classes. In brief, volunteering is a means of keeping fresh in the classroom.

Being a volunteer probation officer involves a host of qualifications too numerous to recount here. Certainly, one learns to listen with the third ear to detect what offenders are saying indirectly (or trying to conceal) rather than saying directly. And since serving as volunteer probation officers involves making recommendations, even giving direct orders to offenders about intimate aspects of their lives, it behooves the volunteer probation officers to know as much as they can about society. (For this reason, sociology continues to be a valuable study for people in correctional work.) At the broadest level, volunteer probation officers come to see how the U.S. economic system of capitalism creates a permanent underclass from which the huge majority of garden-variety offenders come. In conjunction with this, the volunteer probation officer comes to realize how the occupational structure works—how, for example, a drop in the unemployment rate increases the likelihood of offenders getting minimum-wage jobs in the fast food or motel industries.

The volunteer probation officer also comes to understand numerous components of community organization. This information covers everything from local agencies, which may be able to help poor, alcoholic, or drug-addicted offenders, to understanding the subtleties of the operation of the courts, the police department, and the prosecutor's office.

Thus, for a person to be effective as a volunteer probation officer, there is a great deal of information to be absorbed. This information then can be passed on to offenders for their benefit, and it enables the volunteer probation officer to understand offenders' behavior in a realistic context.

A cautionary note is in order. Corrections work is not for the fainthearted volunteer, nor is it for people who demand 100 percent success. Offenders can be difficult to work with, and on occasion are outright hostile. Not all offenders make good on probation or parole: some do commit new offenses and are sent to, or back to, prison. Volunteer probation officers adapt to the idea that whatever they do or do not do, much of the eventual outcome for an offender lies effectively beyond their control. Respect the fact that offenders are responsible for their own destinies. Maybe it is fair to say that working as a volunteer probation officer lends a certain humility to one's perspective.

SUMMARY

This chapter has dealt with the very important task of acquainting the corrections worker with the resources, skills, and desires to become involved that exist in the community. Numerous specialized agencies can help offenders with their day-to-day problems. You cannot be expected to have in your head all the information that these community agencies have gathered. Your task is to recognize offender problem areas and to make the appropriate agency referrals if the problems are not within your area of expertise. Your expertise should be that of a broker matching offenders with agencies.

You also can provide offenders and yourself with much-needed information by organizing a community resource information speakers' program. Such a program can be run periodically to accommodate new offenders. Many offenders find themselves in trouble simply because they do not have access to information about the kind of help that exists in the community to aid them with their problems. These speaker's programs have proven to be most helpful to offenders and corrections workers alike.

Another valuable resource that should not be overlooked is the desire of many individuals in the community to be useful and helpful. These people can be fruitfully incorporated into the correctional enterprise as volunteers. Probation and parole volunteers provide amplification and diversification of services to offenders. Volunteers must be screened, trained, and matched with offenders. Their performance should be monitored by the professional worker to make sure that they are holding offenders responsible and that they are not being manipulated by offenders.

Corrections can be an immensely satisfying career. Your satisfaction will be greatly increased if you learn to use the resources available in your community.

References and Suggested Readings

Allen, H. and C. Simonsen. 2001. *Corrections in America: An Introduction*, 9th edition. Upper Saddle River, New Jersey: Prentice Hall.

Bayse, D. 1993. *Helping Hands: Handbook for Volunteers in Prisons and Jails.* Lanham, Maryland: American Correctional Association.

Boudouris, J. 1996. *Parents in Prison: Addressing the Needs of Families.* Lanham, Maryland: American Correctional Association.

Carlson, E. and E. Parks. 1979. *Critical Issues in Adult Probation: Issues in Probation Management.* Washington, D.C.: U.S. Government Printing Office.

Clark, J. 1975. The Texas Pre-Release Program. In L. Hippchen, ed. *Correctional Classification and Treatment.* Cincinnati, Ohio: Anderson.

Coates, R. 1990. Victim-offender Reconciliation Programs in North America: An Assessment. In B. Galaway and J. Hudson, eds. *Criminal Justice, Restitution, and Reconciliation.* Monsey, New York: Criminal Justice Press.

Cullen, F. and P. Gendreau. 2000. *Assessing Correctional Rehabilitation: Policy, Practice, and Prospects.* In *Criminal Justice 2000.* Washington, DC: National Institute of Justice.

Davis, M. 1996. *9 to 5 Beats Ten to Life: How to (Re)Enter Society.* Lanham, Maryland: American Correctional Association.

Healy, K. 1999. Case Management in the Criminal Justice System. *National Institute of Justice: Research in Action.* Washington, DC: U.S. Department of Justice.

Henningsen, R. 1981. *Probation and Parole.* New York: Harcourt Brace Jovanovich.

Lauen, R. 1997. *Positive Approaches to Corrections: Research, Policy and Practice.* Lanham, Maryland: American Correctional Association.

Lucas, W. 1987. Staff perceptions of volunteers in a correctional program. *Journal of Crime and Justice.* 10:63-78.

Marshall, T. 1990. Results of Research from British Experiments with Restorative Justice. In B. Galaway and J. Hudson, eds. *Criminal Justice, Restitution, and Reconciliation.* Monsey, New York: Criminal Justice Press.

McCarthy, B. R. and B. J. McCarthy. 1984. *Community Based Corrections.* Monterey, California: Brooks/Cole.

McShane, M. and W. Krause. 1993. *Community Corrections.* New York: Macmillian.

Pate, K. 1990. Victim-Offender Reconciliation as Alternative Measures Programs in Canada. In B. Galaway and J. Hudson, eds. *Criminal Justice, Restitution, and Reconciliation.* Monsey, New York: Criminal Justice Press.

Read, E. 1996. *Partners in Change: The 12-Step Referral Handbook for Probation, Parole and Community Corrections.* Lanham, Maryland: American Correctional Association and Hazelden Foundation.

Scheier, I. 1974. The Professional and the Volunteer in Probation: An Emerging Relationship. In G. Killinger and P. Cromwell, eds. *Corrections in the Community.* St. Paul, Minnesota: West Publishing.

Shields, P., C. Chapman, and D. Wingard. 1983. Using volunteers in adult probation. *Federal Probation.* 47:57-64.

Smith, B. 1993. Probation department in Michigan finds volunteers make fine officers. *Corrections Today.* 55:80-82.

Trenczek, T. 1990. A review and assessment of victim-offender reconciliation programs in West Germany. In B. Galaway and J. Hudson, eds. *Criminal Justice, Restitution, and Reconciliation.* Monsey, New York: Criminal Justice Press.

Thurman, Q., J. Zhao, and A. Giacomazzi. 2001. *Community Policing in a Community Era.* Los Angeles: Roxbury.

Umbreit, M. 1994. *Victim Meets Offender: The Impact of Restorative Justice and Mediation.* Monsey, New York: Criminal Justice Press.

Walker, S. 1993. South Carolina volunteer agency plays vital role in corrections. *Corrections Today.* 55:94-100.

Walsh, A. 1985. An evaluation of the effects of adult basic education on rearrest rates among probationers. *Journal of Offender Counseling Services and Rehabilitation.* 9:69-76.

Chapter 14

Offenders' Rights in Casework and Counseling

by Craig Hemmens, J.D., Ph.D.

"Convenience and justice are often not on speaking terms."

Lord Justice Ackner

This chapter is written by Craig Hemmens, who is an assistant professor of criminal justice at Boise State University. He received his B.A. from the University of North Carolina, his J.D. from North Carolina Central University School of Law, and his Ph.D. in criminal justice from Sam Houston State University. His primary research interests are corrections law and criminal procedure.

Introduction

This chapter examines the legal and ethical issues which frequently confront the criminal justice caseworker in the correctional setting and in the community. It provides an overview of the constitutional rights of prisoners, probationers, and parolees, including the right to treatment, the prohibition on "cruel and unusual" punishment, limitations on probation and parole conditions, due process requirements, and the application of the exclusionary rule and *Miranda* warnings to probationers and parolees. Caseworker liability, an emerging area, also is examined. Finally, ethical issues related to the rights of clients and the duties of caseworkers are discussed.

Leading U.S. Supreme Court cases are discussed, but this is an area of the law which is largely bereft of guidance from the high court. It is therefore essential that caseworkers familiarize themselves with the laws of their respective states. There is a great deal of variation in state laws and administrative regulations, particularly in regards to probation and parole conditions and caseworker immunity from liability.

A brief note on legal terminology: a criminal offender possess two types of rights—*substantive rights* and *procedural rights*. *Substantive rights* are those rights created and defined by statute, such as contract law, tort law, and, of course, criminal law. Substantive law prescribes and proscribes various types of conduct. *Procedural rights* are those rights subsumed under the concept of "due process" in the Fifth and Fourteenth Amendments. When it is said that a person is entitled to due process of law, it means there are certain rules and procedures that the state must follow before depriving a person of his or her rights. Essentially, the substantive law delineates the rules by which all members of society must play, while procedural law delineates the rules by which the government must play.

Historical Background

At early common law, and until the middle part of the twentieth century, criminal offenders had few rights. The Bill of Rights, with its protections of individual rights against search and seizure, self-incrimination, and the like, applied only to the federal government, not the states. The exclusionary rule and *Miranda* warnings did not exist. Once incarcerated, individuals lost almost all of their rights and found themselves at the mercy of correctional personnel. Those under community supervision, be it probation or parole, found their rights and opportunities severely circumscribed.

Those convicted of crimes often were treated as "slaves of the state" (*Ruffin v. Commonwealth*, 1871). Most states had "civil death" statutes which stripped convicted individuals of most of their civil rights, such as the right to vote or hold elective office. This loss of rights was justified as a part of the punishment for committing a crime.

Courts took what was referred to as a "hands-off" approach to the rights of prisoners, choosing not to become involved with the affairs of corrections agencies, which were part of the executive branch of government. Courts reasoned that correctional administrators were better equipped to deal with prisoners than judges, and that judicial involvement, through the hearing of inmate complaints, would unnecessarily complicate relations between the executive and judicial branches of government. If prisoners had no rights, then courts need not oversee correctional agencies dealing with prisoners.

Courts also paid scant attention to the rights of probationers and parolees, treating them as essentially equivalent to inmates. Any number of restrictive probation and parole conditions were upheld, with courts often falling back on the rationale that neither probation nor parole was a right, but merely a privilege, something granted by the state, which could be modified or revoked at any time.

By the 1940s, courts began paying closer attention to the rights of prisoners, as part of a growing trend towards increased protection of individual rights. In 1941, the Supreme Court, in *Ex parte Hull*, held that inmates had a right to unrestricted access to federal courts. This decision signaled the beginning of the end of the "hands-off" doctrine and the beginning of the era of judicial intervention in corrections. In 1944, in *Coffin v. Reichard*, a federal district court expanded the scope of habeas corpus to include lawsuits filed by inmates that challenged not whether the state had a right to confine them, but the conditions of their confinement.

The civil rights movement of the 1960s and a change in the membership of the Supreme Court resulted in tremendous changes in criminal procedure and correctional practices. Under Chief Justice Earl Warren, the Court extended a number of protections to criminal defendants, including the exclusionary rule, *Miranda* warnings, and the right to counsel at any "critical stage" of the prosecution. The Supreme Court also began to extend protection of individual rights to those convicted of crimes. The Court, in a line of cases required correctional administrators at all levels, from prison to probation and parole, to accord basic procedural (or due process) rights to criminal offenders.

Following the high court's lead, lower federal courts became more receptive to lawsuits brought by prisoners challenging the conditions of their confinement. In *Holt v. Sarver* (1969), a federal district court in Arkansas determined that inmates could challenge as unconstitutional not merely individual correctional practices, but also the totality of the prison's conditions. This form of suit became known as the "conditions of confinement" lawsuit. Federal district courts, formerly absolute in their deference to the wisdom of correctional administrators, became intimately involved in the monitoring and operation of entire prison systems. In 1976, the Supreme Court, in *Estelle v. Gamble,* held that correctional administrators could be held liable for injury to an inmate if the administrators displayed "deliberate indifference" to the needs or rights of the inmate. While this has proven a fairly difficult standard for inmate plaintiffs to meet, it is nonetheless a far cry from the days of *Ruffin v. Commonwealth,* when inmates were literally seen as "slaves of the state."

Paralleling the increased attention paid by courts to correctional institutions was an increased attention to the rights of those under community supervision. In a series of cases decided during the 1970s, the Supreme Court extended a number of due process rights to probationers and parolees, including the right to a revocation hearing, notice of the charges against the individual, and the right to counsel.

Recently, as the membership of the Supreme Court has become more conservative, the high court has been less receptive to the complaints of inmates, and has declined to extend further the protections accorded inmates and those under community supervision.

Rights of Incarcerated Offenders

The courts have attempted to balance the individual rights of inmates and the authority of correctional administrators. These rights include the Fourth Amendment prohibition on unreasonable searches and seizures, the Fifth Amendment privilege against self-incrimination, the Sixth Amendment right to counsel, and the Fourteenth Amendment's right to be accorded due process of law, whatever that term implies. Other rights examined in some detail by the courts include the right to treatment, and First Amendment rights of association and religious freedom.

RIGHT TO TREATMENT

Treatment involves the cure of a disease or at least the alleviation of pain and suffering. It is a process of diagnosis, intervention, and prognosis (Cohen, 1995). While a right to treatment is not mentioned in the text of the Constitution, courts have made it clear that inmates and those under civil commitment do enjoy a right to treatment. This treatment need not be the best that science has to offer—rather, it is enough if the state provides reasonable care. Under *Estelle v. Gamble* (1976), the state may not be held liable for mere negligent treatment. Liability attaches only if there is evidence akin to recklessness or intentional disregard for the client on the part of the state. Furthermore, the Supreme Court held, in *Washington v. Harper* (1990), that an institutionalized person does not have an absolute right to refuse treatment.

The rationale behind mandating a right to treatment for incarcerated persons is that because the state has restricted their liberty, they are unable to obtain medical services on their own initiative—thus, the state must accept responsibility for their medical well-being. Caseworkers in the institutional setting are not required to do more than is possible, given the limited resources of the institution. A study of inmates indicated that while approximately 80 percent of all inmates are in need of drug and alcohol treatment, less than 20 percent receive treatment while incarcerated, due in large part to the limit on institutional resources (General Accounting Office, 1991). Courts have yet to mandate such treatment.

THE EIGHTH AMENDMENT AND "CRUEL AND UNUSUAL" PUNISHMENT

The Eighth Amendment prohibits "cruel and unusual" punishment. Exactly what is cruel and unusual has changed as society has evolved. The Supreme Court has applied the standard to a variety of situations in corrections, including the death penalty, corporal punishment, and the use of force to control inmates, protect other inmates, or to repel an assault by an inmate.

In general, every prisoner has the right to be free of both offensive bodily contact and the fear of it (Palmer, 1991). Prison officials are permitted to use reasonable force to enforce discipline and to protect themselves and others. The key here is that the force must be reasonable under the circumstances—thus, prison officials may be justified in using extreme force, even deadly force, if the situation warrants it (Hemmens and Atherton, 1999). In addition, the Supreme Court has held that correctional personnel may be liable for failing to prevent harm to an inmate by another inmate, but only if it can be demonstrated that their conduct displayed "deliberate indifference" to the safety of the inmate (*Farmer v. Brennan*, 1994).

While prison officials are allowed to use force, when necessary, to enforce prison regulations, courts have backed away from earlier decisions, which upheld the practice of corporal punishment, or the use of physical force to punish inmates for rule violations. While the Supreme Court never has expressly voided the practice, a number of lower courts have declared corporal punishment unconstitutional (*Jackson v. Bishop*, 1968).

Related to corporal punishment is the age old practice of punishing recalcitrant inmates by placing them in solitary confinement. Courts consistently have rejected the contention that solitary confinement is unconstitutional per se, but they have required that: (1) the conditions of solitary confinement must not be disproportionate to the offense (Palmer, 1991); and (2) since solitary confinement is a punishment above and beyond the punishment of incarceration, basic due process protections must be provided, such as the right to a hearing before being sentenced to solitary confinement (*Sandin v. Conner*, 1995).

ACCESS TO LEGAL SERVICES

Access to the courts was one of the very first constitutional rights that the Supreme Court extended to prisoners, in the 1940 case of *Ex parte Hull*. According to the Court, access to the court system is a basic requirement of due process. The question that courts have dealt with since the decision in *Hull* is what constitutes "access?" The major case in this area is *Johnson v. Avery* (1969), in which the Supreme Court held that a prison regulation which prohibited inmates from assisting other inmates in the preparation of legal materials was unconstitutional, if there was no reasonable alternative by which access to the courts could be obtained. The result is that correctional administrators had to either allow "jailhouse lawyers" to help other inmates, or provide some sort of legal assistance program. Prison officials may restrict the amount of legal materials possessed by an inmate, or the time and place for legal assistance, so long as such limitations are reasonable.

Until recently, it was assumed by many lower courts that another decision of the Supreme Court, *Bounds v. Smith* (1977), required prison administrators to provide inmates with either law libraries or access to persons with legal training. But in 1996, in *Lewis v. Casey*, the Supreme Court clarified its earlier decision, holding that evidence of inadequacies in the delivery of legal services is not enough to justify remedial action by the courts; such action is justified only when an inmate's efforts to pursue a legal claim *in fact* are impaired by lack of access to legal materials.

FREEDOM OF RELIGION

The First Amendment includes several separate individual rights, including the freedom of religion. Regarding the freedom of religion, the Supreme Court has held that prison officials have the right to regulate religious activity to promote valid interests such as security, discipline, and inmate and correctional officer safety. Lower courts generally have deferred to the wisdom of correctional administrators when limitations on religious freedom are based on such grounds. More difficult questions have been what exactly constitutes a "religion," or "religious activity?"

THE FOURTH AMENDMENT

The right of an individual to be free of unreasonable searches and seizures, provided in the Fourth Amendment and made applicable to the states by the due process clause of the Fourteenth Amendment, obviously has limited application to the institutional setting. Inmates are subject to searches of their person, belongings, and cell without warrant or even probable cause. Courts recognize the unique security needs of the institution outweigh the individual rights of the inmate.

DUE PROCESS RIGHTS IN DISCIPLINARY HEARINGS

An area of correctional administration that has received a good deal of attention from the courts is the process by which inmates are disciplined. Discipline is obviously an important element of maintenance of security in the correctional institution. The courts require correctional administrators to provide "due process of law" to inmates involved in disciplinary proceedings. This means that before punishment can be meted out, certain procedures must be followed, to ensure inmates are not being treated unfairly. In *Wolff v. McDonnell* (1974), the U. S. Supreme Court held that due process in prison disciplinary proceedings entails providing (1) inmates with written notice of the charges against them; (2) an opportunity for inmates to present evidence and witnesses in their defense; (3) the assistance of staff or a fellow prisoner, if necessary under the circumstances; and (4) a written statement by the disciplinary board explaining its findings. The Court did not require that the inmate be allowed to cross-examine witnesses, or be provided with counsel.

DUE PROCESS RIGHTS IN PAROLE HEARINGS

Historically, courts in this country have held that the decision to grant or deny a parole or pardon is a matter of executive discretion, implying that courts should not interfere in administrative decision-making. While there is no constitutional right to parole or sentence commutation, the Supreme Court has held that when parole is a possibility, correctional administrators must accord inmates due process. This merely requires that the parole board hold a hearing, and provide the inmate with written reasons for its decision.

In *Greenholtz v. Inmates of Nebraska Penal and Correctional Complex* (1979), the Court held that an inmate has no right to parole, and that a discretionary parole release determination does not create a protected liberty interest. States are not constitutionally required to provide parole. Because there is no entitlement, no protected liberty interest (such as the right to a parole hearing) is created. In *Connecticut Board of Pardons v. Dumschat*, the Court held that a state's practice of granting approximately three-fourths of the applications for commutation of life sentences *did not* create either a "liberty interest" or an "entitlement" so as to require the parole board to explain its reasons for denying an application for commutation.

Rights of Individuals Under Community Supervision

An offender may be released into the community either on probation, or on parole. Probation is a substitute for incarceration of convicted criminals. Probation is defined as "a sentence imposed for commission of crime whereby a convicted criminal offender is released into the community under the supervision of a probation officer in lieu of incarceration" (Black, 1983). Probation has the twin goals of maximizing the liberty of the offender while still protecting the public. It is less costly, and generally more rehabilitative in nature than incarceration.

According to the Supreme Court, the purpose of probation is "to provide an individualized program offering a young or unhardened offender an opportunity to rehabilitate himself without institutional confinement under the tutelage of a probation officer and under the continuing power of the court to impose institutional punishment for his original offense in the event that he abuse the opportunity" (*Roberts v. United States, 1943*).

Parole is a substitute for, and an extension of incarceration. Parole is defined as "a conditional release of a prisoner, generally under supervision of a parole officer, who has served part of the term for which he was sentenced to prison" (Black,1983). Parole has the goal of reintegrating the offender into the community while maintaining some degree of supervision over the individual, thus protecting the public.

CONDITIONS OF PROBATION AND PAROLE

Courts consistently have upheld the use of probation and parole conditions. There are several justifications for imposing probation and parole conditions, including protecting the public, reducing recidivism through deterrence of criminal conduct by the client, promoting alternatives to incarceration, and possibly rehabilitating offenders through closer supervision (Palmer, 1997).

Probation and parole conditions are imposed either by the judge at sentencing, or by a parole board at the parole hearing. While the law in most states suggest conditions to be imposed, the judge or board generally has complete discretion to accept, modify, or reject these conditions.

Surprisingly few statutes specify the goals to be served by probation and parole conditions, but courts have focused on the twin goals of rehabilitation and community protection. These interests are seen by the courts as being of sufficient importance to meet the "compelling state interest" required for abridgement of "fundamental" constitutional rights (Tribe, 1988).

While rehabilitation and public safety often are cited goals, defining these terms with precision is difficult. *Rehabilitation* generally encompasses conditions, which involve treatment, education and reintegration of the offender; *public safety* involves conditions such as a ban on association with criminals, possession of weapons, and a requirement to obey the law.

Probation and parole conditions usually are classified as either general or specific. General conditions are imposed on all; specific conditions are imposed only on some. While judges and parole boards are given tremendous latitude in establishing conditions; in reality, many use a list of previously adopted standard conditions for every individual. Commonly imposed general conditions include requiring the individuals to (1) make periodic reports to their parole officer, (2) notify the officer about changes in employment or residence, (3) obtain permission for out-of-state travel, (4) refrain from possessing firearms, (5) not associate with known criminals, and (6) obey the law.

A special condition is one that is not imposed as a matter of course on all probationers or parolees. Rather, it is tailored to the specific offender. So long as such conditions are reasonable and related to the state's legitimate interest in rehabilitation and/or protection of society, they are likely to be upheld by the courts. A condition which violates a parolee's constitutional rights is invalid even if it has a rehabilitative purpose or protects society.

The imposition of special conditions is not uncommon, as judges and parole boards attempt to tailor the terms of probation or parole to the individual offender. The general rule is that the authority to impose special conditions cannot be delegated to probation officers, although officers often are permitted to determine the precise mode of implementation of a condition. To avoid liability, officers should avoid imposing special conditions, or unilaterally modifying existing conditions.

Considering how many individuals today are on either probation or parole, the amount of litigation concerning the legality of conditions is relatively small. This is likely because the probationer/parolee has agreed to the conditions and is aware of the practical consequences of challenging them. When conditions are challenged, a variety of claims are frequently raised. These include invalid consent, vagueness, unequal enforcement of the law, and infringement on a fundamental right.

The due process clause of the Fourteenth Amendment prohibits the enforcement of vague laws, on the theory that persons cannot conform their conduct if they do not know precisely what is expected of them. Probation and parole conditions often are challenged on the grounds of vagueness, as offenders assert they did not understand the meaning of particular terms. Some conditions are expressed in a very general way, such as "avoid disreputable palaces" or "do not associate with undesirable individuals." Courts generally have held probation and parole conditions to a lesser standard of clarity than statutory provisions, inquiring only as to whether the phrase in question is of common, everyday English usage (del Carmen, 1985).

Unequal enforcement of conditions can be the basis for liability under the equal protection clause of the Fourteenth Amendment. Under this provision, unreasonable distinctions between individuals or classes of individuals are prohibited. The actions of probation and parole officers are sometimes challenged on the grounds of unequal enforcement—the probationer/parolee asserts that he or she has been singled out for harassment by the officer. Courts generally require clear evidence of officer misconduct in these cases (Hemmens and del Carmen, 1997).

In general, probation and parole conditions are valid, so long as they: (1) do not violate the constitution, (2) are reasonable, (3) are unambiguous, and (4) are intended to promote the rehabilitation of the offender and/or the protection of society. When a "fundamental right" is abridged, however, the courts will examine the condition more closely, using what is referred to as "strict scrutiny" review. Under this standard of review, a probation or parole condition is valid only if there is a showing of both (1) a compelling state interest and (2) no less restrictive means of accomplishing the purpose. Rights deemed fundamental by the Supreme Court are found largely in the protections afforded citizens in the Bill of Rights. The First Amendment guarantees of freedom of speech, assembly, and religion are a prime example.

NONASSOCIATION CONDITIONS

A notion likely as old as crime itself is that hanging out with the "wrong crowd" will get a person in trouble. There is support in criminology research for this belief, and it serves as the basis for one of the most common probation and parole conditions, the limitation on association. This condition forbids the offender from having contact with certain persons or types of persons. This limitation is justified on the ground that association with criminals or other "shady" characters will interfere with both the rehabilitation of the offender and reduce public safety. This limitation may apply to a category of persons, such as those with a criminal record, or those who are not "law-abiding" or are of "disreputable or harmful character;" it also may apply to specific, named persons. Nonassociation provisions are authorized by statute in some jurisdictions, and by case law in others.

Nonassociation conditions frequently are challenged as unconstitutional. These challenges fall into one of four categories: (1) the condition is unrelated to the purpose of probation/parole, (2) the condition violates the right of privacy, (3) the language of the condition is too vague, and (4) the condition violates the First Amendment.

Claims that a nonassociation condition is unrelated to the traditional purposes of parole (protection of the public and rehabilitation of the offender) are rarely successful. Courts generally accept without question the assertion that prohibiting contact with criminals and other unsavory types is conducive to public safety and rehabilitation.

Claims that a nonassociation condition violates the right of privacy are also rarely successful, except in some limited circumstances where the nonassociation condition infringed on specific familial rights such as prohibiting a person from living with his or her significant other.

Claims that a nonassociation condition is void because it is vague are sometimes successful. Due process requires that probation and parole conditions be stated clearly enough so that the average person can understand them and know what conduct is and is not permitted. Successful challenges have focused on the language of conditions, which prohibit association with all criminals, without regard for whether the probationer/parolee was aware that the person he or she was associating with had a criminal record.

Claims that a nonassociation condition violates the First Amendment are the most likely to succeed. The First Amendment includes the right of freedom of association; a nonassociation condition clearly infringes on this right. This does not render such conditions invalid, however. Probationers and parolees both enjoy only conditional freedom from confinement, and this freedom comes at the expense of some rights. Courts long have upheld conditions which restrict even "fundamental" rights, such as the freedom of association, so long as the condition is related to a compelling state interest, such as protecting the public or promoting rehabilitation.

The Supreme Court has decided only one case involving the constitutionality of a nonassociation condition. In *Arciniega v. Freeman* the Court interpreted the meaning of a parole condition, which prohibited "association" with other ex-convicts, holding that such a provision did not apply to "incidental" contact" that occurs between ex-convicts in the course of work on a legitimate job. Unresolved by the Court's decision in *Arciniega* was the question of exactly what constitutes "incidental" contact in other situations. Lower courts are left to sort out these issues.

Lower courts have added little to clarify the uncertainty, with most of the decisions involving interpretations of "incidental contact." The lower courts have not strayed far from the Supreme Court's distinction of "incidental contact" and "association." Generally, courts have treated brief, unplanned contact as "incidental," and have treated repeated, intentional contact as "association." Several courts have added the requirement of *scienter*, meaning that the contact must be knowing for it to constitute the association forbidden by the conditions of parole or probation.

There are several areas which pose potential problems regarding limitations on association with other parolees. Often parolees participate in programs composed of individuals with special needs, such as educational programs, vocational training, alcohol and drug treatment, and psychological counseling. Restrictions on association with other parolees presents an obvious problem for these programs. For example, participation in Alcoholics Anonymous by parolees is not uncommon. In this program, members are required to have a sponsor who has similar experiences and maintains a close relationship with the individual. Accordingly, an ex-convict may request another ex-convict to be his or her sponsor. Should this type of association be restricted? If it is not, how would courts differentiate between legitimate self-help organizations and sham organizations created to avoid the restriction on association?

Nonassociation conditions are one of the easiest conditions for probationers and parolees to violate. Most offenders know others with criminal records, or live in an area where they are likely to encounter other offenders. As the facts in *Arciniega* indicate, even offenders who seek to comply with their probation and parole conditions may violate them unintentionally, simply by virtue of working somewhere with other offenders, or by participating in mandatory rehabilitation and reintegration programs.

Clearly, due process requires that offenders be given fair warning as to what conduct will subject them to a deprivation of their liberty. This means probation and parole conditions should be as clear and unambiguous as possible, and that probation and parole officers should take steps to ensure that their clients understand their probation or parole conditions. In the context of nonassociation conditions, this means making sure offenders know the legal meanings of terms such as "association," "incidental contact," and "law-abiding."

TRAVEL CONDITIONS

Probation and parole conditions often are categorized into two groups: reform and control. *Reform conditions* are intended to help in the rehabilitation of the offender, while *control conditions* are intended to aid in the supervision of the offender (Cromwell and del Carmen, 1999). A common probation and parole condition is one which limits in some way the offender's right to travel. This sort of condition is imposed in at least 75 percent of jurisdictions in this country, and comes in a variety of forms. Such a limitation is an example of a control condition.

Restrictions on travel, or more generally the offender's freedom of movement, can be divided into three types: those which prohibit the offender from leaving the jurisdiction, those prohibiting an offender from being at a particular location, and those requiring the offender to be somewhere. Often two or more of these restrictions are combined in the conditions of probation or parole.

Conditions prohibiting the offender from traveling may require the offender stay within the city, county, state, or country which has jurisdiction over the case. Conditions prohibiting the offender from being at a particular place may refer to places where criminal activity is known to occur, or where the offender's presence is likely to lead to trouble or criminal involvement, such as a bar, or the residence of the victim of the offender. Conditions requiring the offender to be somewhere include those which require the offender to live in a particular residence or halfway house, and those which require the offender to be present at treatment or counseling sessions.

Perhaps the most common probation and parole condition is one which requires the offender to remain within a certain geographical area, such as the state or county. Such conditions generally are upheld by the courts. The rationale for upholding such restrictions on the ability to travel include protection of the public and promotion of offender rehabilitation. The public is protected because it is easier to supervise the offender if he or she remains within a limited area. Rehabilitation is fostered because it keeps the offender from going to areas where he or she might be more likely to engage in criminal conduct and because it makes it easier for the probation/parole officer to supervise the offender and help reintegrate the offender into society.

A common condition affecting the freedom of movement is one which requires the offender to be at a particular place at a particular time, such as one in which the offender is required to remain at home during the evening hours. This is a form of curfew. While general curfews for adults are frequently declared unconstitutional by the courts, probation and parole conditions involving a curfew for the offender are often upheld. The justification for upholding a curfew condition is usually that it will protect the public and promote the rehabilitation of the offender by keeping him or her away from places where he or she is more likely to engage in inappropriate and/or illegal behavior.

Probation and parole conditions prohibiting an offender from being in a particular place are not uncommon. For example, an offender might be prohibited from being in a bar, the residence of the victim of his offense, or a school. Courts have struck down such limitations when the state was unable to demonstrate that there is a relationship between the offense and the place prohibited. When the state is able to establish such a relationship, however, courts are likely to uphold the prohibition as fostering rehabilitation and protecting the public.

The right to travel is an ancient one, recognized in English law as early as the Magna Carta (1215). While a right to travel is not specifically mentioned in the Constitution, it is recognized that there exists a constitutional right to interstate travel. The right is derived from Article IV, Section Two of the Constitution, which states that "the citizens of each state shall be entitled to all Privileges and Immunities of Citizens in the several States." The right to travel is a fundamental right, meaning that courts will examine any attempt to restrict it very closely, applying the "strict scrutiny" test, which requires a showing of a "compelling state interest" and that there is no less means of accomplishing the purpose.

There are no U. S. Supreme Court decisions regarding the constitutionality of probation and parole conditions limiting the right to travel. There have been a number of lower federal court decisions and state court decisions involving challenges to such conditions, however. Lower courts long have upheld conditions which restrict even "fundamental" rights, such as the right of travel, so long as the condition is related to a compelling state interest, such as protecting the public or promoting rehabilitation. Probation and parole conditions which impose reasonable restrictions on the ability of the offender to travel or move about usually are upheld, on the ground that they are an appropriate means of both fostering rehabilitation and protecting the public.

While limitations on the freedom of movement are common, such conditions should not be imposed without reason, or without recognition that violation may be all too easy. Requiring an offender to stay away from places where he or she has friends, family, and other ties is an invitation to violation by the offender. Probation and parole officers should work with their clients to ensure the clients fully understand what the limitation on movement means in a practical sense, and to provide ways for clients to conduct activities which foster their rehabilitation and reintegration into society without leading to an unwitting probation or parole violation.

SPEECH CONDITIONS

Probation and parole conditions limiting speech are relatively rare, and most involve probationers who committed crimes while engaged in political demonstrations. Typical conditions bar the making of speeches, distribution of printed materials, and public demonstrations or picketing. Such conditions were not uncommon during the Vietnam War, when political protests occurred with some regularity. Courts have seen a recurrence of such conditions in recent years, largely as a result of antiabortion protests. Some conditions have barred nonpolitical speech. These conditions often are intended to limit the ability of offenders to profit from the publication of materials documenting their criminal exploits.

Courts, recognizing the importance of the freedom of speech, tend to examine restrictions on the right very closely. In general, those cases upholding conditions have focused on the relationship between the condition and the goals of rehabilitation and protection of the public. Cases striking such conditions generally have done so on the ground that they are overbroad, and restrict more speech than is necessary. In *Hoffart v. State* (1985) the court upheld a probation condition prohibiting an antiabortion protestor from entering the establishment that he was picketing against a challenge that such a condition unduly restricted the rights of the offender to engage in a political demonstration. In a similar vein, the court of appeals in *United States v. Turner* (1995) upheld a probation condition preventing an antiabortion protestor from picketing an abortion clinic. The court determined that such a restriction was reasonably related to the goals of probation, including the prevention of further criminal activity and protection of the public.

CONDITIONS MANDATING EDUCATION OR JOB TRAINING

Conditions requiring the offender to participate in educational programming or job training are different from previously discussed conditions in several ways, particularly in that they require the offender to do something, rather than to refrain from doing something. An affirmative act by the offender is required. A common probation and parole condition is the requirement that the offender attend school or an educational program of some kind. The frequency with which this condition is applied is not surprising, given the high value placed on education in American society and the relatively low education level of most offenders.

The type of education required depends on the offender. He or she may be required to attend high school, college, or vocational school, or to participate in programs aimed at allowing the participant to achieve the high school equivalency degree, or General Equivalency Degree. Juvenile offenders may be required to attend school; adult offenders generally are required to attend some form of an adult education program. Other, offense-related educational programs also may be required, such as attendance at an alcohol and drug awareness class, or driver safety class.

The authority to require the offender to participate in educational programs may be found in specific statutes, or under the court and parole board's general authority to impose any condition that is reasonably related to the primary goals of probation and parole—rehabilitation and protection of the public. While the evidence regarding the rehabilitative effects of education programs on recidivism is mixed, historically there has been strong support for such programs. The assumption is that offenders with basic education are less likely to recidivate and more likely to see themselves as members of law-abiding society.

Offenders who either have completed basic educational programs or are in need of a marketable job skill often are required to obtain some form of job training. The justification for such a condition is also similar to the justification for mandatory education—rehabilitation and protection of the public. The assumption is that offenders with job skills will be less likely to return to their criminal ways as they develop a legitimate means of obtaining money.

Several cautions regarding mandating participation in education and job training programs should be mentioned. First, the course of study must not violate the constitutional rights of the offenders, particularly their First Amendment right of freedom of religion. Requiring an offender to attend religious training would likely be considered a violation of the First Amendment. While offenders on probation or parole retain only limited rights, courts look closely at any conditions which impinge on First Amendment rights.

A second caution is that offenders should not be required to participate in educational programs for which they are unprepared or unable to participate in, because of financial constraints or other limitations. This is simply setting the offender up for failure. Probation and parole officers should consider the aptitude and willingness of the offender when making recommendations for educational programming.

CONDITIONS MANDATING MEDICAL TREATMENT

Conditions mandating medical treatment can take several forms, including surgical procedures, psychological treatment, or some type of counseling or therapy. Conditions requiring an offender to undergo some type of surgical procedure are relatively rare, although there have been calls in recent years for greater use of such conditions, at least in regards to sex offenders.

Challenges to conditions mandating medical treatment are based in several different provisions of the Constitution, including the First and Eighth Amendments, and the general right to privacy. These challenges are relatively rare, no doubt in large part because such conditions are themselves rare. Generally, courts have taken the position that a condition requiring medical treatment is not *per se* unconstitutional, so long as the treatment is reasonably related to the goal of rehabilitation. Additionally, courts have noted that the offender always has the option of rejecting such a condition.

Conditions mandating some form of therapy or counseling are much more common than those requiring the offender to undergo a medical procedure. Primarily because these conditions are less physically invasive, they are also much more likely to be upheld by the courts. Additionally, it is often easier to establish a connection between the mandated therapy and the goals of probation and parole.

Conditions requiring the offender to receive some form of therapy or counseling may be authorized by a state statute, or by parole authority regulations. This authorization is frequently vague, merely authorizing "psychological or psychiatric treatment" without providing more specifics. A number of states now provide specific authorization for counseling for sex offenders. Conditions mandating therapy or counseling are quite popular, as there is widespread sentiment that most offenders can benefit from professional attention.

There have been very few challenges to probation and parole conditions mandating therapy or counseling. Courts routinely have rejected such challenges, so long as the treatment is reasonably related to the needs of the offender. Courts have also made it clear that offenders are only required to make reasonable efforts to comply with the treatment condition. Requiring an offender to obtain expensive treatment which he or she clearly cannot afford may be invalidated by the courts.

CONDITIONS MANDATING RESTITUTION

A common probation and parole condition is the requirement that the offender make a payment to the victim. *Restitution* is defined as "an equitable remedy under which a person is restored to his or her position prior to a loss or injury . . . (or) compensation for the wrongful taking of property." It is different from *victim compensation*, where the money is given to the victim by the state. Restitution is paid by the offender to the victim. It is also different from a fine, which is monies paid by the offender to the state and is not treated as compensation. Restitution serves both as atonement for the offender and rehabilitation for the victim.

Restitution has been used for many years. It is mentioned in the Bible as well as the Code of Hammurabi, and received the enthusiastic support of the eighteenth century reformer, Jeremy Bentham. Virtually every jurisdiction allows for the imposition of restitution as a probation condition, while twenty-nine states currently require a court to order restitution to the victim. Restitution has been endorsed in the Model Penal Code, by the American Bar Association, and the National Council on Crime and Delinquency. A 1992 study reported that in a sample of 79,000 probationers, half of all property offenders and a quarter of all violent offenders were ordered to pay restitution as a condition of probation.

It is important to note that restitution may be imposed only by judges, acting either pursuant to a statutory mandate or within the scope of their authority to impose reasonable probation conditions. Probation officers are charged with the responsibility of overseeing the collection of the restitution. Both payment to victim and community service in lieu of payment are included. Restitution is often victim initiated—if the victim does not inform the court of losses suffered, restitution may not be ordered.

Several studies of restitution have revealed that the primary determinant of whether offenders were ordered to make restitution was their ability to pay. Consequently, many offenders are excluded.

Restitution serves a number of purposes. These include (1) providing redress for victims of crime; (2) fostering rehabilitation of the offender; (3) providing accountability for the offender; (4) deterring further criminal activity; (5) serving as an intermediate sanction that is less severe on the offender; (6) reducing demands on the criminal justice system; and (7) reducing the need for vengeance. The sanction is used most often for crimes involving damage to property or economic crimes. It is used much less frequently for violent crimes, as it is difficult to determine the appropriate compensation for such injuries, and it is not seen as an appropriate sanction for such serious offenses.

The authority to require an offender to make restitution has been repeatedly upheld by the courts. Ordinarily, there must be a finding or plea of guilty before restitution can be ordered, although this does not apply to cases involving restitution ordered during the pretrial diversion process. Courts may specify the amount, method of payment, and other conditions relating to restitution. However, the U.S. Supreme Court, in *Bearden v. Georgia*, ruled that probation cannot be revoked because of an offender's inability to pay restitution as a condition of probation when the failure to pay is a result of indigence and not a mere refusal to pay. In this case Bearden was ordered to pay a $500 fine and $200 in restitution, but was unable to find employment and consequently failed to pay either the fine or the restitution. His probation was revoked and he was incarcerated. He argued, and the Supreme Court, per Justice O'Connor, agreed, that the Equal Protection Clause of the Fourteenth Amendment barred the revocation of probation for a nonwillful failure to pay restitution. The Court determined that revocation was proper only if the failure to pay was intentional and the offender did not make a good faith effort to obtain the means to pay.

It sometimes seems as though there are as many probation and parole conditions (and challenges to these conditions) as there are individuals under community supervision. Probation and parole officers can do their job well, however, if they keep in mind a few simple points. First, individuals on probation/parole retain a number of rights, and officers must take care not to abridge these rights. Second, officers have a duty to enforce the conditions of probation and parole, and to do so in an evenhanded, consistent manner. Third, many violations may be avoided if officers make clear to their clients the terms of each condition, as well as their intention to enforce these conditions. Fourth, officers will do well to remember that many probation and parole conditions serve two primary functions at the same time: promotion of offender rehabilitation and reintegration, and protection of society.

Sex Offender Registration, Community Notification, and Civil Commitment

Spurred by media accounts of horrible child sexual assault cases, Congress and the state legislatures in recent years have passed a variety of laws affecting the rights of convicted sex offenders. These laws vary in the details, but focus on three primary objectives: (1) requiring sex offenders to register with local authorities; (2) requiring local law enforcement to notify the community about the presence of sex offenders living in the community; and (3) permitting the state to pursue civil commitment of sex offenders after they have served a period of incarceration. Each of these objectives presents potential legal issues.

Laws affecting sex offenders are often referred to as Meagan's laws, as many of the laws were passed in response to the rape and murder of seven-year old Megan Kanka of New Jersey by a twice-convicted sex offender who lived across the street. The New Jersey legislature and Congress responded by immediately passing legislation affecting sex offenders, and other states soon followed. Much of this legislation was spurred by the Jacob Wetterling Crimes Against Children and Sexually Violent Registration Act, passed by Congress in 1994. This legislation established a national registry system for sex offenders, and required states to pass similar registration and tracking systems or face a loss of federal monies. In particular, the legislation required states to "release relevant information that is necessary to protect the public." Today every state requires the registration of sex offenders, and at least forty-seven states have some form of notification requirement.

While these laws are obviously popular, they are not without controversy. Social scientists have pointed out that there is little empirical proof that such laws reduce recidivism, while legal scholars have suggested the laws may violate any number of constitutional rights, including the ban on *ex post facto laws*, the prohibition on double jeopardy, and the right of privacy.

SEX OFFENDER REGISTRATION

Today all fifty states require that convicted sex offenders register with local authorities. States vary in precisely who is required to register: in some states only those convicted of a sex offense after passage of the registration requirement must comply, while in other states the registration requirement is applied retroactively. Some states require anyone convicted of a sexual offense to register; others also require those convicted of a violent crime against a child to register.

Typical registration requirements include requiring a released offender to register with the local law enforcement agency in the jurisdiction where they are living, to verify their address annually, and to do so for a period of years—often between twenty and thirty years. Failure to comply is a felony, punishable as a new offense.

COMMUNITY NOTIFICATION

Washington was the first state to pass a notification statute, doing so in 1989. The notification movement gained national attention and tremendous momentum with the passage of New Jersey's notification statute, Megan's law, in 1994. Notification statutes were viewed by proponents as a necessary supplement to registration laws, many of which already existed.

There exist a variety of methods of notifying the public. These include public meetings, provision of a written list of offenders, provision of a list on CD-ROM, news releases, and notices targeted to institutions such as schools. Over half the states have or are creating an Internet site devoted to dissemination of sex offender information. More than thirty states allow persons to request information on a specific offender, or to view the sex offender registry at the discretion of local law enforcement officials. States also vary in the determination of which registered sex offenders the public has a right to notice of, with public notice usually limited to those deemed most dangerous.

CIVIL COMMITMENT

The U.S. Supreme Court recently upheld civil commitment of sex offenders in *Kansas v. Hendricks*. Kansas passed legislation in 1994 establishing procedures for the civil commitment of persons who were deemed likely to engage in "predatory acts of sexual violence" due to either a "mental abnormality" or "personality disorder." The statute was applied to Hendricks, after he finished serving a term of imprisonment for child molestation, and he was ordered civilly committed. *Hendricks* challenged his commitment on double jeopardy, *ex post facto*, and due process grounds. In a narrow five-four decision, written by Justice Thomas, the Supreme Court upheld the civil commitment statute. The high court reasoned that neither the double jeopardy nor *ex post facto* clauses applied, as civil commitment was not punitive but regulatory, and these clauses apply only to punishment. There was no due process violation because civil commitment for a mental abnormality did not violate the concept of "ordered liberty."

While only a handful of states (including Arizona, Minnesota, Washington, and Wisconsin) had enacted civil commitment laws prior to the *Hendricks* decision, a number of states have responded by proposing similar legislation.

How sex offenders are managed and supervised is a matter of great concern to the general public, politicians, and criminal justice professionals. Sex offender notification and registration is part of a larger trend towards community justice. Supporters of notification often claim that such laws enable individual citizens to protect themselves against criminal activity. Sex offender laws are also part of the movement to "get tough" on offenders, and are not as far reaching as some proposals. For instance, at least one state, Florida, has passed legislation mandating chemical castration of certain first-time and repeat sex offenders.

Protecting the public from sex offenders and helping offenders with their rehabilitation and reintegration has taken on even greater importance to probation and parole departments as a consequence of the firestorm over registration and notification. There has been a tremendous increase in the resources needed to supervise sex offenders. Unfortunately, there also have been a number of cases involving claims of improper supervision of sex offenders. As a result, the focus is now on containment and control of sex offenders, rather than rehabilitation.

THE FOURTEENTH AMENDMENT AND PROBATION AND PAROLE

Individuals convicted of crime, whether incarcerated or on probation or parole, do not retain the privacy rights enjoyed by the average citizen. Indeed, prisoners have no reasonable expectation of privacy and are subject to warrantless searches based on less than probable cause. This limitation also is evident in regards to probation and parole conditions that impinge on the Fourth Amendment right to be free from "unreasonable" searches and seizures. What may be an unreasonable search when the target is an ordinary citizen may be reasonable when the target is a probationer or parolee. Courts frequently base this distinction on the rationale that a probationer or parolee has a lessened expectation of privacy than the ordinary citizen. There are several policy reasons that support allowing searches of probationers and parolees. These include protecting the public, reducing recidivism through deterrence of criminal conduct by the client, and promoting alternatives to incarceration and, hopefully, rehabilitating offenders by reintegrating them in the community.

Consent to search is one of the most common conditions of probation and parole. The condition generally covers searches conducted by probation or parole officers, and often allows searches by police officers, as well. The scope of the search usually includes the offender's person and property. The terms of the condition may include blanket permission to be searched by caseworkers or law enforcement personnel, or may be limited to searches conducted by the caseworker. While this condition is widespread, it is rarely specifically authorized by statute (Cohen and Gobert, 1992). Instead, the condition usually is justified under the broad discretionary authority of the sentencing court (for probation) or the parole agency (for parole). While this condition is almost always upheld, some courts have struck it down in specific instances where consent to search was not appropriately related to the offense and the background of the offender (Hemmens, Bennett, and del Carmen, 1999).

The Fourth Amendment controls all searches and seizures conducted by state actors, be they police or probation officers. All searches and seizures must be conducted either: (1) based on a warrant, issued upon a showing of "probable cause," or (2) without a warrant, so long as the search is not "unreasonable"—meaning there must be a showing of probable cause and an exigent circumstance or exception, which justifies failure to obtain a warrant. *Exigent circumstances* include such situations as danger to public safety and hot pursuit. Exceptions to the warrant requirement include inventory searches, plain view searches, search incident to arrest, and others. The two exceptions relevant to caseworkers are consent and the special needs of law enforcement.

Consent is a voluntary waiver of a person's Fourth Amendment rights. It may be given expressly, by implication, or by a prior agreement (such as a condition of probation or parole). An interesting, and common, situation is the one in which the terms of probation or parole include a waiver of the right to be free from unreasonable searches and seizures. There are a number of exceptions to the warrant requirement, one of which is consent. So long as consent is freely given, it constitutes a valid waiver of one's Fourth Amendment rights. This waiver need not be informed, or knowing— that is, law enforcement personnel are not required to advise a person that he or she has the right to refuse to consent to a warrantless search. The sole requirement is voluntariness, the absence of coercion or duress. Some of the factors the Court considers in determining whether consent is voluntary include intelligence and age.

Another exception to the warrant requirement which comes into play in probation and parole situations, is the "special needs of law enforcement" exception. Under this exception, the requirement of a warrant and probable cause are determined to interfere too greatly on the government's objective. Courts must balance the degree of intrusion into an individual's right to privacy with the burden on the government. The Court has upheld searches in schools and drug-testing in certain occupations under this exception. In *Griffin v. Wisconsin* (1987), the Court held that a state regulation allowing "reasonable" searches of all probationers was constitutionally valid, on the grounds that the warrant and probable cause requirement would unduly hamper the state's probation system. The Court did not find it necessary to address the issue of the validity of the probationers' consent, since the regulation was upheld under the "special needs" exception.

THE EXCLUSIONARY RULE AND PROBATION AND PAROLE

Until recently, it was unclear whether the exclusionary rule applied to probation and parole revocation hearings, which are generally considered extrajudicial proceedings. The Supreme Court in *Griffin v. Wisconsin* (1987) held that a state regulation allowing warrantless "reasonable" searches and searches based on "reasonable grounds" of probationers was constitutionally valid, on the ground that the warrant and probable cause requirement would unduly hamper the effectiveness of the state's probation system. Lower courts interpreting *Griffin* were split on the applicability of the exclusionary rule to probation and parole revocation hearings where probation and parole officers conduct illegal searches. Finally, during the 1997 term, the high court issued a decision involving the applicability of the exclusionary rule to probation and parole revocation hearings. In *Pennsylvania Board of Probation and Parole v. Scott* (1998) the court, in a five-four decision held that the exclusionary rule does not apply to parole revocation hearings. This is a major victory for probation and parole officers.

PENNSYLVANIA BOARD OF PROBATION AND PAROLE V. SCOTT

Keith Scott was released on parole in September, 1993, after serving ten years for third-degree murder. One of the conditions of his parole was that he would neither own nor possess any weapons. Another condition was that he consent, in advance, to warrantless searches of his person, property, and residence by agents of the Pennsylvania Board of Probation and Parole. Furthermore, he agreed that any evidence seized during such searches could be used in a parole revocation hearing.

About five months after Scott was paroled, three parole officers obtained an arrest warrant for Scott, based on evidence that he had violated several terms of his parole. After arresting Scott they went to his residence, where he lived with his parents, and searched it. In a room adjacent to Scott's bedroom they found several weapons. These were introduced at the revocation hearing. Scott objected to the introduction of the evidence seized during the search of his home, claiming the seizure violated the Fourth Amendment because it was conducted without at least "reasonable suspicion" (as required by *Griffin*). He also claimed that his prior consent to a warrantless search was invalid because it was obtained involuntarily, as a requirement of parole eligibility. The hearing examiner rejected his claims, admitted the seized evidence, and recommitted Scott.

On appeal, the Commonwealth Court of Pennsylvania ruled: (1) the search was unlawful because it was conducted without Scott's consent and was not authorized by any state statutory or regulatory framework ensuring the reasonableness of the officers (per *Griffin*), and (2) the illegally seized evidence should not be admitted at the revocation hearing because the exclusionary rule applied to such proceedings. The Pennsylvania Supreme Court affirmed the lower court, holding that Scott's consent to warrantless searches did not extend to searches conducted without at least "reasonable suspicion," and that the exclusionary rule should apply to parole revocation hearings when parole officers are aware that the subject of their search is a parolee.

The U.S. Supreme Court reversed the decision of the Pennsylvania Supreme Court and held that the exclusionary rule does not apply to parole revocation hearings. Writing for the majority, Justice Thomas emphasized the costs associated with the exclusionary rule, and downplayed the benefits of the rule, particularly in parole revocation hearings. As parole is a "variation on imprisonment of convicted criminals" and parole revocation deprives a parolee "only of the conditional liberty properly dependent on observance of special parole restrictions," Thomas determined that applying the exclusionary rule to parole revocation hearings would significantly alter the revocation process, transforming revocation hearings "from a predictive and discretionary effort to promote the best interests of both parolees and society into trial-like proceedings less attuned to the interests of the parolee."

Thomas stated that the exclusionary rule should not be applied to parole revocation hearings because the purpose of the exclusionary rule is deterrence of unlawful police conduct in the investigation and prosecution of crime, while the purpose of parole is different—to rehabilitate the offender while at the same time to protect the community. Since extension of the exclusionary rule to revocation hearings would not serve these dual purposes, and, in fact, would hamper the effective administration of a parole system, it has no place in revocation hearings.

Writing in dissent, Justice Souter criticized the majority opinion for characterizing the parole officer-parolee relationship as nonadversarial, particularly in instances such as this case, where the parole officers went to Scott's house to search only after they already had arrested him. Souter also noted that deterrence is important when parole officers realize that a criminal trial is unlikely and that all they need to do to have their client returned to prison is to find evidence of a parole violation. In such instances, the parole revocation hearing is likely to be the only forum in which the illegally obtained evidence ever will be offered. Souter's position mirrors that of the minority of lower courts which had held the exclusionary rule applies to parole revocation hearings in large part because parole officers today are more akin to law enforcement than social workers, and hence involved in investigation of criminal activity with the intent to incarcerate the parolee.

The decision in *Scott* is unsurprising, given the high court's reluctance to extend the exclusionary rule beyond the confines of the criminal trial. In *Morrissey v. Brewer* (1972) the Court said that revocation hearings ". . . should be flexible enough to consider evidence including letter, affidavits, and other material that would not be admissible in an adversary criminal trial." This language did not directly mention the exclusionary rule, but did suggest the revocation hearing need not be treated as equivalent to a criminal trial. Furthermore, an overwhelming majority of states already held that the exclusionary rule generally does not apply to probation or parole revocation hearings. The decision in *Scott* not to apply the exclusionary rule follows logically from these prior cases.

The ruling in *Scott* is a major victory for probation and parole officers. It allows the use of evidence, however obtained, in parole revocation hearings. This is an important decision, as parole revocations are becomingly increasingly common as more and more individuals are placed on parole. There are currently in excess of three million people on probation or parole. And while this case dealt only with parole revocation hearings, it is likely the Court would similarly hold the exclusionary does not apply in probation revocation hearings.

CONSENT TO SEARCH

The question which has arisen is whether a waiver of one's Fourth Amendment rights as a condition of probation or parole is truly voluntary, since refusal to waive the right may mean denial of probation or parole, and incarceration. Thus, the individual is effectively caught between a rock and a hard place (or hard time)—give up a constitutional right, or go to prison. Most courts have held that waiver of Fourth Amendment rights as a condition of probation or parole are valid, however (Hemmens, Bennett, and del Carmen, 1998).

Several courts have compared the situation to plea bargaining, which courts have upheld unanimously as noncoercive. Just as the threat of imprisonment hangs over a criminal defendant faced with the choice between going to trial or accepting a plea bargain, the threat of imprisonment hangs over a probation or parole candidate faced with the choice between being imprisoned or accepting the terms of probation or parole. Facing such hard choices, courts have reasoned does not create an unduly coercive atmosphere rendering voluntariness impossible. Rather, it is simply a tough choice, which the individual is being given the opportunity to make. Neither probation nor parole, like plea bargaining, is a constitutional right, after all. Probation and parole are privileges granted by the state, and, as such, are not accorded the same scrutiny as constitutional rights.

Interestingly, there is evidence that some individuals in fact do prefer incarceration to probation or parole. One study of state prisoners found that a substantial number of inmates viewed parole and probation as more onerous than incarceration, and given the choice would rather spend several years in prison than a number of years under community supervision (Crouch, 1993).

PRIVILEGE AGAINST SELF-INCRIMINATION

The Supreme Court has accorded criminal suspects the right to be apprised of their Fifth and Sixth Amendment rights, such as the right to counsel and the privilege against self-incrimination, prior to custodial interrogation. The Court created the so-called *Miranda* warnings because it felt that they were necessary to effectively secure a criminal suspect's privilege against self-incrimination. Prior to the *Miranda v. Arizona* (1966) decision, the Court focused on whether a statement was voluntary—that is, uncoerced by the police. The Court determined in *Miranda* that voluntariness alone was not enough—because an incriminating statement was potentially devastating to a defendant, such statements should be admitted only if they were made freely and with full knowledge of one's constitutional rights.

The Court has refused to extend the *Miranda* warnings to interrogation of probationers or parolees by their caseworkers, however. While the Supreme Court has not directly addressed the issue, most lower courts have held that the *Miranda* warnings are not required before a caseworker speaks with a client, primarily on the rationale that to require the warnings would do serious damage to the relationship between the caseworker and client, creating a law enforcement/interrogation type of atmosphere rather than a counseling type of atmosphere.

While caseworkers are not required to Mirandize their clients before engaging in a routine office visit, a different situation arises when the probation or parole officer has placed the client under arrest. *Miranda* warnings are required whenever someone is in custody and interrogation is about to commence. An ordinary conversation between a client and caseworker does not fall into this category. But once a caseworker has begun investigating a possible crime, and has arrested the client, then *Miranda* warnings are required. The same is true if the caseworker is questioning a client who has been arrested by the police and brought to the caseworker for questioning.

PRIVILEGED COMMUNICATIONS

Courts long have recognized that certain communications should remain confidential, regardless of their probative value in court. Every state has caselaw and statutes according the privilege of confidentiality to certain relationships, such as doctor-patient, husband-wife, lawyer-client, and clergy-parishioner. Confidentiality is not a constitutional right but an evidentiary privilege. This means that the person who enjoys the privilege must exercise it to keep a communication confidential. In other words, the persons must assert the privilege—it will not be extended to them unless they specifically request it.

The importance of privileged communications for criminal justice caseworkers involves their designation, in some states, as counselors. This designation suggests the caseworker-client relationship may be akin to the doctor-patient relationship and that, therefore, communications between a caseworker and a client may be privileged. But most courts have not taken this view. There are exceptions to the doctor-patient privilege, and courts have declined to extend the common law evidentiary privilege of confidentiality to the caseworker-offender relationship, regardless of whether the caseworker is a probation officer or a parole officer. Thus, conversations between a parolee and his or her caseworker are not treated as confidential. The rationale most often proffered for this distinction is that a criminal justice counselor is not a private counselor, but a counselor and a law enforcement agent (*Fare v. Michael C.*, 1979).

In *Jaffee v. Redmond* (1996), the Supreme Court held that there is a psychotherapist-patient privilege with respect to confidential communications. Furthermore, this privilege extends to communications between licensed social workers and patients, as well. While this decision was in accord with the rule in most states, it is potentially significant in that it may open the door for extension of the privilege to other relationships that involve medical/psychological counseling. This could include criminal justice caseworkers. Courts have not yet taken this step, however, and since most criminal justice counselors are not licensed therapists, courts may distinguish them from social workers and psychotherapists on this basis.

RIGHT TO DUE PROCESS IN PROBATION/PAROLE REVOCATION HEARINGS

While those convicted of a crime clearly do not retain all of their rights, the Supreme Court has made it clear that the Fourteenth Amendment's due process clause does apply, not only during incarceration but also at probation and parole revocation hearings. This is a significant change from prior practice.

In *Morrissey v. Brewer* (1972), the Court held that due process required that, at a minimum, parole revocation procedures include: (1) written notice of the claimed parole violation; (2) disclosure to the parolee of the evidence against him or her; (3) an opportunity for the parolee to present evidence and witnesses, and to be heard; (4) the right of the parolee to confront and examine witnesses; (5) a neutral and detached hearing committee; and (6) a written statement by the parole board of the evidence and reasons for revoking parole.

In *Gagnon v. Scarpelli* (1973), the Court held that the requirements for a probation revocation hearing are identical to the requirements for a parole revocation hearing. While the Court admitted that parole and probation are not identical, revocation of probation where a sentence has been imposed previously is fundamentally indistinguishable from revocation of parole.

In *Mempa v. Rhay* (1967), the Court held that the Sixth Amendment right to counsel applies to a combined revocation and sentencing hearing, on the grounds that since the right to counsel attaches at any stage in a criminal proceeding where substantial rights of a criminal defendant are involved, the right should include sentencing.

Caseworker Liability Issues

An emerging area of the law of potential concern to criminal justice caseworkers is the issue of liability, both individual and governmental. There has been a tremendous increase in public concern over the release of potentially dangerous offenders, particularly sexual offenders. At least thirty-four states have enacted laws requiring public notification of the release of certain offenders (Cohen, 1995), and both individual caseworkers and state governments have been held liable for civil damages for negligent release of criminal offenders. At the same time, caseworkers are faced with maintaining a duty to their clients, be they probationers, parolees, or inmates.

It is important to distinguish the different duties owed by a criminal justice caseworker. The caseworker, as a quasi-law-enforcement agent, owes a duty to the public to protect it from harm. This duty applies to caseworkers in both the institutional setting and the community. There is an obligation to keep inmates deemed dangerous away from the public. This duty includes keeping such individuals in secure custody to prevent escape, and to keep such inmates incarcerated until it is determined that they pose no future danger to society. There is also the duty to warn the public when a dangerous person is in the community. A number of states recently have enacted legislation requiring the registration of certain released offenders, as well as notification of the public in general and in some cases, notification of individual victims. Furthermore, community-based criminal justice caseworkers owe a duty to supervise offenders under their care and to report potential dangerousness.

An emerging area of liability is the duty to protect incarcerated inmates from themselves and each other. This traditionally has arisen in the context of inmate-on-inmate assaults, but the AIDS crisis has had an impact on this area. While the Supreme Court reiterated its support for the "deliberate indifference" standard of liability (*Wilson v. Seiter*, 1991), as the spread of communicable diseases such as AIDS and tuberculosis increases in prison, more lawsuits are being filed challenging correctional policies regarding segregation, treatment, and disclosure of information on AIDS-infected inmates (Hammett, Harmon, and Maruschak, 1997; Morse, 2001).

IMMUNITY

At common law, the state could not be sued for civil damages as a result of its actions, regardless of the intent of the state. Under the English doctrine of sovereign immunity, the king, as an agent of God, was incapable of doing wrong; hence, there was no possibility of liability, since there could be no wrongdoing. This doctrine has continued, in watered-down fashion, to the present day, under the theory that the government can be sued only if it consents to the suit, either expressly through statute or constitutional provision.

Most states have some statutory provision waiving their sovereign immunity in certain circumstances. This allows lawsuits to be brought in state court relying on state tort law. A *tort* is a "private or civil wrong or injury other than beach of contract, for which the court will provide a remedy in the form of an action for damages" (Black, 1983).

While the federal and state governments all provide for waiver of their sovereign immunity in some circumstances, this waiver is far from complete. There are three forms of immunity defenses invoked in liability suits: absolute, qualified, and quasi-judicial immunity (Jones and del Carmen, 1992). Under absolute immunity, a lawsuit is dismissed without delving into the merits of the claim itself. Absolute immunity has been applied to legislators, judges, and prosecutors. It generally applies only to officials in the judicial or legislative branches of government.

Where absolute immunity protects officials completely, regardless of motive or intent, qualified immunity protects an official only if the official acted in "good faith." This form of immunity applies only to members of the executive branch of government. Probation and parole officers generally are accorded qualified immunity, although recently some lower courts have become less willing to apply immunity unquestioningly.

Quasijudicial immunity applies to officials who perform both judicial and executive functions. Under this form of immunity, official duties that are essentially nondiscretionary are not protected from liability, while those official duties that are judicial in nature and involve the exercise of discretion are accorded protection from liability. Courts generally have held that the function must be "intimately associated" with the judicial phase of the criminal process for immunity to apply (Jones and del Carmen, 1992). Parole board members generally fall into this protected group. Where qualified immunity is determined by the officer performing the function, quasijudicial immunity is determined by the function itself (del Carmen, 1985).

The importance of the doctrine of sovereign immunity is that it allows a plaintiff to sue not merely the individual caseworker for damages, but to sue the government, as the employer of the individual, under the doctrine of *resondeat superior*. Under this doctrine, an employer may be held liable for the torts of an employee, if these torts are committed in the scope of employment. This doctrine allows plaintiffs to go after the one with "deep pockets," as criminal justice personnel, like other employees, are unlikely to have large resources from which a damage award can be obtained.

Generally speaking, for liability to attach, there must be not only a waiver of sovereign immunity, but proof of inappropriate conduct by the caseworker. In tort law, there are several levels of conduct for which liability may be imposed: strict liability, negligence, and recklessness. In strict liability, liability attaches irrespective of the knowledge of the defendant. This very rarely applies to criminal justice personnel. Usually negligence is not enough to impose liability either. Rather, there must be a showing of recklessness—conduct which displays both serious risk-taking and an awareness of the likelihood of harm. While this may be proven by the civil standard of proof by a mere preponderance of the evidence, rather than the criminal standard of proof beyond a reasonable doubt, it is nonetheless a difficult burden for most plaintiffs to meet.

A common issue involves the decision to release an offender, or the decision not to revoke an offender, and a subsequent criminal act by the offender. Can the caseworker who decided to allow the offender to remain in the community be held liable for damages for the future criminal conduct of the offender? Generally, courts have been reluctant to attach liability in such situations absent a showing of recklessness. In other words, a caseworker who follows established procedure, and who makes an informed discretionary decision will not be held liable if it later turns out to have been a mistaken decision. Courts recognize that predicting future behavior is not foolproof. So long as caseworkers can demonstrate that they have made a good faith effort to make the right decision, liability will not attach. The key is adhering to both existing professional standards and following the legally required steps and procedures. Caseworkers do not always have to be correct, but they do have a duty to acquire and share relevant information, provide the appropriate treatment, and follow any legal requirements (Cohen, 1995). In legal terms, caseworkers have a duty to the public to use reasonable care to prevent a foreseeable risk of harm.

LEGAL REMEDIES FOR HARM

There are several basis for caseworker liability. The most common are state tort law, the Federal Tort Claims Act of 1946, and the Federal Civil Rights Act of 1871 (42 U.S.C. Section 1983). The Federal Tort Claims Act of 1946 waives the sovereign immunity of the federal government in a number of areas, and 42 U.S.C. Section 1983 provides a federal law remedy for injury caused by state actors.

For a plaintiff to succeed under a Section 1983 claim, the defendant must be acting "under color of law," meaning that the injury was a result of misconduct by a state agent acting in his or her role as a state agent. Only individuals may be sued under Section 1983, not corrections departments. In addition, the injury must involve a constitutional or federally protected right. While Section 1983 was passed by Congress in 1871, it was not until 1961, in the case of *Monroe v. Pape*, that the Supreme Court held that the law applied to the violation of civil rights of criminal suspects.

State tort law varies a great deal from state to state; consequently, criminal justice caseworkers are advised to familiarize themselves with the law in their jurisdiction. A tort is a civil wrong. Three conditions must exist for a tort to be proven. First, it must be shown that the defendant owed a duty to the plaintiff. This duty may arise from law, as in the case of contracts, or from the relationship of the plaintiff and defendant. It is this situation which is of most concern to criminal justice caseworkers, as the client-counselor relationship and the counselor-public relationship give rise to certain obligations, including the right to privacy and the duty to warn.

It also must be shown that the defendant not only owed a duty to the plaintiff, but that he or she breached that duty. In legal parlance, there are three forms that this breach of duty may take in regards to state agents. If a caseworker takes an improper action, it is termed *misfeasance*. If the caseworker takes no action or takes a required action but performs it inappropriately, it is referred to as malfeasance.

The third condition for a tort is a demonstration that the injury suffered by the plaintiff was, in fact, the proximate consequence of the defendant's breach of duty. Proximate cause is a legal creation intended to limit liability for damages to consequences which reasonably are foreseeable and related to the defendant's conduct.

Ethical Issues for Caseworkers

Most state statutes provide only a general outline of the duties of probation and parole officers, often speaking in general terms of supervising, counseling, and assisting the offender. Some statutes classify probation and parole officers as law enforcement personnel, while other statutes classify them as social service personnel. This split indicates the variation in perceptions of what the primary task of caseworkers is, and consequently, how caseworkers should interact with their clients.

Because the statutory goals of probation and parole officers are frequently vague, the manner in which a caseworker deals with his or her clients is likely to be determined in large part by the needs of the local agency and outside factors such as public outcry over individual cases. Commentators have identified three different roles that most caseworkers fall into, based on their education, training, and local agency culture. These are the law enforcement model, the therapeutic model, and the synthetic model (Abadinsky, 1982). Under the law enforcement model, caseworkers see their primary role as protecting the public. Under the therapeutic model, caseworkers see their primary role as rehabilitating and aiding the client offender. Under the synthetic model, caseworkers see their primary role as a combination of law enforcement and rehabilitation.

The caseworker is charged, at a minimum, with the twin, and potentially competing, duties of protecting the public by supervising the conduct of the client, and additionally supervising the treatment and rehabilitation of the client. Clearly, there is a potential for role conflict here—what is best for the client may not always be best for the public, and vice versa. How a caseworker reconciles these potentially conflicting goals is determined not only by agency and public pressure, but also by individual ethics. Simply put, the caseworker is faced, on a daily basis, with choosing not just between what is legally required and prohibited, but between what is ethically or morally "right."

The majority of this chapter is taken up with a discussion of the legal rights of criminal justice offenders and the legal duties that these rights create for the criminal justice caseworker. Legal requirements are not the end of the story, however. The law simply provides the parameters of conduct, sketching out the bare minimum that is required of the caseworker. Ethical standards may require more. The caseworker must determine, based on his or her own set of ethics, what sort of conduct is proper. The ethical choices generally revolve around two areas: deciding what is owed to the client, and deciding what is owed to the community. Each of these areas requires the caseworker to make hard choices. When the two areas come into conflict the choice is even more difficult.

There are several ethical duties the criminal justice counselor owes to his or her client. One is the duty to inform the offender of the limitations of their relationship. Thus, a caseworker should inform a client that total confidentiality cannot be assured. Obviously, this ethical duty may limit the development of the relationship, since clients may decide that they cannot divulge all of their activities to the caseworker if doing so may force the caseworker to report them to the authorities.

Criminal justice caseworkers also owe an ethical duty to the client to act in the best interests of the client. Generally, this means providing the opportunity for rehabilitation and treatment, if necessary. An oft-quoted maxim is that the caseworker should "do no harm" to the client. This is a difficult task for the caseworker who is responsible for both helping and supervising the offender.

Perspectives from the Field:
Inmate Rights: Getting the Courts to Listen
By Timothy R. McNeese, J.D.

Tim McNeese has been deputy attorney general for the Idaho Department of Corrections since 1984. He received his bachelor's of science degree from New Mexico State University in 1971, his master's from the University of Colorado in 1975, and his juris doctorate from Gonzaga University in Spokane, Washington in 1980. From 1980 to 1984, Mr. McNeese served as an attorney in the U.S. Army Judge Advocate General's office. He is an adjunct faculty member at Boise State University, teaching methods of legal research for the criminal justice department

In 1984, U.S. District Judge Harold J. Ryan issued a decision in a prisoner civil rights case, which was successfully filed and presented by two inmates, without lawyer assistance, on behalf of the other inmates at the Idaho State Correctional Institution. Judge Ryan found that the Idaho State Correctional Institution was unconstitutionally crowded and that "overcrowding brings on many problems, including idleness, frustration, stress, discomfort, edginess, and fear." He issued a decision which placed population caps on the housing units at Idaho State Correctional Institution. He also ordered such reforms as increases in staffing, improved medical care and dietary programs, clothing modifications, and protection for youthful offenders.

From the perspective of the "jailhouse lawyers," this trial was a tremendous victory. It showed that incarcerated persons with time on their hands, a well-supplied prison law library, and a good cause, could exercise the right of access to courts in a highly effective manner. The good quality of legal representation provided by the two inmate litigants did not go unnoticed by Judge Ryan, who also criticized lawyers who practice in the field of prison law.

In the real world of prison law, representing inmates is not a top priority among attorneys. Except for occasional appearances by attorneys for the American Civil Liberties Union, various Legal Aid Societies, and a handful of others, most inmates use prison law libraries and represent themselves, *pro se* (without a lawyer). The quality and effectiveness of inmate *pro se* representation can be very good. The primary inmate litigant in the previously described case, had a reputation among judges for often dismissing minor legal claims so that he could concentrate on more winnable issues. He also had the exceptional ability to sense the sympathies of the court and the public and to use it for the benefit of the inmate population. Federal court intervention, consent decrees, and court appointed monitors were common in prison cases during the 1980s.

Just a few years ago, the Federal District Court in Idaho estimated that 27 percent of all litigation in federal court involved inmate claims, almost all of which were filed without a lawyer. Although there is no question that many inmate lawsuits have merit, it has been this author's experience that many more are meritless, and some are downright frivolous. The frivolous cases, no doubt, are filed by inmates out of frustration and anger and the desire to get even with a correctional employee or "the system." Many see the court system as a more effective tool to get attention and results than simply filing a written grievance with prison officials. Some are simply ignorant of the law and the function of the courts or do not care.

In an effort to bring to the attention of the public inmate abuses of the court system, the Idaho Attorney General in 1996 joined Attorneys General throughout the country in publishing a list of "most frivolous" inmate lawsuits. A sample of Idaho's most frivolous cases, cited by the Attorney General, included the following:

An inmate obtained a copy of the American Correctional Association magazine left in an employee breakroom. He filled out and mailed to the publisher a card requesting manufacturer's information about prison security and locks. He sued under the First Amendment when the warden refused to let him have the information through the mail.

One inmate sued under the First Amendment because prison policy recognized as "privileged mail," correspondence from attorneys, doctors, and the Governor, but not "dukes, earls, princes, princesses, and the Queen of England." He did not state whether he was expecting any correspondence from these other sources.

An inmate started a prison riot by shattering the glass window on his cell door and filed an Eighth Amendment lawsuit when he cut his foot on the glass fragments in his cell. Another inmate filed a lawsuit because he was ordered to do morning grounds maintenance outside his cellhouse, but was issued only athletic shoes. He wanted a pair of work boots.

One of Idaho's most litigious death row inmates has filed so many meritless legal actions that both the state and federal courts have had to impose the extraordinary sanction of refusing to allow him to file any more lawsuits without first obtaining permission of the court to do so. Inmate litigation of this kind also has resulted in recent state and federal legislation designed to curtail frivolous, time-consuming abuses.

Although Idaho law allows for attorney's fees to be awarded to the state's attorneys when an inmate files a frivolous lawsuit, the reality of prison life is that few inmates have any money in their inmate accounts which can be used to satisfy a judgment awarded against them. Thus, until recently, there has been little to deter an inmate from filing a frivolous action.

In 1996, the state legislature adopted a law which allows for disciplinary detention and loss of inmate privileges to be assessed against inmates who bring a lawsuit which is found to be frivolous or malicious. Additionally, it allows prison and jail officials to collect judgments in frivolous cases from money in an inmate's account and even through the sale of his or her personal property.

In April, 1996, the U.S. Congress passed the Prison Litigation Reform Act of 1995 (PLRA). Among the highlights of this federal legislation is a requirement that no inmate can bring a prison conditions lawsuit in federal court unless he first has exhausted available administrative remedies such as filing a written grievance with the warden, medical staff, and so forth. The Prison Litigation Reform Act additionally states that an inmate claiming to have insufficient money to pay the filing fee for the lawsuit may still be required to pay a partial filing fee, which can be collected in increments whenever money does appear in his or her inmate account.

It is too early to assess the effects of these legislative attempts to correct abuses of the court system by inmates. Frivolous litigation absorbs the court's time and wastes taxpayer dollars. The abundance of these cases in state and federal courts make it extremely difficult for judges to wade through the pleadings to find the ones that are most egregious. Maybe every American is not entitled to his or her day in court anymore, at least according to those who have to pay for it and listen to it.

Summary

This chapter examined an area of criminal justice casework, which many caseworkers probably would like to avoid entirely. The courts in recent years have made the caseworker's job much more difficult, as the rights of criminal offenders, both incarcerated and in the community, have been expanded dramatically. In addition, caseworkers have been held liable for failing to protect the public from the same clients to whom the courts have been according additional rights.

The day has not yet come that a caseworker needs to think like a lawyer, however. If caseworkers can remember a few main points, they should be able to do their job effectively without infringing on the constitutional rights of their clients or incurring liability. Criminal justice offenders do not enjoy the same rights as ordinary citizens. But where rights have been circumscribed, certain procedures still must be followed. This is the essence of the phrase "due process of law." And while caseworkers need not be lawyers, it would be wise to keep abreast of the latest developments in the legal area.

References and Suggested Readings

Abadinsky, H. 1982. *Probation and Parole: Theory and Practice*. Chicago: Nelson-Hall.

Black, H. 1983. *Black's Law Dictionary, 5th Edition*. St. Paul, Minnesota: West Publishing.

Cohen, F. 1995. Liability and Negligent Release. In B. Schwartz and H. Cellini, eds. *The Sex Offender: Corrections, Treatment, and Legal Practices*. Kingston, New Jersey: Civic Research Institute.

Cohen, N., and J. Gobert. 1992. *The Law of Probation and Parole*. Colorado Springs, Colorado: McGraw-Hill.

Collins, W. 2001. *Correctional Law for the Correctional Officer, 3rd edition*. Lanham, Maryland: American Correctional Association.

Cromwell, P. and R. del Carmen. 1999. *Community-Based Corrections*. Belmont, California: Wadsworth.

Crouch, B. 1993. Is incarceration really worse? Analysis of offenders' preferences for prison over probation. *Justice Quarterly*. 10: 67-88.

del Carmen, R. 1985. *Potential Liabilities of Probation and Parole Officers*. Cincinnati, Ohio: Anderson Publishing Company.

General Accounting Office. 1991. *Drug Treatment: State Prisons Face Challenges in Providing Services*. Washington, D.C.: U.S. General Accounting Office.

Hammett, T., P. Harmon, and L. Maruschak. 1997. 1996-1997 *Update: HIV/AIDS, STDs, and TB in Correctional Facilities.* Washington, D.C.: Department of Justice.

Hemmens, C. and E. Atherton. 1999. *Use of Force: Current Practice and Policy.* Lanham, Maryland: American Correctional Association.

Hemmens, C., K. Bennett, and R. del Carmen. 1999. The exclusionary rule does not apply to parole revocation hearings: An analysis of *Pennsylvania Board of Probation and Parole v. Scott. Criminal Law Bulletin.* 35:388-409.

Hemmens, C. and R. del Carmen. 1997. The exclusionary rule in probation and parole revocation proceedings: Does it apply? *Federal Probation 61*(3): 32-39.

Jones, M. and R. del Carmen. 1992. When do probation and parole officers enjoy the same immunity as judges? *Federal Probation.* 56:36-41.

Morse, Christopher. 2001. Mandatory HIV Testing of Youthful Offenders in Adult Correctional Facilities: Time for a Uniform Approach. In E. Rhine and B. Glick, eds. *Journal of Correctional Best Practices: Juveniles in Adult Correctional Systems.* Lanham, Maryland: American Correctional Association.

Palmer, J. 1997. *Constitutional Rights of Prisoners.* Cincinnati, Ohio: Anderson Publishing.

Tribe, L. 1988. *American Constitutional Law.* Minneapolis, Minnesota: West Publishing.

List of Significant Supreme Court Decisions

Arcienga v. Freeman, 404 U.S. 4 (1971).
Bearden v. Georgia, 461 U.S. 660 (1983).
Bounds v. Smith, 430 U.S. 817 (1977).
Coffin v. Reichard, 143 F.2d 443 (6th Cir., 1944).
Connecticut Board of Pardons v. Dumschat, 452 U.S. 458 (1981).
Estelle v. Gamble, 429 U.S. 97 (1976).
Ex parte Hull, 312 U.S. 546 (1941).
Fare v. Michael C., 442 U.S. 707 (1979).
Farmer v. Brennan, 511 U.S. 825 (1994).
Gagnon v. Scarpelli, 411 U.S. 778 (1973).
Greenholtz v. Inmates of Nebraska Penal and Correctional Complex, 442 U.S. 1 (1979).
Griffin v. Wisconsin, 483 U.S. 868 (1987).
Hoffart v. State, 686 S.W.2d 259 (Texas, 1985).
Holt v. Sarver, 309 F.Supp. 362 (E.D. Ark. 1970, aff'd 442 F.2d 304).
In re Gault, 387 U.S. 1 (1967).
In re Winship, 397 U.S. 358 (1970).
Jackson v. Bishop, 404 F.2d 571 (8th Circuit, 1968).
Jaffee v. Redmond, 64 L.W. 4490 (1996).
Johnson v. Avery, 393 U.S. 483 (1969).

Kansas v. Hendricks, 117 S. Ct. 2072 (1997).

Lewis v. Casey, 64 L.W. 4587 (1996).

Mempa v. Rhay, 389 U.S. 128 (1967).

Miranda v. Arizona, 384 U.S. 436 (1966).

Monroe v. Pape, 365 U.S. 167 (1961).

Morrissey v. Brewer, 408 U.S. 471 (1972).

New Jersey v. T.L.O., 469 U.S. 325 (1985).

Pennsylvania Board of Probation and Parole v. Scott, 524 U.S. 357 (1998).

Roberts v. United States, 320 U.S. 264 (1943).

Ruffin v. Commonwealth, 62 Va. 790 (1871).

Sandin v. Conner, 515 U.S. 472 (1995).

United States v. Turner, 44 F.3d 900 (10th Circuit, 1995).

Washington v. Harper, 494 U.S. 210 (1990).

Wilson v. Seiter, 111 S. Ct. 2321 (1991).

Wolff v. McDonnell, 418 U.S. 539 (1974).

Alcohol and the Criminal Offender

If you treat an individual as he is, he will stay as he is. But if you treat him as if he were what he ought to be, he will become what he ought to be and could be.

Wolfgang von Goethe

Although we might talk in very broad and general terms about causes of criminal behavior, theorists should acknowledge that their nominated causes are all subject to the deadening qualification "all other things being equal." It is true, but not very helpful, to describe criminal behavior as irresponsible. Criminal behavior is located somewhere in a dense and messy causal maze, and there are many pathways trodden by those who become involved in the criminal justice system. Many offenders have substance abuse problems, many have character disorders, a few have chemical imbalances, and some are normally responsible individuals who have succumbed to the pressures and urges of the moment. Without specific intervening variables functioning as proximate causes, the more general ultimate causes (whatever they may be) remain hidden.

Note that *proximate causes* are those things that immediately precede an event. *Ultimate causes* are those things that are the furthest removed from the present. Although proximate causes may be quite difficult to work with, they certainly are more amenable to identification and treatment than are ultimate causes.

In this chapter, we will explore alcohol use, abuse, and dependence, the problem most commonly found to be the proximate cause of a variety of crimes, especially violent crimes (Schmalleger, 2001). Wanberg and Milkman (1998) estimated that at least 70 percent of prison inmates are alcohol and/or drug addicted. Alcohol tends to be the drug most often minimized or overlooked by corrections practitioners. We forget that alcohol is a drug, a very powerful and addictive substance. Alcohol is considered such a major player in criminal etiology and crime reduction that we devote an entire chapter to it. You will find few recovering heroin addicts who have not had to overcome a latent alcohol dependency, well after their "shooting" years have passed. Just as often, you will run across the crack cocaine addict who discovers his or her relationship to alcohol after trying to put down the pipe. Cross-addiction, cross-tolerance, and multi-drug use is the reality of offender substance use and abuse.

The Scope of the Addiction Problem

We normally think of illegal drugs when it comes to criminal offender behavior. But, we must train ourselves not to lose sight of the greatest substance abuse threat there is today: alcohol, the legal drug. Alcohol is linked to 94,000 deaths a year versus the "mere" 21,000 fatalities attributable to other drugs (Schmalleger, 2000). The statistical facts are glaring. City police officers spend more than half of their time on alcohol-related offenses. Estimates are that one-third of all arrests in the United States are for alcohol-related offenses (excluding drunk driving, which would significantly increase the percentage of alcohol-related arrests, if included), and that about 75 percent of robberies and 80 percent of homicides involve a drunken offender and/or victim (Masters and Robertson, 1990; Schmalleger, 2001). Alcohol is, at the same time, the most deadly and the most popular of our chemical comforters. We drink to be sociable, to liven up our parties, to feel good, to sedate ourselves, and to anesthetize the pains of life.

Fishman (1986:14-19) estimates that about one out of every ten Americans will develop a serious alcohol-related problem sometime during his or her life, and at least a third, and probably closer to half, of all men and women in prison are alcoholics, or at least heavy drinkers (Read, 1996). The cost of alcohol abuse to society in terms of crime, health, and family and occupational disruption are nothing less than staggering. This cost to the U.S. economy was estimated to be 98.6 billion dollars in 1993, more than the cost of the abuse of any other substance, legal or illegal (DuPont, 1997).

Alcohol is a depressant drug that affects our behavior by inhibiting the functioning of the higher brain centers, the locus of our rational thought processes (the conscience or the superego). As we ingest more alcohol, our behavior becomes less and less inhibited as the rational neocortex surrenders control to the emotions of the more primitive limbic system. Raw basic emotions then are allowed expression without benefit of first being channeled by rational consideration. Given this powerful chemical reaction, and the resultant breakdown in superego functioning, it is no wonder that so much crime is associated with this drug. The rate at which this surrender to raw emotionality occurs depends on a number of variables such as the alcoholic content of the drink and the amount drunk, the speed with which it is drunk, the weight of the drinker, the amount of food in the stomach, and even the time of day.

Abuse Versus Dependence

The difference between an alcohol abuser and an alcoholic or alcohol-dependent person is not always easy to discern. There are myriad definitions of alcohol dependence, those touted by clinicians and academics alike. The most representative of the crucial diagnostic criteria might read as follows: "Alcoholism is a chronic (it endures or recurs unless treated) condition marked by one's progressive (it gets worse if left untreated) incapacity to control alcohol consumption despite psychological, spiritual, social, or physiological life disruptions." This simply means, in layperson's terms, that if you cannot reliably predict what happens to you when you do drink and if the unanticipated negative consequences you experience after drinking are repeated, you are an alcoholic or alcohol dependent. The nonalcoholic heavy drinker will have the wherewithal to stop a self-destructive pattern of drinking in the face of compelling life circumstances such as marital problems, poor job performance, or liver malfunction. The person "dependent" on alcohol (not the occasional "abuser") will be unable to sustain control over time.

Physical dependence means that the body has developed a metabolic demand for a particular substance and rebels violently when it is denied that substance. Alcoholics are not necessarily or normally using alcohol as a means to achieve a "high," but as a means to avoid the terrible physiological pains of withdrawal (alcohol withdrawal can be more life threatening than withdrawal from narcotics). This characteristic dependence should not be confused with "street bum" behavior. Most street bums in trouble with alcohol are probably physically dependent, but there are many more "functioning" alcoholic offenders who do meet the formal criteria for "dependence" but who do not manifest obvious, clearly out-of-control symptoms—at least to all but their innermost circle of family and friends. Alcohol-dependent offenders also may be "maintenance drinkers," adept at keeping sufficient ethanol in their system all day long, so as not to experience withdrawal symptoms. Only rarely might they get "drunk." However, they are seriously alcoholic despite the fact that they do not fit the stereotype for this form of alcohol dependence.

Some Causes

The first stage on the road to alcoholism is obviously taking the first drink. People drink alcohol initially to be "with it," to fit in, and to boost confidence and loosen inhibitions at social gatherings. Alcohol is able to do this because (although it is ultimately a "brain-numbing depressant") at low dosage levels it is actually a stimulant because it raises dopamine levels (Ruden, 1997). It also reduces anxiety, worry, and tension by affecting the neurotransmitter gamma-aminobutyric acid (GAMMA), which is a major inhibitor of stimuli (DuPont, 1997). Alcohol can thus make those of us with worries and who lack confidence relatively carefree and confident, albeit, for a very short time, making it a powerful reinforcer. No wonder alcohol is the world's favorite drug. Given what alcohol does for us in social situations, it is difficult to think about what it might do to us later on. This honeymoon phase with alcohol sometimes leads to getting hooked into a horrendously bad marriage with it, and then to a very painful divorce from it, a process which takes the rest of the person's life.

Type I and II Alcoholics. Given the strong relationship between alcohol and criminal behavior, it is reasonable to suppose that they may have some cause common to both. This is not to imply, needless to say, that alcoholism and criminality are synonymous. Nevertheless, the alcoholism literature contains concepts remarkably similar to some of those addressed in Chapter 3 on the biosocial causes of crime. The distinction made between Type I and Type II alcoholics, for instance, is highly reminiscent of Terrie Moffitt's distinction between adolescent limited and life course persistent offenders. Type II alcoholics can be likened to life-course persistent offenders. They start drinking (and using other drugs) at a very early age, rapidly becoming addicted, and have many character disorders and behavioral problems that *precede* *dopamine → "go get" ect alcohol, sex, candy ecc*

their alcoholism. Type I alcoholics are akin to Moffitt's adolescent-limited offenders. They start drinking later in life than type II's and progress to alcoholism slowly. Type I's typically have families and careers, and if they have character defects, these typically are induced by the alcohol and not permanent (DuPont, 1997).

BIS/BAS and Alcoholism. Another similarity between criminological and alcoholism theorizing is the similarity between reward dominance theory in criminology and the "craving brain" concept in alcoholism theory. The concept of BIS/BAS introduced in Chapter 3 indicated that the behavioral activating system (BAS) is primarily dopamine dominated, that the behavioral inhibiting system (BIS) is primarily serotonin dominated, and that these two systems are "biobalanced" in most people most of the time. There is an old saying among alcoholics that one drink is one too many, and that a hundred drinks are not enough. This seemingly contradictory statement informs us that a single drink activates the pleasure centers in the nucleus accumbens by activating dopamine, but that one drink leads to such a craving for more that even a hundred drinks will not satiate an individual. The saying is a metaphor for what is called the "craving brain" (Ruden, 1997). The craving brain is a reward-dominant brain because it is unbalanced, with dopamine (the "go get it" neurotransmitter) being unopposed by serotonin (the "got it, now stop it") neurotransmitter (Ruden, 1997). The craving brain concept is common to all craving behaviors (eating, gambling, sex, drugs, smoking), and not just to alcoholism. Let us look at another explanation for the problem.

Genetics and Alcoholism. Research increasingly appears to be pointing to the conclusion that addiction to alcohol is at least partially genetic and is related to differential enzyme functioning (Dupont, 1997). Enzymes are protein molecules that serve as catalysts in the chemical conversion of molecules into other types of molecules. Ethanol alcohol is broken down in the liver by enzymes into a molecule called *acetaldehyde* (AcH). AcH produces unpleasant reactions to drinking, such as nausea and headaches, if it is not converted by other enzymes into other molecules that are excreted in the urine. People who metabolize alcohol rapidly, but who have metabolisms that allow for the buildup of AcH, quickly will be sensitized to its unpleasant effects. This natural punishment for drinking makes them less likely to overindulge in the future. AcH, as the first metabolite of alcohol, is thus a built-in guardian against alcoholism. In fact, disulfiram (Antabuse) is used as a treatment for alcoholics because it functions to maintain high levels of AcH in the body by retarding further metabolic reactions (DuPont, 1997). *Isoquinaline → makes become addictive*

AcH combines with several neurotransmitters such as dopamine and serotonin to produce a family of chemicals known as isoquinolines, one of which is a morphine-like substance called *tetrahydropapaveroline* (THP). People whose metabolisms rapidly convert AcH into a number of highly addictive substances (including THP) are far more likely to become alcoholics than people whose metabolisms are less efficient at breaking down AcH. This biophysical line of inquiry could lead to the explanation of why the vast majority of those who drink over a lifetime never become addicted. Perhaps alcohol itself is not inherently addictive, but rather the addiction is to the biosynthetic by-products of alcohol, which are produced differentially in individuals according to the functioning of their metabolic system that is under genetic control. This is not the complete story of the etiology of alcoholism. It only states that among those who do turn to drink, there are some with an inherited predisposition to become addicted.

faster break down quicker you become drunk

Heritable - genetic control genes make enzymes

Assessment, Treatment and Counseling

In view of the high social and financial costs of alcoholism, it is imperative that you make every effort to identify offenders with these problems. Most alcoholics will not readily admit to their condition. They cannot admit, even to themselves, that they have relinquished or have started to relinquish control of their lives to alcohol. Their disease tells them so, tells them they have no problem at all; most are not lying in the traditional sense of the term. They really do believe they are all right. Alcoholics typically lack the choice of accepting reality: every muscle, molecule, and enzyme in their body demands more and more of the substance that carries them forth with life. In contrast, some offenders will overemphasize their drinking, hoping that you and the judge will regard it as a mitigating factor when considering sentencing alternatives. Most often, however, offenders will minimize their consumption pattern.

The ability to identify the alcohol abuser and the alcohol-dependent offender is a skill all criminal justice counselors should strive to acquire. The most obvious indicator of a drinking problem is an arrest record of alcohol-related offenses (drunk driving, drunk and disorderly, and so forth). Ask about the offender's drinking patterns. The frequency and amount of alcohol consumed on a weekly basis, the frequency of legal problems due to drinking, and the amount of time and money spent on drink are all indications of the depth of the problem.

Remember, far more than quantity or frequency of consumption, what really is important is what alcohol does to the person who consumes it. If you discover such patterns, you have an ipso facto case to present to offenders showing that they do have a problem. Point out to offenders that to continue to deny it in the face of such evidence is irrational and unacceptable to you. You are encouraged not to discuss offender alibis designed to convince you that factors other than drinking are responsible for irresponsible behavior. Doing so will result in an argument over the merits of the alibi, possibly leading to reinforcement of the alibi. And, the more people defend their position, the more difficult it becomes to relinquish it.

If you suspect an offender has a drinking problem and you want him or her to admit this problem to themselves, the CAGE Screen Test (Ewing, 1984) affords you this opportunity. CAGE is an acronym for Cut Down, Annoyed, Guilty, Eye-opener. If a person answers "yes" to two or more of the following questions, there is an 88 percent likelihood that the person has an alcohol problem.

1.   Have you ever felt you should CUT DOWN on your drinking?

       When a person feels the need to cut down on drinking, and actually takes steps such as making vows to stop, switching brands, limiting drinking to certain times and places, he or she already has recognized the presence of a problem.

2.   Have you ever felt people ANNOYED you by criticizing your drinking?

       Having someone close to you be annoyed means that they consider the behavior upsetting and problematic, thus providing a basis for reconsidering the behavior. Typical social drinkers do not end up with spouses or others expressing this type of concern.

3.   Have you ever felt bad or GUILTY about your drinking?

Guilt is the psychological equivalent of physical pain—not very pleasant, but very useful. Guilt, like pain, tells us that something is wrong that we should put right. The guilty person knows that his or her life would be better without alcohol, and feels guilty and ashamed about what he or she is doing.

4.   Have you ever had a drink first thing in the morning (an EYE-OPENER) to steady your nerves or to get rid of a hangover?

Number four is a sure giveaway, but two or more positive responses are suggestive of alcoholism.

There are a number of more formal screening tools that you can use to help to identify the offender in trouble with alcohol. One frequently used tool is the *Michigan Alcoholism Screening Test* (MAST). This twenty-four-item yes/no questionnaire should be used only as a corroborative diagnostic aid. Yet, do not rule out alcoholism if the scale score is negative for alcoholism. Offenders certainly can lie on the questionnaire, and verbal and nonverbal cues, such as alcohol-related arrests (which you will know about independently of offenders' responses), may be more valuable with offenders reluctant to disclose the requested information. The questionnaire is best administered in the presence of the criminal justice worker so that he or she can clarify the items, if necessary.

Skilled interviewing is often the most effective way to ascertain whether someone is manifesting signs of alcohol dependence. Do not be afraid to ask very specific questions about the offender's drinking history, weekly pattern, and attitude toward consumption. Focus on using open-ended questions (such as "Tell me exactly what you had to drink Saturday") designed to encourage dialog and expression that may reveal clues about their relationship to the drug, rather than yes or no queries. Do not be shy or feel funny about getting specific about the amount a person consumes. An offender's interpretation of "a beer" could be that forty-two ounce "bumper" of malt liquor, nearly equal to an entire six pack of regular beer. Most community corrections' personnel, including probation and parole officers, use their interviewing, investigative, and assessment skills more than anything else prior to an initial referral for treatment. Often, they have time for little else, let alone the administration of a test instrument, no matter how simple.

Treatment for the alcoholic or problem drinker is a complex affair that may include both medical treatment and psychosocial counseling. The goal is recovery as defined by abstinence, sobriety, and an interest in personal growth. Even more will depend on the relative progression of that person's disease and whether there are complicating coexisting disorders like depression or antisocial personality disorder. Much will depend on the level of the offender's drinking at the time that you first meet him or her.

If the offender is in the chronic stage of alcoholism, hospitalization for detoxification will be necessary. It is most likely, however, that detoxification took place in the jail or at a hospital after the offender's arrest, and you will not have to concern yourself with it. If it did not, secure inpatient medical treatment for the offender. Detoxification in a medical environment is a necessary prerequisite to any future treatment. However, recently, very capable "social" detoxification programs, not located in a medical setting—some even conducted on an outpatient basis—have arisen to provide less costly solutions. If the offender does not have insurance that provides for such treatment, or if welfare authorities cannot provide it, organizations such as the Salvation Army and the Volunteers of America often are successful in securing the necessary treatment. Detoxification is not a treatment for alcoholism. Treatment is a long and difficult process of learning how to sustain complete abstinence from all mood-altering substances.

MUTUAL SELF-HELP GROUPS: ALCOHOLICS ANONYMOUS

There are many different professional addiction treatment resources that reflect particular individual treatment needs: individual counseling, group therapy, motivational interviewing, intensive outpatient facilities, day-treatment programs, longer term residential programs, and many others. Despite all these different therapeutic approaches most, if not all, good clinicians, regardless of their professional orientation, will stress the importance of making good self-help group referrals. These complement the professional treatment most offenders will require.

The best known mutual self-help group, of course, is Alcoholics Anonymous (AA). AA has been called "one of the great success stories of our century" by a group of World Health Organization researchers after studying AA groups in eleven different countries (cited in Alexander, 2000:20). This AA fellowship (a strange "nonorganization" organization really) is a very supportive and totally nonprofessional support group of fellow human beings in trouble with alcohol. They often go to great lengths to help one another, and if used appropriately by the "referrer," AA groups can assist in helping the offender work through his or her denial (Read, 1996).

AA is not a class. AA is not treatment. And AA is not a quick fix. It is a lengthy and often lifetime process of personal transformation. "Old timers" in AA will say to the newcomer, "Sobriety is a process and not an event." The principles of AA eventually become a way of life for many. Initially, the emphasis is on not drinking—one day at a time. Then, the focus shifts toward learning how to achieve sobriety in the sense of balance and serenity. Finally, it should be pointed out that AA is not a religious program. It is, however, a spiritual process, a spiritual program of self-help. Agnostics, atheists, and true believers are all welcome. Unlike religious movements, sects, or denominations, AA holds no preconception or demand for a belief in God.

There is a great deal of typical Rogerian empathy in the meeting rooms of AA. There can be no skirting of the issue in such company. Alcoholic offenders cannot reasonably tell their "bottle-wise" compatriots that they "just don't understand," the way they could tell their nonalcoholic corrections counselors. Fellow AA members will provide offenders not only with support but also visions of the possible. They are role models whose presence serves to emphasize much more strongly than the counselor could that recovery is possible (this role modeling is the social learning component of cognitive-behavioral therapy). Methods of dealing with specific alcohol-related problems are discussed by drawing on the various experiences of those who may have dealt successfully with them. When the solution to a problem is offered by a peer, it is more likely to carry weight than if it is posed by "the Man," who many offenders instinctively distrust and resent.

Genuineness is another Rogerian principle that is a hallmark of AA groups. Most AA participants strongly encourage members to honestly confront their problems, their shortcomings, their responsibilities, and their realities. Although there are no formal leaders, manipulation and game playing are quickly recognized and rejected: "You can't con the cons." Members are encouraged to share with the group their fears, anxieties, hopes, and self-evaluation. This self-disclosure provides the offender with the opportunity to share genuine feelings with others and to build self-esteem and a group identity, qualities sorely lacking in the lives of many persons in trouble with alcohol. As a real added bonus, it has been reported that attending AA actually raises serotonin levels (Gogek, 1994). Not only do raised serotonin levels counteract craving, they also reduce the dysphoric feelings (depression, agitation, hopelessness) described among alcoholics as a "dry drunk" (Ruden, 1997).

Baeklund, Lundwall, and Kissen (1975:305) state it well when they write about their experiences in treating alcoholics: "Over and over we were impressed with the dominant role the patient, as opposed to the kind of treatment used on him, played both in his persistence in treatment and his eventual outcome." Even Herbert Fingarette, who calls the disease model of alcoholism a myth, supports this view: "The consensus of scientific researchers is that willpower and personal strengths do affect the course of a heavy drinker's efforts to control his drinking" (1988:72). So, we return to a central thesis of the various directive counseling theories: the individual, alcoholic, drug addict, criminal, or whatever, only can change his or her destructive behavior by the resolve to accept personal responsibility for his or her behavior. AA is one vehicle that may help the alcoholic to develop that resolve. As William Glasser has put it: "The alcoholic must regain control over his life to satisfy his needs. AA, by itself, cannot satisfy his needs, but it is a way—probably the best way we have available—to get the process started" (1984:132).

Glasser views diseases as arranged on a continuum in terms of the amount of control we have over them. At one end of the continuum is a disease like Huntington's chorea, which is totally genetic. It does not matter how healthy, fit, and strong you otherwise may be, or what you do to try to avoid it, if you have the gene for Huntington's chorea, eventually you will get it. Further down the continuum is cancer. Cancer is a genetic disease, but we can take certain steps to lessen our chances of falling afoul of it by altering our environment (eating right, not smoking, and so forth). Further along the continuum are the various cardiovascular diseases that may be equally under genetic and environmental control. Living a healthy life dramatically reduces our risk of such diseases, even if a genetic predisposition towards them exists. At the other end of the continuum is alcoholism. Glasser concedes that alcoholism is a disease, but asserts that we have considerable control over it. Even if a genetic predisposition exists, if we learn to resist the temptation to drink, the disease cannot manifest itself. Glasser's approach appears to be an eminently sensible compromise between the disease and no-disease models of alcoholism.

The debate about whether addiction, particularly alcoholism, is a "disease-based" condition rages on and on. Most chemical dependency experts, including physicians who are certified "addictionologists," accept it as such with few questions. Among the others, though, there is a real sense of frustration at not being able to identify a single medically scientific and proven cause for the disease of addiction. Based on a recent Supreme Court ruling that the Veterans Administration (VA) may deny certain benefits to alcoholics because their behavior was thought to be the result of "willful misconduct," we sometimes hear that the Supreme Court has ruled that alcoholism is not a disease. The Court is not qualified to rule on such matters, it simply ruled on a matter of law that had to do with the benefit guidelines of the Veterans Administration. As mentioned earlier, the problem is that addiction simply does not have one single cause; it is multifaceted. It is complex, and we do not fully understand it.

Whether or not it is "really" a disease, there are those who feel that the disease model "has little clinical utility, and in fact may interfere with assisting the individual in successfully modifying his or her behavior through implicit communication that substance use is something that is happening to their body rather than something that is within their voluntary control" (Weeks, Moser, and Langevin, 1999:6). This opinion is shared by others, who assert that the disease model fosters dependency and passivity (Parks and Marlatt, 1999). Both these sets of researchers are cognitive-behavioral adherents who strongly support self-reliance and the acceptance of responsibility, thus defining alcoholism as a disease, and the admission of "powerlessness" (step one of the twelve-step program) is counterproductive.

From the author's perspective, there is no doubt that alcoholism is a disease that alters the brain's physiology and functioning. We even can see the differences in the brains of alcoholics versus nonalcoholics through brain imaging techniques (Leshner, 1998). It is a self-induced disease for which the person must accept full responsibility for recovery. Surely admitting being "out of control" and deciding to do something about it is accepting responsibility for changing one's life—a direct confrontation with one's self if there ever was one. And surely believing that one has a disease does not contravene personal efforts to combat it, as legions of cancer and heart patients, among others, can attest.

This author urges that all persons with alcohol-related disorders caught up in the criminal justice system be strongly encouraged to participate in AA. Based on reviews of empirical studies, it has been estimated that about half of those who regularly attend AA meetings with serious intent maintain several years of total abstinence, and that about 60 percent of the remainder "improve to some extent" (U.S. Department of Health and Human Services, 1990:265). Although no figures are available specific to criminal justice offenders, one would not expect their success rate to be this high. When all is said and done, offender motivation remains a crucial variable. As a corrections worker, you have a professional responsibility to do your best to generate this motivation.

Community corrections professionals have recognized the power of these "free" community based self-help programs for many years. In fact, Ed Read, a federal probation officer for the U.S. District Court, in Washington, D.C., who has written and published extensively on addictions, has written a full length book devoted solely on how to access, use, and make proper twelve-step self-help group referrals within the criminal justice system. He is adamant that making these referrals, sometimes over and over again with the same offender in the course of his or her casework, is an irrefutable professional obligation of the corrections worker. In his indispensable book, *Partners in Change*, Read writes: "Why refer every addict or alcoholic? It is almost so simple we forget. We do it because we want to capitalize on what we know is successful, on what we know works out there beyond our office doors" (Read, 1996:5).

Do not hesitate to make attendance at AA (or some alternative sobriety program's) meetings a condition of probation or parole. Experiencing the warm support and caring of fellow travelers may well turn the resistant offender into a motivated client. Insisting that the offender attend AA is another instance of the constructive use of authority. To those who have legal concerns about whether mandatory self-help group attendance violates the Establishment Clause of the First Amendment to the U.S. Constitution, please note the following: In June 1994, U.S. District Judge Gary L. Taylor of the Central District of California (*O'Conner v. State of California*) ruled in favor of the state's Driving Under the Influence (DUI) education and treatment programs that routinely refer offenders to AA and other self-help groups. Significant to this ruling was that the element of personal choice remained intact. Offenders were mandated to attend self-help group meetings, and AA was the recommended vehicle for satisfaction of this condition; however, they were not prevented from using alternative programs, such as Rational Recovery (RR). However, in *Kerr v. Farley* (1996), a federal court judge ruled that offenders' rights are violated by coerced treatment at AA and NA (Narcotics Anonymous) programs.

An alternative to AA meetings outside the probation or parole office is an in-house alcohol program (AA programs in jails, prisons, and halfway houses are "in-house" by definition). The advantage of an in-house program is that officers can closely monitor attendance, participation, and progress. In-house meetings and group counseling sessions are best led by volunteer members of AA and/or community corrections workers who are thoroughly versed in alcohol counseling.

The Lucas County Adult Probation Department has an in-house program called STOP (Sobriety Through Other People). It required STOP clients to (1) attend one in-house AA meeting and at least three others outside the department, (2) attend biweekly in-house group meetings, (3) submit to weekly urinalysis, and (4) meet with the program coordinator once per month. Latessa and Goodman (1989) compared 102 STOP probationers with a control group of 101 other probationers matched for sex, race, and supervision level. STOP clients had more serious criminal histories and much more serious substance abuse problems. STOP offenders had a higher rate of absconding and of technical probation violations, although the authors stress that given the intensity of the treatment regimen and level of surveillance for this group, this was to be expected. The bright spot was that the STOP offenders had 9.2 percent fewer arrests than the regularly supervised offenders, a relatively small difference, but one put in proper perspective when it is realized that alcoholic offenders are particularly susceptible to frequent arrests. As the authors conclude: "The STOP program has demonstrated it is possible to select special-need offenders and deliver increased services in an effective manner" (Latessa and Goodman, 1989:42).

SELF-HELP OPTIONS FOR NONBELIEVERS

There are instances when we encounter offenders who legitimately oppose and resist involvement in the traditional Twelve Step AA model of self-help. For some, usually a distinct minority, their opposition is based not on denial but on genuine philosophical convictions about the recovery process. They may have honestly tried AA but were simply unable to reconcile their own beliefs about religion and/or spirituality with the Twelve Step model.

Rational Recovery (RR) first appeared in the 1980s. It was founded by recovering alcoholics who rejected both the spiritual foundation of the AA Steps as well as the disease concept of alcoholism. RR patterns itself after the writings of Albert Ellis, a pioneer in the field of cognitive psychology and rational emotive behavioral therapy (REBT). Like AA, RR groups vary widely, but they differ in some key respects.

Most RR members attend meetings only once a week, as opposed to the daily attendance schedule encouraged for newcomers to AA. Meetings generally are limited to no more than twelve participants. RR participants believe that problem drinkers make incorrect or shortsighted choices based on emotional states. RR is more time-limited while AA prefers to view itself as indefinite. RR members attend for six- to ten-months and then often stop, sometimes returning to deal with specific crises or relapse. RR members emphasize coming to an understanding of the psychological precursors of their drinking as opposed to developing a relationship with a higher power.

Figure 15.1

A Comparison of AA's Twelve Steps to Sobriety and RR's Equivalents

Alcoholics Anonymous

1. We admitted we were powerless over alcohol–that our lives had become unmanageable.

2. We came to believe that a Power greater than ourselves could restore us to sanity.

3. We made a decision to turn our lives over to the care of God as we understood Him.

4. We made a searching and fearless moral inventory of ourselves.

5. We admitted to God, to ourselves, and to other human beings, the exact nature of our wrongs.

6. We were entirely ready to have God remove all these defects of character.

7. We humbly asked Him to remove our shortcomings.

8. We made a list of all persons we had harmed, and became willing to make amends to them all.

9. We made direct amends to such people wherever possible, except when to do so would injure them or others.

10. We continued to take personal inventory and when we were wrong, promptly admitted it.

11. We sought through prayer and meditation to improve our conscious contact with God, as we understood Him, praying only for knowledge of His will for us and the power to carry that out.

12. Having had a spiritual awakening as a result of these steps, we tried to carry the message to alcoholics and to practice these principles in all our affairs.

* The Twelve Steps are reprinted with the permission of Alcoholics Anonymous World Services, Inc. Permission to reprint the Twelve Steps does not mean that A.A. has reviewed or approved the contents of this publication, nor that A.A. agrees with the views expressed herein. A.A. is a program of recovery from alcoholism only — use of the Twelve Steps in connection with programs and activities which are patterned after A.A., but which address other problems, or in any other non-A.A. context, does not imply otherwise.

** Material from RR reprinted with permission from Rational Recovery Systems, Inc.

Rational Recovery

1. I admit that I have become chemically dependent, and the consequences of the dependency are unacceptable.

2. I accept that, to get better, I will have to refrain from the use of alcohol, because any use very likely will lead to more, and then a return to my previous addiction.

3. I accept that I will likely benefit from some outside help in accomplishing this, because I have been unsuccessful in previous attempts to resist my desire to drink.

4. Although I may have serious personal problems, I still have the capacity to learn about myself, and new ideas and how to achieve a durable and meaningful sobriety.

5. The idea that I need something other than myself upon which to rely is only another dependency idea, and dependency is my original problem.

6. I surrender all ideas of perfection for myself, as I am a fallible, yet very worthwhile, human being.

7. I place a high value on the principles of rationality, learning, objectivity, self-forgiveness, and on my own self-interest.

8. With the passage of time, I will find that refraining from mind-altering drugs is no big thing because they have little intrinsic appeal to a physically and mentally healthy person.

9. Recognizing that there is much more to life than a constant struggle to remain sober, and having gained a reasonable expectation that I can live a meaningful life without alcohol or drugs, I will gradually separate myself from my RR group or therapist, with the understanding that I may return at any time I wish.

10. I accept that there are no perfect solutions to life's problems, and that life is in part a matter of probability and chance, so, therefore, I am willing to take risks to achieve my own self-defined goals.

11. Now certain of my inherent worth, I can take the riskes of loving, for loving is far better than being loved.

12. I recognize the desperate need of others for a rational recovery plan, so I will take these ideas to them, as a way of creating a larger society of sober, rational people.

Another group is Secular Sobriety, which was founded by James Christopher. He was in AA but left over his objection to the spiritual orientation of the Steps and the program's reliance on a higher power. Christopher believes that sobriety is best attained through an emphasis on self-reliance and self-knowledge. Secular Sobriety meetings resemble AA discussion groups. Like AA, Secular Sobriety is based on the premise that alcoholism is a chronic and progressive disease. So, unlike RR members, participants feel they cannot drink because of a physiological rather than psychological abnormality. Additionally, Secular Sobriety groups do not place as much value as AA on the role of sponsorship in the recovery process.

Recognize that few offenders are "believers" in the traditional sense. This is no problem—the majority of all people coming to AA meetings for the first time fit into this category. It is much easier to find an AA meeting these days; RR never has achieved the prominence and widespread availability that AA has realized. Actually, AA's tremendous availability is the biggest difference between it, RR, and Secular Sobriety groups. AA groups are very tolerant of different spiritual beliefs or nonbeliefs, so do not prematurely refer to RR on the basis of an offender's initial expression of resistance.

Medication and Recovery

Disulfiram (sold under the trade name Antabuse) treatment, as a kind of aversion therapy, can be a very useful adjunct to other treatment modalities. As indicated earlier, Antabuse works by maintaining high levels of AcH in the body by retarding its metabolism (DuPont, 1997). Antabuse treatment, administered under medical supervision because it can have harmful, even fatal, effects for people with heart problems, is begun after detoxification. The drug usually is given to the client for several consecutive days along with small doses of alcohol. The unpleasant feelings that accompany drinking alcohol while AcH levels are high act as negative reinforcers. It is hoped that these highly unpleasant consequences associated with alcohol ingestion will be sufficiently aversive to condition the patient from future abuse.

Realize, however, that Antabuse treatment is voluntary on the patient's part. You cannot require it as a condition of supervision. A client who does make the voluntary decision to take Antabuse is taking his or her treatment seriously because he or she also, in effect, has made the decision not to drink during the period that this highly aversive drug remains effective (Antabuse is eliminated from the body very slowly, leaving the body sensitive to alcohol for six to ten days after Antabuse ingestion).

Like most other conditioned responses, however, the effects of Antabuse will be extinguished with the passage of time. It does provide a strong and immediate reason not to drink and thus buys time for the implementation of other types of treatment. It appears to be quite successful when used in conjunction with psychosocial counseling. Billet (1974) reports that 64 percent of a sample of patients who were administered Antabuse in addition to undergoing a comprehensive psychosocial rehabilitation program showed "marked improvement." Only 31 percent of those who were in the same program but who did not receive Antabuse showed a similar level of improvement. Similar results were found in later studies (U.S. Department of Health and Human Services, 1990:266).

In 1996, the U.S. Food and Drug Administration approved the pharmacologic agent naltrexone as a safe and effective adjunct to psychosocial treatments for alcoholism (also for opiate addiction). While certainly not considered a "magic bullet," naltrexone (sold under the trade-name ReVia), promises help to many offenders in their struggle against chronic relapse. It has been claimed that the drug reduces craving and relapse by 50 percent (DuPont, 1997). The National Institute on Alcohol Abuse and Alcoholism (NIAA) recommends that for now, until further study is completed, that only physicians familiar with addiction treatment should prescribe this medication, and only in the context of an alcoholism treatment program. Naltrexone appears to reduce craving in abstinent persons and to block the reinforcing effects of alcohol in patients who drink. This latter effect lessens the likelihood that persons who drink a small amount of alcohol will return to heavy drinking.

The increasing evidence that alcoholism has a strong biological basis is not cause for despair. Marc Schuckit, one of the leading researchers in the biology of alcoholism, has written: "It is unlikely that anyone is predestined to alcoholism or that all those predisposed exhibit the same mechanism of risk" (1989:297). Even those individuals genetically identified as at-risk obviously will not succumb to the disease if they never drink, and individuals who have succumbed can be spared its further ravages if, with the help of caring others, they can move toward sobriety one day at a time."

Perspective from the Field:
Working with the Alcohol-dependent Offender
By Sandra Tebbe

Sandra Tebbe is a probation officer who specializes in working with offenders in trouble with alcohol. She holds master's degrees in both sociology and rehabilitation counseling, and she also is a Certified Alcoholism Counselor. In the past, Ms. Tebbe has specialized in counseling compulsive gamblers on probation.

Alcoholics usually will not recognize that they have a drinking problem. Many cannot recognize it because they find satisfaction in the "loving" concern of those around them. They use this "love" as a means of manipulating their way through an addictive lifestyle. The alcoholics' skillful maneuvers and manipulations do not stop when they commit a crime. Most alcoholic probationers come under supervision expecting the same "loving" concern and the same ignoring, overlooking, and excusing to which they are accustomed.

To help the alcoholic offender, you have to be willing to be rejected. That is what "tough love" is all about, caring enough about clients to hold them totally responsible for their behavior, regardless of whether they like you. Tough love is making each decision carefully to assure that you are not enabling probationers to continue their drinking. This will not make you popular, and it certainly will not make you loved. It is all too easy to ease up a little, to give them some slack, so that they will like you. But you are not the issue. You demonstrate your love for them by holding them responsible for the defeat of their alcoholic conditions.

I started working as a probation officer eight years ago. I coordinate a special state-funded in-house alcohol program. This program provides one of the highest levels of supervision in community corrections and provides for strict and unambiguous correctional consequences for every misbehavior. It has been a good program that teaches what tough love is.

I often am asked, "How can you spend so much time working with alcoholics without getting burned out?" I entered the probation profession at a young age and with idealistic attitudes. It did not take me long to learn how to adapt and survive. Counseling alcoholics means learning how to let go. It does not mean that you stop caring. It means that you must learn that you cannot do it for someone else. It is the realization that you cannot control another person's life or fix their defects. Only they can do that. You have to respect their capacity for control and choice, and allow them to learn from the natural consequences of their behavior.

Most alcoholics have had someone to enable, or make possible, their drinking behavior from the very start. This is one of the reasons that the alcoholic's family, and most everyone else influenced by him or her, becomes "sick." Enabling is usually in the form of continually making excuses for and rescuing the alcoholic from distress. Unfortunately, it is not until alcoholics experience the real pains of their disease that they get around to making a decision to change their lifestyles.

You easily can fall into rescuing behavior with your alcoholic offenders, but you are not doing them any favors if you continue with the enabling patterns they have come to expect. You are not being "nice," "neat," or "loving" to those who need tough love by allowing them to manipulate you and to continue to ruin their lives. Confront them, challenge them, educate them, help them!

Alcoholics almost always will deny their alcoholism. Take Jim, a high-risk probationer of mine. He had been in prison for threatening the life of his baby when police arrived at his home on a domestic dispute call. During the alcohol screening period, Jim stated over and over that he was not an alcoholic: "I don't have to wake up to a drink every day like the drunks on the street. I'm not a weak man. There's lots of times I don't drink."

Jim's defensiveness was a reaction to the many myths associated with alcoholism. Many people think of alcoholics as weak, low-class moral degenerates who lack willpower. My job as his probation officer was to educate him about his disease so that he would open up his mind to treatment. Jim learned through my efforts and through mandatory participation in AA that alcoholism is primarily a physiological disease and that he became addicted because his body is incapable of processing alcohol normally. He also learned that alcoholism is a disease that affects all classes and races. Jim's many family and financial problems did not cause his alcoholism. Rather, his alcoholism undermined his ability to cope, and this inability then exacerbated his problems.

Once Jim learned about his disease, he was better able to deal with it. Jim had to realize that to admit his alcoholism was not to admit that he was a weak or bad person. Through small-group participation and AA attendance, Jim found comfort and support from others with the same problem. These folks "tough loved" Jim into sobriety. Jim has been sober for more than two years now. He has chosen a new life for himself. Although all of his other problems have not disappeared, he is learning how to cope with them without alcohol.

Jim was relatively easy to deal with as alcoholic probationers go. Often, I find that supervising alcoholic probationers means long periods of time waiting for them to "hit bottom." "Hitting bottom" is the term for when alcoholics come to realize that they have gotten about as low as they can go, and that they must change or be forever lost.

A few months ago, one of my probationers hit bottom while sitting in the county jail. John was doing thirty days for his second probation violation, a violation which I easily could have ignored. He had continually denied having a drinking problem, refused to go to AA meetings, and was resentful of authority. This time, however, something was different about John when I visited him in jail. For the first time he did not attempt to rationalize his behavior or blame it on someone else. He was physically sick from withdrawal, homeless, and his wife had left him (a natural consequence of his behavior) because she could not handle his drinking anymore. With a broken spirit, John started to take a hard look at himself and finally asked for help. John is now doing something about his problem. He is one of the several sober probationers in the program, and is one of the many probationers who have learned to love and respect himself through an officer's use of tough love.

Summary

This chapter addresses the most common problem you will encounter in corrections: alcohol use disorders. We defined and discussed the significant challenges posed by offenders in trouble with alcohol. Although researchers have not identified one single cause for alcoholism and consider it a complex and multifaceted condition, there is undoubtedly a strong genetic underpinning for it. We noted the similarity between certain biosocial criminological theories and theories of alcoholism. Alcoholism seems to be at one level a function of the "craving brain," a concept close to reward dominance theory in criminology (discussed earlier in this chapter, and in Chapter 3).

Other scientific evidence on the cause of alcoholism points strongly to the role of the production and metabolism of acetaldehyde (AcH). Antabuse, a drug used in treating alcoholism, functions to maintain high levels of AcH in the bloodstream. This causes the alcoholic to experience the "punishing" physical feelings associated with high alcohol intake. Antabuse is administered to chronic alcoholics in association with intensive psychosocial counseling.

The most successful self-help program that always should be used as a complement to professional treatment is Alcoholics Anonymous (AA). You should endeavor to place every offender with a drinking problem in this organization. It provides members with all the components of a successful counseling relationship (even though it is not "treatment" per se) as outlined by Rogers: positive regard, genuineness, and empathy. Some people, however, object to the "spiritual" nature of AA. For those who are truly resistant, and although not nearly as widely available, offenders could be referred to Rational Recovery or other strictly nonspiritual support groups.

References and Suggested Readings

Alexander, R. 2000. *Counseling, Treatment, and Intervention Methods with Juvenile and Adult Offenders*. Belmont, California: Brooks/Cole.

Baeklund, F., L. Lundwall, and B. Kissen. 1975. Methods for the Treatment of Chronic Alcoholism: A Critical Approach. In R. Gibbons, Y. Israel, H. Kalant, R. Popham, and R. Smart, eds., *Research Advances in Alcohol and Drug Problems*. New York: Wiley.

Billet, S. 1974. Antabuse Therapy. In R. Cantanzaro, ed., *Alcoholism: The Total Treatment Approach*. Springfield, Illinois: Charles C. Thomas.

DuPont, R. 1997. *The Selfish Brain: Learning from Addiction*. Washington, D.C.: American Psychiatric Press.

Ewing, J. 1984. Detecting Alcoholism: The CAGE Questionnaire. *Journal of the American Medical Association*. 252:1905-1907.

Fingarette, H. 1988. *Heavy Drinking: The Myth of Alcoholism as a Disease*. Berkeley, California: University of California Press.

Fishman, R. 1986. *Alcohol and Alcoholism*. New York: Chelsea House.

Glasser, W. 1984. *Control Theory*. New York: Harper and Row.

Gogek, E. 1994. The dry drunk syndrome: Subtype of depression. *American Journal of Psychiatry*. 151:947-948.

Kerr v. Farley, 95 F.3d 472 (1996).

Latessa, E. and S. Goodman. 1989. Alcoholic offenders: Intensive probation program shows promise. *Corrections Today*. 51:38-42.

Leshner, A. 1998. Addiction is a brain disease—and it matters. *National Institute of Justice Journal*. 237:2-6.

O'Connor v. California, 855 F. Supp. 303, 1994

Parks, G and G. Marlatt. 1999. Keeping "What Works" Working: Cognitive-Behavioral Relapse Prevention Therapy with Substance Abusing Offenders. In E. Latessa, ed. *Strategic Solutions: The International Community Corrections Association Examines Substance Abuse*. Lanham, Maryland: American Correctional Association.

Masters, R. and C. Robertson. 1990. *Inside Criminology*. Englewood Cliffs, New Jersey: Prentice-Hall.

Read, E. 1996. *Partners in Change: The 12-Step Referral Handbook for Probation, Parole and Community Corrections*. Lanham, Maryland: American Correctional Association.

Ruden, R. 1997. *The Craving Brain: The Biobalance Approach to Controlling Addictions*. New York: Harper/Collins.

Schmalleger, F. 2001. *Criminal Justice Today, 6th edition.* Upper Saddle River, New Jersey: Prentice Hall.

Schuckit, M. 1989. Biomedical and Genetic Markers of Alcoholism. In H. Goedde and D. Agarwal, eds. *Alcoholism: Biomedical and Genetic Aspects.* New York: Pergamon Press.
_____. AVRT in a Nutshell. *Rational Recovery advertising flyer.* No date.

U.S. Department of Health and Human Services. 1990. *Alcohol and Health.* Washington, D.C.: U.S. Government Printing Office.

Wanberg, K. and H. Milkman. 1998. *Criminal Conduct and Substance Abuse Treatment: Strategies for Self-Improvement.* Thousand Oaks, California: Sage Publications.

Weeks, J., A. Moser, and C. Langevin. 1999. Assessing Substance-Abuse Offenders for Treatment. In E. Latessa, ed. *Strategic Solutions: The International Community Corrections Association Examines Substance Abuse.* Lanham, Maryland: American Correctional Association.

AA
arl Rogers - Empathy
achy fiebie

RR
- Ellis - Rational emotional behavior
- Do when you need a pick up
-

Illegal Drugs and the Criminal Offender

To start thinking about drugs, we need to pose a question of social philoso-phy: what kind of society do we want? Is it a society in which drugs are nec-essary for satisfaction and happiness, or is it a society where they are not necessary?

Maureen Kelleher, Bruce MacMurray, and Thomas Shapiro

Introduction

Although alcohol is a mind-altering drug in common with the other drugs we talk about, we discussed it separately because of the attitude of American society toward alcohol in comparison with nonalcoholic drugs. Alcohol is a legal and socially accept-able form of drugging oneself; marijuana, heroin, LSD, cocaine, and so on are not. It was once thought that respectable middle-class people drink, but only criminals took drugs. Today we see sports and entertainment figures and "respectable" professionals arrested for abuse with some regularity.

According to the U.S. Department of Justice (1991:17), drugs are related to crime in three ways: psychopharmacologically, through economic-compulsivity, and system-ically. In the first instance, psychopharmacologically, crimes are committed because of drug-induced changes in mood and cognitive functioning. Because most drug addicts commit crimes, we should not fall into the trap of concluding from this that drug abuse "causes" criminal behavior. A large body of research (reviewed by McBride and McCoy, 1993) indicates that drug abuse does not appear to initiate a criminal career, although it does increase the extent and seriousness of one. Drug abusers are not "innocents" who are propelled into a criminal career by drugs. Rather, both drug abuse and

Crime/drug addiction → more impulsive

criminality are part of a broader propensity of some individuals to engage in a variety of deviant and antisocial behaviors.

Crimes committed under the influence of drugs (the psychopharmacological component) have less impact on the overall relationship between drugs and crime than those of the economic compulsive and systemic connections. That is, unlike the direct link between alcohol consumption and crime, the link between drug abuse and crime is more indirect. Most drug-related crimes are crimes committed to obtain money to buy drugs, which are very expensive because of their illegal status (the economic-compulsive component). Other crimes are those committed as part of "doing business" in the drug culture (the systemic component). It has been estimated by the Institute for Health Policy that the total cost of addiction to illegal drugs to the U.S. economy was 66.9 billion dollars in 1993, with 46 billion (68.8 percent of the total) being attributable to crime (DuPont, 1997). The U.S. Department of Justice (1991:17) estimated that about 80 percent of the homicides in the District of Columbia in 1988 were drug-related, a staggering increase from the 1985 estimate of 21 percent. The dramatic decline in homicides in the U.S., including the District of Columbia, during the 1990s may have a lot to do with the consolidation of drug gangs (particularly those in the lucrative crack market) and the subsequent end to the territorial wars (Witkin, 1998).

We are not concerned with systemic drug-related crime here; that is more a social and political issue than a corrections issue. We are concerned with the demand side—the users and pushers who will be on our caseloads. Presented in Figure 16.1 are 1990 data from the National Institute of Justice's (1991) Drug Use Forecasting (DUF) research program and its successor, the Arrestee Drug Abuse Monitoring Program (ADAM), which reports 1999 data (National Institute of Justice, 2000). These data forcefully point to the link between drug use and crime in ten of our largest cities. All cities show that more than half of arrestees tested positive for at least one illegal drug in both time periods. Although there is considerable variability among the drugs used within the various cities, cocaine (including crack) is by far the illegal drug abused most frequently. The good news is that, except for Denver, cocaine (including crack) use has dropped in every city, sometimes quite dramatically. This data brings home to the correctional worker just what he or she has to deal with in terms of the supervision and treatment of offenders.

Some Causes of Illegal Substance-related Disorders

Drugs affect brain functioning in one of four ways: (1) they inhibit or slow down the release of chemical neurotransmitters, (2) they stimulate or speed up their release, (3) they prevent the reuptake of transmitters after they have stimulated neighboring neurons, or (4) they break down the transmitters more quickly. It is important to realize that all addictive drugs mimic the actions of normal brain chemistry (Pinel, 2000). Virtually all illegal drugs "have common effects on a single pathway deep within the brain, the mesolimbic reward system" (Leshner, 1998:4). However, these drugs produce more powerful, rapid, and predictable effects on the brain's pleasure centers than are obtained by the normal reward system (the natural action of neurotransmitters in response to our pleasant experiences). Depending on the type of drug taken, the individual's behavior and/or feelings are speeded up or slowed down, intensified or reduced, or stimulated or mellowed. In short, drugs allow us to change an undesirable mood state to one perceived of as more desirable.

Figure 16.1
Drug Use by Male Arrestees

has dropped except Denver

City	% Positive any Drug		Cocaine		Marijuana		Amphetamines		Opiates		PCP	
	1990	1999	'90	'99	'90	'99	'90	'99	'90	'99	'90	'99
Birmingham	69 (21)	64 (15)	50	37	18	39	0	0	7	4	0	0
Chicago	75 (46)	75 (39)	59	42	38	45	0	0	27	20	10	4
Cleveland	65 (22)	71 (24)	49	40	26	43	0	0	4	4	1	10
Dallas	66 (20)	60 (22)	44	34	32	39	0	2	7	5	0	5
Denver	59 (16)	67 (22)	30	41	37	44	1	3	3	3	0	0
Fort Lauderdale	61 (18)	64 (18)	47	41	27	28	0	0	nr	2	0	0
Houston	70 (18)	60 (21)	57	36	21	38	nr	0	6	6	0	6
Los Angeles	70 (28)	62 (20)	54	36	19	32	0	9	16	6	0	2
New York	79 (36)	75 (24)	67	44	38	41	0	0	26	15	4	1
Washington, D.C.	59 (24)	69 (24)	49	38	12	35	nr	1	15	16	6	6

*1990 data from National Institute of Justice's Drug Use Forecasting (1991); 1999 data from National Institute of Justice's Arrestee Drug Abuse Monitoring Program (2000). Figures in parenthesis represent percentage of arrestees testing positive for two or more drugs. nr=not reported. All percentages rounded.

People turn to illegal drugs for many of the same reasons that people turn to alcohol. They may take them initially to be "with it," to be sociable and to conform, to induce pleasure, to escape psychic stress, or to escape chronic boredom. Others are perhaps genetically predisposed to rapidly develop dependency—much the same way some people, given their genetic background, are "sitting ducks" for addiction. Their bodies, their metabolism, and their brain functioning may be different from that of the "normal" person. In these cases, a little "experimentation" with an illegal drug may have far greater negative long-term consequences. Many abuse drugs and become dependent on them because they find little pleasure, comfort, solace, or meaning in their lives. People who confront more pain than pleasure in their daily lives tend to pursue all the artificial comfort they can get. Addicts can become emotionally attached to their substances the way most of us become attached to other people because, generally, their experiences have not prepared them for intimate relationships with others.

A study of drug usage and sexual promiscuity found that lack of parental attachment was a better predictor of both behaviors for men and women than a number of other possibilities (Walsh, 1995). Similarly, looking at the family backgrounds of addicts, Chein and his colleagues (1964:273) remark that, "In almost all addict families, there was a disturbed relationship between the parents, as evidenced by separation, divorce, open hostility, or lack of warmth." The same sentiment is expressed by Burnett (1979:354): "Drug abusers often complain of lack of love and warmth in their homes. An absence of parent 'stroking' in the home will lead to low self-image, which contributes to the susceptibility to drug abuse." Lacking this inner sense of warmth, and self-esteem, addicts think of their pharmacopoeia of fake happiness not in terms of what it does "to" them, but rather in terms of what it does "for" them. We have to break through all their rationalizations, projections, and denials to make them understand the profound difference between *for* and *to*.

Regardless of the type of drug, addiction is not an invariable outcome of drug usage any more than alcoholism is an invariable outcome of drinking. In fact, it appears that most people who experiment with drugs during adolescence do not become addicted (Marlatt *et al.*, 1989). As is the case with alcohol, genetic differences undoubtedly are related to a person's chances of becoming addicted given the same amount of a drug and the same frequency with which it is taken. People differ in the degree of pleasure obtained by a drug, the rate of tolerance, and the type of effect produced (Pinel, 2000).

Illegal Drug Classification   Heroin → depressants

As a corrections worker, you should become familiar with all types of illegal drugs and their effects. However, our mission here precludes any attempt at an exhaustive treatment. What follows is a brief description of the different classes of drugs.

The Depressants. The depressants include the barbiturates/sedatives and the narcotics/opiates. All drugs in this category have the potential for physical and psychological dependence, and all produce *tolerance* (the tendency to require larger and larger doses to produce the same effects after the body adjusts to lower dosages). Depressants range from the relatively mild analgesic sedatives to the insidious narcotics such as heroin. This class of drugs tends to appeal to individuals whose characteristic coping style lean towards isolation, withdrawal, and indifference.

Taking one of the stronger varieties in this category, such as heroin, wafts the individual into a euphoric state of sweet indifference, a state that heroin users describe as the "floats." Intravenous injection of heroin ("mainlining") used to be the most popular method of administering the drug among hard-core addicts. This produces the famous rush, a warm skin flush and orgasmic feeling. After the initial rush, the addict drifts off into a private carefree world for anywhere from three to twelve hours. Needless to say, the problems are still around after the effects wear off, not the least of which is the problem of securing the next rush. This author once supervised a heroin addict who had a $300-per-day habit and who challenged characterization of him as lazy. He said, "Man, we addicts work harder than anybody you know. You try to hustle the streets to come up with that kind of bread every day."

Given the AIDS epidemic and the increasing awareness of the dangers of sharing contaminated "works," many heroin-dependent offenders have shifted to snorting or even smoking heroin and opium. Very disturbing indeed are the reports we receive that indicate heroin smoking and snorting are on the rise, and interestingly, that this increase is not limited to the poor or disenfranchised: middle-income suburban youth are visiting the emergency rooms as well. Another related trend has been the increasing potency of the heroin and opium available on the street. It now is possible to achieve a significant state of intoxication without having to "mainline." Note from the data in Table 16.1 that opium use among arrestees remained fairly stable from 1990 to 1999, going up in some cities, down in others, and remaining more or less the same in others.

This "hustle" is the main reason for heroin addiction's close association with criminal activity. The euphoric state achieved under the influence of heroin is not conducive to effort, criminal or otherwise. Narcotic users are significantly less likely to commit violent crimes than are users of alcohol or stimulants, particularly metham-phetamine and cocaine. In fact, many advocates of decriminalizing or legalizing some or all drugs point to lower levels of drug-related crimes in those countries where free narcotics are supplied to habitual abusers (Walker, 2001).

Heroin is a derivative of morphine, a powerful pain-killer. It is a white or brown-ish powder that usually is dissolved in water and injected. It reliably has been estab-lished that the brain has its own pain-killing substances, endorphins (for "endogenous morphinelike substances"), which are larger and more complex neurotransmitters than those previously discussed, such as dopamine (DuPont, 1997). The presence of these naturally occurring analgesics provide clues to the addictive process. Some have suggested that individuals become heroin addicts because they have insufficient endorphins in the brain to anesthetize naturally the pains of life. In other words, it is not that heroin addicts experience more pains of living than the rest of us, but that they have fewer endorphins. Lacking normal amounts of nature's "tonic" precipitates a search for artificial substitutes to make up the deficit. Frequent injections of heroin affects the body's natural capacity to release endorphins in much the same way that giving individuals too much thyroid extract will eventually cause the body to cease its own production of the thyroid-stimulating hormone, thus turning them into "thyroid junkies." An addict's lower level of natural endorphins is therefore considered a con-sequence rather than a cause of addiction (Pinel, 2000).

There is a great deal of evidence for this. As already mentioned, the brain releas-es neurotransmitters synthesized by genes having the same mood-altering effects (although much weaker) that drugs do. When drugs are ingested, they initially enhance neurotransmission rates, but protracted usage eventually leads to neurotransmitter depletion and ultimate suppression (Frawley, 1987; Gove and Wilmoth, 1992:273). In effect, the genes responsible for synthesizing the particular neurotransmitter(s) effect-ed by the drug shut down because they have been fooled by the exogenous drug into "thinking" that the brain has all that it needs. It is this inoperative endogenous reward system that makes withdrawal from drugs so physically and psychologically painful. Figure 16.2 shows a model of progression from drug experimentation to drug addiction.

Figure 16.2
Model of Progression from Drug Experimentation to Drug Addiction

Dopamine → pleasure → speed up things; enhance what your doing

The Stimulants. The stimulants, primarily amphetamines, methamphetamines, and cocaine, have effects opposite to those of the depressants. They mimic the activity of the sympathetic division of the autonomic nervous system, meaning that they increase arousal and a sense of well being. The stimulants increase the action of norepinepherine and dopamine (the "fight or flight" chemicals), and, thus, are often the drugs of choice for individuals who seek excitement and adventure, the bored, the driven, and the chronically underaroused (Grabowski, 1984). The stimulant class of drugs includes everything from the $3.95 over-the-counter diet pills to the $120 per gram powdered cocaine.

Along with depressants, and alcohol, the use of amphetamines and cocaine have the most immediate association with violent criminal behavior (Fishbein, 2000). Holden (1989:1378) has characterized cocaine as "the most powerful reinforcer known." Cocaine works by blocking the reuptake of the neurotransmitters dopamine and norepinephrine at the synaptic terminals, thus keeping the body in an extended state of arousal. Being highly soluble in fatty tissue, coke is taken up by the brain quickly, producing the familiar euphoric rush. When cocaine is taken intravenously, the rush takes only about fifteen seconds. The strongest and fastest rush comes from smoking "freebase" (the cocaine alkaloid it frees from its acid salt to produce pure cocaine).

A form of smokable cocaine, known as "rock" or "crack," produces intense craving and may be the most addictive substance known (Read, 1992). Crack is manufactured by combining cocaine, baking soda, and water. This mixture is then heated, allowed to cool, and broken into tiny pieces resembling gray slivers of bar soap. Without the elaborate and sometimes dangerous preparations necessary to produce freebase cocaine, crack produces the same high, and its relatively low price makes it attractive to those who formerly resisted the more expensive powdered cocaine. Crack prices range from $5 to $25 for 300 milligrams as opposed to about $120 for a gram (a gram is about the amount of artificial sweetener contained in the typical Equal or Nutrasweet packet) of powdered cocaine. Crack is smoked in cigarettes or in small pipes, and the high, which lasts only about five to ten minutes, comes within eight seconds.

Cocaine addiction is extremely difficult to treat because use of the drug is so rewarding in that it quickly, powerfully, and most importantly, directly affects the brain's pleasure receptors. In the case of crack, it takes effect within seconds of being inhaled, with the high being maintained from five to thirty minutes. Most addicts who have been involved with other kinds of drugs will tell you that cocaine is by far the most desirable. This author once had an offender who spent nine days locked in her room living only on cocaine and water. Her nine-day cocaine holiday cost her $5,000, which she had obtained by trafficking the stuff among her middle-class friends. Cocaine addiction is also very difficult to treat because its nonuse after prolonged use produces a devastating "crash." This is a period of intense anxiety, irritability, and depression that lasts about four days. After prolonged use, the natural activation of the brain's pleasure centers does not occur (depletion and suppression have occurred), making the brain dependent on cocaine to feel any pleasure at all (Visher, 1990:3).

It used to be thought that although cocaine quickly produced tolerance, requiring increasingly greater amounts to obtain the same effects, it did not produce physical dependence. Many individuals do use cocaine on a "recreational" basis without suffering major withdrawal symptoms when not using, but few researchers today deny its addictive power, a power which is especially strong where crack is concerned. Crack addiction develops and progresses faster than any other kind of addiction (Read,

1992:7). The depression and fatigue resulting from the overstimulation of the nervous system creates a tremendous desire for more cocaine to counteract these effects. Since smoking cocaine produces a quicker and stronger high than snorting it, its effect is of shorter duration and the crash is more devastating. If more cocaine is not immediately available, some may resort to alcohol ingestion to help ease the crash.

As we saw from Table 16.1, the number of arrested suspects testing positive for cocaine (including crack in this category) is down dramatically, although it is still the most frequently used of the illegal drugs. This decrease may be attributable to several factors, including severely increased penalties for sale and possession of crack and the extreme danger from others trafficking in the same market. It also shows that many individuals have made a rational decision not to try crack in the first place after surveying the ravages visited on addicts they know. The emerging norm that tells many inner city youth that crack is not "cool," has been attributed to what some researchers call the "younger brother" syndrome (Witkin, 1998). That is, younger members of the community have seen relatives and friends killed or permanently disabled in drug deals gone wrong, and they see others serving long prison sentences, or grow old and emaciated before their time because of their addiction. There are still plenty of crackheads around for us to deal with, however.

Methamphetamine. Methamphetamine or "speed" is the most dangerous of all illegal drugs in terms of its psychopharmacological association with violence. Speed, in its various forms, has reached near-epidemic proportions in some parts of the country, especially the West. It operates on the limbic system to accentuate and accelerate the visual, tactile, auditory, and olfactory impulses. When methamphetamine is taken, users become "wired." They have boundless energy, are super alert, and feel on top of everything. The effects feel so good that they often go on what is called a "run." A run consists of several days on speed without pausing for sleep. Speed is considerably less expensive than cocaine, so a run of five days will cost "only" a few hundred dollars. The price to be paid for the run is that the longer it lasts, the more the feelings of wellbeing turn to hyperactive aggressiveness. The accentuated sensitivity to stimuli, intermixed with fatigue, very easily can produce psychoticlike reactions. This is especially true if the run is being conducted, as it usually is, with several others, all of whom are similarly hypersensitive. Love and beauty and clever conversation will become paranoia, ugliness, hostility, and violent disagreement. This result becomes increasingly more likely as the run is extended and as the available supply of speed peters out.

Offenders dependent on methamphetamine are especially dangerous after the run is over. They find themselves in deep posthigh depressions, their nerves are badly frayed, and they are in desperate need of sleep. They become very argumentative and are susceptible to explosive violence. Any confrontation worsens the depression and leads them on a desperate search for more speed to alleviate the feeling. They will do almost anything to get the next fix and start the vicious cycle spinning again.

A new more potent and more addictive form of methamphetamine, called *ice* or *crystal*, has been added to America's ever-growing illicit pharmacopoeia. Ice is chemically identical to methamphetamine, but, as its name implies, is crystalline in its appearance rather than powdered. It is becoming popular among users of stimulant drugs because of its low price relative to cocaine/crack, its intense and long-lasting high (a high lasting anywhere from seven to twenty-four hours), because it can be smoked rather than injected, and because it is virtually odorless, making for a reduced chance of detection (Nugent, 1990a:4).

crack → hits very quickly
Cheaper cocaine

The Hallucinogens. The hallucinogens are mind-altering drugs such as marijuana and lysergic acid diethylamide (LSD). The smoking of marijuana is so pervasive today that some pay little attention to it; yet, it is safe to say that most criminal justice offenders have tried or continue to smoke marijuana. Its quasi-acceptance can be discerned by reading PSI reports that frequently contain such statements as "With the exception of marijuana, the defendant denies any drug usage." Offenders are often ordered into treatment for marijuana dependency but rarely sent back to prison solely on the basis of such illicit use. There is a tendency on the part of the entire correctional system, sometimes unwittingly, to minimize marijuana use relative to the heavy hitters who use cocaine, crack, and heroin. This is a mistake and we should be doing better.

Those who consider it to be merely a "simple natural weed" akin to tobacco fail to realize the ever-increasing potency of the modern product. Unlike alcohol, which is water soluble and quickly metabolized and excreted from the body, cannabinoids are fat soluble. They penetrate the fatty areas of the body—notably in the brain and the gonads—and remain there for long periods of time. Since only about 10 percent of the THC crosses the blood-brain barrier to produce the marijuana "high," one shudders to think of the damage that the other 90 percent of this powerful chemical is doing to the body. Marijuana is anything but harmless. It has a wide range of subtle, insidious physical and psychological effects, many of which are still to be discovered.

Additionally, marijuana contains hundreds of other chemicals, with unknown effects on the body. The fact that more and more adolescents are experimenting with marijuana, and the research identifies it as a "gateway" drug to other illegal substances, makes minimization of marijuana a dangerous proposition. Note from the data in Table 16.1 that the percentage of arrestees testing positive for marijuana increased considerably from 1990 to 1999.

A more immediately dangerous form of hallucinogen is LSD. In its unadulterated form, LSD is a clear, odorless, and tasteless liquid. It is sold soaked in sugar cubes, in tiny pills, or on saturated blotting paper (microdots). LSD has been termed a psychomimetic drug because its effects sometimes mimic psychosis.

After a period of decline, LSD's usage appears to be increasing again. Today's LSD, however, is only about half as potent as it was during the hippie period. It is a drug primarily favored by those who seek intellectual adventure, the inward-lookers who seek to increase awareness rather than escape it. It causes hyperawareness and a greatly enhanced appreciation of stimuli in the user's perceptual field. LSD does not cause physical dependence, but psychological dependence may occur, and the drug produces tolerance rapidly.

Look-alike drugs, drugs of deception, and designer drugs are ones that fall within the general family of psychoactive substances affecting the brain and central nervous system. We distinguish them from those listed above because they tend to be ever-changing and very hard to pinpoint. Some are not new at all, but are substances from the existing pharmacological pool adapted for street use and abuse. Some are modified "look-alike" drugs made up of nonprescription substances. Most are entirely synthetic, made by underground chemists using increasingly sophisticated equipment and techniques.

A fairly well-known drug on the street today that fits this category is "ecstasy," which is a far more pronounceable, name for 3, 4 methylenedioxymethylamphetamine (MDMA). It is a synthetic substance synthesized from methamphetamine and safrole, which comes from sassafras, nutmeg, or is made from another synthetic called piperonylacetone. Its effects are similar to those produced by both psychedelic drugs such as LSD and stimulants such as methamphetamine. It has been said that persons who enjoy amphetamine-like stimulation and euphoria will gravitate toward "ecstasy." Young people are doing a great deal of "E" at "raves," their surreptitious (at least to parents!) all night dancing parties. As is the case with almost all illegal stimulant drugs, extended use of ecstasy can lead to psychosis (Pinel, 2000).

Case Study
Confessions of a Recovered Addict
Anonymous

This piece was written by one of the author's ex-students who found that love, both tough and tender, was the answer to her many addictions. She is now a drug abuse counselor—and a good one.

We all know what drug and alcohol addiction is, but I was addicted to just about everything that kicked my pleasure centers into gear—booze, drugs of all kinds, food, tobacco, and sex. You might say that I have an addictive personality. This is no story about a ghetto child, for I'm the product of an upper middle-class background.

At my "sweet sixteen" stage of life, I discovered men. I was fresh out of a private Catholic girls' school, and men, a lot of them, were what I wanted. I would go out to the naval air station in Lemore, California, to dance, drink, and to find a man who would go to bed with me while the rest of my chums were at a high school football game or at some other "square" function.

I was drinking heavily by the time I was eighteen, and I was also beginning to turn on to various drugs. When I graduated from high school, I didn't go onto college like most of my friends. I went to a home for unwed mothers. We were counseled there for our promiscuous ways, but the subject of drug and alcohol abuse was never addressed. But this was 1968, and nobody thought about addiction among "young ladies." After all, heroin addiction belonged in the ghetto, and alcoholics were all dirty old men rolling in the gutters of skid row.

At this period in my life, I sought men out only for sex; "meaningful relationships" were for squares. Besides, who would want to love a 280-pound woman anyway? (Remember, food was another of my addictions). Not too many wanted to sleep with one either, so I found myself "buying" a man for a gram of coke or a few drinks. I didn't really get pleasure from sex, and often I actually would get physically sick when thinking about what I was doing. I realize now that I just wanted someone to hold me, and if sex was the price, so be it. This is not much different from being willing to suffer hangovers and withdrawal pains from my other addictions.

Throughout the late sixties, through the seventies and into the eighties, sex, drugs, and rock n' roll were a way of life for me. I was desperate for love, but thought I could only get it from stuffing myself with food, booze, pills, or penises. I spent my entire inheritance of $250,000 (I told you I was no pauper) in the mad service of these addictions. It's a horrible feeling to wake up in the morning thinking that the only things that would make the new day bearable were my addictions. This lifestyle cost me my health, the respect of my family, my self-respect, and the opportunity to get an education and lead a normal life. I can't even bear children now because the various venereal diseases I've had have destroyed this capacity.

One event in my life was instrumental in turning it around for me. I was in an automobile accident in which both the driver and I were drunk and high. I received a broken jaw and a few other things, but was out of the hospital and back running the bar I owned within six weeks. But by now, the cops were on to me. I was doing a little drug dealing from my bar, and was stupid enough to sell $1,800 worth of coke to an undercover officer. I was busted the next day and held in jail until my trial date. There, I spent three months without drugs, alcohol, sex, or excessive amounts of food.

The judge sentenced me to five years probation, a $4,000 fine, and 120 hours of community service. I also was ordered to pay back the "buy money." My probation officer was a real "knuckle dragger," an ex-cop. He made it plain to me that his only job was to put me back in jail if I screwed up. I did my community service hours and visited my parole officer weekly. I began to see him as the caring father who I never had, actually enjoying the discipline involved in doing my community service and following my parole officer's orders. He and I became as friendly as a probationer and her officer could be. He was a very positive influence in my life, getting me interested in enrolling in college and pursuing a career in criminal justice.

I am now off probation, have my degree in criminal justice, and am married to a very loving man. I have not touched either alcohol or drugs since I was busted, have given up smoking, am down to a respectable weight of 165 at 5' 6", and my husband is the only man I've had sex with, or wanted to have sex with, in the past six years. I still see and talk with my probation officer, and I still volunteer at the agency where I did my community service. I want to devote my life's work to helping those poor lost souls on the same mad path to hell that I once walked, a path now made even more dangerous by the appearance of the AIDS virus. There is a life after addiction if only you can find love and give it in return. I first found it in the cold stare of my probation officer, and then in the arms of my loving husband and the soft smiles of his two children.

Identification and Treatment Considerations

Everything said about alcoholism treatment has general application to other drug treatment. Attempts to rehabilitate drug abusers have been impeded by the pessimistic attitude "once an addict, always an addict." This attitude partly may be a function of society's more negative perceptions of drug addicts in relation to its perceptions of alcoholics. Although addiction is certainly a chronic condition, and periods of relapse are to be expected, the corrections worker should not share the common attitudes of hopelessness and stigma (Parks and Marlatt, 1999).

Like alcoholics, many drug abusers and addicts are reluctant to admit that they have a drug problem unless they feel that you may consider their problem to be a mitigating factor against some form of punitive reaction. If drug abusers do not admit their dependency during the initial interview, they will tend to do whatever they can to hide it while under supervision. It is important that you identify any existing drug problem during your initial contacts. There are several signs that can assist you in this endeavor. Some researchers (Weekes, Moser, and Langevin, 1999), however, feel that denial is not such a problem with hard-core offenders, who are largely inured to concerns of stigma.

The most obvious first step is to check the record for a history of drug-related arrests or previous drug treatment. Ask the offender to explain involvement with drugs at those times. This may lead into an admission of current usage. If you suspect narcotics usage, look for tracks on their hands and arms, which they conceal, even in summer, by wearing long sleeves. Does the offender wear sunglasses to your office to conceal constricted and fixed pupils? Is the offender drowsy and "laid back" during visits? If the offender's nose is frequently running or eyes watering, it may indicate that he or she is late in getting a fix. Does the offender scratch himself or herself and complain of frequent sickness? Does the offender have difficulty concentrating and frequently arrive late or miss appointments?

The abuser of stimulants is somewhat harder to detect by behavior in your office. As opposed to the narcotics addict, the stimulant abuser may display an excited, hyperactive, and talkative demeanor, which may sometimes degenerate into hostility and irritability. This will be particularly in evidence if you tell offenders that you suspect their drug abuse and order them to go to a clinic for a urinanalysis. All offenders whom you suspect of drug abuse should be made to undergo urinalysis at frequent but always random intervals.

Research studies strongly suggest that regular urine testing in conjunction with intensive supervision is more effective in reducing recidivism among probationers and parolees than if they are intensely supervised without urine testing (Speckart, Anglin, and Deschenes, 1989; Anglin, Speckart, and Deschenes, 1989). As indicated above, urinalysis should be performed on a random basis because veteran users know how to beat it for most drugs. Cocaine, for instance, is detectable in the urine for only up to forty-eight to seventy-two hours, often even less if the user "flushes" (consumes large quantities of water to dilute concentration of foreign substances per unit of urine).

The on-site, relatively immediate, drug testing methodology has advanced by leaps and bounds in recent years. There are "kits," portable machines, and testing cups, all with various advantages and disadvantages in terms of practical value. Staff must determine their particular office's needs, meet the various company representatives, and do the cost-pricing research, accordingly. Although still fairly expensive, and this may change over time, hair analysis shows promising results. Unlike most all the other drug testing methodology, examining hair samples can provide information about an offender's drug use over time, often dating back years.

An even better alternative may be the sweat patch. This patch may be applied like a bandage by the supervising officer to the offender's arm, and it may be worn for up to fourteen days. The patch is resistant to environmental contaminants and is tamper-evident (it cannot be tampered with undetected). The pad collects and contains various residues from the offender's sweat left behind after it evaporates, including residues from consumed drugs (Baerand and Booher, 1994). Probation and parole officers taking part in a field trial of the patch conclusively endorsed it over traditional urinalysis because of its gender-neutral convenience and the elimination of the need to handle urine samples. The patch is more expensive than urinalysis, but since it may cover the same period as two or three analyses, it may be more cost effective over the long run (Vito, 1999).

THERAPEUTIC COMMUNITIES

Offenders in trouble with illegal drugs have the same full range of treatment options open to them as do alcoholics. Interestingly, research and experience has shown that since many criminal offenders addicted to illegal drugs are also struggling with characterological disorders, or personality disorders, including the "antisocial" type, longer-term residential treatment facilities seem to offer the best hope for treatment success. Part of the problem with many inner city, disenfranchised offenders who fall within this population is that instead of rehabilitation, these individuals require exposure to something much more basic: habilitation. They need a total long-term cultural change, with the opportunity to learn new values, behavior, and cognition.

The use of therapeutic communities in the treatment of drug abuse has been popular since 1959, when its most famous representative, Synanon, was established. Therapeutic communities are total treatment environments isolated from the rest of society, as far as is practical. According to a leading researcher on therapeutic communities, their essential dynamic "is mutual self-help. Thus the day-to-day activities are conducted by the residents themselves. In their jobs, groups, meetings, recreation, personal, and social time, it is residents who continually transmit to each other the main messages and expectations of the community" (cited in Hooper, Lockwood, and Inciardi, 1993:291). The amount of time residents spend in therapeutic communities ranges from six months to two years.

In such settings, addicts receive support, feedback, and information in an accepting, caring, honest, and empathetic way. They learn that if tensions and stresses arise, a refocusing of the primary stress in their lives (addiction) will place the secondary tensions and stresses in proper perspective. They will gather reservoirs of self-esteem with renewed feelings of self-control. The regaining of self-esteem and a sense of self-control is considered essential for drug addicts (Frawley, 1987). Learning self-forgiveness through positive and negative peer pressure, and from the positive examples of those peers, the addicts then will be able to focus their anger and negative talk on the substance that holds them in its grip, rather than on themselves. Self-worth, which is the product of both self-forgiveness and the elimination of negative self-talk, eventually will emerge.

Therapeutic communities are considered to be the most successful of drug rehabilitation programs, but they typically require "a highly structured, long-term (eight-to-twelve months) residential program, which includes a highly confrontational form of group therapy, resocialization, progressive responsibility, and gradual reentry into the community" (Lightfoot, 1999:55). They are not panaceas, nor are they suited for all addicts. As with treatment for alcoholism, success or lack of success will depend a great deal on the personality attributes addicts bring with them to the therapeutic process.

The structure and intense pressure experienced in the therapeutic community leads to a large number of dropouts (either voluntary, or removal is initiated by staff or peers in the community). In one study of a prison-based therapeutic community, it was found that even among those who did complete the program, only 54.5 percent were drug free after six months of completion. This was significantly better than the 34.4 percent in a work-release control group, however. On a more positive note, 90.9 percent who completed the therapeutic community and were part of a postrelease outreach program were found to be drug free during the same period (Hooper,

Lockwood, and Inciardi, 1993:305). These results underscore the need for ongoing treatment and support for drug addicts over an extensive period of time.

MUTUAL SELF-HELP GROUPS

Among the many nonresidential mutual support options available today are Narcotics Anonymous (NA) and Cocaine Anonymous (CA), two twelve-step fellowship groups located throughout the world and modeled after AA. No matter what your "evidence," if you have the slightest suspicion that someone is in trouble with illegal drugs, refer them to these experts. They have been there. They know how to achieve abstinence, and they know how to sustain their positive arrest-free lifestyle. Again, the author recommends Ed Read's book, *Partners in Change* (1996), for a complete and very practical explanation of how these programs function. Needless to say, programs like Rational Recovery (RR) and Secular Sobriety also are available for referrals.

PHARMACOLOGICAL TREATMENTS

Arguing that addiction is a brain disease, Alan Leshner, director of the National Institute on Drug Abuse, states that: "If we understand addiction as a prototypical psychobiological illness, with critical biological, behavioral, and social context components, our treatment strategies must include biological, behavioral, and social context elements" (1998:5). The biological elements are the various drug antagonists (drugs that inhibit the effects of other drugs). Opponents of pharmacotherapy argue that it merely substitutes one drug for another and it, therefore, is not a treatment. But advocates of this method of treatment counter that it enhances and augments, not replaces, traditional methods of treatment and is more cost effective and immediate (Nugent,1990b). Nugent also argues that "Drug users are often emotionally unstable; pharmacotherapeutics regulate them, making them more receptive to counseling and rehabilitation" (1990b:6). This author agrees. After all, we pharmacologically attempt to regulate schizophrenics and others suffering from syndromes associated with chemical imbalances in the brain. First we try to stabilize their brain chemistry, and then their lives.

Among the various drug therapies, the best known and most widely used is *methadone* maintenance. Some authorities feel that this method should be used only after psychotherapeutic methods have been tried and failed because methadone creates its own dependence. However, it is extremely successful in blocking the withdrawal pains of heroin without producing any rewarding euphoria or rush of its own. Best of all, the heroin addict on a methadone program can function normally in the community. Although addicts retain their physical dependence on a narcotic (methadone), they defeat their psychological craving for heroin and no longer have to engage in criminal activity to avoid withdrawal. Addicts typically report to a clinic daily to drink their methadone mixed with orange juice. Methadone appears fairly successful as a treatment method. Kaplan (1991:3) states that "Methadone maintenance 'works' for around 30 or 40 percent of the addicts who undergo treatment. Moreover, the arrest rate of addicts drops dramatically when they enter methadone treatment."

If psychological craving for heroin exists, narcotic antagonists such as *Cyclazocine* and *Naloxone* are available to offset the craving. They do not possess the narcoticlike properties of methadone, but they do produce rapid detoxification. These antagonists block the desirable effects of heroin and, like Antabuse, should be used in conjunction with intensive counseling designed, as always, to get offenders to exert control over their own lives, and to behave responsibly. A recent study of more than 1,600 cocaine addicts in treatment in 11 U.S. cities found that 77 percent remained cocaine free in the year following treatment, with relapse incidents being highly related to severity of patient problems and shorter stays (less than 90 days) in treatment (Simpson, et al., 1999).

Desipramine is a drug that has been used experimentally in the treatment of cocaine addicts within the context of a full treatment plan that may include counseling and dietary changes. It has a claimed success rate in keeping addicts from craving the drug for up to nine months. This is quite an advance over the use of other methods, which have reported records of only fifteen days. But desipramine is not a magic bullet, and must be used as an adjunct to other therapies.

The newest antagonistic drug is *buprenorphine*, which can be used to treat both cocaine and heroin addiction, and potential addiction to other drugs as well. It has several other advantages, not the least of which is that it is nonaddictive and safe (Ling *et al.*, 1996). Unlike methadone and other therapeutic drugs, buprenorphine is not likely to create an illicit drug market because its opiate effects are weak (Nugent, 1990b:6).

Interestingly, the effects of the various antagonists have been found to differ across genders. For males, methadone is found to be more effective than buprenorphine in treating opiate addiction, while for females the opposite was the case. For cocaine addiction, buprenorphine was superior to methadone for males, but methadone was superior to buprenorphine for females (Oliveto, *et al.*, 1999).

There are quite a few complications involved with the pharmacological treatment of drug addiction. These complications are not your affair, however. Your responsibility is to become familiar with medical facilities that dispense these antagonistic drugs in the event that you are faced with a particularly intractable offender with whom all else has failed.

Do not be put off by arguments that these drugs "only treat symptoms, not the cause." The symptoms are precisely those aspects with which we are most immediately concerned. Much of medicine is concerned with "treating symptoms" while the body's natural defenses are marshaled to attack the cause. In fact, apart from the infectious diseases, medicine has very few "cures." Ailments such as heart disease, diabetes, and arthritis, just like alcoholism, are never cured. Drugs designed to alleviate these medical problems help people cope by minimizing the destructive effects of symptoms associated with the problems in people's lives.

Further, do not be disheartened by those who tell you that it is practically "impossible" to wean substance abusers successfully from their problems, or by those who will assert that voluntary acquiescence on the part of the offender is "absolutely necessary" for successful treatment. A number of studies of troops returning from Vietnam show that many men were able to kick their habits *regardless* of whether they were treated. One study found that 43 percent of a sample of 600 returning soldiers reported an addiction to heroin. Although some reported occasional use in the United States, only 12 percent of those reporting addiction in Vietnam relapsed to addiction levels back in the United States. Once they were back home, "removed from the pressures of war and once more in the presence of family and friends and opportunities for constructive activity, these men felt no need for heroin" (Peel, 1978:65). This is an instructive statement about the power of attachment, commitment, and involvement to generate responsible behavior.

Of the second pessimistic assertion, the majority of chemically dependent people who have been successfully treated were forced into treatment against their will.

They did not necessarily want to discontinue their chemical usage, but certain crises in their lives forced them to accept help. It is true that the vast majority of people being treated for substance abuse have very large bootprints impressed on their backsides. But so what? Being involved with the criminal justice system because of substance abuse should be crisis enough to generate the beginnings of motivation in some offenders, and the experiences undergone in the treatment program may motivate others. Two recent reviews of the United States (Farabee, Pendergast, and Anglin, 1998) and United Kingdom (Barton, 1999) literature on coerced substance abuse treatment concluded that such treatment leads to positive reductions in abuse, even greater reductions in some cases than among voluntary clients, presumably because of the threat of criminal justice sanctions.

As a corrections worker who is probably not trained in direct clinical techniques, most likely you will not be directly involved in the treatment of alcohol or other drug-dependent offenders. However, you will be indirectly involved by being a knowledgeable broker about available programs in your community, insisting on frequent urine testing (or other equivalent test) of offenders not in residential treatment, and above all, by holding offenders strictly responsible for remaining alcohol and drug free. Treating offenders with substance abuse problems is a team effort, and you do your part by effective offender monitoring and serving as a liaison with treatment agencies, according to the principles of good case management.

Summary

Looking at illegal drug abuse and addiction, we noted that illegal drug users bear the added burden of the crime associated with their use. Illegal drugs cost a lot of money and generally precipitate great risks on the part of the dependent or potentially dependent offender.

Drug classification is important to understand. The depressants range from the relatively mild analgesic sedatives to the more challenging narcotics like heroin and opium. Since purity levels have risen, and offenders are worried about dirty needles, many more are snorting or smoking these drugs as opposed to injecting them intravenously. The stimulants, of course, have the opposite effect. Crack cocaine and methamphetamine are powerfully addictive substances ravaging some parts of the country with their enticing capacity to generate a stimulating sense of well-being. Marijuana, actually classified as an hallucinogen, is far more potent today than ever before. And unfortunately, studies are showing that young people and others, including a very large segment of the offender population, are heavily involved with marijuana.

Identification and assessment of offenders in trouble with illegal drugs and alcohol is a critical component of your job. And although drug dependent offenders respond to the full range of treatment resources available, therapeutic communities (TCs) seem particularly suited to many of them. As always, referral to mutual self-help support groups like Narcotics Anonymous (NA), Cocaine Anonymous (CA), and Rational Recovery (RR) should be routine in every case, and accompany any other professional treatment referral.

REFERENCES AND SUGGESTED READINGS

Anglin, M., G. Speckart, and E. Deschenes. 1989. *Reexamining the Effects of Probation and Parole on Narcotics Addiction and Property Crime: Final Report*. National Institute of Justice, Washington, D.C.: U.S. Department of Justice.

Baerand, J. and J. Booher. 1994. The patch: A new alternative for drug testing in the criminal justice system. *Federal Probation*. 58:29-33.

Barton, A. 1999. Breaking the crime/drugs cycle: The birth of a new approach? *The Howard Journal*. 38:144-157.

Burnett, M. 1979. Understanding and Overcoming Addictions. In S. Eisenberg and L. Patterson, eds. *Helping Clients with Special Concerns*. Chicago: Rand McNally.

Chein, I., G. Gerhard, R. Lee, and E. Rosenfeld. 1964. *The Road to Narcotics, Delinquency and Social Policy*. New York: Basic Books.

DuPont, R. 1997. *The Selfish Brain: Learning from Addiction*. Washington, D.C.: American Psychiatric Press.

Farabee, D., M. Pendergast, and M. Anglin. 1998. The effectiveness of coerced treatment for drug-abusing offenders. *Federal Probation*. 109:3-10.

Fishbein, D. 2000. Neuropsychological function, drug use, and violence. *Criminal Justice and Behavior*. 27:139-159.

Frawley, P. 1987. Neurobehavioral model of addiction. *The Journal of Drug Issues*. 17:29-46.

Gove, W. and C. Wilmoth. 1992. Risk, Crime, and Neurophysiologic Highs: A Consideration of Brain Processes that May Reinforce Delinquent and Criminal Behavior. In L. Ellis and H. Hoffman, eds. *Crime in Biological, Social, and Moral Contexts*. Westport, Connecticut: Praeger.

Grabowski, J. 1984. *Cocaine: Pharmacology, Effects and Treatment of Abuse*. Washington, D.C.: National Institute of Drug Abuse.

Holden, C. 1989. Street-wise crack research. *Science*. 246:1376-1381.

Hooper, R., D. Lockwood, and J. Inciardi. 1993. Treatment techniques in corrections-based therapeutic communities. *The Prison Journal*. 73:290-306.

Kaplan, J. 1991. Heroin. *National Institute of Justice Crime File* (NCJ # 97225). Washington, D.C.: U.S. Department of Justice.

Leshner, A. 1998. Addiction is a brain disease—and it matters. *National Institute of Justice Journal*. 237:2-6.

Lightfoot, L. 1999. Treating Substance Abuse and Dependence in Offenders: A Review of Methods and Outcomes. In E. Latessa, ed. *Strategic Solutions: The International Community Corrections Association Examines Substance Abuse.* Lanham, Maryland: American Correctional Association.

Ling, W., D. Wesson, C. Charuvastra, and J. Klett. 1996. A controlled trial comparing buprenorphine and methadone maintenance in opioid dependance. *Archives of General Psychiatry.* 53:401-407.

Marlatt, G., J. Baer, D. Donovan, and D. Kivlanhan. 1989. Addictive behaviors: Etiology and treatment. *Annual Review of Psychology.* 39:223-252.

McBride, D. and C. McCoy. 1993. The drugs-crime relationship: An analytical framework. *The Prison Journal.* 73:257-278.

Narcotics Control Technical Assistance Program. 1990. Future Drug Testing Kits. *NCTAP News.* October. 4:1.

National Institute of Justice. 1991. *Annual Report on Adult Arrestees: Drugs and Crime in America's Cities.* Washington, D.C.: U.S. Department of Justice.

_____. 2000. 1999 *Annual Report on Drug Use Among Adult and Juvenile Arrestees.* Washington, D.C.: United States Department of Justice.

Nugent, E. 1990a. *Ice:* The New Cold War. *NCTAP News.* January. 3:1-4.

_____. 1990b. Pharmacotherapy. *NCTAP News.* April. 3:6-7.

Oliveto, A., A. Feingold, R. Schottenfeld, P. Jatlow, and T. Kosten. 1999. Desipramine in opioid-dependent cocaine abusers maintained on buprenorphine vs methadone. *Archives of General Psychiatry.* 56:812-820.

Parks, G. and G. Marlatt. 1999. Keeping "What Works" Working: Cognitive-Behavioral Relapse Prevention Therapy with Substance Abusing Offenders. In E. Latessa, ed. *Strategic Solutions: The International Community Corrections Association Examines Substance Abuse.* Lanham, Maryland: American Correctional Association.

Peel, S. 1978. Addiction: The analgesic experience. *Human Nature.* 1:61-66.

Pinel, J. 2000. *Biopsychology, 4th edition.* Boston: Allyn and Bacon.

Read, E. 1992. Euphoria on the rocks: Understanding crack addiction. *Federal Probation.* 56:3-11.

_____. 1996. *Partners in Change: The 12-Step Referral Handbook for Probation, Parole and Community Corrections.* Lanham, Maryland: American Correctional Association and Hazelden Foundation.

Simpson, D., G. Joe, B. Fletcher, R. Hubbard, and D. Anglin. 1999. A National Evaluation of Treatment Outcomes for Cocaine Dependence. *Archives of General Psychiatry.* 56:505-514.

Speckart, G., M. Anglin, and E. Deschenes. 1989. Modeling the longitudinal impact of legal sanctions on narcotics use and property crime. *Journal of Quantitative Criminology.* 5:33-56.

U.S. Department of Justice. 1999. *Annual Report of Drug Use Among Adult and Juvenile Arrestees.* Washington, D.C.: Bureau of Justice Statistics.

_____. 2000. 1999 *Violent Crime in the United States.* Washington, D.C.: Bureau of Justice Statistics.

Visher, C. 1990. Incorporating drug treatment in criminal sanctions. *NIJ Reports.* Summer, 1-7.

Vito, G. 1999. What Works in Drug Testing and Monitoring. In E. Latessa, ed. *Strategic Solutions: The International Community Corrections Association Examines Substance Abuse.* Lanham, Maryland: American Correctional Association.

Walker, S. 2001. *Sense and Nonsense about Crime and Drugs.* Belmont, California: Wadsworth.

Walsh, A. 1995. Parental attachment, drug use, and facultative sexual strategies. *Social Biology.* 42:95-107.

Weeks, J., A. Moser, and C. Langevin. 1999. Assessing Substance-Abusing Offenders for Treatment. In E. Latessa, ed. *Strategic Solutions: The International Community Corrections Association Examines Substance Abuse.* Lanham, Maryland: American Correctional Association.

Witkin, G. 1998. The crime bust. *U.S. News and World Report.* May 25.

Chapter 17

The Sex Offender

Sex offenders had better not be viewed as horrible, villainous criminals who have to be harshly punished. . . . They can, rather, be diagnosed either as relatively healthy individuals who are rash enough to get into occasional difficulty, or a more seriously disturbed person whose sexual behavior puts them in frequent conflict with the law.

Albert Ellis

Sex and American Society

Sexual offenses encompass such a wide range of behaviors that you reasonably may question the wisdom of placing all of them in a single category. After all, the exhibitionist is as different from the rapist as the check forger is from the armed robber. If you live in a state that has antisodomy laws, and many states still do, you might even be guilty of felonious behavior for which you could be imprisoned if you engage in oral or anal sex (in some states, with a member of either sex), even with your consenting spouse. However, we will be concerned just with those sexual offenses that involve a true offender/victim relationship, such as rape and child molesting; that is, behavior that almost universally is considered to be a serious breach of lawful behavior rather than relatively mild deviations from sanctioned behavior.

The sex offender and his (sex offenders are almost invariably male) behavior have to be viewed in the context of his culture. Few things interest Americans more than sex. Our culture is shot through with sexual themes. Billions of dollars are spent every year on cosmetics, hairstyling, breath mints, health spas, and so forth, to make us appear sexually attractive. Ears are pierced, lips painted, underarms sprayed, necklines lowered, and skirts raised, and young men advertise their wares by pouring their salon-tanned limbs into shrunken jeans. Goaded on by the wizards of Madison Avenue, many of us have fallen prey to the notion that we are less than good Americans if we are not supremely sexual beings.

Counteracting this pressure toward sexual expression is the highly puritanical strain that exists in American culture. The sensitivity of the American legal system to sexual behavior, extending even into the marital bed, is made evident by Robertson (1987:251): "The laws [pertaining to sex] have few parallels in the modern world outside of the Soviet Union and some of its satellites. Western European nations have generally abandoned similar legislation, in some cases as long as a century ago." Thus, Americans are simultaneously pushed toward sexual expression by a permissively erotic market and then pulled back again by a restrictive code of sexual morality. It is against this background that the sex offender is defined and punished.

The Public Image of the Sex Offender

We Americans do not like sex offenders. They are the only group of offenders we keep in prison under indefinite civil commitment laws *after* they have completed their criminal sentences, a practice which was given the seal of approval by the U.S. Supreme Court in *Kansas v. Henrick*, (1997). Practices such as this, as well as notification and registration laws, set sex offenders apart from other offenders. As a society, we appear to be convinced that the sex criminal is a brutally depraved and oversexed monster who spends his time haunting dirty movies and teenage hangouts; an incurable, spiritually disfigured "dirty old man." He is a "species apart," either a "super male" in an interminable state of tumescence or a pathetic and evil old man searching for sparks of sensuality in the unwilling arms of a child. Although such characteristics are sometimes true, the criminal justice worker must not harbor such stereotypes.

No common denominator distinguishes all sex offenders. Unlike the typical robber or burglar, sex offenders are businessmen, physicians, teachers, attorneys, police officers, and ministers, as well as unskilled laborers and "street people." In terms of their crimes, a sex offender can be everything from a sexual sadist who uses his penis to defile and degrade his victim to the gentle and unassuming church deacon who "playfully" touches a neighborhood child where he should not. There are certainly differences between the sex offender whose passion for his new date exceeds her expectations and the rapist who attacks with equal intensity the nubile homecoming queen and the octogenarian cripple—differences that will affect your recommendations and treatment strategies. Likewise, there is the father who feels that he has the lordly "right of the first night" with a succession of his offspring versus the father who offends once and is then mortified by what he has done.

Rape and Rapists *rape decreasing*

Forcible rape is defined in the Federal Bureau of Investigation's Uniform Crime Reports (UCR) as: "the carnal knowledge of a female forcibly and against her will" (Federal Bureau of Investigation, 1999:23). According to this report, there were 93,103 reported rapes in 1998, a 12.5 decrease from the 102,096 reported in 1994. Even though rape rates have been decreasing steadily since 1990, rape is still perhaps the most underreported of all crimes, probably because of the fear and embarrassment suffered by its victims. Indeed, the National Crime Victimization Survey (NCVS) for the same year showed 333,000 reported rapes (U.S. Department of Justice, 1999). In other words, the NCVS data show more than three-and-one-half times the number of rapes than the

NCVS shows more rapes

UCR. No doubt that rape is an excruciatingly traumatic event for its victims, the effects of which may last long after any physical scars have healed. This can be true even if the perpetrator is known to the victim as an acquaintance, boyfriend, date, or even as a spouse.

The views of the rapist in professional literature run the gamut, with many of the opinions being strongly colored by such nonobjective factors as personal morality and sexual politics. Each view, of course, fits some rapists, but no view fits all rapists. There are those who regard rape as being symptomatic of some dark psychological disturbances and others who see it simply as part of a complex of cultural values that emphasize macho masculinity, power, aggression, and violence. The first of these views is exemplified by the work of Drzasga,who explains rape as an act performed by "degenerate male imbeciles" seeking to satisfy "sadistic and aggressive desires for sexual dominance" (1960:57). In this perspective, rape is a violent rather than a sexual act in which the penis is substituted for the gun or knife. This view may be accurate in some unknown percentage of rape cases, but to ascribe such motivations across the board is to commit what philosophers call the logical fallacy of *affirming the consequent*. Affirming the consequent means that having observed the consequences of an action, we infer that they were the motivations of the actor. Thus, we observe that the rapist asserts his dominance over his victim and in doing so humiliates, defiles, and degrades her. It is unwarranted, however, to assume that this outcome necessarily constituted his motivations for his crime.

The common assertion that "there is nothing sexual about rape" may be politically correct, but it ignores the fact that if intercourse were accomplished, the sexual component of the act is the only one of which we can be sure—everything else is conjecture. We have no direct access to a rapist's motivations beyond the sexual. Many imprisoned rapists eventually will convince a counselor that their motivations were to degrade and defile their victims. But do they do this because those were indeed their motivations, or do they do it because they have learned that the way to obtain parole points is to tell officials what they think officials want to hear? "Confess your crime, confront your crime, understand the motives for your crime, and show remorse for your crime." These are the conditions of the parole game that inmates soon learn. Is it really only coincidence that sophisticated criminals always seem to explain their behavior in accordance with the contemporary academic explanation?

While it is true that the feminist perspective generally has rejected the idea of sexual motivation for rape, some feminists now recognize the sexual motivation for rape, claiming that the "not sex" argument was initially necessary to emphasize that women got no pleasure out of being raped (Gilmartin, 1994; Herman, 1990). Very few American females (about 18 percent) and even fewer males (about 9 percent) believe that rape is committed because of nonsexual motives such at hatred and anger (Hall, 1987).

Finally, the clinical perspective (the perspective of those engaged in the assessment and treatment of rapists) remains tied to the notion that rape is primarily sexually motivated (Barbaree and Marshall, 1991). Science rather than sexual politics should be the guide to the "true" nature of this horrible crime. In a plea to depoliticize rape, Craig Palmer asserts that the "not sex" explanation prevents researchers from learning more about the phenomenon of rape, and this occurs "at the expense of an increased number of rape victims" (1994:59). Palmer's point is that if we misidentify the motives of rapists, we compromise treatment plans for the rapist as well as efforts at rape prevention. This is what should concern us most as corrections workers.

Operant behavior If you do something & get what you want then will try it again

Lee Ellis supplies voluminous evidence to support his contention, that rape is "sexually motivated, and that aggressiveness and dominating behavior exhibited by rapists largely reflect tactics rather than goals" (1991:632). However, he agrees that the drive to possess and control is a motive, although it is secondary to the sex drive. He states that in the overwhelming majority of acquaintance rapes, force is used only after other tactics (pleading, use of alcohol, claims of love) have failed, making it difficult to claim that rape is "nonsexual." He also points out that rape exists in a number of non-human animal species, making it difficult to claim that similar behavior in human males is motivated by hatred of females, or is the result of socialization.

While Ellis claims that the *motivation* for rape is unlearned (the sex drive and the drive to possess and control are considered the products of evolutionary selection forces), the specific behavior surrounding it is learned. The mechanisms he proposes are not cultural modeling, but rather those of operant conditioning. The raw basics of operant conditioning boil down to stating that behavior that is rewarded tends to be repeated, and punished behavior tends to become extinguished. He contends that males who have successfully employed "pushy" tactics to gain sexual favors have been reinforced in that behavior. The early reinforcements may have been little more than a necking or petting session, but if he learns that each time he escalates his pushiness that he gains greater sexual access, his behavior gradually will be shaped in ways that eventually could lead to rape.

Thus, it appears that the majority of rapes are motivated by misdirected and misguided sexual desires rather than by dark, sadistic, and disturbed psychological motivations far removed from sex. It is readily granted, however, that male dominance feelings are an integral part of sexual relations, whether consensual or otherwise. Perhaps rape is best viewed as a fusion of sex and aggression because both sexual and aggressive behavior appear to be mediated by the same neurological substrates, and both are facilitated/activated by the same sex steroids (Marshall and Barbaree, 1990). As a corrections worker, you will be doing offenders a disservice if you succumb uncritically to pat interpretations that sound esoteric but may well be empty. Perhaps the best way to view someone accused of rape is suggested by Albert Ellis (1986) in the epigraph to this chapter; that is, unless there is evidence to the contrary, he should be viewed as a relatively psychologically healthy individual who has committed a very odious crime.

The other dominant interpretation of rape, more sociological in orientation, is the view that rapists are simply following learned cultural behavior. Although rape is "socially regarded as intolerable, it has its origins in approved patterns of interaction between the sexes" (Robertson, 1987:259). Others view rape as indicative of a general hatred of women that characterizes the behavior of "normal" adult men (Clark and Lewis, 1977:140). This is a gratuitously harsh view of all men, and one that sees rape as an unfortunate manifestation of a general principle defining the relationship between the sexes. It is, furthermore, contradicted by the ethnographic record that indicates that "rape is universally discouraged by moral traditions" (Thornhill and Palmer, 2000:173).

In this author's experience working with rapists, he learned that most rapes involve offenders and victims who are acquainted with one another. Many men who are convicted of rape under these circumstances are enamored of traditional masculine values. They value sexual prowess and tend to hold the "whore/madonna" image of women. They have difficulty understanding how their victims could be so ungrateful as to accuse them of rape. They feel that once a woman's initial protestations are overcome in a forceful "masculine" way, just like the romantic heroes in the movies, then she should just melt into their arms. After all, in the world of veiled sexual messages it is "common knowledge" to them that "no" really means "yes."

Here is an excerpt from a presentence investigation report in which the processing officer is commenting on the statement of a defendant convicted of raping his sister-in-law. This defendant came home drunk one night (rape is often associated with alcohol), dragged his seventeen-year-old sister-in-law into his bedroom, told his sleeping wife to get up and get out, and proceeded to rape her sister:

It is clear from the defendant's explicit statement that he does not deny the charge.

On the contrary, one almost gets the impression that he rather enjoyed writing his statement, which depicts him as an accomplished lover and mentor to the sexually naive. "How can this be rape?" he asks in an aggrieved tone of voice. He believes that his amorous designs were pursued fully in accord with the rules of the game; i.e., in the"masculine" way of his subculture. For him the crime was little more than an "assault with a friendly weapon." It strains this officer's imagination to think of the defendant as venting his sexual passions on an unwilling girl whose mother was in the next room fully aware of what was going on. Not only that, he had the audacity to ask his wife to vacate her bed so that he could do his thing in comfort.

Rapists such as this young man use aggression as a means to an end, not as an end in itself. Many of them might not have gone on to complete the act if they did not harbor stereotypes of women as sexual playthings who "really" want to "be taken," even if they do put up a little token resistance. Many date rapes and acquaintance rapes would not occur if males who engage in this kind of behavior rid themselves of such stereotypes. Females also would do well to divest themselves of their own stereotypes of femininity. Talking to many victims of date and acquaintance rape often reveals that they tend to be passive, nonassertive types with traditional views of the relationship between the sexes. Counselors at rape crisis centers frequently will state that many rapes can be avoided if women forcefully assert their rights to their own bodies.

There are rapists who do become more sexually aroused when victims fight back, and may even be impotent without such stimuli. They may prefer violent to consensual sex, and their primary motive may well be to defile and humiliate. Such rapes tend to be stranger rapes and are thus more terrifying and physically injurious to the victim. Rapists of this type tend to have marked feelings of inadequacy and inferiority and powerlessness, and tend to be highly sexed and socially inadequate (Ellis, 1991). Unlike the typical date or acquaintance rapist, stranger rapists tend to have histories of other violent crimes (Adler, 1984).

Most studies of rapists concentrate on the violent rapist. We do know with relative certainty that among these subjects violence is an important component of the sexual excitement they obtain from their crimes in much the same way that whips and other devices arouse masochists and sadists, and enemas arouse klismaniacs. This pattern of preferential violence is determined by comparing penile responses of convicted rapists with those of nonrapists when exposed to sexual stimuli with a strong violence content. Penile response is measured by a device called a penile plethysmograph, which is rather like a blood pressure gauge. The penile plethysmograph measures the pressure of blood in the penis to ascertain how sexually excited subjects become when exposed to auditory and/or visual stimuli depicting various sexual situations. Violent rapists become significantly more aroused than nonrapists or nonviolent rapists when exposed to this material (Barbaree, Marshall, and Lantheir, 1979; Quinsey and Chaplin, 1982).

Most men will show some penile response to a variety of sexual stimuli, especially novel stimuli, even if they consider it deviant and would not engage in such behavior. The value of the penile plethysmograph lies not only in comparing the responses of convicted rapists with those of "normal" males, but also in comparing rapists' penile responses to stimuli depicting violent sex to their responses to stimuli depicting nonviolent consensual sex. For instance, if a rapist achieves a 30 percent erection when viewing nonviolent sex and one of 80 percent when viewing violent sex, we can conclude both that he is more interested in violent than consensual sex and that he is probably a dangerous individual. Likewise, if a man has a 90 percent erection in response to sexual stimuli involving young boys and one of only 5 percent to stimuli involving adult females, we can conclude that he is a homosexual pedophile—the penis, unlike its owner, finds it difficult to lie (Earls and Proulx, 1987).

Such findings do seem to indicate that the violent rapist is "sick" in that he apparently needs violence to complete the sexual act. Strangely enough, rape is not listed as a sexual deviation in the *Diagnostic and Statistical Manual of Mental Disorders*, fourth edition (DSM-IV) of the American Psychiatric Association (APA). The American Psychiatric Association apparently does not see any clearly defined syndrome associated with rape that could be called "rapism" in the same way that they identify conditions like exhibitionism and pedophilia. Violent rapists simply may be violent men who take what they want, whether it be money or sex. Their sexual offenses appear to be part of a pattern of violent criminality. However, the criminal justice worker's primary concern should be the safety of the public. Accordingly, individuals who exhibit patterns of violent behavior should be placed in custodial care for as long as the law allows.

A STATISTICAL LOOK AT STRANGER VERSUS DATE/ACQUAINTANCE RAPE

Data on sex offenders reveal some remarkable differences between stranger and date/acquaintance rape that suggest that these offenses generally are committed by quite psychologically different men (Walsh, 1983). Victims of stranger rape were significantly older, ranging in age from fifteen to seventy-one. The age range of victims of date/acquaintance rape was much smaller (fourteen through forty-four), as would be expected in a dating context. Stranger rapists had significantly more serious criminal histories, were of significantly lower class, and were significantly younger (an average of twenty-two years versus an average of thirty-one). Eighty percent of the victims of stranger rape were physically harmed, as opposed to 33.3 percent of the date/acquaintance category; 73 percent used some kind of weapon, as opposed to 21 percent of the others, and 66.7 percent were drug and/or alcohol addicts, as opposed to 12 percent of the others. Like other such studies, these data emphasize the qualitative differences that can exist among acts of rape and its perpetrators.

Unlike stranger rape, which almost by definition involves the perpetrator's expectation of violence, as previously noted, in most instances of date rape, force is used only after various other nonviolent tactics have been tried (Koss and Leonard, 1984; Ellis, 1991). Of course, this data should not be construed as minimizing date rape. All forms of rape psychologically injure the victim, regardless of whether or not physical injuries were sustained.

ASSESSMENT AND TREATMENT OF RAPISTS

Public outrage at rapists and child molesters has made the idea of treatment rather than administration of swift punishment for sex offenders a very unpopular idea. However, Gendreau and Ross (1987) point out that the realization that most incarcerated sex offenders eventually will be released has generated a demand for treatment to insure a successful reintegration into the community. From their review of a number of studies dealing with sex offender treatment programs, Gendreau and Ross (1987) are cautiously optimistic. Most studies did report a gratifying rate of success when comparing results from treated and untreated offenders. Although none of these studies dealt with the violent rapist, the general impression gleaned from their totality is that incest and heterosexual child molesters showed the most treatment success, and homosexual child molesters performed worst (Gendreau and Ross, 1987).

A recent review of 12 meta-analyses (a meta-analysis is an examination of a large number of studies of the same type to gain an overall impression) covering a total of 356 different studies found that 9 of the meta-analyses were positive (treatment "works"), 3 were inconclusive, but none were negative (Lotke, 1996:2). A more recent review of 79 studies with a total of 10,988 sex offenders found an overall recidivism rate of 13 percent among treated offenders compared to 18 percent for untreated offenders (Alexander, 1999). Recidivism was defined as rearrest for a sexual offense. While this percentage difference does not seem much, it still represents a lot of women and children who remained unvictimized.

The assessment and treatment of sexual offenders almost always is conducted by mental health teams. If the sentencing judge feels that an offender's crime or his record of sexual offenses warrant it, he will be referred to a diagnostic center, or to individual psychologists or psychiatrists in communities lacking such a specialized center. Typically, the offender is administered a series of tests such as the MMPI, and an IQ test, and he undergoes a series of psychosocial interviews. The judge and the PSI investigator are provided with the results of these tests, a diagnosis, treatment prognosis, and a sentencing recommendation. A recent study suggests that the diagnosis tends to be a reflection of behavior (such as a nonviolent child molester labeled as a "passive-aggressive pedophile"), and the prognosis and sentencing recommendation are entirely a function of the severity of the offense and of the offender's criminal history (Walsh, 1990).

Treatment for the violent rapist is extremely difficult and the results discouraging. Alexander's (1999) study cited above found a recidivism rate of 20.1 percent for treated rapists compared to 23.7 percent for untreated rapists. These rates went up to 29.3 percent after five years for treated offenders (no data was available for untreated offenders). Many treatments such as aversive conditioning (a method of treatment by which an offender is shown sexually arousing pictures in conjunction with some sort of punishing stimuli, such as an electric shock or some foul-smelling substance) have been drastically curtailed in the United States because of civil rights considerations (Marsh and Walsh, 1995).

Therapeutic castration appears to be the most effective form of treatment. A review of European literature involving 2,055 sex-offending castrates followed over periods of time as long as 20 years found extremely low recidivism rates ranging from 0 to 7.4 percent (Bradford, 1990). As we have seen, studies of violent rapists in the United States show that they have much higher rates of known recidivism regardless of whether treated (with methods other than surgical or drug intervention) or not

andocre — blocks receptors *Better than "Depo"*
Depro — Provera — *Problem → side effects*

(Alexander, 1999). The castration research offers strong support for those who favor theories of rape that emphasize hormonal factors (coupled with inadequate socialization) in the etiology of rape, such as Ellis (1991). Although surgical castration has been tried in the United States, it has been discontinued for civil rights reasons.

It remains to be seen how the courts ultimately will view chemical castration by the use of drugs such as medroxyprogesterone (Depo-Provera) or cyproterone acetate (Andocur) of offenders with excessive sex drives that place them at risk for reoffending. Depo-Provera reduces libido by drastically reducing testicular production of testosterone, and Andocur does the same thing by blocking testosterone receptors (Emory, Cole and Meyer, 1992). Such drugs have been called "limbic-hypothalamic tranquilizers" because they "allow the offender to concentrate on his psychosocial problems without the distracting fantasies and urges accompanying androgen-driven limbic-hypothalamic activity" (Marsh and Walsh, 1995:87).

In other words, these drugs reduce the level of the male sex hormone testosterone, which leads to a diminution of arousal or responsiveness to sexuality and violence. With the activity of the more primitive brain area (the limbic system) dampened, the counselor can concentrate on combating neocortical weaknesses ("thinking errors"). We should note that castration does not eliminate the sex drive, and that a castrate can become aroused with a willing partner's patient stimulation. What is greatly reduced is a sex offender's excessive and compulsive desires. Chemical castration was mandated into law in California in 1997, and several other states have initiated similar measures (Schmalleger, 2001). However, the constitutionality of such measures has yet to be fully tested in the courts.

Whereas the convicted violent rapist nearly always is incarcerated, the date or acquaintance rapist tends to get probation more often than imprisonment. The treatment of the latter type of rapist while on probation should center around group counseling sessions to correct "thinking errors" in which stereotypical images of women are brought out into the open and discussed. Educating males to accept women as equals who have the right to say "no" can go a long way toward preventing a reoccurrence. As we have seen, it is a sad fact that many men do actually believe that women "ask for it" if they accept a date or willingly engage in any physical behavior. Egocentric thinking (believing that everyone thinks as we do) leads some men to the conclusion that, "Hey, I'm aroused and ready to go so she must be, too." The kind of men who tend to believe these things and to commit date rape are masculine males in the traditional "macho" sense of the word (Bernard et al., 1985)—"Real men don't take no for an answer." Given this, the probation officer also should consider thinking errors as they relate to the date rapist's conceptions of what a "real man" is. The questioning and challenging techniques of Rational Emotive Behavior Therapy (REBT) and a healthy dose of bibliotherapy (both discussed in Chapter 11) should prove useful in this regard.

Exercises such as the one concerning the victim experience in the chapter on institutional counseling can be used fruitfully here. Movies can be shown that reveal the psychological trauma that accompanies rape. In the spirit of restorative justice, it is better yet to have a rape victim speak to the group about her experience and about how it affected her life. Select the victim carefully, however. You do not want a victim who spouts trendy sexual politics and who defines rape as everything from violent sexual assault to sexual innuendo and jokes. Nor do you want one who flays the group and denigrates all men because of her experience. Although such a response from a victim is quite understandable, the group will act defensively against her and refuse to take her seriously. If this does become the group's reaction, the whole exercise probably will have done more harm than good. Local rape crisis centers usually have a number of strong victims willing to talk to various groups about their experiences in a dispassionate way. Needless to say, if alcohol were involved in the incident, attention to that problem area also should be part of the offender's treatment.

CHILD MOLESTERS

A *child molester* is a person (overwhelmingly a male) who uses children to gratify his sexual urges. A child molester may or may not be a true pedophile (a person who is literally a "lover of children"). Most individuals convicted of molesting children apparently prefer adult sex but have opportunistically taken advantage of a child, but pedophiles are preferentially sexually attracted to children, sometimes exclusively (Langevin, 1990). Some child molesters are offenders who take advantage of any form of sexual gratification immediately available to them, regardless of age, sex, or even at times, of species. Child molestation tends to be associated with three age categories: the teen years, the mid to late thirties, and the mid fifties and older.

Teenage molesters tend to be socially withdrawn and of lower intelligence than the average teenager. Intercourse is rarely attempted by these young molesters. Sexual activity tends to take the form of kissing and the manual manipulation of the genitals. The victim most often is known to the offender, and the act can be viewed as a form of sexual curiosity on the part of a teenager who is too self-effacing to attempt to satisfy it with consenting persons of his own age.

Those offenders in their mid to late thirties are more likely than not to be married. Quite often the victim is a stepchild of the offender. Having a stepfather is the strongest single predictor of sexual abuse for girls, and the greatest predictor for boys is living in a father-absent home (Glaser and Frosh, 1993). Not infrequently, the molestation can go on for quite some time. The offender usually is able to maintain the ongoing "relationship" by telling his victim that the child's mother would get mad if she found out, or that the child probably would be placed in a juvenile detention center or a foster home if the offense became known. The initial act of molestation is likely to occur when the offender finds himself unemployed for an extended period of time, has been drinking, or finds that his normal sex life has soured. One study of child molesters found that 34.3 percent of them were unemployed at the time of their offense (Walsh, 1994). This is about five times the average unemployment rate for males over a six-year period in the jurisdiction from which the data were obtained.

The molester of fifty-five and older is usually a man without any prior contact with the law. He recently may have suffered the loss of his wife by death or divorce and finds himself quite lonely. It is extremely rare that such offenders will use any kind of force to gain compliance. They usually will use promises of rewards such as money or candy to persuade victims to do their bidding. As with teenage molesters, actual intercourse rarely figures in the sexual activity of this group. Also, they tend to be deeply ashamed and remorseful when their activity is discovered, and they are the least likely of all offenders to offend again.

Molesters who offend against male children tend more to be true pedophiles than are their heterosexual counterparts. Walsh (1994) found that 34.7 percent of the homosexual molesters were diagnosed as pedophiles, as opposed to 13.2 percent of the heterosexuals. They were also more likely to be strangers to their victims (26.5 percent, versus only 4.8 percent of the heterosexual offenders). On the one hand, homosexual offenders were much less likely (4.1 percent) to use force or the threat of force to gain compliance than were the heterosexuals (19.2 percent). On the other hand, they were more than twice as likely to have a prior conviction for molesting (49 percent versus 22.1 percent). However, in 21.6 percent of those prior molestations, the victims were females. It may be thus more accurate to call these men bisexual pedophiles.

Rapists Versus Child Molesters.

[handwritten: lower class] *[handwritten: higher class]*

According to Groth (1979), both rapists and child molesters are threatened by normal adult sexuality. The difference is that the rapist attacks the source of the threat and the child molester retreats from it by turning to safer substitutes (children). Many child molesters are shy and introverted and haunted by feelings of inadequacy, which may prevent them from interacting sexually with mature adults (Bartol, 1995). It is not unusual to see cases in which an offender carried on an affectionate "affair" with a child for long periods of time (Walsh, 1988). The emotional investment quite often appears to extend beyond sexuality. However misdirected the attachment, the child is valued as a person and a "lover." In contrast, the target for the rapist is just an object or symbol upon whose body he seeks to satisfy his selfish needs. It is rare that the child molester attempts sexual penetration, whereas such penetration, as the primordial symbol of conquest, is the ultimate aim of the rapist. Only 14 percent of the author's sample of child molesters vaginally or anally penetrated their victims, as opposed to 69 percent of the combined stranger and date/acquaintance rapists. Oral sex (61 percent) was the primary kind of sexual activity engaged in by the child molesters, with 25 percent having only manual sexual contact with their victims.

Among other interesting comparisons, the rapists had far more serious criminal histories despite being significantly younger (average age of twenty-eight versus an average of thirty-seven for the molesters). The child molesters were of significantly higher social class. Occupationally, molesters ranged from laborers to ministers and physicians. The rapists were almost all in lower-status occupations, if working at all. Seventy-two percent of the molesters had been married at some stage in their lives, with 42 percent being married at the time of their offenses. The identical marriage figures for the rapists were 58 and 30 percent, respectively. Ninety percent of the child molesters were related to or acquainted with their victims, as opposed to 61 percent of the rapists, and 63 percent had previous sexual contact with their victims, as opposed to 23.8 percent of the rapists. None of the molesters used a weapon; 30 percent of the rapists did.

Clearly, a sharp line divides the rapist from the child molester. Most child molesters, child rapists (strangers who attempt or accomplish genital intercourse) excepted, tend to have a strong stake in conformity. If the offense was not violent or if the offender has no previous record of similar behavior indicative of an abiding interest in children as sexual targets, he usually can be considered a good probation risk. But given the level of seriousness attached to this kind of behavior, it is imperative that a thorough investigation into the offender's background be conducted prior to making any recommendations to that effect. Needless to say, the findings and recommendations of mental health professionals should be read and considered very carefully.

[handwritten: homo - pedophile]

Assessment and Treatment of Child Molesters → good probation canada

One in three women and one in ten men claim to have been sexually assaulted by the age of thirteen by someone they know, and it has been estimated that 70 percent of prostitutes and 80 percent of female drug abusers were sexually abused by a family member (Rush, 1980:5). Although these figures are highly suspect because of the extremely variable way that "sexual assault" is defined in different studies, the problem of the sexual assault of children is still an urgent one.

Unfortunately, there is an aura of "nothing works" pessimism surrounding the treatment of child molesters. Laws mandating registration for convicted child molesters, and those requiring that neighbors be informed when a convicted child molester moves into a neighborhood, make it clear that, understandably, the public is more concerned with punishment and surveillance than with treatment. Most probation and parole officers have neither the time nor the training to counsel child molesters, and even those criminal justice workers whose exclusive role is counseling will find it difficult to treat them without more expert help. It therefore is necessary to gain some idea of the treatment modalities available for sex offenders in your community.

An excellent book on this topic written by two probation officers is available from the American Correctional Association: *Supervision of the Sex Offender* by Georgia Cummings and Maureen Buell (1997). Chapters concern the presentence investigation report, relapse prevention as a supervision strategy, tools for assessing compliance and control, sex-offender treatment, and others.

A variety of treatment modalities have been implemented by public and private agencies. According to Brecher (1978), those most frequently implemented rely almost exclusively on group therapy, interpersonal communication skills, and psychoeducational programs (such as social and self-control skills). The efficacy of such modalities in terms of recidivism rates has been questioned by a number of researchers (Romero and Williams, 1983) who have failed to find statistically significant differences in recidivism rates between sex offenders on probation who received treatment and a control groups of offenders who did not. This would seem to indicate that either the treatment modalities themselves are not successful, or else treatment had been initiated without a proper assessment of the condition to be treated. Psychometric assessment by itself has been shown to be of limited utility for the assessment, classification, and treatment of sexual offenders (Hall *et al.*, 1986; Hall and Proctor, 1987).

According to Greer and Stuart (1983) a "state of the art" sexual abuse treatment program would include tools for physiological assessment of sexual arousal patterns in addition to psychosocial assessment and treatment. Such tools are the penile plethysmograph and the polygraph. Several researchers have reported the superiority of penile tumescence measures to assess and classify sex offenders, as well as for a tool for treatment (Marshall and Christie, 1981; Avery-Clark and Laws, 1984). The rationale for the use of these tools is simple: any meaningful treatment must be preceded by an adequate assessment of an offender and his full and open disclosure of the nature and extent of his sexual proclivities.

As Lundell (1987:2) states: "All therapists concur that effective treatment only can begin when the full extent of the offender's history of sexual deviant behavior is known." Without polygraph information it is doubtful if the treatment providers will get this history. For instance, one study found that the number of victims admitted t

Hetro - one time offender least likely to offend.
Homo pedaphile hardest to control.

by child molesters increased from an average of 1.87 at the intake interview to 2.85 when required to take a polygraph (Lester and Hurst, 2000). A more dramatic discrepancy was found in a small unpublished study at a sex abuse clinic where this author is a consultant. This study found that molesters admitted to an average of 1.5 victims at intake, and 9.1 after polygraph confirmation.

Self-disclosure does not mean that if the offender discloses his sexual sins and peccadillos that he necessarily will benefit from the emotional "catharsis," although he may well do so. While it is axiomatic that the offender cannot be properly confronted (nor can he confront himself) until the full extent of his offending behavior is out in the open, other purposes are attached to the effort to elicit full disclosure. Additional victims who are identified through the disclosure process may be contacted and invited to come in for victim counseling. Many sexual abuse treatment centers consider the contacting of previously unknown victims to be a vital part of their mandate since it is well known that untreated victims are candidates for future psychological problems, including becoming offenders themselves (Smith and Monastersky, 1986; Walsh, 1988).

The SANE Therapeutic Program

This section briefly outlines one such "state of the art" treatment program known as SANE (Sexual Abuse Now Ended) that has gained national attention (Marsh and Walsh, 1995). SANE is a victim-oriented program based on the philosophy of "restitution therapy," a concept that falls under the umbrella of restorative justice. Treatment for the offender is regarded as a privilege and is designed to repair the damage done to the sexually abused victim in a "clarification" process. Clarification is the process by which the sex offender accepts and communicates to his victim his responsibility for his crime, thereby eliminating much of the shame and guilt experienced by victims of sexual abuse.

Through treatment of one-to-five years in duration, the offender is taught to restructure the thought processes that have allowed him to commit his crime, and to develop a genuine empathy for how his victim experienced his sexual abuse. Rational Emotive Behavior Therapy and group counseling are used to help offenders unlearn thinking errors and to acquire more appropriate thinking patterns.

The SANE program does not accept offenders who are violent, who show clear evidence of brain damage or psychosis, or who deny the charge against them. Because this is a confrontational program, it is of little use to confront offenders who deny the existence of anything to confront. Offenders who deny accusations of child molestation generally have higher recidivism rates than either treated or nontreated offenders who admit their offenses (Marshall and Barbaree, 1988).

Upon intake, the offender completes a demographic and sexual history questionnaire (augmented by his presentence investigation report), and is required to complete a battery of psychological tests. These tests are sent to one of SANE's consulting psychologists to determine diagnosis, amenability to treatment, appropriate treatment modality, and reoffending risk. Clinical staff then ascertain whether the offender has given his therapists a complete accounting of his sexual history. This process is facilitated by periodic polygraph assessments. The offender then must recognize and diminish his sexual arousal to deviant sexual activity as assessed through periodic penile plethysmograph testing, which should show a progressive decrease in penile blood volume when he is exposed to deviant sexual stimuli.

The offender is terminated from the program successfully only when he has (1) revealed all victims as indicated by passing his polygraph examinations, (2) when he has recognized and confronted his deviant arousal patterns revealed by plethysmograph tests, (3) his penile arousal to nondeviant sexual material is greater than it is to deviant sexual material, and (4) his therapist has determined that the offender has accepted his full responsibility for his actions and has made "emotional restitution" to his victim or victims.

Perspective from the Field:
SANE Solutions to Sexual Offending
By Kim Batt-Lincoln

Kim Batt-Lincoln has been program director of the SANE Solutions to Physical and Sexual Abuse program for the past seven years. She holds a master's degree in community counseling from the College of Idaho and is a Licensed Professional Counselor in the State of Idaho. Prior to working at the SANE program, Ms. Batt-Lincoln worked for the Idaho Department of Corrections as a presentence investigator, preparole instructor, and the coordinator of a women's program.

Our American society has a remarkable intolerance for sexual offenders as compared to other criminals. There appears to be a variety of reasons for this intolerance. First, the majority of Americans are uncomfortable broaching the topic of human sexuality in any form, whether healthy or unhealthy. In fact, as a result of our cultural mores, it would appear that most sexual experiences in our society are "shame based"; hence, the sexual offender becomes a perfect "dumping ground" for all the sexual shame we have stored up.

Second, victims of child sexual abuse can be severely traumatized. Sexual abuse is a major contributing factor to an array of other social problems, such as substance abuse, adult criminality, teen pregnancy, and serious mental disorders. The trauma created by child sexual abuse can be so terribly profound because it is about betrayal by the only person(s) a child can trust. The offender is most often a father, stepfather, brother, or other relative. Thus, we empathize with the fact that sexual abuse shatters a small child's perception that the world is a safe and secure place, sometimes forever. Sexual abuse offends a society whose heritage strongly supports family values.

Third, the popular media has contributed a great deal to our society's panacea for sex offending, best described by such clichés as "lock 'em up and throw away the key," and the other popular solution laughingly referred to as "shotgun therapy." Of course, the media only prints stories about the most heinous crimes of child sexual abuse. They portray all sex offenders as predatory pedophiles, lurking in the bushes, waiting to jump out and grab children and then proceeding to commit acts of sexual violence. Nothing could be further from the truth! During the author's seven years with the SANE program, only 10 to 15 percent of the referrals were pedophiles (offenders who prefer sex with children). The vast majority of sexual offenders are incredibly inadequate human beings with low self-esteem, few social skills, a fear of intimacy, and a lack of accurate information differentiating sex from love.

Lastly, previously inadequate therapeutic methods have lent credence to public opinion that "sex offenders aren't treatable." Ten-to-twenty years ago when we sent sex offenders to insight-oriented psychotherapy this, in fact, was the case—recidivism rates were just as high for treated as for untreated offenders. The profession of sex offender treatment, as endorsed by the Association for the Treatment of Sexual Abusers (ATSA) has evolved into a highly structured treatment modality involving cognitive restructuring, use of polygraph and penile plethysmograph as assessment instruments, aversive conditioning to reduce deviant arousal, and relapse prevention techniques. Research evaluations regarding the effectiveness of different therapies are fraught with methodological difficulties but are showing that sex offender treatment really does work over the long term.

If we as a society continue to react emotionally to the problem of child sexual abuse, we circumvent effective solutions to the problem. This author has made it her life's work to continue to fight the problem of sexual abuse in Idaho through education, counseling, and rationality; however, there remains much work to be done to combat society's punitive response to dealing with this problem. After all, most incarcerated offenders eventually get out of prison and live among us.

Perspective from the Field:
Sex-offender Treatment: An Inside View
By Raymond W. Schuenemann

Ray Schuenemann is a prison inmate serving a sixty-nine-year sentence in Arizona. An obsessive-compulsive neurosis stemming from childhood abuse was both the motivator for his adult offenses as well as the source of his lifelong successes. Active in high school sports and student government, he was a senior class officer. Within sixteen months of enlisting in the Marines, he was promoted to sergeant. He graduated summa cum laude from the University of Houston, is a licensed plumber in two states, and has held a Secret security clearance. His eight-year marriage was solemnized in the Salt Lake Temple and produced one son. He exposed himself compulsively from the age of four. Nine days after returning from Vietnam, he entered a woman's apartment for sex. A year later, he confessed this to authorities and was charged with burglary. He spent the next eight years (1971 to 1979) on Texas prison farms, followed by six months on parole. In 1987, at the age of thirty-eight, he was convicted of five sexual assaults, four attempts, and three related burglaries. The sixty-nine-year sentence was too long to allow him into treatment, but he cooperated by admitting to offenses for which others were doing time, and he was admitted into the Fairbanks program. He graduated from the Sex Offender Treatment Program in 1992 and is now serving the remainder of his sentence. He will be eighty-four years old when he gets out.

Fairbanks Correction Center's sex-offender treatment program combines education and therapy enabling men to grow from past conditioning to learn self-management. Core subjects, program format, and key features are described to inform the public, policymakers, victims, and prospective offenders about what goes on in a successful treatment program. Prior to the sex offender treatment program, I was skeptical about sex offender treatment which looked like a waste of time and money. Sex offenders were "other people" who deserved prison punishment to deter them from offending.

In truth, offenders grow only through education, with professional help in order to develop self-control. Each offender's personal motivation for offending must be diagnosed and specifically treated. Without professional help and deliberate social training, offenders have no chance of defying the laws of human behavior to miraculously change for the better. My gratitude for the sex-offender treatment program comes from perspectives denied to therapists because I know what it is like to be forcibly separated from family, to be an abused child, a perpetrator, and an adult living in either self-disgust or in prison. In healing, I also rely on my religious faith.

A sex crime is a symptom of a problem within a perpetrator. Sex itself is never the root cause. Offenses are the by-product of poor self-esteem, lack of social skills, faulty attitudes, childhood abuse, mental illness, misdirected legitimate needs, and causes generally summed up as inappropriate behavior connected to sex and aggression. Offenders are made, but fortunately they can be unmade with proper diagnosis and training.

The Fairbanks Correction Center's sex-offender treatment program is composed of four parts, three in-jail phases: I-beginner, II-intermediate, III-advanced, with phase IV being aftercare in the community for one year. The in-jail portion was designed to last eighteen months, six in each phase, but the few men who graduated generally needed two years or longer to complete all the requirements. In the fifteen-year history of the sex offender treatment program in Alaska, there only have been about fifty graduates from Phase III. It took me three years to graduate. Twenty-four hours a day, each offender lives under intense scrutiny by peers, therapists, and prison employees. Three years is comparable to the total actual number of months spent in high school, or in college gaining a bachelor's degree. Think of your growth and quantum leaps of development during those periods of your own life.

Core Subjects: Prison-based sex offender treatment programs in different states teach common fundamentals such as victim awareness, behavior patterns, examining unresolved childhood issues, relapse prevention, and thinking errors. Each core subject holds different value in treatment depending on what motivated an offender. The backbone of the Fairbanks Correction Center's sex offender treatment program was cognitive behavioral therapy concerning thinking errors, weekly homework, monthly presentations, and phase assignments. The premise underlying thinking errors is that behavior follows from thoughts; therefore, conscious thinking guides us to better choices. Each offender learns to recognize both his thought patterns and their consequences.

Victim awareness is a study of the harmful effects our behavior can have on others. People can be harmed physically, mentally, emotionally, spiritually, socially, and have their lives drastically altered. Rarely is harm intentional in sex offenses, but serious harm is almost always the outcome. This has to be brought to men's attention, and for this sensitivity to develop there are two prerequisites. First, a man has to recognize his own emotions and understand their function. Offenders are stunted emotionally, generally due to childhood abuse. Second, before a man can feel empathy for others, he has to feel sympathy for himself.

People are creatures of habit; our behavior follows cycles. Poor self-image leads to depression, withdrawal, acting out, guilt, pushing guilt away, false confidence, and another turn of the cycle. The sex-offender treatment program helps each man identify his pattern and then teaches him coping skills to get out of unhealthy spirals. Self-understanding was the goal, for as Carl Rogers said, "The degree of self-understanding is perhaps the most important factor in predicting the individual's behavior."

✗ Offenders are made by their childhood experiences. To some degree, all of us are products of a community. There are specific reasons why some abused children grow up to be offenders while others do not. Offenders learn a different code of right and wrong from what happened to them and what they saw modeled. It is okay for offenders to learn that they were victims and that they must take responsibility to counteract those adverse affects by wholesome, growth-developing self-management. These offenders have learned faulty attitudes that erroneously gave them permission to act-out. Some children are abused to such a degree that major mental illness is inflicted. In my case, treatment for an obsessive-compulsive disorder was essential for reformation.

Relapse prevention is an itemized plan for wholesome living. The plan reviews an offender's strengths and weaknesses, and then lists tempting situations which he must avoid. Allowing for mistakes (called "lapses"), the plan calls upon the offender's known coping skills to get him out of lapses so they do not escalate into a *relapse*, a law violation.

Program Format Sex-offender treatment program offenders are taught in more than one way. Repeated learning events reinforce the lessons. Offenders are organized into closed groups of ten, which meet for an hour, five days a week. Ten minutes at the beginning of each group session are allocated for "individual issues" in which men are called to task by their peers for any misconduct. With twenty group-working days per month, each member is responsible for two days of presentations on subjects assigned by a therapist. Day and night group members monitor other members' behavior throughout the institution.

Each month each of the three therapists holds a private office meeting with each offender. One-on-one sessions focus on any issue the therapist chooses. Therapists take time with each man to determine why he has gone wrong, and then tailor an individualized treatment plan, as well as talk about individual concerns. Meeting notes are kept in each offender's file.

Each individual must complete a daily treatment journal. Events, thoughts, and feelings of that day are recorded along with examinations of past trauma. This journal is a key to discovery, insight, and growth. Each month a therapist reviews the journals and writes comments and suggestions. Also for that phase, evaluations are done by group members, therapists, and the treatment team. Treatment team evaluators include the prison classification officer, a parole officer, and sometimes ranking correctional officers. Questions from these savvy average citizens reflect society's concerns. All aspects of the offender's life are subject to inquisitorial inspection.

Small groups of four to fifteen men convene on their own time in personal rooms, the dayroom, or classrooms, on weekends and evenings for further study including: human sexuality, goal imagery, childhood abuse, motivation, and gaps in the sex-offender treatment program itself. Leading a subgroup gives each Phase III client-facilitator the additional experience of mastering the subject, because nobody learns like the teacher.

The sex offender treatment program office is filled with pertinent reading material. Bibliotherapy is great for those men who can learn from self-help psychology books, including articles from victims. There are more texts and publications available from the staff psychologist.

Informal socialization is perhaps the most subtle and effective way of teaching prosocial behavior. Prison employees and therapists maintain wholesome living conditions in the wing where all 31 program participants live apart from the 200-man general population. This provides an oasis for repentance and rehabilitation, because each man adhered, more or less voluntarily, to the same values and goals and was committed to the same ways and means of achieving them. Everybody worked on everybody else to file off the rough edges. Conversations and publications were kept to wholesome standards, in contrast to elsewhere in prison.

Key Features Some features of sex offender treatment programs deserve specific recognition for their effectiveness. Upon entering the program each offender takes a psychological profile battery of tests. In Phase III, they retake the same battery to measure any improvement. Explaining your test results to the group is a two-day presentation, scheduled after privately reviewing the scores with a therapist.

Classes promoted by prison administrators dovetail with the sex-offender treatment program. Each support program teaches correct principles and gives offenders an opportunity to serve and to practice prosocial behavior. A list of supporting classes includes: drug and alcohol counseling, Adult Children of Alcoholics, alternatives to violence, the learning center, religious services, assertiveness training, institutional jobs, talking circle, craft shop, Jaycees, Veteran's Affairs workshops for war veterans and others suffering from posttraumatic stress disorder, peer group counseling, and others.

Some people learn the value of talking in their family. Others do not; it is not modeled for them. They learn to keep their mouths shut, to be secretive, or simply not to talk. Until a person learns how to actively listen and how to talk assertively, expressing true feelings, and verbally processing the day's events, he does not know how wonderful it is, how it paves the way for meeting daily needs. Legitimate emotional needs motivate every bit of human behavior. People sometimes resort to indirect means such as crime to meet their needs. Awareness of legitimate needs helps men to fulfill these needs directly through socially approved channels.

Those in sex-offender treatment programs must perform different behaviors and practice them in real situations such as using coping skills and being properly assertive in crises. Demonstrating change is a phase requirement judged by group members and therapists. This is not just an academic program; practical skills such as work responsibility and getting along well with others have to be proven over years. When I asked therapists if this treatment works, they gave me a printed article which said that our sex-offender treatment program was based on one in Oregon where the overall program effectiveness was 95 percent of the offenders were free of new sex crime convictions and 96 percent were free of any new felony.

Summary

Few criminal types arouse our passion for punishment more than the sex offender. Sex offenses are perhaps the most underreported of all major crimes, but we should not put all sex offenders into a common basket. The rapist differs dramatically from the child molester, and stranger rapists and acquaintance rapists also differ considerably. The majority of rapists appear to be traditional macho males who believe in the notion that "no" means "yes." They rarely respect women as autonomous human beings who have absolute rights to their own bodies. There are rapists (usually strangers to their victims) who appear to require violence and victim degradation for their perverted satisfaction–you will find this type of rapist to be rare in comparison with the acquaintance/date rapist.

Treatment of rapists in community corrections should center around discussions of sex roles, images of women, and the victim's experience. Usually, rapists who are imprisoned are those who are violent. Their treatment must be more intense and specialized, and, therefore, tends to be administered by psychiatrists and psychologists. Child molesters are, in the main, weak and lonely individuals. Only occasionally will you run into a true pedophile. Child molesters tend to be concentrated in three age categories: the teens, mid to late thirties, and the mid fifties and older. There are usually some special conditions contributing to child molestation, such as mental deficiency, unemployment, and loneliness. Just as there are some major demographic differences between acquaintance and stranger rapists, there are major differences between rapists and child molesters. The biggest differences are the average ages of the two groups and the rapists' greater propensity to use force.

The treatment of child molesters is best accomplished within specialized sex abuse clinics. One such program we examined uses physiological assessment tools—the penile plethysmograph and the polygraph—to assess, treat, and monitor the offender.

REFERENCES AND SUGGESTED READINGS

Adler, C. 1984. The convicted rapist: A sexual or a violent offender? *Criminal Justice and Behavior*. 11:157-177.

Alexander, M. 1999. Sexual offender treatment efficacy revisited. *Sexual Abuse: A Journal of Research and Treatment*. 11:101-116.

Avery-Clark, C. and D. Laws. 1984. Differential erection response patterns of sexual child abusers to stimuli describing activities with children. *Behavior Therapy*. 15:71-83.

Barbaree, H. and W. Marshall. 1991. The role of male sexual arousal in rape: Six models. *Journal of Consulting and Clinical Psychology*. 59:621-630.

Barbaree, H., W. Marshall, and R. Lanthier. 1979. Deviant sexual arousal in rapists. *Behavior Research and Therapy*. 17:215-222.

Bartol, C. 1995. Criminal Behavior: *A Psychosocial Approach, third edition.* Englewood Cliffs, New Jersey: Prentice Hall.

Bernard, J., S. Bernard, and M. Bernard. 1985. Courtship violence and sex-typing. *Family Relations*. 34:573-576.

Bradford, J. 1990. The Antiandrogen and Hormonal Treatment of Sex Offenders. In W. Marshall, D. Laws, and H. Barbaree, H., eds. *Handbook of Sexual Assault: Issues, Theories, and Treatment of the Offender*. New York: Plenum.

Brecher, E. 1978. *Treatment Programs for Sex Offenders*. Washington, D.C.: U.S. Government Printing Office.

Cummings, G. and M. Buell. 1997. *Supervision of the Sex Offender*. Safer Society Press. Available from the American Correctional Association, Lanham, Maryland.

Clark, L. and D. Lewis. 1977. *Rape: The Price of Coercive Sexuality*. Toronto: The Woman's Press.

Drzasga, J. 1960. *Sex Crimes*. Springfield, Illinois: Charles C. Thomas.

Earls, C. and J. Proulx. 1987. The differentiation of francophone rapists and non-rapists using penile circumferential measures. *Criminal Justice and Behavior*. 13: 419-429.

Ellis, A. 1986. The Sex Offender. In H. Toch, ed. *Psychology of Crime and Criminal Justice*. Prospect Heights, Illinois: Waveland Press.

Ellis, L. 1991. A synthesized (biosocial) theory of rape. *Journal of Consulting and Clinical Psychology*. 59:631-642.

Emory, L., C. Cole, and W. Meyer. 1992. The Texas experience with DepoProvera: 1980-1990. *Journal of Offender Rehabilitation*. 18:125-139

Federal Bureau of Investigation. 1999. 1999 *Uniform Crime Reports*. Washington, D.C.: U.S. Department of Justice.

Gendreau, P. and R. Ross. 1987. Revivification of rehabilitation: Evidence from the 1980s. *Justice Quarterly*. 4:349-406.

Gilmartin, P. 1994. *Rape, Incest, and Child Sexual Abuse: Consequences and Recovery*. New York: Garland.

Glaser, D. and S. Frosh. 1993. *Child Sex Abuse*. Toronto: University of Toronto Press.

Greer, J. and I. Stuart. 1983. *The Sexual Aggressor: Current Perspectives and Treatment*. New York: Van Nostrand Reinhold.

Groth, A. 1979. *Men Who Rape*. New York: Plenum.

Hall, E. 1987. Adolescents' perceptions of sexual assault. *Journal of Sex Education and Therapy*. 13:37-42.

Hall, G., R. Maiuro, P. Vitaliano, and W. Proctor. 1986. The utility of the MMPI with men who have sexually assaulted children. *Journal of Consulting and Clinical Psychology*. 54:493-496.

Hall, G. and W. Proctor. 1987. Criminological predictors of recidivism in a sexual offender population. *Journal of Consulting and Clinical Psychology*. 55:111-112.

Herman, J. 1990. Sex Offenders: A Feminist Perspective. In W. Marshall, D. Laws, and H. Barbaree, eds. *Handbook of Sexual Assault: Issues, Theories, and Treatment of the Offender*. New York: Plenum.

Kansas v. Hendricks 138 U.S. 521 (1997).

Koss, M. and K. Leonard. 1984. Sexually Aggressive Men: Empirical Findings and Theoretical Implications. In N. Malamuth and E. Donnerstein, eds. *Pornography and Sexual Aggression*. New York: Academic Press.

Langevin, R. 1990. Sexual Anomalies and the Brain. In W. Marshall, D. Laws, and H. Barbaree, eds. *Handbook of Sexual Assault: Issues, Theories, and Treatment of the Offender*. New York: Plenum.

Lester, D. and G. Hurst. 2000. Treating Sex Offenders. In P. Van Vooris, M. Braswell, and D. Lester, eds. *Correctional Counseling and Rehabilitation*. Cincinnati, Ohio: Anderson.

Lotke, E. 1996. Sex offenders: Can treatment work? *Corrections Compendium*. 21:1-3.

Lundell, R. 1987. The Utility of Polygraph Testing in the Treatment of Sex Offenders. Paper presented at the annual conference of the Association for the Behavioral Treatment of Sexual Abusers. Portland, Oregon.

Marsh, R. and A. Walsh. 1995. Physiological and psychosocial assessment and treatment of sex offenders: A comprehensive victim-oriented program. *Journal of Offender Rehabilitation*. 22:77-96.

Marshall, W. and H. Barbaree. 1988. The long-term evaluation of a behavioral treatment program for child molesters. *Behavior Research and Therapy*. 26:499-511.

_____. 1990. An Integrated Theory of the Etiology of Sexual Offending. In W. Marshall, D. Laws, and H. Barbaree, eds. *Handbook of Sexual Assault: Issues, Theories, and Treatment of the Offender*. New York: Plenum.

Marshall, W. and M. Christie. 1981. Pedophilia and aggression. *Criminal Justice and Behavior*. 8:145-158.

Palmer, C. 1994. Twelve Reasons Why Rape Is Not Sexually Motivated: A Skeptical Examination. In R. Francoeur, ed. *Taking Sides: Clashing Views on Controversial Issues in Human Sexuality.* Guilford, Connecticut: Dushkin.

Quinsey, V. and T. Chaplin. 1982. Penile responses to nonsexual violence. *Criminal Justice and Behavior.* 9:372-381.

Robertson, I. 1987. *Sociology.* New York: Worth.

Romero, J. and L. Williams. 1983. A Comparative Study of Group Psychotherapy and Intensive Probation Supervision with Sex Offenders. *Federal Probation.* 47:36-42.

Rush, S. 1980. *Best Kept Secrets.* New York: McGraw-Hill.

Schmalleger, F. 2001. *Criminal Justice Today, sixth ed.* Upper Saddle River, New Jersey: Prentice Hall.

Smith, W. and C. Monastersky. 1986. Assessing juvenile sexual offenders' risk for reoffending. *Criminal Justice and Behavior.* 13:115-140.

Thornhill, R. and C. Palmer. 2000. *A Natural History of Rape: Biological Bases of Sexual Coercion.* Cambridge, Massachusettes: MIT Press.

U.S. Department of Justice. 1999. *Criminal Victimization, 1998.* Washington, D.C.: Bureau of Justice Statistics.

Walsh, A. 1983. *Differential Sentencing Patterns Among Felony Sex Offenders and Non-Sex Offenders.* Ann Arbor, Michigan: University Microfilms International.

_____. 1988. Lessons and concerns from a case study of a "scientific molester." *Corrective and Social Psychiatry and Journal of Behavior Technology, Methods, and Therapy.* 34:18-23.

_____. 1990. Twice labeled: The effects of psychiatric labeling on the sentencing of sex offenders. *Social Problems.* 37:375-389.

_____. 1994. Homosexual and heterosexual child molestation: Case characteristics and sentencing differentials. *International Journal of Offender Therapy and Comparative Criminology.* 38:339-353.

Chapter 18

Mentally Ill and Mentally Deficient Offenders

Our task now is to begin to understand that the causes of mental health problems are as varied as their manifestations. Some are physical. Some are emotional. Some are rooted in social and environmental conditions. Most are a complex combination of these and other factors, some of which are unknown.

President's Commission on Mental Health

Mentally ill and mentally deficient offenders pose a particularly difficult set of challenges for the correctional worker. A survey of New York probation officers found that working with mentally ill and mentally deficient offenders presented them with their greatest difficulties (Wertlieb and Greenberg, 1989). For new correctional workers used to dealing with only "fully rational" people in their daily lives, their first acquaintance with mentally ill or deficient offenders comes as quite a shock. Nevertheless, they must be prepared to deal effectively with offenders who are especially ill-equipped to respond positively to their problems.

A 1999 Bureau of Justice study found that 16 percent of prison and jail inmates suffer some sort of mental illness, and that 547,800 mentally ill offender were on probation or parole (Ditton, 1999). These figures do not include mentally deficient (IQ of 70 or below) offenders, who are estimated to constitute 10 percent of prison populations (Schmalleger, 2001). Although no similar figures are available for the number of community corrections offenders who are mentally deficient, many are functioning at an intellectual level that makes them difficult and frustrating people with whom to work. To be forewarned is to be forearmed, so the more you learn about such offenders before meeting them the better prepared you will be. Some of you might even find

351

the challenge so interesting and rewarding that you might decide to specialize in this type of offender.

↳ Too much dopamine
SCHIZOPHRENICS *1 out of every 100 draws*

You will run into a variety of mentally ill offenders in corrections. Space limitations preclude any comprehensive treatment of mental illness, making it necessary to concentrate on the illness most associated with offending (psychopathy is not considered an illness since psychopaths are able to function well, if not morally, in society). According to Palermo, Gumz, and Liska (1992:55), schizophrenics probably account for more criminal offenses than all other mental patients combined. Thus, the discussion of mental illness is limited to this group.

In the early 1980s it was estimated that 170,000 schizophrenics lived at home with their families and that 120,000 were on the streets without any permanent home (Department of Health and Human Services, 1981:21-22). With an incidence of this magnitude, you can expect to have two or three offenders who have been diagnosed as schizophrenic on your caseload at any one time (schizophrenics commit crimes, too). With the increase in concern for patients' rights and the decarceration movement, the criminal justice system is absorbing much of the mentally ill population (Schmalleger, 2001).

Schizophrenics are extremely difficult to supervise in a community corrections setting, and they frequently end up seriously violating their conditions of probation or parole and being consigned to prison. Schizophrenics are not, however, a homogeneous category of individuals. There are various medically defined subtypes, which need not concern us here. The most severely impaired schizophrenics are hospitalized, so those with whom you may be dealing are able to function minimally outside a mental institution.

As well as being differentiated behaviorally and symptomatically, schizophrenics also may be differentiated by the pathway they took to their condition. The most serious form is *process schizophrenia*, a condition that develops insidiously over a long period of time. These are individuals whose histories show an early inability to function normally, to make friends, to handle school work, and to behave acceptably. The second type is *reactive schizophrenia*, sufferers of which may not have a history of psychological and social dysfunction. Their descent into schizophrenia is usually marked by the onset of an acutely stressful experience. Bill Bloggs was characterized in his psychological evaluation as "being in the early stage of reactive schizophrenia," a condition no doubt related to the stress of his arrest and incarceration (sometimes termed *jailhouse psychosis*). Research evidence bears out the proposition that being incarcerated, especially for the first time, can bring out symptoms of mental disorder not previously in evidence (Gibbs, 1987).

The "four A's" are used by mental health professionals to identify schizophrenia (American Psychiatric Association, 1994). These are *autism* (living in a subjective fantasy world), *ambivalence* (simultaneous conflicting feelings), inappropriate *affect* (emotions and feelings that are not congruent with the situation), and loose *associations* (the connection of an experience or idea with an unrelated experience or idea). Although schizophrenia most often is diagnosed long before an offender is seen by a community corrections worker, be on the lookout for evidence of any of these four A's. If you encounter them, make a referral to the local diagnostic and treatment center.

It is extremely difficult for the average person to have any idea what the schizophrenic experience is like. To obtain an inkling, think of the scariest and most vivid

Dopamine

C

dreams you have ever had. When we are in a dream state, our neurons are active making random connections (Peterson, 1997). These connections are not being made in response to external stimuli as they do when we are awake; since we are unconscious during sleep, there are none. The brain has an inherent need for structure, to make sense of the information coming into it from the outside in the form of electrochemical impulses. During sleep it does the best that it can to generate order from this chemical chaos by drawing on past experiences stored in its memory banks. But since the brain impulses are haphazard, darting from one memory to others that may be quite unrelated, the images they generate are less than coherent.

Both the dream and schizophrenic states are evoked from a very private reality, which may be scary and quite incoherent. The difference—and what a difference it is— is that when we dream, we wake up, are aware that we were dreaming, and begin to respond "normally" to stimuli from the outside world. Schizophrenics must remain in the scary and incoherent private world trying to make sense out of a neurochemical cascade that has little or no connection with external reality. In sum, schizophrenics have great difficulties in filtering information, and focusing their attention and responding appropriately to environmental stimuli (Pinel, 2000).

CAUSALITY

The causes of schizophrenia, and even its objective existence, long have been hotly debated. In this author's undergraduate days, radical environmentalists dismissed schizophrenia as a myth, or as a diagnostic "grab bag" used against poor people of whose behavior we disapproved. This viewpoint was radically wrong, for schizophrenia is an identifiable entity. The most compelling evidence comes from the radioisotope brain scans of positron emission tomography (PET). PET scans use computer imaging techniques similar to those of the more familiar CAT scans. Whereas CAT scans reveal information about brain structure, PET scans provide information about brain functioning. Injecting radioactive glucose isotopes reveals a biochemical map of neurometabolism as the glucose is converted into energy. This technique produces distinct neurological maps of normal, schizophrenic, and manic-depressive individuals (Pinel, 2000). These identifiable differences in brain functioning indicate an objective physical reality corresponding to the condition we call schizophrenia.

An earlier clue to the chemical basis for schizophrenia came with the advent of the antipsychotic drugs such as Haloperidol and Clozapine, which work by blocking the neurotransmitter dopamine at the synapse. All antipsychotic drugs are effective, but a number of patients are neurologically treatment-resistant (Hales, Yudofsky and Talbot, 1996). Clozapine works well in such cases but carries a significant risk of seizures (Hales, Yudofsky and Talbot, 1996).

A literature review of the various antipsychotic drugs concluded that they have differing effects on the various cognitive deficits suffered by schizophrenics, and thus medication should be specifically tailored to the severity of each individual's symptoms (Meltzer and McGurk, 1999). All antipsychotic drugs work more effectively for symptoms such as hallucinations, delusions, and incoherence, which represents increased neural activity, than for symptoms such as decreased neural activity, such as withdrawal, lack of warmth, and blunted emotions (Pinel, 2000).

Schizophrenia, viewed at the molecular level, seems to be a function of one of three possible conditions: (1) an excess of dopamine, (2) a deficiency of an enzyme called monoamine oxidase, which removes dopamine by oxidation after it has performed its excitatory function, or (3) an excess of dopamine receptors in the brain (Pinel, 2000). Any one of these conditions (or a combination of all three) would cause the hyperstimulation of the brain characteristic of schizophrenia. It also has been noted that high doses of amphetamines can produce symptoms mimicking psychosis by stimulating the secretion of dopamine (Pinel, 2000). If any offenders show schizophrenic symptoms, it may be a good idea to check his or her substance abuse history for excessive use of stimulants and hallucinogens.

Linking the schizophrenic syndrome to brain structure and functioning and genetic predisposition does not preclude strong environmental input. The 1995 *International Congress on Schizophrenia Research* summarized the past decade's research by concluding that "genetic factors determine predispositions to schizophrenia, but environmental factors are required for expression of the illness" (Buckley *et al.*, 1996:458). The genes with which we enter the world (genotype) interact with the environment to produce the organism we recognize as "me" (phenotype). Genes are not expressed in a vacuum; many require a particular environment in order to be expressed in the direction of their predisposition.

Regardless of genetic predisposition, schizophrenia occurs in the brain; and brain structure and function are particularly sensitive to input from the environment. One biologically oriented researcher, in stating that we must search for such environmental factors, further states that: "These factors are most likely found in the family and in the sociocultural environment in which the child becomes schizophrenic" (Freier, 1986:154). A commonly held developmental picture of schizophrenics found in study after study is that they tend to come from homes lacking in security and love, although such opinions regarding this form of supposed environmental causality are rarely found in schizophrenia literature today.

It very well may be that extreme adverse events experienced in early childhood change the physical structures of our pleasure and pain centers to determine thresholds for activation and shutdown (Perry and Pollard, 1998). Liebowitz (1983:46-47) is among those who think that limbic thresholds for pleasure and displeasure are determined by early experiences. If our early experiences were loving ones, our pleasure centers in the future will be activated easily. In contrast, "People in whom painful childhood experiences are constantly stirred up are experiencing bombardment of their displeasure centers, rendering them more vulnerable and more likely to experience new events as painful as well" (Liebowitz, 1983:47). This analysis certainly fits in with the withdrawal, isolation depression, and anhedonia (inability to experience pleasure) so characteristic of the schizophrenic.

There are many possible pathways to schizophrenia, and we certainly do not want to fall into the trap of blaming every developmental outcome on parental behavior. Many of the negative parental events observed among families of schizophrenics may be effects of schizophrenia rather than a cause. Some children bring personalities and temperaments with them to the socialization process that are not conducive to forming a loving relationship. Even the most loving of parents may become frustrated and eventually turn away when their best efforts are rebuffed continually by their mentally ill children—schizophrenia can develop even in "model" loving families.

The Link Between Mental Illness and Crime

After several decades of denying that there was any link between mental illness and crime, the psychiatric community has reversed its stance. Many of the studies that led to the conclusion that there was no link between crime and mental illness were conducted during the period when individuals with serious mental illnesses were routinely institutionalized for very long periods of time, and often even for life. The deinstitutionalization movement in the 1960s shifted many such persons into the community and resulted in greater visibility and higher arrest rates for the mentally ill (Bartol, 1995:148; Marzuk, 1996).

Even with the new evidence there is some reluctance to affirm the link between crime and mental illness out of fear of further stigmatizing an already highly stigmatized group. However, the evidence cannot be dismissed or ignored, especially by correctional workers charged with supervising the mentally ill. One review found that out of eighty-six studies that examined the relationship between mental illness and criminal/antisocial behavior, in seventy-nine studies (92 percent) the relationship was positive, six studies were nonsignificant, and only one study was negative; that is, mental illness was associated with lower levels of criminal and antisocial behavior in this study (Ellis and Walsh, 2000).

Two studies found that the incidence of violence was up to five-times greater among people with serious mental problems (mostly schizophrenics and manic depressives) than among people with no diagnosis of mental illness after controlling for many demographic factors (Link *et al.*, 1992; Swanson, 1994). Similarly, a Danish study of more than 300,000 individuals followed to age forty-three found that persons with histories of psychiatric hospitalization were three to eleven times more likely to have criminal convictions than people with no psychiatric history (Hodkins *et al.*, 1996). A well-controlled British study found that male schizophrenics had three times as many convictions for violent crimes than nonpsychotic criminals in a control group (Beck and Wencel, 1998). After reviewing many studies of the link between mental illness and violence, Marzuk concluded that:

> [W]e must recognize that the link is a real one and that it persists even after controlling for demographic . . . variables. The link appears strongest for the severe mental illnesses, particularly those involving psychosis, and, as for those persons without diagnosed mental illness, it is increased by the use of alcohol and other psychoactive substances. It is likely that active symptoms, particularly distorted perceptions, faulty reasoning, and distorted modulation of affect are more important than the label of a specific diagnosis (1996:484).

However, the vast majority of the mentally ill are nonviolent, and they are more likely to be victims of violence than perpetrators (Marzuk, 1996:485). The mentally ill most at risk include the homeless, those who use alcohol and other drugs, and those who do not take their antipsychotic medication (Lykken, 1995). Nonpsychotic patients who remain connected to other human beings and who faithfully take their medication are probably less dangerous than the average person (Bartol, 1995). Most of the worst killers in American history were morally rather than mentally "sick." Most of the truly scary people this author has met in his days in the field were not mental patients, and most of the mental patients he has met seemed much more scared and anxious than dangerous. Nonetheless, the correctional worker must be aware that if the situation is right, the mentally ill offender is at greater risk for committing violence than is the typical offender.

Treatment

The treatment of schizophrenics is primarily a medical concern. The corrections worker is involved as a community resource broker and as a medication monitor. Most schizophrenics are quite manageable and cooperative as long as they are taking their antipsychotic medication. The difficulty has always been to make sure that they take it. They are quite prone to "forgetting" their daily dose, and some who may be willing to take it one day will be unwilling to take it the next day for fear that they are being "poisoned," or because of its side effects. You may be able to circumvent schizophrenic offenders' ambivalence about daily pill taking by negotiating an agreement for treatment with the long-acting drug Prolixin. This drug is injected every two or three weeks, and the medication is gradually released over that time. One usually can enlist the help of a family member to drive the patient to the community health clinic for this treatment every two weeks or so.

Again, be cautioned against the old "treating symptoms rather than causes" argument. Drugs no more cure schizophrenia than insulin cures diabetes. But who would deny insulin to the diabetic? Antipsychotic drugs do for schizophrenics what insulin does for diabetics. They stabilize biological functions, and by doing so they help the sufferer to cope. They enable schizophrenics to control desires to act out their delusions. The combination of appropriate medication and individual and family counseling has shown good results with schizophrenics who have been properly assessed as being able to benefit from such a regimen (Spaulding, *et al.*, 1999).

Sometimes schizophrenics who do not suffer too severely from the disorder are able to stabilize their lives through a supportive marriage and the acquisition of some work skills. You cannot play Cupid, but you can try to obtain employment for schizophrenic offenders in sheltered workshops. Sheltered workshops provide an opportunity for individuals to learn work skills, gather self-esteem, and become somewhat independent in a protective work setting that is not as demanding as a regular work setting. Such work shelters also provide counseling and instruction on such work-related activities as grooming, timekeeping, work habits, following instructions and orders, and getting along with fellow employees. Most larger cities have at least one such workshop in the community, but the final decision about admissions belongs to their administrators. If you have an offender who you feel is a likely candidate for admission to a work shelter, you should accompany the offender on a visit so that you can learn about its program and of the administrators' reasons for granting or denying the offender a place.

Remember, schizophrenics' perceptions of reality, however distorted, are as real to them as your vivid dreams are to you while you are experiencing them. Schizophrenics have withdrawn from the common reality because it is too painful and threatening, so they have a vested interest in maintaining their own. You should not argue with their reality, but this restraint does not preclude your pointing out its disadvantages or comparing it with your own reality in a gentle and reassuring manner. On no account should you validate their reality by pretending to participate in it, and you should not accept their condition as hopeless.

MILWAUKEE'S COMMUNITY SUPPORT PROGRAM

A "model" community-based program for schizophrenics is Milwaukee's Community Support Program (CSP). The program's primary objective is: "to keep persons afflicted with chronic mental illnesses out of local jails and hospitals and to help them live independently" (McDonald and Teitelbaum, 1994:8). The program receives most of its clients from the courts and probation agencies in the area, although some are referred from elsewhere. Like all good criminal justice programs, the Community Support Program adopts a "carrot and stick" approach to managing its clientele. It does everything that it can to help offenders live independently and within the law, but noncompliance with directives often results in withdrawal of services or a new court appearance. The principal kinds of services provided to Community Support Program participants are therapeutic, financial management, and housing assistance.

Therapeutic services include both medical and psychosocial services. Offenders are given a full medical examination upon entry and closely monitored thereafter. The primary medical service is the provision of antipsychotic medication five days per week. After nurses verify that offenders have taken their medication, offenders are given a chit which they turn in at the cashier's window where they receive their daily monetary allowance. Failure to take medication results in nonpayment of this allowance. It is surprising how so many notoriously reluctant patients suddenly become motivated to take their medication when there is an immediate cash reward for doing so.

The Community Support Program is able to reward offenders for taking their medication because it is the legal recipient of each offender's social security and disability benefits. The program pays all offenders' fixed expenses such as rent and utilities, with the rest doled out after each dose of medication. Financial management services are particularly useful for mentally ill offenders who are poorly prepared to manage their own finances and often are preyed on by thieves who know when social security checks are delivered. Full-time financial advisers maintain offenders' accounts and work out budgets and other money management techniques with them to maintain the relative stability of their cash flow.

The third major component of the program is housing assistance. Many offenders come to the program lacking any type of stable accommodation. Housing specialists at the Community Support Program indicate that they are able to find stable housing for offenders with relative ease because landlords like the idea of regular payments coming directly from the program rather than having to chase down renters every month.

Space does not permit more than this bare-bones description of this program that appears to be the probation/parole officer's dream. Such a program in any jurisdiction would prove a tremendous asset to the criminal justice worker who could not possibly supply the services supplied by Community Support Program. The program illustrates that it is possible to supervise mentally ill offenders in the community quite successfully and relatively inexpensively. While this program (which began in 1978) has not been formally evaluated, its continued funding from state and local government as well as high praise from the local judiciary and probationary agencies, speak of the high esteem in which the program is held (McDonald and Teitelbaum, 1994:9).

The Mentally Deficient Offender → 50% on case load

Intellectual functioning as measured by IQ tests, after a long period of neglect in terms of its relationship with criminal activity, is making a strong comeback (Hirschi and Hindelang, 1977; Moffitt and Silva, 1988). This author agrees with Wilson and Herrnstein's opinion that "criminology acted rashly when, in the 1930s, it virtually ceased considering IQ as a significant correlate of criminal behavior, for it was just at that moment in the evolution of mental testing that the tests were beginning to yield solid data on the cognitive predispositions toward offending" (1985:159).

Although many criminologists still believe that IQ tests are biased, a decade's worth of research conducted by geneticists, psychometricians, and developmental psychologists led the prestigious National Academy of Sciences to insist that they are not (Seligman, 1992:155), and an overwhelming proportion of more than 1,000 experts surveyed by Snyderman and Rothman (1988) agreed. More recently, the American Psychological Association's Task Force on Intelligence reiterated that IQ tests were not biased, and that variation in genes has a very large influence on variance in intelligence (Neisser et al., 1995). Given this new interest in IQ, and given that IQ scores are the assessment measurements most readily available (and probably the most useful) to correction workers, it is necessary to know what these scores have to tell us.

The most widely used IQ tests are the Revised Wechsler Intelligence Scale for Children (WISC-R) and the Wechsler Adult Intelligence Scale (WAIS). As we saw in Chapter 3, these scales are divided into verbal and performance subtests, providing measures of verbal IQ (VIQ) and performance IQ (PIQ). PET scan studies have shown that the neurological processes engaged when subjects are administered the different IQ subscales are lateralized to opposite hemispheres of the brain (Chase et al., 1984; Duara et al., 1984). In other words, different sides of the brain are involved depending on whether the individual is working a problem that engages verbal or performance IQ skills.

VIQ and PIQ subtests are alternated and are administered in the following order:

Verbal Scale	Performance Scale
1. Information	2. Picture completion
3. Similarities	4. Picture arrangement
5. Arithmetic	6. Block design
7. Vocabulary	8. Object assembly
9. Comprehension	10. Coding (or mazes)

All ten subtests as a whole are measures of general intelligence in that they measure an individual's capacity to think rationally, act purposefully, and to deal effectively with his or her environment. They attempt to measure such things as long and short-term memory, concentration, computational skills, verbal abstractions, awareness of and openness to one's culture and its norms, manual dexterity, visual/spatial acuity, and adaptability. However, there is no one-to-one relationship between the two subscales; they measure somewhat different domains of intelligence, with the performance scale providing an assessment for those whose family backgrounds do not promote verbal skills. Note that both subscales contribute about equally to an individual's full-scale IQ score.

Most sociological studies linking IQ to crime and delinquency have viewed IQ as a unitary phenomenon. That is, IQ studies have tended to correlate full-scale IQ with various measures of crime and delinquency. Such a conceptualization of IQ may obscure as much about the IQ/delinquency relationship as it reveals. Full-scale IQ (FIQ) is obtained by summing VIQ and PIQ scores and dividing by two. For example, if an individual has a VIQ score of 100 and a PIQ score of 90, his or her FIQ is (100 + 90)/2 = 95. The reason that the use of FIQ might distort the IQ/delinquency relationship is that offenders typically show a greater deficit in VIQ than they do in PIQ relative to general population norms. Combining the two subscales to obtain FIQ has the effect of making the overall IQ mean scores for the general and delinquent populations somewhat more equal than they would otherwise be (Herrnstein, 1989:3), thus leading to the under-estimation of the influence of cognitive variables on delinquency.

Low VIQ individuals may be viewed as somewhat more prone to violence and aggression because they lack verbal skills that mediate between a stimulus and a response. Daniel Goleman discusses this issue in his best-selling book: *Emotional Intelligence* (1996). Joseph (1982) has noted that the motor areas of the cortex mature earlier than areas involved with thought processes, making for speedy responses to stimuli on the part of infants and young children that are not mediated by thought processes. As children mature, there is increasing communication between the verbal and visual-spatial hemispheres of the brain, and their responses to stimuli are slowed while the left brain processes and interprets motor behavior initiated by the right brain. Initially, this is an "after the fact" interpretive process, but with increasing language acquisition and socialization, children eventually are able to foresee their response before they react. In other words, there is an ever-increasing engagement of the left hemisphere in the processing, organization, and appropriate inhibition of emotional transmissions received from the right brain.

The efficiency with which the verbal qualities of the left hemisphere performs its interpretive and inhibitory task varies considerably from person to person. This variability appears to be greatly influenced by early environmental experience. There is stiff competition within the infant's rapidly branching neurons for synaptic connections, and those neurons that are activated most frequently are those that firmly establish themselves (Smith, 1993). To borrow a couple of metaphors from transactional analysis, established neuronal connection patterns function as "memory tapes" playing over and over in the head until they become a "life script" governing our interactions with others.

Children who have strong visual-spatial capabilities relative to their verbal capabilities may tend to retain some of the unmediated rapidity of response to stimuli that is characteristic of the immature brain. As such children grow older, they retain their childhood priorities for instant pleasure and self-gratification without having developed the "self-talk" necessary to generate a sense of discipline, responsibility, and a recognition of the rights of others. When we have a young child who processes information this way, we have a "brat" who slaps playmates and steals their candy. A juvenile or an adult using similar cognitive processes may be a delinquent or a criminal who steals, assaults, robs, and rapes. The cognitive processes of the immature child and the delinquent or criminal are the same, but the content of those cognitions becomes much more threatening as the person becomes older, stronger, and more ambitious in the pursuit of self-gratification.

Some researchers have linked low VIQ to levels of interpersonal maturity using the *I-level* ("I" for "interpersonal maturity") system (Andrew, 1980). This system proposes that cognitive and personality integration follows a sequential pattern in normal human development, and sets up seven I-levels. Level one is the most basic (for example, the character of Lenny from the novel *Of Mice and Men*), and the extremely rare level seven is considered the ideal (perhaps only someone like Mother Teresa falls into this category). Criminals generally fall into levels two through five, with level five so rarely present among criminals that generally, only levels two through four are used to assess delinquent and criminal subjects (Austin, 1981:187). Work with abused children also has found that interpersonal maturity is linked to cognitive maturity measures (Trickett, 1993).

As might be expected, interpersonal maturity varied positively with VIQ in Andrew's (1980) study. Level two subjects, subjects in which the only system of cognitive reference appear to be themselves and their personal needs, had a mean VIQ of 78.7. Level three subjects, those who have internalized some social rules but who use them to manipulate, had a mean VIQ of 90.4. Level four subjects, who tend to be neurotic and acting-out because of conflicts between personal needs and social rules that have been more strongly internalized than other I-level subjects, had a VIQ mean of 98.4. These VIQ differences were partly mediated by age, with younger children naturally being more cognitively immature. However, the significant effect (p < .001) remained when controlling for age.

The main determinants of I-level appear to be verbal intelligence, so much so that Austin (1975) has suggested that the I-level system measures intelligence plus "moral orientation" more so than social maturity (as measured by the Jesness Immaturity Scale). Intellectual maturity is probably a necessary, if not sufficient, condition for moral maturity, and moderate correlations (in the mid .40s range) consistently have been found between moral reasoning and IQ (Kohlberg, 1984).

Moral orientation, of course, means moral reasoning, and moral reasoning involves making decisions about what is acceptable behavior and what is not. A deficit in moral orientation also means a mental fixation on egocentric thinking and short-run hedonism, patterns of thought more congruent with infantile and early childhood brain development than that of the mature adult. What this suggests is that individuals with a deficit in left-brain VIQ relative to right-brain PIQ have a tendency to act out rather than think out in a variety of situations. In a sense, then, violent and aggressive behavior is a form of visual/spatial ability that is unregulated by verbal ability among individuals lacking in internal moral standards of conduct.

It was noted earlier that Andrew (1980) found VIQ to be related to interpersonal maturity using the I-level system. In an earlier study of 122 probationers, Andrew (1974) found that interpersonal maturity was even more closely related to the P>V discrepancy marker (described in Chapter 3) than to VIQ. The most mature probationers (I-level 4) had a mean P > V discrepancy of 4.41 points, the I-level 3 probationers had a mean discrepancy of 7.33 points, and the I-level 2's had a mean of 17.78. It is clear that low verbal intelligence alone cannot account for interpersonal immaturity, and that a high PIQ relative to an individual's VIQ also plays an important part.

It also is clear that as correctional workers, you often will have to deal with mentally deficient individuals. Mental deficiency does not mean mental retardation (variably defined, but usually those with IQs of seventy or below). The former term connotes a correctable deficiency in mental functioning; the latter connotes an impairment (possibly organic) of the ability to learn. Although mentally retarded individuals are overrepresented in the criminal justice system in comparison to their number in the general population, they are rarely found on a probation/parole officer's caseload (Lampert, 1987). Offenders with mental deficiencies, however, will be represented in relatively large numbers. These people have the mental capacity to commit crimes but are deficient in the capacity to forge a responsible lifestyle for themselves.

A number of reviews have characterized the IQ-criminality relationship as ubiquitous and robust (Stattin and Klackenberg-Larson, 1993; Lynam, Moffitt, and Stouthhammer-Loeber, 1993). Nevertheless, perhaps because of mainstream sociology's distaste for explanations having to do with individual differences, sociological criminology has tended to avoid the issue of the link between IQ and criminality, or even to consider the topic taboo (Gordon, 1980). It is considered particularly distasteful if those individual differences are linked to genetic factors. This is not the place to get into the bitter issue of the nature versus nurture issues of intelligence.

Suffice it to say, evidence from behavioral genetics indicates that about 60 percent of the variance in IQ scores is attributable to genetic factors, which leaves about 40 percent attributable to environmental and genetic/environmental interaction factors (Neisser *et al.*, 1995; Snyderman and Rothman, 1988; Seligman, 1992; Rushton and Ankney, 1996). No matter what our natural intellectual endowment may be, it is stretched or suppressed by a host of environmental factors such as low birth weight, malnutrition, lack of stimulation, and abuse and neglect (Bronfenbrenner and Ceci, 1994).

Abuse and neglect appear to have a particularly deleterious effect on IQ. This author (Walsh, 1990) found that children who were illegitimate and abused and neglected had both the lowest average VIQ (83.02) and highest average PIQ (102.24) among four cross-classified groups of juvenile delinquents. These findings lend support to the hypothesis developed in Chapter 3 that abuse and neglect can lead to elevated PIQ scores relative to VIQ scores through the possible effect of abuse and neglect in dampening autonomic nervous system response. A review of the literature by Salzinger and her colleagues (1991) found across various studies that abuse and neglect has a serious negative impact on IQ levels.

How Does IQ Affect Criminality?

Ellis and Walsh (2000) report that 130 out of 159 studies (82 percent) found a negative relationship between IQ and criminal and antisocial behavior (the lower the IQ the greater involvement in such behavior), 24 found nonsignificant results (mostly in self-report studies), and 5 actually reported a positive relationship. Demonstrating a link between IQ and crime is not the same as demonstrating a causal link. Perhaps intelligence is only linked to crime because only the less intelligent criminals get caught. The so-called differential detection hypothesis proposes exactly that; in other words, lower IQ offenders are overrepresented in the criminal justice system because of their inability to avoid detection. Moffitt and Silva's (1988) review of Hirschi and Hindelang's (1977:583) evidence concluded that such arguments "are not supported by the available evidence."

To further explore this issue, Moffitt and Silva obtained juvenile arrest and IQ data for every male born in a certain area of New Zealand over a period of one year. They divided the males into three groups: (1) self-reported delinquents who actually had a juvenile record, (2) self-reported delinquents who officially were undetected (they were unknown to the police), and (3) self-reported nondelinquents. All self-reports were cross-checked with police records for accuracy. They found that the two delinquent groups (detected and undetected) did not differ significantly from each other on mean FIQ, VIQ, or PIQ. This indicates that undetected delinquents were no "brighter" than their detected peers. Both delinquent groups, however, had significantly lower FIQ and VIQ means than the nondelinquent group. The two delinquent groups did not differ from the nondelinquent group on PIQ, however, which again emphasizes the superiority of PIQ relative to VIQ among delinquents.

This still does not demonstrate a direct effect of IQ on crime and delinquency. Rather, low intelligence may exert its influence indirectly through a long chain of other negative factors. The most likely sequence of events is shown in Figure 18.1.

Figure 18.1

Effect of IQ on Crime and Delinquency

This chain indicates that individuals with low IQ's tend to do rather poorly in school, which may lead to frustration, low self-esteem, and negative labeling by teachers. These outcomes have the effect of increasing the probability that low IQ people will drop out of school and associate with others ("bad company") with similar characteristics and experiences. This results in a number of frustrated and alienated young men (and increasingly, young women) of limited intelligence and achievement hanging around together on street corners with nothing to do, and as we all know, "The devil finds work for idle hands."

The other possibility is that IQ has a more direct effect. A national cohort study found that IQ scores at age four (long before children accumulate school experiences) predict later delinquency (Lipsitt, Buka, and Lipsitt, 1990). In other words, poor cognitive skills and conduct problems are evident before children enter school, and poor school performance is another manifestation of these disabilities. This evokes the cognitive and temperamental deficits of Terrie Moffitt's life-course persistent offenders discussed in Chapter 3.

A LOOK AT THE INTELLECTUAL FUNCTIONING OF CORRECTIONAL OFFENDERS

Figure 18.2 compares percentages in a sample of 376 Ohio adult male felons and a sample of 513 Idaho juvenile delinquents with percentages of the general population within seven IQ levels. The figure provides some indication of the distribution of IQ levels with which the correctional helper can expect to work, although neither sample constitutes a random sample. The mean IQ of the adult sample is 93.5, and the mean IQ of the delinquent sample is 93.7. These figures are somewhat higher than the 10-point gap (100 being the American mean IQ) that Herrnstein (1989) says is consistently found between offenders and nonoffenders. However, the national mean includes the offender population, which means that if we excluded offenders in the calculation of the national mean it may be close to 103 (Herrnstein, 1989). In light of what was said earlier about the problem of combining VIQ and PIQ to obtain FIQ, it is interesting to note that the mean VIQ and PIQ scores of the juvenile sample were 90.5 and 97.6, respectively. The former is significantly different from the population mean, but the latter is not. Separate VIQ-PIQ scores were not obtained from the adult sample.

The figure provides comfort for those of us who believe in the concept of rehabilitation. Mindful of the limitations of the samples, what conclusions can we draw? It is clear that more than half of the subjects in both samples are within the normal range (90-110) of intelligence. Also note that above average intelligence (IQs over 110) is relatively incompatible with the criminal activity most of us will be dealing with (this is not to deny that corporate crime, committed by high-IQ executives, is considered by many to be more costly than street crime, but such activity usually is dealt with under administrative rather than criminal law).

Figure 18.2

Comparison of Population Norms on IQ with
Scores of a Criminal Sample

IQ Level	Descriptions/ Anticipations	Percentage of general population	Percentage of criminal sample	Percentage of delinquent sample
65 and below	Defective: needs special education, can function in protected situation.	2.2	0.5	3.5
66-79	Borderline: slow learner, can perform routine work under close supervision.	6.7	13.3	10.2
80-90	Dull normal: can function independently but needs vocational training.	16.1	25.0	23.2
91-110	Normal: can complete high school and some college-level work, has few vocational limitations.	50.0	56.6	51.6
111-119	Bright: no limitations	16.1	2.4	9.2
120-127	Superior: no limitations	6.7	2.1	1.2
128 and above	Very superior: no limitations	2.2	0.5	0.4

* General population norms adapted from Wechsler. 1944. *The Measurement of Adult Intelligence*. Baltimore: Williams and Wilkins.

Only 5 percent of the adult criminals and 4 percent of the delinquents had IQs over 110, whereas 25 percent of the population have IQs that high. At the other end of the scale, those with IQs less than the normal range are overrepresented in both samples. They constitute 38.3 and 37.6 percent of the adult and juvenile samples, respectively, as opposed to the 25 percent we would expect if IQ and criminal activity were unrelated variables. Nevertheless, with the possible exception of the "defectives," all the offenders in the samples possess the intellectual capacity to be educable and/or trainable. This also means that they have the capacity to be taught to act responsibly. Be aware that IQ does not represent the individual's problem-solving capacity. Correctional workers are advised to consider offenders' IQ scores, especially at the lower levels, as a reflection of their minimal rather than maximal level of functioning.

Of course, low intelligence does place limitations on what a person can achieve, but with a caring, involved, optimistic, and demanding helper, most offenders can be taught to behave responsibly and can be motivated to make the best of their capacities. If you do not make this belief an integral part of your operational style, then perhaps your talents would be better employed in some other line of work.

Special Problems Working with Mentally Deficient Offenders

There are no glaring differences between mentally deficient offenders and other offenders; intellectual functioning is a matter of degree, not of kind. Yet, because of their deficiencies, many such offenders cannot express themselves adequately or indicate their needs, which often makes it difficult for the corrections worker to identify the appropriate services they may require. There are other concerns and difficulties you should be aware of when dealing with mentally deficient offenders. Some of the most important are outlined below.

The Nature of Today's Economy: For this discussion, "mentally deficient" are those at any level below the "dull-normal" cutoff IQ score of 80 (Bowker and Schweid, 1992). Terms such as "retardation" or "mental deficiency" are defined relative to the level of intellectual functioning needed for meaningful participation in society. In labor-intensive agricultural and industrial societies there is ample opportunity for low IQ individuals to earn a living wage, and thus participate meaningfully in their societies. However, as we move into the less labor-intensive postindustrial age, the intellectual demands of the workplace have become increasingly complex. The more difficult those demands become, the level of intellectual functioning required to meet them becomes higher. The competition for jobs leads employers to demand ever-increasing educational achievement, regardless of whether college preparation really is required to do the job. Thus, for those at the lower-level of IQ, it becomes more frustrating for them to find and maintain employment that pays a living wage. Such unfortunate facts about the modern economy make the community brokerage aspect of correctional work more difficult, but not impossible.

Self-esteem Maintenance: Most people are well aware of their limitations and do not need others to remind them of what they are. Few things are more self-esteem deflating than to be told that you are "stupid." Many offenders adopt their tough and aggressive veneer to resist others applying the "stupid" label to them (Carbonell and Perkins, 2000). You must never imply by word, deed, or gesture, that mentally deficient offenders are anything less than valuable human beings. It is particularly important that you establish a warm supportive relationship with mentally deficient offenders because they tend to operate more from an emotional rather than an intellectual frame of reference (but you are reminded to take care that they do not become overly dependent on you).

Offenders are easier to deal with if they feel that you value their humanity. However, it is easy to become frustrated and angry at offenders who continually fail to follow instructions. They must be held accountable for such failures, but you should never say things like, "God! I've told you over and over; wassamatter, are you stupid or somethin'?" Be firm, but be cognizant of the person's need to maintain his or her sense of self-worth.

The Self-consistency Motive: Have you ever nodded knowingly in class when catching your professor's eye to acknowledge that you are following what he or she is saying when, in fact, you did not have a clue? Although you missed the chance to have the point clarified, it was probably more important to you to maintain the impression for yourself and others that you are a person who "catches on." Some low-functioning offenders, likewise, are inclined to nod in response to what you might consider simple instructions when they actually are quite confused. They fear that to constantly ask for clarification would upset their (and your) tenuous hold on the image of themselves as "not stupid." One study of New York probation officers found that many of them complained that "special needs" offenders frequently did not understand their instructions (Wertlieb and Greenberg, 1989:10-17). So, do not assume that mentally deficient offenders fully understand your instructions just because they smile and nod at you.

Patience is a Virtue: It should be obvious that patience is especially virtuous in dealing with such offenders. Instructions should be imparted slowly in simple language, and offenders should be asked to repeat them one at a time "just to make sure I know I'm telling you right, Jack." Remember, limited intelligence usually means a limited time horizon, so make sure that any instructions are capable of being fulfilled in reasonably short order. Pay special attention to balancing (not overtaxing) treatment efforts. Be especially concrete and specific, and proceed slowly. The techniques of reality therapy are perhaps best suited to working with the mentally deficient offender. Its emphasis on specificity, concreteness, and "one-step-at-a-time" appears tailor-made for offenders lacking in the kind of talking and reasoning skills required for rational emotive therapy counseling or the analytical skills required to do structural analysis in transactional analysis.

Personal Hygiene: Bathing and other habits or personal hygiene are not particularly important items on the agendas of most mentally deficient offenders. Ignorance of such matters often leads to disgust and ostracism from others, which may further exacerbate the person's low self-esteem. Poor hygiene and dress can prevent a person from obtaining even the most menial of jobs. There is no excuse for poor hygiene habits in today's society. Make sure that the offender understands this. It would be especially useful in this regard to be aware of special community agencies that work with such problems among the mentally deficient.

Case Study:
Portrait of a Schizophrenic

Greg was a frail, good-looking man of twenty-four when I first met him. He had two prior convictions for misdemeanor vandalism and was in my office now convicted of felony vandalism. Greg had this nasty habit of throwing chunks of rock through plate glass windows.

He was extremely difficult to interview for he manifested all the classic symptoms of the schizophrenic. He sat staring at me with flat affect, his hygiene was poor, and he did not particularly care what I had to say to him. I was able to find out that his life revolved around the TV set, in front of which he spent practically every waking hour. He wasn't fussy about which programs he watched, but he was concerned that whatever channel it happened to be, it must not be changed. Each of his vandalism charges stemmed from arguments with his mother or some other family member over changing channels. The upshot of those arguments was that his mother would throw him out of the house. When that occurred, Greg would proceed to the closest business establishment with a big glass window, put a brick through it, and sit down among the debris to await the arrival of the police. This tactic yielded him a place to sleep and another TV at which he could stare.

I took Greg back home after the presentence investigation interview since he had just been released from the county jail and was penniless. I also wanted to get a feel for his environment. Upon meeting his mother, I soon formed an opinion of her as a dominating, egocentric, and manipulative shrew. She flatly informed me that the only reason that her son was welcome in her house was his $200 monthly disability check.

His four brothers were likewise unfriendly and cruel. Since Greg was much smaller than his brothers, and a "wacko" to boot, he was a convenient target for their verbal and physical aggression. It seemed to me that rather than involving himself with those who rejected him and offered him no love, Greg had withdrawn into a semicatatonic world of dials and plastic people. The characters on the screen could not rebuff him as real people could. I came to view his reactions to channel switching as an attempt to protect somehow the existence of those benign characters on the screen.

I learned that Greg was seeing a psychiatrist at a local center who was prescribing Thorazine for him. Unfortunately, family members never made it much of their business to make sure that Greg took his medication as directed. I was able to persuade his mother to request that his psychiatrist place him on Prolixin if medically advisable, arguing that for a small investment of her time (driving Greg to the center for his injection twice a month) she could enjoy a semblance of peace in the house. And, more important for her, she could be assured of the uninterrupted flow of his disability checks. I also suggested that to avoid future problems she might consider buying Greg his own TV set.

Greg's mother did both of these things, and peace reigned for about nine months. Greg reported at my office on time twice a month and was fairly agreeable. Visits to his home revealed that things were still the same in terms of the family's treatment of Greg. He still was picked on and rejected, even beaten, by other family members, even though his own behavior had improved rather remarkably.

Then, I received a call from the mental health center informing me that Greg had missed his last two appointments with them. He was also a week late reporting to me. I decided to go to his home to find out what was happening. I was informed that two weeks prior to my visit Greg had gotten into a fight with his older brother and had stabbed him. Although the wound was superficial and the police had not been called, Greg panicked and fled from the house. I never heard from Greg again. Had he remained in my city, he surely would have been arrested again and I would have seen him. As far as I know, Greg is still out there somewhere among the hordes of loveless and rejected individuals who aimlessly wander the streets of our big cities. Greg's case is an example of how one's best efforts can sometimes come to less than an ideal ending. We have to accept failures as well as successes and learn from them both.

Perspective from the Field:
Never a Dull Moment with a Mental Health Caseload
By William D. Smith

William Smith has been an adult supervision probation officer in Santa Cruz County, California, for the past seven years. A graduate of San Francisco State University in psychology, Mr. Smith formerly worked as a group counselor at Juvenile Hall in Santa Cruz.

My job as a probation officer with a mental health clientele involves intense supervision of fifty-five individuals suffering from various types of schizophrenia and bipolar disorders. They all are court-ordered to take their prescribed psychotropic medications, to follow all mental health directives, and to follow all the usual probation terms and conditions. Their crimes range from relatively minor misdemeanors to bank robbery and assault with a deadly weapon. In this unique position, I work closely with a variety of mental health professionals to prevent recidivism and relapses into chronic states of mental deterioration. About 70 percent of my time is spent in contact with probationers in my office or in the field, about 20 percent in court appearances and writing probation violations, and about 10 percent in meetings with mental health staff.

Bipolar individuals are most problematic when they are in their manic phase. During this phase they are hyper, "on top of the world," and have delusions of grandeur. A term that best describes the manic person is "in your face." Such people sometimes can go without sleep for several days and not realize they have deteriorated. A few of my bipolar probationers can function fairly well at their "baseline" level of functioning, and a few can maintain part-time jobs or attend college. However, most of them are chronic sufferers who are unemployed and on social security.

The two most common reasons why mental health offenders relapse are that they fail to take their medication and/or they abuse alcohol and/or drugs. Such relapses often lead to reoffending or expensive in-patient stays at mental health facilities. People choose not to take their medication for a variety of reasons, but mostly because of the many negative side-effects, which can include abnormal weight gain, liver and kidney damage, male impotency, and a general impairment of functioning. Manic patients may go off their medication just to experience the manic high, and others to avoid the stigma of the "mentally ill" label. Some offenders who begin to feel "normal" while on their medication will stop because they feel that they do not need it any more. Yet, the vast majority of schizophrenics and those with bipolar disorders need to be on medication for the rest of their lives.

One patient/offender with a long history of failing to take her medication because of side effects is Jan, a forty-year-old paranoid schizophrenic who was diagnosed in her early twenties. She was on probation for setting fire to her parents' curtains believing that she was ridding the house of demons. After she had been on my caseload for about two months, I paid a home visit and found her wearing a robe with a white towel wrapped around her head. She claimed that she was "Queen Holiness Heinous," queen to "David Shang-Hai-Shek." I tried to get her into a short-term treatment program but she was turned away after claiming to be "Mrs. Jesus Christ." Because of this, I had to arrest her and place her in the mental health unit at the county jail so that we could stabilize her and get her back on medication. Several weeks after her jail stay, I had to arrest her again for failing to take her medicine. Her brother had called me because she had fixated on watching the "Chinese T.V. station," although she does not understand a word of Chinese. Following this and other such incidents, I asked that her medication be administered by injection. It has now been approximately seven months since she started receiving her monthly shots without any further incidents of instability.

Another chronic schizophrenic on my caseload is a forty-two-year-old male named Doug. He has been on probation for about two years for abusing his wife, who is also schizophrenic. Six months ago, Doug was admitted into the local mental health unit after trying to commit suicide by swallowing his bottle of psychiatric pills. Doug told me that he had done this because he had abused his wife again, felt guilty about it, and was afraid of going back to jail. The combination of fear and guilt caused him to experience hallucinations regarding jail inmates who were threatening that they were going to eat him alive. I assured him that I would not send him back to jail, as he was already in his own mental prison. After his release from the hospital, he was transferred to an open psychiatric facility for one month. Doug is presently living with his wife in a board and care facility. They both attend couples counseling, and so far, this appears to have had a positive impact on their relationship.

Other outcomes are not so positive. For example, take twenty-seven-year-old Steve who was placed on probation in 1995 for shattering his college professor's jaw and cheekbone with an axe handle. Steve had done this because he thought that the professor was spreading rumors about him. Although placed in a state mental hospital for six months and in the county jail for one year, he continued to harbor animosity against the professor. After several months on probation and employed part-time as a gas station attendant, I received calls from others telling me that Steve was acting outlandishly and was telling everyone that he wanted to hurt the professor again. Additionally, Steve was observed on the professor's college campus, which was a violation of his "stay away" order. Because of this, Steve was arrested and ordered to complete six months in the state hospital. Stories such as this are worrisome and feed into the popular belief that the mentally ill are violent and dangerous. However, this is the exception, not the rule, and for the most part, the mentally ill are nonthreatening.

In summary, there is literally never a dull moment on my job. The key assets to doing this job are patience and a sense of realism about what you can and cannot accomplish. At least 80 percent of the offenders on my caseload have violated their probation at least once during the five years I have been working this caseload. However, I do not view this as indicative of low success. My success indicators are the safety of the public and the safety and welfare of the offenders.

Summary

Unless their departments have a specialized caseload of mentally ill offenders, most probation and parole officers are likely to get at least one or two individuals of this type on their caseloads at any one time. The "four A's"—autism, ambivalence, inappropriate affect, and loose associations—are used to identify schizophrenics. Schizophrenia also can be identified today by the use of the PET scan, which reveals the brain's functioning, as opposed to its structure.

At the physiological level, schizophrenia appears to be a function of an excess of various chemical neurotransmitters, or perhaps an excess of receptors for those neurotransmitters. There are also strong indicators that the development of schizophrenia requires environmental input as well as biological. The most common background item associated with schizophrenia is a history of childhood love deprivation, although schizophrenia may appear in the most loving of families. Your job in dealing with schizophrenics is to act as a medication monitor and to put them in touch with various community agencies, such as sheltered workshops and specialized counseling services.

Intelligence, as measured by IQ tests, once again is becoming of interest to criminologists. Modern research fairly reliably has determined that IQ tests are not biased and that intelligence levels are strongly influenced by genetics. High IQ tends to be relatively incompatible with crime (at least with street-level crime), and the mentally deficient commit a disproportionate amount of crime. Nevertheless, most delinquents and criminals are in the normal (90-110) range of intelligence, and, therefore, intellectually capable of profiting from counseling, education, and training.

Low IQ offenders present some special supervision difficulties. One of the major problems you may face is helping them to secure work in an increasingly technological, and thus intellectually demanding, society. Pay special attention to the self-esteem and self-consistency needs of such offenders, and be very patient with them. All instructions should be phrased as simply and as concretely as possible to avoid misunderstanding.

References and Suggested Readings

American Psychiatric Association. 1994. *Diagnostic and Statistical Manual of Mental Disorders, 4th edition*. Washington, D.C.: American Psychiatric Association.

Andrew, J. 1974. Delinquency, the Wechsler P>V sign, and the I-level system. *Journal of Clinical Psychology*. 30:331-335.

_____. 1980. Verbal IQ and the I-level classification system for delinquents. *Criminal Justice and Behavior*. 7:193-202.

Austin, R. 1975. Construct validity of I-level classification. *Criminal Justice and Behavior*. 2:113-129.

_____. 1981. I-level and the Rehabilitation of Delinquents. In P. Kratcoski, ed. *Correctional Counseling and Treatment*. Monterey, California: Roxbury.

Bartol, C. 1995. *Criminal Behavior: A Psychosocial Approach*. Englewood Cliffs, New Jersey: Prentice-Hall.

Beck, J. and H. Wencel. 1998. Violent crime and Axis I psychopathology. In A. Skodel, ed. *Psychopathology and Crime. Washington*, D.C.: American Psychiatric Press.

Bowker, A. and R. Schweid. 1992. Habilitation of the Retarded Offender in Cuyahoga *County. Federal Probation*. 56:48-52.

Bronfenbrenner, U. and S. Ceci. 1994. Heredity, Environment, and the Question "How"—A First Approximation. In R. Plomin and G. McClearn, eds. *Nature, Nurture, and Psychology*. Washington, DC: American Psychological Association.

Buckley, P., R. Buchanan, S. Schulz, and C. Tamminga. 1996. Catching up on schizophrenia: The fifth international congress on schizophrenia research. Warm Springs, Virginia. April 8-12, 1995. *Archives of General Psychiatry*. 53:456-462.

Carbonell, J. and R. Perkins. 2000. Diagnosis and Assessment of Criminal Offenders. In P. Van Vooris, M. Braswell, and D. Lester, eds. *Correctional Counseling and Rehabilitation*. Cincinnati, Ohio: Anderson.

Chase, T., P. Fedio, N. Foster, R. Brooks, G. Di Chiro, and L. Mansi. 1984. Wechsler adult intelligence scale performance: Cortical localization of fluorodeoxyglucose F 18 positron emission tomography. *Archives of Neurology*. 41:244-247.

Department of Health and Human Services. 1981. *Toward a National Plan for the Chronically Mentally Ill.* DHHS publication No (ADM) 81-1077. Washington, D.C.: Department of Health and Human Services.

Ditton, P. 1999. *Mental Health and Treatment of Inmates and Probationers.* Washington, D.C.: Bureau of Justice Statistics.

Duara, R., C. Grady, J. Haxby, D. Ingvar, L. Sokoloff, R. Margolin, R. Manning, N. Cultler, and S. Rapoport. 1984. Human brain glucose utilization and cognitive function in relation to age. *Annals of Neurology.* 16:702-713.

Ellis, L. and A. Walsh. 2000. *Criminology: A Global Perspective.* Boston: Allyn and Bacon.

Freier, M. 1986. The Biological Bases of Criminal Behavior. In P. Greenwood, ed., *Intervention Strategies for Chronic Juvenile Offenders.* New York: Greenwood.

Gibbs, J. 1987. Symptoms of psychopathology among jail inmates: The effects of exposure to the jail environment. *Criminal Justice and Behavior.* 14:288-310.

Goleman, D. 1996. *Emotional Intelligence.* New York: Bantam Books.

Gordon, H. 1980. Research on Race and Delinquency: Taboo or Not Taboo? In E. Sagarin, ed., *Taboos in Criminology.* Beverly Hills, California: Sage.

Hales, R., S. Yudofsky, and J. Talbot. 1996. *Textbook of Psychiatry.* Washington, D.C.: American Psychiatric Association Press.

Herrnstein, R. 1989. Biology and Crime. *National Institute of Justice Crime File,* NCJ 97216. Washington, D.C.: U.S. Department of Justice.

Hirschi, T. and M. Hindelang. 1977. Intelligence and delinquency: A revisionist review. *American Sociological Review.* 42:571-587.

Hodkins, S., S. Mednick, P. Brennan, F. Schulsinger, and M. Engberg. 1996. Mental disorder and crime: Evidence from a Danish birth cohort. *Archives of General Psychiatry.* 53:489-496.

Joseph, R. 1982. The neuropsychology of development: Hemispheric laterality, limbic language, and the origins of thought. *Journal of Clinical Psychology.* 38:4-33.

Kohlberg, L. 1984. *The Psychology of Moral Development: The Nature and Validity of Moral Stages.* New York: Harper and Row.

Lampert, R. 1987. The mentally retarded offender in prison. *The Justice Professional.* 2:60-70.

Liebowitz, M. 1983. *The Chemistry of Love.* New York: Berkeley Books.

Link, B., H. Andrews, and F. Cullen. 1992. The violent and illegal behavior of mental patients reconsidered. *American Sociological Review.* 57:275-292.

Lipsitt, D., S. Buka, and L. Lipsitt. 1990. Early intelligence scores and subsequent delinquent behavior: A prospective study. *American Journal of Family Therapy.* 18:197-208.

Lykken, D. 1995. *The Antisocial Personalities.* Hillsdale, New Jersey: Lawrence Erlbaum.

Lynam, D., T. Moffitt, and M. Stouthamer-Loeber. 1993. Explaining the relation between IQ and delinquency: Class, race, test motivation, school failure, or self-control? *Journal of Abnormal Psychology.* 102:187-196.

Marzuk, P. 1996. Violence, crime, and mental illness: How strong a link? *Archives of General Psychiatry.* 53:481-486.

McDonald, D. and M. Teitelbaum. 1994. Managing mentally ill offenders in the community: Milwaukee's community support program. Washington, D.C.: *National Institute of Justice.*

Meltzer, H. and S. McGurk. 1999. The effects of clozapine, risperidon, and olanzapine on cognitive function in schizophrenia. *Schizophrenia Bulletin.* 25:233-255.

Moffitt, T. and P. Silva. 1988. IQ and delinquency: A test of the differential detection hypothesis. *Journal of Abnormal Psychology.* 97:330-333.

Neisser, U., G. Boodoo, T. Bouchard, A. Boykin, N. Brody, S. Ceci, D. Halpern, J. Loehlin, R. Perloff, R. Sternberg, and S. Urbina. 1995. *Intelligence: Knowns and Unknowns: Report of a Task Force Established by the Board of Scientific Affairs of the American Psychological Association.* Washington, D.C.: American Psychological Association.

Palermo, G., E. Gumz, and F. Liska. 1992. Mental illness and criminal behavior revisited. *International Journal of Offender Therapy and Comparative Criminology.* 36:53-61.

Perry, B. and R. Pollard. 1998. Homeostasis, stress, trauma, and adaptation: A neurodevelopmental view of childhood trauma. *Child and Adolescent Psychiatric Clinics of America.* 733-51.

Peterson, C. 1997. *Psychology: A Biopsychosocial Approach.* New York: Longman.

Pinel, J. 2000. *Biopsychology, fourth edition.* Boston: Allyn and Bacon.

Rushton, J. and C. Ankney. 1996. Brain size and cognitive ability: Correlations with age, sex, social class, and race. *Psychonomic Bulletin and Review.* 3:21-36.

Salzinger, S., R. Feldman, M. Hammer, and M. Rosario. 1991. Risk for physical child abuse and the personal consequences for its victims. *Criminal Justice and Behavior.* 18:64-81.

Schmalleger, F. 2001. *Criminal Justice Today, 6th edition.* Upper Saddle River, New Jersey: Prentice Hall.

Seligman, D. 1992. *A Question of Intelligence: The IQ Debate in America.* New York: Birch Lane.

Smith, D. 1993. Brain, environment, heredity, and personality. *Psychological Reports.* 72:3-13.

Snyderman, M. and S. Rothman. 1988. *The IQ Controversy, the Media, and Public Policy.* New Brunswick, New Jersey: Transaction Books.

Spaulding, W., S. Fleming, D. Reed, M. Sullivan, D. Storzbach, and M. Lam. 1999. Cognitive functioning in schizophrenia: Implications for psychiatric rehabilitation. *Schizophrenia Bulletin.* 25:275-289.

Stattin, H. and I. Klackenberg-Larsson. 1993. Early language and intelligence development and their relationship to future criminal behavior. *Journal of Abnormal Psychology.* 102:369-378.

Swanson, J. 1994. Mental Disorder, Substance Abuse, and Community Violence. In J. Monahan and H. Steadman, eds. *Violence and Mental Disorders: Developments in Risk Assessment.* Chicago, Illinois: University of Chicago Press.

Trickett, P. 1993. Maladaptive development of school-aged physically abused children: Relationship with the child-rearing context. *Journal of Family Psychology.* 7:134-137.

Walsh, A. 1990. Illegitimacy, child abuse and neglect, and cognitive development. *Journal of Genetic Psychology.* 151:279-285.

Wechsler, D. 1944. *The Measurement of Adult Intelligence.* Baltimore: Williams and Wilkins.

Wertlieb, E. and M. Greenberg. 1989. Strategies for working with special-needs probationers. *Federal Probation.* 53:10-17.

Wilson, J. and R. Herrnstein. 1985. *Crime and Human Nature.* New York: Simon and Schuster.

Chapter 19

The Juvenile Delinquent

The logic of concentrating on treating the youngest of offenders is inescapable. There is almost universal agreement by crime experts of every persuasion that the roots of criminal behavior are often embedded in very early life. If past experience piles up around the offender in cumulative fashion, early roots . . . can soon grow too large to unearth.

Hans Toch

Legal Background

Those who aspire to work in juvenile probation services must become familiar with the differences between the adult and juvenile systems. However, be aware that in a growing number of states the age at which youth are waived into the adult system and tried and sentenced as adults is becoming lower. This, too, has implications for caseworkers in both the adult and juvenile system. In the juvenile system, juveniles are never called criminals, even when they commit criminal acts. Juvenile acts that are forbidden by law are called "delinquent" acts. The term *delinquent* comes from a Latin term meaning to "leave undone." The connotation is that the juvenile delinquent has *not done* something that he or she was supposed to (behave lawfully) rather than *done* something he or she was not supposed to do. The difference is subtle, but reflects the rehabilitative rather than punitive thrust of American juvenile justice. In fact, in some states, juveniles are not put on probation but enrolled in aftercare, and their probation officer becomes their aftercare worker or counselor.

Juveniles enjoy or, depending on your perspective, suffer, a special status in society and in its justice system. They are expected not to do a number of things adults have a right to do, such as smoke, drink, drive automobiles, leave home, and ignore the wishes of their parents. They also are expected to do a number of things that adults may ignore, such as attend school, obey curfews, and obey their parents. If juveniles violate any of these do and don't rules, they can be charged with having committed a *status offense*—an act of commission or omission applicable only to juveniles. Status offenses are the most frequently dealt with offenses in the juvenile system (Heck, 2000).

The special status of juveniles in the juvenile justice system rests on the concept of *parens patriae*. This terms literally means "father of his country," and practically means that the state may take over the supervision of a child under legal disability and act as a substitute for his or her parents. Underlying this concept is the philosophy that if the child misbehaves, his or her parents are to blame. In such an event, the state may assume responsibility for the child, diagnose the problem, and take appropriate remedial action. This responsibility can be in the form of juvenile probation services, with the child remaining in the parental home, or a court order may be issued removing the child from the parental home and placing him or her in a state facility (detention center or group home).

All actions of the juvenile courts and its officers, at least in theory, are supposed to be "in the best interests of the child." The juvenile courts do not have trials. They have "hearings" or "adjudication hearings." The child does not plead guilty or not guilty; he or she "admits" or "denies" the charge. The court never finds the child "guilty," but rather makes "a finding of fact." The "finding of fact" can be either that he or she is delinquent (that is, in a condition requiring the intervention and care of the state), or is not delinquent. A presentence investigation report is not written, a "predisposition" or "social inquiry" report is. The courts never sentence the child, rather they "dispose" of the matter, and they seek rehabilitation rather than punishment (Heck, 2000). You should not be misled by all these euphemisms into the belief that juveniles should not be held responsible for their conduct.

However, the American criminal justice system has been criticized severely of late for failing to control juvenile crime and for coddling juveniles. This has resulted in tremendous increases in *waivers to adult court* (transfer of jurisdiction from juvenile to adult court for processing as an adult). All states have provisions for waivers, but between 1979 and 1995, eight states enacted mandatory waiver statutes for serious violent crimes in legislative attempts to reduce discretion of juvenile courts and to show that legislators are not "soft on crime" (Fritsch and Hemmens, 1995:32).

Why so Much Delinquency?

Juvenile delinquency in the United States has been called a "growth industry" (Romig, Cleland, and Romig, 1989). But delinquency is not unique to the United States; juvenile misbehavior occurs everywhere, and is everywhere "bemoaned." Plato, in his *Republic*, soundly condemned the behavior of the youth of his time; and William Shakespeare puts the following words into the mouth of a shepherd in *The Winter's Tale*: "I would there be no age between ten and three-and-twenty, or that youth would sleep out the rest; for there is nothing in the between but getting wenches with child, wronging the ancientry, stealing, fighting" (Act III, Scene III). But these observations do not diminish the urgency of the problem in the contemporary United States. Those ancient Greek or Elizabethan youngsters, or youngsters anywhere else for that matter, never ran around drugged to their eyeballs, wielding automatic weapons, and killing, raping, and robbing for fun—situations that occur all too often in American inner cities.

bemoaned → complained about!

Antisocial behavior is caused by various factors presented in Chapters 2 and 3. However, there are certain factors unique to juvenile delinquency. Most of the juveniles involved in delinquency do not become adult criminals (Moffitt, 1993). During the youthful period of life, the probability of antisocial behavior increases dramatically, but it diminishes in later periods.

CAUSALITY: BIOLOGICAL FACTORS

A look at graphs depicting age and crime rates from around the world, and as far back as such graphs have been drawn, show a dramatic surge in offending shortly after the average age of male puberty, a peak at ages sixteen and seventeen, and a slow, steady decline thereafter (Gottfredson and Hirschi, 1990). In Chapter 3 we saw that the vast majority of offenders limited their offending to adolescence (the period from puberty to maturity), a period in which strong testosterone-driven physical drives and abilities outrun neurophysiological maturity. It has long been known that early-maturing boys confronting their "raging hormones" with a less mature brain than their age mates engage in more antisocial behavior than late maturing boys (Buchanan, Eccles, and Becker, 1993), and the same finding has also been reported for girls (Caspi et al., 1993).

Two recent magnetic resonance imaging (MRI) studies (Giedd et al., 1999; Sowell et al., 1999) confirm what parents always have known—adolescents are a couple of doughnuts shy of a dozen in the cognitive area. These studies show that the prefrontal cortex (PFC) is the most immature area of a teen's brain. As we saw in Chapter 3, the prefrontal cortex serves functions such as making reasoned judgments and modulating emotions arising from the limbic system. MRI data show that this link between the limbic system and the prefrontal cortex is often tenuous among adolescents (Baird, et al, 1998), which is probably why they rely on raw emotions to evaluate situations more so than adults. Perhaps it is no wonder that teens so often misinterpret the intentions of others, and often seem to be moody.

These kinds of studies suggest that the age effect on offending is a function of two biosocial processes on opposite trajectories, one of which (the pubescent hormonal surges) holds temporary sway over the other (neurological maturity). Consistent with this suggestion, it has been found that testosterone levels at puberty do effect future problem behavior, but only for boys entering puberty significantly earlier than is the norm (Drigotas and Udry, 1993).

As we also saw in Chapter 3, these biological effects are compounded in modern societies in which people are entering puberty earlier than ever (mostly because of improved nutrition), and in which longer periods of formal preparation are required to participate meaningfully in the workforce. This "maturity gap" gives birth to many of the psychological and environmental causes of delinquency discussed below.

Among the many other problems associated with delinquency is attention deficit with hyperactivity disorder (ADHD). Despite the tendency of some to dismiss ADHD as the medicalization of childish "high spirits," it is clearly identifiable as much more than that. Ellis and Walsh (2000) found ninety-nine studies in which attention deficit with hyperactivity disorder was positively related to delinquent and criminal behavior, and only one (for drug offenses) in which no significant relationship was reported.

Children affected by attention deficit with hyperactivity disorder have extremely short attention spans and are prone to extreme boredom, are restlessness, have low levels of inhibitory control and great impulsiveness, have difficulties with peers, frequently exhibit disruptive behavior, and are academic underachievers. Although obviously it is true that most children manifest some of these symptoms at one time or another, and it is probably true that attention deficit with hyperactivity disorder is overdiagnosed, the symptoms of children affected by attention deficit with hyperactivity disorder amass to form a syndrome (eight out of fourteen symptoms are required for diagnosis), and their symptoms are chronic and more severe (Weiss, 1991).

Attention deficit with hyperactivity disorder affects somewhere between 2 and 9 percent of the childhood population and is four or five times more prevalent in males than in females (Levy, *et al.*, 1997). Although the precise cause of attention deficit with hyperactivity disorder is not known, fifteen twin studies and two adoption studies show that genetics is a factor (Ellis and Walsh, 2000). The heritability (recall that heritability is a measure of the degree to which a trait is under genetic control) of attention deficit with hyperactivity disorder is exceptionally high compared to other behavioral disorders. It is reported to range between .75 to .91, and the findings are robust regardless of whether the disorder is considered to be a categorical trait (a discrete, either/or disorder) or continuous trait (a matter of degree rather than something one has or has not), and regardless of the cutoff criteria applied (Levy, *et al.*, 1997).

Some children diagnosed with attention deficit with hyperactivity disorder show EEG patterns of underarousal (slow brain waves) similar to adult psychopaths (Lynam, 1996). Such a brain wave pattern is experienced subjectively as boredom, which motivates the person to seek or create environments containing more excitement. Hyperactivity can be normalized temporarily by methylphenidate (Ritalin), which is a mild stimulant drug.

Although stimulants have the effect of *increasing* activity for those individuals without attention deficit with hyperactivity disorder, they have a calming or normalizing affect on those suboptimally aroused by raising the activity of the brain's sensory mechanisms (principally, the reticular activating system (RAS)) to normal levels. This relieves boredom because the brain becomes more attentive to features of the child's environment previously ignored, and the child becomes less disruptive, less obnoxious to peers, and can focus more on schoolwork.

Child delinquents affected by attention deficit with hyperactivity disorder are more likely than delinquents not affected by it to persist in their antisocial ways as adults, but this probability rises dramatically for affected children also diagnosed with *conduct disorder* (CD). *Conduct disorder* is defined as "the persistent display of serious antisocial actions [assaulting, stealing, setting fires, behaving with cruelty toward animals] that are extreme given the child's developmental level and have a significant impact on the rights of others" (Lynam, 1996:211). Attention deficit with hyperactivity disorder and conduct disorder are found to occur together in 30 to 50 percent of cases (reviewed in Lynam, 1996). Lynham (1996:22) describes the trajectory from attention deficit with hyperactivity disorder to criminality, stating that the co-occurrence of attention deficit with hyperactivity disorder and conduct disorder:

> may tax the skills of parents and lead to the adoption of coercive child rearing techniques, which in turn may enhance the risk of antisocial behavior. Entry into school may bring academic failure and increase the child's frustration, which may increase his or her level of aggressive behavior. Finally, the peer rejection associated with hyperactivity may lead to increased social isolation and conflict with peers.

CAUSALITY: PSYCHOLOGICAL FACTORS

As we have seen, neurological and hormonal changes during adolescence often make the period between childhood and adulthood a confusing one. In the United States, where we keep individuals in the dependent role of childhood longer than any other nation, it is a particularly trying period. This strange and sometimes frightening stage of life we call adolescence has been considered everything from a normal developmental period accompanied by a few mild disturbances experienced by about half of all teenagers (Buchanan, Eccles and Becker, 1993), to a stage of life that is very emotionally disturbing for just about all teenagers (Moffitt, 1993). From a review of the literature, Udry (1990:2) lists the following changes that typically occur among high-school age adolescents: "They complete puberty, [have] lower academic achievement values, increased values of independence, increased tolerance for violation of adult standards, decreased religiosity, decline in church attendance, increased reported alcohol and drug use, and increased sexual activity." Except for the completion of puberty, these changes are not likely to be welcomed by parents and other authority figures, and they certainly represent a gap between biological and social maturity that must be bridged.

In psychologist Erik Erikson's (1963) *Eight Ages of Man* model of human psychosocial development, he identifies eight stages in the human life cycle in which individuals are confronted with new challenges and interactions with themselves and with their environment. Each of these stages involve crises that can lead to opposite (positive or negative) personality outcomes depending on how the crises are confronted and resolved. Adolescence is identified as a stage in which the two polar outcomes are *identity* versus *role confusion*. In reality, of course, these outcomes are never either/or dichotomies. Most teenagers emerge from this stage situated somewhere on a shifting continuum.

During this stage, young people start asking philosophical questions about themselves: "Who am I?" "What is my place, and where am I going?" "What does this or that person think of me?" They also start to form opinions and theories and ask questions about many aspects of their environment that they formerly took for granted. Their surging hormones, abundant energies, and new questioning orientation make them impatient, action orientated, and imbued with an aura of omnipotence. If, thanks to loving parents, they were successful in navigating previous developmental states (trust versus mistrust, autonomy versus doubt, initiative versus guilt, and industry versus inferiority), they will emerge with a positive identity ("I'm OK, you're OK") and very little role confusion.

If mistrust, doubt, guilt, and inferiority were previous outcomes, role confusion is the likely outcome of this stage. To seek out an identity, they will turn away from neglectful parents and toward others in the same sorry boat as themselves. Needless to say, such a strategy is not a good one, for with these groups come negative identities—"delinquent," "doper," "punk"—but even a negative identity is better than no identity at all as long as it is accepted by the groups to which we belong.

Even youths from well-adjusted homes often conform more with their peers' expectations than with their parents' during adolescence. This is a normal part of growing up and part of finding one's own way in life. The trick is to find the right set of peers. Well-loved youths generally will be prosocial and will seek the company of others like themselves, but children who do not find love, support and supervision at home may resort to groups outside the family, and these groups are often deviant

(Rodkin, et al, 2000). About two-thirds of the children who run away from home do so in response to parental abuse (Hyde and Hyde, 1985:2). Rejected children, being unsure of themselves, often will overidentify with the heroes of cliques and crowds, or with the heroes the media provides for them to hold themselves together.

CAUSALITY: ENVIRONMENTAL FACTORS

Sometimes, institutions of higher learning employ those who call themselves moral relativists or situational ethicists, and who believe that no one person's system of values is inherently superior to any other's. They do not believe that moral or ethical absolutes should govern our social behavior. However, the moral vacuum that our society has created produces over one million illegitimate births each year in the United States to teens barely past menarche. Eventually, many of these children become part of the horde of gang members who infest our cities and bankrupt our hospitals' trauma centers.

With our country's diminishing emphasis on the institutions of family and religion, increasingly behavior, attitudes, and values have come under the influence of other forces. A good case can be made that we have abrogated much of the responsibility for socializing our young to peer groups and to television, both of which represent immature and often antisocial visions of reality. Groups have a morality and direction of their own that is often radically different from the sum of their individual parts. Already unsure of identity and direction, juveniles in peer groups defer to the collective judgment. With internalized standards submerged in groups, and with responsibility diffused among them, sometimes we see horrible manifestations of anti-social "group think" such as "gang banging" and "wilding" (packs of young males running wild, attacking and destroying people and/or property).

Television, the other half of the socialization equation, provides youth with models and standards of behavior, selling greed, hedonism, impatience, and impulsivity ("Go out and buy this or that and you will feel great and the boys/girls will love you. Do it now!"). Our youth grow up seeing all kinds of complex problems solved in one hour (often by violent means) with six commercial breaks designed to sell children TV-land's version of the good life. Is it any wonder that our children and youth become narcissistic, lower their thresholds for violence, become desensitized to the suffering of others, and have difficulty delaying gratification? And don't forget, these cultural factors are superimposed on a neurophysiology designed for action.

The themes of many television programs and movies often appear as though they were produced by some malignant juvenocracy specifically to challenge traditional notions of decency and good character. Teachers are portrayed as helpless, bumbling idiots who are easily manipulated, intimidated, and outsmarted by crude (but "cool") teenagers. Youths who study and behave respectably are characterized as "nerds" or "geeks," and are ostracized by the Beavis and Butt-Head in-crowd.

Parents either are archetypal versions of the 1950s "square" or they are hypocrites (which in reality, unfortunately, is all too often the case) who indulge their own hedonistic impulses (sexual, chemical, and so forth) while condemning those of their children, such as the dysfunctional family portrayed in the movie American Beauty. On television, the family warmth of Ozzie and Harriet (although smarmy and unrealistic) has been replaced by the renowned families of Al and Peggy Bundy, and Homer and Marge Simpson, who are equally unrealistic and totally dysfunctional.

To this equation, add the music that interests teens nowadays—a metallic cacophony that still is unable to disguise increasingly misogynistic and violent lyrics.

[handwritten: ADHD → Stimulants / 2-9% have ADHD]

An article in *Salon Magazine* that questions why critics are so kind to rapper Marshall Mathers (also known as Eminem) states:

> The Marshall Mathers LP debuted at No. 1 in blockbuster style. The aggressively demented album, which features the white rapper weaving rapid-fire tales about rape, faggots, bitches, drug overdoses and throat cuttings, sold 1.7 million copies in just seven days . . . the most successful showing by a rapper ever (*Salon*, 2000).

On MTV, children watch videos that are blatantly violent and pornographic (many actually casting porn stars since these women are willing to do whatever the artists in the videos request), and are shown feature programs where obnoxious self-indulgence is promoted, while sensitivity, responsibility, altruism, and other indications of decency and character are pooh-poohed.

Meanwhile, the entertainment industry has been targeted for promoting violent material to children. Movie studios have admitted that they test-market R-rated movies to children as young as nine, and have agreed to discontinue this practice, allowing underage children to test R-rated movies only if accompanied by an adult. And the video game industry has been questioned in Senate hearings concerning a rash of school shootings, including those in Colorado by Eric Harris and Dylan Klebold, and in Kentucky by Michael Carneal, all of whom were said to be fans of ultraviolent video games.

Effective Supervision of the Juvenile Delinquent

[handwritten: DISCIPLINE, ACCEPT THEMSELVES, EMOTIONS & feelings THEMSELVES AND OTHERS. + relationships MAKING CHOICES SOLVE PROBLEMS,]

A child's psychosocial development must involve at least the nine requirements outlined below. Love is essential, of course, but it is not enough. Although the primary responsibility for meeting these requirements rests with the parents, when a child is placed in the care of the state, responsibility partly rests on the juvenile probation officer and/or detention officer/group home counselor. The requirements presented below should serve juvenile correctional workers as a minimal working model for understanding their juvenile offenders and for meeting their needs. "Child" is the usual term in juvenile probation for an offender of any age who has not reached the age of majority.

1. **Children need discipline**: The cornerstone of raising children to healthy and responsible adulthood is discipline. An undisciplined child is either smothered with unconditional love, making the child a spoiled brat who excuses himself or herself for everything, or is an unloved child, an unruly child, and probably a child who will grow up to be an unconscionable adult. This author considers discipline to be "applied love" (or "tough love," if you prefer).

Although there are components of punishment in discipline, the two terms are not synonymous. Juvenile delinquents have suffered far more than their share of punishment, but have received little discipline. Forcing children to follow rules by inflicting pain—hitting, punching, yelling, screaming, hog-tying, and other forms of humiliation—is punishment. Looking into the family histories of delinquents, you will find many arbitrary rules have been applied inconsistently. If mom or dad feel good on Friday (pay day), the violation of rule X perhaps is overlooked. If they feel bad on "blue" Monday, the same violation is severely punished. It is no wonder the child is confused and comes to view punishment more as a function of parental mood than of rule violation. Children soon learn that getting caught rather than breaking rules is the thing to be avoided.

On the other hand, discipline "always starts with trying to teach children to follow reasonable rules through negotiation. . . . Discipline involves the sanctions of the loss of either freedom or privileges until the child is willing to negotiate" (Glasser, 1984:197). Children must know the rules, what is expected of them, and the guidelines they must follow. This does not imply that the household should be democratic in that the child's wishes are given equal status to those of the parents. Children lack the maturity to be given such privileges. Rather, it should be a benevolent dictatorship in which the best interests of the child are given every consideration. There are few children who would not benefit from increased expectations such as doing chores around the house, having more common courtesy, participating in family functions, and so on. Living up to reasonable expectations gives children a sense of participation in common goals, a sense of accomplishment, a sense of being needed for one's contributions, and the beginnings of a success identity.

If the child violates any of these expectations, he or she must be allowed to suffer the natural consequences. Although these sanctions should not be severe or designed to humiliate, they should be applied swiftly and with absolute certainty. Of course, the imposed sanctions are punitive in the sense that the children do not welcome them. However, since both the rules and the consequences of violating them are agreed to before the violation occurs, children retain feelings of control over their life that are absent in households that alternate arbitrarily between permissiveness and punishment. If delinquents lack this sense of control, Glasser asserts that they should be "treated with strict but creative probation where they would learn to regain control of their lives" (1984:198).

2. **Children must learn learn how to understand and accept themselves**. The development of a realistic and positive self-concept is a must for all of us, and is the goal of all interpersonal counseling. It is the juvenile probation officer/aftercare worker's role, in corroboration with children's families, teachers, and other interested parties, to help them to accomplish this. These efforts should be coordinated by the juvenile probation officer/aftercare worker, with special attention to assure that individual efforts are not working at cross purposes. Consistent discipline related to reasonable rules gives children structure, predictability, and the ability to think about an outcome in the abstract and then to select a behavior that will achieve it. This is called self-discipline. The sooner this structure and predictability is in place, the sooner the children can build their self-concept around it.

3. **Children must become aware of and learn how to understand their emotions and feelings**. This is, of course, part of the process of acquiring a realistic sense of self and of self-control—the ability to select the appropriate response to a feeling from a number of possibilities. When children are aware of their feelings and understand them for what they are, they can respond to them more appropriately. For instance, a frustrated adolescent may respond with terms such as, "I hate you," or, "I could kill you." These are immature labels and they are putting on feelings not well understood. Hopefully, what is meant is that "I don't like what you've done," rather than "I hate you," and "I would very much like you to stop," rather than "I could kill you." Whenever children inappropriately label their emotional feelings, these feelings should be explored in a patient, caring, and nonauthoritarian fashion. Even more so than an adult offender, juveniles will "shut down" if they perceive an attitude of "I know best." You

do "know best," but children must come to this conclusion themselves. The better children relate to you, the sooner this will happen.

4. **Children must understand the feelings and emotions of others**. Basically, this involves the ability to empathize with the feelings and concerns of others. Several studies have implicated the lack of empathy to delinquent behavior (Farrington, 1989; Lykken, 1995). Inappropriately socialized children live only in their own emotionally egocentric worlds, and they blame other people or circumstances for their antisocial behavior. If such children constantly feel angry, hostile, mean, and uncaring, they will take it for granted that it is natural to feel that way, and, therefore, think everyone else feels that way, too. With the realization that this is not so, the children perceive alternatives and pay attention to positive role models who can exchange their caring, compassion, and understanding for the children's anger and hostility.

All children know when they have been hurt, and they all know that they do not like it. They must learn that other people have feelings too, and that these feeling must be respected. Sometimes their lack of maturity does not allow them to realize that mom and dad may be deeply hurt by their troublesome behavior. This is more often the ignorance of immaturity than the "I don't care" of malice. Empathy training in group sessions may afford them this realization. Getting a child enrolled in team sports, a church group, or organizations such as scouts, or if appropriate, a Big Brother/Big Sister program, goes a long way to show them that many people do care.

All communities contain their share of truly physically and mentally disadvantaged youngsters. A program that would be advantageous to both these youngsters and to delinquents could be set up and supervised by a probation officer. Delinquents would be assigned to help handicapped youngsters. This could involve everything from wheeling chair-bound youngsters around the local shopping mall to helping them read. Handicapped youngsters obviously would benefit, and so would their delinquent helpers. They would achieve a measure of empathy with the truly disadvantaged, and would gain a feeling of accomplishment, community involvement, and enhanced self-esteem. As a lot of us know, it is often much more rewarding to give than to receive, and research supports the notion that empathy training is useful in reducing aggressive behavior (Romig, Cleland, and Romig, 1989:131).

5. **Children must learn to establish positive interpersonal relationships**. "Bad companions" often are blamed by juveniles and parents alike for getting juveniles into trouble. The obvious answer to this is to forbid juvenile delinquents from associating with other juvenile delinquents. But, like so many other things, this is much easier said than done. As with adolescent romantic relationships, to forbid is to drive the parties further into each other's arms (the "Romeo and Juliet" effect). Birds of a feather do flock together, and if we want to stop the flocking, we have to clip some feathers. We have to teach children, and provide them with, positive prosocial alternatives to the birds with whom they currently are flying. We have to discover their prosocial interests and make them as exciting as "raising hell." They have to learn to relate to more mature peers, to cooperate through teamwork, and learn how to settle conflicts peacefully.

Sports, such as those offered at Police Athletic Leagues and at various probation departments, are an excellent vehicle for teaching a child teamwork, competence, and self-esteem through positive and constructive endeavors. Bill Wakefield (1991) provides us with information on a low-cost athletic program for delinquents, which significantly increased these attributes among participants. He organized a running program staffed by volunteer coaches, and with running gear donated by local athletic stores (you will be surprised how generous businesses can be when asked for a good cause). He reports increased pride in the youths, both in terms of achievement and body image, as they covered increasing distances, a greater sense of group cohesion, and less "acting out." Successfully completing a run of some distance garners the all-important approval of their peers for socially acceptable behavior, and, at the same time, the approval of authority figures. Wakefield's study shows that "treating" troubled children means more than just sitting in an office trying to reason with them. Of course, running releases endorphins, which creates a sense of pleasure.

6. **Children must understand the processes involved in making choices and decisions and in solving problems**. All of us are constantly making choices and decisions; delinquents just make too many bad ones. Making positive choices depends on the knowledge we have of the consequences of making them (the remote as well as the immediate consequences) rather than of making an alternative decision, and on the control we feel that we have over our lives that allows us to make relatively independent choices. As has been pointed out, an unloved and undisciplined child will turn to peer groups for affiliation and attention, the members of which, having had similar experiences, will likewise lack the ability to make positive decisions. Choices and decisions within such a peer group will be made under antisocial pressure, and will be made on the basis of gut emotions unalloyed by thoughts of remote consequences. Children must be taught to make their own decisions, and the task of parents and probation officers is to seek and achieve a sound balance between supporting the child's decision and making sure these decisions are responsible ones.

7. **Children need positive values and ideals with which to guide their lives**. Values are the vital core of society, the cement that holds it together, without which social life would be literally meaningless ("anomie"). Values have to be taught; children need to know what goals are worth striving for, what ideas are worthy of being preserved, what is important in life, and how they should lead a good life. As we have seen, many positive values are being mercilessly assaulted in the popular media. Some people view values such as the golden rule, honor, and personal integrity as hopelessly old fashioned and restrictive of personal liberty. On the contrary, values set us free by anchoring our lives in a meaningful sense of community and provide us with guidelines for social living. Children who never learn the value of values trudge through life caring for little else other than the immediate gratification of their selfish impulses.

Juvenile correctional workers in some jurisdictions called "careworkers" should serve as role models for their offenders by emphasizing in word and deed that positive prosocial value are indispensable. In an effort to "identify" with offenders, you should never—except perhaps jokingly—adopt their mannerisms and speech. This does not mean that you always should look cold and professional and use language that smells of old books. A little contemporary vernacular is fine, but stay away from delinquent slang that expresses antisocial values such as "geek," "fink," "NARC," "pigs," and "bad mutha." The use of such language by the correctional worker gilds it with an aura of legitimacy. This might be "identifying" with offenders, but is not the point of the whole process to get them to identify with you and the prosocial values you are supposed to embody?

8. **Children must learn to appreciate the value of education and work**. We all know the tremendous value of education and work, but we will never get the message over to delinquents who are convinced otherwise by preaching to them. They have heard it all before and rejected it, so they are not likely to buy it from you. We tend to reject and belittle the things we feel that we do not understand or feel we cannot

master. This happens even in college, where presumably students do have a belief in the value of education.

Although many delinquents have attention deficit disorders and other learning disabilities, there are few reasons why healthy children should not be able to master the typical American high school curriculum. But students need to know and understand *why* education is important and *what it can do for them*. Many barely literate student athletes knuckle down to study under "no pass, no play" rules. A recent television news item reported that youths who drop out of school in Virginia cannot obtain a driver's license. Given the importance of driving for teenagers, no prizes are offered for guessing what has happened to Virginia's dropout rate—it declined substantially. Yes, it is coercion (discipline), but we are all coerced to some extent. How many of you reading this are in college for no other reason than being possessed of an insatiable desire to acquire knowledge for its own sake? You are probably in college because you have made a contract with yourself to forego immediate gratification for the greater rewards that you know education brings with it. You have learned the lesson; others can too.

We often think of police officers as "bustin' 'em" and probation officers as "trustin' 'em." But police officers and probation officers can work, in conjunction with school authorities, as a three-pronged team to help troubled children. An innovative program implemented by the Boise (Idaho) Police Department has been in operation for more than twenty-five years in various Boise elementary and high schools. Plainclothes Boise police officers are assigned to schools as school resource officers. These officers, because of the authority inherent in the police role, often can be more effective than school authorities in dealing with hostile and uncooperative youths and parents because they cannot be intimidated by them the way teachers and school counselors can (Scheffer, 1987:38-39). School resource officers are very effective not only in detecting and deterring school crime, but also in counseling and helping many troubled youths. As for the attitude of youths toward the police in these schools,

> The interviews with students revealed a positive humanistic view of police and their role in society, a high degree of trust in the resource officer and a clear indication that many students have altered their attitudes concerning wrong-doing as well as how they think about the functions and motives of the police (1987:85).

This is a heartening attitude from teenagers, many of whom have had little contact with caring police officers, and whose attitudes toward the police are usually ones of fear, contempt, and disrespect. Turning kid's heads around about the most visible symbols of authority goes a long way to turning their heads around about all reasonable authority. If your city has such a program, as a juvenile probation officer, you should find out all you can about it and use this valuable resource to its fullest.

9. **Children need a sense of responsibility for their actions and lives.** This whole book is more or less about the development of a sense of responsibility. Responsibility means disciplined action—having chores to do around the house, doing your schoolwork, occupying your time with meaningful activities, giving to others, and so on. It means having a positive self-concept around which you can organize your life and pursue meaningful and socially useful goals. It also means having the maturity to know when you are wrong and being willing to accept the consequences for your

actions without rancor. Even some law-abiding adults have problems with this, so be patient with your young delinquent charges.

The imposition of community service and restitution orders goes a long way to help develop a sense of responsibility in juvenile offenders. Repaying the community through putting in useful work hours with a nonprofit organization can give children a sense of usefulness as contributing members to the community they have offended. It also places the children in the company of prosocial others from whom they may learn valuable lesson. Both community service and restitution are integral components of the restorative justice philosophy.

Monetary restitution in the amount appropriated by the child also should be assessed. Thorvaldson (1980:22) views restitution as reparation ("repairing" damage done) performed for justice's sake and to teach offenders moral values. In other words, in addition to being simple justice for the victim, the child learns that you cannot get something for nothing. Sometimes the payment of restitution presents a problem for a child who is below the age requirement for legal employment. If children cannot pay restitution themselves, the court may order the parents or guardians to do so because they are financially and legally responsible for their children. Research indicates that, by and large, relatively mature offenders identify restitution as right and proper and see its reparative and rehabilitative intent, while low-maturity offenders tend to see it as punitive (Van Vooris, 1985). Your task is to convince all offenders who are ordered to pay restitution of the morality and responsibility of such an order.

DIFFERENT STROKES FOR DIFFERENT FOLKS

Nothing works uniformly for everyone. This is particularly true of juveniles who come to you in various stages of maturity and from various backgrounds. You need to treat subcultural delinquents who view the gang as an extension of the family differently from neurotic delinquents, who may be from fairly functional families, and then, both these types have to be treated differently from sociopathic delinquents. From the well-established finding that delinquents who begin offending before puberty become the most frequent and serious offenders, you certainly should be aware that these children need very special attention.

There are many ways that delinquents could be classified for treatment purposes; far too many, in fact, for an attempt at any exhaustive coverage here. Unless your department has routine testing of its children by psychologists, and unless you are well versed in interpreting these tests and translating the information imparted into treatment action, you may be in the self-defeating position of treating all offenders alike. It is useful, however, to know something about offenders' treatment potential and how they might differ among themselves vis-a-vis this potential. For instance, take the differences between extroverts (people whose attention and interests are directed predominantly toward what is outside the self) and introverts (people whose are predominantly inward looking and introspective). Extroverts condition less well than introverts because they are typically suboptimally aroused. For this same reason, extroverts do less well in school and are more likely to be delinquent than introverts (Wilson and Herrnstein, 1985). Just in terms of the extroversion/introversion dimension, then, you would expect different treatment strategies to follow.

But how do you know at what level of maturity offenders are, or if they are introverts or extroverts? You could learn the dynamics of I-level interviewing as described by Ruth Masters (1994) if you have the time, or you could read a book or articles on the subject to sensitize yourself to this system. There are also various scales in the literature that tap the concepts of sensation-seeking and introversion/extroversion. But unless your department allows for time and funds to pursue these strategies, you are on your own. This is not as bad as it sounds. After two or three sessions with offenders, you should have a pretty good idea about their maturity levels and how they are situated along the introversion/extroversion continuum. Additionally, you usually will have access to a piece of information that may serve as an adequate proxy for these intellectual and personality attributes.

As indicated in Chapter 3, one of the most readily available tests for corrections workers is the Wechsler performance-verbal IQ profile, which is correlated with the I-level classification system (Masters, 1994). Although the V > P intellectual profile (high maturity level/introvert) is rare among delinquent and criminal populations, if a child with such a profile becomes seriously delinquent, he or she may be more psychologically disturbed than other delinquents. Walsh, Petee, and Beyer (1987) found that V > P children who do become delinquent are more seriously involved in it than are intellectually balanced (P = V) children, but less so than P > V children.

The implication is that while subcultural delinquents may be "normal" children reacting to criminogenic environments, the delinquency of V > P children may have its origins in some psychological disturbance rather than in outside factors. You should have children with a significant V > P profile psychologically tested by a competent psychologist. Do not, of course, treat the Wechsler test as a classification panacea. Interpret it with caution, and only if the subscale scores are significantly discrepant (12-15 points or higher). If the examining mental health professionals uncover some disturbance, they are the ones to treat it. You also need to get their input on how you should handle the child.

Even then, cognitive imbalance must be interpreted within an environmental context. In higher socioeconomic environments, where resistance to crime is high, we should expect individual differences in physiology and neurology to have a greater impact on antisocial behavior than environmental factors. In lower socioeconomic environments, where resistance to crime is low, expect that the disabilities of those environments to have more impact than individual differences (Nachshon and Denno, 1987). One study showed that measured environmental variables were unable to account for any significant variance in violent delinquency after P>V had explained all that it could, while the opposite pattern was observed among juveniles from disadvantaged socioeconomic environments (Walsh, 1991). With so many factors to be considered, you can see why prediction and classification is such a tricky business.

Family Counseling

An added dimension of difficulty in juvenile probation work not encountered in adult correctional work is the necessity of dealing with the children's parents, who can be more difficult to handle than their children. As a juvenile probation officer/caseworker, you may not only be confronted with resistance and hostility from the child but also from the child's parents. If the child comes from a negative family situation in which there is parental criminality and substance abuse, you are not likely to receive much voluntary cooperation. If the parents care little or not at all for the child or his or her future, they are not likely to understand why you should, and if they come to believe that you do, they may consider you a "sucker." Your home visits and telephone calls may be considered just another hassle they have to endure. They also may be concerned that you might uncover many negative aspects of the family's lifestyle (such as drug dealing or physical and sexual abuse) that may further incur the wrath of the adult authorities.

You may experience some parental hostility and resistance even if the child comes from a relatively healthy family. Parents may feel threatened by your probing of the family dynamics. They may feel it an unwarranted intrusion into their private lives, and perhaps as an effort to pin the blame for their child's predicament on them. They also may seek to protect the child from you, believing that he or she is a blameless victim of circumstances or the bad influence of friends (it is always someone else's kid who causes the trouble). This is particularly devastating to your efforts to help the child who may come to view the relationship as "us against them" (he or she and the parents against you and probation services, in general). This reinforces any feeling that the child has that he or she is being picked on, after all, "Mom and dad think so." Such parents are doing nothing if not enabling their child's delinquent behavior.

Nevertheless, the juvenile probation officer needs, and should insist on, parental support in working with children. Parents must be made to understand that their role and responsibility is not diminished when their children are placed on probation. On the contrary, parental supervision is even more critical during this period. It is the parents, not the probation officer, who handle routine day-to-day discipline in the home. Parents have to realize that their cooperation during this period is of the utmost importance, and they should be supplied with general guidelines relating to the direction that this cooperation should take. This cooperation should include such things as attending appointments with the juvenile probation officer when requested, arranging transportation for their child's appointments, reporting violations of probation rules, enforcing consistent discipline, and working with their child on the conditions of probation, including family counseling.

The involvement of the family in the rehabilitative effort has been considered a "must" (Bleckman and Vryan, 2000). The child is embedded in a family, so if the family system is dysfunctional it is of little use concentrating on the individual child, who is only a minor part of the whole. If the juvenile court is to function "in the best interests of the child," it must have jurisdiction over the family so that its decisions can be enforced. The juvenile court is vested with the authority to order parents, under pain of contempt of court, to receive counseling. This could take the form of simple parental effectiveness training (PET) in which parents are schooled in the art of parenting, or it could be designed to explore, in conjunction with their child, the family dynamics that are contributing to the child's misbehavior.

Because the family is an interlocking system containing a number of complicated relationships, effective family counseling is more difficult than individual counseling. The maximum number of paired relationships in any family can be obtained by: total pairs = $[N(N-1)]/2$, where N is the number of people in the family. If the Evans family consists of mom, dad, and five children, the total number of possible paired relationships existing in that family is $[(7)(6)]/2 = 21$. That is, twenty-one interacting pairs, which is just the beginning! There are many other combinations consisting of groups greater than two. These relationships may include everything from genuine love to genuine hatred, all existing within a single household. So, you can see why family counseling is a specialty that should be attempted only by those with special training in that area. Any attempt to engage in it on the part of a corrections worker unschooled in its techniques may do more harm than good.

Some well-funded jurisdictions have family crisis units directly responsible to the juvenile court, but if your department lacks such a luxury, you must be aware of counselors in the community to whom you can refer the family. Even short-term family counseling—focusing on clarity of family communication, limit setting, contract negotiation, conflict resolution, and the presentation of alternative problem solving strategies—have been shown to decrease delinquent behavior (Robins and Szapocznik, 2000). These same types of programs also have been found to have positive effects on the prevention of younger sibling delinquency. In other words, an improvement in family dynamics spills over to prevent delinquency in younger children who, while not delinquent at the time that the counseling took place, are at risk of becoming so.

The (relatively) short-term Prosocial Family Therapy System described by Bleckman and Vryan (2000) is a comprehensive system with very encouraging results. However, it works on a family-by-family basis and requires master's level counselors. The great majority of juvenile probation departments have neither the time for such individualized counseling nor the appropriate treatment staff. As frequently stressed, if the child's family is in need of such counseling, refer, refer, refer.

Family intervention counseling is clearly a very valuable part of delinquency prevention and treatment. It is more realistic than individual counseling in a juvenile setting because it takes place in a context in which children are fully immersed, and because it enlists the treatment aid of (hopefully) more mature adults who are in full legal control of the delinquent child. It often forces parents and children to engage in what they both want, but lack the knowledge and insight to initiate themselves. The value of family counseling is stressed by the chief counselor of a family crisis center in Akron, Ohio, in the following way:

> Our experience has shown that both the parents and the children who are referred to the center are pleading for help, and although they at first appear reluctant to become involved in family counseling and resist it, they eventually come around. The children, especially the girls, are trying to find a way to get along with their parents. Communication has broken down, the girl may want to tell her parents how she feels but cannot do so because opportunities are not available or she is afraid they won't understand. Often the acting-out behavior of these girls is a way of finally gaining their parents' attention. A setting which forces the parents and child to communicate is a welcome relief (quoted in Kratcoski and Kratcoski, 1979:359).

Assessing the Child's Needs

The first thing you have to do when you are presented with new juvenile offenders is to find out as much as you can about them. In addition to the information you may have at your disposal from various sources, such as school counselors, teachers, and parents, you need to get a "feel" for your offenders from an assessment interview. Figure 19.1 provides a suggested interview guide by which you can learn something about the children and their family and peers. The interview topics were developed around the nine components for healthy psychosocial development, previously addressed. When you have learned something about the children's needs, you will have to obtain a commitment with the children and their family to cooperate with you in the rehabilitative effort. You then have to match the children's needs with the available resources in your community whose business it is to address these needs, making very sure that you do not undertax or overtax the children's coping resources or those of the family. Treatment plans for juveniles then can be developed and implemented in a fashion similar to the process outlined in this chapter.

Figure 19.1
An Assessment Guide for Juvenile Delinquents and Their Needs

ATTITUDES AND ATTRIBUTES

- What is your perception of the child's self-worth?
- Does the child frequently feel depressed, angry, or rejected?
- Does the child lie and/or manipulate facts and situations?
- Does the child accept the validity of society's value system?
- Does the child express empathy toward others?
- What are the child's full-scale, verbal, and performance IQ scores, and is there a significant (12 or more points) discrepancy between his/her verbal and performance scores?
- Does the child have any positive goals in life?

BEHAVIOR

- Do the child's behavior patterns indicate age-appropriate maturity and sense of responsibility?
- Do the child's behavior patterns indicate extroversion/introversion?
- Does the child show the ability to defer gratification and control impulses?
- Does the child show appropriate remorse for delinquent acts?
- Does the child abuse alcohol/drugs, and why (peer pressure, reduce inhibitions, kill emotional pain)?
- What is the child's offense pattern (violent, sexual, stealing, related to substance abuse, status offenses) and does it evidence an increasing pattern of seriousness?
- Does the child have any hobbies or engage in sports?
- Is the child sexually active?

SCHOOL BEHAVIOR AND ATTITUDES

- How does the child perform in school? Does the child live up to his or her potential as indicated by IQ scores and teachers' perceptions?
- Does he or she put adequate effort into studies?
- Does the child have a learning disability that contributes both to low self-esteem and school difficulties?
- What is the child's attitude toward school and his or her teachers?
- Does the child have frequent absences (excused or unexcused)?
- Does the child sufficiently appreciate the value of education?

FAMILY DYNAMICS

- Does the child feel attached to parents and siblings or does he or she feel rejected?
- What is the attitude of parents toward the child?
- Is there evidence of abuse and neglect in the family?

- Do parents know the difference between punishment and discipline, and which do they use?
- Does the child speak and behave very differently when in the company of parents versus when he or she is not?
- What family stresses (financial, occupational, legal, emotional, and so forth) exist, and how are they being dealt with?
- Do parents and siblings model illegal and irresponsible behavior?
- Do parents encourage, support, and reinforce desired behavior?
- Do parents monitor school performance and take an active part in the child's school interests?
- Do adequate communications skills exist in the family?
- Do parents expect too little or too much from the child?

PEER GROUPS

- Does the child associate with delinquent peers?
- Does the child have any nondelinquent friends?
- Do the child's peers model illegal behavior?
- How dependent on the peer group is the child for his or her feelings of support, attachment, acceptance, and direction.
- Has there been a recent drastic change in the child's dress and appearance (tattoos, color of clothes, hair style) suggesting a deepening integration into a gang subculture?
- What are the peer group's typical nondelinquent activities, and are they constructive or destructive?
- What was the peer influence (if any) on the current offense?

Perspective from the Field:
The Workaday World of a Juvenile Probation Officer
By Grace J. Balazs

Grace J. Balazs is a juvenile probation officer in Ada County, Idaho. A graduate of Boise State University in Criminal Justice, Ms. Balazs formerly worked as a presentence investigator for Ada County's Fourth District felony court and as a cocounselor for a sexual abuse clinic.

I wrote a *Perspective from the Field* for the first edition of this book shortly after I became a juvenile probation officer, which was ten years ago. In reviewing that perspective, I was surprised and pleased that my attitude and commitment has not changed. I still believe that the profession is full of challenges, and is not the typical 8:00 to 5:00 job. The pay is not exceptional, the stress is high, and time constraints and paperwork abound. I believe I've become wiser and more effective in doing my job, but I am perhaps still a bit naive in my belief that the kids we see at "juvey" are basically good kids who have made bad choices. Juveniles haven't changed much over the past ten years; many of their crimes are still committed out of stupidity and peer pressure, and they want acceptance and self-esteem. There are those juveniles who commit crimes because it is in their nature, and there are those who commit them because they have been environmentally conditioned. I believe that the child's home environment and their parents' lifestyles play a major role in determining the child's behavior.

What I have observed over the years is that children sorely lack self-respect, and have little respect for parents (and adults in general), authority (police, courts), or the rights and property of others, and there is little comprehension of conscience, or healthy guilt and remorse. Also, I see lack of respect for education. It is sad to see a child's commitment to school erode because of poor attendance, poor grades, and poor behavior. Parents often seem helpless to do anything to make their children appreciate education or make them comply with rules. Every day I see children as old as seventeen who can hardly read or write. I hear young girls calling themselves "sluts" and "whores," and permitting themselves to be sexually active—the only way they know to gain acceptance. Altercations between children and (step)parents are not uncommon. I wonder if "respect" will ever again be something we will value?

The responsibilities of a probation officer are not only to the court, but to the juvenile, his or her parents, and to the community. Attempts are made to redirect the juvenile's behavior by offering him or her and their families a variety of resources both within and outside of the probation offices. The Ada County Juvenile Court uses the balanced approach, which incorporates (1) accountability, (2) community protection, and (3) competency development, with victim rights, compensation, and protection being a priority.

A juvenile probation officer's work is extremely necessary. I can think of nothing more worthwhile than making a contribution towards turning a troubled child's life around. However, the job is also very tough, and sometimes frustrating. Juvenile probation officers run into many absurd situations that make them shake their heads and wonder how children and families are able to cope. For instance, I've had one seventeen-year-old girl who has already had three pregnancies, and one fourteen-year-old girl who explained with relish, and perhaps a little pride, that she had been tested for the HIV-virus! Most juveniles that come through "juvey" already have experienced many trials and traumas on a fairly regular basis. Many of these youths are survivors of dysfunctional families with a wide range of problems. These problems may be anything from physical abuse and neglect, to parents who enable their kids delinquency by not providing them with behavioral boundaries.

I have a boy on probation who has experienced physical, mental, and chemical abuse for most of his life. This sixteen year-old was abandoned by his mother at the age of four. He was raised by a "wicked stepmother" who did not want him in her home, and did all she could to deprive this youngster of love and affection. The boy's father had a serious alcohol problem, which interfered with employment and added to the family's stress. More stress led to more drinking and to more anger, which was directed at the boy. As a consequence, the boy became a user of chemicals himself, got into fights, had numerous problems in school, and constantly ran away from home. After being labeled as a "worthless no-account," he was told that he was no longer welcome in their home.

It seemed almost inevitable that this child would be turned over to the custody of the state; however, after some telephone investigation, I located his biological mother's whereabouts in another state. That was the easy part; the challenge was yet to come, for how do you attempt to reunite a relationship after twelve years? How does a child talk comfortably with a woman who abandoned him twelve years ago, and his only knowledge of her reflects a criminal record for drug abuse and prostitution? A lesson learned—you never assume anything. This woman, a recovering alcoholic, was turning her life around and had been steadily employed for four years. She was overjoyed at the prospect of seeing her son again. The "official" story was that she had abandoned her son. *Her* story was that her husband had taken him from her because of her chemical abuse, and that she did not know how to go about getting him back.

Through an interstate compact (an agreement by one state to take over the supervision of another state's case) the boy was reunited with his mother after twelve years without contact and with a head full of questions and misinformation. It appears to be a happy ending, but who knows what will happen in both their lives?

As a juvenile probation officer, I have to work with families to support their efforts to rehabilitate their children. Probably one of the most challenging tasks is working with dysfunctional and difficult families. Such families are a problem because, even if the child is afforded the resources to help facilitate positive change, he or she must return to a family environment where our best efforts may be sabotaged.

Unlike dealing with adult offenders, where you need only to attend to the adults themselves, when dealing with juvenile delinquents you must face their parents as well. This is no easy task, for many are hostile toward the system, including the juvenile probation officer. Many of them provide slim sources of strength, tough love, or guidance to their offspring. It is not uncommon for parents simply to want the court to lock their children up and to throw away the key. They may be angry and frustrated with their children, but this is no solution. Other parents will take the opposite stance, claiming that their child is without flaw of character, and dispute the evidence against him or her. There are also parents who will fight and argue against every effort you make toward helping their child.

Every once in a while, some parents will take the initiative and seek help for their children. There are those who appreciate what you are doing, who will cooperate with your efforts, and perhaps even give you a "thanks." Such instances almost seem unnatural. Parents present the juvenile probation officer with as much of a problem as the youths in many instances.

The family of an offender who was molested by her "Uncle Jose" when she was six years-old, contains a father who is a homosexual, and whose sister is brain damaged as a result of being dropped on her head as an infant. This fourteen year-old girl hates her mother for reasons she will not articulate, but whom she identifies as the source of her troubles. This offender is recovering from a major chemical dependency, but insists "I don't need counseling; I've worked it all out." I know this is not true, and that it is imperative to work through feelings and issues and to establish new boundaries through counseling. She has lived with a series of foster families, and although she wears a fake smile, I wonder what's going on in her mind and how psychologically sound she really is.

All case scenarios are not as interesting or challenging as these. Most of my offenders are youths who have made mistakes, but are quite pleasant. They will never see the inside of "juvey" again after their probation has expired. Although many of the kids I meet are able to creatively manipulate and twist the facts, and some are cons in the making, I can honestly say that I have not met a kid yet who I did not believe had some type of saving quality. Only once have I had an offender who made me so angry that I lost my "cool." At the next meeting, however, he was a pussycat, so I assume that I said something right to him to bring the relationship back to a working situation.

The agency here in Boise is a small community working for the best interests of the juvenile. We are a close-knit group, and the camaraderie I feel is one of the best experiences I've known. I believe that the prosecutors, public defenders, judges, clerical staff, juvenile probation officers, intake staff, and detention staff, are all here because they care about young people. I have personally received much satisfaction knowing that I am doing my part assisting young offenders with their rehabilitation and making my community a safe and pleasant place to live.

Summary

A corrections professional in juvenile services has perhaps the most demanding and important job in the criminal justice field. As Hans Toch indicated in the epigraph of this chapter, the juvenile officer gets individuals at a crucial juncture; the time before their criminal roots are too deeply embedded. If through your caring efforts you can wrench these roots from their criminogenic soil, you have performed a great service both to the child and to your community. Edwards and Nuckols (1991:40) provide us with a statement that all juvenile officers should stamp in their minds: "Working with high-risk children and adolescents is a long, long walk with many disappointments. It is important to know that no matter how horrible the environment, the fact remains that children respond to love, although it's a cliché, one person can make a difference in the life of a child."

Working with juveniles presents some special problems (and opportunities) not found among adult criminal populations. Despite the sometimes overwhelming nature of juvenile delinquency, the official ideology of the juvenile court is frankly rehabilitative and avoids many of the stigmatizing terms ("criminal," "defendant", "trial," "guilty," and so forth) used in the adult system.

With the realization that most delinquents do not become adult felons, certain psychological and environmental factors were identified as possible causal factors in delinquency. Adolescence was described as a trying time for many youngsters, caught as they are in a "time warp" between childhood and adulthood. It is a time during which they are trying to distance themselves from the authority of their parents and to find their own identities. This attempt often is made under the influence of the peer group and the entertainment media, both of which often model antisocial attitudes and behaviors.

Then, the effective supervision of juveniles was addressed, with emphasis placed on the essential requirements for the healthy psychosocial development of children. Loving discipline is the first essential requirement. Such discipline differs from punishment, and lays a foundation for a responsible lifestyle. Other requirements addressed were the children's acceptance of themselves and of their emotions and feelings, their understanding of the feelings of others, and the process of making decisions, problem-solving, and establishing positive interpersonal relationships. Values, education, and a responsible lifestyle also were addressed.

The idea of treating different individuals differently, addressed in earlier chapters, was expanded, with emphasis on two dimensions: maturity level and extroversion/introversion, and on the Wechsler P > V test to form a preliminary impression of where the child fits along these dimensions. Caution was urged when making interpretations, noting that any interpretation should take the environmental context into account.

Family counseling is the most important component of a delinquent's treatment. We cannot deal effectively with delinquency until delinquency-generating factors that may be present in the family are defined and confronted. Although many families are reluctant to get involved in counseling, they must be involved in it, and the juvenile probation officer/careworker's task is to make sure that they do become involved and come to appreciate its values. Many families and delinquents welcome the opportunity to learn how to communicate more effectively, and studies have shown that family counseling is useful and productive.

The chapter ended with a guide for a needs assessment interview to help corrections workers get a feel for offenders and their environmental situations. With an assessment being made, the next step is to match the children's needs with available community resources to help them.

References and Suggested Readings

American Correctional Association. 1996. *Correctional Issues: Juvenile Justice Programs and Trends*. Lanham, Maryland: American Correctional Association.

Baird, A., S. Gruber, D. Fein, L. Maas, R. Steingard, P. Renshaw, B. Cohen, and D. Yurgelun-Todd. 1998. Functional magnetic resonance imaging of facial affect recognition in children and adolescents. *Journal of the Academy of Child and Adolescent Psychiatry*. 38:195-199.

Bleckman, E. and K. Vryan. 2000. Prosocial family therapy: A manualized preventative intervention for juvenile offenders. *Aggression and Violent Behavior*. 5:343-378.

Buchanan, C., J. Eccles, and J. Becker. 1993. Are adolescents the victims of raging hormones? Evidence for activational effects of hormones on moods and behavior at adolescence. *Psychological Bulletin*. 111:62-107.

Caspi, A., D. Lynam, T. Moffitt, and P. Silva. 1993. Unraveling girls' delinquency: Biological, dispositional, and contextual contributions to adolescent misbehavior. *Developmental Psychology*. 29:19-30.

Cullen, M. and J. Wright. 1996. *Cage Your Rage for Teens: A Guide to Anger Control*. Lanham, Maryland: American Correctional Association.

Drigotas, S. and J. Udry. 1993. Biosocial models of adolescent problem behavior: Extension to panel sesign. *Social Biology*. 40:1-7.

Edwards, D. and C. Nuckols. 1991. Identifying kids at high risk. *Adolescent Counselor*. 3:25- 40.

Ellis, L. and A. Walsh. 2000. *Criminology: A Global Perspective*. Boston: Allyn and Bacon.

Erickson, E. 1963. *Childhood and Society*. New York: Norton.

Farrington, D. 1989. Psychobiological factors in the explanation and reduction of juvenile delinquency: Genetics, intelligence, morality, and personality. *Today's Delinquent*. 8:37-51.

Fritsch, E. and C. Hemmens. 1995. Juvenile waiver in the United States 1979-1995: A comparison and analysis of state waiver statutes. *Juvenile and Adult Family Court Journal*. 46:17- 35.

Giedd, J., J. Blumenthal, N. Jeffries, F. Castellanos, H. Liu, A. Zijenbos, T. Paus, A. Evans, and J. Rapoport. 1999. Brain development during childhood and adolescence: A longitudinal MRI study. *Nature Neuroscience*. 2:861-863.

Glasser, W. 1984. *Control Theory: A New Explanation of How We Control Our Lives*. New York: Harper and Row.

Glick, B. and A. Goldstein. 1995. *Managing Delinquency Programs that Work*. Lanham, Maryland: American Correctional Association.

Gottfredson, M. and T. Hirschi. 1990. *A General Theory of Crime*. Stanford, California: Stanford University Press.

Heck, C. 2000. Civil Law and Juvenile Justice. In A. Walsh and C. Hemmens, eds. *From Law to Order: The Theory and Practice of Law and Justice*. Lanham, Maryland: American Correctional Association.

Hyde, M. and L. Hyde. 1985. *Missing Children*. New York: Franklin Watts.

Kratcoski, P. and L. Kratcoski. 1979. *Juvenile Delinquency*. Englewood Cliffs, New Jersey: Prentice-Hall.

Levy, F., D. Hay, M. McStephen, C. Wood, and I. Waldman. 1997. Attention-deficit hyperactivity disorder: A category or a continuum? Genetic analysis of a large-scale twin study. *Journal of the American Academy of Child and Adolescent Psychiatry*. 36:737-744.

Lykken, D. 1995. *The Antisocial Personalities*. Hillsdale, New Jersey: Lawrence Erlbaum.

Lynam, D. 1996. Early identification of chronic offenders: Who is the fledgling psychopath? *Psychological Bulletin*. 120:209-234.

Masters, R. 1994. *Counseling Criminal Justice Offenders*. Thousand Oaks, California: Sage.

Moffitt, T. 1993. Adolescent-limited and life-course-persistent antisocial behavior: A developmental taxonomy. *Psychological Review*. 100:674-701.

Nachshon, I. and D. Denno. 1987. Violent Behavior and Cerebral Hemisphere Function. In S. Mednick, T. Moffitt, and S. Sack, eds. *The Causes of Crime: New Biological Approaches*. Cambridge: University of Cambridge Press.

Office of Juvenile Justice and Delinquency Protection. 1996. Juvenile Offenders and Victims: 1996 *Update on Violence*. Washington, D.C.: U.S. Government Printing Office.

Robins, M. and J. Szapocznik. 2000. Brief strategic family therapy. *Juvenile Justice Bulletin*. April: 1-11.

Rodkin, P., T. Farmer, R. Pearl, and R. Van Acker. 2000. Heterogeneity of popular boys: Antisocial and prosocial configurations. *Developmental Psychology*. 36:14-24.

Romig, D., C. Cleland, and L. Romig. 1989. *Juvenile Delinquency: Visionary Approaches*. Columbus, Ohio: Merrill.

Salon Magazine (www.salon.com). *Invisible Man*. E. Boehlert. June 7, 2000.

Scheffer, M. 1987. *Policing From the Schoolhouse: Police-School Liaison and Resource Officer Programs*. Springfield, Illinois: Charles C. Thomas.

Sowell, E., P. Thompson, C. Holmes, T. Jernigan, and A. Toga. 1999. In vivo evidence for post-adolescent brain maturation in frontal and striatal regions. *Nature Neuroscience*. 2:859-861.

Thorvaldson, S. 1980. Toward the Definition of the Reparative Aim. In J. Hudson and B. Gallaway, eds. *Victims, Offenders, and Alternative Sanctions*. Lexington, Massachusetts: Lexington Books.

Udry, J. 1990. *Biosocial Models of Adolescent Problem Behaviors. Social Biology*. 37:1-10.

Van Vooris, P. 1985. Restitution outcome and probationers' assessments of restitution. *Criminal Justice and Behavior*. 12: 259-287.

Wakefield, B. 1991. Delinquency, exercise, and self-esteem: A look at a new program for high risk youth. *Paper presented at the 1991 annual meeting of the Academy of Criminal Justice Sciences*. Nashville, Tennessee.

Walsh, A. 1991. *Intellectual Imbalance: Love Deprivation and Violent Delinquency: A Biosocial Perspective*. Springfield, Illinois: Charles C. Thomas.

Walsh, A., T. Petee, and J. Beyer. 1987. Intellectual imbalance: Comparing high verbal and high performance IQ delinquents. *Criminal Justice and Behavior*. 14:370-379.

Weiss, G. 1991. Attention-deficit hyperactivity disorder. In M. Lewis, ed. *Child and Adolescent Psychiatry: A Comprehensive Textbook*. Baltimore: Williams and Wilkins.

Wilson, J. and R. Herrnstein. 1985. *Crime and Human Nature.* New York: Simon and Schuster.

Chapter 20

The Female Offender

Counselors of women must intervene with delicate balance. The goal is to help women adapt to transitions and resolve ambiguities in their own individual ways and according to their own values while also helping them move beyond where they are in order to become independent, autonomous human beings.

Nancy Schlossberg and Laura Kent

Gender Differences in Criminality

No doubt, across time, national boundaries, and type of crime, females commit far fewer crimes than males. In 1999, there were 84,427 women imprisoned in state and federal prisons, which constituted 6.5 percent of all prison inmates in the United States (Beck and Mumola, 1999). From international crime data, Wilson and Herrnstein (1985:104) conclude that "Males are five to fifty times [depending on the country] more likely to be arrested as are females." Prostitution (which is really male driven) is the only crime in which females dominate, and they are almost never arrested for other sex crimes such as child molestation. The gap between the sexes in the United States is widest for violent crimes. In 1999, females constituted 17 percent of all arrests for violent crimes and 29 percent of all arrests for property crimes (FBI, 1999). However, between 1970 and 1990, a period in which the male arrest rate increased by 19 percent, the female arrest rate increased almost 32 percent, mainly for drug and property offenses (Steffensmeier, 1995).

THE MALE CHIVALRY HYPOTHESIS

Are these huge discrepancies in male/female crime an accurate reflection of actual sex differences in behavior or of something else? Some feminist criminologists (for example, Simon, 1975) view the relationship between gender and crime largely as a function of differential reporting and differential application of formal arrests rather than actual differences in male and female criminality. In other words, there is a bias in favor of women that disposes victims not to report crimes committed against them by women, and a similar bias in the "chivalrous" criminal justice system, which is revealed in the unwillingness of police officers to arrest women and in the unwillingness of the courts to convict.

To test this hypothesis, Hindelang (1979) compared Uniform Crime Report (UCR) data and National Victimization Survey (NVS) data for the years 1972 through 1976. He found that the official and self-reported rates of victimization accorded extremely well with one another, especially for violent crimes. The percentage of females arrested for simple assault as indicated by the Uniform Crime Report was identical with the National Victimization Survey data at 14 percent. For robbery (Uniform Crime Report = 7 percent, NVS = 4 percent) and aggravated assault (Uniform Crime Report = 13 percent, NVS = 8 percent), official reporting was greater than survey reporting, a finding that runs directly contrary to the chivalry hypothesis. Hindelang's study provides confidence that arrest data are quite accurate with respect to the gender characteristics of offenders.

The Family Background of Female Offenders

Since female criminality is comparatively rare, it would seem to follow that females who become criminal are more atypical of their gender than criminal males are atypical of theirs. As Herrnstein (1989:20) points out, "there are fewer female offenders than male, but they are more deviant [than nonoffending females] psychologically, both intellectually and in personality." The reasoning is that since females generally tend to be more conformist in their behavior than males, the criminal threshold is much higher for females than for males. That is, it takes greater frequency and/or severity of the experiences typically related to criminal behavior to propel females over the line dividing deviance from nondeviance than it does for males.

Although there is a relative dearth of studies of female crime and delinquency, what studies there are tend to support the contention that female offenders come from more dysfunctional families than their male counterparts. For instance, one study found that: "There was more mother-adolescent conflict/hostility and a trend for more parental conflict/hostility in families of female delinquents than in the families of male delinquents" (Henggeler, Edwards, and Borduin, 1987:206). Other studies among female prison inmates have found that they had been subjected to physical and sexual abuse (either as children or by husbands and boyfriends) at rates exceeding three to four times the national rate (Daley and Argeriou, 1997; Crawford, 1988).

Summing up her study of 240 girls committed to the California Youth Authority, Rosenbaum (1989:38) states: "Not only did these girls suffer from their parents' broken marriages and multiple relationships, alcoholism, and mental illness, but they typically lacked the nurturing youth require." In a study of male and female adult sociopaths, Cloninger, Reich, and Guze (1975:20) state that there existed "many kinds of more frequent disruptive home experiences in female sociopaths compared to male sociopaths." It has also been found that females are less sensitive than males to criminogenic factors in the environment that are located outside the family, such as poverty and peer influences (Walsh, 1991). Because females are apparently more resistant to criminogenic environmental influences (in other words, it takes more to push them "over the line"), a number of theorists have hypothesized that there is probably a stronger genetic component involved for women who engage in crime than there is for males who engage in crime (Campbell, 1999; Mealey, 1995; Raine, 1993).

Looking back on the material on intellectual imbalances among males in Chapter 3, it is interesting to note how the delinquent girls compare with the boys in terms of intellectual imbalance. Of the seventy-four girls in our sample, forty-five (60.8 percent) were P=V, and twenty-nine (39.2 percent) were P>V imbalanced. None of the girls showed the V>P imbalanced profile, further emphasizing the atypicality of female delinquents. Since the P>V profile is also overrepresented among female delinquents, with the V>P profile being completely absent, we have further evidence that P>V is a marker of antisocial behavior, and V>P is a marker of conforming behavior (Walsh, 1991).

Causality: Structural

As in so many "sensitive" areas of criminology, heated debate surrounds the issue of why we observe such a criminality gender gap. Some writers, citing the ideology that always seems to intrude into the issue of gender differences in criminality (such as nature versus nurture, sexism, the role of the feminist movement), indicate that to even explore the issue borders on the taboo (Scarr, 1993). Not to explore an issue because it may cause psychic pain for some is to agree with those who feel that ignorance might be bliss, which is sheer nonsense. The best approach is to admit that no single cause of the gender gap exists, and that the issue is not one of nature versus nurture but rather nature *via* nurture. Feminist explanations of female crime revolve around the influence of the woman's liberation movement. According to some authorities, as women enter the job market in greater numbers, opportunities for committing crime increase proportionately.

Feminist criminology has two major concerns: (1) Do the traditional male-centered theories of crime apply to women? and (2) What explains the universal fact that females are far less involved in crime and other forms of antisocial behavior than males? Only the second concern is relevant to us here. Feminist criminologists' explanations for the large gender gap in criminality rest heavily on traditional sociological notions of the power of socialization. Males are socialized to be assertive, aggressive, ambitious, and dominant, which are admirable qualities if prosocially directed, but also may be conducive to crime in some situations. Females, on the other hand, are socialized to be passive, nurturing, "ladylike," and home- and family-oriented, qualities which are negatively related to criminality. This viewpoint suggests that if females were socialized in the same way as males and had similar roles and experiences, gender differences in criminality would disappear. We will address this point later, but for now we will briefly examine what feminists mean by examining female criminal behavior from a feminist point of view.

In asserting the inadequacy of mainstream ("malestream"?) theories to explain female crime, feminists are not saying that females do not face, nor are they insensitive to, the same kinds of pressures that influence male criminality. What they are saying is that females often face situations that are more or less *specific to their gender* that may lead to crime, but which are ignored too often by mainstream criminology. For instance, shoplifting has been considered an extension of the legitimate shopping role of females (Smart, 1976:5), and prostitution as an illegitimate extension of the legitimate role of a wife (Morris, 1987:29). While these examples may seem to stretch concepts to a breaking point (and the second one is downright insulting to married women), many feminists take them very seriously.

Two gender-specific accounts of female criminality are *criminalizing girls' survival* and *victim-precipitated homicide*. In the first instance, it has been shown that girls are far more likely than boys to be sexually victimized, especially by family members (Walsh, 1994). This victimization leads to a variety of psychological and behavioral responses such as depression, anger, anxiety, promiscuity, truancy, and running away from home (Chesney-Lind, 1995). The first runaway offense probably will result in the girl being returned to the conditions she sought to escape, reinforcing her belief that "nobody cares," and strengthening her resolve not to get caught again. In order not to be caught again and to survive, the girl may steal food, money, or clothing, may use and sell drugs, and may prostitute herself. These "survival behaviors" probably will result in arrest and may precipitate lifetime patterns of criminal behavior (Chesney-Lind, 1995:84). According to Chesney-Lind, patriarchy (as expressed in male-centered family dynamics) combines with paternalism (as expressed in official reactions to female runaways) to force girls into "lives of escaped convicts" (1995:84).

Victim-precipitated homicide (a homicide in which the victim initiates the sequence of events leading to his or her murder) is the second gender-specific theory. This concept begins with the fact that homicides committed by males are mostly intrasexual while most committed by females are intersexual. This suggests that the causes of homicide might be very different for females and males, but how? It has long been noted that African-American women are second only to African-American men in the rate of arrest for homicide in the United States (Barak, 1998; Mann, 1995). Most instances of black female homicide involve women killing their husbands or lovers in self-defense situations (Mann, 1995). Assaults by African-American males on their wives and lovers tend to be more frequent, violent, and injurious than assaults by males of other races (Rasche, 1995), but black victims are less willing or able to make use of agencies dealing with spousal abuse (Rasche, 1995). Consequently, African-American women often resort to the use of deadly weapons to protect themselves.

The sequence of events leading to victim-precipitated homicide typically is described as follows: The frustrations experienced by African-American males in American society often lead to violent assaults on their wives/lovers. Because these wives/lovers have less access to social agencies, and may be taken less seriously if they have, they may resort to violence to protect themselves (Mann, 1995; Rasche, 1995). Thus, women who kill in self-defense situations are considered by feminist criminologists to be victims of a classist, racist, and sexist society, as well as victims of a black subculture that has a high level of tolerance of violence.

Causality: Biological

Increased opportunities provide an adequate explanation for the increase in female property crime over the past few decades, but these opportunities have not resulted in a similar dramatic increase in female violent crime. Even for crime in general, the data generally run counter to feminist theories. For example, a review of the recent literature found that as gender equality increased, females have tended to commit fewer rather than more crimes relative to males (Ellis and Walsh, 2000).

As long as we continue to view the commission of any crime as simply a function of differential opportunities and ignore certain biological differences between the sexes, we will remain puzzled regarding the gender gap. Males are simply more "prepared" to do violence than females whether we look at children, adolescents, or adults, and regardless of the culture in which it takes place (Barash and Lipton, 2001; Campbell, 1999). As Dianna Fishbein (1992:100) summed up the issue of socialization versus biology as it pertains to male and female differences in crime rates, "[C]ross cultural studies do not support the prominent role of structural and cultural influences of gender-specific crime rates as the type and extent of male versus female crime remains constant across cultures."

In her presidential address to the American Sociological Association, Alice Rossi admonished her colleagues to pay attention to the findings of the biological and neurological sciences if their theories about sex and gender are to be viable (1984:4). Rossi's admonition is particularly important if the sex difference we are attempting to understand is a propensity for violence. We know that male and female brains have certain structural differences, and are differentially sensitive to the various steroid hormones that increase the probability of the expression of violence and aggression (Fishbein, 1992; Lopreatto and Crippen, 1998). As Olweus *et al.* (1988:268) have pointed-ed out: "There is little doubt that circulating levels of testosterone during the fetal stage have profound organizational effects on the brain of human and nonhuman primate males. These effects include an increased readiness to engage in aggressive behavior."

The biological evidence points to a neurohormonal foundation for sex-typical (not sex-specific) social behavior, including criminal behavior. A review of the behavior and personality characteristics of the various types of genetic and chromosomal intersex anomalies (Turner's, Klinefelter's and XYY syndromes, androgen insensitivity syndrome, and congenital adrenal hyperplasia) concluded that the further we depart from "pure" femininity (defined as the complete absence of androgen activity) along the intersex continuum, the more deviant and antisocial both personality and behavior tend to become (Walsh, 1995a). This should not be taken to mean that hormonal factors have a *necessary* connection with violence, or that violence does not occur absent of hormonal influence. A more thorough examination of the biological bases of sex differences in criminality is contained in Walsh (1995b).

One of the benefits of examining female criminality apart from male criminality is that it cautions against simplistic biological or environmental determinism. Both biological and environmental factors contribute to criminality, with biological factors being more important in some cases and environmental factors in others. The black/white comparison of homicide rates highlights the role of the biology of sex differences (in both black and white communities, males have a much higher homicide rate than females) and the role of sociocultural factors (black females have a higher homicide rate than white males).

"Dr. Jekyll and Ms. Hyde":
Portrait of a Violent Woman

One of the most memorable cases this author ever had was that of a well-educated thirty-year-old 5' 1", 110 pound woman, "Jane." She had gotten into a vicious fight with her husband. With the help of a butcher knife, which she embedded in his chest, she got the better of him. She then left the house, and returned some minutes later to have another go at him. By that time, her husband had staggered into a bedroom for his pistol, with which he shot her in the chest and shoulder. Both parties were taken to the hospital, he with a collapsed lung, she to have her right breast removed. Jane was arrested for aggravated assault.

Looking at Jane's record, it was clear that until the age of twenty-seven she was the picture of propriety and conformity, with only two traffic tickets on her rap sheet. After the age of twenty-seven, her sheet began to resemble that of an aggressive psychopath, with ten assaults recorded (including the present offense). The stories behind those assaults revealed that she had assaulted her parents several times, driven her car at police officers when they attempted to arrest her, chased a woman who she accused of having an affair with her husband with an ice pick, and threatened her husband's employer with a gun. These attacks had grown in number and severity over the several months before the stabbing of her husband.

To all who knew her, it seemed as though this sweet and dedicated daughter, wife, and mother had been transformed overnight into a raging monster. She was only an occasional drinker, but her aggressive outbursts did not coincide with her drinking; she did not use any kind of illicit substances, and her family could not identify any tension or stresses in her environment that had occurred prior to the onset of her bizarre behavior. But she certainly had them now. The custody of her children had been awarded to her husband, her right breast had been shot off, and she was facing sentencing for aggravated assault for which she could receive four to twenty-five years in prison.

This author met Jane in the county jail in the course of conducting a PSI interview. She was quite depressed, but articulate and cooperative, and she did not seem the least bit dangerous. Before being placed in jail, she had been placed in a local psychiatric hospital for ten weeks. They had done the usual psychiatric workups on her and concluded that she was "rather severely maladjusted, extremely impulsive, and in dire need of psychiatric care." There was no attempt to explain Jane's apparent "Dr. Jekyll and Ms. Hyde" behavior or its rather abrupt onset at age twenty-seven. Instead, they had chosen a series of adjectives describing her emotional state at the time of the commission of her assaults, which *described* her behavior, but did not *explain* it.

In a conclusion that was fully consistent with Jane's diagnosis, the psychiatric team recommended "due process" (which meant incarceration) with extensive psychiatric treatment. Initially, this author agreed with them. But Jane said one thing that made him reconsider. Her assaultive behavior always seemed to occur around the time of her menstrual period. She also had mentioned this to her psychiatrist, but since this was the late 1970s, the heyday of strict environmentalist explanations for all kinds of behavior, he dismissed it as an "old wive's tale." Studies by psychiatrist Katharina Dalton implicated the role of premenstrual tension syndrome (PMS) in violent crime among women.

Further reading revealed that PMS had been successfully used as a defense in many European courts. The author discussed these things with the sentencing judge and indicated that here we have the basis for medical treatment. The judge allowed two extra weeks to complete the presentence investigation report, during which the author sought a physician to corroborate "this PMS stuff" and to treat her. Although PMS is a well-known syndrome today, there were still a lot of physicians in the 1970s who agreed with her psychiatrist that PMS was an old wive's tale. One biologically oriented psychiatrist prescribed progesterone hormone therapy for Jane. She remained in the county jail for an additional two months while the psychiatrist assessed the effectiveness of the treatment. Her behavior during that time was sufficiently good for the judge to take a chance with her and, much to the chagrin of her husband, he released her on probation.

While on probation, Jane received physical therapy for her arm, which had withered somewhat due to the effects of her gunshot wound, and she continued with her progesterone treatments. She obtained employment, and she became reconciled with her parents. Although her husband retained custody of their children, Jane was allowed previously denied visitation rights. Not once during her four-year period of probation did Jane feel the urge to assault anyone, and she was a very cooperative probationer.

Looking back on this case, the author was successful in sustaining his point of view. However, from Jane's perspective, it was a tragedy. Because of an accident of physiology, she lost her husband and the custody of her children, became estranged from her parents, had her right breast shot off, and had been imprisoned in psychiatric wards and jails. Her unpleasant story may well have continued on the same track had the author been unable to find a psychiatrist not afraid to go up against the conventional wisdom of the time. The simple administration of progesterone turned Ms. Hyde back into the much more appealing Dr. Jekyll. It is indeed a pity that it came so late.

Counseling Female Offenders

Some readers may wonder why it is necessary to devote a separate chapter to the female offender: "Aren't women people too, with the same motives and frailties of men?" Doesn't it 'ghettoize' females to treat them separately?" Can't women benefit from the same kinds of counseling and treatment that men get?" Judith Resnik (1983:109) goes so far as to say that prison inmates should not be classified by sex because, "sexual segregation does harm to the emerging, but still fragile, societal value of sexual equality," and some counseling theorists believe that men and women should not be treated differently in counseling for much the same reasons (Spiegel, 1979). Although these arguments have some validity, few people take this view today, either in terms of sex segregation or in terms of the use of different counseling modalities for women. Like it or not, women are different from men in certain respects that demand different (but not unequal) treatment. The American Psychological Association (APA) recognizes this, and has set forth a series of principles that they consider to be essential for the counseling of women. Those principles having applicability to correctional settings are summarized and paraphrased from Corey (1986:341).

First and foremost, any individual counseling women should be knowledgeable and sensitized to the biological, psychological, and social issues that have an impact on women. In other words, there are differences between the sexes that make a difference, and these differences should not be ignored in the name of political correctness. It follows from this, according to the American Psychological Association, that the counselor must be aware that models and treatment modalities developed for male offenders may not be applicable to females. This obviously does not mean that females do not benefit from the counseling skills of a warm and concerned counselor in the same way that men do. It simply means that there are *additional* considerations.

Counselors must be sensitive to issues of sexism in their language and behavior. Male counselors must be as professional with their female offenders as they are with their male offenders. Using such endearments as "honey" or "babe" sends messages that may not be received in the same spirit that they were sent. Women who are sensitive to the women's movement will take this as a sexist attempt to denigrate them and keep them in their place. More traditional women may take it as a sexual come-on. In either case, you have damaged the professional relationship. A power relationship exists between the criminal justice worker and the offender, and males supervising and counseling females should be aware of the possibility of sexual activity between the worker and his offender. This possibility must be avoided, but it will be more difficult to accomplish if you give female offenders the impression that you have more than a professional interest in them. These are all points made previously in this book, but they are well worth repeating here.

Edward Scott's long experience with counseling female offenders leads him to believe that they present special and unique challenges. He writes that he has never met a female criminal in a counseling setting who has had a healthy attitude about human relationships. In agreement with many feminist criminologists, Scott believes that this is primarily due to the negative experiences with males that most female offenders have had (1977:216). He further states that many such women may be hostile toward male counselors, making the male counselor the target for past abuses (this is not necessarily open hostility, but rather an attitude of "passive aggressiveness"). However, he further believes a male counselor is preferable to a female counselor because female offenders must be allowed to work through their relationship problems, which he considers to be the main obstacle that they have to circumvent (1977:217).

Feminist Counseling

Feminist counselors would strongly disagree with Scott on at least two issues. First, they insist that female counselors (of a feminist persuasion) are more effective with female offenders than males. According to Jocelyn Chaplin, the first phase of feminist counseling is the "mothering" phase. Although she asserts that men are just as capable of mothering as women, because only females have been socialized into that role in our patriarchal society, only female counselors can adequately engage in this trust-building phase (1988). Second, feminist counselors would argue that it is precisely because female offenders have had such bad experiences with male relationships that male counselors would be ineffective in building trust. They also might fear that Scott's "working through their relationship problems" means that women will be persuaded to further adjust to the status quo and remain in subordinate positions (Enns, 1993). Women certainly have issues with power imbalances, and the counseling relationship probably will be perceived as just another instance in which the offender is in a subordinate position (Alexander, 2000).

A number of important differences exist between traditional and feminist counseling. Feminist counselors use a number of traditional counseling theories, which they tailor to fit feminist philosophy by stripping them of what are considered their male-centered biases (Chaplin, 1988). Another important difference is that while traditional counseling theories encourage their adherents to adopt a value-free stance, feminist counseling is unabashedly ideological and encourages its adherents to adopt a value-laden activism (Enns, 1993). "Consciousness raising" is considered necessary to free women from the shackles of patriarchy, which, as we have seen, many feminists see as the "cause" of women's offending.

A corollary of consciousness raising is that offenders are taught how to separate the external and internal sources of their problems. In other words, offenders should not blame themselves for the problems they have which arise from institutionalized sexism, sex-role socialization, patriarchy, and so forth (Worell and Remer, 1992). Recognizing external sources of our problems is an aid in both reducing guilt and anxiety associated with self-blame and in knowing what steps to take to change those sources. A battered woman who is empowered by the knowledge that she is not to blame for her victimization, and who comes to value herself as an independent person who does not need her batterer's "support," may take steps to terminate the relationship before either she or her batterer is murdered.

Externalizing blame should not always be seen as an inappropriate defense mechanism or as "copping out." It is entirely appropriate to divest yourself of responsibility for bad things that happen to you if they are truly the result of the actions of others. As discussed earlier, the trouble is that many of us have a built-in bias to readily accept suggestions that exonerate us. Women never should blame themselves for their own battering, or for using whatever methods they must to defend themselves. However, this author would have severe reservations about any counselor telling a female thief, forger, drug addict, child abuser, or whatever, that all her actions and problems can be laid at the door of our sexist and patriarchal society. There is a real danger that such "consciousness raising" will serve as an exculpatory factor, and thus be counterproductive. If the offender is truly blameless, however, the question for the feminist counselor now becomes: "Now that you have correctly attributed blame, what are you going to do about it?"

FEMINIST COUNSELING TECHNIQUES

Feminist counselors employ a variety of techniques in common with traditional counselors such as role playing and bibliotherapy. This description is limited to only those techniques relatively unique to feminist theory as described by Judith Worrell and Pam Remer (1992). It is apparent from these descriptions that feminist counselors must have knowledge of the sociology of sex roles and be conversant in assertiveness-training skills.

Sex-role Analysis: Sex role analysis often is done in a group context and is designed to explore sex roles and the messages they imply and show how the consequences of these roles (both positive and negative) affect women. Offenders are invited to identify how they have internalized these messages and then decide which of these messages they would like to change. Women may be requested to ask themselves questions such as: "What are the costs and benefits of continuing to adopt this particular sex role for me?" "Are the internalized messages related to this role really congruent with my innermost feelings, or are they strongly at odds with them?"

Power Analysis: Power analysis extends sex-role analysis by increasing offenders' awareness of sex-based power differentials (how do sex-role stereotypes affect the male/female use of power?). It also is designed to empower offenders to be able to influence factors external to themselves that are affecting their lives.

Assertiveness Training: To become empowered is to stand up for yourself, to refuse to be exploited psychologically or physically by others who have influence on your life. To achieve this goal, it is necessary to receive assertiveness training. Being assertive is not the same as being aggressive. Indeed, asserting one's right to be treated with respect may be the very thing needed to avoid aggressive confrontation in the future. It always struck this author that women who killed their husbands or lovers were typically (but not always) very passive types who finally snapped under frequent abuse (*see also* Wojda and Rowse, 1997).

Reframing and Relabeling: *Reframing* refers to a shift in the frame of reference used to view the offenders' problems. *Relabeling* refers to a change in the name or evaluation of offenders' characteristics and behaviors, usually from negative (based on male-centered norms) to positive (based on female-centered norms). From the feminist perspective, reframing concerns a shift from the individual to the sociopolitical system. This is the most controversial aspect of feminist counseling. It would be unacceptable by other counseling theories; not because our sociopolitical system is beyond criticism, but because if blame lies outside of ourselves, then change only can come when that external thing changes, which may be never. Blame shifting to the sociopolitical system is not the same as identifying specific relationships negatively affecting one's life. Relationships with specific persons can be changed readily; the "system" obviously cannot.

Special Concerns of Women in Prison

Drug related offenses landed the majority of women offenders behind bars (Schmalleger, 2001). Women seem particularly susceptible to cocaine abuse (mostly in the form of crack). The ADAM drug use data discussed in Chapter 16 showed that in almost every reporting city, the percentage of female arrestees testing positive for cocaine was greater than the percentage of male arrestees. This does *not* mean that more women abuse cocaine than men. It means that among the much lower number of women who are arrested, more test positive than among the men who are arrested.

Those who believe that separate standards for males and females perpetuate sexism may be happy to learn that no special efforts have been made to design prison classification systems for females. Systems designed for male prisoners have been applied to women without change (Clements, 1986). Clements considers this "benign neglect" that simply reflects the reality that only about 6.6 percent of incarcerated individuals are women, and that female inmates are less violent, more cooperative, and less escape prone. The attitude seems to be, "Why make special efforts for such a small and relatively well behaved group when we are faced with the horrendous problems of male inmates." It is not that female inmates cause staff no trouble at all. It appears from a number of studies that female inmates commit more disciplinary offenses than male inmates during the first year of incarceration, although these offenses are far less serious and may reflect less tolerance of female misbehavior on the part of correctional staff (Lindquist, 1980).

Part of the reason that females may commit more disciplinary offenses is the abysmal state of correctional programs available for females in prison, and for the special pains of imprisonment they may feel (Pollock-Byrne, 1990). Programs for women tend to be overwhelmingly sex stereotyped, emphasizing clerical work, food service, and cosmetology, or aimed at housekeeping skills such as cooking and sewing, with few programs offering employable skills (Kratcoski and Babb, 1990). According to some critics, such programs serve to reinforce social roles and expectations of women as servants of others, feelings of dependency in women, and low self-esteem (Welch, 1996:215). There obviously is nothing remiss, however, in providing parental effectiveness training for women who may be deficient in this area. As opposed to being sexist, this simply reflects the fact that women do the vast majority of parenting, and the fact that female offenders are not the best parents in the world (Flanagan, 1996:50; Boudouris, 1996).

Adding to the normal pains of imprisonment is the fact that most female inmates have children under the age of eighteen. One national survey found that while only 20 percent of female inmates were currently married, 73 percent of them had children (Glick and Neto, 1977). A more recent study found that 80 percent of incarcerated women had children, and 62 percent of those were single parents (Schmalleger, 2001). The pains of imprisonment for inmate mothers are described by Vetter and Silverman:

> Imprisonment for the inmate mother has a twofold adverse effect. In addition to the emotional loss and pangs of separation suffered by the mother, she faces the prospect of endless worry over the care and custody of her children. . . . If there is no father or close relative to assume responsibility for looking after the children, the most likely result is that the children's care will be taken over by a social welfare agency and the children may be placed in a foster home or put up for adoption (1986:228).

In general, male inmates do not suffer the same emotional pangs over separation from their children. Writing of the male inmate's separation from their children, Scott (1977:219) says: "He walks away with ease—and at times, pride—from children he has fathered." Moreover, while some husbands and boyfriends take responsibility for their children while the children's mothers are incarcerated, they are exceptions to the rule (Schmalleger, 2001). The special concerns of inmate mothers always should be foremost in the minds of institutional counselors and caseworkers.

The discussion of unwed motherhood raises a particularly thorny issue for the correctional worker with female offenders of childbearing age. Out-of-wedlock births present the United States with a tremendous burden, and have been called "the new American dilemma" (Garfinkel and McLanahan, 1986:1). Illegitimacy brings with it a plethora of problems for both mother and child, not the least of which is the huge increase in the probability of lifelong poverty (Moynihan, 1992; Hamburg, 1993; Wilson, 1993). Traditionally, conservatives put the blame for illegitimacy on moral irresponsibility and "generous" welfare payments that enable jobless women to bear illegitimate children and still get by, while liberals talk about the hardening of poverty in this country that has produced unemployable males who are poor marriage prospects, or the horrendous homicide rate among young black males that leaves black women with fewer prospective spouses.

These structural arguments doubtless have merit, but, once again, offer no help to the correctional worker. Yet, we may be able to do our bit in preventing at least some out-of-wedlock births by keeping in mind Gottfredson and Hirschi's (1997:33) focus on illegitimacy as the policy recommendations deducible from their self-control theory.

They write that: "Delaying pregnancy among unmarried girls would probably do more to affect the long-term crime rates than all the criminal justice programs combined." This is not a statement of moral condemnation. It is a statement that recognizes the importance of the reproductive team of mother and father to the healthy development of offspring.

It seems that young girls and women who consciously chose to bear illegitimate children without adequate means to support them, or who irresponsibly failed to take proper precautions, are in need of intensive counseling. As emphasized by many sociologists, the breakdown of the family and of traditional morality have turned values on their head. Just as it is "cool" for many males to deal drugs and father numerous illegitimate offspring, it is a mark of status for some females to become mothers (Kondracke, 1991:187). A young girl lacking in love and affection now has her own child upon whom she can pour out her love, and who has to love her in return. Otherwise stated, she is getting her love and worthiness needs met in the best way she knows how.

For some that consider morality to be a quaint, old-fashioned word with little modern relevance, they will consider any efforts to try to change reproductive behavior an intrusion of privacy. However, attempting to inculcate some sort of responsibility as it is defined by therapists such as Ellis and Glasser is not simply morality. Clearly, it is irresponsible and irrational (in the reality-therapy sense of long-term consequences) to produce illegitimate children for most women. Research indicates that among many unwed mothers, there is much pride and love initially, but that when the child begins to explore and put verbal demands on them, love gives way to "rather severe rejection" (Wilson and Herrnstein, 1985:239). The effects of this rejection and other factors typically surrounding illegitimate birth among the poor are severe and criminogenic (Herrnstein, 1989; Messner and Sampson, 1991; Walsh, 1991, 1995b).

Without moralizing about sexual behavior (a lost cause, anyway), the correctional worker might point out the many downsides of unwed motherhood. Many unwed mothers already know who they are emotionally, but they may lack the verbal skills to bring these realizations to consciousness. These young women and others who are not yet mothers have to find alternative means to fulfill their needs for love and worthiness, and to realize that it is not smart to reproduce without thinking what the future holds for them and their offspring. If their pregnancies are more a functional lack of taking proper precautions than a conscious desire to reproduce, a referral to the local family planning agency for counseling and birth-control devices may be appropriate. Community agencies offering parenting skills also are useful in this context. Given the cultural pressures arrayed against you, however, do not expect much success in your efforts.

For a variety of reasons, female inmates are more isolated from the outside world than male inmates. Kratcoski and Babb's study of seven U.S. Bureau of Prison facilities found that 50 percent of female inmates never had visitors compared with 25 percent of the men (1990:269). This may be due to a greater number of male inmates being married compared to female inmates, a greater propensity among women to visit their menfolk in prison, or perhaps a greater geographical isolation of women's facilities. The isolation of female inmates from significant others is particularly disturbing in light of findings indicating that female self-esteem is more dependent on loving relationships than is male self-esteem (Walsh and Balazs, 1990).

Whatever the reasons may be for greater female isolation, "correctional experts agree that inmates who maintain contact with their spouses and families are likely to experience fewer adjustment problems than those who do not have family support" (Kratcoski and Babb, 1990: 278). Correctional counselors and caseworkers should be sensitive to the visitation patterns of female inmates and attempt to compensate for their isolation from the outside world.

Positive Rehabilitative Aspects of Female Offenders

So far, all seems negative. As a group, female criminals have suffered more abuse and neglect than male criminals. They appear to be more atypical of their sex than males are of theirs. If imprisoned, they seem to adjust less well initially, have fewer programs to occupy their time, and have emotional problems involving separation from children and other loved ones that apparently exceed the pain felt by men similarly separated. What about the positive aspects of dealing with female offenders?

First, in general, females tend to possess more of the attributes that contribute to a prosocial lifestyle, such as empathy and altruism, than males. For instance, genetic studies have shown that females are inherently more altruistic than males (Rushton et al., 1986). The authors attribute this difference to the influence of genes on sex-hormone secretion patterns. We see evidence of a greater "decency" among women even when we compare interpersonal relationship patterns in male and female institutions. Within male prisons, rape and brutality are rife, with rape being used to humiliate and dominate as much as to relieve sexual tension. On the other hand, coerced sexuality in female prisons is a very rare thing. Female inmates tend to form close emotional relationships, get "married," and form "families." Additionally, "much of what has been described as prison homosexuality does not even include a sexual relationship. Rather, the women involved receive the affection and attention they need in a dyad with sexual connotations" (Pollock-Byrne, 1990:144).

Second, females receive very little peer support for their criminality. There are no accolades for being tough and street smart for females as there often are for males. As destructive as they may be, males do receive some psychic rewards from likeminded others, but such rewards are not forthcoming for females. Consequently, females are less comfortable with a deviant identity, less committed to criminal values, and psychologically more motivated to change their behavior (Warren, 1986).

Third, female offenders appear to have better intellectual skills than male offenders. Studies involving the I-level classification system (see Chapter 19) indicate that, as a group, female offenders tend to fall into higher maturity levels than male offenders (Warren, 1986). Similarly, a study of all male and female inmates in North Carolina (Joesting, Jones, and Joesting, 1975) found that female inmates had a significantly higher mean IQ (100.5) than male inmates (85.5). It was also found in this study that males scored significantly higher on all except three of the MMPI subscales indicative of psychological and characterological problems. In no instance was the female mean significantly higher than the male mean.

These studies safely can be generalized to all female offenders because they reflect general sex differences typically found among nonoffender samples. It is fairly well established that the female brain matures earlier than the male brain, that girls talk earlier than boys, that there are fewer mentally retarded females than mentally retarded males, and females of all ages generally do better than males on standardized tests of verbal skills (Moir and Jessel, 1991). It follows from this that most females will be better candidates for counseling methods that emphasize cognitive skills. Thus, female offenders seem to be in a better position intellectually than male offenders to seek and to use information about themselves and their situations so that they may change and become prosocial and independent human beings. You can help them to do this if you understand the special disabilities and stresses suffered by women in a society that still tends to afford women second-class status.

Summary

Although some women can be as dangerous and as criminal as men, females, in general, are much less crime prone. Greater participation in the workforce provides women with increasing opportunities to commit crimes such as fraud and embezzlement. While female rates of such "economic" crimes are increasing faster than male rates, they are still much smaller.

Numerous studies have shown that females who do become criminal have suffered a greater frequency and/or intensity of many of the negative environmental factors that are said to increase the probability of criminal activity than do male criminals. They tend to have suffered more physical, sexual, and psychological abuse, parental substance abuse, parental neglect, and have come from poorer homes and homes that are more likely to be broken. Yet, it appears that women have a higher threshold against antisocial behavior than men.

Feminist criminologists wish to look at female criminality in light of the experiences that color the female world. Some feminists view female crime as extensions of normal female roles, while others concentrate on how patriarchy and sexism can lead to it. We examined "criminalizing girls' survival" and "victim-precipitated homicide" as examples of the latter.

Females are less socially and biologically "prepared" to do violence than men. Greater nonviolence among women is probably attributable to neurohormonal factors. Although there is some disagreement as to whether female offenders should be treated differently in terms of counseling, the American Psychological Association and feminist counselors believe that they should. Many problems leading females to commit crimes are the result of their relationships with males, making it unreasonable to expect female offenders to respond positively to male counselors. Feminist counseling tailors traditional counseling theories to feminist philosophy and is unabashedly ideological. Feminist counseling seeks to raise consciousness among its clientele by techniques such as sex role and power analysis, assertiveness training, and reframing and relabeling.

Females appear to have greater adjustment problems when incarcerated. This includes unwed motherhood, the lack of meaningful programs, and a greater isolation from the outside world—problems greater than those suffered by males. The disabilities of unwed motherhood, both for the mother and her child, were emphasized and require attention by the criminal justice worker.

On the positive side, many female characteristics make female offenders better candidates for rehabilitation than male offenders. Females are less comfortable with a deviant lifestyle, are more altruistic, have higher maturity levels, and higher IQ's than male offenders. Thus, although women suffer greater social disabilities than men and are less well serviced by the criminal justice system on the whole, their personal characteristics may be viewed as affording them greater rehabilitative potential.

Perspective from the Field:
The Special Challenge of the Female Offender
By Cydnee J. Heyrend

After a career in a variety of criminal justice positions, Cydnee Heyrend became the superintendant of the Boise Community Work Center for women in 1988. The Work Center functions as a halfway house providing a safe, secure, and humane environment that promotes respect and dignity for inmates and staff while recognizing the need to provide programs that specifically address women's issues. This facility is the first in Idaho committed to providing a comprehensive program for the needs of female offenders and served as the model for Idaho's new women's prison, which opened in 1993.

In dealing with the female offender, one of the most compelling issues and differences between the male and female is in the "processing" of information. The male inmate appears to have been socialized and trained to accept more easily a monosyllabic answer. However, the female offender demands processing and dialog about any given situation. This necessitates a staff that is open to explaining the reasons for a "no"; the reasons for policies and procedures, rules and regulations, or referrals. In an institution, if the staff does not take the time to give the offender these explanations, you can pretty well bet that within a course of one hour, you will not have just one upset, disgruntled, or frustrated woman, but an entire tier.

Female offenders tend to be very literal. Besides extended explanations, simple verbal comments by staff members can upset or defuse a situation dramatically. Emotional issues of women are close to the surface and can be triggered at any given time by an external variable. Therefore, prior to making a judgment or answering a question, it is paramount that the staff member assess the situation and the female's emotional and cognitive level and endeavor to determine the ramifications of their interaction.

For the male staff members, this type of interaction becomes even more complex. Knowing that a great percentage of female offenders are dealing with codependency issues and a strong probability of prior abuse by male family members, the training for male staff members becomes a critical issue. Training must include progressive and active approaches to determine a healthy role model and training in the subtleties of manipulation, which these women have used with males to survive.

When a woman offender enters a correctional institution, the staff must be prepared to deal with her complexities. Anger management and stress reduction programs must be developed to resolve bitterness, anxiety over the loss of her children, shame, and the fear of the future. The staff must be alert to the physical health of the woman, gynecological status, prenatal and postpartum care, birth control, and of course the AIDS virus. We also place an emphasis on the sensitive issues of physical and sexual abuse or domestic violence. It is very important to remember that the majority of female offenders, like men, are alcohol and substance abusers and should receive appropriate programming. Additionally, a well-balanced mental health treatment program must be devised to maintain the appropriate security concerns, primarily because female offenders become more self-abusive rather than destructive toward the facility or staff.

Realizing that the female offender most likely will become the sole support of her family and children, programming must address educational and vocational training. Placement in these programs is emphasized as part of their return to the community. Resocialization at an improved level financially is as important as improvement emotionally. More recognition should be placed on the female offenders' individualized program plan to include parenting skills, child development, and educational programs. Facilities should include a parent-child visitation room and a children's playroom to provide training for both mother and child in a supervised program.

From my experience in dealing with offenders of both sexes, I can say that the female offender is more complex and demanding. Working with female offenders, therefore, requires great attention and appropriate decision making. It focuses on creativity and demands changes of a predominantly male system. Interaction is more intense with female offenders but allows the greatest possible opportunity for change. It necessitates knowledge of the offender and knowledge of the community so that the transition from incarceration to resocialization may be accomplished.

The future for female offenders will be determined by the professional staff that have the cognizance, dedication, and realization that the female offender is different and deserves specific programs to answer her long-unaddressed needs.

References and Suggested Readings

Alexander, R. 2000. *Counseling, Treatment, and Intervention Methods with Juvenile and Adult Offenders.* Belmont, California: Brooks/Cole.

American Correctional Association. 1990. *Female Offender: What Does the Future Hold?* Lanham, Maryland: American Correctional Association.

_____. 1993. *Female Offenders: Meeting the Needs of a Neglected Population.* Lanham, Maryland: American Correctional Association.

_____. 2000. *2000 Juvenile and Adult Correctional Departments, Institutions, Agencies, and Paroling Authorities Directory.* Lanham, Maryland: American Correctional Association.

Barak, G. 1998. *Integrating Criminologies.* Boston: Allyn and Bacon.

Barash, D. and J. Lipton. 2001. Making Sense of Sex. In D. Barash, ed. *Understanding Violence.* Boston: Allyn and Bacon.

Beck, A. and C. Mumola. 1999. Prisoners in 1998. Washington, D.C.: *Bureau of Justice Statistics.*

Blinn, Cynthia, ed. 1997. *Maternal Ties: A Selection of Programs for Female Offenders.* Lanham, Maryland: American Correctional Association.

Boudouris, J. 1996. *Parents in Prison: Addressing the Needs of Families.* Lanham, Maryland: American Correctional Association.

Campbell, A. 1999. Staying alive: Evolution, culture, and women's intrasexual aggression. *Behavioral and Brain Sciences*. 22:203-214.

Chaplin, J. 1988. *Feminist Counseling in Action*. Beverly Hills, California: Sage.

Chesney-Lind, M. 1995. Girls, Delinquency and Juvenile Justice: Toward a Feminist Theory of Young Women's Crime. In B. Price and N. Sokoloff, eds. *The Criminal Justice System and Women: Offenders, Victims, and Workers*. New York: McGraw-Hill.

Clements, C. 1986. *Offender Needs Assessment*. Lanham, Maryland: American Correctional Association.

Cloninger, C., T. Reich, and S. Guze. 1975. The multifactorial model of disease transmission: Sex differences in the familial transmission of sociopathy (antisocial behavior). *British Journal of Psychiatry*. 127: 11-22.

Corey, G. 1986. Theory and Practice in Counseling and Psychotherapy. Monterey, California: Brooks/Cole.

Crawford, J. 1988. *Tabulation of a Nationwide Survey of Female Offenders*. Lanham, Maryland: American Correctional Association.

Daley, M., and M. Argeriou. 1997. Characteristics and treatment needs of sexually abused pregnant women in drug rehabilitation: The Massachusetts MOTHERS Project. *Journal of Substance Abuse Treatment*. 14:191-196.

Dalton, K. 1964. *The Premenstrual Syndrome*. Springfield, Illinois: Charles C. Thomas.

Ellis, L., and A. Walsh. 2000. *Criminology: A Global Perspective*. Boston: Allyn and Bacon.

Enns, C. 1993. Twenty years of feminist counseling and therapy: From naming biases to implementing multifaceted practice. *The Counseling Psychologist*. 21:3-87.

Federal Bureau of Investigation. 1999. *Uniform Crime Reports 1998*. Washington, D.C.: U.S. Government Printing Office.

Fishbein, D. 1992. The psychobiology of female aggression. *Criminal Justice and Behavior*. 19:9-126.

Flanagan, L. 1996. Meeting the special needs of females in custody: Maryland's unique approach. *Federal Probation*. 59:49-53.

Garfinkel, I. and S. McLanahan. 1986. *Single Mothers and their Children: A New American Dilemma*. Washington, D.C.: The Urban Institute.

Glick, R. and V. Neto. 1977. *National Study of Women's Correctional Programs*. Washington, D.C.: U.S. Government Printing Office.

Gottfredson, M. and T. Hirschi. 1997. National crime control policies. In M. Fisch, ed. *Criminology* 97/98. Guilford, Connecticut: Dushkin Publishing.

Hamburg, D. 1993. The American family transformed. *Society.* 30:60-90.

Henggeler, S., J. Edwards, and C. Borduin. 1987. The family relations of female juvenile delinquents. *Journal of Abnormal Child Psychology.* 15:199-209.

Herrnstein, R. 1989. The individual offender. *Today's Delinquent.* 8:5-35.

Hindelang, M. 1979. Sex differences in criminal activity. *Social Problems.* 27:143-154.

Joesting, J., N. Jones, and R. Joesting. 1975. Male and female inmates' differences on MMPI scales and revised beta IQ. *Psychological Reports.* 37:471-474.

Kondracke, M. 1991. The Two Black Americas. In K. Finsterbusch, ed. *Sociology* 91/92. Guilford, Connecticut: Dushkin.

Kratcoski, P. and S. Babb. 1990. Adjustment of older inmates: An analysis of institutional structure and gender. *Journal of Contemporary Criminal Justice.* 6:264-281.

Lindquist, C. 1980. Prison discipline and the female offender. *Journal of Offender Counseling, Services and Rehabilitation.* 4:305-318.

Lopreato, J., and T. Crippen. 1999. *Sociology in Crisis: The Need for Darwin.* New Brunswick, New Jersey: Transaction.

Mann, C. 1995. Women of Color in the Criminal Justice System. In B. Price and N. Sokoloff, eds. *The Criminal Justice System and Women: Offenders, Victims, and Workers.* New York: McGraw-Hill.

Mahan, M., ed. 2000. *Female Offenders and Community Corrections: From Assessment to Assistance: What Works.* Lanham, Maryland: American Correctional Association.

Mealey, L. 1995. The sociobiology of sociopathy: An integrated evolutionary model. *Behavioral and Brain Sciences.* 18:523-59.

Messner, S. and R. Simpson. 1991. The sex ratio, family disruption, and rates of violent crime: The paradox of demographic structure. *Social Forces.* 69:693-713.

Moir, A. and D. Jessel. 1991. *Brain Sex: The Real Differences Between Men and Women.* New York: Lyle Stuart.

Morris, A. 1987. *Women and Criminal Justice.* Oxford: Basil Blackwell.

Morton, Joann B., ed. 1998. *Complex Challenges, Collaborative Solutions: Programming for Adult and Juvenile Female Offenders*. Lanham, Maryland: American Correctional Association.

Moynihan, D. 1992. How the Great Society Destroyed the American Family. *Public Interest*. 108:53-64.

Olweus, D., A. Mattson, D. Schalling, and H. Low. 1988. Circulating testosterone levels and aggression in adolescent males: A causal analysis. *Psychosomatic Medicine*. 50:261-272.

Pollock-Byrne, J. 1990. *Women, Prison, and Crime*. Pacific Grove, California: Brooks/Cole.

Raine, A. 1993. *The Psychopathology of Crime: Criminal Behavior as a Clinical Disorder*. San Diego: Academic Press.

Rasche, E. 1995. Minority Women and Domestic Violence: The Unique Dilemmas of Battered Women of Color. In B. Price and N. Sokoloff, eds. *The Criminal Justice System and Women: Offenders, Victims, and Workers*. New York: McGraw-Hill.

Resnik, J. 1983. Should Prisoners Be Classified by Sex? In J. Doig, ed. *Criminal Corrections: Ideals and Realities*. Lexington, Massachusetts: Lexington Books.

Rosenbaum, J. 1989. Family dysfunction and female delinquency. *Crime and Delinquency*. 35:31-41.

Rossi, A. 1984. Gender and parenthood: American Sociological Association, 1983 Presidential Address. *American Sociological Review*. 49:1-19.

Rushton, J., D. Falker, M. Neale, D. Nias, and H. Eysenck. 1986. Altruism and aggression: The heritability of individual differences. *Journal of Personality and Individual Differences*. 6:1192-1198.

Scarr, S. 1993. Biological and cultural diversity: The legacy of Darwin for diversity. *Child Development*. 63:1-9.

Schmalleger, F. 2001. *Criminal Justice Today*, 6th ed. Upper Saddle River, New Jersey: Prentice Hall.

Scott, E. 1977. Women criminals: Therapy with female offenders. *International Journal of Offender Therapy and Comparative Criminology*. 21:208-220.

Simon, R. 1975. *Women, Crime, and Criminology*. London: Routledge and Kegan Paul.

Smart, C. 1976. *Women, Crime, and Criminology: A Feminist Critique*. London: Routledge and Kegan Paul.

Spiegel, S. 1979. Separate principles for counseling women: a new form of sexism. *The Counseling Psychologist*. 8:49-50.

Steffensmeier, D. 1995. Trends in Female Crime: It's Still a Man's World. In B. Price and N. Sokoloff, eds. *The Criminal Justice System and Women Offenders, Victims and Workers*. New York: McGraw-Hill

Vetter, H. and I. Silverman. 1986. *Criminology and Crime: An Introduction*. New York: Harper and Row.

Walsh, A. 1991. *Intellectual Imbalance, Love Deprivation and Violent Delinquency: A Biosocial Perspective*. Springfield, Illinois: Charles C. Thomas.

_____. 1994. Homosexual and heterosexual child molestation: Case characteristics and sentencing differentials. *International Journal of Offender Therapy and Comparative Criminology*. 38:339-353.

_____. 1995a. *Biosociology: An Emerging Paradigm*. Westport, Connecticut: Praeger.

_____. 1995b. Genetic and cytogenetic intersex anomalies: Can they help us to understand gender differences in deviant behavior? *International Journal of Offender Therapy and Comparative Criminology*. 39:151-166.

Walsh, A. and G. Balazs. 1990. Love, sex, and self-esteem. *Free Inquiry in Creative Sociology*. 18:37-41.

Warren, M. 1986. The Female Offender. In H. Toch, ed. *Psychology of Crime and Criminal Justice*. Prospect Heights, Illinois: Waveland.

Welch, M. 1996. *Corrections: A Critical Approach*. New York: McGraw-Hill.

Wilson, J. 1993. On gender. *Public Interest*. 112:3-26.

Wilson, J. and R. Herrnstein. 1985. *Crime and Human Nature*. New York: Simon and Schuster.

Wojda, R. and J. Rowse, with photographs by G. Wojda. 1997. *Women Behind Bars*. Lanham, Maryland: American Correctional Association.

Worell, J. and P. Remer. 1992. *Feminist Perspectives in Therapy: An Empowerment Model for Women*. New York: John Wiley.

The Elderly Offender

by Grace J. Balazs

If society has little place for the elderly man/woman in general, it has even less place for the elderly prisoner or ex-convict.

Delores Golden

This chapter was written by Grace J. Balazs. Ms. Balazs was graduated from Boise State University with a degree in criminal justice. She is currently a juvenile probation officer for Ada County, Idaho. She formerly worked as a presentence investigator for the Ada County adult felony courts and as a cofacilitator for a sexual offender program in Boise. Ms. Balazs has conducted research on the elderly offender, has published in the area of self-esteem, and she is listed in *Who's Who Among American University Students*.

Scope of the Problem

The elderly criminal offender has received relatively little attention in the criminal justice system or in the criminological literature. "Criminological gerontology is highly neglected, if not completely nonexistent" (Krause and Schafer, 1971:3). This neglect is probably due to there being so few elderly inmates. However, we can expect an increase in interest in the elderly offender as the American population ages. It is expected that 16 percent of the American population will be fifty years of age or older by the year 2005 (Kratcoski, 2000).

There is a problem in defining the term "elderly" in a criminal justice context. In the larger society, the term usually is reserved for those who have achieved senior citizen status; that is, those aged sixty-five or older. But age is relative, and anyone over the age of thirty is considered "old" in prison settings (Chaiklin and Fultz, 1985). In some systems, the term *geriatric* has been applied to inmates as "young" as fifty-nine, regardless of the presence or absence of health problems (Snarr, 1996). Alston points out that the literature on the "older offender" has referred to age groups ranging from forty to sixty-five, and adds that these discrepant definitions make generalizations difficult (1986). The Uniform Crime Report (1999) defines older offenders as those fifty-five years of age or older. Given the this plethora of definitions, the term "elderly" will be variably defined in this chapter.

According to a U.S. Department of Justice report (Beck and Mumola, 1999), the proportion of inmates aged thirty-five to fifty-four ("old" by prison standards) grew from 25 percent in 1986 to 40 percent in 1998. The neglect of the elderly offender in terms of criminal justice policy also can be attributed to the reluctance of criminal justice administrators to allocate scarce funds for special programs aimed at a small category of offenders who present them with few problems, at least as far as supervision is concerned. As McCarthy and Langworthy (1987:8) point out: "As we have found from research on female offenders, small numbers and the designation of an offender group as a 'nonproblem' may lead to lack of agency attention."

As of 1998, the over sixty-fives accounted for only 12 percent of the total U.S. population, so even when we adjust for the number of over sixty-fives in the general population, they still are very much underrepresented among criminal offenders. However, there is evidence that elderly criminal activity has been increasing steadily over the past few decades, with the over 55 prison population doubling nationally from 13,800 inmates in 1988 to 39,000 in 1998 (Schmalleger, 2000).

In Florida, for instance, while the total prison population has grown 25 percent over the past few years, inmates aged fifty or older have increased 51 percent (Snarr, 1996:130). The latest national figures show that the number of male inmates over age fifty-five increased by 47 percent from 1996 to 1998 (from 18,064 to 34,204) and female inmates over age fifty-five increased by 57 percent (from 643 to 1,482) (American Correctional Association, 2000:32). This increase in elderly incarceration rates, however, must be interpreted in light of the much lower base rates of the elderly.

Some Causes of Elderly Crime

If we examine the causes of crime among elderly offenders with long criminal histories, the social or personal situations that moved them in criminal directions when they were young are presumably the same ones that influence them today. They may be successful career criminals who continue to receive psychic and financial rewards from crime, which they consider to be preferable to those they feel that they could receive from leading a "straight" life. Since most criminals "mature" out of crime by the time they are forty, if not well before that (Jolin and Gibbons, 1987), we have to assume that offenders who continue the criminal lifestyle past this age are either "successful" criminals or else are immature individuals who lack the requisite insight to engage in the midlife reassessment process that most of us go through, criminal or not. Of course, some elderly criminals simply have found their "comfort zone" in prison, and are proud of their criminal exploits and values (Graham, 1992). One person described many older criminals as "jitterbug celebrities proud of their fifty-year mandatory minimums" (Chaneles, 1995:556).

However, what about offenders who enter the criminal justice system for the first time at an advanced age? Why, after presumably leading a conventional life up to that point, do they become involved with crime for the first time long after most former criminals have matured out of it? From a biological perspective, some suggest that chronic brain syndrome associated with age may lead to loss of inhibitions against illegal sexual behavior, such as exhibitionism and child molestation, and against aggression. However, this explanation would account for only a very small proportion of elderly criminal behavior. Abnormal brain functioning that is secondary to old age (such as Alzheimer's disease) is far less common than many people think, and has a typical onset age of around age seventy (Twining, 1988:28).

From a more psychological point of view, Weigand and Burger (1979) see many of the frustrations of old age—poverty, loss of occupational status, and boredom—combined with situational factors such as loneliness and liquor, to create opportunities for sexual acting-out and/or violence. The problem may be a declining range of personal contacts, which may lead to emotional intensity and conflict.

A study of MMPI profiles of older prison inmates found them to be less psychopathic than younger inmates, but much more neurotic (Panton, 1976/1977). Commenting on these profiles, Panton states: "They appeared to have limited ability to cope with emotional stress and appeared to have difficulty in personal adaptability and resourcefulness" (1976/1977:207). Since elderly first-time offenders apparently have led conventional lifestyles up to the point of committing their crimes, it is possible that any and all of these causal factors may have contributed to the sudden onset of their criminal behavior. The spontaneity and impulsiveness of the crimes of the elderly first offender (Goetting, 1983) also point to the possibility that the infirmities of age played an important role in the criminal act.

Having said this, it should be emphasized that there is no geriatric crime wave occurring in this country. Much of the increase in the incarceration rate among the elderly has to do with the "get tough" policies of the 1980s and 1990s, which saw the emergence of habitual offender statutes, mandatory minimum sentences, and longer sentences (Schmallager, 2000). Very few older people are arrested for committing the major index offenses (murder, rape, robbery, and so forth). In fact, Steffensmeier (1989:299) points out that more than 85 percent of elderly arrests in 1984 were for either alcohol-related offenses such as driving while intoxicated or petty thievery, with males accounting for most of the drinking arrests and females for most of the petty theft offenses.

Maturing Out of Crime

Why are the elderly, even the elderly who were formerly criminals, less crime-prone than the young? Some of us may think of crime as a physical occupation requiring strength and stamina, attributes that decline with age, so criminals desist from crime as they age because they no longer can cut the mustard. As appealing as this simple explanation may be, it widely misses the mark. Maximum endurance can be maintained into the mid-thirties; strength does not usually peak until the late thirties to early forties, and the coordination of a fifty-year-old man is about on par with that of a man half his age (Donnelly et al., 1991:80). In most cases, most formerly criminal men withdraw from crime before the age of forty, an age long before any normal person becomes infirm or enfeebled (Jolin and Gibbons, 1987:240).

The accelerating decrease in criminal activity after its peak during the midteens has been noted in all countries ever since crime statistics have been kept (Ellis and Walsh, 2000). This suggests that something "law like" is occurring. Baldwin (1990) addresses this issue by focusing on average age-graded levels of arousal at different developmental periods, and finds that these levels closely mirror the age/crime curve. Infants are often confronted by novel stimuli that surpass their optimal arousal level and become distressed as a result. Children become habituated to more and more stimuli and need higher levels of sensory input to be optimally aroused as they age.

The need for arousal is greatest during adolescence when ratios of behavior-facilitating dopamine and the behavior-moderating serotonin favor dopamine. As we age, habituation sets in as formerly novel occurrences become commonplace. As we age further, even formerly optimal levels of neurological arousal become aversive to many of us, and we take pains to reduce the level of stimuli to more tranquil levels. Baldwin does not claim that the neurohormonal mechanisms underlying sensory reinforcement and habituation is all that we need to know to understand the age-related crime levels.

Related to Baldwin's theory are findings from five different countries showing that age brings with it a decrease in personality traits positively related to antisocial behavior and increases in personality traits negatively related to antisocial behavior (McCrae et al., 2000). McCrae and his colleagues state that: "From age 18 to 30 there are declines in Neuroticism, Extraversion, and openness to experience, and increases in Agreeableness and Conscientiousness; after age 30 the same trends are found, although the rate of change seems to decrease" (2000:183). Thus, shifting neurohormonal ratios are related to shifting personality patterns as we age, and these shifting patterns are in the direction of prosocial behavior.

From a social-psychological perspective, Steffensmeier (1989) provides us with some insight as to why the elderly are so much less crime-prone than the young. The elderly are likely to experience changes in role expectations and in their aspirations and goals, so that they no longer strive for the same level of material fulfillment and recognition that they sought when younger. In effect, the major sources of reinforcement for criminal behavior—money, sex, status, intense and lasting hostility toward others, and antisocial peer pressure—are absent or relatively weak in old age. Shifting contingencies and opportunities thus result in decreasing reinforcements for antisocial behavior and increasing reinforcements for prosocial behavior.

The physiological and social/psychological explanations complement each other. We would expect to witness a reduction in the kinds of behavior Steffensmeier mentions on the basis of neurohormonal changes alone. Along with these changes, there is a growing psychological maturity, more opportunities to develop ties with the conventional world, more reasonable (scaled-down) ambitions, and an increase in conservatism that all aging individuals seem to develop (Jolin and Gibbons, 1987).

The Elderly Behind Bars

Although based on minimal evidence, there is some indication that elderly offenders, all other things being equal, are treated more leniently than their younger counterparts, and that the general public expects it to be so (McCarthy and Langworthy, 1987:10). For instance, Stephen Hucker's (1984) comparison of elderly and younger minor sex offenders found that older offenders were less likely to be sent to prison (1 percent versus 27 percent), but also less likely to receive counseling (33 percent versus 50 percent) in either prison or community-based settings. Of course, the criminal justice system has limits to its sentencing flexibility for the elderly who violate societal rules and regulations. The elderly do not expand these limits merely because of their age and the perplexities that accompany the aging individual.

Surprisingly, a relatively large proportion of incarcerated elderly offenders, particularly first offenders, are there for committing violent offenses, at least in proportion to their numbers relative to their youthful peer inmates (Chaiklin and Fultz, 1985). Regardless of the crimes that put them in prison, the management of the elderly is an issue with which correctional institutions must contend. The prison milieu adds to physical and psychological woes, and to the confusion and disorder of the truly geriatric individual. On the other hand, the elderly are not generally a management problem, are generally quite cooperative with the prison staff, get along well with other inmates, and accumulate significantly lower numbers of disciplinary write-ups than youthful and middle-aged inmates (Goetting, 1983:299).

PRISON PROGRAMS FOR THE ELDERLY

Public representatives and correctional leaders are hard pressed to support specific programs designed for the incarcerated elderly offender. Such tailor-made programs are considered unrealistic, and are low on the hierarchy of priorities in a system in which the bulk of its offenders are young men (Alston 1986:219). There is also the constant strain on the correctional budget and its other resources, including community services, and volunteer and counseling programs. The expense of medical care and maintenance of the elderly inmate already constitute a severe strain on the correctional budget quite apart from any special geriatric nonessential services and programs. Additionally, complying with the Americans with Disabilities Act, which disproportionately applies to older offenders, is a major financial and management burden on the correctional system (Morton and Anderson, 1996). According to Schmalleger (2000), it costs an average of $69,000 per year to incarcerate a man more than fifty-five years of age; this is over three times the average ($20,000) for younger offenders.

Of course, many students of the elderly inmate experience feel that prison programs for the elderly are necessary. For instance, Chaiklin and Fultz write:

> The emphasis in most correctional training and placement programs often has been on youthful offenders. As an unfortunate consequence, older offenders experience proportionately greater hardship in the civilian labor force. There is an obvious need for special programs emphasizing job placement and community-based treatment to aid older offenders (1985:27).

One serious problem associated with the lack of programs for the elderly is that it can hurt their chances of parole. Participation in prison programs contributes greatly to positive parole decisions for inmates (Alston, 1986:219). Of course, this is not a problem for older offenders who are fit and who enjoy good health, but basketball and boxing are programs that do not appeal to our older population either inside or outside prison walls. Additionally, the elderly offender is not particularly motivated to participate in vocational-type programs because they feel that they have "done their time" in the work force already (Goetting, 1983:298).

A study by C. Eamon Walsh (1992) found that elderly inmates express different prison environment needs from those expressed by younger inmates. Whereas younger inmates wanted lots of activity and stimulation in prison, the elderly sought more structure and predictability, and wanted to be insulated from the noise and intrusion of the younger inmates. Their main concerns were for more preventive medical attention and help in maintaining family ties and support. In short, Walsh found that the differing needs and concerns of the old and the young in prison are essentially the same differences as that between the young and old on the outside.

As it is now, the elderly are not seen as constituting a unique group of individuals, as are women and juveniles, for instance. Once upon a time, both women and juveniles were not treated differently from male offenders either, but as we began to realize their unique situations, we began to deal with them differently. Perhaps we will view the elderly as a unique population some time in the future also. We certainly do appear to need such special programs, for as Krajick has written: "They are a corrections problem, they are a parole problem, they are a welfare problem, they are a mental health problem, and no one takes care of them" (1979:36).

Psychological Aspects of Incarceration

Being sentenced to prison has to be a traumatic experience, especially for the elderly first offender. The elderly are supposed to be wise, serene, and to have reached a point in their lives at which respect and deference is expected from the young. But elderly inmates find themselves in an environment in which they are constantly ordered around by young correctional officers, and "constantly hustled and cheated by younger inmates" (Chaneles 1995:51). Elderly offenders have reached a stage in life in which they are compelled to look back on their lives and arrive at some sort of evaluation, as we all must do eventually. The need to evaluate oneself must be felt more intensely for the incarcerated geriatric offender whose life has been turned upside down.

Erik Erikson best described this process of self-evaluation in his "eight ages of man" model of socialization (Yablonsky and Haskell, 1988:122-124). According to Erikson, after individuals have proceeded through multiple stages of life in which they have to establish new basic orientations to the self and to the social world, they ultimately are confronted with conceptualizing their entire lives and being. Erikson refers to this particular facet as the stage of "ego identity versus despair." Undergoing this stage, individuals find a sense of resignation and perhaps wisdom from the circumstances of their lives. Alternatively, they may find only disgust or bitter resentment. The prison environment in which elderly offenders find themselves obviously can have a substantial effect on how they resolve this final life-stage.

Panton's (1976/1977) research has shown that the elderly criminal is more likely to be psychologically characterized as neurotic rather than psychotic or psychopathic. Their psychological problems are more ones of loneliness, lack of self-esteem, and those associated with medical disabilities such as Alzheimer's disease. Chaiklin and Fultz's (1985) sample of older inmates found that half of them had IQs below 90, and that 25 percent were receiving some sort of psychiatric treatment. They further indicated that "A comprehensive workup on this group would show that their mental health is as poor as their physical health. They survive because, in its own way, prison provides a supportive and structured life" (1985:29).

Inabilities, such as decreased stamina and strength, the inability to endure discomfort, and fatigue and memory loss are additional disabilities that may be suffered by the elderly. Health problems, such as arthritis, strokes, infections, imbalanced blood chemistries, and insufficient and improper medications are daily concerns (Chaiklin and Fultz, 1985). The inability to deal with such problems and concerns may become preoccupations of the elderly, which may plunge them further into depression and despair. On the other hand, Goetting (1983:295) indicates that several studies have shown that elderly inmates report only slightly less life satisfaction than do senior citizens in free society. However, this could be because elderly inmates have learned to have fewer expectations about themselves and their lot in life.

Female inmates fifty-five and older constitute a much smaller percentage of all female prisoners than do their male counterparts. For white males, the rate is 96 per 100,000, while for white females it is only 3 per 100,000 (Gilliard and Beck, 1998). The corresponding figures for African-Americans is 505 and 18, respectively (Gilliard and Beck, 1998). However, although there are far fewer older female inmates than older male inmates, they appear to have more difficulty adjusting to institutional life. Kratcoski (2000) points out that older females are less likely than their male counterparts to receive visitors, participate in structured activities, less likely to form friendships with other inmates, and are more likely to have health problems. All of this is exacerbated by the general tendency of prison authorities to concentrate program resources on males, who are perceived as being in greater need of them.

Supervising the Elderly Offender on Probation/Parole

Most elderly offenders are given a suspended sentence and placed on probation, as are most other convicted offenders (Robin, 1990:505). There are at least four elderly offenders under community supervision for every one elderly offender in prison (McCarthy and Langworthy, 1987:9). In general, probation and parole departments find no difficulty in maintaining supervision of the elderly offender (McCarthy and Langworthy, 1987:18). Basically, the elderly do not cause much trouble, and often are placed on inactive supervision status (mailed-in reports). However, at times, the truly geriatric offender is senile, thus causing a different kind of problem for their probation and parole officers.

Most are on probation or parole for crimes against persons, primarily sexual crimes such as child molestation, and many are granted probation for crimes, which probably would have resulted in incarceration for younger offenders (McCarthy and Langworthy, 1987; Shichor, 1988). Female elderly offenders constituted about one-fourth of the offenders in these studies, and were convicted primarily of welfare fraud. About two-thirds of the elderly offenders in these studies never finished high school, and more than half were unemployed and had incomes below the poverty level.

Although it has been said that most elderly offenders present few supervision problems, criminal justice workers should be aware of certain aspects of their supervision. Foremost among these aspects is being on guard against negative or preconceived stereotypical attitudes toward them based on their age ("ageism"). As in any other instance of bias based on visible characteristics, such as sex or race, harboring age bias severely limits a counselor's effectiveness. This does not mean that you should not be aware of and pay attention to real differences that separate the aged from the young. Ageism, as well as sexism and racism, does not mean that you ignore basic differences. Rather, these "isms" reflect attitudes that go beyond what the data warrant—to assert some kind of inferiority in the class of people identified. In other words, you should be aware of the limiting factors involved with advanced age, but by no means must you assume that advanced age *automatically* limits offenders in their activities (some sixty-five-year- olds are physically and mentally more fit than some twenty-five-year-olds), in their attitudes toward change, or their ability to change.

Active listening is particularly important with very elderly offenders. Many of the concerns voiced in the discussion of the mentally deficient offender are applicable to the elderly offender, albeit for different reasons. You must be prepared to take more time with them because decreased speed in processing information is one of the most universal facts of aging (Twining, 1988:49). Although elderly offenders' verbal skills are barely affected by aging, they need just a little more time to process what you are saying, so your normal rate of discourse may present a problem for them. They may be reluctant to ask you to frequently repeat what you have said, so you must anticipate this additional need. If you do not, you may be faced with a lot of miscommunication and confusion.

Also, be aware of the possibility of some hearing loss among truly elderly offenders, many of whom may not be able to afford corrective devices. If this is the case, you will have to moderate the tone of your speech somewhat without giving offenders the impression that you are shouting at them. Elderly people are more prone to more anxiety than the young (Twining, 1988:51), so you must be careful that your efforts to make yourself heard do not reflect themselves in your agitated looks or your barking tone. Many older people try to cover up hearing loss by faking or "bluffing" hearing because they fear negative ageist reactions from others. Such people have been found to have significantly more negative self-concepts than older people who realistically accept their impairment (Blackwell and Levey, 1986).

Some elderly offenders play on hearing loss, whether or not it is an impairment that they actually have. Many of them try to use hearing impairment an excuse for infractions, claiming that it caused them to misunderstand a situation or instruction or to make a bad decision based on misperceived information (Shichor, 1988:171). Do not add to the negative self-concepts of "bluffers" by ridiculing them and pointing out their bluffs, neither should you allow a hearing impairment to constitute an excuse for not following instructions. Rather, you might point out that there is no need to engage in such behavior, that you fully understand and accept their impairment, and that you do not mind repeating yourself any time that it is necessary. Make sure they also know that it is their responsibility to make sure that they have heard and understood your instructions.

Older people quite rightly feel that they have achieved a stage in life that entitles them to a certain special respect and dignity. As we have seen, many elderly offenders often feel especially poorly about themselves for having acquired a criminal label. Along with this loss of self-respect, imagine how embarrassing it must be to have a great part of their lives controlled by an officer who, in all likelihood, is half his or her age. Never subject elderly offenders to condescension by talking down to them as if they were children, although extra patience sometimes may be required when dealing with those who may have some impairment in their cognitive functioning. Unless requested to do otherwise, always show your respect by referring to older inmates as "Mr.", "Mrs.", or any such title they may prefer. While it is necessary to respect the dignity of all offenders, it is especially necessary to respect the dignity of those who have come to expect it in their "golden years."

If you are supervising elderly parolees, be aware of some of the special difficulties they face. The imprisoned elderly offender's reentry into the community is a matter that can be quite confusing, filled with anxiety, embarrassment, and a mixture of excitement and depression (Studt, 1973:43). (The readjustment problem was dramatically presented in the movie, Tough Guys. These wise old cons were released into a world that bewildered them after serving thirty years inside. A similar theme occurs for Brooks and Red in *The Shawshank Redemption*.) If parolees have no support from friends and significant others, such as family members, their reassimilation into the community can be painful and difficult. This is true for parolees of any age, but perhaps particularly so for elderly parolees. Carroll states: "Many have lost or outlived their families. They may have no homes or job skills. Who hires an older person anyway, much less an ex-con? They have no savings or medical insurance, and may not know how to take advantage of welfare programs" (1989:70).

The ability of the elderly offender to function outside the criminal justice system is of great concern, especially if they have become institutionalized. Consequently, being set free with next to no resources poses a threat for these individuals because of their dependency on the institution. It is something of a natural impulse to want to go that extra mile for an older person, but you must not let them transfer their dependency on the institution to dependency on you. As is the case with your other offenders, do things with them rather than for them. Elderly individuals must learn to draw on reserves of physical and mental attributes, which do not come easily to them anymore. The parole agent must be aware of this and of the resources in his or her community that may ease the elderly parolee's transition into a world that may be quite different from the one left behind some years ago.

Alcoholism and problem drinking are a particular problem among elderly criminal justice offenders (McCarthy and Langworthy, 1987). According to Fishman (1986:65-66), increasing age leads to an increasing likelihood of alcohol abuse among the elderly, who are suffering problems of social isolation, bereavement, ill health, low self-esteem, and the side effects of medication. Many elderly people take to drinking much more frequently than they did when they were younger because it serves as a substitute for what they have lost. Alcohol may be seen as replacing lost friends, dulling the psychic pains of bereavement, and the physical pains of ill health, and temporarily bolstering self-esteem.

Fishman (1986:66) believes that problem drinking among the elderly ideally should not be treated in mainstream alcoholism programs (this is particularly true if the problem drinking is of recent onset, situational, and related to the problems of old age). He feels that they are best treated through counseling and increased social involvement with age peers. Furthermore, he feels that the prognosis for successful treatment is good for late-onset elderly problem drinkers if treated in this fashion. Fishman's message to correctional workers can be viewed as emphasizing that narrow and uniform approaches to alcohol treatment will not suffice, and that you must be sensitive to special classes of offenders who need to be treated outside the usual methods.

Another aspect of ageism is the notion that "you can't teach old dogs new tricks." While it is true that older individuals tend to resist change more than younger individuals, it is wrong to assume that older people cannot develop new components of their lives if enough motivation is generated. You just need a bit more flexibility in your approach with older inmates. As Twining (1988:177) puts it: "It is no good having a few standard solutions to problems and then just picking the one that seems to fit best. This might not work too badly for younger people, but it is no good for people who are older." Whatever your "solutions" might be, above all treat elderly inmates with the dignity they especially deserve, while remembering that the elderly are your future.

Case Study: The Elderly Inmate:
A View From the Inside

Mr. "Frank James" is a sixty-three-year-old inmate at the Idaho State Correctional Institution. His incarceration is for the sexual abuse of his fifteen-year-old stepdaughter, for which he received a sentence of five-to-ten years. Frank believes that he is serving a life sentence because of his age and poor health. Mr. James has severe emphysema, which requires him to be practically inseparable from an oxygen supply day and night. He does not berate the court for his incarceration, but questions the severity of his sentence given his lack of previous convictions.

Mr. James is a personable gentleman; he is quiet and courteous, and does not appear to be disturbed in his present environment. His social history reflects only a tenth-grade education, and he admits that he has a bad conduct discharge from the Army. He has been married five times, with the longest marriage lasting nine years and the shortest lasting just over one year. He is presently unmarried, and has no communication with any of his ex-wives or nine children. His victim is presently living in a foster home in another state, and he resents the fact that he was not consulted on this matter.

Presently, he is in denial about the offense, and he stated that he had told his daughter that if the occasion should arise where he was confronted with such an accusation, he simply would deny the charge. He is involved in a sex-offender therapy group and told me that he "knows" the psychologist thinks he is lying and that no progress will be made until he admits the offense, yet Mr. James remains consistent in his denial.

When asked to describe the world of an elderly offender, one of the first things he said was that most offenders do not have a support system of individuals on the outside. This is even more evident for the elderly, whether they are incarcerated or not. Families neglect their elderly for many different reasons. He identifies himself as one of those neglected individuals. His sole contact is his elderly mother who lives in Nebraska and is seriously ill.

Mr. James says that he functions quite well in prison and gets along with both older and younger prisoners. He finds that the prison provides adequate accommodations for his medical needs, although he states that it is often a "hassle" to obtain medical care, and thus not worth the effort to seek it out. He sees a doctor in prison much less frequently than he did on the outside, indicating that he spent thirty days in the hospital before being sent to prison while the institution made arrangements for his health care.

Mr. James has taken the attitude of "live and let live" at the institution. He cooperates with prison officials, and does not pry into the business of other offenders. He also has not let the prison environment affect his state of mind. He says that he feels much the same as he did on the outside, and never suffers from depression, although he acknowledges that this is unusual for the elderly offender.

Mr. James is housed with a group of fifteen-to-twenty individuals who range in age between sixty and eighty years old. Their age does not exclude these men from associating with other inmates at the institution, but many just seek to be left alone to serve out their sentence. Television and cards are popular pastimes among these men.

Mr. James has not explored the entire facility, restricting himself to the area of his cell block. He chooses to take his meals at his cell block because this is more convenient for him in terms of mobility and personal comfort. He seldom finds it necessary to visit the commissary at the institution, and receives no money from outside the prison, which would allow him to make purchases there. He does not feel particularly deprived, however, and feels that his needs are adequately met without having to supplement them.

Mr. James does not think that it is necessary to have correctional institutions designed specifically for the elderly, especially not if the purpose is to separate the elderly from younger offenders. He feels that younger inmates have a positive affect on the older inmates because morale is usually higher among the older men when free association is permitted. Mixing with younger men, says Mr. James, is uplifting, and provides the elderly offender with mental and physical stimulation. He also feels that older offenders act as a "stabilizing influence" on the "younger bucks" inside the walls. This mixture of ages is the closest thing the inmates have to a community atmosphere, the likes of which, many of these men may not see for some time. However, he says that the prison environment can get you down quick enough in one way or another.

Mr. James' time is pretty much his own, with his day beginning when he chooses. Breakfast is served at the dining room at 7:00 A.M., but he rarely gets up that early. Instead, he asks for his breakfast to be brought to the cell block around 9:00 A.M., after he is up and about. His day is not demanding. He functions at his own pace because many of the prison's activities are of no interest to him. The exception to this is that he likes to work with leather, and and seems quite proud of the fact that he has learned to make so many practical articles. It disappoints him that the items cannot be put up for sale at the prison site or in the community, since it would be nice to have some extra cash created by the motivation that comes from this sense of accomplishment. This hobby is the only pastime that adds variety to his day. The rest is routine: get up, watch television, play cards, eat meals, lights out. Although lights are out officially at 10:00 P.M., he reads until 1.30 A.M., thanks to the individual lights that are in each room.

Mr. James stated several times that his routine does not vary much from what it did at home. He was relatively inactive then, with limited employment because of his disability. The lack of privacy is the thing that bothers him most, "but what can be done about that in a place like this when one is under continual guard?" He does not care much for his cell mate, either, but goes with the flow and does not make an issue about something he cannot change. He does not want to cause trouble, stating that it is better to work together and avoid controversy so that correctional officers do not lock down the cell block.

Frank James will continue to serve his time with little change in his routine, and he says that he has little to worry about inside or outside the institution since he lacks personal obligations outside the prison that require his attention. When he is released, he plans to live in Nebraska with his mother, if she is still alive. If not, he is familiar with the services available through the housing authorities, food programs, welfare, and Medicare, to adequately sustain him for the rest of his life.

Perspective from the Field:
Golden Years and Iron Gates
By Kenneth L. Faiver MPH, MLIR

Kenneth L. Faiver is president of Correctional Health Resources, Inc., a firm which recruits doctors and other health care staff for prisons and jails. Active as a consultant in correctional health care issues, he is a senior accreditation surveyor for the National Commission on Correctional Health Care and the author of *Health Care Management Issues in Corrections*. In addition, he was the administrator of health services for the Michigan Department of Corrections for sixteen years and served as chief medical coordinator for Puerto Rico's prison system for three years. He holds master's degrees in theology, in labor, industrial relations, and in public health, and was a Pew doctoral fellow in public health.

Until a very few years ago, even large prison systems had only a handful of inmates above seventy-five years of age. In fact, there were not very many prisoners older than sixty. The median age of most prison populations was in the mid-twenties. It is a relatively new phenomenon in the United States to find large numbers of elderly persons behind bars.

The few gray heads and wrinkled faces belonged to old-timers serving life sentences who already had spent many years behind bars. "Prisonwise" and mellowed by their years, they wanted to do "quiet time." They often were respected and looked up to by the younger crowd. Indeed, the old-timer sometimes became a "pet" of staff and of other inmates, as well. People made allowances when they were slow in line or became mixed up or confused. There were willing hands to push wheelchairs or to assist with other needs.

Things are different today. Not only are there more elderly prisoners than ever before, they are aging, or "greying" as it has been called. Judges are giving felons longer sentences. Parole and pardon boards are reluctant to release inmates to the community. With the growing number of senior citizens in the free world, it is to be expected that the number of those who commit crimes will increase, as well.

Some older persons suffering from mental problems used to live out their days in state mental institutions. However, now that most mental hospitals across the country have been closed, many of these people are homeless. They sleep on park benches; in doorways and abandoned houses; or under bridges. When they become too much of a public nuisance, they are arrested. Several such arrests incur longer sentences. Sometimes elderly persons who lack adequate means of support intentionally seek shelter from the cold and from hunger by committing acts which are likely to result in arrest and incarceration.

Whatever the reason—and there are many—elderly inmates are no longer the rare exceptions which used to inspire respect and assistance and protection. Instead, they have become a "bother"—a nuisance. In addition, they themselves are annoyed by the loud voices and loud music so common among younger inmates. These younger, predatory types show little respect and take advantage of older inmates, hurting or abusing them, teasing them, and taking or damaging their property. Moreover, officers are required to enforce rules equitably and may not be able to allow for special accommodations due to the slowness, confusion, or disability that frequently accompanies the aging process.

Besides the increasing number of elderly in prisons, one must take into account the past lifestyles of those elderly inmates (smoking, poor diet, poverty, minimal access to health care), and then the need for increased resources—to include personnel, funding and facilities—to care for them, in record numbers, becomes obvious. According to Jonathan Turley, the founder of Project for Older Prisoners (POPS), a Washington, D.C. advocacy group, "The geriatric prison population has very specialized needs that most facilities are very poorly suited to handle. The result is that most gerontological problems go untreated until they are chronic" (Schreiber, 1999). One elderly inmate costs an average of $69,000 per year to care for, which is two to three times the cost for other inmates (Drummond, 1999). Although the percent of prisoners age fifty and older is estimated at only 5.7 percent, more than 55 percent of inmates are between the ages of thirty and forty-nine, and are serving, on average, twenty-four year sentences (Schreiber, 1999; Hollis, 1999). In Virginia, more than $61 million annually is spent on only 891 inmates, or 3 percent of the total inmate population, and a special facility to house the infirm and elderly inmate population has room for 200—about one-fourth of Virginia's eligible inmates (Holman, 1999).

Some states have begun addressing the issue. For instance, in Columbia, South Carolina the first private medical prison opened in October 1999. Pennsylvania quickly followed suit by contracting out the building and operation of a 700-inmate medical prison for an estimated pricetag of $45 million. Texas currently is converting part of a state prison into a sixty-bed geriatric center. An example of how the influx of elderly inmates is affecting states that are less prepared is Michigan. In 1996, their only facility equipped to accommodate elderly offenders had 85 beds, and yet more than 600 prisoners in the state qualified to be there (French, 1996).

Some Solutions

The number of inmates requiring assistance with activities of daily living (dressing, feeding, bathing, using the toilet, walking) will continue to increase. Some of these will require nursing home care. Those who are incontinent will need to be diapered and bathed frequently. These are costly, highly labor-intensive services. Disorders such as Alzheimer's disease and organic brain syndrome resulting from the aging process also place major burdens on caregivers. The Americans with Disabilities Act makes it clear that appropriate accommodations must be made, even in prisons, to meet the needs of physically and mentally disabled persons.

More and more persons will reach the end of their lives while under sentences. Some of them do not need to die in prison. Especially as they become disabled or terminally ill, depending on a number of factors, many will no longer represent a real threat or danger to society. Under such circumstances, consideration should be given to seeking approval from the parole board or the governor for release in a time-sensitive manner. Special laws may be necessary in some states to enable or facilitate compassionate release.

For those who cannot be released, humane environments should be prepared for the terminally ill. Hospices in the free world can serve as a model. People associated with the hospice movement are often happy to provide advice and valuable assistance for replication of features of this program in the prisons.

Prisons need a specific policy concerning "do not resuscitate" orders, advance directives, and durable power of attorney. It is appropriate to respect the inmate's wishes and to permit death with dignity. Legal advice should be sought in preparing the policy, and due care must be observed to ensure that the terminal patient (or properly constituted representative) provides witnessed informed consent and that there is no coercion. Where feasible, family members should be consulted. The chaplain also may be helpful. It is clearly unacceptable to do as one facility administrator recently said: "We don't bother with DNR orders here. We just run a slow code."

Secure extended-care facilities, or nursing homes, may need to be developed. A number of systems already have done this. However, if these were planned and established at a time when the number of elderly and chronically disabled inmates was far less, they are likely no longer adequate. Besides in-house units, nursing home beds also can be contracted in the community. It also may be feasible to parole them to a secure nursing home—possibly with an electronic tether.

Specialized housing for the elderly, perhaps in a low-security unit constructed near a prison medical complex, may be a cost-effective solution to some difficult management problems. One or more social workers should be assigned to assist in prerelease research and preparations for discharge, including Medicaid/Medicare enrollment, identifying shelter and support systems, or reestablishing linkage with family members.

Summary

Until quite recently, little attention has been paid to the elderly offender. Because they are very much underrepresented among our criminal population, they have been considered something of a "nonproblem." However, the proportion of our elderly citizens under some form of correctional supervision is rising as our society ages.

Several issues regarding the elderly offender were raised, including the definition of "elderly," which has been defined differently in various studies. Given the youthful nature of our criminal population, anyone more than thirty is considered old in prison, but we have not considered anyone below fifty as old. We also looked at some possible reasons why, after a lifetime of noncriminal behavior, many elderly individuals commit crime. These reasons ranged from the biological impairments sometimes accompanying old age, to the social and psychological problems of the elderly.

The elderly behind bars are not considered to be a behavioral problem. Probably for this reason (and in common with female inmates), there are very few programs specifically aimed at them. The main problem for the institutional correctional people presented by the elderly is financial. Because of the plethora of health problems suffered by the elderly, it costs about $69,000 a year or more to maintain a person in prison who is fifty years of age or older.

Perhaps partly because of this, many elderly offenders who may otherwise have been incarcerated are being diverted into community corrections. Yet, they present relatively few supervision problems to probation/parole officers. We noted some specific aspects of community supervision, such as problem drinking and hearing impairment, as well as the importance of treating elderly offenders with respect and dignity while also holding them accountable.

References and Suggested Readings

Alston, L. 1986. *Crime and Older Americans.* Springfield, Illinois: Charles C. Thomas.

American Correctional Association. 2000. *2000 Juvenile and Adult Correctional Departments, Institutions, Agencies and Paroling Authorities Directory.* Lanham, Maryland: American Correctional Association.

Baldwin, J. 1990. The role of sensory stimulation in criminal behavior, with special attention to the age peak in crime. In L. Ellis and H. Hoffman, eds., *Crime in Biological, Social, and Moral Contexts.* New York: Praeger.

Beck, A. and C. Mumola. 1999. *Prisoners in 1998.* Washington, D.C.: Bureau of Justice Statistics.

Blackwell, D. and L. Levey. 1986. Hearing impairment, self-concept, and morale among the elderly. *Free Inquiry in Creative Sociology.* 15:21-26.

Carroll, G. 1989. Growing old behind bars. *Newsweek.* November 20.

Chaiklin, H. and L. Fultz. 1985. The service needs of older offenders. *The Justice Professional.* 1:26-33.

Chaneles, S. 1995. Growing old behind bars. In K. Haas and G. Alpert, eds., *The Dilemmas of Corrections.* Prospect Heights, Illinois: Waveland.

Donnelly, S., J. Kane, M. Thigpen, and D. Thigpen. 1991. It's coming back to me now. *Time.* 22:78-80.

Drummond, T. 1999. Cellblock seniors: They have grown old and frail in prison. Must they still be locked up? *Time Magazine,* June 14-21. Reprinted at www.mapinc.org/drugnews/v99/n653/a12.html.

Ellis, L. and A. Walsh. 2000. *Criminology: A Global Perspective.* Boston: Allyn and Bacon.

Favier, K. 1998. *Health Care Management Issues in Corrections.* Lanham, Maryland: American Correctional Association.

Fishman, R. 1986. *Alcohol and Alcoholism.* New York: Chelsea House.

French, R. 1996. State Taxpayers Feel Pinch of Aging Prison Population. *The Detroit News.* www.detnews.com/menu/stories/42072.htm.

Gilliard, D. and A. Beck. 1998. *Prisoners in 1997.* Washington, D.C.: Bureau of Justice Statistics.

Goetting, A. 1983. The elderly in prisons: Issues and perspectives. *Journal of Research in Crime and Delinquency*. 20:291-309.

Graham, G. 1992. *The One-eyed Man is King. Seattle, Washington: Gordon Graham and Company.*

Hollis, M. 1999. Tough Sentences Leave Florida with Prisons Filled with Aged, Ailing Criminals. *The Sun Sentinel.* www.sunsentinel.com/news/daily.

Holman, B. 1999. Old Men Behind Bars. *The Washington Post*, July 25. Reprinted at www.sentencing.org/v2i2.html.

Hucker, S. 1984. Psychiatric Aspects of Crime in Old Age. In E. Newman et al., eds., *Elderly Criminals*. Cambridge: Oelgeschlager, Gunn and Hain.

Jolin, A., and D. Gibbons. 1987. Age patterns in criminal involvement. *International Journal of Offender Therapy and Comparative Criminology*. 31:237-260.

Krajick, K. 1979. Growing old in prison. *Corrections Magazine*. March: 33-39.

Kratcoski, P. 2000. Older Inmates: Special Programming Concerns. In P. Kratcoski, ed., *Correctional Counseling and Treatment*. Prospect Heights, Illinois: Waveland Press.

Krause, E. and S. Schafer. 1971. Prisoners of Age, Final Report to the National Institute of Mental Health. Washington, D.C.: *National Institute of Mental Health*.

McCarthy, B. and R. Langworthy. 1987. Older offenders on probation and parole. *Journal of Offender Counseling, Services, and Rehabilitation*. 12:7-25.

McCrae, R., P. Costa, F. Ostendorf, A. Angleitner, M. Hrebickova, M. Avila, J. Sanz, M.Sanchez-Bernardos, M. Kusdil. R. Woodfield, P. Saunders and P. Smith. 2000. Nature over nurture: Temperament, personality, and life span development. *Journal of Personality and Social Psychology*, 78:173-186.

Morton, J. and J. Anderson. 1996. Implementing the Americans with Disabilities Act for Inmates. *Corrections Today*. 86, 58-90, 140-141.

Panton, J. 1976/1977. Personality characteristics of aged inmates within a state prison population. *Offender Rehabilitation*. 1:207.

Robin, G. 1990. *Introduction to the Criminal Justice System*. New York: Harper and Row.

Schmalleger, F. 2000. *Criminal Justice Today*. Upper Saddle River, New Jersey: Prentice Hall.

Schreiber, C. 1999. Behind Bars: Aging Prison Population Challenges Correctional Health Systems. *Nurse Week*. www.nurseweek.com/features/99-7/prison.html.

Shichor, D. 1984. The Extent and Nature of Lawbreaking by the Elderly: A Review of Arrest Statistics. In E. Newman, D. Newman, and M. Gerwitz, eds., *Elderly Criminals*. Cambridge, Massachusetts. Oelgeschlager, Gunn, and Hain.

_____. 1988. An exploratory study of elderly probationers. *International Journal of Offender Therapy and Comparative Criminology*. 32:163-174.

Snarr, R. 1996. *Introduction to Corrections*. Madison, Wisconsin: Brown and Benchmark.

Steffensmeier, D. 1989. The invention of the "new" senior citizen criminal. *Research on Aging*. 9:281-311.

Studt, E. 1973. Reintegration from the Parolee's Perspective. In Reintegration of the Offender into the Community. Washington, D.C.: *National Institute of Law Enforcement and Criminal Justice*.

Twining, C. 1988. *Helping Older People: A Psychological Approach*. New York: Wiley.

United States Department of Justice. 1989. *Monday Morning Highlights*. Washington, D.C.: United States Department of Justice.

Walsh, C. 1992. Aging Inmate Offenders: Another Perspective. In C. Hartjen and E. Rhine, eds., *Correctional Theory and Practice*. Chicago: Nelson/Hall.

Weigand, N. and J. Burger. 1979. The elderly offender and parole. *The Prison Journal*. 59:48-57.

Yablonsky, L. and M. Haskell. 1988. *Juvenile Delinquency*. New York: Harper and Row.

Chapter 22

Epilog

The professional application of the knowledge, tools, and techniques presented in this book will, I believe, assist you in supervising and helping those unfortunate lives that it one day may be you privilege to touch. It is an awesome responsibility to be charged with helping, befriending, and rectifying the attitudes and behaviors of another human being. Never cease examining and improving yourself or learning everything you can about your profession. Make wise use of the numerous community resources available to aid you in this endeavor.

However, never lose sight of the fact that the most important person in the rehabilitative effort is the offender. You must not fall into the trap of doing things for and to offenders; rather, you should do things with them. We wish to foster offender responsibility through self-reliance. An overemphasis on providing everything for the offender, beyond the initial stage, is not congruent with this aim and tends to encourage offender dependence. It is fine if offenders lean on you a little, but only if they lean in order to lift themselves up to responsibility.

The experienced worker may be excused for asking how all these concepts, suggestions, and techniques realistically can be put to work given the constraints imposed by time and large caseloads. The judicious management of caseloads requires organization and a thorough knowledge of the clientele. This is best accomplished by proper offender classification based on presentence investigation information. Proper classification and risk and needs assessment enable you as the officer to determine which offenders are most in need of your attention. Many offenders on the average caseload require little, if any, "treatment" beyond occasional reporting and the officer's monitoring of daily arrest sheets. These low-risk/low-needs offenders are often "situational" offenders whose trip through "the system" can be sufficient to teach them the errors of their ways. The time you save by having minimal contact with these offenders can be put to good use by concentrating on more problematic offenders. Knowledge and proper use of community resources, and of the skills and motivations of volunteers, will strengthen your efforts. There is always enough time for organized, efficient, and caring criminal justice workers to do the job they have chosen. Few vocations are more psychologically rewarding and uplifting.

Appendix

SOCIAL HISTORY QUESTIONNAIRE _____

Prior to your next appearance in court for final disposition, the Adult Probation Department must complete a presentence investigation for the judge. This presentence investigation includes information about your background that the judge will take into consideration when deciding whether to place you on probation or not. Please completely fill out this questionnaire, and if you have any questions concerning the questionnaire, feel free to ask. The information that you provide will be confidential in that only the Probation Department and the judge will be allowed to see it. Upon completion of this questionnaire, please return it to the person who gave it to you.

GENERAL INFORMATION:

FULL NAME:_____

PRESENT ADDRESS:_____

TELEPHONE #:_____

PLACE OF BIRTH:_____

DATE OF BIRTH:_____

SOCIAL SECURITY NO.:_____

SOCIAL HISTORY QUESTIONNAIRE (continued) _____

FAMILY:
Please list the members of your family, including parents, brothers, sisters, spouse, and children.

NAME	RELATIONSHIP	AGE	ADDRESS
PARENTS:			
BROTHERS & SISTERS:			
WIFE/HUSBAND:			
CHILDREN:			

Have you ever been married before? Yes / No

Date of wedding:

Date of divorce:

EDUCATION:

Please list what schools you have attended (elementary, secondary, college, and job training programs).

SCHOOL	DATES ATTENDED	HIGHEST GRADE COMPLETED

EMPLOYMENT:

Please list in order your job history. If employed at the present time, please note where and the name of your supervisor.

EMPLOYER	ADDRESS	DATE STARTED	DATE LEFT	REASON

Spouse's Current Employer:

SOCIAL HISTORY QUESTIONNAIRE (continued) _____

MILITARY HISTORY:
Please note the following information:

Branch of Service:_____

Date of Entry:_____

Date of Discharge:_____

Type of Discharge:_____

Location of Service:_____

_____

HEALTH:
Please make a statement as to your general state of health. Do you have any medical problems, are you under a doctor's care, or are you on medication? Please note below:

PRIOR RECORD: **BIR #**   **FBI #**
If you have been arrested before, either as a juvenile or adult, please list these arrests. Also, please note what happened in court after these arrests. Please note if you have been on probation or parole before, or if you are under any supervision at the present time.

SOCIAL HISTORY QUESTIONNAIRE (continued)_____

Please fill in the following list of information:

1. **Housing costs:** Weekly:_____ or monthly: _____

2. **Food costs:** Weekly: _____ or monthly: _____

3. **Approximate Monthly Cost of Utilities:**

   A. Telephone: _____
   B. Gas: _____
   C. Water: _____
   D. Electric: _____

4. **Loan Payments:**

   A.

   B.

   C.

   D.

   E.

5. **Other Miscellaneous Costs:**

   A.

   B.

   C.

   D.

   E.

SOCIAL HISTORY QUESTIONNAIRE (continued) _____

Print in your own words a statement concerning the offense. What did you do, when, who was involved, why, did you repay the victim?, etc.

Stop Here.

CLIENT MANAGEMENT CLASSIFICATION ASSESSMENT INSTRUMENT _____

The purpose of CMC is to provide the probation professional with an efficient and effective case management system. CMC includes procedures for developing individualized strategies for the quality supervision of adult offenders. This process is accomplished through the completion of the three system components: an assessment procedure, a supervision planning process, and supervision according to one of five distinct strategies, depending on individualized case needs. It is not to be used with juveniles nor for any other than its stated purpose.

CMC INSTRUCTIONS

There are four parts to the CMC assessment instrument. Whenever possible, the following sequence (A to D) should be followed.

A. Attitude interview (45 items)
B. Objective history (11 items)
C. Behavioral observations (8 items)
D. Officer impressions of contributing factors (7 items)

The Attitude Section

Column One:

A SEMI-STRUCTURED INTERVIEW with suggested questions has been developed to elicit attitude information about the offense, the offender's background, and about present plans and problems. The average interview takes about forty-five minutes and the scoring about five minutes.

Use a **natural, open** conversational style of interviewing that is comfortable for both you and the probationer. If the probationer presents some important or interesting information requiring follow-up, feel free to do so before returning to the structured sequence. While stressing free-flowing communication, some structuring is required to ensure the reliability and validity of the instrument. Therefore, make every effort to **preserve the meaning of the questions** when transposing them into your own words.

In the interview, each section is introduced by one or two open-ended questions, which are intended to encourage discussion on a particular subject. If the information needed to score the items is not obtained from the open-ended questions, one or two specific questions are provided for each item. If those questions fail to elicit the needed information, continue to inquire with increasingly direct questions unless you see the word -STOP-. "-STOP-" means to discontinue inquiry (except to repeat or clarify a misunderstood question).

For some items, "a" and "b" questions are included. If the "b" question is asterisked (*), always ask it unless the answer to the "a" makes the "b" questions meaningless (e.g., "no" to question 10a). If question "b" is not asterisked, ask it if the needed information was not elicited from question "a."

Column Two:

THE ITEM OBJECTIVES AND RESPONSES are listed in column two. Many times the suggested questions will approach the item objective in an indirect manner in order to elicit the most valid response.

Column Three:

A SCORING GUIDE is included to provide criteria and assistance in scoring ambiguous responses. When scoring, you must choose only one alternative for each item. If you cannot choose an alternative, do not rate the item.

CMC (continued) _____

Attitudes About Offense

Could you tell me about the offense that got you into trouble?

QUESTIONS	RESPONSES	SCORING GUIDE
1a. How did you get involved in this offense?	1. Motivation for committing the offense (a) emotional motivation (e.g., anger, sex offense, etc.)	1. a. -Using drugs -Assault (not for robbery)
1b. (If denied) What did the police say that you did?	(b) material (monetary) motivation	b. -Prostitution -Car theft (except for joy riding) -Selling drugs (including to support a habit)
	(c) both emotional and material motivation	c. -Stealing from parents for revenge -Stealing primarily for peer acceptance -Man who won't pay alimony primarily because he's angry with his ex-wife
2a. How did you decide to commit the offense? 2b. Could you tell me more about the circumstances that led up to the offense?	2. Acceptance of responsibility for current offense (a) admits committing the offense and doesn't attempt excuses (b) admits committing the offense but emphasizes excuses (e.g., drinking, influence by friends, family problems, etc.) (c) denies committing the offense	2. a. Explains circumstances but takes responsibility b. Blames circumstances and does not take responsibility c. Probationers who deny any significant aspect of the offense are scored "c" (e.g., the probationer admits that he helped to jimmy a car window but denies responsibility for removing valuables because his friends removed them).

CMC (continued)

QUESTIONS	RESPONSES	SCORING GUIDE
3a. Looking back at the offense, what is your general feeling about it? -STOP-	3. Expression of guilt about current offense (a) expresses guilt feelings or spontaneous empathy toward victim (b) expresses superficial or no guilt (c) victimless crime	3. a. Probationer must feel some personal shame and regret (not just verbalization to impress the officer). b. -"I feel bad because now I have a record." -"People are disappointed in me." (Indicates some regret but not necessarily guilt.) -"I know it was wrong." (Emphasis is on having done wrong, but not on feeling bad because one has done wrong.) c. -Using drugs -Sexual activities between consenting adults

Offense pattern

I'd like to talk to you about your prior offenses. Have you been in trouble before? (Obtain a *complete* picture of probationer's offense style, including current offense, when scoring items 5-8.)

QUESTIONS	RESPONSES	SCORING GUIDE
4a. What prior offenses have you been convicted of? *4b. Were you ever in trouble as a juvenile?(List on grid below)	4. Offense and severity (a) no prior offenses (Skip items 5, 6, 7, and 8.) (b) mainly misdemeanors (c) no constant pattern (d) mainly felonies	4-8. Include juvenile and serious traffic offenses (e.g., drunk driving). Don't count dismissals. 4. Use only prior offenses. b. Should not be used if probationer has more than two serious felonies. (Use choice "c" or "d.") d. Over 50% of probationer's offenses are felonies.

CMC (continued) _____

QUESTIONS	RESPONSES	SCORING GUIDE
5a. Have you ever been armed or hurt someone during these offenses? *5b. Did you ever threaten anyone?	5. Was probationer ever involved in an offense where he (she) was armed, assaultive, or threatened injury to someone? (a) yes (b) no	5-8. Use current and prior offense factors to score 5-8.
6a. How did you decide to commit these offenses? 6b. Did you plan these offenses beforehand? (Discuss offenses individually until a clear pattern emerges).	6. Offenses were *generally* (a) planned (b) no consistent pattern (c) impulsive	6. Officer's judgement based on all factors. a. -Exhibitionist who drives around in a car looking for a girl to whom to expose himself. b. -Person who decides to commit an offense, then drinks to build courage. c. -Exhibitionist who is driving to work, suddenly sees a girl, and pulls over and exposes himself. -Person gets drunk and into a bar fight.
7. Were you drinking or on drugs when you committed this offense?	7. Percent of offenses committed while drinking or on drugs (a) never (b) 50% or less (c) over 50%	7. Count offenses where there was *any* chemical use regardless of whether person was intoxicated or not.
8. Did you do the offense alone or with others?	8. Offenses were *generally* committed (a) alone (b) no consistent pattern (c) with accomplices	

CMC (continued) _____

Offense	(Item 4) Fel./Misd.	(Item 5) Assaultive?	Circumstances of Offense	(Item 6) Planned?	(Item 7) Chemicals?	(Item 8) Accomplices?

School and Vocational Adjustment

Now, I'd like to find out some things about your background. Let's begin with school. How did you like school?

QUESTIONS	RESPONSES	SCORING GUIDE
9. What was your favorite subject in school? -STOP-	9. Favorite subject (a) vocational (b) academic (c) gym (d) no favorite subject	9. a. -Business course. b. -Music or art.
10a. Did you have a favorite teacher in high school? 10b. What did you like about him (her)?	10. Attitude toward teachers (a) no favorite teacher (b) teacher chosen because of certain qualities that the probationer admired (c) teacher chosen because of close personal relationship with the teacher	10. b. -"She would help kids." c. -"She would help me."

CMC (continued)

QUESTIONS	RESPONSES	SCORING GUIDE
11a. How far did you go in school? 11b. Did you have any problems with schoolwork? (If probationer did not graduate from high school, find out why not.)	11. Probationer's school performance (a) no problems (b) learning problems (difficulty performing schoolwork) (c) lack of interest, behavior, or other problems	11. a. Don't use for probationer who didn't complete high school. b. For probationer whose learning problems result from a lack of capacity (not just from lack of interest or behavioral problems). If probationer has both a lack of capacity *and* behavioral problems, score "b." Lack of capacity takes precedence when scoring.
12. Now, I'd like to know about your work history. What kinds of jobs have you had? (Find out actual job responsibilities. Use grid on next page.)	12. Primary vocation (a) unskilled labor (b) semi-skilled (c) skilled labor or white collar (d) no employment history (homemaker) (Skip 13 & 14) (e) student or recent graduate (Skip 13 & 14)	12. a. -Average person could do job without training. -Probationer's been in the job market for over six months, but has no employment history. (Also score items 13 and 14.) c. Job requires some training and/or experience. d. For homemaker, use prior vocational history, if any. If none, check "d" and skip items 13 and 14. e. Probationer was recently (within six months) a student and hasn't had the opportunity to establish an employment pattern. (Skip items 13 and 14.)

CMC (continued) _____

QUESTIONS	RESPONSES	SCORING GUIDE
13a. How long did you work on your most recent job? 13b. How long between that job and your previous job? (Start with most recent job and go backwards, until a clear pattern emerges. Use grid for 12 - 14.)	13. Percent of working life where probationer was employed full-time (a) over 90% (b) over 50% to 90% (c) 50% or less	13. "Working Life..." i.e., time period society would expect one to be working. Subtract time in school, institutions, etc.
14a. What was your reason for leaving your most recent job? 14b. Have you had any trouble getting jobs?	14. Primary vocational problem (a) none (Can be used only if item 13 is scored "a.") (b) problems due to lack of skills or capacity (c) attitude or other problems	14. a. Don't use "a" if working less than 90% c. -"Because of my drinking problem."

(Item 12) (Start with most recent) Jobs and Job Responsibilities	(Item 13a) Duration	(Item 14a) Reason for Leaving
(Item 13b) Unemployment Interval		
(Item 13b) Unemployment Interval		
(Item 13b) Unemployment Interval		

Correctional Assessment, Casework and Counseling

CMC (continued) _____

QUESTIONS	RESPONSES	SCORING GUIDE
15a. Where do you live now? 15b. Have you moved around much? (Deal with time period after probationer turned 18.)	15. Living stability background (a) essentially stable living arrangements (b) some unstable periods (c) essentially unstable living arrangements	15. Consider what is stable for the probationer's age group.
16a. Have you had any trouble supporting yourself or received welfare? 16b. (If applicable) How did you support yourself when you were unemployed?	16. History of being self-supporting (a) probationer has usually been self-supporting (b) probationer has had several periods where he (she) wasn't self-supporting (c) probationer has essentially not been self-supporting	16. Illegal activities and welfare are not counted as self-supporting. For probationer who has not had the opportunity to support her/himself (e.g., homemaker or person living with relative), estimate the likelihood of (her) his being able to support (her) himself.

CMC (continued) _____

FAMILY ATTITUDES

Now I'd like to know about your childhood. Can you tell me what it was like?

QUESTIONS	RESPONSES	SCORING GUIDE
17a. How do (did) you get along with your father? 17b. How do you feel about your father?	17. Present feelings toward father (a) close (b) mixed or neutral (c) hostile	17. In multi-father families, use the person whom the probationer identifies as father. b. -"We get along" (without implication of closeness)
18a. If you did something wrong as a teenager, how did your father handle it? 18b. What kind of discipline did he use?	18. Type of discipline father used (during probationer's teenage years) (a) verbal or privilege withdrawal (b) permissive (generally let probationer do as he (she) pleased) (c) physical	18. If the probationer didn't live with father or father figure during at least part of his (her) adolescent years, do not rate item 18. b. -"He always left it to mom."
19a. How do (did) you get along with your mother? 19b. How do you feel about your mother?	19. Present feelings towards mother (a) close (b) mixed or neutral (c) hostile	19. In multi-mother families, use the person whom the probationer identifies as mother. b. -"We get along" (without implication of closeness).
20a. If you did something wrong as a teenager, how did your mother handle it? 20b. What kind of discipline did she use?	20. Type of discipline mother used (during probationer's teenage years) (a) verbal or privilege withdrawal (b) permissive (generally let probationer do as he (she) pleased) (c) physical	20. If the probationer didn't live with mother or mother figure during at least part of his (her) adolescent years, do not rate item 20. b. -"She always left it to Dad."

CMC (continued) _____

QUESTIONS	RESPONSES	SCORING GUIDE
21a. Were you ever abused by either of your parents? 21b. Did either of them ever go overboard on the punishment? -STOP-	21. Was probationer ever physically abused by a biological, step, or adoptive parent? (a) yes (b) no	21. Item 21 should be based on facts described and not whether the client felt abused. a. -cuts on face -severe body bruises -sexual abuse -locked in closet or starved for unusual periods of time
22a. How would your parents have described you as a child (before you were a teenager)? *22b. Did both of your parents see you the same way?	22. Parental view of probationer (prior to adolescence) (a) good child (b) problem child (c) parents differed	22. a. -No special problems. -"Like anybody else." b. -"My parents were always complaining about me." -Seen as "strange kid."
23. How would you describe yourself as a child (before you were a teenager)?	23. As a child, probationer describes self as (a) good child (normal or average) (b) problem child	23. Accept what the probationer says even if his (her) behavior does not match his (her) perception. (Examples from item 22 apply here.)
24a. How do you get along with your brothers and sisters? 24b. How do you feel about them?	24. General feelings toward siblings (a) close (b) neutral or mixed (c) hostile (d) no siblings	24. Include half-siblings; exclude step-siblings. b. -"Like some, not others."
25. Would you describe your early childhood (before you were a teenager) as happy or unhappy? -STOP-	25. General attitude toward childhood (a) happy (b) not happy	25. Accept the probationer's view.

CMC (continued) _____

QUESTIONS	RESPONSES	SCORING GUIDE
26. If you could change anything about your childhood, what would you change?	26. Satisfaction with childhood (a) basically satisfied (would change little) (b) dissatisfied with material aspect (c) dissatisfied with self, family, or emotional climate	26. c. -"I should've gone to school."
27. Can you describe your father's personality? (If answer is unclear, ask probationer to describe another person he (she) knows well.)	27. Probationer's description of personality (a) multi-faceted (b) superficial (e.g., "good," "bad," "nice," etc.)	27. The focus of this item is the *complexity* with which the probationer views people. The ability to describe attributes, or explain the reasons for behavior, is being measured. "Superficial" indicates a lack of capacity to perceive depth in personality and not just an evasion of the question. One or two complex statements are sufficient for an "a" score. a. -"Ambitious and honest." -"Sensitive to others." -"Dad was strict because that is the way he was brought up." b. -"No good drunk" (with no further explanation). -"Kind." -"Don't know."

CMC (continued) _____

Interpersonal Relations

Let's talk about your friends. Do you spend much time with them?

QUESTIONS	RESPONSES	SCORING GUIDE
28a. What are your friends (associates) like? *28b. Have any of them been in trouble with the law? (If probationer has no current associates, use prior associates.)	28. Probationer's associates are (a) essentially non-criminal (b) mixed (c) mostly criminal	28. Don't count marijuana use (alone) as criminal. a. Don't use "a" if probationer committed offense(s) with accomplices.
29a. How do you get along with your friends? *29b. How do they act toward you?	29. In interaction with friends, probationer is (a) used by others (b) withdrawn (c) other problems (d) normal	29. This item should be based on *officer's judgement* of the quality of the probationer's interactions. If the officer thinks the probationer is used by friends even though the probationer thinks he (she) gets along "ok," check choice "a."
30a. Do you have a closest friend? *30b. What do you like best about him (her)? -STOP-	30. Description of probationer's relationship with his (her) closest friend (a) talk (share feelings) or help each other (b) do things together (less emphasis on talking or sharing feelings) (c) has none	30. a. -"We do things for each other." -"We're like brothers." b. -"He's a hunter too."
31. Are you satisfied with the way you get along with people?	31. Satisfaction with interpersonal relationships (a) feels satisfied (b) feels dissatisfied	31. Accept the probationer's statement.

CMC (continued) _____

QUESTIONS	RESPONSES	SCORING GUIDE
32. In general, do you tend to trust or to mistrust people? -STOP-	32. General outlook toward others (a) basically trusting (b) mixed or complex view (c) basically mistrusting	32. b. A complex view of people (e.g., trusts in some situations and not in others) -"I trust people too much." -"It takes a while to get to know them."
33a. Can you tell me about your relationships with women (men)? *33b. Do you generally go out with a lot of women (men) or date the same person for long periods?	33. Probationer's opposite sex relationship pattern generally is (a) long-term (over six months) or serious relationships (b) short- and long-term relationships (c) short-term, less emotionally involved relationships, or little dating experience	33. c. Short-term relationships with no solid commitments to persons of the opposite sex
34. In your relationship with your wife/girlfriend (husband/boyfriend), who tends to make the decisions?	34. In opposite sex interactions, probationer generally (a) dominates (b) is average or adequate (c) is nonassertive or dominated	34. *Officer's judgement:* Do not accept the probationer's response without exploring his (her) relationships or seeing how some specific decisions are made (e.g., who decides what to do or with whom to socialize; who controls the money).

CMC (continued) _____

Feelings

Now, I'd like to ask you about your feelings. Have you had any problems handling your feelings?

QUESTIONS	RESPONSES	SCORING GUIDE
35. Do you consider yourself to be a nervous (or anxious) person? -STOP-	35. Does probationer view self as a nervous person? (a) yes (b) no	35. Accept the probationer's statement. a. -"I worry a lot." -"I'm hyperactive."
36a. What kind of things get you depressed? 36b. What do you do when you're feeling depressed? (If denies, find out how he (she) keeps from getting depressed.)	36. What does probationer do when feeling depressed? (a) seeks someone to talk to, or tries to figure it out (b) seeks an activity to distract self (c) drinks or uses drugs (d) isolates self	36. b. -"Forget about them." -"Watch T.V." d. -"I pray." -"I go to sleep."
37a. Have you ever thought seriously about hurting or killing yourself? 37b. (If probationer says yes to above) Have you ever tried it?	37. Self-destructive behavior (a) never seriously contemplated suicide (b) has had definite thoughts of suicide (c) has attempted it	37. c. Requires overt action that resulted in self-harm or clear intent toward suicide.
38a. What do you do when you are feeling angry with people? 38b. Have you ever hurt anybody when you were angry?	38. In handling anger, probationer (a) is physically aggressive (b) avoids expression to others or has trouble expressing anger appropriately (c) responds appropriately	38. Based on all sources of reliable information (e.g., offense history) and not just on probationer's statement: Physically aggressive problems should take precedence in scoring. If probationer says, "I leave," find out if/how he (she) deals with the anger later. b. -"I break things."

CMC (continued) _____

QUESTIONS	RESPONSES	SCORING GUIDE
39a. Can you describe your personality? 39b. What do you like and what do you dislike about yourself? -STOP-	39. In describing self, probationer (a) emphasizes strength (b) emphasizes inadequacy (probationer tends to downgrade self) (c) can't describe self	39. If the probationer gives both positive and negative statements about (him) herself, *choose the one emphasized most.* If the positive and negative have equal emphasis, choose the first response given. c. Choice "c" is designed to identify the probationer who is incapable of showing *insight* or *complexity* into (him) herself; e.g., "I'm okay" (and can't elaborate); "I'm nice"; "I get into too much trouble"; etc.
40. (No questions asked. Rate your impression of probationer's openness in discussing feelings.)	40. Openness in discussing feelings (a) discusses as openly as able (b) is evasive or superficial	40. a. If the officer felt that the probationer was fairly straightforward in talking about his (her) feelings. b. If the officer thought the probationer was evasive or superficial.

CMC (continued) _____

Plans and Problems

QUESTIONS	RESPONSES	SCORING GUIDE
41. Aside from your legal problems, what is the biggest problem in your life right now? -STOP-	41. What does the probationer view as his (her) most important problem area right now? (a) personal (b) relationships (c) vocational-educational (including employment) (d) financial (e) no big problems presently (Score item 42 as "a")	41. a. Probationer names several important problems -Drinking or drugs -"Get my head together." b. -"Get things straightened our with my fiancee." -"Try to get along better with my parents."
42. How do you expect this problem (from item 41) to work out?	42. Attitude toward solving problems (a) optimistic; expects to succeed (Include 41. e) (b) unclear (c) pessimistic; expects to fail	42. a. -"O.K., because I've got a better paying job." b. -"O.K., I hope." -"I'll be O.K. if I get a better paying job." c. Probationer is pessimistic about outcome or can't figure out a solution.
43a. What goals do you have for the future? *43b. What are your plans for achieving your goals? -STOP-	43. Future plans (a) short-term goals (most goals can be fulfilled within about six months) or no goals (b) unrealistic goals (c) realistic, long-term goals (most goals are well-developed and extend beyond six months)	43. a. -"Just live day to day." Poorly developed goals with no plans for achieving them b. -Strange, way-out, or impossible-to-achieve goals c. Probationer is able to (1) set a goal within the realm of possibility and (2) list the steps necessary to achieve the goal.

CMC (continued) _____

QUESTIONS	RESPONSES	SCORING GUIDE
44. (No question asked. Rate the item based on follow-through on jobs, education, training programs, treatment programs, etc., based on all sources.)	44. Probationer usually sticks with, or completes, things he (she) begins. (a) yes (b) no	44. Compare to the average probationer.
45a. How will being on probation affect your life? 45b. What do you expect to get from being on probation? -STOP-	45. Probationer's general expectations about supervision (a) no effect (b) monetary, counseling, or program help (c) hopes supervision will keep him (her) out of trouble (d) negative expectations (e) mixed or unclear expectations	

CMC (continued) _____

Objective Background Items

Instructions: Ask direct questions to obtain the following information.

QUESTIONS	SCORING GUIDE

Legal History

1. Age of earliest court appearance:
   (a) 14 or younger
   (b) 15-17
   (c) 18-22
   (d) 23 or older

46. Include juvenile offenses and serious traffic offenses (e.g., drunk driving, hit and run). Exclude divorce, custody proceedings, etc.

2. Number of prior offenses:
   (a) none
   (b) 1-3
   (c) 4-7
   (d) 8 or more

47. Exclude the probationer's present offense in rating this item. Include juvenile and serious traffic offenses.

3. Number of commitments to state or federal correctional institutions:
   (a) none
   (b) 1
   (c) 2 or more

48. Include juvenile commitments.

4. Time spent under probation or parole supervision:
   (a) none
   (b) 1 year or less
   (c) over 1 year; up to 3 years
   (d) over 3 years

49. Include juvenile supervision.
   a. Use "a" for new probationer.

Medical History

5. (Circle all applicable choices.)
   (a) frequent headaches, back, or stomach problems
   (b) serious head injuries
   (c) prior psychiatric hospitalization
   (d) outpatient psychotherapy
   (e) none of the above

50. a. Vague complaints not diagnosed by a physician
   b. Skull fractures
      Head injuries that required treatment (beyond X-ray)
   d. Professional inpatient or outpatient drug/alcohol treatment

CMC (continued) _____

QUESTIONS	SCORING GUIDE

School History

6. Highest grade completed:
   (a) 9th or below
   (b) 10th to 12th
   (c) high school graduate (exclude GED)
   (d) some post-high school training leading
       toward a degree

7. Did probationer ever receive special education or remedial help in school?
   (a) yes
   (b) no

                             52. Include special programs for learning
                                   deficiencies (rather than behavior problems).
                                   Do not include English-as-a-second-language.

Family History

8. Probationer was raised primarily by:
   (a) intact biological family
   (b) other

                             53. Choice "a" requires *both natural parents* in
                                   an intact home until probationer reached
                                   about 16 years of age.

9. Did either parent have a history of
   (Circle all applicable choices):
   (a) being on welfare
   (b) criminal behavior
   (c) psychiatric hospitalization
   (d) suicide attempts
   (e) drinking problems
   (f) none of the above

                             54. Includes step and adoptive parents.

10. Have siblings (including half- and step-
    siblings) ever been arrested?
    (a) none
    (b) some
    (c) most
    (d) not applicable

Marital Status

11. Currently probationer is:
    (a) single (never married)
    (b) single (separated or divorced)
    (c) married (including common-law)

————————————— END INTERVIEW —————————————

CMC (continued) _____

Behavioral Patterns

Instructions: Rate the following behaviors as observed during the interview. Use (b) for the average probationer. Use (a) and (c) for distinct exceptions to the average.

1. **Grooming and Dress**

    (a) Below Average   (b) Average   (c) Above Average

2. **Self-confidence**

    (a) Lacks Confidence   (b) Average   (c) Overly Confident

3. **Attention Span**

    (a) Easily Distractable   (b) Average   (c) Very Attentive

4. **Comprehension**

    (a) Below Average   (b) Average   (c) Above Average

5. **Thought Processes**

    (a) Sluggish   (b) Average   (c) Driven (Accelerated)

6. **Affect**

    (a) Depressed   (b) Average   (c) Elated

7. **Self-disclosure**

    (a) Evasive   (b) Average   (c) Very Open

8. **Cooperation**

    (a) Negativistic   (b) Average   (d) Eager to Please

CMC (continued)

Impressions

Instructions: On the continuum below, rate the significance of each factor with regard to the probationer. Did (does) this problem contribute to the probationer's legal difficulties? At least one item must be rated a "1" and at least one item must be rated a "5."

A. SOCIAL INADEQUACY

Socially inept. Unable to perceive the motives and concerns of others. Unable to survive in society and care for self.

(1) (2) (3) (4) (5)

Socially adept. Able to assert self and to perceive the motives and concerns of others. Able to survive in society and care for self.

Do not merely rate performance on social situations. Rate ABILITY.

B. VOCATIONAL INADEQUACY

Lacks the capacity to obtain and maintain relatively permanent and reasonably paying employment.

(1) (2) (3) (4) (5)

Has the capacity to obtain and maintain relatively permanent and reasonably paying employment.

Do not merely rate job performance. Rate CAPACITY.

C. CRIMINAL ORIENTATION

Criminal behavior is an acceptable and common part of the probationer's life and s/he attempts to live off crime without trying to make it in a pro-social way.

(1) (2) (3) (4) (5)

Criminal behavior is not an acceptable nor common part of his/her life, nor does s/he attempt to live off of crime without trying to make it in a pro-social way.

Do not merely rate the frequency of offenses. Rate VALUES and ORIENTATION.

D. EMOTIONAL FACTORS

Emotional problems (e.g., chemical dependency, sex, fear, depression, low self-esteem, anxiety, self-destructiveness) contributed highly to the offense (pattern).

(1) (2) (3) (4) (5)

Emotional factors did not contribute significantly to the offense (pattern).

CMC (continued) _____

E. FAMILY HISTORY PROBLEMS

Parental family problems in childhood and adolescence contributed significantly to the offense (pattern).

(1) (2) (3) (4) (5)

Parental family problems of childhood and adolescence did not contribute significantly to the offense (pattern).

F. ISOLATED SITUATIONAL (TEMPORARY CIRCUMSTANCES)

Unusual or temporary circumstances in the probationer's life, which are unlikely to be repeated, contributed significantly to the offense.

(1) (2) (3) (4) (5)

Offense is not a result of unusual or temporary circumstances (i.e., offense is part of a continuing pattern).

Do not merely rate infrequency of offenses. Rate OVERALL PATTERN.

G. INTERPERSONAL MANIPULATION

Uses, controls, and/or manipulates others to gain his/her own ends with little regard for the welfare of others.

(1) (2) (3) (4) (5)

Misuse of others, manipulation, and control did not contribute significantly to offense (pattern).

CMC (continued) _____

Supervision Planning

STEP 1: FORCE FIELD ANALYSIS: Using all resources available, identify the strengths/resources and problems/weaknesses, if any, that pertain to each area in reference to the probationer and his (her) primary environment.

Area	Rank	Strength/Resource	Problem/Weakness	Rank
Present offense				
Offense pattern				
Correctional history				
Education				
Mental ability				
Employment record				
Vocational skills				
Finances				
Residential stability				
Family history				
Interpersonal skills				
Companions				
Intimate relationships				
Emotional stability				
Drugs & alcohol				
Plans & goals				
Probation expectations				
Sexual behavior				
Health				
Values & attitudes				

STEP 2: PRIORITIZATION: Apply the following criteria to the above in order to rank the four most important areas relative to the probationer's legal difficulties: the relative strength, the alterability, the relative speed with which change can occur, and the interdependency with other areas.

CMC (continued) _____

STEP 3: TENTATIVE SUPERVISION PLAN: Using the priority areas from step B, "pencil in" tentative goals, objectives, and action plans. Use Supervision Guidelines as a resource.

1.   Problem Statement: _____
_____

      Long-range Goal:_____
_____

      Short-range Objectives:_____
_____ Date Achieved:_____
_____ Date Achieved:_____
_____

      Probationer Action Plan:_____
_____
_____
_____
_____

      Officer/Referral Action Plan:_____
_____
_____
_____

2.   Problem Statement:_____
_____

      Long-range Goal:_____
_____

      Short-range Objectives:_____
_____ Date Achieved:_____
_____ Date Achieved:_____

      Probationer Action Plan:_____
_____
_____
_____
_____

      Officer/Referral Action Plan:_____
_____
_____

STEP 4: FINAL PLAN: Negotiate the above with the probationer and modify accordingly.

CMC (continued) _____

REASSESSMENT PLAN: Revise at routine intervals or when special circumstances so indicate.

1.   Problem Statement:_____

    Long-range Goal:_____

    Short-range Objectives:_____

    _____ Date Achieved:_____

    _____ Date Achieved:_____

    Probationer Action Plan:_____

    Officer/Referral Action Plan_____

2.   Problem Statement:_____

    Long-range Goal:_____

    Short-range Objectives:_____

    _____ Date Achieved:_____

    _____ Date Achieved:_____

    Probationer Action Plan:_____

    Officer/Referral Action Plan:_____

FELONY SENTENCING WORKSHEET _____

Defendant's Name:_____ Case No. _____

OFFENSE RATING

1. Degree of Offense

Assess points for the one most serious offense or its equivalent for which offender is being sentenced, as follows: 1st degree felony = 4 points; 2nd degree felony = 3 points; 3rd degree felony = 2 points; 4th degree felony = 1 point. _____

2. Multiple Offenses

Assess 2 points if one or more of the following applies: (A) offender is being sentenced for two or more offenses committed in different incidents; (B) offender is currently under a misdemeanor or felony sentence imposed by any court; or (C) present offense was committed while offender on probation or parole. _____

3. Actual or Potential Harm

Assess 2 points if one or more of the following applies: (A) serious physical harm to a person was caused; (B) property damage or loss of $300 or more was caused; (C) there was a high risk of any such harm, damage, or loss, though not caused, (D) the gain or potential gain from theft offense(s) was $300 or more, or (E) dangerous ordnance or a deadly weapon was actually used in the incident, or its use was attempted or threatened. _____

4. Culpability

Assess 2 points if one or more of the following applies: (A) offender was engaging in continuing criminal activity as a source of income or livelihood, (B) offense was part of a continuing conspiracy to which offender was party, or (C) offense included shocking and deliberate cruelty in which offender participated or acquiesced. _____

5. Mitigation

Deduct 1 point for each of the following, as applicable: (A) there was substantial provocation, justification or excuse for offense; (B) victim induced or facilitated offense, (C) offense was committed in the heat of anger, and (D) the property damaged, lost, or stolen was restored or recovered without significant cost to the victim. _____

NET TOTAL = OFFENSE RATING _____

OFFENDER RATING

1. Prior Convictions

Assess 2 points for each verified prior felony conviction, any jurisdiction. Count adjudications of delinquency for felony as convictions. _____

Assess 1 point for each verified prior misdemeanor conviction, and jurisdiction. Count adjudications of delinquency for misdemeanor as convictions. Do not count traffic or intoxication offenses or disorderly conduct, disturbing the peace, or equivalent offenses. _____

2. Repeat Offenses

Assess 2 points if present offense is offense of violence, sex offense, theft offense, or drug abuse offense, and offender has one or more prior convictions for same type of offense. _____

3. Prison Commitments

Assess 2 points if offender was committed on one or more occasions to a penitentiary, reformatory, or equivalent institution in any jurisdiction. Count commitments to state youth commission or similar commitments in other jurisdictions. _____

4. Parole and Similar Violations

Assess 2 points if one or more of the following applies: (A) offender has previously had probation or parole for misdemeanor or felony revoked; (B) present offense committed while offender on probation or parole, (C) present offense committed while offender free on bail; or (D) present offense committed while offender in custody. _____

5. Credits

Deduct 1 point for each of the following as applicable: (A) offender has voluntarily made bona fide, realistic arrangements for at least partial restitution; (B) offender was age 25 or older at time of first felony conviction; (C) offender has been substantially law-abiding for at least 3 years; and (D) offender lives with his or her spouse or minor children or both and is either a breadwinner for the family or, if there are minor children, a housewife. _____

NET TOTAL = OFFENDER RATING _____

FELONY SENTENCING WORKSHEET (continued)

Indicated Sentence

Circle the box on the chart where the offense and offender ratings determined on the previous page intersect. This indicates a normal sentencing package. If the indicated sentence appears too severe or too lenient for the particular case, do not hesitate to vary from the indicated sentence. In that event, however, list the reasons for the variance in the space provided on the next page.

		OFFENDER RATING			
	0 - 2	**3 - 5**	**6 - 8**	**9 - 11**	**12 OR MORE**
6 OR MORE	Impose one of three lowest minimum terms.	Impose one of three highest minimum terms.	Impose one of three highest minimum terms.	Impose one of two highest minimum terms. Make at least part of multiple sentences consecutive.	Impose highest minimum term. Make at least part of multiple sentences consecutive.
	No probation.	No probation.	No probation.	No probation.	No probation.
5	Impose one of three lowest minimum terms. Some form of probation indicated only with special mitigation.	Impose one of three lowest minimum terms. No probation.	Impose one of three highest minimum terms. No probation.	Impose one of three highest minimum terms. No probation.	Impose one of two highest minimum terms. Make at least part of multiple sentences consecutive. No probation.
4	Impose one of two lowest minimum terms. Some form of probation indicated.	Impose one of three lowest minimum terms. Some form of probation indicated only with special mitigation.	Impose one of three lowest minimum terms. No probation.	Impose one of three highest minimum terms. No probation.	Impose one of three highest minimum terms. No probation.
3	Impose one of two lowest minimum terms. Some form of probation indicated.	Impose one of two lowest minimum terms. Some form of probation indicated.	Impose one of three lowest minimum terms. Some form of probation indicated only with special mitigation.	Impose one of three lowest minimum terms. No probation.	Impose one of three highest minimum terms. No probation.
0 - 2	Impose lowest minimum term. Some form of probation indicated.	Impose one of two lowest minimum terms. Some form of probation indicated.	Impose one of two lowest minimum terms. Some form of probation indicated.	Impose one of three lowest minimum terms. Some form of probation indicated only with special mitigation.	Impose one of three lowest minimum terms. No probation.

(Left side label: **OFFENSE RATING**)

FELONY SENTENCING WORKSHEET (continued)_____

PROBATION AVAILABILITY

Sometimes the preceding chart will indicate probation when it is forbidden by law in the particular case. Before recommending or imposing sentence in any case, consult the statutes for probationability and check the boxes below if applicable.

☐ **OFFENDER IS A REPEAT OFFENDER OR A DANGEROUS OFFENDER.** See RC 2929.01 for definitions. Probation for drug treatment permitted in limited cases under RC 2951.04 (B) (3).

☐ **OFFENSE IS NON-PROBATIONAL PER SE.** Indicates aggravated murder, murder, rape, felonious sexual penetration, any offense committed while armed with a firearm or dangerous ordnance, and any offense in which a sentence of "actual incarceration" is required.

SENTENCE IMPOSED; VARIANCES

ACTUAL SENTENCE IMPOSED
Term imposed each count, and fine if any

_____

_____

_____

_____

☐ Committed to serve sentence.

☐ Committed but shock probation possible.

☐ Other probation granted (describe)

_____

_____

REASONS FOR VARIANCE
If the actual sentence imposed varies from the disposition indicated on the chart in any respect, state the reasons for the variance.

_____

_____

_____

_____

_____

_____

_____

_____

CLIENT RISK AND NEED ASSESSMENT SURVEY

DEPARTMENT OF CORRECTIONS
DIVISION OF PROBATION & PAROLE

Client No. _____   Client Name: _____

Officer No. _____

CLIENT RISK ASSESSMENT

Instructions: Enter numerical rating in box at right.

1. TOTAL NUMBER OF PRIOR FELONY CONVICTIONS:
(include juvenile adjudications, if known):
a. None.. Enter 0
b. One.. Enter 2
c. Two or more .... Enter 4

2. PRIOR NUMBER OF PROBATION/PAROLE SUPERVISION PERIODS:
(include juvenile, if known):
a. None.. Enter 0
b. One or more .... Enter 4

3. PRIOR PROBATION/PAROLE REVOCATIONS:
(adult only)
a. None.. Enter 0
b. One or more .... Enter 4

4. AGE AT FIRST KNOWN CONVICTION OR ADJUDICATION:
(include juvenile, if known)
a. 24 years or older ....Enter 0
b. 20 through 23 years ....Enter 2
c. 19 years or younger...Enter 4

5. HISTORY OF ALCOHOL ABUSE:
a. No history of abuse ....Enter 0
b. Occasional or prior abuse ....Enter 2
c. Frequent current abuse..Enter 4

6. HISTORY OF OTHER SUBSTANCE ABUSE:
(prior to incarceration for parolees):
a. No history of abuse ....Enter 0
b. Occasional or prior abuse ....Enter 1
c. Frequent current abuse..Enter 2

CLIENT RISK AND NEED ASSESSMENT SURVEY (continued)_____

7. AMOUNT OF TIME EMPLOYED IN LAST 12 MONTHS:
(prior to incarceration for parolees; based on 35-hr. week):
a. 7 months or more .... Enter 0
b. 4 months through 6 months .... Enter 1
c. Less than 4 months .... Enter 2
d. Not applicable... Enter 0

8. AGENT IMPRESSION OF OFFENDER'S ATTITUDE:
a. Motivated to change; receptive to assistance .... Enter 0
b. Dependent or unwilling to accept responsibility...................................... Enter 3
c. Rationalizes behavior, negative; not motivated to change....................... Enter 5

9. RECORD OF CONVICTION FOR SELECTED OFFENSES:
(include current offense; add categories and enter total):
a. None of the following... Enter 0
b. Burglary, Theft, Auto Theft, Robbery .... Add 2
c. Forgery, Deceptive Practices (Fraud, Bad Check, Drugs) .... Add 3

10. ASSAULTIVE OFFENSES:
Crimes against persons, which include use of weapon, physical force, threat of force, all sex crimes, and vehicular homicide.
Yes/No (circle one)

Total Score (Range: 0-34):

CLIENT RISK AND NEED ASSESSMENT SURVEY (continued) _____

CLIENT NEED ASSESSMENT

Instructions: Enter numerical rating in box at right.

1. ACADEMIC/VOCATIONAL SKILLS:
   a. High school or above skill level .... Enter 0
   b. Has vocational training, additional not needed/desired .... Enter 1
   c. Has some skills; additional needed/desired.. Enter 3
   d. No skills; training needed.. Enter 5

2. EMPLOYMENT:
   a. Satisfactory employment for 1 year or longer.. Enter 0
   b. Employed; no difficulties reported; or homemaker, student, retired, or disabled and
      unable to work ....Enter 1
   c. Part-time, seasonal, unstable employment or needs additional employment; unemployed, but
      has a skill .... Enter 4
   d. Unemployed & virtually unemployable; needs training... Enter 7

3. FINANCIAL STATUS:
   a. Longstanding pattern of self-sufficiency... Enter 0
   b. No current difficulties...Enter 1
   c. Situational or minor difficulties.. Enter 4
   d. Severe difficulties ....Enter 6

4. LIVING ARRANGEMENTS (within last six months):
   a. Stable and supportive relationships with family or others in living group .... Enter 0
   b. Client lives alone or independently within another household... Enter 1
   c. Client experiencing occasional, moderate interpersonal problems within living group ..... Enter 4
   d. Client experiencing frequent and serious interpersonal problems within living group....... Enter 6

5. EMOTIONAL STABILITY:
   a. No symptoms of instability.. Enter 1
   b. Symptoms limit, but do not prohibit adequate functioning .... Enter 5
   c. Symptoms prohibit adequate functioning.. Enter 8

6. ALCOHOL USAGE (Current):
   a. No interference with functioning.. Enter 1
   b. Occasional abuse; some disruption of functioning; may need treatment .... Enter 4
   c. Frequent substance abuse; serious disruption; needs treatment.. Enter 7

7. OTHER SUBSTANCE USAGE (Current):
   a. No interference with functioning... Enter 1
   b. Occasional substance abuse, some disruption of functioning; may need treatment........... Enter 4
   c. Frequent substance abuse; serious disruption; needs treatment.. Enter 6

CLIENT RISK AND NEED ASSESSMENT SURVEY (continued)_____

8. REASONING/INTELLECTUAL ABILITY:
a. Able to function independently .... Enter 1
b. Some need for assistance; potential for adequate adjustment............................ Enter 4
c. Deficiencies suggest limited ability to function independently .... Enter 7

9. HEALTH
a. Sound physical health, seldom ill... Enter 1
b. Handicap or illness interferes with functioning on a recurring basis .... Enter 2
c. Serious handicap or chronic illness; needs frequent medical care...................... Enter 3

10. AGENT'S IMPRESSION OF CLIENT'S NEEDS:
a. None... Enter 0
b. Low .... Enter 1
c. Moderate .... Enter 4
d. High .... Enter 6

Total Score (Range 5-61)

SCORING AND OVERRIDE

Instructions: Check appropriate block.

SCORE-BASED SUPERVISION LEVEL: ☐ Maximum ☐ Medium ☐ Minimum

Check if there is an override: ☐ Explain: _____

FINAL CATEGORY OF SUPERVISION: ☐ Maximum ☐ Medium ☐ Minimum

APPROVED:_____
    (Supervisor Signature and Date)   Agent

Date Supervision Level Assigned: MONTH: DAY: YEAR:

RISK ASSESSMENT SCORING GUIDE

This scale emphasizes behavior while on supervision. The reassessment is based on behavior since the last classification form was completed.

1. Total number of prior felony convictions (include juvenile adjudications if known).

   A. Do not count present offense. The item refers to prior convictions.
   B. Multiple convictions are counted as separate offenses.
   C. For juveniles, this includes only behavior that would be a felony if committed by an adult.

2. Prior number of probation/parole supervision periods (include juvenile, if known).

   A. Revocation hearings that result in a continuance are not counted as a new period of probation/parole.
   B. For juvenile records count only those periods of probation that follow an actual adjudication.
   C. Note: The officer needs only one prior probation/parole in order to move client out of the 0 category. It is not necessary to know the total number of revocations that may have occurred.

3. Prior probation/parole revocations - (adult only)

   A. Disposition of the court or board must be revocation, even though the client may later be reinstated or immediately granted a new parole/probation.

4. Age at first known conviction or adjudication, include juvenile if known.

   A. Convictions may be for a felony or misdemeanor.
   B. Exclude routine traffic, such as: speeding, stop sign, parking violations, etc. Include convictions for DUI, Reckless Driving, Careless Driving, etc.
   C. For juvenile, include only those instances where a person has actually been adjudicated for a crime they could be convicted of if they were an adult.

5. History of alcohol abuse.

   A. This item should be interpreted to mean "in the last 36 months."
   B. The officer is not to make a judgment based simply on number of drinks consumed per day or information of that nature; rather, does the client's drinking interfere with his/her ability to function and meet day-to-day demands. Indications of problems in this area would thus include such things as arriving for work late due to a hangover, frequent drunken quarrels at home or work, excessive expenditure on alcohol, etc. Alcohol-related arrests should generally be coded as indications of serious problems.

RISK ASSESSMENT SCORING GUIDE (continued) _____

    C. Probationers/parolees being supervised for a crime such as DUI Manslaughter should automatically be scored as 4.

6.   History of other substance abuse.

    A. The officer should interpret this item to mean "in the last 36 months." The scoring of this item is similar to that of the alcohol item with one difference. The officer must bear in mind that drug usage may, in itself, be a violation of the law and thus is much more threatening to the client's remaining out of legal trouble. The officer should be attuned to other problems stemming from legal drug use as well. In this regard, prescriptions that the client has should be scrutinized in terms of both frequency and duration of usage.

7.   Amount of time employed in the last 12 months (prior to any incarceration based on a 35-hour week).

    A. A person will receive a 0 in this category if he has been employed for seven or more months, averaging at least 35 hours per week during the last 12 months.

    A person will receive a score of 1 if he has been employed four to six months, averaging a 35-hour week during the last 12 months.

    A client will receive a 2 if he has been employed less than four months throughout the past twelve months.

    B. Part-time employment should be averaged. If a client has been employed for the past twelve months working 20 hours per week, he would receive a score of 1.

    C. Students are scored non-applicable, even though they may have been working part-time. Use non-applicable if in the officer's judgment, there are valid reasons why the client could not have been employed, as in situations of extended illness, disability, or are retired and receiving a monthly retirement check.

8.   Current Living Situation: This area can only be determined after a home visit has been conducted.

    A. A person will receive a 0 in this category if his present living situation is stable. There must be an adequate income and no serious family disturbances such as fights that require law enforcement or outside parties to calm the incident. Takes pride in the appearance of his/her residence.

    B. A person will receive a 3 if there is an inadequate income in the home, occasional serious argument, which may require outside assistance to calm, and/or cluttered living area.

RISK ASSESSMENT SCORING GUIDE (continued)

    C. A person will receive a 5 if any of the following conditions exist: (1) there is little, if any, income coming into the home; (2) there are fights that require law enforcement assistance to calm; (3) there is separation or divorce; (4) there is a dirty, cluttered home; (5) child protective has investigated abuse or neglect or any other serious incident that creates disorganization or stress.

9.   Agent's impression of offender's attitude.

    A. This term is inherently subjective. The officer will find scoring easier if he/she focuses on the phrase "motivated to change." Does this client recognize the need for change, and does he/she accept the responsibility for change? Are there any indications that he/she is beginning to make initial behavior changes? The difference between a score of 3 or 5 would be the client's motivation to change.

10.   Record of conviction for selected offenses (include current offense—add categories and enter total).

    A. This category includes convictions, felony or misdemeanant, during the past five years.

    B. The only possible answers are 0, 2, 3, or 5. If the item does not apply, enter 0. The only way to receive 5 points is to have at least one offense that receives 2 points plus one that receives 3 points.

11.   Violent or assaultive offenses within the last five years.

    A. This category receives no points. If yes is checked, the client may be classified maximum regardless of the number of points acquired.

    B. If a client was committed to a treatment for custody, exclude the time spent in those facilities as part of the last five years, unless the client was convicted for a new offense.

    C. For parolees, count assaultive offenses occurring five years prior to incarceration.

    D. An assaultive offense is defined as an offense against a person that involves the use of a weapon, physical force or threat of force, all forcible felonies, and all sex crimes.

    E. The current offense is counted if it is assaultive.

NEEDS ASSESSMENT SCORING GUIDE _____

INTRODUCTION

The needs assessment form has been constructed to provide a standardized information base from which programs may be developed. Its purpose is to serve as a tool in making objective classification decisions.

The items and scores on the instrument are based on agent's time required to deal with the various problem areas and levels. The basic idea behind the scoring of each item is the same: to what extent, if any, is the client's ability to function in the day-to-day world impaired. The needs assessment instrument differs from the risk assessment instrument in that both positive and negative points are awarded.

The form is designed to indicate areas of programming need and to distinguish among those clients who definitely need programming, those that may require some programming, and those who need no programming in each designated area. The needs assessment form has not been designed to make classification a more rigid, mechanical, or routine process, nor is its purpose to eliminate client input. In those areas where programming is definitely needed or may be needed, the agent should discuss with the client the various program options and the nature of each program. After reviewing the needed programming and the options available, the probation/parole officer should formulate a supervision plan.

The usefulness of the needs assessment instrument is largely dependent on the quality of information relied upon.

The goal of the needs assessment instrument is to eliminate subjectivity and the personal interpretation from the classification decision-making process. The new classification process will consist of decisions based on objective criteria. It is believed that this process will be beneficial to both the probation and parole officer who must justify their decisions and to clients being classified who demand fairness.

1. ACADEMIC AND VOCATIONAL SKILLS

The item focuses on functional skills rather than actual academic credentials. Therefore, a skilled craftsman may receive zero even though he or she may have little formal education. The individual's ability to make his or her way in the world is an important consideration. College, high school diploma, or G.E.D. may not be enough—ability must be shown.

(a) High school or above skill level (demonstrates ability) ....Enter 1
(b) Has vocational training; additional not needed/desired (adequate skills)..........................Enter 1
(c) Has some skills; additional needed/desired, low skill level, may have high school diploma
   or G.E.D. but demonstrates difficulty reading and writing. Real difficulty filling out written reports or job applications. Has ability to do better..Enter 3
(d) No skills; training needed, minimal-retarded, special education classes or unable to read,
   write, or do simple mathematical computations..Enter 5

2. EMPLOYMENT

The probation/parole officer must look beyond simple employment/unemployment in rating the item. Under-employment should be taken into account as should "unsatisfactory" employment. An example of "unsatisfactory"

NEEDS ASSESSMENT SCORING GUIDE (continued) _____

employment would be a client with a serious alcohol problem and repeated alcohol-related offenses who is employed as a bartender. In order to score this item, the probation/parole officer must establish a firm employment chronology. While attempting to do so, the agent should be particularly sensitive to gaps in employment.

    (a) Satisfactory employment for one year or longer, likes the job, salary sufficient to pay for basic needs, education or vocational background. ....Enter 0

    (b) Employed; no difficulties reported, or homemaker, student, retired, or disabled and unable to work, chance for upward advancement with current employer. ....Enter 1

    (c) Part-time, seasonal, unstable employment and needs additional employment; unemployed, but has a skill, job has no future. ....Enter 4

    (d) Unemployed and virtually unemployable; needs training, large gaps in employment, culturally handicapped, self-employment highly questionable. ....Enter 7

3. FINANCIAL STATUS

Does the client have the skills to handle the simple financial responsibilities of everyday life such as maintaining a checking account and preparing a personal budget?

    (a) Long-standing pattern of self-sufficiency, well-off. ....Enter 0

    (b) No current difficulties, providing—not overextending, no serious indebtedness. ....Enter 1

    (c) Situational or minor difficulties, employed but not making it, difficulty in paying court obligations, overextending, difficulty paying bills...Enter 4

    (d) Severe difficulties, welfare, can't pay court obligations, bankruptcy. ....Enter 6

4. LIVING ARRANGEMENTS (Within the last six months)

    (a) Stable and supportive relationship with family or other living group, marriage intact—no history of separation; both parents together, no prior criminal record for other family member, good attitude toward spouse/parents...Enter 0

    (b) Client lives alone or independently within another household, relatively stable, getting along, no noticeable problems. ....Enter 1

    (c) Client experiencing occasional, moderate interpersonal problems with living group, disorganized, recognize problems exist, motivated to change. ....Enter 4

    (d) Client exhibiting frequent and serious interpersonal problems within living group, children removed, recently separated or divorced (within two years); history of bad marriage; extensive prior criminal records of family members; sexual abuse; lack of control; abusive drinking; domestic violence. ....Enter 6

5. EMOTIONAL STABILITY

Guides for the probation/parole officer in regard to this item are as follows: Does the client deal with anger appropriately? Does he/she exhibit excessive anxiety or become immobilized by stress? Ability to cope with day-to-day life situations is a concern here. The 5 score would be used for a neurotic client, with 8 reserved for those with psychotic characteristics.

(a) No symptoms of instability; no apparent stress, well-adjusted ....Enter 1
(b) Symptoms limit, but do not prohibit adequate functioning; neurotic, mild symptoms of
    depression, anxiety, or acting out, occasional abuse of alcohol or other drugs ....Enter 5
(c) Symptoms prohibit adequate functioning; psychotic, severe symptoms of depression,
    anxiety, or acting out, frequent use of alcohol or other drugs; suicidal ....Enter 8

6. ALCOHOL USAGE (Current)

As on the risk assessment instrument, "interference with functioning" is the key here. Parole/probation officers are to avoid moral judgments regarding alcohol use and focus instead on the role of alcohol in the client's life. Alcohol-related driving offenses receive a 7.

(a) No interference with functioning, no alcohol abuse..Enter 1
(b) Occasional abuse; some disruption of functioning; may need treatment; gets
    "drunk" by own definition twice a month or more; some disruption in functioning
    when drinking (whether or not "drunk") with family, work, socially, etc. Minor al-
    cohol-related offenses ....Enter 4
(c) Frequent abuse; serious disruption; needs treatment; drinks regularly although never or
    rarely gets "drunk"; has withdrawal symptoms if stops drinking; has physical symptoms of
    alcoholism; memory lapse, blackouts, passing out; serious disfunction at work; absen-
    teeism, fired, fights with co-workers or other supervisors or customers; with family, be-
    comes violent, neglectful, abusive toward spouse, children, parents, can't pay bills,
    separation occurrence; past driving record involving alcohol; present offense or any arrests
    within the past five years involving alcohol before or during ....Enter 7

7. OTHER SUBSTANCE ABUSE (Current)

The scoring of this item is to be accomplished in the same manner as the "drug usage" item in the risk assessment instrument. A 4 score would apply to clients convicted of marijuana possession while the 6 would refer to present involvement with the drug.

(a) No interference with functioning, no abuse...Enter 1
(b) Occasional substance abuse; some disruption of functioning; may need treatment; con-
    victed of marijuana possession, but no longer using..Enter 4
(c) Frequent substance abuse; serious disruption; needs treatment; addiction or recent use of
    marijuana, narcotics, medication as not prescribed; conviction for possession or intent to
    deliver; deals in selling of drugs...Enter 6

8. REASONING/INTELLECTUAL ATTITUDE

This item looks at organic cognitive capacity as opposed to emotional ability, hence the problem level relates to the possibility of retardation. Is the client mentally alert or able to function effectively?
(a) Able to function independently; appears to be average intelligence. Can comprehend
    what is being said in normal conversation. Can read and comprehend rules of proba-
    tion/parole .... Enter 1

NEEDS ASSESSMENT SCORING GUIDE (continued) _____

    (b) Some need for assistance; potential for adequate adjustment; has difficulty in completing forms without assistance; has difficulty understanding written or verbal communication; has difficulty using or reading a clock, ruler, calendar, dictionary; has difficulty in following directions; emphasis on difficulty in comprehension ....Enter 4

    (c) Deficiencies suggest limited ability to function independently; borderline mental retardation; client cannot function independently; client receives SSI benefits for reason due to developmental disabilities; client is employed in shelter work house ....Enter 7

9. HEALTH

The probation/parole officer should take mental health into account (particularly in the case of the substance abuser), as well as the presence of physical handicaps. Alcoholism or drug abuse is automatically 2 points.

    (a) Sound physical health; seldom ill; no problems. ....Enter 1

    (b) Handicap or illness interferes with functioning on a reoccurring basis; client may have a condition that restricts employment, requires occasional medical attention (high blood pressure, heart condition, epilepsy, missing limb, back problems, etc.) ....Enter 2

    (c) Serious handicap or chronic illnesses; needs frequent medical care; client has a condition that severely restricts employment and program participation. He/she requires frequent medical attention and may be on medication (blindness, serious heart conditions, terminal illness, deafness, paralysis, etc.) ....Enter 3

10. AGENT'S IMPRESSION OF CLIENT'S NEEDS

This is designed to accommodate the agent's subjective impressions.

    (a) None. ....Enter 0

    (b) Low ....Enter 1

    (c) Moderate..Enter 4

    (d) High...Enter 6

PRINCIPLES OF CLASSIFICATION

The foundation of classification is a system—the organized and established procedure for combining an interdependent group of events into a unified whole. A system entails the coming together of all components to produce a product: classification. The type of system that exists will determine the type of classification that exists. The *process* by which classification is effected is an integral part of the product. If the process (embodied in the policy and procedure manual) changes, then the classification decisions will change.

Any classification system must operate on the basis of valid principles; those presented below describe the factors necessary for a classification system to exist (Solomon 1980). (In addition, the 14 principles listed below make up the criteria for a classification system assessment tool for evaluating basic system functioning. Specific methods for use of the principles as an assessment tool are discussed in Section 5, *Prison Classification: A Model Systems Approach.*) It is important to note that the following principles must apply to the *entire* prison system, including women and youthful offender institutions and programs.

1. There must be a clear definition of goals and objectives of the total correctional system.

Traditionally, security and custody have been the primary goals and objectives of correctional systems. While most also have rehabilitation as a goal, it is secondary to security and custody, as the latter comprise the primary public mandate to corrections. Humane care and treatment, however, should be integral to all systems.

Prior to attempting to design a classification process or other system-wide program, the Department of Corrections must be very clear as to its own goals and objectives (its function, purpose, and priorities). These should be realistic and understandable to both staff and inmates.

Within these goals, a classification system can be developed to sort those inmates whose identified needs fall within the agency's objectives. Only after conceptualizing its own goals can a correctional system develop a rational classification process.

2. There must be detailed written procedures and policies governing the classification process.

An essential component for a classification decision-making model is a policy statement that sets forth the Department of Corrections' goals, objectives, and purposes for the new classification system. For example, when developing its new classification system in 1979, the Minnesota Department of Corrections based the system on eight departmental "principles" regrading classification. These principles, in order of importance to Minnesota's Department of Corrections, are:

- Minimize risk to the public
- Minimize risk to other inmates and institution staff
- Minimize breaches of security
- Minimize system risk
- Minimize security levels
- Maximize fairness (similar offenders treated in a similar manner)
- Maximize the objective and quantitative nature of all classification criteria
- Maximize inmate understanding of the classification system and inmate participation in program decisions

PRINCIPLES OF CLASSIFICATION (continued)

Policies such as Minnesota's should be included in a comprehensive departmental classification policy manual. The American Correctional Association (ACA) Manual of Standards for Adult Correctional Institutions (1977) calls "essential" (Standard No. 4373) a ". . . classification manual containing all the classification policies and detailed procedures for implementing policies; this manual is made available to all staff involved with classification and is reviewed at least annually and updated as necessary."* The manual must be written clearly and concisely and *must* be understood by classification personnel. The policies contained in the manual should deal with such classification issues as:

- Initial inmate classification and reclassification
- Instructions regarding the makeup of classification committees, units, and teams and the full responsibilities of each
- Definitions of various committees' responsibilities for custody, employment, and vocational/program assignments
- Instructions concerning potential changes in an inmate's program
- Procedures relating to inmate transfer from one program to another and from one institution to another
- Content of the classification interview
- Method of documentation of decisions made

Since classification policies must be dynamic, constantly subject to change and revision as the classification process is continuously evaluated, the classification manual should be prepared in such a manner as to provide for easy update. (An important caution here is that the length of the manual is not necessarily correlated with its quality.)

3. The classification process must provide for the collection of complete, high-quality, verified, standardized data.

The classification system must define the data needed and the format in which it is to be collected and analyzed. High-quality, standardized data is essential to a valid statistical base for classification decision making and for correlation of prediction and need factors.
Complete and verified data permits:

- Equitable determinations based on particular factors of individual cases
- Similar decisions among individual classification analysts on roughly comparable cases
- Quantitative analysis of trends in classification decision making for individual facilities or the Department of Corrections as a whole

Through its technical assistance projects, NIC has found that the quantity and quality of offender data (criminal history, personal and family background, etc.) available to teams when the classification decision must be made are frequently less than adequate, and sometimes entirely unusable. Forms often are incomplete, some data collected are of questionable relevance, and much information is subject to broad interpretation because of its qualitative (narrative) nature.

---

*This standard has since been superseded by Standard 3-4282, which states: "Written policy, procedure, and practice provide for a written inmate classification plan. The plan specifies the objectives of the classification system and methods for achieving them, and it provides a monitoring and evaluation mechanism to determine whether the objectives are being met. The plan is reviewed at least annually and updated as needed." Standards for Adult Correctional Institutions, Third edition, 1990.

PRINCIPLES OF CLASSIFICATION (continued) _____

In many of the systems studied, NIC found that no specific guidelines were given to field staff regarding the collection of offender background data necessary for a valid classification decision. Without specific and objective guidelines, field staff are not likely to prepare reports sufficiently comprehensive and reliable to be used in an empirically valid statistical analysis.

4. **Measurement and testing instruments used in the classification decision-making process must be valid, reliable, and objective.**

The numerous legal grievances filed by inmates in recent years charging that classification decision-making processes are discriminatory, biased, or invalid point up the necessity to ensure that any tests administered to inmates have been validated for reliability as predictors of custody and/or program needs. In addition, correctional departments must be able to demonstrate that the testing processes are objective, logical, and fundamentally fair and are designed to meet the needs of both the inmates and the institution. By the same token, tests designed for other purposes should not be used to classify inmates (I.Q. tests, personality inventories).

In mid-1979, NIC sponsored a national survey of screening and classification processes, which assessed the current state-of-the-art in the design and utilization of classification instruments for decision making (American Justice Institute 1979). The survey found that correctional agencies have been shifting from subjective judgments to standardized instruments for classification decision making. The instruments being used are printed forms containing a fixed set of weighted criteria that provide an overall offender summary score. Considerations of this score in the process assists the classification team in making more uniform and consistent decisions that are less subject to legal challenge. (North Carolina and Minnesota submitted their instruments for legal review prior to implementation.) In some states, the forms are used both for custody and needs decision making.

5. **There must be explicit policy statements structuring and checking the discretionary decision-making powers of classification team staff.**

A corrections department must establish clear guidelines governing the discretionary decision-making powers of classification team staff. Otherwise, the department leaves itself open to allegations of unfairness, arbitrariness, and bias.

Discretionary powers of classification staff remain unstructured in too many systems. One example of the resultant problems was provided by a state corrections department in a grant application to NIC: "There is a very broad range of subjective and informal criteria used by those responsible for the classification of inmates; each person involved in the classification process has internalized his own set of significant variables, has established the relative importance of each of these variables according to his own value scale, and applies these standards in the classification decision on a case-by-case basis.

While discretion cannot and should not be completely eliminated, steps can be taken to designate boundaries within which classification decisions will be made, thus eliminating too broad discretionary power of individuals. A system in which the classification processes, rules, policies, findings, and reasons are open to scrutiny can further serve to check discretion.

Structuring and checking discretion is the responsibility of the Department of Corrections' central office. This responsibility is carried out by:

PRINCIPLES OF CLASSIFICATION (continued)

- Direction and supervision of the classification process by high-level central office personnel
- Establishment of procedures for interinstitutional transfer, including review by central office staff and an appeal procedure and administrative review of difficult cases
- Establishment of procedures for central office monitoring and evaluation of the classification process to ensure that it is operating according to policy
- Establishment of procedures for consideration of mitigating or aggravating factors in decision making
- Initiation of policy pertaining to classification, inmate programs/treatment, and casework, including a classification manual
- Selection, training, and supervision of counselors and other classification staff members

6. **There must be provision for screening and further evaluating inmates who are management problems and those who have special needs.**

This necessary function, also the responsibility of the Department of Corrections' central office, must be included in any model classification system.

Inmates who are management problems and require special considerations in placement and programming fall into several categories:

- Those who require protection and separation because they may be in danger from other inmates
- Those who, by reason of their offense, criminal record, or institutional behavior require particularly close supervision
- Those who received unusual publicity because of the nature of their crime, arrest, or trial or who were involved in criminal activities of a sophisticated nature, such as organized crime

The most dangerous inmates must be separated from the less violent individuals; thus, the classification process, by necessity, needs to include procedures to determine which inmates are potentially dangerous, such as those who have a history of assaultive or predatory behavior.

In addition to screening and further evaluating inmates who are management problems, the correctional system's central office must provide for inmates who have special needs. Those individuals who, through effective screening, are shown to require special program assignments and monitoring include, but are not limited to, the aged and infirm, the mentally ill and retarded, and those with special medical problems.

7. **There must be provisions to match offenders with programs; these provisions must be consistent with risk classification needs.**

This process involves the establishment of clear, operational definitions of the various types of offenders and available institutional programs. But risk as well as need factors must be considered when decisions are being made.

Thus, NIC recommends that the classification process be directed toward:

- Identifying and evaluating the factors underlying each inmate's needs
- Recommending programs and activities for inmates according to their *specific* needs and the availability of resources

PRINCIPLES OF CLASSIFICATION (continued) _____

- Developing and recording the necessary data to support services and long-range program planning

To fulfill these tasks, it is necessary to identify and utilize *all* programs that are available to each individual inmate. This function can be accomplished through a systematic classification of the offender and subsequent development of a program plan specifically designed for him/her.

8. There must be provision to classify each inmate at the least restrictive custody level.

This model classification system component targets the prevalent problem of overclassification. Eliminating overclassification is among the most significant objectives of new classification systems being designed and implemented in Minnesota, Tennessee, New York, and other states.

The first step involved here is developing specific criteria for differential custody assignments. Equally crucial is the second step of ensuring that both staff and inmates are aware of these criteria.

NIC recommends that clearly understandable custody definitions and supervision guidelines be applied system-wide. At a minimum, definitions should be given for (1) the traditional levels of custody—maximum, close, medium, and community and (2) the different uses of segregation (especially disciplinary segregation). A basic premise is that every inmate should be in the lowest custody believed suitable for adequate supervision and warranted by his/her behavior.

9. There must be provision to involve the inmate in the classification process.

Each new inmate should be provided with a copy of the custody criteria; a written explanation of the classification process; and a written explanation of the health care, employment, vocational training, education, transfer, and special programs available, including the selection criteria for each.

In addition, the correctional system should provide for classification teams at each institution so the inmate can participate in the classification decision-making process. ACA standard No. 4374 [Standard 3-4284, Third edition, 1990] calls for "maximum involvement of . . . the inmate in classification reviews." The inmate should be present except, perhaps, during deliberations of the classification team.

10. There must be provisions for systematic, periodic reclassification hearings.

Providing for reclassification on a regularly scheduled basis is another "essential" standard (No. 4376)[Standard 3-4287, Third edition, 1990] recommended by the ACA. Periodic review and reclassification is a cornerstone of any model classification system.

In reporting on its study of the classification process at the Tennessee Department of Corrections, NIC suggested the adoption of the following reclassification guidelines:

- Review/reclassification within two weeks following the inmate's transfer from another institution within the system
- Review every three months for inmates serving terms of 18 months or less
- Review every six months for inmates serving terms of 18 months and one day to five years
- Annual review for inmates serving terms of five years of more (NIC now recommends review every six months.)

PRINCIPLES OF CLASSIFICATION (continued) _____

If suitable manpower is available, reviews can be conducted on a more frequent basis. Optimally, inmates should be permitted to initiate reviews of their progress, status, and programming (ACA "important" Standard No. 4379)[Standard 3-4290, Third edition, 1990].

11. The classification process must be efficient and economically sound.

An empirically based classification system should enable the Department of Corrections to handle large numbers of offenders efficiently through a grouping process based on needs and risk. This can be accomplished by using modern technology to assist in the storage, correlation, and retrieval of data, although use of a computer should not be essential.

An efficient, economically sound classification system also makes effective use of other components of the criminal justice system, as well as social service agencies, for the provisions of offender data (such as information obtained for pre-sentence reports).

The development of a model classification system should involve cooperating with other agencies to devise a standard reporting format for offender information, preferably one that elicits quantitative data insofar as possible.

12. There must be provisions to continuously evaluate and improve the classification process.

Any true process continuously strives to improve itself through feedback, evaluation, and action to correct deficiencies. Thus, the model classification system, if it is to be effective, must be able to continuously improve to meet the changing needs of the inmate population and the correctional system as a whole. It must be responsive to emerging knowledge and professional understanding of the classification process. The system must also be responsive to staff and inmate input.

13. Classification procedures must be consistent with constitutional requisites.

The central office must keep abreast of litigation applicable to its jurisdiction in order to ensure the continued legality of its classification policies, procedures, and decisions. Most state Departments of Correction have a legal section that can be of assistance in this area.

14. There must be an opportunity to gain input from administration and line staff when undertaking development of a classification system.

In summary, the hallmark of classification is *the non-capricious assignment of individuals.* In order to accomplish equity in custody, security, program and treatment determination, and placement, a system reflecting the above principles must exist. Furthermore, it must be utilized.

A basic tenet to classification takes the idea of non-capricious placement a step further. As stated earlier, classification seeks to determine the placement of individuals in accord with their various correctional needs. Each of these outcomes may be accomplished separately, but it is only when they are combined into a comprehensive process that strives for equity and objectivity that we define it as classification. Since equity and objectivity are goals, principles and procedures should be employed that reflect these aims.

INITIAL INMATE CLASSIFICATION _____

Custody

Name:_____ Number:_____
　　　Last　　　　　　First　　　　　　MI
Classification Caseworker:_____ Date:_____

1. HISTORY OF INSTITUTIONAL VIOLENCE   Score:_____
(Jail of Prison, code most serious within last five years)
None 0
Assault and battery not involving use of a weapon or resulting in serious injury 3
Assault and battery involving use of a weapon and/or resulting in serious injury or death 7

2. SEVERITY OF CURRENT OFFENSE   Score:_____
(Refer to the *Severity of Offense Scale* on p. 303. Score the most serious offense if there are multiple
convictions.)
Low 0
Low moderate 1
Moderate 2
High 4
Highest.. 6

3. PRIOR ASSAULTIVE OFFENSE HISTORY   Score:_____
(Score the most severe in inmate's history. Refer to the *Severity of Offense Scale*.)
None, low, or low moderate 0
Moderate... 2
High 4
Highest.. 6

4. ESCAPE HISTORY (Rate last 3 years of incarceration)   Score:_____
No escapes or attempts (or no prior incarcerations) 0
An escape or attempt from minimum or community custody, no actual or threatened violence:
　　Over 1 year ago 1
　　Within the last year.. 3
An escape or attempt from medium, or above custody, or an escape from minimum or community custody
with actual or threatened violence:
　　Over 1 year ago 5
　　Within the last year..7

CLOSE CUSTODY SCORE (Add items 1 through 4)
(If score is 10 or above, inmate should be assigned to close custody. If score is under 10, complete items 5 through
8 and use medium/minimum scale.)

490

INITIAL INMATE CLASSIFICATION (continued)

5. ALCOHOL/DRUG ABUSE
Score:_____
None 0
Abuse causing occasional legal and social adjustment problems 1
Serious abuse, serious disruption of functioning 3

6. CURRENT DETAINER
Score:_____
None 0
Misdemeanor detainer... 1
Extradition initiated - misdemeanor... 3
Felony detainer.. 4
Extradition initiated - felony 6

7. PRIOR FELONY CONVICTIONS
Score:_____
None 0
One 2
Two or more 4

8. STABILITY FACTORS
Score:_____
(Check appropriate box(s) and combine for score.)
Age 26 or over... -2
High school diploma or GED received... -1
Employed or attending school (full or part-time) for six months or longer at time of arrest.......-1

MINIMUM/MEDIUM SCORE (Add items 1 through 8.)
**Total
Score:_____**
MEDIUM/MINIMUM SCALE:
Medium Custody 7-22
Minimum Custody... 6 or less

INITIAL INMATE CLASSIFICATION (continued) _____

Severity of Offense Scale

(From Massachusetts Superior Court Sentencing Guidelines Project, 1979)

6 POINTS:

- Armed assault in a dwelling
- Armed robbery while masked
- Armed robbery
- Arson in a dwelling place, night, occupied
- Burglary, being armed
- Kidnapping to extort
- Murder*
- Rape
- Robbery
- Stealing by confining or putting in fear

5 POINTS:

- Extortion
- Incest
- Kidnapping
- Manslaughter
- Mayhem

4 POINTS:

- Arson (Note: not Arson as listed above)
- Breaking and entering, nighttime
- Burglary, not being armed
- Burning to defraud
- Burning insured property
- Burning real property
- Carrying a firearm+
- Common receiver
- Indecent A&B child under 14
- Mfg., dist., or poss. with intent to dist., Class A&B

INITIAL INMATE CLASSIFICATION (continued)

3 POINTS:
- Assault and battery to collect a loan
- Assault and battery with a dangerous weapon
- Assault with intent to murder, maim
- Assault with intent to rob while being armed
- Attempt to murder by poisoning
- Breaking and entering in the daytime

Attempt or accessory before the fact of an offense receives the same score as the substantive offense.

*Score only if prior offense.

+If present offense, score only if *not* most serious offense.

INITIAL INMATE CLASSIFICATION (continued) _____

Assessment of Needs

NAME:_____ NUMBER:_____

      Last   First   MI

CLASSIFICATION CHAIRMAN:_____

DATE:_____

TEST SCORES:

                                                                          I.Q.:_____

                                                                          Reading:_____

                                                                          Math:_____

NEEDS ASSESSMENT: Select the answer that best describes the inmate.

HEALTH: Code:_____

1. Sound physical health, seldom ill.

2. Handicap or illness that interferes with functioning on a recurring basis.

3. Serious handicap or chronic illness, needs frequent medical care.

INTELLECTUAL ABILITY: Code:_____

1. Normal intellectual ability, able to function independently.

2. Mild retardation, some need for assistance.

3. Moderate retardation, independent functioning severely limited.

BEHAVIORAL/EMOTIONAL PROBLEMS: Code:_____

1. Exhibits appropriate emotional responses.

2. Symptoms limit adequate functioning, requires counseling, may require medication.

3. Symptoms prohibit adequate functioning, requires significant intervention, may require medication or separate housing.

ALCOHOL ABUSE:

                                                 Code:_____

1. No alcohol problem.

2. Occasional abuse, some disruption of functioning.

3. Frequent abuse, serious disruption, needs treatment.

INITIAL INMATE CLASSIFICATION (continued)_____

DRUG ABUSE: Code:_____

   1. No drug problem.   2. Occasional abuse, some   3. Frequent abuse, serious
                                  disruption of functioning.   disruption, needs treatment.

EDUCATIONAL STATUS: Code:_____

   1. Has high school diploma   2. Some deficits, but potential for   3. Major deficits in math and/or
      or GED.   high school diploma or GED.   reading, needs remedial programs.

VOCATIONAL STATUS: Code:_____

   1. Has sufficient skills to   2. Minimal skill level, needs   3. Virtually unemployable, needs
      obtain and hold   enhancement.   training.
      satisfactory employment.

Correctional Assessment, Casework and Counseling

INITIAL INMATE CLASSIFICATION (continued) _____

Initial Classification Summary
1. Override Considerations   Code:_____
  - **Custody Classification**
    1. None
    2. Inmate Needs Protection
    3. Temporary Placement-Pending Investigation
    4. Temporary Placement-Punitive Isolation
    5. Temporary Placement-Suicide Threat   Score:_____
    6. Other, Specify:
                                                              I.Q._____
    _____
                                                    Score:_____ Reading:_____
    _____
                                                              Math:_____

2. Custody Level Assignment: Code:_____
    1. Community
    2. Minimum
    3. Medium
    4. Close
    5. Maximum
    6. Protective Custody
    7. Other, Specify:
                                                              Code:_____
    _____
                                                    Score:_____
    _____
                                                              Code:_____
    _____
                                                    Score:_____

3. Facility Assignment: Code:_____

4. Program Recommendations   Score:_____
    (In order of priority)
                                                              Code:_____

	Program Code	Enrollment Code*
_____	___	___
_____	___	___
_____	___	___
_____	___	___

Code:_____

Score:_____ Code:_____

INITIAL INMATE CLASSIFICATION (continued)_____

5. Work Recommendations:

	Work Code	Inmate Skills	Skill Code
_____	____	_____	____
_____	____	_____	____
_____	____	_____	____
_____	____	_____	____
_____	____	_____	____

Score:_____   Code:_____

Score:_____   Code:_____

Score:_____

TOTAL SCORE:_____

*Enrollment Code

Program available = 1

Program currently at capacity/unavailable = 2

Program needed but does not exist at required custody level = 3

Inmate refuses program = 4

CORRECTIONAL ADJUSTMENT CHECKLIST (CACL) _____

Name and number of inmate:_____

Name of person completing this checklist: _____

Your position:_____ Date completed:_____

Instructions: Please indicate which of the following behaviors this inmate exhibits. If the behavior describes the inmate, circle the "1." If it does not, circle the "0." *Please complete every item.*

0	1	1. Worried, anxious
0	1	2. Tries, but cannot seem to follow directions
0	1	3. Tense, unable to relax
0	1	4. Socially withdrawn
0	1	5. Continually asks for help from staff
0	1	6. Gets along with the hoods
0	1	7. Seems to take no pleasure in anything
0	1	8. Jittery, jumpy; seems afraid
0	1	9. Uses leisure time to cause trouble
0	1	10. Continually uses profane language; curses and swears
0	1	11. Easily upset
0	1	12. Sluggish and drowsy
0	1	13. Cannot be trusted at all
0	1	14. Moody, brooding
0	1	15. Needs constant supervision
0	1	16. Victimizes weaker inmates
0	1	17. Seems dull and unintelligent
0	1	18. Is an agitator about race
0	1	19. Continually tries to con staff
0	1	20. Impulsive; unpredictable
0	1	21. Afraid of other inmates
0	1	22. Seems to seek excitement
0	1	23. Never seems happy
0	1	24. Doesn't trust staff
0	1	25. Passive; easily led

CORRECTIONAL ADJUSTMENT CHECKLIST (continued) _____

0	1	26. Talks aggressively to other inmates
0	1	27. Accepts no blame for any of his troubles
0	1	28. Continually complains; accuses staff of unfairness
0	1	29. Daydreams; seems to be mentally off in space
0	1	30. Talks aggressively to staff
0	1	31. Has a quick temper
0	1	32. Obviously holds grudges; seeks to "get even"
0	1	33. Inattentive; seems preoccupied
0	1	34. Attempts to play staff against one another
0	1	35. Passively resistant; has to be forced to participate
0	1	36. Tries to form a clique
0	1	37. Openly defies regulations and rules
0	1	38. Often sad and depressed
0	1	39. Stirs up trouble among inmates
0	1	40. Aids or abets others in breaking the rules
0	1	41. Considers himself unjustly confined

Source: Herbert C. Quay, Ph.D.

Correctional Assessment, Casework and Counseling

RAW SCORE FORM: CORRECTIONAL ADJUSTMENT CHECKLIST (CACL) _____

Name and number of inmate:_____

Name of person completing this checklist:_____

Your position:_____ Date completed:_____

Instructions: For each "1" circled on the Correctional Adjustment Checklist, place a checkmark on the line corresponding to the item number. Add the checkmarks to obtain the Raw Score for each group.

Group			
I	**II**	**IV**	**V**
			1._____
		2._____	3._____
		4._____	5._____
6._____		7._____	8._____
9._____			
10._____			11._____
		12._____	
13._____		14._____	
15._____			
16._____		17._____	
18._____	19._____		
20._____			21._____
22._____		23._____	
	24._____	25._____	
26._____			
27._____	28._____	29._____	
30._____			
31._____			
32._____		33._____	
	34._____	35._____	
36._____			
37._____			38._____
39._____			
40._____	41._____		

Total (Raw Score): _____ _____ _____ _____

Source: Herbert C. Quay, Ph.D.

500

CHECKLIST FOR THE ANALYSIS OF
LIFE HISTORY RECORDS OF ADULT OFFENDERS (CALH) _____

Name and number of inmate:_____

Name of person completing this checklist:_____

Your position:_____ Date started: _____

Instructions: Circle each behavior trait that describes this inmate's life history.

1. Has few, if any, friends
2. Thrill-seeking
3. Preoccupied; "dreamy"
4. Uncontrollable as a child
5. Has expressed guilt over offense
6. Expresses need for self-improvement
7. Socially withdrawn
8. Weak, indecisive, easily led
9. Previous local, state, or federal incarceration
10. Tough, defiant
11. Irregular work history (if not a student)
12. Noted not to be responsive to counseling
13. Gives impression of ineptness, incompetence in managing everyday problems in living
14. Supported wife and children
15. Claims offense was motivated by family problems
16. Close ties with criminal elements
17. Depressed, morose
18. Physically aggressive (strongarm, assault, reckless homicide, attempted murder, mugging, etc.)
19. Apprehension likely due to "stupid" behavior on the part of the offender
20. Single marriage
21. Expresses feelings of inadequacy, worthlessness
22. Difficulties in the public schools
23. Suffered financial reverses prior to commission of offense for which incarcerated
24. Passive, submissive
25. Bravado, braggart
26. Guiltless; blames others
27. Expresses lack of concern for others

Source: Herbert C. Quay, Ph.D

Correctional Assessment, Casework and Counseling

RAW SCORE FORM: LIFE HISTORY CHECKLIST (CALH) _____

Name and number of inmate: _____

Name of person completing this checklist:_____

Your position: _____ Date completed: _____

Instructions: For each item circled on the Checklist for the Analysis of Life History Records of Adult Offenders, place a checkmark on the line corresponding to the item number. Add the checkmarks to obtain the Raw Score for each group.

	Group	
I	**III**	**IV**
		1. _____
2. _____		
		3. _____
4. _____		
	5. _____	
	6. _____	
		7. _____
		8. _____
9. _____		
10. _____		
11. _____		
12. _____		13. _____
	14. _____	
	15. _____	
16. _____		17. _____
18. _____		19. _____
	20. _____	
		21. _____
22. _____	23. _____	
		24. _____
25. _____		
26. _____		
27. _____		

Total (Raw Score): _____ _____ _____

Source: Herbert C. Quay, Ph.D.

502

RAW SCORE TO NORMALIZED T-SCORE CONVERSIONS
FOR CORRECTIONAL ADJUSTMENT CHECKLIST (CACL)_____

Scale I		Scale II		Scale IV		Scale V	
Raw score	T-score	Raw score	T-score	Raw score	T-score	Raw score	T-score
0	41	0	44	0	40	0	39
1	49	1	54	1	47	1	46
2	53	2	59	2	51	2	50
3	56	3	62	3	54	3	54
4	58	4	65	4	56	4	57
5	59	5	70	5	59	5	61
6	60			6	61	6	65
7	61			7	63	7	71
8	62			8	65		
9	63			9	69		
10	64			10	73		
11	65			11	78		
12	66						
13	67						
14	68						
15	69						
16	71						
17	73						
18	76						

RAW SCORE TO NORMALIZED T-SCORE CONVERSIONS FOR LIFE HISTORY CHECKLIST (CALH)

Scale I		Scale III		Scale IV	
Raw score	T-score	Raw score	T-score	Raw score	T-score
0	35	0	39	0	39
1	43	1	47	1	47
2	47	2	52	2	53
3	51	3	58	3	58
4	55	4	64	4	62
5	58	5	70	5	66
6	61	6	76	6	70
7	64			7	74
8	67			8	82
9	71			9	90
10	75				
11	82				

CLASSIFICATION PROFILE FOR ADULT OFFENDERS _____

Name and number of inmate: _____

Name of person completing this profile: _____

Your position: _____   Date: _____

	Scale	Raw Score	T-score
1. Correctional Adjustment Checklist (CACL)	I	_____	_____
	II	_____	_____
	IV	_____	_____
	V	_____	_____
Checklist for the Analysis of Life History Records (CALH)	I	_____	_____
	III	_____	_____
	IV	_____	_____

	Scale	CACL T-score	CALH T-score	Final T-score
2. Combined Scores	I	_____ +	_____ ÷ 2 =	_____
	II	_____	=	_____
	III		_____ =	_____
	IV	_____ +	_____ ÷ 2 =	_____
	V	_____	=	_____

3. Assignment

_____ Group I   _____ Group III   _____ Group IV
_____ Group II   _____ Group V

CLASSIFICATION PROFILE FOR ADULT OFFENDERS (continued)_____

Instructions:

1. Transfer Totals from Raw Score forms onto appropriate Raw Score lines.
   Using the appropriate conversion table, convert each Raw Score to a T-score.
   - If two CACLS are used per inmate, convert all Raw Scores to T-scores; then add the T-scores obtained for each scale and divide the sum by 2.
2. List the final CACL and CALH T-scores on the appropriate lines in the Combined Scores section.
   - For Scales I and IV, add the T-scores and divide by 2.
3. Use the highest Final T-score to make the final assignment.
   If the two scores are tied, use the following tie-breaker rules:
   - If Group I and Group II are tied for highest,
     —and there is one housing unit for *both* groups, assign to Heavy.
     —and there is one housing unit for *each* group, assign for the best balance or use of available housing.
   - If Group IV and Group V are tied for highest,
     —and there is one housing unit for both groups, assign to Light.
     —and there is one housing unit for each group, assign for the best balance or use of available housing.
   - If Group I *or* Group II are tied with any other group, assign to Heavy.
   - If Group IV *or* Group V are tied with Group III, assign to Light.

(Note: Before using any tie-breaker rules, recheck all scoring and calculations.)

Index

E

volunteers and clients, matching
by type of relationship, 257
Fine, contrasted with restriction, 275
Fire setting, 43
First Amendment, 265, 267, 270
and nonassociation, 271
and participation in education and
job training, 274
Fishbein, Dianna, 401
Fixation, 169
Florida, elderly inmates in, 418
Force, use of, 266
42 USC Section 1983, 140
Fourteenth Amendment, 139, 278-280
Fourth Amendment, 265, 267, 279, 281
Free association, 265
Free will, 237
and probation/parole revocation
hearings, 283-284
Freeman, Dr. Robert, 24, 59
Freud, Sigmund, 166
Friendship and criminals, 38
Frivolous lawsuits, 289

G

Gagnon v. Scarpelli, 284
Gall's phrenology, 45
Games People Play, 185
Gamma-aminobutyric acid, 295
Gang affiliations, 151
GATB, *see* General Aptitude Test
Battery (GATB)
GED (General Equivalency Degree), 113,
249
Gender
and criminality, 397ff
and drug antagonists, 324
Gendreau, P., 3, 162, 335
Gene/environment correlation, 33-34
Gene/environment interaction, 34, 35
General Aptitude Test Battery (GATB),
144, 145

General Equivalency Degree (GED),
see GED
General strain theory, 16
Genuineness, 172, 299
Geriatric offenders, *see* Elderly

offenders
Germany, victim-offender reconciliation
program in, 253
Gibbons, Don, 32
Glasser, William, 39, 193, 194, 206, 300,
406
founder of reality therapy, 192
Glick, Barry, 221
Goffman, I. 225
Goethe, Wolfgang von, 293
Golden, Delores, 417
Goldstein, Arnold, 221
Goleman, Daniel, 359
Gottfredson, Michael, 23, 407
Graham, Gordon, 221, 227
*Greenholtz v. Inmates of Nebraska
Penal and Correctional
Complex*, 268
Griffin v. Wisconsin, 279-280
Group,
definition of, 228-229
Group counseling, 46, 225ff
advantages of, 242
catharsis, 232
for child molesters, 339
competency development, 10
components of, 230-234
definition, 230-233
difficult group members, 238-241
disruption of, 245
disadvantages of, 242
empathy training, 236
exercises in, 241, 243
goals of, 229-230
group therapy contrasted with,
231
leading of, 10
member selection, 229-230
at mental health center, 248
planning for, 229
in prison, 243-244
reality orientation, 231-232
selection of group members,
229-230
self-disclosure in, 233
size of, 232
topics for, 234-238
withdrawn member, 240-241
Guilt, lack of among psychopaths, 33

H

Halfway houses, 249
Hallucinogens, 318-319
Haloperidol, 353
Hare, Robert, 44
Health Care Management Issues in Corrections, 428
Health insurance policies, 249
Helling v. McKinney, 140
Hemmens, Craig, 263
Heritability, 144
    ADHD, of, 376
    IQ, of, 361
Heroin, 314-315
Heyrend, Cydnee J., 411
Hirschi, Travis, 20, 193, 407
Hoffart v. State, 273
Holt v. Sarver, 265
Homeless, accommodations for, 250
Hospice care for inmates, 429
Hospitals as substance abuse centers, 248
Hostility, *see* Resistant/reluctant offenders
Housing assistance, 357
Hudson v. Palmer, 140
Human Development Training Institute, 227
Human Synergistics Lifestyle Inventory, 145-146
Humor of correctional worker, 57
Hungary, crime in, 13

I

Ice, *see* Methamphetamine
Idaho, 10
Idaho State Correctional Institution, 288
I-level System, 359-360, 384
    of females, 409
Illegitimacy, 361, 378, 407-408
Indiana, victim-offender reconciliation program in, 253
Inmate code, 225-227
Immunity from liability, 284-286
Impulse control, 32
Incidental contact, 272

Informants, protection of, 151
Information processing, male versus female, 411
Initial Inmate Classification, 490-497
Inmates, number of in federal prison, 124; *see also* Female offenders; Offenders
Innovation (in anomie theory), 15-16
Intellectualization, 169
Intensive care units and quality of relationship, 178
Intensive supervision, 131
International Association of Justice Volunteerism, 250
International Congress on Schizophrenia Research, 354
Internet, sex offender notification, 278
Interpersonal intrusiveness, 216-217
Interrogation, 73, 87ff
    back door approach, 92
    bluffing, 91-92
    interviews versus, 73, 88
    leading questions, 90
    Miranda warnings, and, 88, 282-283
    preparation for, 89
    professionalism in, 89-90
    style, 89-90,
    termination of, 92
Interstate Compact, 391
Interviews, 73ff
    active listening, 75, 424
    arguing, avoiding, 78
    authority, 83
    closed questions, 75-76
    conducting of, 83-85
    counseling, contrasted with, 164-165
    daydreaming, avoiding, 78
    detouring, avoiding, 78
    exercises in, 93-94
    familiarity with case, 80, 81
    hostility, dealing with, 84
    interrogations versus, 73, 88
    interrupting, 88
    listening, 77-78
    open questions, 75, 76
    physical surroundings for, 80
    probing, 76

Religion,
freedom of, 267
training in, 274
Reluctant/resistant offender, 84,
194-196
Remer, Pam, 405-406
Reproductive success, 37, 38
Resistance, 195-196, 238-239
Resource allocation, 47
Respect, lack of in juveniles, 390
Respondeat superior, 285
Responsibility, 408
lack of in psychopaths, 32
and reality therapy, 193
reattributing, 237-238
in youth, 383
Responsivity principle, 127-128
Restitution, 254, 275-276, 384
Restorative justice, 6-11, 247, 253
for rape victim, 336-337
Reticular activating system (RAS), 36,
37, 376
Retreatism (in anomie/strain theory),
15
Retributive justice/just deserts, 6, 7, 10
Reward dominance theory, 34-36
Rhodes v. Chapman, 140
Right to counsel, 265; *see also* Sixth
Amendment
Rights of offenders, 264ff
access to legal services, 265, 267
cruel and unusual punishment,
freedom from, 266
due process, 264, 265
parole hearings and, 268
procedural rights, 264, 265
self-incrimination, 265, 282-283
substantive rights, 264
treatment refusal right, 266
treatment rights, 265-266
under community supervision,
268-272
Risk and needs assessment, 125-126,
151, 473-476
Risk taking of criminals, 23
scoring guide for, 477-483
Ritalin, 376,
Ritualism (in anomie/strain theory), 15
Rock, *see* Cocaine

Rogers, Carl, 178, 208
and AA, 299-300
client-centered approach, 170-172
Role reversal in group counseling, 236
Ross, Robert R., 221, 335
Rossi, Alice, 401
RR, *see* Rational Recovery
Ruffin v. Commonwealth, 264, 265
Rule breaking in lifestyle theory, 216
Run (of speed) defined, 317

S

Sadist, 241
Salvation Army, 251, 299
Samenow, Stanton, 207, 215, 243
Sandin v. Conner, 266
SANE (Sexual Abuse Now Ended)
therapeutic program, 340-342
Scared Straight, 7
Schizophrenia, 352-357
antipsychotic drugs, 353, 356
case study, 365-366
causes of, 353-354
medication and treatment, 435,
456
Milwaukee Community Support
Program, 356-357
numbers of, 352
process versus reactive, 352
Schlosslberg, Nancy, 397
Schrink, Jeffrey, 56
Schuckit, Marc, 305
Schuenemann, Raymond W., 342
Scienter, 271
Scott, Edward, 404
Searches and seizures, 265, 267, 279-
282; *see also* Fourth
Amendment
Secular Sobriety, 302, 304
Selective intervention, 129-130
Self-centeredness of psychopaths, 33
Self-concept, 53ff, 380
client-centered therapy and,
170-171
of correctional counselors, 54
of offenders, 23, 54
self-disclosure, and 64-66
self-esteem and, 55-56

Voting rights, 264

W

Waivers (of juveniles to adult court), 374
Wakefield, Bill, 381-382
Walnut Street Prison, 140, 141
Walsh, C., 421-422
Walters, Glen, 215
Warrant for searches, 279
Washington v. Harper, 266
Washington State
    civil commitment of sex offenders in, 278
    sex offender registration, 277
Wechsler Adult Intelligence Scale (WAIS), 145, 358, 399
Wechsler P>V test, 43, 360, 385
Weekend detention, 10
Welfare agencies, 249-250
West, Marilyn, 117
Whitehead, Lindsey, 178
Wilson v. Seiter, 284
Wisconsin civil commitment of sex offenders, 278
Wisconsin Bureau of Community Corrections, 124
WISC-R, Revised Weschler Intelligence Scale for Children, 358
Wolff v. McDonnell, 267-268
Women offenders, *see* Female offenders
Work, value of, 382-383
Worrell, Judith, 405-406

Y

Yochelson, Samuel, 207, 215, 243
Younger brother syndrome, 317

About the Author

Anthony Walsh, Ph.D. is a professor of criminal justice at Boise State University in Idaho. He has had field experience as a police officer and as a probation officer. His primary interests are in the biosocial bases of behavior, criminology, criminal justice assessment, and statistics. His latest books are *From Law to Order: The Theory and Practice of Law and Justice* with Craig Hemmens, published by the American Correctional Association (2000); *Criminology: A Global Perspective* with Lee Ellis, published by Allyn and Bacon (2000), and *Essential Statistics for the Social and Behavioral Sciences* with Jane Ollenburger published by Prentice Hall (2000).